THE STATISTICS AND CALCULUS WITH PYTHON WORKSHOP

A comprehensive introduction to mathematics in Python for artificial intelligence applications

Peter Farrell, Alvaro Fuentes, Ajinkya Sudhir Kolhe, Quan Nguyen, Alexander Joseph Sarver, and Marios Tsatsos

Packt

THE STATISTICS AND CALCULUS WITH PYTHON WORKSHOP

Authors: Peter Farrell, Alvaro Fuentes, Ajinkya Sudhir Kolhe, Quan Nguyen, Alexander Joseph Sarver, and Marios Tsatsos

Reviewers: Achint Chaudhary, Amit Chaurasia, Rohan Chikorde, Sanjin Dedic, Tim Hoolihan, Ravi Ranjan Prasad Karn, and Alberto Manzini

Managing Editors: Madhunikita Sunil Chindarkar

Acquisitions Editors: Manuraj Nair, Royluis Rodrigues, Kunal Sawant, Sneha Shinde, Archie Vankar, Karan Wadekar, and Alicia Wooding

Production Editor: Shantanu Zagade

First published: August 2020

Production reference: 1170820

ISBN: 978-1-80020-976-3

Published by Packt Publishing Ltd.

Livery Place, 35 Livery Street

Birmingham B3 2PB, UK

EXPERIENCE THE WORKSHOP ONLINE

Thank you for purchasing the print edition of *The Statistics and Calculus with Python Workshop.* Every physical print copy includes free online access to the premium interactive edition. There are no extra costs or hidden charges.

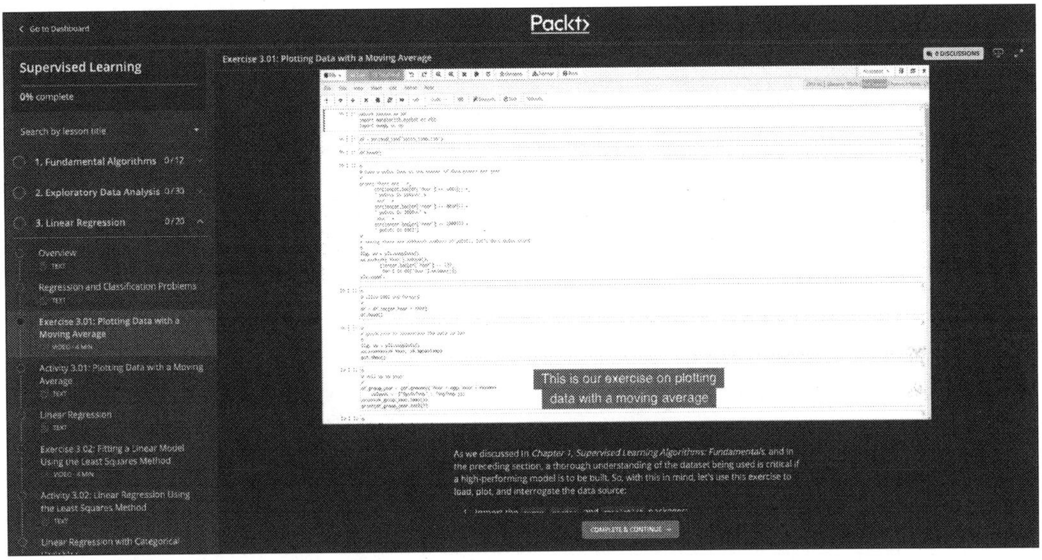

Figure A: An example of the companion video in the Workshop course player (dark mode)

With the interactive edition you'll unlock:

- **Screencasts**: Supercharge your progress with screencasts of all exercises and activities.
- **Built-In Discussions**: Engage in discussions where you can ask questions, share notes and interact. Tap straight into insight from expert instructors and editorial teams.
- **Skill Verification**: Complete the course online to earn a Packt credential that is easy to share and unique to you. All authenticated on the public Bitcoin blockchain.
- **Download PDF and EPUB**: Download a digital version of the course to read offline. Available as PDF or EPUB, and always DRM-free.

To redeem your free digital copy of *The Statistics and Calculus with Python Workshop* you'll need to follow these simple steps:

1. Visit us at https://courses.packtpub.com/pages/redeem.
2. Login with your Packt account, or register as a new Packt user.
3. Select your course from the list, making a note of the three page numbers for your product. Your unique redemption code needs to match the order of the pages specified.
4. Open up your print copy and find the codes at the bottom of the pages specified. They'll always be in the same place:

EXERCISE 4.02: PERFORMING MISSING VALUE ANALYSIS FOR THE DATAFRAMES

In this section, we will be implementing a missing value analysis on the first DataFrame to find the missing values. This exercise is a continuation of *Exercise 4.01, Importing Data into DataFrames*. Follow these steps to complete this exercise:

1. Import the **missingno** package:

```
# To analyze the missing data
!pip install missingno
import missingno as msno
```

2. Find the missing values in the first DataFrame and visualize the missing values in a plot:

```
# Missing Values in the first DataFrame
msno.bar(dataframes[0],color='red',labels=True,sort="ascending")
```

A B 2 1 C

Figure B: Example code in the bottom-right corner, to be used for free digital redemption of a print workshop

5. Merge the codes together (without spaces), ensuring they are in the correct order.
6. At checkout, click **`Have a redemption code?`** and enter your unique product string. Click **`Apply`**, and the price should be free!

Finally, we'd like to thank you for purchasing the print edition of *The Statistics and Calculus with Python Workshop*! We hope that you finish the course feeling capable of tackling challenges in the real world. Remember that we're here to help if you ever feel like you're not making progress.

If you run into issues during redemption (or have any other feedback) you can reach us at workshops@packt.com.

Table of Contents

Chapter 6: Matrices and Markov Chains with Python 299

Chapter 12: Intermediate Calculus with Python 589

PREFACE

ABOUT THE BOOK

Are you looking to start developing artificial intelligence applications? Do you need a refresher on key mathematical concepts? Full of engaging practical exercises, *The Statistics and Calculus with Python Workshop* will show you how to apply your understanding of advanced mathematics in the context of Python.

The book begins by giving you a high-level overview of the libraries you'll use while performing statistics with Python. As you progress, you'll perform various mathematical tasks using the Python programming language, such as solving algebraic functions with Python starting with basic functions, and then working through transformations and solving equations. Later chapters in the book will cover statistics and calculus concepts and how to use them to solve problems and gain useful insights. Finally, you'll study differential equations with an emphasis on numerical methods and learn about algorithms that directly calculate values of functions.

By the end of this book, you'll have learned how to apply essential statistics and calculus concepts to develop robust Python applications that solve business challenges.

AUDIENCE

If you are a Python programmer who wants to develop intelligent solutions that solve challenging business problems, then this book is for you. To better grasp the concepts explained in this book, you must have a thorough understanding of advanced mathematical concepts, such as Markov chains, Euler's formula, and Runge-Kutta methods as the book only explains how these techniques and concepts can be implemented in Python.

ABOUT THE CHAPTERS

Chapter 1, *Fundamentals of Python*, introduces you to the Python language. You will learn how to use Python's most integral data structures and control flows, as well as picking up best practices for programming-specific tasks such as debugging, testing, and version control.

Chapter 2, *Python's Main Tools for Statistics*, introduces the ecosystem of scientific computing and visualization in Python. These discussions will revolve around the specific Python libraries that facilitate these tasks, such as NumPy, pandas, and Matplotlib. Hands-on exercises will help you practice their usage.

Chapter 3, Python's Statistical Toolbox, describes the theoretical basics of statistical analysis. You will learn about the fundamental components in the field of statistics, namely the various types of statistics and statistical variables. This chapter also includes a brief overview of a wide range of different Python libraries and tools that can help to facilitate specialized tasks, such as SymPy, PyMC3, and Bokeh.

Chapter 4, Functions and Algebra with Python, discusses the theoretical foundation of mathematical functions and algebraic equations. These discussions are also accompanied by interactive exercises that present corresponding tools in Python that can streamline and/or automate various procedures, such as drawing function graphs and solving equations and systems of equations.

Chapter 5, More Mathematics with Python, teaches you the basics of sequences, series, trigonometry, and complex numbers. While these can prove to be challenging theoretical topics, we will consider them from a different practical perspective, specifically via practical applications such as financial analysis and 401(k)/retirement calculations.

Chapter 6, Matrices and Markov Chains with Python, introduces you to the concepts of matrices and Markov chains. These are mathematical objects commonly used in some of the most popular applications of mathematics, such as artificial intelligence and machine learning. The chapter is coupled with the hands-on activity of developing a word predictor.

Chapter 7, Doing Basic Statistics with Python, marks the start of the portion of this book where we specifically focus on statistics and statistical analysis. This chapter introduces the process of exploratory data analysis and, in general, using simple statistical techniques to interpret a dataset.

Chapter 8, Foundational Probability Concepts and Their Applications, dives deeper into complex statistical concepts, such as randomness, random variables, and using simulations as a technique to analyze randomness. This chapter will help you become more comfortable working with statistical problems that involve randomness.

Chapter 9, Intermediate Statistics with Python, wraps up the topic of statistics by iterating over the most important theories in the field, such as the law of large numbers and central limit theorem, as well as commonly used techniques, including confidence intervals, hypothesis testing, and linear regression. With the knowledge you'll gain in this chapter, you will be ready to tackle many real-life statistical problems using Python.

Chapter 10, Foundational Calculus with Python, begins the topic of calculus by discussing more involved concepts, such as the slope of a function, the area under a curve, optimization, and solids of revolution. Typically considered as complicated problems in mathematics, these concepts are explained in an intuitive and hands-on manner with the help of Python.

Chapter 11, More Calculus with Python, tackles more complex topics in calculus, namely, the calculation of arc lengths and surface areas, partial derivatives, and series expansions. Once again, we will be able to see the power of Python in helping us approach these advanced topics, which normally can be quite challenging for many students.

Chapter 12, Intermediate Calculus with Python, concludes the book with some of the most interesting topics in calculus, such as differential equations, the Euler method, and the Runge-Kutta method. These methods present an algorithmic approach to solving differential equations, which is particularly applicable in Python as a computational tool.

CONVENTIONS

Code words in text, database table names, folder names, filenames, file extensions, pathnames, dummy URLs, user input, and Twitter handles are shown as follows:

"To do this, we can use the **`with`** keyword together with the **`open()`** function to interact with the text file."

A block of code is set as follows:

```
if x % 6 == 0:
    print('x is divisible by 6')
```

In some cases, a line of code is immediately followed by its output. These cases are presented as follows:

```
>>> find_sum([1, 2, 3])
6
```

In this example, the executed code is the line which begins with **>>>**, and the output is the second line (**6**).

In other cases, the output is shown separately from the code block, for ease of reading.

Words that you see on the screen, for example, in menus or dialog boxes, also appear in the text like this: "When you click on the **Fetch Images** button, the images appear with authors' names."

New terms and important words are shown like this: "Write the returned list to the same input file in a new line in the same **comma-separated values** (**CSV**) format".

CODE PRESENTATION

Lines of code that span multiple lines are split using a backslash (\ ). When the code is executed, Python will ignore the backslash, and treat the code on the next line as a direct continuation of the current line.

For example:

```
history = model.fit(X, y, epochs=100, batch_size=5, verbose=1, \
                    validation_split=0.2, shuffle=False)
```

Comments are added into code to help explain specific bits of logic. Single-line comments are denoted using the **#** symbol, as follows:

```
# Print the sizes of the dataset
print("Number of Examples in the Dataset = ", X.shape[0])
print("Number of Features for each example = ", X.shape[1])
```

Multi-line comments are enclosed by triple quotes, as shown below:

```
"""
Define a seed for the random number generator to ensure the
result will be reproducible
"""
seed = 1
np.random.seed(seed)
random.set_seed(seed)
```

SETTING UP YOUR ENVIRONMENT

Before we explore the book in detail, we need to set up specific software and tools. In the following section, we shall see how to do that.

SOFTWARE REQUIREMENTS

You'll also need the following software installed in advance:

- OS: Windows 7 SP1 64-bit, Windows 8.1 64-bit or Windows 10 64-bit, macOS, or Linux
- Browser: Latest version of Google Chrome, Firefox, or Microsoft Edge
- Python 3.7
- Jupyter Notebook

INSTALLATION AND SETUP

Before you start this book, you will need to install Python (3.7 or above) and Jupyter, which are the main tools that we will be using throughout the chapters.

INSTALLING PYTHON

The best method to install Python is via the environment manager Anaconda, which can be downloaded from https://docs.anaconda.com/anaconda/install/. Once Anaconda has been successfully installed, you can follow the instructions at https://docs.conda.io/projects/conda/en/latest/user-guide/tasks/manage-environments.html to create a virtual environment for this project within which Python can be run.

Unlike other methods of installing Python, Anaconda offers an easy-to-navigate interface that also takes care of most low-level processes when Python and its libraries are to be installed.

Following the instructions above, you can create a new environment named **`workshop`** using the command **`conda create -n workshop python=3.7`**. To activate the new environment, run **`conda activate workshop`**. For the next steps, you will need to activate this environment every time you need to test the code.

In this workshop, every time a new library is used that has not already been installed, that library can be installed using the **`pip install [library_name]`** or **`conda install [library_name]`** commands.

PROJECT JUPYTER

Project Jupyter is open source, free software that gives you the ability to run code written in Python and some other languages interactively from a special notebook, similar to a browser interface. It was born in 2014 from the **IPython** project and has since become the default choice for the entire data science workforce.

To install the Jupyter Notebook inside the **`workshop`** environment, just run **`conda install -c conda-forge notebook`**. For more information about Jupyter installation, go here: https://jupyter.org/install.

At https://jupyterlab.readthedocs.io/en/stable/getting_started/starting.html, you will find all the details you need to know how to start the Jupyter Notebook server. In this book, we use the classic notebook interface.

Usually, we start a notebook from the Anaconda Prompt with the **`jupyter notebook`** command.

Start the notebook from the directory where you choose to download the code files to in the following *Installing the Code Bundle* section.

For example, if you have installed the files in the macOS directory **`/Users/YourUserName/Documents/ The-Statistics-and-Calculus-with-Python-Workshop`**, then in the CLI you can type **`cd /Users/YourUserName/Documents/The-Statistics-and-Calculus-with-Python-Workshop`** and run the **`jupyter notebook`** command. The Jupyter server will start and you will see the Jupyter browser console:

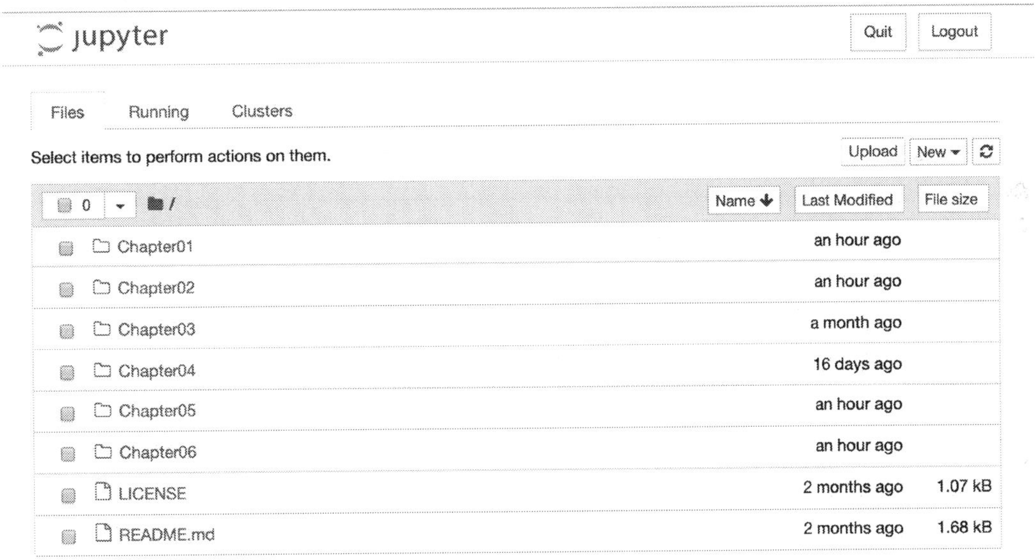

Figure 0.1: Jupyter browser console

Once you are running the Jupyter server, click on **`New`** and choose **`Python 3`**. A new browser tab will open with a new and empty notebook. Rename the Jupyter file:

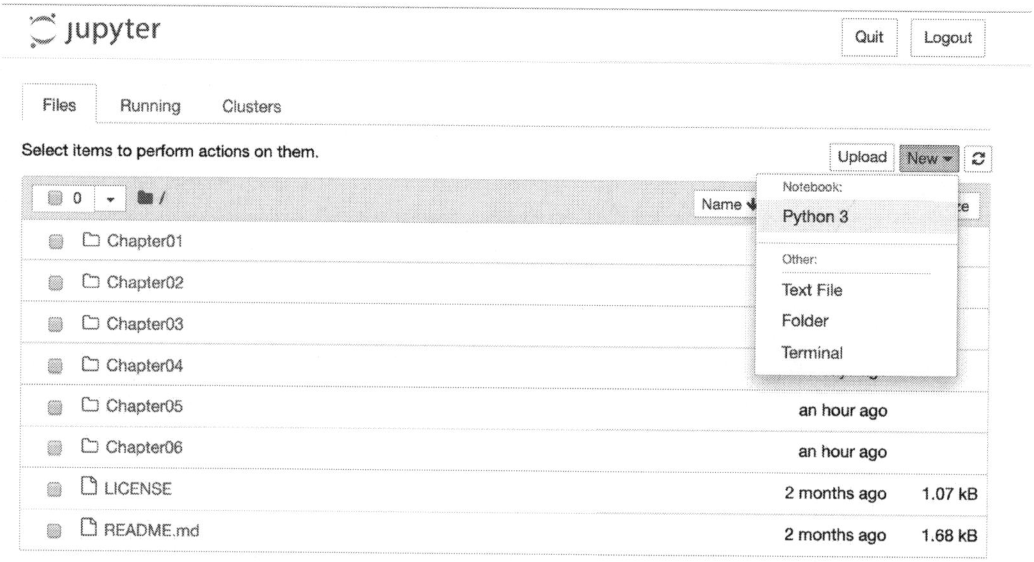

Figure 0.2: Jupyter server interface

The main building blocks of Jupyter notebooks are cells. There are two types of cells: **`In`** (short for input) and **`Out`** (short for output). You can write code, normal text, and Markdown in **`In`** cells, press *Shift* + *Enter* (or *Shift* + *Return*), and the code written in that particular **`In`** cell will be executed. The result will be shown in an **`Out`** cell, and you will land in a new **`In`** cell, ready for the next block of code. Once you get used to this interface, you will slowly discover the power and flexibility it offers.

When you start a new cell, by default, it is assumed that you will write code in it. However, if you want to write text, then you have to change the type. You can do that using the following sequence of keys: *Esc* | *M* | *Enter*. This will convert the selected cell to the **Markdown** (**M**) cell type:

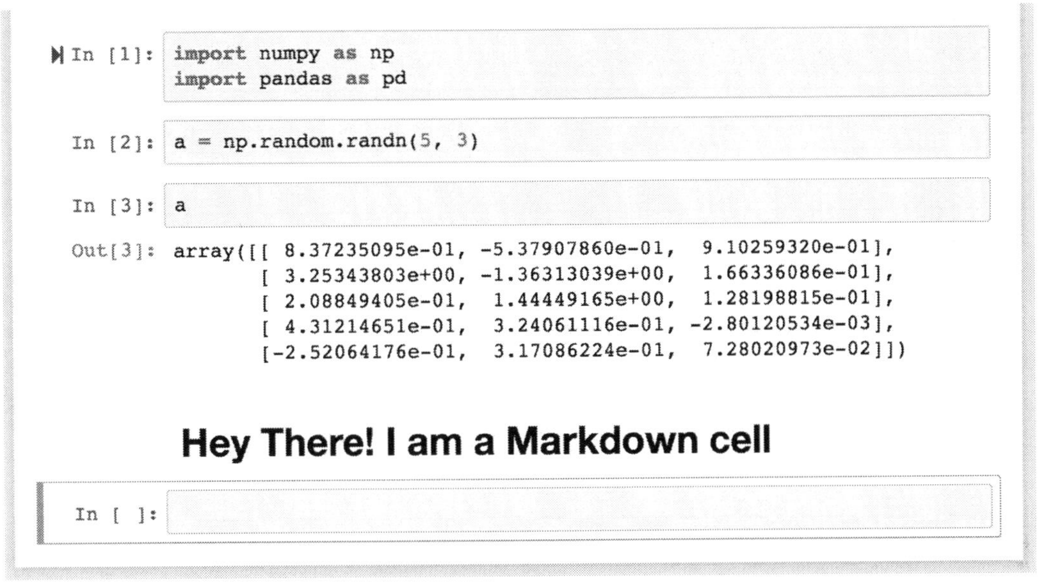

In [1]: import numpy as np
import pandas as pd
In [2]: a = np.random.randn(5, 3)
In [3]: a
Out[3]: array([[8.37235095e-01, -5.37907860e-01, 9.10259320e-01],
[3.25343803e+00, -1.36313039e+00, 1.66336086e-01],
[2.08849405e-01, 1.44449165e+00, 1.28198815e-01],
[4.31214651e-01, 3.24061116e-01, -2.80120534e-03],
[-2.52064176e-01, 3.17086224e-01, 7.28020973e-02]])
Hey There! I am a Markdown cell
In [ ]:

Figure 0.3: Jupyter Notebook

When you are done with writing some text, execute it using *Shift* + *Enter*. Unlike the case with code cells, the result of the compiled Markdown will be shown in the same place as the **`In`** cell.

To get a *cheat sheet* of all the handy key shortcuts in Jupyter, go to https://packt.live/33sJuB6. With this basic introduction, we are ready to embark on an exciting and enlightening journey.

Installing Libraries

`pip` comes pre-installed with Anaconda. Once Anaconda is installed on your machine, all the required libraries can be installed using **`pip`**, for example, **`pip install numpy`**. Alternatively, you can install all the required libraries using **`pip install -r requirements.txt`**. You can find the **`requirements.txt`** file at https://packt.live/3gv0zhb.

The exercises and activities will be executed in Jupyter Notebooks. Jupyter is a Python library and can be installed in the same way as the other Python libraries – that is, with **`pip install jupyter`**, but fortunately, it comes pre-installed with Anaconda. To open a notebook, simply run the command **`jupyter notebook`** in the Terminal or Command Prompt.

ACCESSING THE CODE FILES

You can find the complete code files of this book at https://packt.live/3kcWZe6. You can also run many activities and exercises directly in your web browser by using the interactive lab environment at https://packt.live/2PpqDOX.

We've tried to support interactive versions of all activities and exercises, but we recommend a local installation as well for instances where this support isn't available.

If you have any issues or questions about installation, please email us at **`workshops@packt.com`**.

1

FUNDAMENTALS OF PYTHON

OVERVIEW

This chapter reviews the basic Python data structures and tools that will be used in future discussions. These concepts will allow us to refresh our memory regarding Python's most fundamental and important features, while simultaneously preparing us for advanced topics in later chapters.

By the end of this chapter, you will be able to use control flow methods to design your Python programs and initialize common Python data structures, as well as manipulate their content. You will solidify your understanding of functions and recursion in Python algorithm design. You will also be able to facilitate debugging, testing, and version control for Python programs. Finally, in the activity at the end of this chapter, you will create a Sudoku solver.

INTRODUCTION

Python has enjoyed an unprecedented increase in popularity and usage in recent years, especially in mathematics, which is the main topic of this chapter. However, before we delve into the advanced topics in mathematics, we will need to solidify our understanding of the fundamentals of the language.

This chapter will offer a refresher on the general concepts of Python; the topics covered will allow you to be in the best position for later discussions in this book. Specifically, we will be reviewing elementary concepts in general programming such as conditionals and loops, as well as Python-specific data structures such as lists and dictionaries. We will also discuss functions and the algorithm design process, which is an important part in any medium or large Python project that includes mathematics-related programs. All of this will be done through hands-on exercises and activities.

By the end of this chapter, you will be well positioned to tackle more complex, interesting problems in later chapters of this book.

CONTROL FLOW METHODS

Control flow is a general term that denotes any programming syntax that can redirect the execution of a program. Control flow methods in general are what allow programs to be dynamic in their execution and computation: depending on the current state of a program or its input, the execution of that program and thus its output will dynamically change.

IF STATEMENTS

The most common form of control flow in any programming language is conditionals, or **`if`** statements. **`if`** statements are used to check for a specific condition about the current state of the program and, depending on the result (whether the condition is true or false), the program will execute different sets of instructions.

In Python, the syntax of an **`if`** statement is as follows:

```
if [condition to check]:
    [instruction set to execute if condition is true]
```

Given the readability of Python, you can probably already guess how conditionals work: when the execution of a given program reaches a conditional and checks the condition in the **`if`** statement, if the condition is true, the indented set of instructions *inside* the **`if`** statement will be executed; otherwise, the program will simply skip those instructions and move on.

Within an **`if`** statement, it is possible for us to check for a composite condition, which is a combination of multiple individual conditions. For example, using the **`and`** keyword, the following **`if`** block is executed when both of its conditions are satisfied:

```
if [condition 1] and [condition 2]:
    [instruction set]
```

Instead of doing this, we can use the **`or`** keyword in a composite condition, which will display positive (true) if either the condition to the left or to the right of the keyword is true. It is also possible to keep extending a composite condition with more than one **`and`/`or`** keyword to implement conditionals that are nested on multiple levels.

When a condition is not satisfied, we might want our program to execute a different set of instructions. To implement this logic, we can use **`elif`** and **`else`** statements, which should immediately follow an **`if`** statement. If the condition in the **`if`** statement is not met, our program will move on and evaluate the subsequent conditions in the **`elif`** statements; if none of the conditions are met, any code inside an **`else`** block will be executed. An **`if...elif...else`** block in Python is in the following form:

```
if [condition 1]:
    [instruction set 1]
elif [condition 2]:
    [instruction set 2]
...
elif [condition n]:
    [instruction set n]
else:
    [instruction set n + 1]
```

This control flow method is very valuable when there is a set of possibilities that our program needs to check for. Depending on which possibility is true at a given moment, the program should execute the corresponding instructions.

EXERCISE 1.01: DIVISIBILITY WITH CONDITIONALS

In mathematics, the analysis of variables and their content is very common, and one of the most common analyses is the divisibility of an integer. In this exercise, we will use **if** statements to consider the divisibility of a given number by 5, 6, or 7.

Perform the following steps in order to achieve this:

1. Create a new Jupyter notebook and declare a variable named **x** whose value is any integer, as shown in the following code:

```
x = 130
```

2. After that declaration, write an **if** statement to check whether **x** is divisible by 5 or not. The corresponding code block should print out a statement indicating whether the condition has been met:

```
if x % 5 == 0:
    print('x is divisible by 5')
```

Here, **%** is the modulo operator in Python; the **var % n** expression returns the remainder when we divide the **var** variable by the number, **n**.

3. In the same code cell, write two **elif** statements to check whether **x** is divisible by 6 and 7, respectively. Appropriate **print** statements should be placed under their corresponding conditionals:

```
elif x % 6 == 0:
    print('x is divisible by 6')
elif x % 7 == 0:
    print('x is divisible by 7')
```

4. Write the final **else** statement to print out a message stating that **x** is not divisible by either 5, 6, or 7 (in the same code cell):

```
else:
    print('x is not divisible by 5, 6, or 7')
```

5. Run the program with a different value assigned to **x** each time to test the conditional logic we have. The following output is an example of this with **x** assigned with the value **104832**:

```
x is divisible by 6
```

6. Now, instead of printing out a message about the divisibility of **x**, we would like to write that message to a text file. Specifically, we want to create a file named **output.txt** that will contain the same message that we printed out previously.

   To do this, we can use the **with** keyword together with the **open()** function to interact with the text file. Note that the **open()** function takes in two arguments: the name of the file to write to, which is **output.txt** in our case, and **w** (for write), which specifies that we would like to write to file, as opposed to reading the content from a file:

```
if x % 5 == 0:
    with open('output.txt', 'w') as f:
        f.write('x is divisible by 5')
elif x % 6 == 0:
    with open('output.txt', 'w') as f:
        f.write('x is divisible by 6')
elif x % 7 == 0:
    with open('output.txt', 'w') as f:
        f.write('x is divisible by 7')
else:
    with open('output.txt', 'w') as f:
        f.write('x is not divisible by 5, 6, or 7')
```

7. Check the message in the output text file for its correctness. If the **x** variable still holds the value of **104832**, your text file should have the following contents:

```
x is divisible by 6
```

In this exercise, we applied the usage of conditionals to write a program that determines the divisibility of a given number by 6, 3, and 2 using the `%` operator. We also saw how to write content to a text file in Python. In the next section, we will start discussing loops in Python.

> **NOTE**
>
> The code lines in the **`elif`** block are executed sequentially, and breaks from sequence, when any one of the conditions is true. This implies that when x is assigned the value 30, once **`x%5==0`** is satisfied, **`x%6==0`** is not checked.
>
> To access the source code for this specific section, please refer to https://packt.live/3dNflxO.
>
> You can also run this example online at https://packt.live/2AsqO8w.

LOOPS

Another widely used control flow method is the use of loops. These are used to execute the same set of instructions repeatedly over a specified range or while a condition is met. There are two types of loops in Python: **`while`** loops and **`for`** loops. Let's understand each one in detail.

THE WHILE LOOP

A **`while`** loop, just like an **`if`** statement, checks for a specified condition to determine whether the execution of a given program should keep on looping or not. For example, consider the following code:

```
>>> x = 0
>>> while x < 3:
...     print(x)
...     x += 1
0
1
2
```

In the preceding code, after **x** was initialized with the value **0**, a **while** loop was used to successively print out the value of the variable and increment the same variable at each iteration. As you can imagine, when this program executes, **0**, **1**, and **2** will be printed out and when **x** reaches **3**, the condition specified in the **while** loop is no longer met, and the loop therefore ends.

Note that the **x += 1** command corresponds to **x = x + 1**, which increments the value of **x** during each iteration of the loop. If we remove this command, then we would get an infinite loop printing **0** each time.

THE FOR LOOP

A **for** loop, on the other hand, is typically used to iterate through a specific sequence of values. Using the **range** function in Python, the following code produces the exact same output that we had previously:

```
>>> for x in range(3):
...     print(x)
0
1
2
```

The **in** keyword is the key to any **for** loop in Python: when it is used, the variable in front of it will be assigned values inside the iterator that we'd like to loop through sequentially. In the preceding case, the **x** variable is assigned the values inside the **range(3)** iterator—which are, in order, **0**, **1**, and **2**—at each iteration of the **for** loop.

Instead of **range()**, other types of iterators can also be used in a Python **for** loop. The following table gives a brief summary of some of the most common iterators to be used in **for** loops. Don't worry if you are not familiar with the data structures included in this table; we will cover those concepts later in this chapter:

Iterator	**What is iteratively returned in a for loop**	**Example**
`range(a, b [, step])`	Numbers between `a` (inclusively) and `b` (exclusively), apart from an amount equal to `step` (the default value of which is 1).	`range(1, 6, 2)` will iteratively return `1`, `3`, and `5` in a `for` loop.
A Python list	Elements in the list in order.	`[1, 3, 2, 4]` will iteratively return `1`, `3`, `2`, and `4` in a `for` loop.
A Python tuple	Elements in the tuple in order.	`(1, 3, 2)` will iteratively return `1`, `3`, and `2` in a `for` loop.
A Python dictionary	Keys in the dictionary in order.	`{'a': 1, 'b': 2, 'c': 3}` will iteratively return `'a'`, `'b'`, and `'c'` in a `for` loop.
A Python string	Characters in the string in order.	`'Hello, world!'` will iteratively return `'H'`, `'e'`, `'l'`, ..., `'d'`, and `'!'` in a `for` loop.
A Python set	Elements in the set in any order.	`{1, 3, 2, 4}` might iteratively return `1`, `3`, `2`, and `4` in a `for` loop.
`enumerate(iterator)`	Elements in the `iterator` parameter with their corresponding index.	`enumerate(['a', 'b', 'c'])` will iteratively return `(0, 'a')`, `(1, 'b')`, and `(2, 'c')`.
`zip(a, b, ...)`	Parallel elements in `a`, `b`, ... in tuples, in order.	`zip([1, 3, 2], ('a', 'b', 'c'))` will iteratively return `(1, 'a')`, `(3, 'b')`, and `(2, 'c')` in a `for` loop.

Figure 1.1: List of datasets and their examples

It is also possible to nest multiple loops inside one another. While the execution of a given program is inside a loop, we can use the **break** keyword to exit the current loop and move on with the execution.

EXERCISE 1.02: NUMBER GUESSING GAME

For this exercise, we will put our knowledge of loops to practice and write a simple guessing game. A target integer between 0 and 100 is randomly selected at the beginning of the program. Then, the program will take in user inputs as guesses of what this number is. In response, the program will print out a message saying **Lower** if the guess is greater than the actual target, or **Higher** if the opposite is true. The program should terminate when the user guesses correctly.

Perform the following steps to complete this exercise:

1. In the first cell of a new Jupyter notebook, import the **random** module in Python and use its **randint** function to generate random numbers:

```
import random
true_value = random.randint(0, 100)
```

   Every time the **randint()** function is called, it generates a random integer between the two numbers passed to it; in our case, an integer between 0 and 100 will be generated.

   While they are not needed for the rest of this exercise, if you are curious about other functionalities that the random module offers, you can take a look at its official documentation at https://docs.python.org/3/library/random.html.

> **NOTE**
>
> The rest of the program should also be put in the current code cell.

2. Use the **input()** function in Python to take in the user's input and assign the returned value to a variable (**guess**, in the following code). This value will be interpreted as the guess of what the target is from the user:

```
guess = input('Enter your guess: ')
```

3. Convert the user input into an integer using the **int()** function and check it against the true target. Print out appropriate messages for all possible cases of the comparison:

```
guess = int(guess)

if guess == true_value:
    print('Congratulations! You guessed correctly.')
elif guess > true_value:
    print('Lower.')  # user guessed too high
else:
    print('Higher.')  # user guessed too low
```

> **NOTE**
>
> The # symbol in the code snippet below denotes a code comment. Comments are added into code to help explain specific bits of logic.

4. With our current code, the **int()** function will throw an error and crash the entire program if its input cannot be converted into an integer (for example, when the input is a string character). For this reason, we need to implement the code we have inside a **try...except** block to handle the situation where the user enters a non-numeric value:

```
try:
    if guess == true_value:
        print('Congratulations! You guessed correctly.')
    elif guess > true_value:
        print('Lower.')  # user guessed too high
    else:
        print('Higher.')  # user guessed too low

# when the input is invalid
except ValueError:
    print('Please enter a valid number.')
```

5. As of now, the user can only guess exactly once before the program terminates. To implement the feature that would allow the user to repeatedly guess until they find the target, we will wrap the logic we have developed so far in a **`while`** loop, which will break if and only if the user guesses correctly (implemented by a **`while True`** loop with the **`break`** keyword placed appropriately).

   The complete program should look similar to the following code:

```
import random

true_value = random.randint(0, 100)

while True:
    guess = input('Enter your guess: ')

    try:
        guess = int(guess)

        if guess == true_value:
            print('Congratulations! You guessed correctly.')
            break
        elif guess > true_value:
            print('Lower.')  # user guessed too high
        else:
            print('Higher.')  # user guessed too low

    # when the input is invalid
    except ValueError:
        print('Please enter a valid number.')
```

6. Try rerunning the program by executing the code cell and test out different input options to ensure that the program can process its instructions nicely, as well as handle cases of invalid inputs. For example, the output the program might produce when the target number is randomly selected to be 13 is as follows:

```
Enter your guess: 50
Lower.
Enter your guess: 25
Lower.
Enter your guess: 13
Congratulations! You guessed correctly.
```

In this exercise, we have practiced using a **while** loop in a number guessing game to solidify our understanding of the usage of loops in programming. In addition, you have been introduced to a method of reading in user input and the **random** module in Python.

> **NOTE**
>
> To access the source code for this specific section, please refer to https://packt.live/2BYK6CR.
>
> You can also run this example online at https://packt.live/2CVFbTu.

Next, we will start considering common Python data structures.

DATA STRUCTURES

Data structures are types of variables that represent different forms of information that you might want to create, store, and manipulate in your program. Together with control flow methods, data structures are the other fundamental building block of any programming language. In this section, we will go through some of the most common data structures in Python, starting with strings.

STRINGS

Strings are sequences of characters that are typically used to represent textual information (for example, a message). A Python string is denoted by any given textual data inside either single- or double-quotation marks. For example, in the following code snippet, the **a** and **b** variables hold the same information:

```
a = 'Hello, world!'
b = "Hello, world!"
```

Since strings are roughly treated as sequences in Python, common sequence-related operations can be applied to this data structure. In particular, we can concatenate two or more strings together to create a long-running string, we can iterate through a string using a **for** loop, and individual characters and substrings can be accessed using indexing and slicing. The effects of these operations are demonstrated in the following code:

```
>>> a = 'Hello, '
>>> b = 'world!'
```

```
>>> print(a + b)
Hello, world!

>>> for char in a:
...     print(char)
H
e
l
l
o
,
 # a blank character printed here, the last character in string a

>>> print(a[2])
l

>>> print(a[1: 4])
ell
```

One of the most important features that was added in Python 3.6 was f-strings, a syntax to format strings in Python. Since we are using Python 3.7, we can avail this feature. String formatting is used when we would like to insert the value of a given variable into a predefined string. Before f-strings, there were two other formatting options, which you may be familiar with: %-formatting and **`str.format()`**. Without going into too much detail, these two methods have a few undesirable characteristics, and f-strings was therefore developed to address those problems.

The syntax for f-strings is defined with curly brackets, **`{`** and **`}`**. For example, we can combine the printed value of a variable using an f-string as follows:

```
>>> a = 42
>>> print(f'The value of a is {a}.')
The value of a is 42.
```

When a variable is put inside the f-string curly brackets, its **`__str__()`** representation will be used in the final printed output. This means you can obtain further flexibility with f-strings by overwriting and customizing the dunder method, **`__str__()`**, while working with Python objects.

Common numeric formatting options for strings such as specifying the number of digits after the decimal or datetime formatting can be done in f-strings using the colon, as demonstrated here:

```
>>> from math import pi
>>> print(f'Pi, rounded to three decimal places, is {pi:.3f}.')
Pi, rounded to three decimal places, is 3.142.

>>> from datetime import datetime
>>> print(f'Current time is {datetime.now():%H:%M}.')
Current time is 21:39.
```

Another great thing about f-strings is that they are faster to render and process than the other two string formatting methods. Next, let's discuss Python lists.

LISTS

Lists are arguably the most used data structure in Python. It is Python's own version of an array in Java or C/C++. A list is a sequence of elements that can be accessed or iterated over in order. Unlike, say, Java arrays, elements in a Python list do not have to be of the same data structure, as demonstrated here:

```
>>> a = [1, 'a', (2, 3)]  # a list containing a number, a string, and a tuple
```

> **NOTE**
>
> We'll talk more about tuples in the next section.

As we have discussed previously, elements in a list can be iterated over in a `for` loop in a similar way as characters in a string. Lists can also be indexed and sliced in the same way as strings:

```
>>> a = [1, 'a', (2, 3), 2]
>>> a[2]
(2, 3)
>>> a[1: 3]
['a', (2, 3)]
```

There are two ways to add new elements to a Python list: **append()** inserts a new single element to the end of a list, while list concatenation simply concatenates two or more strings together, as shown here:

```
>>> a = [1, 'a', (2, 3)]
>>> a.append(3)
>>> a
[1, 'a', (2, 3), 3]

>>> b = [2, 5, 'b']
>>> a + b
[1, 'a', (2, 3), 3, 2, 5, 'b']
```

To remove an element from a list, the **pop()** method, which takes in the index of the element to be removed, can be used.

One of the operations that make Python lists unique is list comprehension: a Pythonic syntax to efficiently initialize lists using a **for** loop placed inside square brackets. List comprehension is typically used when we want to apply an operation to an existing list to create a new list. For example, say we have a list variable, **a**, containing some integers:

```
>>> a = [1, 4, 2, 9, 10, 3]
```

Now, we want to create a new list, **b**, whose elements are two times the elements in **a**, in order. We could potentially initialize **b** as an empty list and iteratively loop through **a** and append the appropriate values to **b**. However, with list comprehension, we can achieve the same result with a more elegant syntax:

```
>>> b = [2 * element for element in a]
>>> b
[2, 8, 4, 18, 20, 6]
```

Furthermore, we can even combine conditionals inside a list comprehension to implement complex logic in this process of creating Python lists. For example, to create a list of twice the elements in **a** that are odd numbers, we can do the following:

```
>>> c = [2 * element for element in a if element % 2 == 1]
>>> c
[2, 18, 6]
```

Another Python data structure that is very often contrasted with list is tuple, which we will discuss in the next section. However, before moving forward, let's go through an exercise on a new concept: multi-dimensional lists/arrays.

Multi-dimensional arrays, also known as tables or matrices (and sometimes tensors), are common objects in the field of mathematics and machine learning. Given the fact that elements in a Python list can be any Python objects, we can model arrays that span more than one dimension using lists in a list. Specifically, imagine that, within an overarching Python list, we have three sublists, each having three elements in it. This object can be thought of as a 2D, 3 x 3 table. In general, we can model *n*-dimensional arrays using Python lists that are nested inside other lists *n* times.

EXERCISE 1.03: MULTI-DIMENSIONAL LISTS

In this exercise, we will familiarize ourselves with the concept of multi-dimensional lists and the process of iterating through them. Our goal here is to write logic commands that dynamically display the content of a 2D list.

Perform the following steps to complete this exercise:

1. Create a new Jupyter notebook and declare a variable named **a** in a code cell, as follows:

```
a = [[1, 2, 3], [4, 5, 6], [7, 8, 9]]
```

   This variable represents a 3 x 3 2D table, with the individual sublists in the list representing the rows.

2. In a new code cell, iterate through the rows by looping through the elements in list **a** (do not run the cell just yet):

```
for row in a:
```

3. At each iteration in this **for** loop, a sublist in **a** is assigned to a variable called **row**. We can then access the individual cells in the 2D table by indexing the individual rows. The following **for** loop will print out the first element in each sublist, or in other words, the number in the first cell of each row in the table (**1**, **4**, and **7**):

```
for row in a:
    print(row[0])
```

4. In a new code cell, print out the values of all the cells in table **a** by having a nested **for** loop, whose inner loop will iterate through the sublists in **a**:

```
for row in a:
    for element in row:
        print(element)
```

   This should print out the numbers from 1 to 9, each in a separate row.

5. Finally, in a new cell, we need to print out the diagonal elements of this table in a nicely formatted message. To do this, we can have an indexing variable — **i**, in our case — loop from **0** to **2** to access the diagonal elements of the table:

```
for i in range(3):
    print(a[i][i])
```

Your output should be 1, 5, and 9, each in a separate row.

> **NOTE**
>
> This is because the row index and the column index of a diagonal element in a table/matrix are equal.

6. In a new cell, change the preceding **print** statements using f-strings to format our printed output:

```
for i in range(3):
    print(f'The {i + 1}-th diagonal element is: {a[i][i]}')
```

This should produce the following output:

```
The 1-th diagonal element is: 1
The 2-th diagonal element is: 5
The 3-th diagonal element is: 9
```

In this exercise, we have combined what we have learned about loops, indexing, and f-string formatting to create a program that dynamically iterates through a 2D list.

> **NOTE**
>
> To access the source code for this specific section, please refer to https://packt.live/3dRP8OA.
>
> You can also run this example online at https://packt.live/3gpg4al.

Next, we'll continue our discussion about other Python data structures.

TUPLES

Declared with parentheses instead of square brackets, Python tuples are still sequences of different elements, similar to lists (although the parentheses can be omitted in assignment statements). The main difference between these two data structures is that tuples are immutable objects in Python—this means they cannot be mutated, or changed, in any way after their initialization, as shown here:

```
>>> a = (1, 2)
>>> a[0] = 3  # trying to change the first element
Traceback (most recent call last):
    File "<stdin>", line 1, in <module>
TypeError: 'tuple' object does not support item assignment
>>> a.append(2)  # trying to add another element
Traceback (most recent call last):
    File "<stdin>", line 1, in <module>
AttributeError: 'tuple' object has no attribute 'append'
```

Given this key difference between tuples and lists, we can utilize these data structures accordingly: when we want a sequence of elements to be immutable for any number of reasons (for example, to ensure the logical integrity functions), a tuple can be used; if we allow the sequence to be able to be changed after its initialization, it can be declared as a list.

Next, we will be discussing a common data structure in mathematical computing: sets.

SETS

If you are already familiar with the mathematical concept, the definition of a Python set is essentially the same: a Python set is a collection of unordered elements. A set can be initialized with curly brackets, and a new element can be added to a set using the **add()** method, like so:

```
>>> a = {1, 2, 3}
>>> a.add(4)
>>> a
{1, 2, 3, 4}
```

Since a set is a collection of Python elements, or in other words, an iterator, its elements can still be iterated over using a **for** loop. However, given its definition, there is no guarantee that those elements will be iterated in the same order as they are initialized in or added to the set.

Furthermore, when an element that already exists in a set is added to that set, the statement will have no effect:

```
>>> a
{1, 2, 3, 4}
>>> a.add(3)
>>> a
{1, 2, 3, 4}
```

Taking the union or the intersection of two given sets are the most common set operations and can be achieved via the **`union()`** and **`intersection()`** methods in Python, respectively:

```
>>> a = {1, 2, 3, 4}
>>> b = {2, 5, 6}
>>> a.union(b)
{1, 2, 3, 4, 5, 6}
>>> a.intersection(b)
{2}
```

Finally, to remove a given element from a set, we can use either the **`discard()`** method or the **`remove()`** method. Both remove the item passed to them from a set. However, if the item does not exist in the set, the former will not mutate the set, while the latter will raise an error. Just like tuples and lists, you can choose to use one of these two methods in your program to implement specific logic, depending on your goal.

Moving on, the last Python data structure that we will be discussing in this section is dictionaries.

DICTIONARIES

Python dictionaries are the equivalent of hash maps in Java, where we can specify key-value pair relationships and perform lookups on a key to obtain its corresponding value. We can declare a dictionary in Python by listing out key-value pairs in the form of **`key: value`**, separated by commas inside curly brackets.

For example, a sample dictionary containing students' names mapped to their final scores in a class may look as follows:

```
>>> score_dict = {'Alice': 90, 'Bob': 85, 'Carol': 86}
>>> score_dict
{'Alice': 90, 'Bob': 85, 'Carol': 86}
```

In this case, the names of the students (**'Alice'**, **'Bob'**, and **'Carol'**) are the keys of the dictionary, while their respective scores are the values that the keys are mapped to. A key cannot be used to map to multiple different values. The value of a given key can be accessed by passing the key to the dictionary inside square brackets:

```
>>> score_dict['Alice']
90
>>> score_dict['Carol']
86
>>> score_dict['Chris']
Traceback (most recent call last):
  File "<stdin>", line 1, in <module>
KeyError: 'Chris'
```

Note that in the last statement in the preceding snippet, **'Chris'** is not a key in the dictionary, so when we attempt to access its value, **KeyError** is returned by the Python interpreter.

Changing the value of an existing key or adding a new key-value pair to an existing dictionary can be done using the same syntax:

```
>>> score_dict['Alice'] = 89
>>> score_dict
{'Alice': 89, 'Bob': 85, 'Carol': 86}
>>> score_dict['Chris'] = 85
>>> score_dict
{'Alice': 89, 'Bob': 85, 'Carol': 86, 'Chris': 85}
```

Similar to list comprehension, a Python dictionary can be declared using dictionary comprehension. For instance, the following statement initializes a dictionary mapping integers from **-1** to **1** (inclusively) to their respective squares:

```
>>> square_dict = {i: i ** 2 for i in range(-1, 2)}
>>> square_dict
{-1: 1, 0: 0, 1: 1}
```

As we can see, this dictionary contains the key-value pairs **x** – **x ** 2** for every **x** between **-1** and **1**, which was done by placing the **for** loop inside the initialization of the dictionary.

To delete a key-value pair from a dictionary, we would need to use the **del** keyword. Say we would like to delete the **'Alice'** key and its corresponding value. We would do this like so:

```
>>> del score_dict['Alice']
```

Attempting to access a deleted key will cause the Python interpreter to raise an error:

```
>>> score_dict['Alice']
KeyError: 'Alice'
```

One of the most important aspects of Python dictionaries to keep in mind is the fact that only immutable objects can be dictionary keys. In the examples so far, we have seen strings and numbers as dictionary keys. Lists, which can be mutated and changed after initialization, cannot be used as dictionary keys; tuples, on the other hand, can.

EXERCISE 1.04: SHOPPING CART CALCULATIONS

In this exercise, we will use the dictionary data structure to build a skeletal version of a shopping application. This will allow us to review and further understand the data structure and the operations that can be applied to it.

Perform the following steps to complete this exercise:

1. Create a new Jupyter notebook and declare a dictionary representing any given items available for purchase and their respective prices in the first code cell. Here, we'll add three different types of laptops with their prices in dollars:

```
prices = {'MacBook 13': 1300, 'MacBook 15': 2100, \
          'ASUS ROG': 1600}
```

> **NOTE**
>
> The code snippet shown here uses a backslash (\ ) to split the logic across multiple lines. When the code is executed, Python will ignore the backslash, and treat the code on the next line as a direct continuation of the current line.

2. In the next cell, initialize a dictionary representing our shopping cart. The dictionary should be empty at the beginning, but it should map an item in the cart to how many copies are to be purchased:

```
cart = {}
```

3. In a new cell, write a **while True** loop that represents each step of the shopping process and asks the user whether they would like to continue shopping or not. Use conditionals to handle different cases of the input (you can leave the case where the user wants to continue shopping until the next step):

```
while True:
    _continue = input('Would you like to continue '\
                      'shopping? [y/n]: ')

    if _continue == 'y':
        ...
    elif _continue == 'n':
        break
    else:
        print('Please only enter "y" or "n".')
```

4. Inside the first conditional case, take in another user input to ask which item should be added to the cart. Use conditionals to increment the count of the item in the **cart** dictionary or handle invalid cases:

```
    if _continue == 'y':
        print(f'Available products and prices: {prices}')
        new_item = input('Which product would you like to '\
                         'add to your cart? ')

        if new_item in prices:
            if new_item in cart:
                cart[new_item] += 1
            else:
                cart[new_item] = 1
        else:
            print('Please only choose from the available products.')
```

5. In the next cell, loop through the **cart** dictionary and calculate the total amount of money the user has to pay (by looking up the quantity and price of each item in the cart):

```
# Calculation of total bill.
running_sum = 0
for item in cart:
    running_sum += cart[item] * prices[item]  # quantity times price
```

6. Finally, in a new cell, print out the items in the cart and their respective amount in different lines via a **for** loop and at the end the total bill. Use an f-string to format the printed output:

```
print(f'Your final cart is:')
for item in cart:
    print(f'- {cart[item]} {item}(s)')
print(f'Your final bill is: {running_sum}')
```

7. Run the program and experiment with different carts to ensure our program is correct. For example, if you were to add two MacBook 13s and one ASUS ROG to my shopping cart and stop, the corresponding output would be as follows:

```
In [5]: print(f'Your final cart is:')
        for item in cart:
            print(f'- {cart[item]} {item}(s)')
        print(f'Your final bill is: {running_sum}')

        Your final cart is:
        - 2 MacBook 13(s)
        - 1 ASUS ROG(s)
        Your final bill is: 4200
```

Figure 1.2: Output of the shopping cart application

And that concludes our shopping cart exercise, through which we have familiarized ourselves with the use of dictionaries to look up information. We have also reviewed the use of conditionals and loops to implement control flow methods in a Python program.

> **NOTE**
>
> To access the source code for this specific section, please refer to https://packt.live/2C1Ra1C.
>
> You can also run this example online at https://packt.live/31F7QXg.

In the next section, we will discuss two integral components of any complex program: functions and algorithms.

FUNCTIONS AND ALGORITHMS

While functions denote a specific object in Python programming with which we can order and factor our programs, the term *algorithm* typically refers to the general organization of a sequence of logic to process its given input data. In data science and scientific computing, algorithms are ubiquitous, commonly taking the form of machine learning models that are used to process data and potentially make predictions.

In this section, we will discuss the concept and syntax of Python functions and then tackle some example algorithm-design problems.

FUNCTIONS

In its most abstract definition, a function is simply an object that can take in an input and producing an output, according to a given set of instructions. A Python function is of the following form:

```
def func_name(param1, param2, ...):
    [...]
    return [...]
```

The **def** keyword denotes the start of a Python function. The name of a function can be anything, though the rule is to avoid special characters at the beginning of the name and to use snake case. Between the parentheses are the parameters that the function takes in, which are separated by commas and can be used inside the indented code of the function.

For example, the following function takes in a string (though this requirement is unspecified) and prints out a greeting message:

```
>>> def greet(name):
...     print(f'Hello, {name}!')
```

Then, we can call this function on any string that we want and achieve the effect that we intended with the instruction inside the function. If we somehow mis-specify the arguments that a function takes in (for example, the last statement in the following code snippet), the interpreter will return an error:

```
>>> greet('Quan')
Hello, Quan!
>>> greet('Alice')
Hello, Alice!
>>> greet()
Traceback (most recent call last):
  File "<stdin>", line 1, in <module>
TypeError: greet() missing 1 required positional argument: 'name'
```

It is important to note that any local variables (variables declared inside a function) cannot be used outside of the scope of the function. In other words, once a function finishes its execution, none of its variables will be accessible by other code.

Most of the time, we would want our functions to return some sort of value at the end, which is facilitated by the **`return`** keyword. As soon as a **`return`** statement is executed, the execution of a program will exit out of a given function and return to the parent scope that called the function. This allows us to design a number of dynamic logic sequences.

For example, imagine a function that takes in a Python list of integers and returns the first element that is divisible by 2 (and returns **`False`** if there is no even element in the list):

```
def get_first_even(my_list):
    [...]
    return  # should be the first even element
```

Now, the natural way to write this function is to loop through the elements in the list and check for their **2**-divisibility:

```
def get_first_even(my_list):
    for item in my_list:
        if item % 2 == 0:
            [...]
    return  # should be the first even element
```

However, if and when the condition is met (that is, when the current element we are iterating over is divisible by **2**), that very element should be the return value of the function, since it is the first element in the list that is divisible by **2**. This means we can actually return it within the **`if`** block (and finally return **`False`** at the end of the function):

```
def get_first_even(my_list):
    for item in my_list:
        if item % 2 == 0:
            return item
    return False
```

This approach is to be contrasted with an alternative version where we only return the element that satisfies our condition at the end of the loop, which will be more time-consuming (execution-wise) and require an additional check as to whether there is an even element in the input list. We will examine a variation of this logic in depth in the next exercise.

EXERCISE 1.05: FINDING THE MAXIMUM

Finding the maximum/minimum of an array, or list, is a common exercise in any introductory programming class. In this exercise, we will consider an elevated version of the problem, in which we need to write a function that returns the index and the actual value of the maximum element within a list (if tie-breaking is needed, we return the last maximum element).

Perform the following steps to complete this exercise:

1. Create a new Jupyter notebook and declare the general structure of our target function in a code cell:

```
def get_max(my_list):
    ...

    return ...
```

2. Create a variable that keeps track of the index of the current maximum element called **running_max_index**, which should be initialized to **0**:

```
def get_max(my_list):
    running_max_index = 0

    ...

    return ...
```

3. Loop through the values in the parameter list and their corresponding indices using a **for** loop and the **enumerate** operation:

```
def get_max(my_list):
    running_max_index = 0

    # Iterate over index-value pairs.
    for index, item in enumerate(my_list):
        [...]

    return ...
```

4. At each step of the iteration, check to see if the current element is greater than or equal to the element corresponding to the running indexing variable. If that is the case, assign the index of the current element to the running maximum index:

```
def get_max(my_list):
    running_max_index = 0

    # Iterate over index-value pairs.
    for index, item in enumerate(my_list):
        if item >= my_list[running_max_index]:
            running_max_index = index

    return [...]
```

5. Finally, return the running maximum index and its corresponding value as a tuple:

```
def get_max(my_list):
    running_max_index = 0

    # Iterate over index-value pairs.
    for index, item in enumerate(my_list):
        if item >= my_list[running_max_index]:
            running_max_index = index
    return running_max_index, my_list[running_max_index]
```

6. In a new cell, call this function on various lists to test for different cases. An example of this is as follows:

```
>>> get_max([1, 3, 2])
(1, 3)
>>>  get_max([1, 3, 56, 29, 100, 99, 3, 100, 10, 23])
(7, 100)
```

This exercise helped us review the general syntax of a Python function and also offered a refresher on looping. Furthermore, variations of the logic that we considered are commonly found in scientific computing projects (for example, finding the minimum or an element in an iterator that satisfies some given conditions).

> **NOTE**
>
> To access the source code for this specific section, please refer to https://packt.live/2Zu6KuH.
>
> You can also run this example online at https://packt.live/2BUNjDk.

Next, let's discuss a very specific style of function design called *recursion*.

RECURSION

The term **recursion** in programming denotes the style of solving a problem using functions by having a function recursively call itself. The idea is that each time the function is called, its logic will take a small step toward the solution of the problem, and by doing this many times, the original problem will be finally solved. The idea is that if we somehow have a way to translate our problem into a small one that can be solved in the same way, we can repeatedly break down the problem to arrive at the base case and ensure that the original, bigger problem is solved.

Consider the problem of computing the sum of *n* integers. If we somehow already have the sum of the first *n - 1* integers, then we can simply add the last number to that sum to compute the total sum of the *n* numbers. But how can the sum of the first *n - 1* numbers be computed? With recursion, we once again assume that if we have the sum of the first *n - 2* numbers, then we add in that last number. This process repeats until we reach the first number in the list, and the whole process completes.

Let's consider this function in the following example:

```
>>> def find_sum(my_list):
...     if len(my_list) == 1:
...             return my_list[0]
...     return find_sum(my_list[: -1]) + my_list[-1]
```

We can see that, in the general case, the function computes and returns the result of adding the last element of the input list, **`my_list[-1]`**, to the sum of the sublist without this last element **`my_list[: -1]`**, which is in turn computed by the **`find_sum()`** function itself. Again, we rationalize that if the **`find_sum()`** function can somehow solve the problem of summing a list in a smaller case, we can generalize the result to any given non-empty list.

Handling the base case is therefore an integral part of any recursive algorithm. Here, our base case is when the input list is a single-valued one (checked by our **`if`** statement), in which case we should simply return that very element in the list.

We can see that this function correctly computes the sum of any non-empty list of integers, as shown here:

```
>>> find_sum([1, 2, 3])
6
>>> find_sum([1])
1
```

This is a somewhat basic example, as finding the sum of a list can be easily done by maintaining a running sum and using a `for` loop to iterate over all the elements in the input list. In fact, most of the time, recursion is less efficient than iteration, as there is significant overhead in repeatedly calling function after function in a program.

However, there are situations, as we will see in the following exercise, where, by abstracting our approach to a problem to a recursive algorithm, we can significantly simplify how the problem is solved.

EXERCISE 1.06: THE TOWER OF HANOI

The Tower of Hanoi is a well-known mathematical problem and a classic application of recursion. The problem statement is as follows.

There are three disk stacks where disks can be placed in and n disks, all of different sizes. At the beginning, the disks are stacked in ascending order (the largest at the bottom) in one single stack. At each step of the game, we can take the top disk of one stack and put it at the top of another stack (which can be an empty stack) with the condition that no disk can be placed on top of a disk that is smaller than it.

We are asked to compute the minimum number of moves necessary to move the entire stack of n disk from one stack to another. While the problem can be quite complex if we think about it in a linear way, it becomes simpler when we employ a recursive algorithm.

Specifically, in order to move the n disks, we need to move the top $n - 1$ disks to another stack, move the bottom, biggest disk to the last stack, and finally move the $n - 1$ disks in the other stack to the same stack as the biggest disk. Now, imagine we can compute the minimum number of steps taken to move $(n - 1)$ disks from one stack to another, denoted as $S(n - 1)$, then to move n disks, we need $2\ S(n - 1) + 1$ steps.

That is the recursively analytical solution to the problem. Now, let's write a function to actually compute this quantity for any given n.

Perform the following steps to complete this exercise:

1. In a new Jupyter notebook, define a function that takes in an integer named **n** and returns the quantity that we arrived at previously:

```
def solve(n):
    return 2 * solve(n - 1) + 1
```

2. Create a conditional in the function to handle the base case where **n = 1** (note that it only takes one step to move a single disk):

```
def solve(n):
    if n == 1:
        return 1

    return 2 * solve(n - 1) + 1
```

3. In a different cell, call the function on different inputs to verify that the function returns the correct analytical solution to the problem, which is $2^n - 1$:

```
>>> print(solve(3) == 2 ** 3 - 1)
True
>>> print(solve(6) == 2 ** 6 - 1)
True
```

Here, we are using the **==** operator to compare two values: the returned value from our **solve()** function and the analytical expression of the solution. If they are equal, we should see the Boolean **True** printed out, which is the case for both comparisons we have here.

While the code in this exercise is short, it has illustrated the point that recursion can offer elegant solutions to a number of problems and has hopefully solidified our understanding of the procedure of a recursive algorithm (with the general step and a base case).

> **NOTE**
>
> To access the source code for this specific section, please refer to https://packt.live/2NMrGrk.
>
> You can also run this example online at https://packt.live/2AnAP6R.

With that, we'll move on and start discussing the general process of algorithm design in the next section.

ALGORITHM DESIGN

Designing algorithms is actually something that we have been doing all along, especially in this section, which is all about functions and algorithms: discussing what a functional object should take in, how it should process that input, and what output it should return at the end of its execution. In this section, we will briefly discuss some practices in a general algorithm-design procedure and then consider a somewhat complex problem called the *N-Queens problem* as an exercise.

While writing Python functions, some programmers might choose to implement subfunctions (functions within other functions). Following the idea of encapsulation in software development, a subfunction should be implemented when it is only called by instructions within another function. If this is the case, the first function can be viewed as a helper function of the second and therefore should be placed *inside* that second function. This form of encapsulation allows us to be more organized with our programs/code and ensure that if a piece of code does not need to use the logic within a given function, then it should not have access to it.

The next point of discussion involves recursive search algorithms, which we'll look at in the next exercise. Specifically, when an algorithm is recursively trying to find a valid solution to a given problem, it can reach a state in which there are no valid solutions (for example, when we are trying to find an even element in a list of only odd integers). This leads to the need for a way to indicate that we have reached an invalid state.

In our find-the-first-even-number example, we chose to return **`False`** to indicate an invalid state where our input list only consists of odd numbers. Returning some sort of flag such as **`False`** or `0` is actually a common practice that we will follow in later examples in this chapter as well.

With that in mind, let's jump into the exercise of this section.

EXERCISE 1.07: THE N-QUEENS PROBLEM

Another classic algorithm-design problem in mathematics and computer science, the N-Queens problem asks us to place *n* queen pieces in the game of chess on an *n* x *n* chessboard so that no queen piece can attack another. A queen can attack another piece if they share the same row, column, or diagonal, so the problem is essentially finding a combination of locations for the queen pieces so that any two given queens are in different rows, columns, and diagonals.

For this exercise, we will design a *backtracking* algorithm that searches for a valid solution to this problem for any positive integer, *n*. The algorithm is as follows:

1. Given the requirements of the problem, we argue that in order to place *n* pieces, each row of the chessboard needs to include exactly one piece.
2. For each row, we iteratively go through all the cells of that row and check to see whether a new queen piece can be placed in a given cell:

   a. If such a cell exists, we place a piece in that cell and move on to the next row.

   b. If a new queen piece cannot be placed in any cell in the current row, we know that we have reached an invalid state and thus return **`False`**.
3. We repeat this process until a valid solution is found.

The following diagram describes how this algorithm works with *n = 4*:

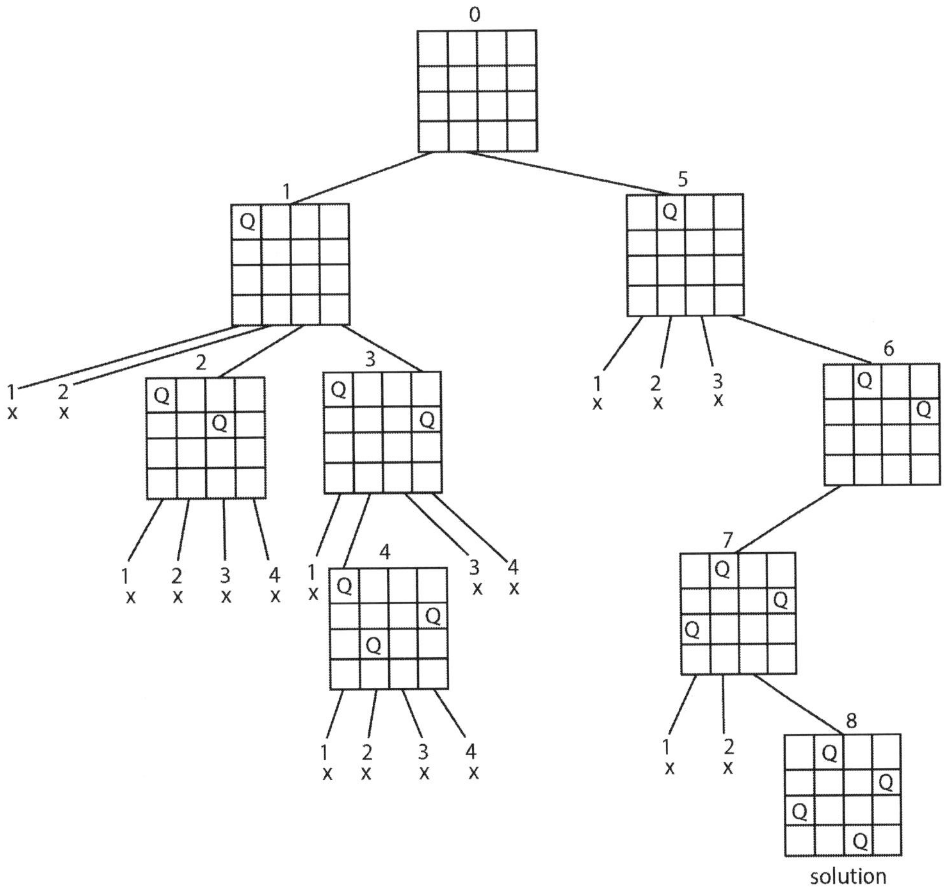

Figure 1.3: Recursion with the N-Queens problem

Now, let's actually implement the algorithm:

1. Create a new Jupyter notebook. In its first cell, declare a variable named **N** to represent the size of our chessboard, as well as the number of queen pieces we need to place on the board:

```
N = 8
```

2. A chessboard will be represented as a 2D, *n* x *n* list with 0 representing an empty cell and 1 representing a cell with a queen piece. Now, in a new code cell, implement a function that takes in a list of this form and print it out in a nice format:

```
# Print out the board in a nice format.
def display_solution(board):
    for i in range(N):
        for j in range(N):
            print(board[i][j], end=' ')
        print()
```

   Note that the **end=' '** argument in our **print** statement specifies that instead of ending the printed output with a newline character, it should simply be a space character. This is so that we can print out the cells in the same row using different **print** statements.

3. In the next cell, write a function that takes in a board, a row number, and a column number. The function should check to see whether a new queen piece can be placed on this board at the location given by the row and column numbers.

   Note that since we are iteratively placing pieces rows to rows, each time we check to see whether a new piece can be placed at a given location, we only need to check for the rows above the location:

```
# Check if a queen can be placed in the position.
def check_next(board, row, col):
    # Check the current column.
    for i in range(row):
        if board[i][col] == 1:
            return False

    # Check the upper-left diagonal.
    for i, j in zip(range(row, -1, -1), \
                    range(col, -1, -1)):
```

```
        if board[i][j] == 1:
            return False

    # Check the upper-right diagonal.
    for i, j in zip(range(row, -1, -1), \
                    range(col, N)):
        if board[i][j] == 1:
            return False

    return True
```

4. In the same code cell, implement a function that takes in a board and a row number. This function should go through all the cells in the given row and check to see whether a new queen piece can be placed at a particular cell (using the **check_next()** function written in the preceding step).

   For such a cell, place a queen in that cell (by changing the cell value to **1**) and recursively call the function itself with the next row number. If a final solution is valid, return **True**; otherwise, remove the queen piece from the cell (by changing it back to **0**).

   If, after we have considered all the cells of the given row, no valid solution is found, return **False** to indicate an **invalid** state. The function should also have a conditional at the beginning to check for whether the row number is larger than the board size **N**, in which case we simply return **True** to indicate that we have reached a valid final solution:

```
def recur_generate_solution(board, row_id):
    # Return if we have reached the last row.
    if row_id >= N:
        return True

    # Iteratively try out cells in the current row.
    for i in range(N):
        if check_next(board, row_id, i):
            board[row_id][i] = 1

            # Return if a valid solution is found.
            final_board = recur_generate_solution(\
                board, row_id + 1)
```

```
            if final_board:
                return True

            board[row_id][i] = 0

    # When the current board has no valid solutions.
    return False
```

5. In the same code cell, write a final solver function that wraps around the two functions, **`check_next()`** and **`recur_generate_solution()`** (in other words, the two functions should be subfunctions of the function we are writing). The function should initialize an empty 2D *n* x *n* list (representing the chessboard) and call the **`recur_generate_solution()`** function with row number 0.

   The function should also print out the solution at the end:

```
# Generate a valid solution.
def generate_solution():
    # Check if a queen can be placed in the position.
    def check_next(board, row, col):
        [...]

    # Recursively generate a solution.
    def recur_generate_solution(board, row_id):
        [...]

    # Start out with en empty board.
    my_board = [[0 for _ in range(N)] for __ in range(N)]
    final_solution = recur_generate_solution(my_board, 0)

    # Display the final solution.
    if final_solution is False:
        print('A solution cannot be found.')
    else:
        print('A solution was found.')
        display_solution(my_board)
```

6. In a different code cell, run the overarching function from the preceding step to generate and print out a solution:

```
>>> generate_solution()
A solution was found.
1 0 0 0 0 0 0 0
0 0 0 0 1 0 0 0
0 0 0 0 0 0 0 1
0 0 0 0 0 1 0 0
0 0 1 0 0 0 0 0
0 0 0 0 0 0 1 0
0 1 0 0 0 0 0 0
0 0 0 1 0 0 0 0
```

Throughout this exercise, we have implemented a backtracking algorithm that is designed to search for a valid solution by iteratively making a move toward a potential solution (placing a queen piece in a safe cell), and if the algorithm somehow reaches an invalid state, it will *backtrack* by undoing its previous move (in our case, by removing the last piece we placed) and looking for a new move to make. As you can probably tell, backtracking is closely related to recursion, and that is why we chose to implement our algorithm using a recursive function, thus consolidating our understanding of the general concept.

> **NOTE**
>
> To access the source code for this specific section, please refer to https://packt.live/2Bn7nyt.
>
> You can also run this example online at https://packt.live/2ZrKRMQ.

In the next and final section of this chapter, we will consider a number of administrative tasks in Python programming that are often overlooked, namely debugging, testing, and version control.

TESTING, DEBUGGING, AND VERSION CONTROL

It is important to note that, in programming, the actual task of writing code is not the only element of the process. There are other administrative procedures that play important roles in the pipeline that are often overlooked. In this section, we will discuss each task one by one and consider the process of implementing them in Python, starting with testing.

TESTING

In order to make sure that a piece of software that we have written works as we intended and produces correct results, it is necessary to put it through specific tests. In software development, there are numerous types of testing that we can apply to a program: integration testing, regression testing, system testing, and so on. One of the most common is unit testing, which is our topic of discussion in this section.

Unit testing denotes the focus on individual small units of the software, as opposed to the entire program. Unit testing is typically the first step of a testing pipeline—once we are reasonably confident that the individual components of our program are working correctly, we can move on to test how these components work together and see whether they produce the results we want (with integration or system testing).

Unit testing in Python can be easily implemented using the **`unittest`** module. Taking an object-oriented approach, **`unittest`** allows us to design tests for our programs as Python classes, making the process more modular. Such a class needs to inherit from the **`TestCase`** class from **`unittest`**, and individual tests are to be implemented in separate functions, as follows:

```
import unittest


class SampleTest(unittest.TestCase):
    def test_equal(self):
        self.assertEqual(2 ** 3 - 1, 7)
        self.assertEqual('Hello, world!', 'Hello, ' + 'world!')

    def test_true(self):
        self.assertTrue(2 ** 3 < 3 ** 2)
        for x in range(10):
            self.assertTrue(- x ** 2 <= 0)
```

In the **SampleTest** class, we placed two test cases where we want to check whether two given quantities are equal or not using the **assertEqual()** method in the **test_equal()** function. Here, we test whether $2^3 - 1$ is indeed equal to 7, and whether string concatenation in Python is correct.

Similarly, the **assertTrue()** methods used in the **test_true()** function test for whether the given parameter is evaluated **True** or not. Here, we test whether 2^3 is less than 3^2, and whether the negative of perfect squares of integers between 0 and 10 are non-positive.

To run the tests we have implemented, we can use the following statement:

```
>>> unittest.main()
test_equal (__main__.SampleTest) ... ok
test_true (__main__.SampleTest) ... ok

----------------------------------------------------------------------
Ran 2 tests in 0.001s

OK
```

The produced output tells us that both of our tests returned positive. One important side note to keep in mind is that if you are running a unit test in a Jupyter notebook, the last statement needs to be as follows:

```
unittest.main(argv=[''], verbosity=2, exit=False)
```

As a result of the fact that the unit tests are to be implemented as functions in a Python class, the **unittest** module also offers two convenient methods, **setUp()** and **tearDown()**, which are to be run automatically before and after each test, respectively. We will see an example of this in our next exercise. For now, we will move on and talk about debugging.

DEBUGGING

The term *debugging* literally means the removal of one or many bugs from a given computer program, thus making it work correctly. In most cases, a debugging process follows a failed test where it is determined that there is a bug in our program. Then, to debug the program, we need to identify the source of the error that caused the test to fail and attempt to fix the code related to that error.

There are multiple forms of debugging that a program might employ. These include the following:

- **Print debugging**: Arguably one of the most common and elementary methods of debugging, print debugging involves identifying the variables that might play a role in causing the bug, placing `print` statements for those variables at various places in our program so that we can track the changes in the values of those variables. Once a change in the value of a variable is found to be undesirable or unwanted, we look at where specifically that `print` statement is in the program and therefore (roughly) identify the location of the bug.
- **Logging**: If instead of printing the values of our variables to standard output, we decide to write the output to a log file, this is called logging. Logging is often done to keep track of specific events taking place in the execution of the program we are debugging or simply monitoring.
- **Tracing**: To debug a program, we, in this case, will follow the low-level function calls and execution stack of the program when it executes. By looking at the order in which variables and functions are used from that low-level perspective, we can identify the source of the error as well. Tracing can be implemented in Python using the `sys.settrace()` method from the `sys` module.

In Python, it is quite easy to employ print debugging, as we simply need to use `print` statements. For more complex functionalities, we can use a debugger, a module/library that is specifically designed for debugging purposes. The most dominant debugger in Python is the built-in `pdb` module, which used to be run via the `pdb.set_trace()` method.

Starting from Python 3.7, we can opt for a simpler syntax by placing calls to the built-in `breakpoint()` function. At each place where a `breakpoint()` function is called, the execution of the program will pause and allow us to inspect the behavior and current characteristics of the program, including the values of its variables.

Specifically, once the execution of the program reaches a **`breakpoint()`** function, an input prompt will appear, where we can enter a **`pdb`** command. There are many commands that you can take advantage of that are included in the documentation of the module. Some notable commands are as follows:

- **`h`**: For *help*, which prints out the complete list of commands you can use.
- **`u/d`**: For *up* and *down*, respectively, which move the running frame count one level in a direction.
- **`s`**: For *step*, which executes the instruction that the program is currently at and pauses at the first possible place in the execution. This command is very useful in terms of observing the immediate effect of a line of code on the state of the program.
- **`n`**: For *next*, which executes the instruction that the program is currently at and only pauses at the next instruction in the current function and when the execution is returned. This command works somewhat similarly to **`s`**, though it skips through instructions at a much higher rate.
- **`r`**: For *return*, which continues the execution until the current function returns.
- **`c`**: For *continue*, which continues the execution until the next **`breakpoint()`** statement is reached.
- **`ll`**: For *longlist*, which prints out the source code for the current instruction.
- **`p [expression]`**: For *print*, which evaluates and prints out the value of the given expression

Overall, once the execution of a program is paused by a **`breakpoint()`** statement, we can utilize a combination of the preceding different commands to inspect the state of the program and identify a potential bug. We'll look at an example of this in the following exercise.

EXERCISE 1.08: TESTING FOR CONCURRENCY

In this exercise, we will consider a well-known bug in concurrency- or parallelism-related programs called a *race condition*. This will serve as a nice use case to try out our testing and debugging tools. Since the integration of **pdb** and other debugging tools is still underdeveloped in Jupyter Notebooks, we will be working with **.py** scripts in this exercise.

Perform the following steps to complete this exercise:

1. The setup of our program (which is implemented in the following steps) is as follows. We have a class that implements a counter object that can be manipulated by multiple threads in parallel. The value of an instance of this counter object (stored in its **value** attribute, initialized to **0**) is incremented every time its **update()** method is called. The counter also has a target that its value should be incremented to. When its **run()** method is called, multiple threads will be spawned. Each thread will call the **update()** method, thus incrementing its **value** attribute a number of times that is equal to the original target. In theory, the final value of the counter should be the same as the target, but we will see that this is not the case due to a race condition. Our goal is to apply **pdb** to track the changes of variables inside this program to analyze this race condition.

2. Create a new **.py** script and enter the following code:

```
import threading
import sys; sys.setswitchinterval(10 ** -10)

class Counter:
    def __init__(self, target):
        self.value = 0
        self.target = target
    def update(self):
        current_value = self.value
        # breakpoint()
        self.value = current_value + 1

    def run(self):
        threads = [threading.Thread(target=self.update) \
                                   for _ in range(self.target)]
        for t in threads:
            t.start()
```

```
    for t in threads:
        t.join()
```

This code implements the **Counter** class that we discussed earlier. Note that there is a line of code that sets the switch interval of our system; we will discuss this later.

3. With the hope that the value of a **counter** object should be incremented to its true target, we will test its performance with three different target values. In the same **.py** script, enter the following code to implement our unit tests:

```
import unittest

class TestCounter(unittest.TestCase):
    def setUp(self):
        self.small_params = 5
        self.med_params = 5000
        self.large_params = 10000

    def test_small(self):
        small_counter = Counter(self.small_params)
        small_counter.run()
        self.assertEqual(small_counter.value, \
                         self.small_params)

    def test_med(self):
        med_counter = Counter(self.med_params)
        med_counter.run()
        self.assertEqual(med_counter.value, \
                         self.med_params)

    def test_large(self):
        large_counter = Counter(self.large_params)
        large_counter.run()
        self.assertEqual(large_counter.value, \
                         self.large_params)


    if __name__ == '__main__':
        unittest.main()
```

Here, we can see that in each testing function, we initialize a new **`counter`** object, run it, and finally compare its value with the true target. The targets for the test cases are declared in the **`setUp()`** method, which, as we mentioned previously, is run before the tests are carried out:

```
Run this Python script:test_large (__main__.TestCounter) ... FAIL
test_med (__main__.TestCounter) ... FAIL
test_small (__main__.TestCounter) ... ok

======================================================================
FAIL: test_large (__main__.TestCounter)
----------------------------------------------------------------------
Traceback (most recent call last):
    File "<ipython-input-57-4ed47b9310ba>", line 22, in test_large
    self.assertEqual(large_counter.value, self.large_params)
AssertionError: 9996 != 10000

======================================================================
FAIL: test_med (__main__.TestCounter)
----------------------------------------------------------------------
Traceback (most recent call last):
    File "<ipython-input-57-4ed47b9310ba>", line 17, in test_med
    self.assertEqual(med_counter.value, self.med_params)
AssertionError: 4999 != 5000

----------------------------------------------------------------------
Ran 3 tests in 0.890s

FAILED (failures=2)
```

As you can see, the program failed at two tests: **`test_med`** (where the final value of the counter was only 4,999 instead of 5,000) and **`test_large`** (where the value was 9,996 instead of 10,000). It is possible that you might obtain a different output.

4. Rerun this code cell multiple times to see that the result might vary.

5. Now that we know there is a bug in our program, we will attempt to debug it. Reimplement our **Counter** class by placing a **breakpoint()** statement between the two instructions in the **update()** method, as shown in the following code, and rerun the code cell:

```
class Counter:
    ...

    def update(self):
        current_value = self.value
        breakpoint()
        self.value = current_value + 1

    ...
```

6. In the main scope of our Python script, comment out the call to the unit tests. Instead, declare a new **counter** object and run the script using the Terminal:

```
sample_counter = Counter(10)
sample_counter.run()
```

Here, you will see a **pdb** prompt appear in the Terminal (you might need to press *Enter* first to make the debugger proceed):

```
-> self.value = current_value + 1(Pdb)
> /Users/quannguyen/PycharmProjects/PythonMath-Packt/Chapter01/Exercise1.8/counter.py(14
)update()
-> self.value = current_value + 1
> /Users/quannguyen/PycharmProjects/PythonMath-Packt/Chapter01/Exercise1.8/counter.py(14
)update()
-> self.value = current_value + 1


> /Users/quannguyen/PycharmProjects/PythonMath-Packt/Chapter01/Exercise1.8/counter.py(14
)update()
-> self.value = current_value + 1> /Users/quannguyen/PycharmProjects/PythonMath-Packt/Ch
apter01/Exercise1.8/counter.py(14)update()
-> self.value = current_value + 1


(Pdb) █
```

Figure 1.4: pdb interface

7. Input **ll** and hit *Enter* to see where in the program we are pausing:

```
(Pdb) ll
  9         def update(self):
 10             current_value = self.value
 11             breakpoint()
 12  ->         self.value = current_value + 1
```

   Here, the output indicates that we are currently pausing between the two instructions that increment the value of our counter inside the **update()** method.

8. Hit *Enter* again to return to the **pdb** prompt and run the **p self.value** command:

```
(Pdb) p self.value
0
```

   We can see that the current value of the counter is **0**.

9. Return to the prompt and enter the **n** command. After this, use the **p self.value** command again to inspect the value of the counter:

```
(Pdb) n
--Return--
> <ipython-input-61-066f5069e308>(12)update()->None
-> self.value = current_value + 1
(Pdb) p self.value
1
```

10. We can see that the value has been incremented by 1. Repeat this process of alternating between **n** and **p self.value** to observe that the value stored in **self.value** is not updated as we proceed through the program. In other words, the value typically stays at 1. This is how the bug manifests itself in large values of the counter, as we have seen in our unit tests.

11. Exit the debugger using *Ctrl* + *C*.

> **NOTE**
>
> To access the source code for this specific section, please refer to https://packt.live/2YPCZFJ.
>
> This section does not currently have an online interactive example and will need to be run locally.

For those who are interested, the bug of our program stems from the fact that multiple threads can increment the value of the counter at roughly the same time, overwriting the changes made by one another. With a large number of threads (such as 5,000 or 10,000, which we have in our test cases), the probability of this event taking place becomes higher. This phenomenon, as we mentioned previously, is called a race condition, and it is one of the most common bugs in concurrent and parallel programs.

Aside from demonstrating some **pdb** commands, this exercise also illustrates the fact that it is necessary to design tests to cover different situations. While the program passed our small test with the target being 5, it failed with larger values of the target. In real life, we should have the tests for a program to simulate a wide range of possibilities, ensuring that the program still works as intended, even in edge cases.

And with that, let's move on to the last topic of this chapter, version control.

VERSION CONTROL

In this section, we will briefly talk about the general theory behind version control and then discuss the process of implementing it with Git and GitHub, arguably the most popular version control systems in the industry. Version control is to a programming project what backing up data is to regular files. In essence, version control systems allow us to save our progress in a project separately from our local files so that we can come back to it later on, even if the local files are lost or damaged.

With the functionalities that current version control systems such as Git and GitHub provide, we can also do a lot more. For example, the branching and merging features from these systems offer their users a way to create multiple versions of a common project so that different directions can be explored; the branch that implements the most preferred direction will then be merged with the main branch in the end. Additionally, Git and GitHub allow work between users on their platform to be seamless, which is greatly appreciated in team projects.

To understand the available features that we can take advantage of with Git and GitHub, let's go through the following exercise.

EXERCISE 1.09: VERSION CONTROL WITH GIT AND GITHUB

This exercise will walk us through all of the steps necessary to get started with Git and GitHub. If you do not have any experience working with version control yet, this exercise will be beneficial to you.

Perform the following steps to complete this exercise:

1. First, if you haven't already, register for a GitHub account by going to https://www.github.com/ and sign up. This will allow you to host the files that you want to version control on their cloud storage.

2. Go to https://git-scm.com/downloads and download the Git client software for your system and install it. This Git client will be responsible for communicating with the GitHub server. You know if your Git client is successfully installed if you can run the **git** command in your Terminal:

```
$ git
usage: git [--version] [--help] [-C <path>] [-c <name>=<value>]
           [--exec-path[=<path>]] [--html-path] [--man-path] [--info-
path]
           [-p | --paginate | -P | --no-pager] [--no-replace-objects]
[--bare]
           [--git-dir=<path>] [--work-tree=<path>]
[--namespace=<name>]
           <command> [<args>]
```

Otherwise, your system might need to be rebooted for the installation to take full effect.

3. Now, let's start the process of applying version control to a sample project. First, create a dummy folder and generate a Jupyter notebook and a text file named **input.txt** with the following content in it:

```
1,1,1
1,1,1
```

4. In the first cell of the Jupyter notebook, write a function called **add_elements()** that takes in two lists of numbers and adds them up element-wise. The function should return a list that consists of the element-wise sums; you can assume that the two parameter lists are of the same length:

```
def add_elements(a, b):
    result = []
    for item_a, item_b in zip(a, b):
        result.append(item_a + item_b)

    return result
```

5. In the next code cell, read in the **input.txt** file using a **with** statement and extract the last two lines of the file using the **readlines()** function and list indexing:

```
with open('input.txt', 'r') as f:
    lines = f.readlines()

last_line1, last_line2 = lines[-2], lines[-1]
```

Note that in the **open()** function, the second argument, **'r'**, specifies that we are reading in the file, as opposed to writing to the file.

6. In a new code cell, convert these two strings of text input into lists of numbers, first using the **str.split()** function with the **','** argument to isolate the individual numbers in each line, and then the **map()** and **int()** functions to apply the conversion to integers element-wise:

```
list1 = list(map(int, last_line1[: -1].split(',')))
list2 = list(map(int, last_line2[: -1].split(',')))
```

7. In a new code cell, call **add_elements()** on **list1** and **list2**. Write the returned list to the same input file in a new line in the same **comma-separated values** (**CSV**) format:

```
new_list = add_elements(list1, list2)

with open('input.txt', 'a') as f:
    for i, item in enumerate(new_list):
        f.write(str(item))

        if i < len(new_list) - 1:
            f.write(',')
        else:
            f.write('\n')
```

Here the **'a'** argument specifies that we are writing to append a new line to the file, as opposed to reading and overwriting the file completely.

8. Run the code cell and verify that the text file has been updated to the following:

```
1,1,1
1,1,1
2,2,2
```

9. This is the current setup of our sample project so far: we have a text file and a Python script inside a folder; the script can alter the content of the text file when run. This setup is fairly common in real-life situations: you can have a data file that contains some information that you'd like to keep track of and a Python program that can read in that data and update it in some way (maybe through prespecified computation or adding new data that was collected externally).

   Now, let's implement version control in this sample project.

10. Go to your online GitHub account, click on the plus sign icon (**+**) in the top-right corner of the window, and choose the **`New repository`** option, as illustrated here:

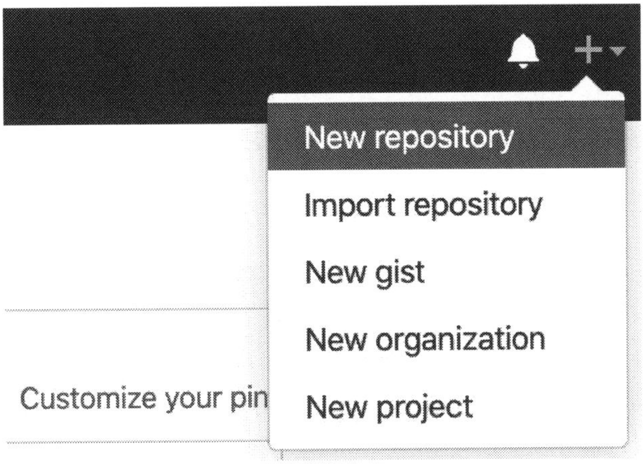

Figure 1.5: Creating a new repository

Input a sample name for your new repository in the form and finalize the creation process. Copy the URL to this new repository to your clipboard as we will need it later.

This, as the name suggests, will create a new online repository that will host the code we want to version control.

11. On your local computer, open your Terminal and navigate to the folder. Run the following command to initialize a local Git repository, which will be associated with our folder:

```
$ git init
```

12. Still in the Terminal, run the following command to add everything in our project to Git and commit them:

```
git add .
git commit -m [any message with double quotes]
```

Instead of **`git add .`**, you can replace **`.`** with the names of the files that you want to register with Git. This option is helpful when you only want to register a file or two, as opposed to every file you have in a folder.

13. Now, we need to link our local repository and the online repository that we have created. To do that, run the following command:

```
git remote add origin [URL to GitHub repository]
```

Note that "origin" is simply a conventional nickname for the URL.

14. Finally, upload the locally registered files to the online repository by running the following command:

```
git push origin master
```

15. Go to the website for the online repository to verify that the local files we created have indeed been uploaded to GitHub.

16. On your local computer, run the script included in the Jupyter notebook and change the text file.

17. Now, we would like to commit this change to the GitHub repository. In your Terminal, run the following commands again:

```
git add .
git commit
git push origin master
```

18. Go to or refresh the GitHub website to verify that the change we made the second time has also been made on GitHub.

With this exercise, we have walked through a sample version control pipeline and seen some examples of how Git and GitHub can be used in this respect. We also saw a refresher on the process of reading and writing to files in Python using the **with** statement.

> **NOTE**
>
> To access the source code for this specific section, please refer to https://packt.live/2VDS0IS.
>
> You can also run this example online at https://packt.live/3ijJ1pM.

This also concludes the last topic of the first chapter of this book. In the next section, we have provided an activity that will serve as a hands-on project that encapsulates the important topics and discussions we have gone through in this chapter.

ACTIVITY 1.01: BUILDING A SUDOKU SOLVER

Let's test what we have learned so far with a more complex problem: writing a program that can solve Sudoku puzzles. The program should be able to read in a CSV text file as input (which contains the initial puzzle) and output the complete solution to that puzzle.

This activity serves as a warmup consisting of multiple procedures that are common in scientific computing and data science projects, such as reading in data from external files and manipulating that information via an algorithm.

1. Use the **`sudoku_input_2.txt`** file from the GitHub repository of this chapter as the input file for our program by copying it to the same location as the Jupyter notebook you will be creating in the next step (or create your own input file in the same format where empty cells are represented with zeros).

2. In the first code cell of a new Jupyter notebook, create a **`Solver`** class that takes in the path to an input file. It should store the information read from the input file in a 9 x 9 2D list (a list of nine sublists, each of which contains the nine values of individual rows in the puzzle).

3. Add a helper method that prints out the puzzle in a nice format, as follows:

```
-----------------------
0 0 3 | 0 2 0 | 6 0 0 |
9 0 0 | 3 0 5 | 0 0 1 |
0 0 1 | 8 0 6 | 4 0 0 |
-----------------------
0 0 8 | 1 0 2 | 9 0 0 |
7 0 0 | 0 0 0 | 0 0 8 |
0 0 6 | 7 0 8 | 2 0 0 |
-----------------------
0 0 2 | 6 0 9 | 5 0 0 |
8 0 0 | 2 0 3 | 0 0 9 |
0 0 5 | 0 1 0 | 3 0 0 |
-----------------------
```

4. Create a **`get_presence(cells)`** method in the class that takes in any 9 x 9 2D list, representing an unsolved/half-solved puzzle, and returns a sort of indicator regarding whether a given number (between 1 and 9) is present in a given row, column, or quadrant.

For instance, in the preceding example, the returned value of this method should be able to tell you that 2, 3, and 6 are present in the first row, while no number is present in the second column.

5. Create a **`get_possible_values(cells)`** method in the class that also takes in any 2D list representing an incomplete solution and returns a dictionary, whose keys are the locations of currently empty cells and the corresponding values are the lists/sets of possible values that those cells can take.

   These lists of possible values should be generated by taking into account whether a number is present in the same row, column, or quadrant as a given empty cell.

6. Create a **`simple_update(cells)`** method in the class that takes in any 2D incomplete solution list and calls the **`get_possible_values()`** method on that list. From the returned value, if there is an empty cell that holds only one possible solution, update that cell with that value.

   If such an update does happen, the method should call itself again to keep updating the cells. This is because after an update, the list of possible values for the remaining empty cells might change. The method should return the updated 2D list in the end.

7. Create a **`recur_solve(cells)`** method in the class that takes in any 2D incomplete solution list and performs backtracking. First, this method should call **`simple_update()`** and return whether or not the puzzle is completely solved (that is, whether or not there are empty cells in the 2D list).

   Next, consider the possible values of the remaining empty cells. If there are empty cells remaining and you have no possible values, return a negative result to indicate that we have reached an invalid solution.

   On the other hand, if all cells have at least two possible values, find the cell that has the fewest number of possible values. Loop through these possible values, sequentially fill them in the empty cell, and call **`recur_solve()`** inside itself with the updated cells to implement the recursive nature of the algorithm. At each iteration, return whether the final solution is valid. If no valid final solution is found via any of the possible values, return a negative result.

8. Wrap the preceding methods in a **solve()** method, which should print out the initial puzzle, pass it to the **recur_solve()** method, and print out the returned solution from that method.

   For example, with the preceding puzzle, a **Solver** instance, when **solve()** is called, will print out the following output.

   Initial puzzle:

```
-----------------------
0 0 3 | 0 2 0 | 6 0 0 |
9 0 0 | 3 0 5 | 0 0 1 |
0 0 1 | 8 0 6 | 4 0 0 |
-----------------------
0 0 8 | 1 0 2 | 9 0 0 |
7 0 0 | 0 0 0 | 0 0 8 |
0 0 6 | 7 0 8 | 2 0 0 |
-----------------------
0 0 2 | 6 0 9 | 5 0 0 |
8 0 0 | 2 0 3 | 0 0 9 |
0 0 5 | 0 1 0 | 3 0 0 |
-----------------------
```

   Solved puzzle:

```
-----------------------
4 8 3 | 9 2 1 | 6 5 7 |
9 6 7 | 3 4 5 | 8 2 1 |
2 5 1 | 8 7 6 | 4 9 3 |
-----------------------
5 4 8 | 1 3 2 | 9 7 6 |
7 2 9 | 5 6 4 | 1 3 8 |
1 3 6 | 7 9 8 | 2 4 5 |
-----------------------
3 7 2 | 6 8 9 | 5 1 4 |
8 1 4 | 2 5 3 | 7 6 9 |
6 9 5 | 4 1 7 | 3 8 2 |
-----------------------
```

EXTENSIONS

1. Go to the *Project Euler* website, https://projecteuler.net/problem=96, to test out your algorithm against the included puzzles.

2. Write a program that generates Sudoku puzzles and includes unit tests that check whether the solutions generated by our solver are correct.

NOTE

The solution for this activity can be found on page 648.

SUMMARY

This chapter introduced the most fundamental building blocks of Python programming: control flow, data structures, algorithm design, and various housekeeping tasks (debugging, testing, and version control). The knowledge that we have gained in this chapter will prepare us for discussions in future chapters, where we'll learn about other more complex and specialized tools in Python. In particular, in the next chapter, we will talk about the main tools and libraries that Python offers in the fields of statistics, scientific computing, and data science.

2

PYTHON'S MAIN TOOLS FOR STATISTICS

OVERVIEW

This chapter presents a practical introduction to the main libraries that most statistics practitioners use in Python. It will cover some of the most important and useful concepts, functions, and **Application Programming Interfaces** (**APIs**) of each of the key libraries. Almost all of the computational tools that will be needed for the rest of this book will be introduced in this chapter.

By the end of this chapter, you will understand the idea behind array vectorization of the NumPy library and be able to use its sampling functionalities. You'll be able to initialize pandas DataFrames to represent tabular data and manipulate their content. You'll also understand the importance of data visualization in data analysis and be able to utilize Python's two most popular visualization libraries: Matplotlib and Seaborn.

INTRODUCTION

After going through a refresher on the Python language in the previous chapter, we are now ready to tackle the main topics of this book: mathematics and statistics.

Among others, the general fields of computational mathematics and statistics can be broken up into three main tool-centric components: representation and engineering; analysis and computation; and finally, visualization. In the ecosystem of the Python programming language, specific libraries are dedicated to each of these components (namely, pandas, NumPy, Matplotlib, and Seaborn), making the process modular.

While there might be other similar packages and tools, the libraries that we will be discussing have been proven to possess a wide range of functionalities and support powerful options in terms of computation, data processing, and visualization, making them some of a Python programmer's preferred tools over the years.

In this chapter, we will be introduced to each of these libraries and learn about their main API. Using a hands-on approach, we will see how these tools allow great freedom and flexibility in terms of creating, manipulating, analyzing, and visualizing data in Python. Knowing how to use these tools will also equip us for more complicated topics in the later chapters of this workshop.

SCIENTIFIC COMPUTING AND NUMPY BASICS

The term **scientific computing** has been used several times in this workshop so far; in the broadest sense of the term, it denotes the process of using computer programs (or anything with computing capabilities) to model and solve a specific problem in mathematics, engineering, or science. Examples may include mathematical models to look for and analyze patterns and trends in biological and social data, or machine learning models to make future predictions using economic data. As you may have already noticed, this definition has a significant overlap with the general fields of data science, and sometimes the terms are even used interchangeably.

The main workhorse of many (if not most) scientific computing projects in Python is the NumPy library. Since NumPy is an external library that does not come preinstalled with Python, we need to download and install it. As you may already know, installing external libraries and packages in Python can be done easily using package managers such as pip or Anaconda.

From your Terminal, run the following command to use pip to install NumPy in your Python environment:

```
$ pip install numpy
```

If you are currently in an Anaconda environment, you can run the following command instead:

```
$ conda install numpy
```

With these simple commands, all the necessary steps in the installation process are taken care of for us.

Some of NumPy's most powerful capabilities include vectorized, multi-dimensional array representations of objects; implementation of a wide range of linear algebraic functions and transformations; and random sampling. We will cover all of these topics in this section, starting with the general concept of arrays.

NUMPY ARRAYS

We have actually already come across the concept of an array in the previous chapter, when we discussed Python lists. In general, an array is also a sequence of different elements that can be accessed individually or manipulated as a whole. As such, NumPy arrays are very similar to Python lists; in fact, the most common way to declare a NumPy array is to pass a Python list to the **`numpy.array()`** method, as illustrated here:

```
>>> import numpy as np
>>> a = np.array([1, 2, 3])
>>> a
array([1, 2, 3])
>>> a[1]
2
```

The biggest difference we need to keep in mind is that elements in a NumPy array need to be of the same type. For example, here, we are trying to create an array with two numbers and a string, which causes NumPy to forcibly convert all elements in the array into strings (the **`<U21`** data type denotes the Unicode strings with fewer than 21 characters):

```
>>> b = np.array([1, 2, 'a'])
>>> b
array(['1', '2', 'a'], dtype='<U21')
```

Similar to the way we can create multi-dimensional Python lists, NumPy arrays support the same option:

```
>>> c = np.array([[1, 2, 3], [4, 5, 6], [7, 8, 9]])
>>> c
array([[1, 2, 3],
       [4, 5, 6],
       [7, 8, 9]])
```

> **NOTE**
>
> While working with NumPy, we often refer to multi-dimensional arrays as matrices.

Apart from initialization from Python lists, we can create NumPy arrays that are in a specific form. In particular, a matrix full of zeros or ones can be initialized using **np.zeros()** and **np.ones()**, respectively, with a given dimension and data type. Let's have a look at an example:

```
>>> zero_array = np.zeros((2, 2))  # 2 by 2 zero matrix
>>> zero_array
array([[0., 0.],
       [0., 0.]])
```

Here, the tuple **(2, 2)** specifies that the array (or matrix) being initialized should have a two-by-two dimension. As we can see by the dots after the zeros, the default data type of a NumPy array is a float and can be further specified using the **dtype** argument:

```
>>> one_array = np.ones((2, 2, 3), dtype=int)  # 3D one integer matrix
>>> one_array
array([[[1, 1, 1],
        [1, 1, 1]],

       [[1, 1, 1],
        [1, 1, 1]]])
```

All-zero or all-one matrices are common objects in mathematics and statistics, so these API calls will prove to be quite useful later on. Now, let's look at a common matrix object whose elements are all random numbers. Using **np.random.rand()**, we can create a matrix of a given shape, whose elements are uniformly sampled between 0 (inclusive) and 1 (exclusive):

```
>>> rand_array = np.random.rand(2, 3)
>>> rand_array
array([[0.90581261, 0.88732623, 0.291661   ],
       [0.44705149, 0.25966191, 0.73547706]])
```

Notice here that we are not passing the desired shape of our matrix as a tuple anymore, but as individual parameters of the **np.random.rand()** function instead.

If you are not familiar with the concept of randomness and random sampling from various distributions, don't worry, as we will cover that topic later on in this chapter as well. For now, let's move forward with our discussion about NumPy arrays, particularly about indexing and slicing.

You will recall that in order to access individual elements in a Python list, we pass its index inside square brackets next to the list variable; the same goes for one-dimensional NumPy arrays:

```
>>> a = np.array([1, 2, 3])
>>> a[0]
1
>>> a[1]
2
```

However, when an array is multi-dimensional, instead of using multiple square brackets to access subarrays, we simply need to separate the individual indices using commas. For example, we access the element in the second row and the second column of a three-by-three matrix as follows:

```
>>> b = np.array([[1, 2, 3], [4, 5, 6], [7, 8, 9]])
>>> b
array([[1, 2, 3],
       [4, 5, 6],
       [7, 8, 9]])
>>> b[1, 1]
5
```

Slicing NumPy arrays can be done in the same way: using commas. This syntax is very useful in terms of helping us access submatrices with more than one dimension in a matrix:

```
>>> a = np.random.rand(2, 3, 4)  # random 2-by-3-by-4 matrix
>>> a
array([[[0.54376986, 0.00244875, 0.74179644, 0.14304955],
        [0.77229612, 0.32254451, 0.0778769 , 0.2832851 ],
        [0.26492963, 0.5217093 , 0.68267418, 0.29538502]],
       [[0.94479229, 0.28608588, 0.52837161, 0.18493272],
        [0.08970716, 0.00239815, 0.80097454, 0.74721516],
        [0.70845696, 0.09788526, 0.98864408, 0.82521871]]])
>>> a[1, 0: 2, 1:]
array([[0.28608588, 0.52837161, 0.18493272],
       [0.00239815, 0.80097454, 0.74721516]])
```

In the preceding example, **`a[1, 0: 2, 1:]`** helps us to access the numbers in the original matrix, **`a`**; that is, in the second element in the first axis (corresponding to index **`1`**), the first two elements in the second axis (corresponding to **`0: 2`**), and the last three elements in the third axis (corresponding to **`1:`**). This option is one reason why NumPy arrays are more powerful and flexible than Python lists, which do not support multi-dimensional indexing and slicing, as we have demonstrated.

Finally, another important syntax to manipulate NumPy arrays is the **`np.reshape()`** function, which, as its name suggests, changes the shape of a given NumPy array. The need for this functionality can arise on multiple occasions: when we need to display an array in a certain way for better readability, or when we need to pass an array to a built-in function that only takes in arrays of a certain shape.

We can explore the effect of this function in the following code snippet:

```
>>> a
array([[[0.54376986, 0.00244875, 0.74179644, 0.14304955],
        [0.77229612, 0.32254451, 0.0778769 , 0.2832851 ],
        [0.26492963, 0.5217093 , 0.68267418, 0.29538502]],

       [[0.94479229, 0.28608588, 0.52837161, 0.18493272],
        [0.08970716, 0.00239815, 0.80097454, 0.74721516],
        [0.70845696, 0.09788526, 0.98864408, 0.82521871]]])
>>> a.shape
(2, 3, 4)
>>> np.reshape(a, (3, 2, 4))
```

```
array([[[0.54376986, 0.00244875, 0.74179644, 0.14304955],
        [0.77229612, 0.32254451, 0.0778769 , 0.2832851 ]],

       [[0.26492963, 0.5217093 , 0.68267418, 0.29538502],
        [0.94479229, 0.28608588, 0.52837161, 0.18493272]],

       [[0.08970716, 0.00239815, 0.80097454, 0.74721516],
        [0.70845696, 0.09788526, 0.98864408, 0.82521871]]])
```

Note that the **`np.reshape()`** function does not mutate the array that is passed in-place; instead, it returns a copy of the original array with the new shape without modifying the original. We can also assign this returned value to a variable.

Additionally, notice that while the original shape of the array is **`(2, 3, 4)`**, we changed it to **`(3, 2, 4)`**. This can only be done when the total numbers of elements resulting from the two shapes are the same *(2 x 3 x 4 = 3 x 2 x 4 = 24)*. An error will be raised if the new shape does not correspond to the original shape of an array in this way, as shown here:

```
>>> np.reshape(a, (3, 3, 3))
-------------------------------------------------------------
ValueError                    Traceback (most recent call last)
...
ValueError: cannot reshape array of size 24 into shape (3,3,3)
```

Speaking of reshaping a NumPy array, transposing a matrix is a special form of reshaping that *flips* the elements in the matrix along its diagonal. Computing the transpose of a matrix is a common task in mathematics and machine learning. The transpose of a NumPy array can be computed using the **`[array].T`** syntax. For example, when we run **`a.T`** in the Terminal, we get the transpose of matrix **a**, as follows:

```
>>> a.T
array([[[0.54376986, 0.94479229],
        [0.77229612, 0.08970716],
        [0.26492963, 0.70845696]],

       [[0.00244875, 0.28608588],
        [0.32254451, 0.00239815],
        [0.5217093 , 0.09788526]],

       [[0.74179644, 0.52837161],
        [0.0778769 , 0.80097454],
```

```
        [0.68267418, 0.98864408]],

       [[0.14304955, 0.18493272],
        [0.2832851 , 0.74721516],
        [0.29538502, 0.82521871]]]])
```

And with that, we can conclude our introduction to NumPy arrays. In the next section, we will learn about another concept that goes hand in hand with NumPy arrays: vectorization.

VECTORIZATION

In the broadest sense, the term **vectorization** in computer science denotes the process of applying a mathematical operation to an array (in a general sense) element by element. For example, an add operation where every element in an array is added to the same term is a vectorized operation; the same goes for vectorized multiplication, where all elements in an array are multiplied by the same term. In general, vectorization is achieved when all array elements are put through the same function.

Vectorization is done by default when an applicable operation is performed on a NumPy array (or multiple arrays). This includes binary functions such as addition, subtraction, multiplication, division, power, and mod, as well as several unary built-in functions in NumPy, such as absolute value, square root, trigonometric functions, logarithmic functions, and exponential functions.

Before we see vectorization in NumPy in action, it is worth discussing the importance of vectorization and its role in NumPy. As we mentioned previously, vectorization is generally the application of a common operation on the elements in an array. Due to the repeatability of the process, a vectorized operation can be optimized to be more efficient than its alternative implementation in, say, a **`for`** loop. However, the trade-off for this capability is that the elements in the array would need to be of the same data type—this is also a requirement for any NumPy array.

With that, let's move on to the following exercise, where we will see this effect in action.

EXERCISE 2.01: TIMING VECTORIZED OPERATIONS IN NUMPY

In this exercise, we will calculate the speedup achieved by implementing various vectorized operations such as addition, multiplication, and square root calculation with NumPy arrays compared to a pure Python alternative without vectorization. To do this, perform the following steps:

1. In the first cell of a new Jupyter notebook, import the NumPy package and the **`Timer`** class from the **`timeit`** library. The latter will be used to implement our timing functionality:

```
import numpy as np
from timeit import Timer
```

2. In a new cell, initialize a Python list containing numbers ranging from 0 (inclusive) to 1,000,000 (exclusive) using the **`range()`** function, as well as its NumPy array counterpart using the **`np.array()`** function:

```
my_list = list(range(10 ** 6))
my_array = np.array(my_list)
```

3. We will now apply mathematical operations to this list and array in the following steps. In a new cell, write a function named **`for_add()`** that returns a list whose elements are the elements in the **`my_list`** variable with **`1`** added to each (we will use list comprehension for this). Write another function named **`vec_add()`** that returns the NumPy array version of the same data, which is simply **`my_array + 1`**:

```
def for_add():
    return [item + 1 for item in my_list]


def vec_add():
    return my_array + 1
```

4. In the next code cell, initialize two **Timer** objects while passing in each of the preceding two functions. These objects contain the interface that we will use to keep track of the speed of the functions.

   Call the **repeat()** function on each of the objects with the arguments 10 and 10—in essence, we are repeating the timing experiment by 100 times. Finally, as the **repeat()** function returns a list of numbers representing how much time passed in each experiment for a given function we are recording, we print out the minimum of this list. In short, we want the time of the fastest run of each of the functions:

```
print('For-loop addition:')
print(min(Timer(for_add).repeat(10, 10)))

print('Vectorized addition:')
print(min(Timer(vec_add).repeat(10, 10)))
```

   The following is the output that this program produced:

```
For-loop addition:
0.5640330809999909
Vectorized addition:
0.006047582000007878
```

   While yours might be different, the relationship between the two numbers should be clear: the speed of the **for** loop addition function should be many times lower than that of the vectorized addition function.

5. In the next code cell, implement the same comparison of speed where we multiply the numbers by **2**. For the NumPy array, simply return **my_array * 2**:

```
def for_mul():
    return [item * 2 for item in my_list]

def vec_mul():
    return my_array * 2

print('For-loop multiplication:')
print(min(Timer(for_mul).repeat(10, 10)))

print('Vectorized multiplication:')
print(min(Timer(vec_mul).repeat(10, 10)))
```

Verify from the output that the vectorized multiplication function is also faster than the **for** loop version. The output after running this code is as follows:

```
For-loop multiplication: 0.5431750800000259
Vectorized multiplication: 0.005795304000002943
```

6. In the next code cell, implement the same comparison where we compute the square root of the numbers. For the Python list, import and use the **math.sqrt()** function on each element in the list comprehension. For the NumPy array, return the expression **np.sqrt(my_array)**:

```
import math

def for_sqrt():
    return [math.sqrt(item) for item in my_list]

def vec_sqrt():
    return np.sqrt(my_array)

print('For-loop square root:')
print(min(Timer(for_sqrt).repeat(10, 10)))

print('Vectorized square root:')
print(min(Timer(vec_sqrt).repeat(10, 10)))
```

Verify from the output that the vectorized square root function is once again faster than its **for** loop counterpart:

```
For-loop square root:
1.1018582749999268
Vectorized square root:
0.01677640299999439
```

Also, notice that the **np.sqrt()** function is implemented to be vectorized, which is why we were able to pass the whole array to the function.

This exercise introduced a few vectorized operations for NumPy arrays and demonstrated how much faster they are compared to their pure Python loop counterparts.

> **NOTE**
>
> To access the source code for this specific section, please refer to https://packt.live/38l3Nk7.
>
> You can also run this example online at https://packt.live/2ZtBSdY.

That concludes the topic of vectorization in NumPy. In the next and final section on NumPy, we'll discuss another powerful feature that the package offers: random sampling.

RANDOM SAMPLING

In the previous chapter, we saw an example of how to implement randomization in Python using the **`random`** library. However, the randomization in most of the methods implemented in that library is uniform, and in scientific computing and data science projects, sometimes, we need to draw samples from distributions other than the uniform one. This area is where NumPy once again offers a wide range of options.

Generally speaking, random sampling from a probability distribution is the process of selecting an instance from that probability distribution, where elements having a higher probability are more likely to be selected (or drawn). This concept is closely tied to the concept of a random variable in statistics. A random variable is typically used to model some unknown quantity in a statistical analysis, and it usually follows a given distribution, depending on what type of data it models. For example, the ages of members of a population are typically modeled using the normal distribution (also known as the bell curve or the Gaussian distribution), while the arrivals of customers to, say, a bank are often modeled using the Poisson distribution.

By randomly sampling a given distribution that is associated with a random variable, we can obtain an actual realization of the variable, from which we can perform various computations to obtain insights and inferences about the random variable in question.

We will revisit the concept and usage of probability distributions later in this book. For now, let's simply focus on the task at hand: how to draw samples from these distributions. This is done using the **`np.random`** package, which includes the interface that allows us to draw from various distributions.

For example, the following code snippet initializes a sample from the normal distribution (note that your output might be different from the following due to randomness):

```
>>> sample = np.random.normal()
>>> sample
-0.43658969989465696
```

You might be aware of the fact that the normal distribution is specified by two statistics: a mean and a standard deviation. These can be specified using the **`loc`** (whose default value is **`0.0`**) and **`scale`** (whose default value is **`1.0`**) arguments, respectively, in the **`np.random.normal()`** function, as follows:

```
>>> sample = np.random.normal(loc=100, scale=10)
>>> sample
80.31187658687652
```

It is also possible to draw multiple samples, as opposed to just a single sample, at once as a NumPy array. To do this, we specify the **`size`** argument of the **`np.random.normal()`** function with the desired shape of the output array. For example, here, we are creating a 2 x 3 matrix of samples drawn from the same normal distribution:

```
>>> samples = np.random.normal(loc=100, scale=10, size=(2, 3))
>>> samples
array([[ 82.7834678 , 109.16410976, 101.35105681],
       [112.54825751, 107.79073472,  77.70239823]])
```

This option allows us to take the output array and potentially apply other NumPy-specific operations to it (such as vectorization). The alternative is to sequentially draw individual samples into a list and convert it into a NumPy array afterward.

It is important to note that each probability distribution has its own statistic(s) that define it. The normal distribution, as we have seen, has a mean and a standard deviation, while the aforementioned Poisson distribution is defined with a λ (lambda) parameter, which is interpreted as the expectation of interval. Let's see this in an example:

```
>>> samples = np.random.poisson(lam=10, size=(2, 2))
>>> samples
array([[11, 10],
       [15, 11]])
```

Generally, before drawing a sample from a probability distribution in NumPy, you should always look up the corresponding documentation to see what arguments are available for that specific distribution and what their default values are.

Aside from probability distribution, NumPy also offers other randomness-related functionalities that can be found in the **random** module. For example, the **np.random.randint()** function returns a random integer between two given numbers; **np.random.choice()** randomly draws a sample from a given one-dimensional array; **np.random.shuffle()**, on the other hand, randomly shuffles a given sequence in-place.

These functionalities, which are demonstrated in the following code snippet, offer a significant degree of flexibility in terms of working with randomness in Python in general, and specifically in scientific computing:

```
>>> np.random.randint(low=0, high=10, size=(2, 5))
array([[6, 4, 1, 3, 6],
       [0, 8, 8, 8, 8]])
>>> np.random.choice([1, 3, 4, -6], size=(2, 2))
array([[1, 1],
       [1, 4]])
>>> a = [1, 2, 3, 4]
>>> for _ in range(3):
...         np.random.shuffle(a)
...         print(a)
[4, 1, 3, 2]
[4, 1, 2, 3]
[1, 2, 4, 3]
```

A final important topic that we need to discuss whenever there is randomness involved in programming is reproducibility. This term denotes the ability to obtain the same result from a program in a different run, especially when there are randomness-related elements in that program.

Reproducibility is essential when a bug exists in a program but only manifests itself in certain random cases. By forcing the program to generate the same random numbers every time it executes, we have another way to narrow down and identify this kind of bug aside from unit testing.

In data science and statistics, reproducibility is of the utmost importance. Without a program being reproducible, it is possible for one researcher to find a statistically significant result while another is unable to, even when the two have the same code and methods. This is why many practitioners have begun placing heavy emphasis on reproducibility in the fields of data science and machine learning.

The most common method to implement reproducibility (which is also the easiest to program) is to simply fix the seed of the program (specifically its libraries) that utilizes randomness. Fixing the seed of a randomness-related library ensures that the same random numbers will be generated across different runs of the same program. In other words, this allows for the same result to be produced, even if a program is run multiple times on different machines.

To do this, we can simply pass an integer to the appropriate seed function of the library/package that produces randomness for our programs. For example, to fix the seed for the **random** library, we can write the following code:

```
>>> import random
>>> random.seed(0)  # can use any other number
```

For the random package in NumPy, we can write the following:

```
>>> np.random.seed(0)
```

Setting the seed for these libraries/packages is generally a good practice when you are contributing to a group or an open source project; again, it ensures that all members of the team are able to achieve the same result and eliminates miscommunication.

This topic also concludes our discussion of the NumPy library. Next, we will move on to another integral part of the data science and scientific computing ecosystem in Python: the pandas library.

WORKING WITH TABULAR DATA IN PANDAS

If NumPy is used on matrix data and linear algebraic operations, pandas is designed to work with data in the form of tables. Just like NumPy, pandas can be installed in your Python environment using the pip package manager:

```
$ pip install pandas
```

If you are using Anaconda, you can download it using the following command:

```
$ conda install pandas
```

Once the installation process completes, fire off a Python interpreter and try importing the library:

```
>>> import pandas as pd
```

If this command runs without any error message, then you have successfully installed pandas. With that, let's move on with our discussions, beginning with the most commonly used data structure in pandas, **`DataFrame`**, which can represent table data: two-dimensional data with row and column labels. This is to be contrasted with NumPy arrays, which can take on any dimension but do not support labeling.

INITIALIZING A DATAFRAME OBJECT

There are multiple ways to initialize a **`DataFrame`** object. First, we can manually create one by passing in a Python dictionary, where each key should be the name of a column, and the value for that key should be the data included for that column, in the form of a list or a NumPy array.

For example, in the following code, we are creating a table with two rows and three columns. The first column contains the numbers 1 and 2 in order, the second contains 3 and 4, and the third 5 and 6:

```
>>> import pandas as pd
>>> my_dict = {'col1': [1, 2], 'col2': np.array([3, 4]),'col3': [5, 6]}
>>> df = pd.DataFrame(my_dict)
>>> df
    col1    col2    col3
0   1       3       5
1   2       4       6
```

The first thing to note about **`DataFrame`** objects is that, as you can see from the preceding code snippet, when one is printed out, the output is automatically formatted by the backend of pandas. The tabular format makes the data represented in that object more readable. Additionally, when a **`DataFrame`** object is printed out in a Jupyter notebook, similar formatting is utilized for the same purpose of readability, as illustrated in the following screenshot:

```
In [2]: import pandas as pd

        my_dict = {'col1': [1, 2], 'col2': np.array([3, 4]),
                   'col3': [5, 6]}

        df = pd.DataFrame(my_dict)
        df
```

Out[2]:

	col1	col2	col3
0	1	3	5
1	2	4	6

Figure 2.1: Printed DataFrame objects in Jupyter Notebooks

Another common way to initialize a **DataFrame** object is that when we already have its data represented by a 2D NumPy array, we can directly pass that array to the **DataFrame** class. For example, we can initialize the same DataFrame we looked at previously with the following code:

```
>>> my_array = np.array([[1, 3, 5], [2, 4, 6]])
>>> alt_df = pd.DataFrame(my_array, columns=['col1', 'col2', 'col3'])
>>> alt_df
   col1    col2    col3
0  1       3       5
1  2       4       6
```

That said, the most common way in which a **DataFrame** object is initialized is through the **pd.read_csv()** function, which, as the name suggests, reads in a CSV file (or any text file formatted in the same way but with a different separating special character) and renders it as a **DataFrame** object. We will see this function in action in the next section, where we will understand the working of more functionalities from the pandas library.

ACCESSING ROWS AND COLUMNS

Once we already have a table of data represented in a **DataFrame** object, there are numerous options we can use to interact with and manipulate this table. For example, the first thing we might care about is accessing the data of certain rows and columns. Luckily, pandas offers intuitive Python syntax for this task.

To access a group of rows or columns, we can take advantage of the **loc** method, which takes in the labels of the rows/columns we are interested in. Syntactically, this method is used with square brackets (to simulate the indexing syntax in Python). For example, using the same table from our previous section, we can pass in the name of a row (for example, **0**):

```
>>> df.loc[0]
col1    1
col2    3
col3    5
Name: 0, dtype: int64
```

We can see that the object returned previously contains the information we want (the first row, and the numbers 1, 3, and 5), but it is formatted in an unfamiliar way. This is because it is returned as a **Series** object. **Series** objects are a special case of **DataFrame** objects that only contain 1D data. We don't need to pay too much attention to this data structure as its interface is very similar to that of **DataFrame**.

Still considering the **loc** method, we can pass in a list of row labels to access multiple rows. The following code returns both rows in our example table:

```
>>> df.loc[[0, 1]]
   col1   col2   col3
0  1      3      5
1  2      4      6
```

Say you want to access the data in our table column-wise. The **loc** method offers that option via the indexing syntax that we are familiar with in NumPy arrays (row indices separated by column indices by a comma). Accessing the data in the first row and the second and third columns:

```
>>> df.loc[0, ['col2', 'col3']]
col2    3
col3    5
Name: 0, dtype: int64
```

Note that if you'd like to return a whole column in a **DataFrame** object, you can use the special character colon, **:**, in the row index to indicate that all the rows should be returned. For example, to access the **'col3'** column in our **DataFrame** object, we can say **df.loc[:, 'col3']**. However, in this special case of accessing a whole column, there is another simple syntax: just using the square brackets without the **loc** method, as follows:

```
>>> df['col3']
0    5
1    6
Name: col3, dtype: int64
```

Earlier, we said that when accessing individual rows or columns in a **DataFrame**, **Series** objects are returned. These objects can be iterated using, for example, a **for** loop:

```
>>> for item in df.loc[:, 'col3']:
...     print(item)
5
6
```

In terms of changing values in a **DataFrame** object, we can use the preceding syntax to assign new values to rows and columns:

```
>>> df.loc[0] = [3, 6, 9]  # change first row
>>> df
    col1    col2    col3
0   3       6       9
1   2       4       6
>>> df['col2'] = [0, 0]  # change second column
>>> df
    col1    col2    col3
0   3       0       9
1   2       0       6
```

Additionally, we can use the same syntax to declare new rows and columns:

```
>>> df['col4'] = [10, 10]
>>> df.loc[3] = [1, 2, 3, 4]
>>> df
   col1   col2   col3   col4
0  3      0      9      10
1  2      0      6      10
3  1      2      3      4
```

Finally, even though it is more common to access rows and columns in a **DataFrame** object by specifying their actual indices in the **loc** method, it is also possible to achieve the same effect using an array of Boolean values (**True** and **False**) to indicate which items should be returned.

For example, we can access the items in the second row and the second and fourth columns in our current table by writing the following:

```
>>> df.loc[[False, True, False], [False, True, False, True]]
   col2   col4
1  0      10
```

Here, the Boolean index list for the rows **[False, True, False]** indicates that only the second element (that is, the second row) should be returned, while the Boolean index list for the columns, similarly, specifies that the second and fourth columns are to be returned.

While this method of accessing elements in a **DataFrame** object might seem strange, it is highly valuable for filtering and replacing tasks. Specifically, instead of passing in lists of Boolean values as indices, we can simply use a conditional inside the **loc** method. For example, to display our current table, just with the columns whose values in their first row are larger than **5** (which should be the third and fourth columns), we can write the following:

```
>>> df.loc[:, df.loc[0] > 5]
   col3   col4
0  9      10
1  6      10
3  3      4
```

Again, this syntax is specifically useful in terms of filtering out the rows or columns in a **DataFrame** object that satisfy some condition and potentially assign new values to them. A special case of this functionality is find-and-replace tasks (which we will go through in the next section).

MANIPULATING DATAFRAMES

In this section, we will try out a number of methods and functions for **DataFrame** objects that are used to manipulate the data within those objects. Of course, there are numerous other methods that are available (which you can find in the official documentation: https://pandas.pydata.org/pandas-docs/stable/reference/api/pandas.DataFrame.html). However, the methods given in the following table are among the most commonly used and offer great power and flexibility in terms of helping us to create, maintain, and mutate our data tables:

Method	**Effects**
`rename(self[, axis, ...])`	Changes the labels of the rows or columns
`fillna(self[, method, ...])`	Replaces empty cells (that contain `NA`/`NaN` values) using a specific method
`replace(self, to_replace=None, value=None)`	Replaces cells that contain the value passed to `to_replace` by the value passed to `value`
`drop(self[, labels, axis, ...])`	Drops specific rows or columns from the data table
`pd.concat(objs, axis=0, join='outer', ...)`	Concatenates pandas objects along the specified axis
`sort_values(self, by[, axis, ascending, ...])`	Sorts by values along the specified axis
`pd.read_csv()`	Reads a CSV text file and returns the corresponding `DataFrame` object
`to_csv()`	Writes a `DataFrame` object to file as a CSV text file

Figure 2.2: Methods used to manipulate pandas data

The following exercise will demonstrate the effects of the preceding methods for better understanding.

EXERCISE 2.02: DATA TABLE MANIPULATION

In this hands-on exercise, we will go through the functions and methods included in the preceding section. Our goal is to see the effects of those methods, and to perform common data manipulation techniques such as renaming columns, filling in missing values, sorting values, or writing a data table to file.

Perform the following steps to complete this exercise:

1. From the GitHub repository of this workshop, copy the **Exercise2.02/dataset.csv** file within the **Chapter02** folder to a new directory. The content of the file is as follows:

```
id,x,y,z
0,1,1,3
1,1,0,9
2,1,3,
3,2,0,10
4,1,,4
5,2,2,3
```

2. Inside that new directory, create a new Jupyter notebook. Make sure that this notebook and the CSV file are in the same location.

3. In the first cell of this notebook, import both pandas and NumPy, and then read in the **dataset.csv** file using the **pd.read_csv()** function. Specify the **index_col** argument of this function to be **'id'**, which is the name of the first column in our sample dataset:

```
import pandas as pd
import numpy as np

df = pd.read_csv('dataset.csv', index_col='id')
```

4. When we print this newly created **DataFrame** object out, we can see that its values correspond directly to our original input file:

```
     x    y     z

id
0    1    1.0   3.0
1    1    0.0   9.0
2    1    3.0   NaN
3    2    0.0   10.0
4    1    NaN   4.0
5    2    2.0   3.0
```

   Notice the **NaN** (**Not a Number**) values here; **NaN** is the default value that will be filled in empty cells of a **DataFrame** object upon initialization. Since our original dataset was purposefully designed to contain two empty cells, those cells were appropriately filled in with **NaN**, as we can see here.

   Additionally, **NaN** values are registered as floats in Python, which is why the data type of the two columns containing them are converted into floats accordingly (indicated by the decimal points in the values).

5. In the next cell, rename the current columns to **'col_x'**, **'col_y'**, and **'col_z'** with the **rename()** method. Here, the **columns** argument should be specified with a Python dictionary mapping each old column name to its new name:

```
df = df.rename(columns={'x': 'col_x', 'y': 'col_y', \
                        'z': 'col_z'})
```

   This change can be observed when **df** is printed out after the line of code is run:

```
     col_x    col_y    col_z
id
0    1        1.0      3.0
1    1        0.0      9.0
2    1        3.0      NaN
3    2        0.0      10.0
4    1        NaN      4.0
5    2        2.0      3.0
```

6. In the next cell, use the **fillna()** function to replace the **NaN** values with zeros. After this, convert all the data in our table into integers using **astype(int)**:

```
df = df.fillna(0)
df = df.astype(int)
```

The resulting **DataFrame** object now looks like this:

```
    col_x    col_y    col_z
id
0   1        1        3
1   1        0        9
2   1        3        0
3   2        0        10
4   1        0        4
5   2        2        3
```

7. In the next cell, remove the second, fourth, and fifth rows from the dataset by passing the **[1, 3, 4]** list to the **drop** method:

```
df = df.drop([1, 3, 4], axis=0)
```

Note that the **axis=0** argument specifies that the labels we are passing to the method specify rows, not columns, of the dataset. Similarly, to drop specific columns, you can use a list of column labels while specifying **axis=1**.

The resulting table now looks like this:

```
    col_x    col_y    col_z
id
0   1        1        3
2   1        3        0
5   2        2        3
```

8. In the next cell, create an all-zero, 2 x 3 **DataFrame** object with the corresponding column labels as the current **df** variable:

```
zero_df = pd.DataFrame(np.zeros((2, 3)),
                       columns=['col_x', 'col_y', \
                                'col_z'])
```

The output is as follows:

```
   col_x   col_y   col_z
0  0.0     0.0     0.0
1  0.0     0.0     0.0
```

9. In the next code cell, use the **pd.concat()** function to concatenate the two **DataFrame** objects together (specify **axis=0** so that the two tables are concatenated vertically, instead of horizontally):

```
df = pd.concat([df, zero_df], axis=0)
```

Our current **df** variable now prints out the following (notice the two newly concatenated rows at the bottom of the table):

```
   col_x   col_y   col_z
0  1.0     1.0     3.0
2  1.0     3.0     0.0
5  2.0     2.0     3.0
0  0.0     0.0     0.0
1  0.0     0.0     0.0
```

10. In the next cell, sort our current table in increasing order by the data in the **col_x** column:

```
df = df.sort_values('col_x', axis=0)
```

The resulting dataset now looks like this:

```
   col_x   col_y   col_z
0  0.0     0.0     0.0
1  0.0     0.0     0.0
0  1.0     1.0     3.0
2  1.0     3.0     0.0
5  2.0     2.0     3.0
```

11. Finally, in another code cell, convert our table into the integer data type (the same way as before) and use the **to_csv()** method to write this table to a file. Pass in **'output.csv'** as the name of the output file and specify **index=False** so that the row labels are not included in the output:

```
df = df.astype(int)
df.to_csv('output.csv', index=False)
```

The written output should look as follows:

```
col_x, col_y, col_z
0,0,0
0,0,0
1,1,3
1,3,0
2,2,3
```

And that is the end of this exercise. Overall, this exercise simulated a simplified workflow of working with a tabular dataset: reading in the data, manipulating it in some way, and finally writing it to file.

> **NOTE**
>
> To access the source code for this specific section, please refer to https://packt.live/38ldQ8O.
>
> You can also run this example online at https://packt.live/3dTzkL6.

In the next and final section on pandas, we will consider a number of more advanced functionalities offered by the library.

ADVANCED PANDAS FUNCTIONALITIES

Accessing and changing the values in the rows and columns of a **`DataFrame`** object are among the simplest ways to work with tabular data using the pandas library. In this section, we will go through three other options that are more complicated but also offer powerful options for us to manipulate our **`DataFrame`** objects. The first is the **`apply()`** method.

If you are already familiar with the concept of this method for other data structures, the same goes for this method, which is implemented for **`DataFrame`** objects. In a general sense, this method is used to apply a function to all elements within a **`DataFrame`** object. Similar to the concept of vectorization that we discussed earlier, the resulting **`DataFrame`** object, after the **`apply()`** method, will have its elements as the result of the specified function when each element of the original data is fed to it.

For example, say we have the following **DataFrame** object:

```
>>> df = pd.DataFrame({'x': [1, 2, -1], 'y': [-3, 6, 5], \
                       'z': [1, 3, 2]})
>>> df
    x   y   z
0   1   -3  1
1   2   6   3
2   -1  5   2
```

Now, say we'd like to create another column whose entries are the entries in the **x_squared** column. We can then use the **apply()** method, as follows:

```
>>> df['x_squared'] = df['x'].apply(lambda x: x ** 2)
>>> df
    x   y   z   x_squared
0   1   -3  1   1
1   2   6   3   4
2   -1  5   2   1
```

The term **lambda x: x ** 2** here is simply a quick way to declare a function without a name. From the printed output, we see that the **'x_squared'** column was created correctly. Additionally, note that with simple functions such as the square function, we can actually take advantage of the simple syntax of NumPy arrays that we are already familiar with. For example, the following code will have the same effect as the one we just considered:

```
>>> df['x_squared'] = df['x'] ** 2
```

However, with a function that is more complex and cannot be vectorized easily, it is better to fully write it out and then pass it to the **apply()** method. For example, let's say we'd like to create a column, each cell of which should contain the string **'even'** if the element in the **x** column in the same row is even, and the string **'odd'** otherwise.

Here, we can create a separate function called **parity_str()** that takes in a number and returns the corresponding string. This function can then be used with the **apply()** method on **df['x']**, as follows:

```
>>> def parity_str(x):
...     if x % 2 == 0:
...         return 'even'

...     return 'odd'

>>> df['x_parity'] = df['x'].apply(parity_str)
>>> df
   x   y   z  x_squared   x_parity
0  1  -3   1  1           odd
1  2   6   3  4           even
2 -1   5   2  1           odd
```

Another commonly used functionality in pandas that is slightly more advanced is the **pd.get_dummies()** function. This function implements the technique called one-hot encoding, which is to be used on a categorical attribute (or column) in a dataset.

We will discuss the concept of categorical attributes, along with other types of data, in more detail in the next chapter. For now, we simply need to keep in mind that plain categorical data sometimes cannot be interpreted by statistical and machine learning models. Instead, we would like to have a way to translate the categorical characteristic of the data into a numerical form while ensuring that no information is lost.

One-hot encoding is one such method; it works by generating a new column/attribute for each unique value and populating the cells in the new column with Boolean data, indicating the values from the original categorical attribute.

This method is easier to understand via examples, so let's consider the new **'x_parity'** column we created in the preceding example:

```
>>> df['x_parity']
0     odd
1    even
2     odd
Name: x_parity, dtype: object
```

This column is considered a categorical attribute since its values belong to a specific set of categories (in this case, the categories are **odd** and **even**). Now, by calling **pd.get_dummies()** on the column, we obtain the following **DataFrame** object:

```
>>> pd.get_dummies(df['x_parity'])
   even   odd
0  0      1
1  1      0
2  0      1
```

As we can observe from the printed output, the **DataFrame** object includes two columns that correspond to the unique values in the original categorical data (the **'x_parity'** column). For each row, the column that corresponds to the value in the original data is set to **1** and the other column(s) is/are set to **0**. For example, the first row originally contained **odd** in the **'x_parity'** column, so its new **odd** column is set to **1**.

We can see that with one-hot encoding, we can convert any categorical attribute into a new set of binary attributes, making the data readably numerical for statistical and machine learning models. However, a big drawback of this method is the increase in dimensionality, as it creates a number of new columns that are equal to the number of unique values in the original categorical attribute. As such, this method can cause our table to greatly increase in size if the categorical data contains many different values. Depending on your computing power and resources, the recommended limit for the number of unique categorical values for the method is 50.

The **value_counts()** method is another valuable tool in pandas that you should have in your toolkit. This method, to be called on a column of a **DataFrame** object, returns a list of unique values in that column and their respective counts. This method is thus only applicable to categorical or discrete data, whose values belong to a given, predetermined set of possible values.

For example, still considering the **'x_parity'** attribute of our sample dataset, we'll inspect the effect of the **value_counts()** method:

```
>>> df['x_parity'].value_counts()
odd     2
even    1
Name: x_parity, dtype: int64
```

We can see that in the **'x_parity'** column, we indeed have two entries (or rows) whose values are **odd** and one entry for **even**. Overall, this method is quite useful in determining the distribution of values in, again, categorical and discrete data types.

The next and last advanced functionality of pandas that we will discuss is the **groupby** operation. This operation allows us to separate a **DataFrame** object into subgroups, where the rows in a group all share a value in a categorical attribute. From these separate groups, we can then compute descriptive statistics (a concept we will delve into in the next chapter) to explore our dataset further.

We will see this in action in our next exercise, where we'll explore a sample student dataset.

EXERCISE 2.03: THE STUDENT DATASET

By considering a sample of what can be a real-life dataset, we will put our knowledge of pandas' most common functions to use, including what we have been discussing, as well as the new **groupby** operation.

Perform the following steps to complete this exercise:

1. Create a new Jupyter notebook and, in its first cell, run the following code to generate our sample dataset:

```
import pandas as pd

student_df = pd.DataFrame({'name': ['Alice', 'Bob', 'Carol', \
                                    'Dan', 'Eli', 'Fran'],\
                           'gender': ['female', 'male', \
                                      'female', 'male', \
                                      'male', 'female'],\
                           'class': ['FY', 'SO', 'SR', \
                                     'SO',' JR', 'SR'],\
                           'gpa': [90, 93, 97, 89, 95, 92],\
                           'num_classes': [4, 3, 4, 4, 3, 2]})
student_df
```

This code will produce the following output, which displays our sample dataset in tabular form:

	name	gender	class	gpa	num_classes
0	Alice	female	FY	90	4
1	Bob	male	SO	93	3
2	Carol	female	SR	97	4
3	Dan	male	SO	89	4
4	Eli	male	JR	95	3
5	Fran	female	SR	92	2

Most of the attributes in our dataset are self-explanatory: in each row (which represents a student), **name** contains the name of the student, **gender** indicates whether the student is male or female, **class** is a categorical attribute that can take four unique values (**FY** for first-year, **SO** for sophomore, **JR** for junior, and **SR** for senior), **gpa** denotes the cumulative score of the student, and finally, **num_classes** holds the information of how many classes the student is currently taking.

2. In a new code cell, create a new attribute named **'female_flag'** whose individual cells should hold the Boolean value **True** if the corresponding student is female, and **False** otherwise.

   Here, we can see that we can take advantage of the **apply()** method while passing in a lambda object, like so:

```
student_df['female_flag'] = student_df['gender']\
                            .apply(lambda x: x == 'female')
```

   However, we can also simply declare the new attribute using the **student_df['gender'] == 'female'** expression, which evaluates the conditionals sequentially in order:

```
student_df['female_flag'] = student_df['gender'] == 'female'
```

3. This newly created attribute contains all the information included in the old **gender** column, so we will remove the latter from our dataset using the **drop()** method (note that we need to specify the **axis=1** argument since we are dropping a column):

```
student_df = student_df.drop('gender', axis=1)
```

Our current **DataFrame** object should look as follows:

	name	class	gpa	num_classes	female_flag
0	Alice	FY	90	4	True
1	Bob	SO	93	3	False
2	Carol	SR	97	4	True
3	Dan	SO	89	4	False
4	Eli	JR	95	3	False
5	Fran	SR	92	2	True

4. In a new code cell, write an expression to apply one-hot encoding to the categorical attribute, **class**:

```
pd.get_dummies(student_df['class'])
```

5. In the same code cell, take this expression and include it in a **pd.concat()** function to concatenate this newly created **DataFrame** object to our old one, while simultaneously dropping the **class** column (as we now have an alternative for the information in this attribute):

```
student_df = pd.concat([student_df.drop('class', axis=1), \
                        pd.get_dummies(student_df['class'])], axis=1)
```

The current dataset should now look as follows:

	name	gpa	num_classes	female_flag	JR	FY	SO	SR
0	Alice	90	4	True	1	0	0	0
1	Bob	93	3	False	0	0	1	0
2	Carol	97	4	True	0	0	0	1
3	Dan	89	4	False	0	0	1	0
4	Eli	95	3	False	0	1	0	0
5	Fran	92	2	True	0	0	0	1

6. In the next cell, call the **groupby()** method on **student_df** with the **female_flag** argument and assign the returned value to a variable named **gender_group**:

```
gender_group = student_df.groupby('female_flag')
```

As you might have guessed, here, we are grouping the students of the same gender into groups, so male students will be grouped together, and female students will also be grouped together but separate from the first group.

It is important to note that when we attempt to print out this **GroupBy** object stored in the **gender_group** variable, we only obtain a generic, memory-based string representation:

```
<pandas.core.groupby.generic.DataFrameGroupBy object at  0x11d492550>
```

7. Now, we'd like to compute the average GPA of each group in the preceding grouping. To do that, we can use the following simple syntax:

```
gender_group['gpa'].mean()
```

The output will be as follows:

```
female_flag
False     92.333333
True      93.000000
Name: gpa, dtype: float64
```

Our command on the **gender_group** variable is quite intuitive: we'd like to compute the average of a specific attribute, so we access that attribute using square brackets, **[' gpa ']**, and then call the **mean()** method on it.

8. Similarly, we can compute the total number of classes taking male students, as well as that number for the female students, with the following code:

```
gender_group['num_classes'].sum()
```

The output is as follows:

```
female_flag
False     10
True      10
Name: num_classes, dtype: int64
```

Throughout this exercise, we have reminded ourselves of some of the important methods available in pandas, and seen the effects of the **groupby** operation in action via a sample real-life dataset. This exercise also concludes our discussion on the pandas library, the premier tool for working with tabular data in Python.

> **NOTE**
>
> To access the source code for this specific section, please refer to https://packt.live/2NOe5jt.
>
> You can also run this example online at https://packt.live/3io2gP2.

In the final section of this chapter, we will talk about the final piece of a typical data science/scientific computing pipeline: data visualization.

DATA VISUALIZATION WITH MATPLOTLIB AND SEABORN

Data visualization is undoubtedly an integral part of any data pipeline. Good visualizations can not only help scientists and researchers find unique insights about their data, but also help convey complex, advanced ideas in an intuitive, easy to understand way. In Python, the backend of most of the data visualization tools is connected to the Matplotlib library, which offers an incredibly wide range of options and functionalities, as we will see in this upcoming discussion.

First, to install Matplotlib, simply run either of the following commands, depending on which one is your Python package manager:

```
$ pip install matplotlib
$ conda install matplotlib
```

The convention in Python is to import the **`pyplot`** package from the Matplotlib library, like so:

```
>>> import matplotlib.pyplot as plt
```

This **`pyplot`** package, whose alias is now **`plt`**, is the main workhorse for any visualization functionality in Python and will therefore be used extensively.

Overall, instead of learning about the theoretical background of the library, in this section, we will take a more hands-on approach and go through a number of different visualization options that Matplotlib offers. In the end, we will obtain practical takeaways that will be beneficial for your own projects in the future.

SCATTER PLOTS

One of the most fundamental visualization methods is a scatter plot – plotting a list of points on a plane (or other higher-dimensional spaces). This is simply done by means of the **`plt.scatter()`** function. As an example, say we have a list of five points, whose x- and y-coordinates are stored in the following two lists, respectively:

```
>>> x = [1, 2, 3, 1.5, 2]
>>> y = [-1, 5, 2, 3, 0]
```

Now, we can use the **plt.scatter()** function to create a scatter plot:

```
>>> import matplotlib.pyplot as plt
>>> plt.scatter(x, y)
>>> plt.show()
```

The preceding code will generate the following plot, which corresponds exactly to the data in the two lists that we fed into the **plt.scatter()** function:

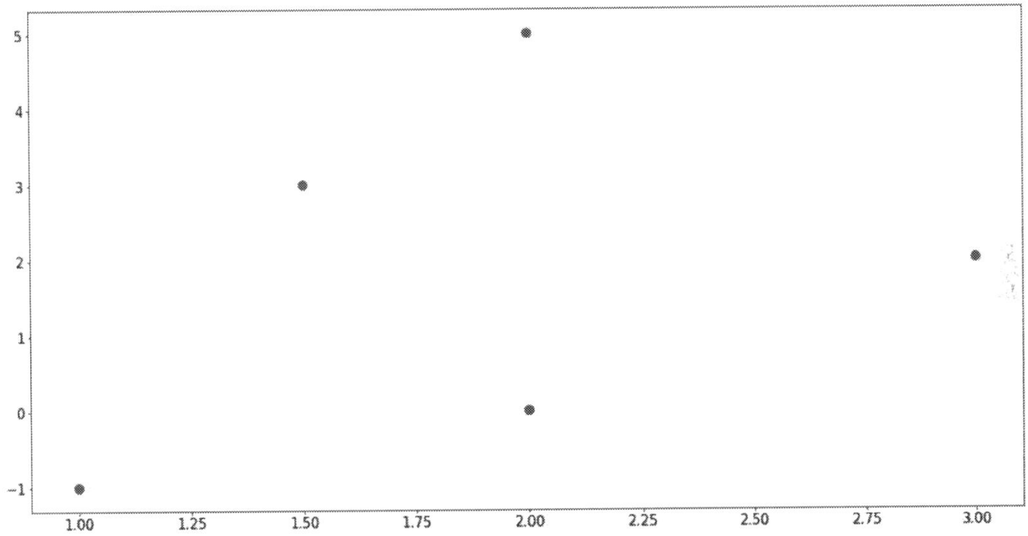

Figure 2.3: Scatter plot using Matplotlib

Note the **plt.show()** command at the end of the code snippet. This function is responsible for displaying the plot that is customized by the preceding code, and it should be placed at the very end of a block of visualization-related code.

As for the **plt.scatter()** function, there are arguments that we can specify to customize our plots further. For example, we can customize the size of the individual points, as well as their respective colors:

```
>>> sizes = [10, 40, 60, 80, 100]
>>> colors = ['r', 'b', 'y', 'g', 'k']

>>> plt.scatter(x, y, s=sizes, c=colors)
>>> plt.show()
```

The preceding code produces the following output:

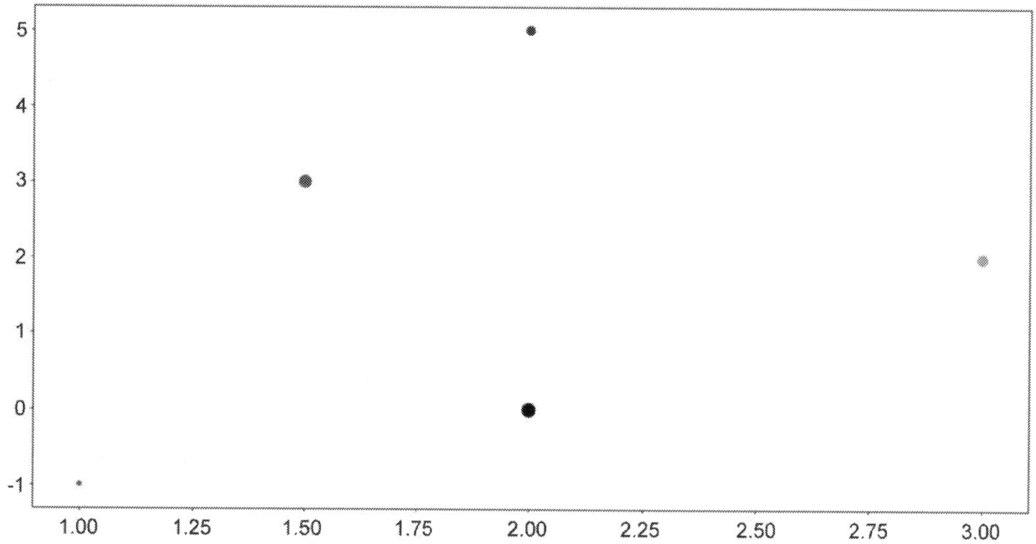

Figure 2.4: Scatter plots with size and color customization

This functionality is useful when the points you'd like to visualize in a scatter plot belong to different groups of data, in which case you can assign a color to each group. In many cases, clusters formed by different groups of data are discovered using this method.

> **NOTE**
>
> To see a complete documentation of Matplotlib colors and their usage, you can consult the following web page: https://matplotlib.org/2.0.2/api/colors_api.html.

Overall, scatter plots are used when we'd like to visualize the spatial distribution of the data that we are interested in. A potential goal of using a scatter plot is to reveal any clustering existing within our data, which can offer us further insights regarding the relationship between the attributes of our dataset.

Next, let's consider line graphs.

LINE GRAPHS

Line graphs are another of the most fundamental visualization methods, where points are plotted along a curve, as opposed to individually scattered. This is done via the simple **`plt.plot()`** function. As an example, we are plotting out the sine wave (from 0 to 10) in the following code:

```
>>> import numpy as np

>>> x = np.linspace(0, 10, 1000)
>>> y = np.sin(x)

>>> plt.plot(x, y)
>>> plt.show()
```

Note that here, the **`np.linspace()`** function returns an array of evenly spaced numbers between two endpoints. In our case, we obtain 1,000 evenly spaced numbers between 0 and 10. The goal here is to take the sine function on these numbers and plot them out. Since the points are extremely close to one another, it will create the effect that a true smooth function is being plotted.

This will result in the following graph:

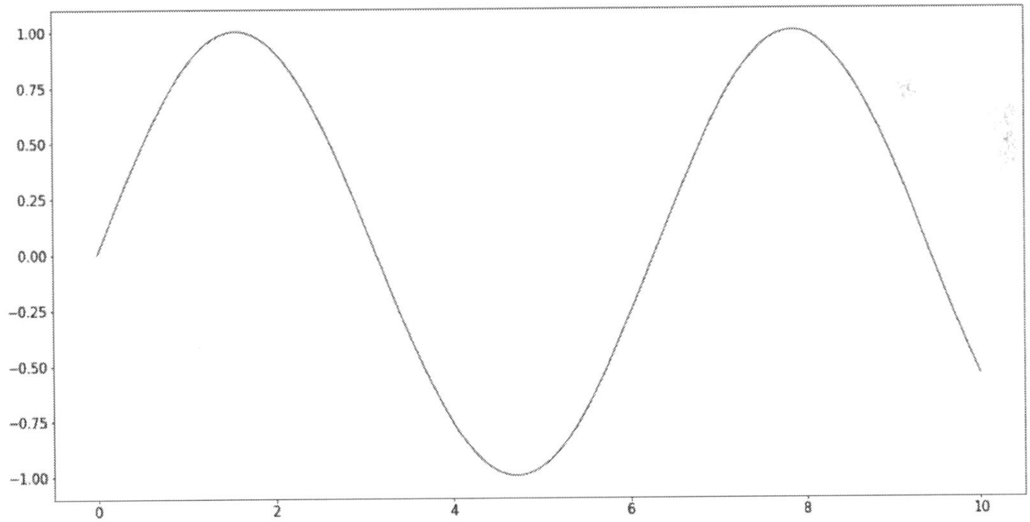

Figure 2.5: Line graphs using Matplotlib

Similar to the options for scatter plots, here, we can customize various elements for our line graphs, specifically the colors and styles of the lines. The following code, which is plotting three separate curves (the $y = x$ graph, the natural logarithm function, and the sine wave), provides an example of this:

```
x = np.linspace(1, 10, 1000)

linear_line = x
log_curve = np.log(x)
sin_wave = np.sin(x)

curves = [linear_line, log_curve, sin_wave]
colors = ['k', 'r', 'b']
styles = ['-', '--', ':']

for curve, color, style in zip(curves, colors, styles):
    plt.plot(x, curve, c=color, linestyle=style)

plt.show()
```

The following output is produced by the preceding code:

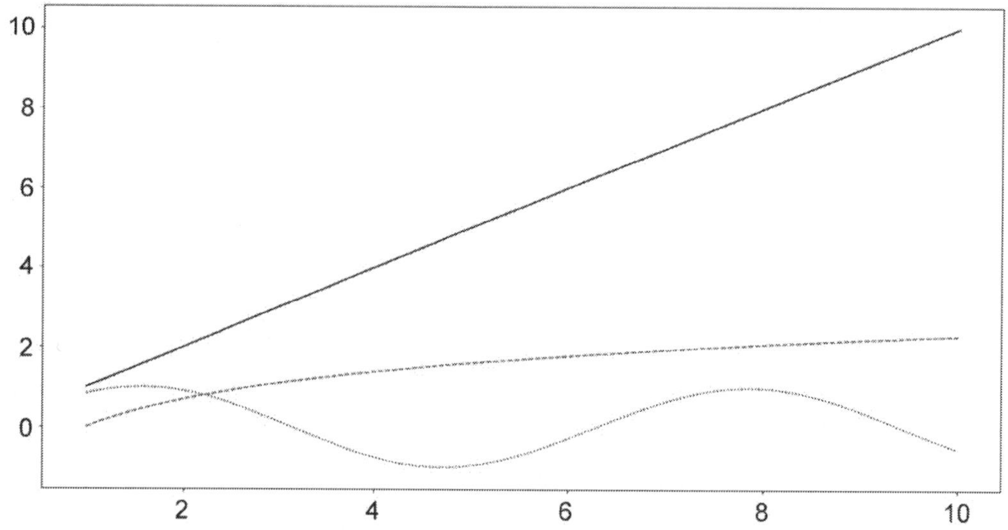

Figure 2.6: Line graphs with style customization

> **NOTE**
>
> A complete list of line styles can be found in Matplotlib's official documentation, specifically at the following page: https://matplotlib.org/3.1.0/gallery/lines_bars_and_markers/linestyles.html.

Generally, line graphs are used to visualize the trend of a specific function, which is represented by a list of points sequenced in order. As such, this method is highly applicable to data with some sequential elements, such as a time series dataset.

Next, we will consider the available options for bar graphs in Matplotlib.

BAR GRAPHS

Bar graphs are typically used to represent the counts of unique values in a dataset via the height of individual bars. In terms of implementation in Matplotlib, this is done using the **plt.bar()** function, as follows:

```
labels = ['Type 1', 'Type 2', 'Type 3']
counts = [2, 3, 5]

plt.bar(labels, counts)
plt.show()
```

The first argument that the **plt.bar()** function takes in (the **labels** variable, in this case) specifies what the labels for the individual bars will be, while the second argument (**counts**, in this case) specifies the height of the bars. With this code, the following graph is produced:

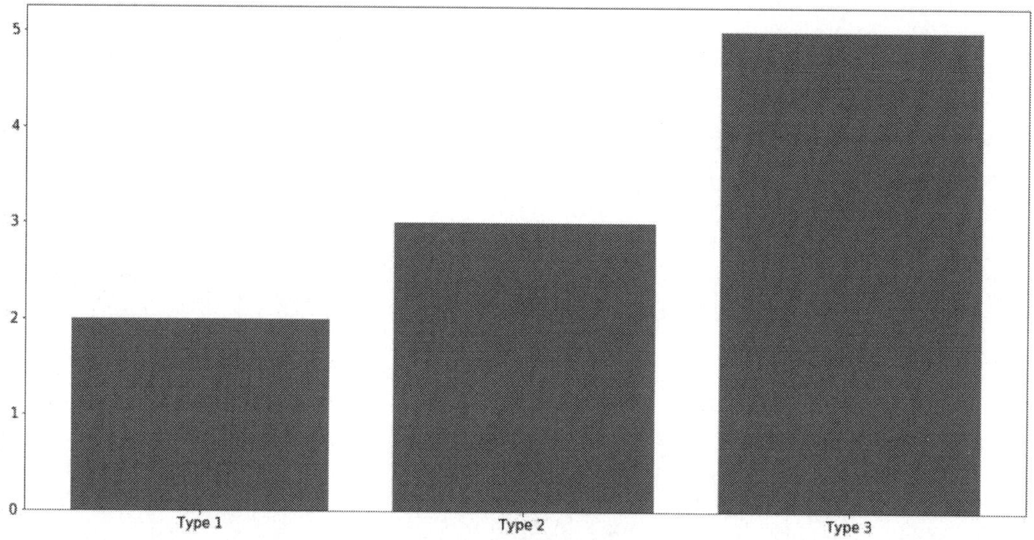

Figure 2.7: Bar graphs using Matplotlib

As always, you can specify the colors of individual bars using the **c** argument. What is more interesting to us is the ability to create more complex bar graphs with stacked or grouped bars. Instead of simply comparing the counts of different data, stacked or grouped bars are used to visualize the composition of each bar in smaller subgroups.

For example, let's say within each group of **Type 1**, **Type 2**, and **Type 3**, as in the previous example, we have two subgroups, **Type A** and **Type B**, as follows:

```
type_1 = [1, 1]  # 1 of type A and 1 of type B
type_2 = [1, 2]  # 1 of type A and 2 of type B
type_3 = [2, 3]  # 2 of type A and 3 of type B

counts = [type_1, type_2, type_3]
```

In essence, the total counts for **Type 1**, **Type 2**, and **Type 3** are still the same, but now each can be further broken up into two subgroups, represented by the 2D list **counts**. In general, the types here can be anything; our goal is to simply visualize this composition of the subgroups within each large type using a stacked or grouped bar graph.

First, we aim to create a grouped bar graph; our goal is the following visualization:

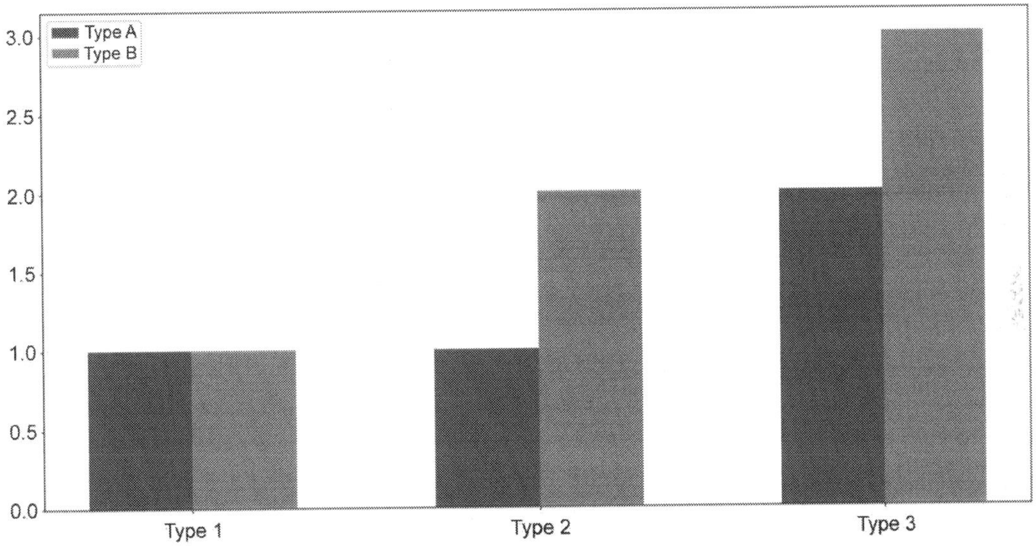

Figure 2.8: Grouped bar graphs

This is a more advanced visualization, and the process of creating the graph is thus more involved. First, we need to specify the individual locations of the grouped bars and their width:

```
locations = np.array([0, 1, 2])
width = 0.3
```

Then, we call the **plt.bar()** function on the appropriate data: once on the **Type A** numbers (**[my_type[0] for my_type in counts]**, using list comprehension) and once on the **Type B** numbers (**[my_type[1] for my_type in counts]**):

```
bars_a = plt.bar(locations - width / 2,
  [my_type[0] for my_type in counts], width=width)
bars_b = plt.bar(locations + width / 2,
  [my_type[1] for my_type in counts], width=width)
```

The terms **`locations - width / 2`** and **`locations + width / 2`** specify the exact locations of the **`Type A`** bars and the **`Type B`** bars, respectively. It is important that we reuse this **`width`** variable in the **`width`** argument of the **`plt.bar()`** function so that the two bars of each group are right next to each other.

Next, we'd like to customize the labels for each group of bars. Additionally, note that we are also assigning the returned values of the calls to **`plt.bar()`** to two variables, **`bars_a`** and **`bars_b`**, which will then be used to generate the legend for our graph:

```
plt.xticks(locations, ['Type 1', 'Type 2', 'Type 3'])
plt.legend([bars_a, bars_b], ['Type A', 'Type B'])
```

Finally, as we call **`plt.show()`**, the desired graph will be displayed.

So, that is the process of creating a grouped bar graph, where individual bars belonging to a group are placed next to one another. On the other hand, a stacked bar graph places the bars on top of each other. These two types of graphs are mostly used to convey the same information, but with stacked bars, the total counts of each group are easier to visually inspect and compare.

To create a stacked bar graph, we take advantage of the **`bottom`** argument of the **`plt.bar()`** function while declaring the non-first groups. Specifically, we do the following:

```
bars_a = plt.bar(locations, [my_type[0] for my_type in counts])
bars_b = plt.bar(locations, [my_type[1] for my_type in counts], \
                 bottom=[my_type[0] for my_type in counts])

plt.xticks(locations, ['Type 1', 'Type 2', 'Type 3'])
plt.legend([bars_a, bars_b], ['Type A', 'Type B'])

plt.show()
```

The preceding code will create the following visualization:

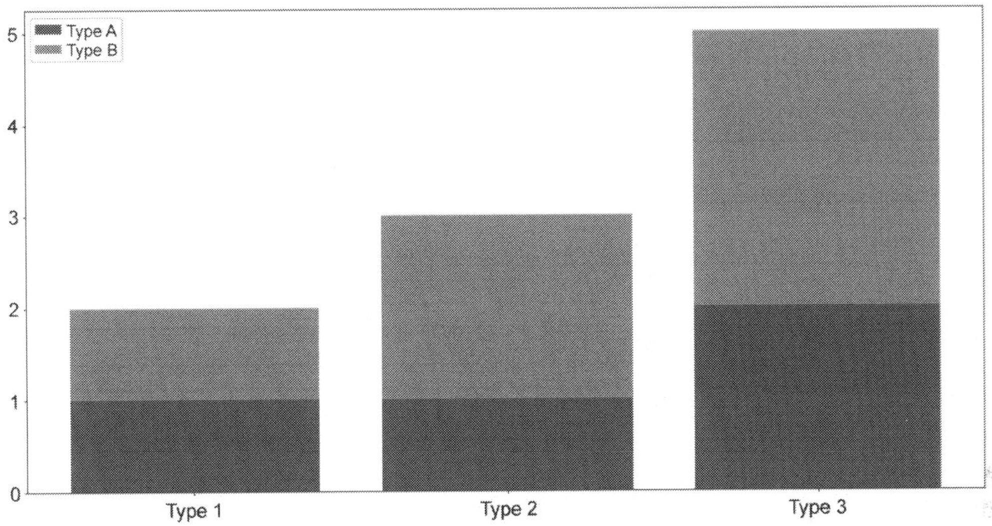

Figure 2.9: Stacked bar graphs

And that concludes our introduction to bar graphs in Matplotlib. Generally, these types of graph are used to visualize the counts or percentages of different groups of values in a categorical attribute. As we have observed, Matplotlib offers extendable APIs that can help generate these graphs in a flexible way.

Now, let's move on to our next visualization technique: histograms.

HISTOGRAMS

A histogram is a visualization that places multiple bars together, but its connection to bar graphs ends there. Histograms are usually used to represent the distribution of values within an attribute (a numerical attribute, to be more precise). Taking in an array of numbers, a histogram should consist of multiple bars, each spanning across a specific range to denote the amount of numbers belonging to that range.

Say we have an attribute in our dataset that contains the sample data stored in **`x`**. We can call **`plt.hist()`** on **`x`** to plot the distribution of the values in the attribute like so:

```
x = np.random.randn(100)

plt.hist(x)
plt.show()
```

The preceding code produces a visualization similar to the following:

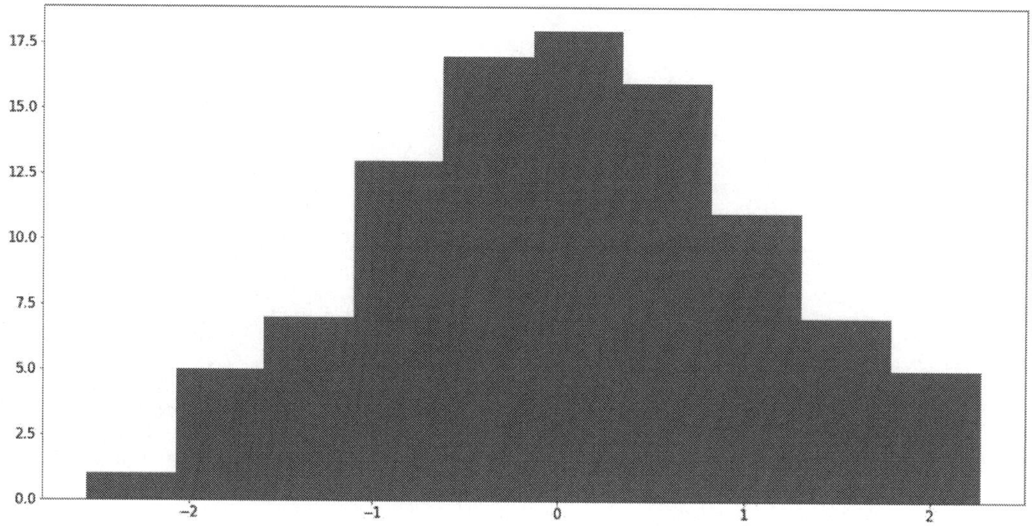

Figure 2.10: Histogram using Matplotlib

> **NOTE**
>
> Your output might somewhat differ from what we have here, but the general shape of the histogram should be the same—a bell curve.

It is possible to specify the **`bins`** argument in the **`plt.hist()`** function (whose default value is 10) to customize the number of bars that should be generated. Roughly speaking, increasing the number of bins decreases the width of the range each bin spans across, thereby improving the granularity of the histogram.

However, it is also possible to use too many bins in a histogram and achieve a bad visualization. For example, using the same variable, **`x`**, we can do the following:

```
plt.hist(x, bins=100)
plt.show()
```

The preceding code will produce the following graph:

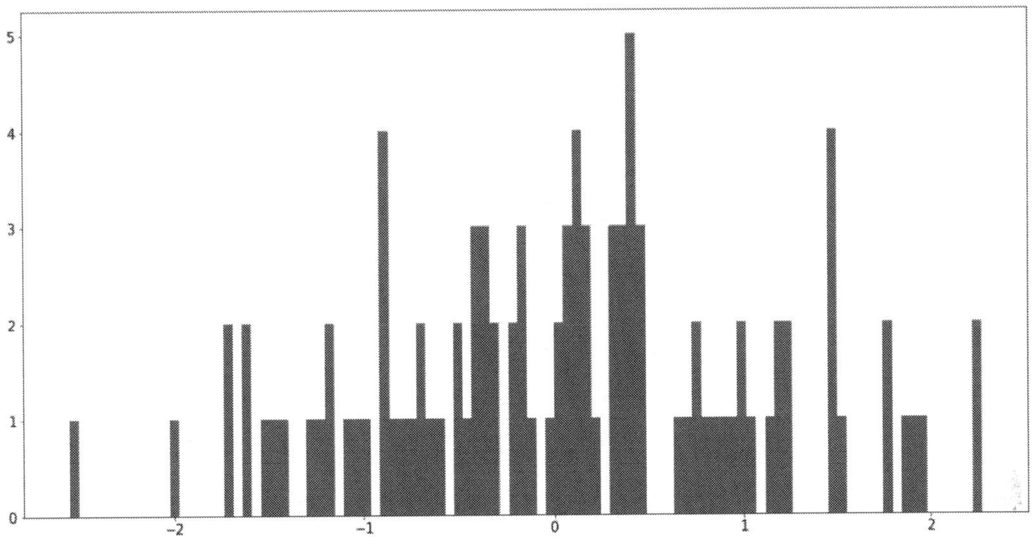

Figure 2.11: Using too many bins in a histogram

This visualization is arguably worse than the previous example as it causes our histogram to become fragmented and non-continuous. The easiest way to address this problem is to increase the ratio between the size of the input data and the number of bins, either by having more input data or using fewer bins.

Histograms are also quite useful in terms of helping us to compare the distributions of more than one attribute. For example, by adjusting the **`alpha`** argument (which specifies the opaqueness of a histogram), we can overlay multiple histograms in one graph so that their differences are highlighted. This is demonstrated by the following code and visualization:

```
y = np.random.randn(100) * 4 + 5

plt.hist(x, color='b', bins=20, alpha=0.2)
plt.hist(y, color='r', bins=20, alpha=0.2)
plt.show()
```

The output will be as follows:

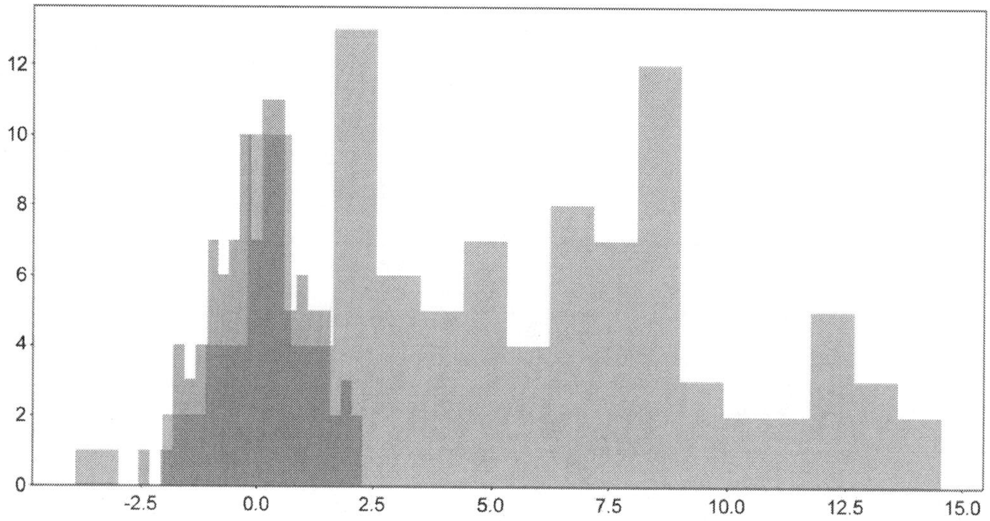

Figure 2.12: Overlaid histograms

Here, we can see that while the two distributions have roughly similar shapes, one is to the right of the other, indicating that its values are generally greater than the values of the attribute on the left.

One useful fact for us to note here is that when we simply call the **`plt.hist()`** function, a tuple containing two arrays of numbers is returned, denoting the locations and heights of individual bars in the corresponding histogram, as follows:

```
>>> plt.hist(x)
(array([ 9.,  7., 19., 18., 23., 12.,  6.,  4.,  1.,  1.]),
   array([-1.86590701, -1.34312205, -0.82033708, -0.29755212,
           0.22523285, 0.74801781,  1.27080278,  1.79358774,
           2.31637271,  2.83915767, 3.36194264]),
  <a list of 10 Patch objects>)
```

The two arrays include all the histogram-related information about the input data, processed by Matplotlib. This data can then be used to plot out the histogram, but in some cases, we can even store the arrays in new variables and use these statistics to perform further analysis on our data.

In the next section, we will move on to the final type of visualization we will be discussing in this chapter: heatmaps.

HEATMAPS

A heatmap is generated with a 2D array of numbers, where numbers with high values correspond to hot colors, and low-valued numbers correspond to cold colors. With Matplotlib, a heatmap is created with the **`plt.imshow()`** function. Let's say we have the following code:

```
my_map = np.random.randn(10, 10)

plt.imshow(my_map)
plt.colorbar()
plt.show()
```

The preceding code will produce the following visualization:

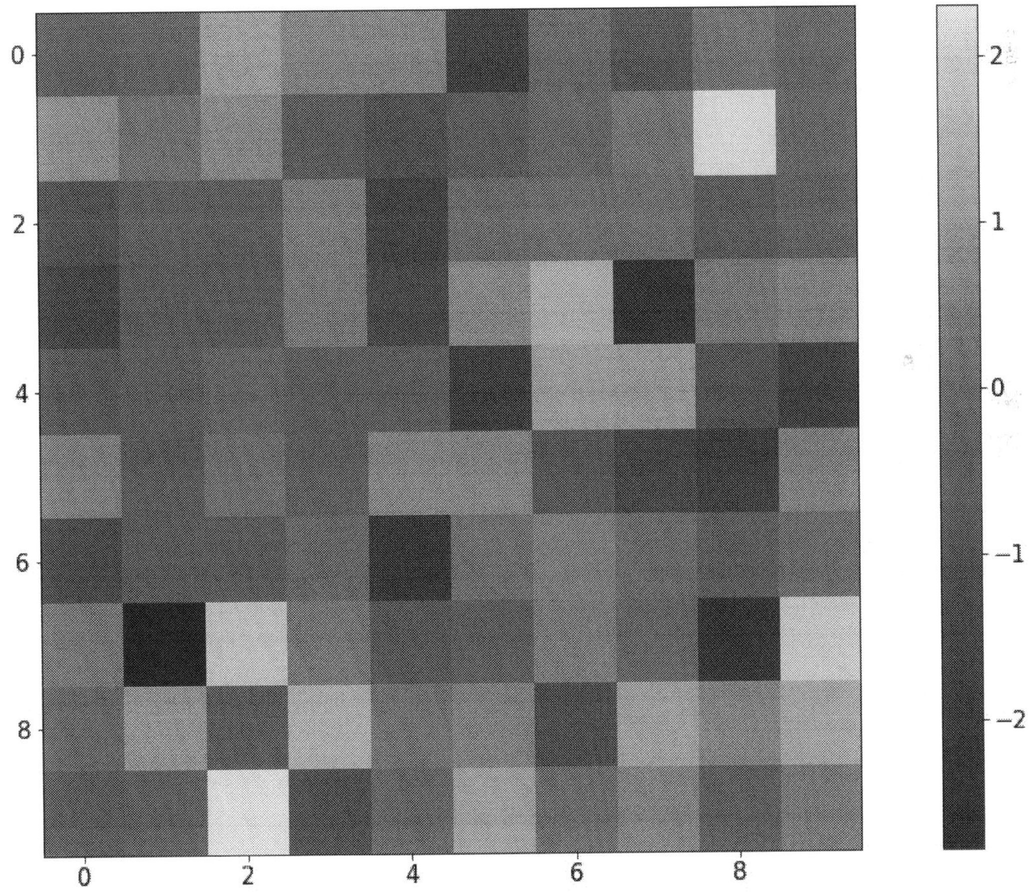

Figure 2.13: Heatmap using Matplotlib

Notice that with this representation, any group structure in the input 2D array (for example, if there is a block of cells whose values are significantly greater than the rest) will be effectively visualized.

An important use of heatmaps is when we consider the correlation matrix of a dataset (which is a 2D array containing a correlation between any given pair of attributes within the dataset). A heatmap will be able to help us pinpoint any and all attributes that are highly correlated to one another.

This concludes our final topic of discussion in this section regarding the visualization library, Matplotlib. The next exercise will help us consolidate the knowledge that we have gained by means of a hands-on example.

EXERCISE 2.04: VISUALIZATION OF PROBABILITY DISTRIBUTIONS

As we briefly mentioned when we talked about sampling, probability distributions are mathematical objects widely used in statistics and machine learning to model real-life data. While a number of probability distributions can prove abstract and complicated to work with, being able to effectively visualize their characteristics is the first step to understanding their usage.

In this exercise, we will apply some visualization techniques (histogram and line plot) to compare the sampling functions from NumPy against their true probability distributions. For a given probability distribution, the **probability density function** (also known as the **PDF**) defines the probability of any real number according to that distribution. The goal here is to verify that with a large enough sample size, NumPy's sampling function gives us the true shape of the corresponding PDF for a given probability distribution.

Perform the following steps to complete this exercise:

1. From your Terminal, that is, in your Python environment (if you are using one), install the SciPy package. You can install it, as always, using pip:

```
$ pip install scipy
```

   To install SciPy using Anaconda, use the following command:

```
$ conda install scipy
```

   SciPy is another popular statistical computing tool in Python. It contains a simple API for PDFs of various probability distributions that we will be using. We will revisit this library in the next chapter.

2. In the first code cell of a Jupyter notebook, import NumPy, the **stats** package of SciPy, and Matplotlib, as follows:

```
import numpy as np
import scipy.stats as stats
import matplotlib.pyplot as plt
```

3. In the next cell, draw 1,000 samples from the normal distribution with a mean of **0** and a standard deviation of **1** using NumPy:

```
samples = np.random.normal(0, 1, size=1000)
```

4. Next, we will create a **np.linspace** array between the minimum and the maximum of the samples that we have drawn, and finally call the true PDF on the numbers in the array. We're doing this so that we can plot these points in a graph in the next step:

```
x = np.linspace(samples.min(), samples.max(), 1000)
y = stats.norm.pdf(x)
```

5. Create a histogram for the drawn samples and a line graph for the points obtained via the PDF. In the **plt.hist()** function, specify the **density=True** argument so that the heights of the bars are normalized to probabilistic values (numbers between 0 and 1), the **alpha=0.2** argument to make the histogram lighter in color, and the **bins=20** argument for a greater granularity for the histogram:

```
plt.hist(samples, alpha=0.2, bins=20, density=True)
plt.plot(x, y)
plt.show()
```

The preceding code will create (roughly) the following visualization:

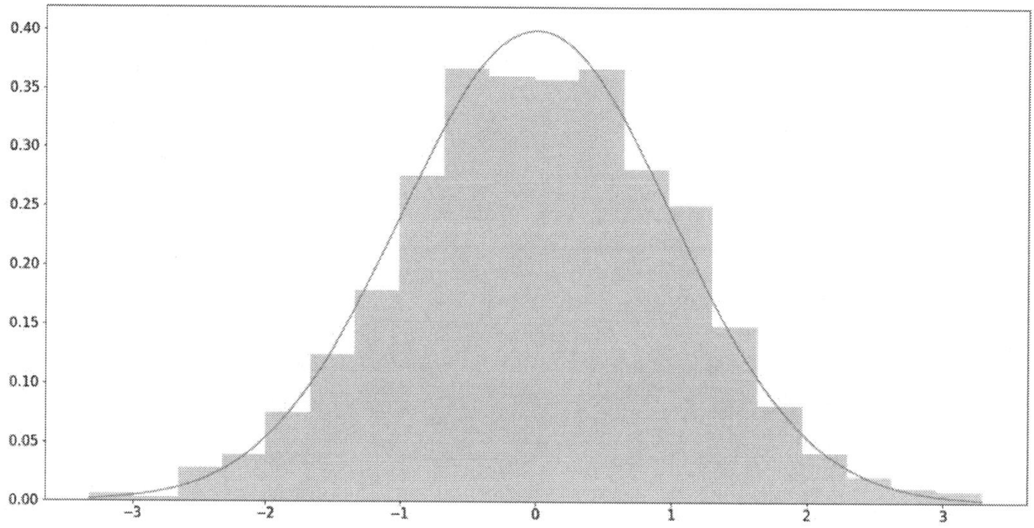

Figure 2.14: Histogram versus PDF for the normal distribution

We can see that the histogram for the samples we have drawn fits quite nicely with the true PDF of the normal distribution. This is evidence that the sampling function from NumPy and the PDF function from SciPy are working consistently with each other.

> **NOTE**
>
> To get an even smoother histogram, you can try increasing the number of bins in the histogram.

6. Next, we will create the same visualization for the Beta distribution with parameters (2, 5). For now, we don't need to know too much about the probability distribution itself; again, here, we only want to test out the sampling function from NumPy and the corresponding PDF from SciPy.

   In the next code cell, follow the same procedure that we followed previously:

```
samples = np.random.beta(2, 5, size=1000)
x = np.linspace(samples.min(), samples.max(), 1000)

y = stats.beta.pdf(x, 2, 5)

plt.hist(samples, alpha=0.2, bins=20, density=True)
plt.plot(x, y)
plt.show()
```

   This will, in turn, generate the following graph:

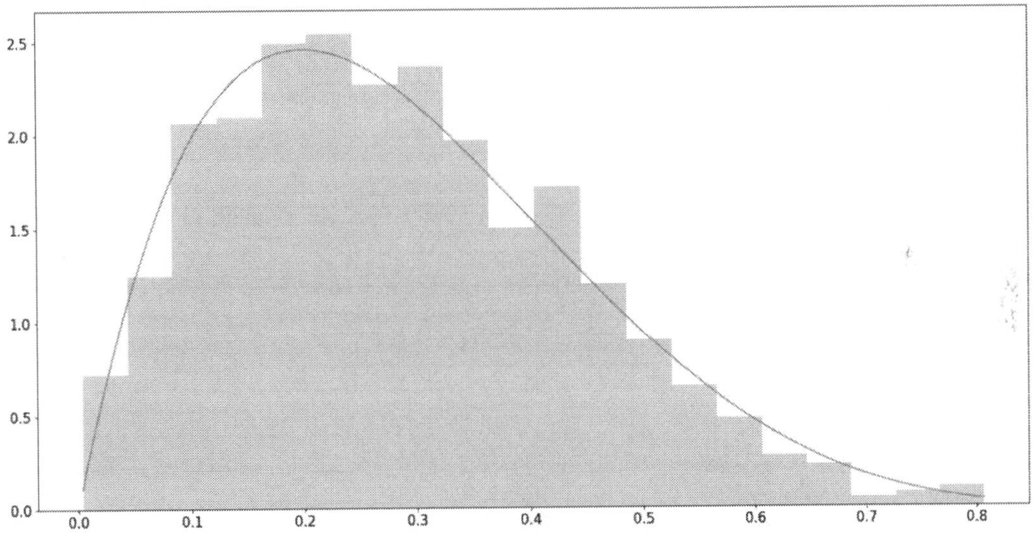

Figure 2.15: Histogram versus PDF for the Beta distribution

7. Create the same visualization for the Gamma distribution with parameter α = 1:

```
samples = np.random.gamma(1, size=1000)
x = np.linspace(samples.min(), samples.max(), 1000)
y = stats.gamma.pdf(x, 1)

plt.hist(samples, alpha=0.2, bins=20, density=True)
plt.plot(x, y)
plt.show()
```

The following visualization is then plotted:

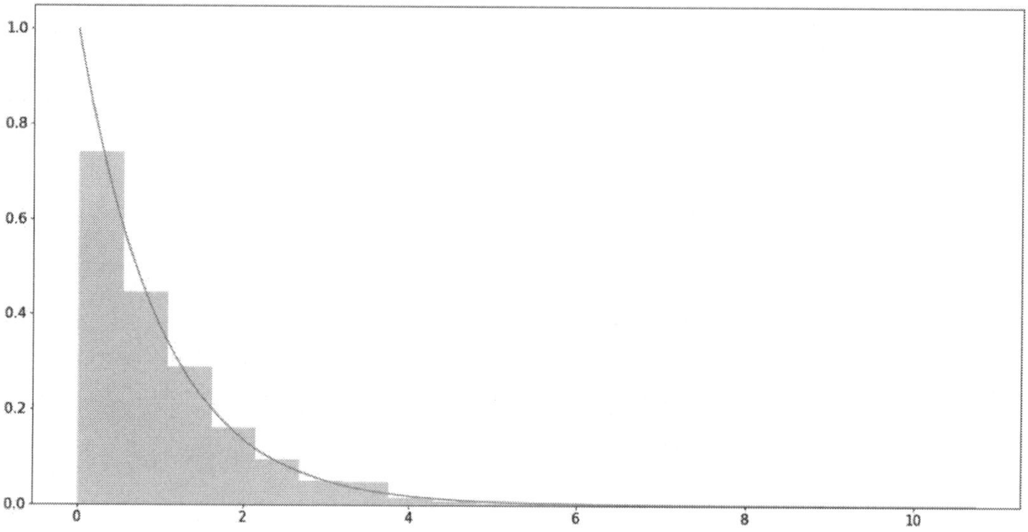

Figure 2.16: Histogram versus PDF for the Gamma distribution

Throughout this exercise, we have learned to combine a histogram and a line graph to verify a number of probability distributions implemented by NumPy and SciPy. We were also briefly introduced to the concept of probability distributions and their probability density functions.

> **NOTE**
>
> To access the source code for this specific section, please refer to https://packt.live/3eZrEbW.
>
> You can also run this example online at https://packt.live/3gmjLx8.

This exercise serves as the conclusion for the topic of Matplotlib. In the next section, we will end our discussion in this chapter by going through a number of shorthand APIs, provided by Seaborn and pandas, to quickly create complex visualizations.

VISUALIZATION SHORTHAND FROM SEABORN AND PANDAS

First, let's discuss the Seaborn library, the second most popular visualization library in Python after Matplotlib. Though still powered by Matplotlib, Seaborn offers simple, expressive functions that can facilitate complex visualization methods.

After successfully installing Seaborn via pip or Anaconda, the convention programmers typically use to import the library is with the **sns** alias. Now, say we have a tabular dataset with two numerical attributes, and we'd like to visualize their respective distributions:

```
x = np.random.normal(0, 1, 1000)
y = np.random.normal(5, 2, 1000)

df = pd.DataFrame({'Column 1': x, 'Column 2': y})
df.head()
```

Normally, we can create two histograms, one for each attribute that we have. However, we'd also like to inspect the relationship between the two attributes themselves, in which case we can take advantage of the **jointplot()** function in Seaborn. Let's see this in action:

```
import seaborn as sns

sns.jointplot(x='Column 1', y='Column 2', data=df)
plt.show()
```

As you can see, we can pass in a whole **DataFrame** object to a Seaborn function and specify the elements to be plotted in the function arguments. This process is arguably less painstaking than passing in the actual attributes we'd like to visualize using Matplotlib.

The following visualization will be generated by the preceding code:

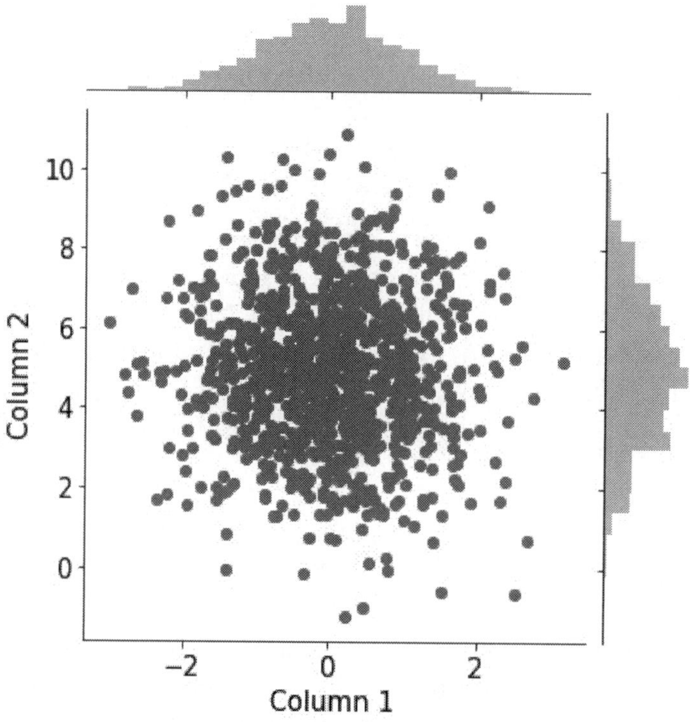

Figure 2.17: Joint plots using Seaborn

This visualization consists of a scatter plot for the two attributes and their respective histograms attached to the appropriate axes. From here, we can observe the distribution of individual attributes that we put in from the two histograms, as well as their *joint* distribution from the scatter plot.

Again, because this is a fairly complex visualization that can offer significant insights into the input data, it can be quite difficult to create manually in Matplotlib. What Seaborn succeeds in doing is building a pipeline for these complex but valuable visualization techniques and creating simple APIs to generate them.

Let's consider another example. Say we have a larger version of the same student dataset that we considered in *Exercise 2.03*, *The Student Dataset*, which looks as follows:

```
student_df = pd.DataFrame({
    'name': ['Alice', 'Bob', 'Carol', 'Dan', 'Eli', 'Fran', \
             'George', 'Howl', 'Ivan', 'Jack', 'Kate'],\

    'gender': ['female', 'male', 'female', 'male', \
               'male', 'female', 'male', 'male', \
               'male', 'male', 'female'],\

    'class': ['JR', 'SO', 'SO', 'SO', 'JR', 'SR', \
              'FY', 'SO', 'SR', 'JR', 'FY'],\

    'gpa': [90, 93, 97, 89, 95, 92, 90, 87, 95, 100, 95],\

    'num_classes': [4, 3, 4, 4, 3, 2, 2, 3, 3, 4, 2]})
```

Now, we'd like to consider the average GPA of the students we have in the dataset, grouped by class. Additionally, within each class, we are also interested in the difference between female and male students. This description calls for a grouped/stacked bar plot, where each group corresponds to a class and is broken into female and male averages.

With Seaborn, this is again done with a one-liner:

```
sns.catplot(x='class', y='gpa', hue='gender', kind='bar', \
            data=student_df)
plt.show()
```

This generates the following plot (notice how the legend is automatically included in the plot):

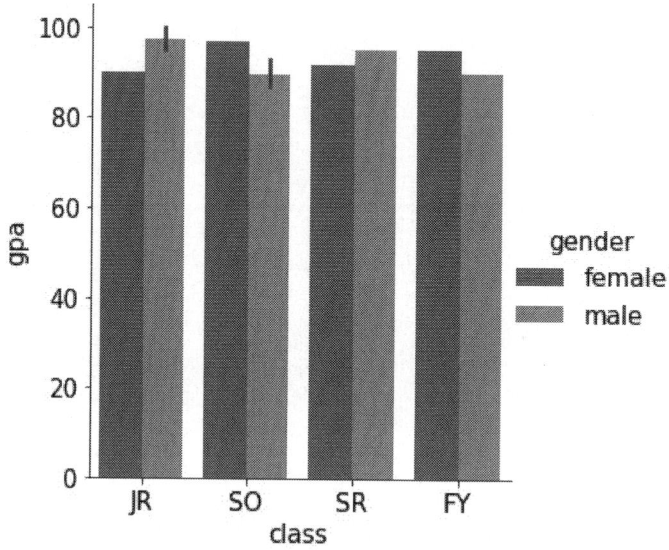

Figure 2.18: Grouped bar graph using Seaborn

In addition to Seaborn, the pandas library itself also offers unique APIs that directly interact with Matplotlib. This is generally done via the **`DataFrame.plot`** API. For example, still using our **`student_df`** variable we used previously, we can quickly generate a histogram for the data in the **`gpa`** attribute as follows:

```
student_df['gpa'].plot.hist()
plt.show()
```

The following graph is then created:

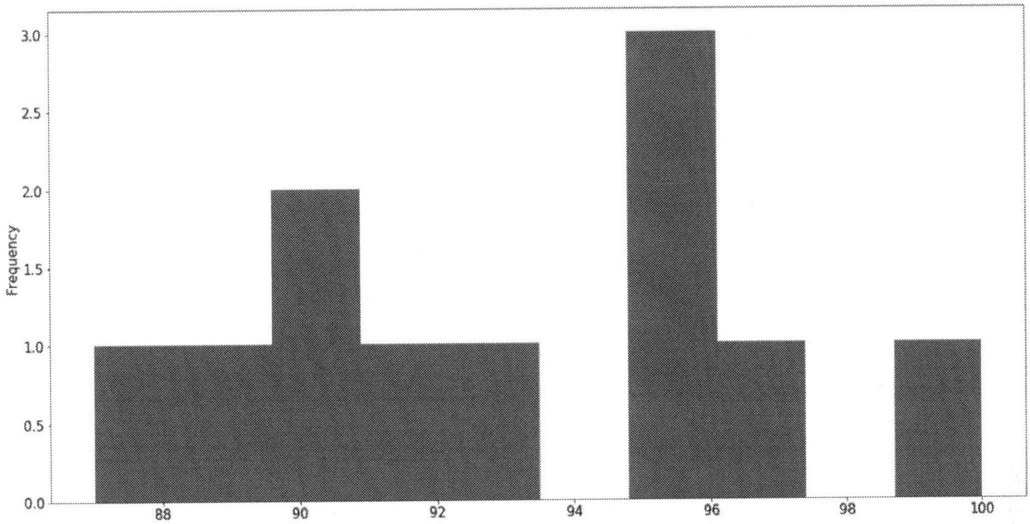

Figure 2.19: Histogram using pandas

Say we are interested in the percentage breakdown of the classes (that is, how much of a portion each class is with respect to all students). We can generate a pie chart from the class count (obtained via the **`value_counts()`** method):

```
student_df['class'].value_counts().plot.pie()
plt.show()
```

This results in the following output:

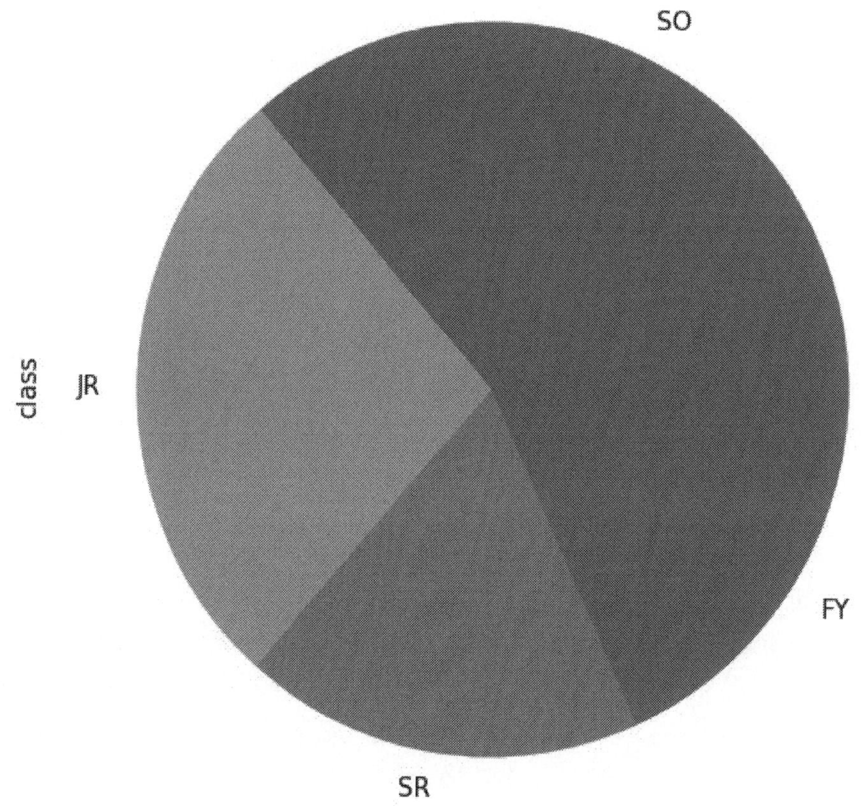

Figure 2.20: Pie chart from pandas

Through these examples, we have an idea of how Seaborn and Matplotlib streamline the process of creating complex visualizations, especially for **`DataFrame`** objects, using simple function calls. This clearly demonstrates the functional integration between various statistical and scientific tools in Python, making it one of the most, if not the most, popular modern scientific computing languages.

That concludes the material to be covered in the second chapter of this book. Now, let's go through a hands-on activity with a real-life dataset.

ACTIVITY 2.01: ANALYZING THE COMMUNITIES AND CRIME DATASET

In this activity, we will practice some basic data processing and analysis techniques on a dataset available online called *Communities and Crime*, with the hope of consolidating our knowledge and techniques. Specifically, we will process missing values in the dataset, iterate through the attributes, and visualize the distribution of their values.

First, we need to download this dataset to our local environment, which can be accessed on this page: https://packt.live/31C5yrZ

The dataset should have the name **`CommViolPredUnnormalizedData.txt`**. From the same directory as this dataset text file, create a new Jupyter notebook. Now, perform the following steps:

1. As a first step, import the libraries that we will be using: pandas, NumPy, and Matplotlib.
2. Read in the dataset from the text file using pandas and print out the first five rows by calling the **`head()`** method on the **`DataFrame`** object.
3. Loop through all the columns in the dataset and print them out line by line. At the end of the loop, also print out the total number of columns.
4. Notice that missing values are indicated as **`'?'`** in different cells of the dataset. Call the **`replace()`** method on the **`DataFrame`** object to replace that character with **`np.nan`** to faithfully represent missing values in Python.
5. Print out the list of columns in the dataset and their respective numbers of missing values using **`df.isnull().sum()`**, where **`df`** is the variable name of the **`DataFrame`** object.
6. Using the **`df.isnull().sum()[column_name]`** syntax (where **`column_name`** is the name of the column we are interested in), print out the number of missing values in the **`NumStreet`** and **`PolicPerPop`** columns.
7. Compute a **`DataFrame`** object that contains a list of values in the **`state`** attribute and their respective counts. Then, use the **`DataFrame.plot.bar()`** method to visualize that information in a bar graph.

8. Observe that, with the default scale of the plot, the labels on the x-axis are overlapping. Address this problem by making the plot bigger with the **`f, ax = plt.subplots(figsize=(15, 10))`** command. This should be placed at the beginning of any plotting commands.

9. Using the same value count **`DataFrame`** object that we used previously, call the **`DataFrame.plot.pie()`** method to create a corresponding pie chart. Adjust the figure size to ensure that the labels for your graph are displayed correctly.

10. Create a histogram representing the distribution of the population sizes in areas in the dataset (included in the **`population`** attribute). Adjust the figure size to ensure that the labels for your graph are displayed correctly.

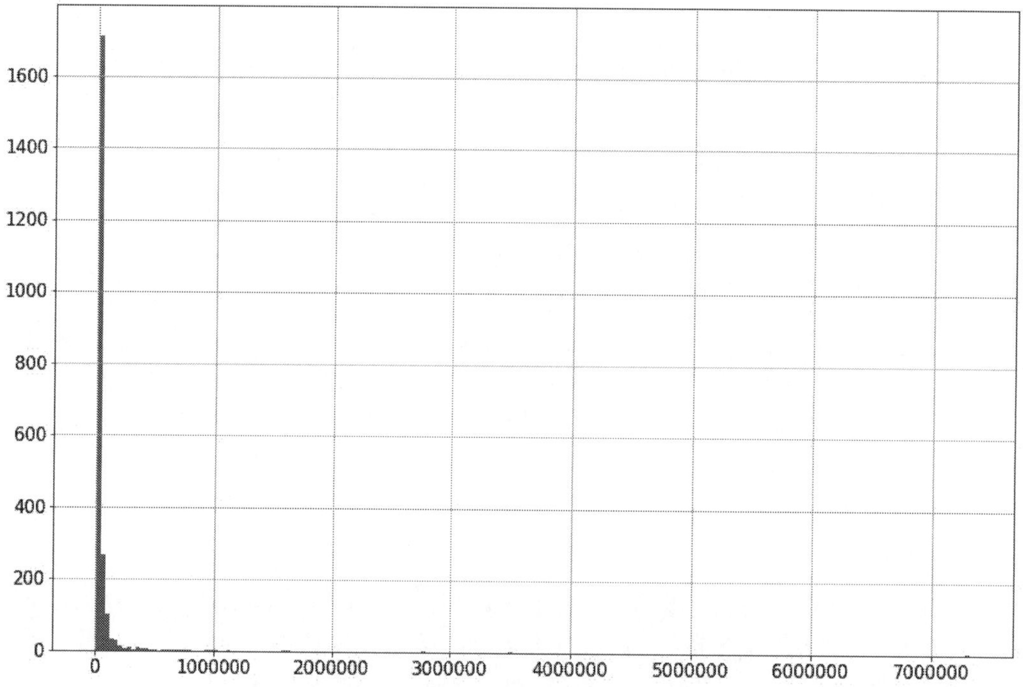

Figure 2.21: Histogram for population distribution

11. Create an equivalent histogram to visualize the distribution of household sizes in the dataset (included in the `householdsize` attribute).

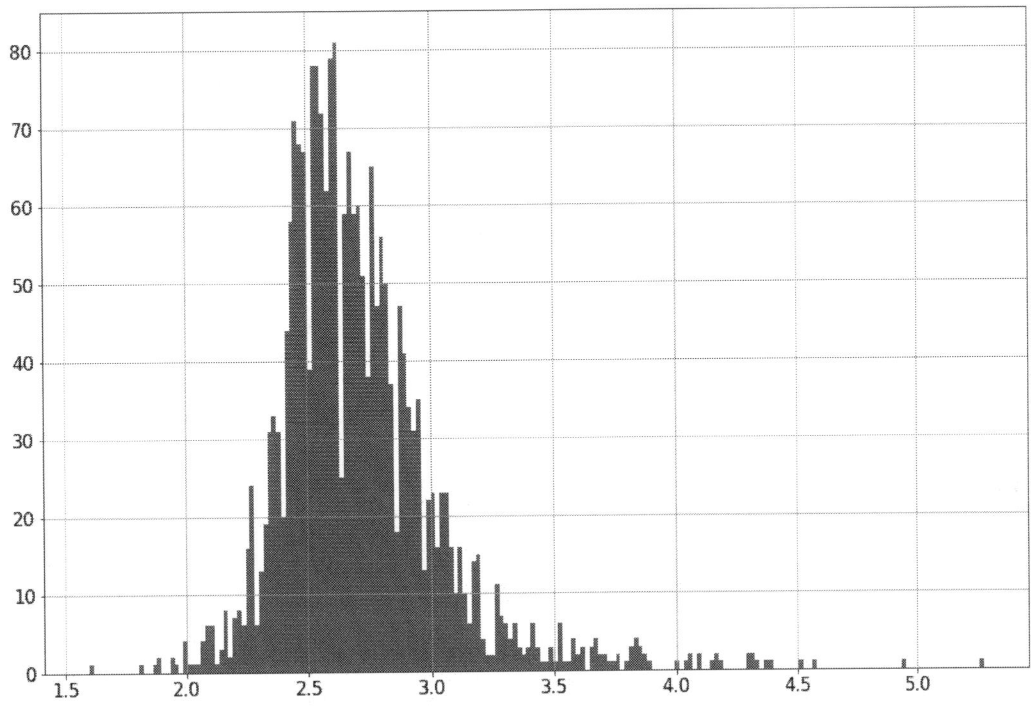

Figure 2.22: Histogram for household size distribution

> **NOTE**
>
> The solution to this activity can be found on page 653.

SUMMARY

This chapter went through the core tools for data science and statistical computing in Python, namely, NumPy for linear algebra and computation, pandas for tabular data processing, and Matplotlib and Seaborn for visualization. These tools will be used extensively in later chapters of this book, and they will prove useful in your future projects. In the next chapter, we will go into the specifics of a number of statistical concepts that we will be using throughout this book and learn how to implement them in Python.

3

PYTHON'S STATISTICAL TOOLBOX

OVERVIEW

In the previous chapter, we learned about the three main libraries in Python that help us facilitate various tasks in our statistics/machine learning projects. This chapter, in turn, initiates the formal topic of statistics and its relevant concepts. While it contains a number of theoretical discussion points, we will also employ intuitive examples and hands-on coding activities to help facilitate understanding. What we learn in this chapter will then prepare us for later statistics-related chapters in this workshop.

By the end of this chapter, you will understand the fundamental concepts in statistics and statistical methods. You'll also be able to carry out various statistics-related tasks using Python tools and libraries, and will have had an overview of a number of advanced statistics libraries in Python, such as statsmodels and PyMC3.

INTRODUCTION

So far, we have learned how to use the Python language, especially three of its core libraries—NumPy, pandas, and Matplotlib, for statistics and data science. However, in order to fully take advantage of these tools, we will need to have a solid theoretical understanding of statistics itself. By knowing the idea behind statistical tests and techniques, we will be able to utilize the tools that Python offers more effectively.

It is true that in statistics and machine learning, libraries in Python offer great options—from data cleaning/processing to modeling and making inferences. However, a fundamental understanding of statistics is still required so that we can make initial decisions regarding what kinds of techniques should be used in our process, depending on the data we have.

As such, in this chapter, we will learn about core concepts in statistics such as , inference, sampling, variables, and so on. We will also be introduced to a wide range of Python tools that can help facilitate more advanced statistical techniques and needs. All of this will be demonstrated with hands-on discussions and examples.

AN OVERVIEW OF STATISTICS

In this section, we will briefly discuss the goal of the overarching field of statistics and talk about some of its fundamental ideas. This conversation will set the context for the subsequent topics in this chapter and this book.

Generally speaking, statistics is all about working with data, be it processing, analyzing, or drawing a conclusion from the data we have. In the context of a given dataset, statistics has two main goals: describing the data, and drawing conclusions from it. These goals coincide with the two main categories of statistics — descriptive statistics and inferential statistics — respectively.

In descriptiv**e statistics**, questions are asked about the general characteristics of a dataset: What is the average amount? What is the difference between the maximum and the minimum? What value appears the most? And so forth. The answers to these questions help us get an idea of what the dataset in question constitutes and what the subject of the dataset is. We saw brief examples of this in the previous chapter.

In **inferential statistics**, the goal is to go a step further: after extracting appropriate insights from a given dataset, we'd like to use that information and infer on unknown data. One example of this is making predictions for the future from observed data. This is typically done via various statistical and machine learning models, each of which is only applicable to certain types of data. This is why it is highly important to understand what types of data there are in statistics, which are described in the next section.

Overall, statistics can be thought of as a field that studies data, which is why it is the foundation for data science and machine learning. Using statistics, we can understand the state of the world using our sometimes-limited datasets, and from there make appropriate and actionable decisions, made from the data-driven knowledge that we obtain. This is why statistics is used ubiquitously in various fields of study, from sciences to social sciences, and sometimes even the humanities, when there are analytical elements involved in the research.

With that said, let's begin our first technical topic of this chapter: distinguishing between data types.

TYPES OF DATA IN STATISTICS

In statistics, there are two main types of data: categorical data and numerical data. Depending on which type an attribute or a variable in your dataset belongs to, its data processing, modeling, analysis, and visualization techniques might differ. In this section, we will explain the details of these two main data types and discuss relevant points for each of them, which are summarized in the following table:

Features	**Categorical data**	**Numerical data**
Characteristic	Discrete values	Continuous values
Ordinality	No	Yes
Modeling	Categorical/discrete probability distributions	Continuous probability distributions
Data processing	One-hot encoding	Scaling and normalization
Descriptive statistics	Mode	Mean and standard deviation
Predictive modeling	Classification	Regression
Visualization techniques	Pie charts and bar graphs	Histograms, line graphs, and scatter plots

Figure 3.1: Data type comparison

For the rest of this section, we will go into more detail about each of the preceding comparisons, starting with categorical data in the next subsection.

CATEGORICAL DATA

When an attribute or a variable is categorical, the possible values it can take belong to a predetermined and fixed set of values. For example, in a weather-related dataset, you might have an attribute to describe the overall weather for each day, in which case that attribute might be among a list of discrete values such as **"sunny"**, **"windy"**, **"cloudy"**, **"rain"**, and so on. A cell in this attribute column *must* take on one of these possible values; a cell cannot contain, for example, a number or an unrelated string like **"apple"**. Another term for this type of data is *nominal data*.

Because of the nature of the data, in most cases, there is no ordinal relationship between the possible values of a categorical attribute. For example, there is no comparison operation that can be applied to the weather-related data we described previously: **"sunny"** is neither greater than or less than **"windy"**, and so on. This is to be contrasted with numerical data, which, although we haven't discussed it yet, expresses clear ordinality.

On the topic of differences between data types, let's now go through a number of points to keep in mind when working with categorical data.

If an unknown variable that is a categorical attribute is to be modeled using a probability distribution, a categorical distribution will be required. Such a distribution describes the probability that the variable is one out of *K* predefined possible categories. Luckily for us, most of the modeling will be done in the backend of various statistical/machine learning models when we call them from their respective libraries, so we don't have to worry about the problem of modeling right now.

In terms of data processing, an encoding scheme is typically used to *convert* the categorical values in an attribute to numerical, machine-interpretable values. As such, string values, which are highly common in categorical data, cannot be fed to a number of models that only take in numerical data.

For example, some tend to use the simple encoding of assigning each possible value with a positive integer and replacing them with their respective numerical value. Consider the following sample dataset (stored in the variable named **weather_df**):

```
weather_df
```

The output will be as follows:

	temp	weather
0	55	windy
1	34	cloudy
2	80	sunny
3	75	rain
4	53	sunny

Now, you could potentially call the **map()** method on the **weather** attribute and pass in the dictionary **{'windy': 0, 'cloudy': 1, 'sunny': 2, 'rain': 3}** (the **map()** method simply applies the mapping defined by the dictionary on the attribute) to encode the categorical attribute like so:

```
weather_df['weather_encoded'] = weather_df['weather'].map(\
                                {'windy': 0, 'cloudy': 1, \
                                 'sunny': 2, 'rain': 3})
```

This DataFrame object will now hold the following data:

```
weather_df
```

The output is as follows:

	temp	weather	weather_encoded
0	55	windy	0
1	34	cloudy	1
2	80	sunny	2
3	75	rain	3
4	53	sunny	2

We see that the categorical column **weather** has been successfully converted to numerical data in **weather_encoded** via a one-to-one mapping. However, this technique can be potentially dangerous: the new attribute implicitly places an order on its data. Since *0 < 1 < 2 < 3*, we are inadvertently imposing the same ordering on the original categorical data; this is especially dangerous if the model we are using specifically interprets that as truly numerical data.

This is the reason why we must be careful when transforming our categorical attributes into a numerical form. We have actually already discussed a certain technique that is able to convert categorical data without imposing a numerical relationship in the previous chapter: one-hot encoding. In this technique, we create a new attribute for every unique value in a categorical attribute. Then, for each row in the dataset, we place a **1** in a newly created attribute if that row has the corresponding value in the original categorical attribute and **0** in the other new attributes.

The following code snippet reiterates how we can implement one-hot encoding with pandas and what effect it will have on our current sample weather dataset:

```
pd.get_dummies(weather_df['weather'])
```

This will produce the following output:

	cloudy	rain	sunny	windy
0	0	0	0	1
1	1	0	0	0
2	0	0	1	0
3	0	1	0	0
4	0	0	1	0

Among the various descriptive statistics that we will discuss later in this chapter, the mode — the value that appears the most — is typically the only statistic that can be used on categorical data. As a consequence of this, when there are values missing from a categorical attribute in our dataset and we'd like to fill them with a central tendency statistic, a concept we will define later on in this chapter, the mode is the only one that should be considered.

In terms of making predictions, if a categorical attribute is the target of our machine learning pipeline (as in, if we want to predict a categorical attribute), classification models are needed. As opposed to regression models, which make predictions on numerical, continuous data, classification models, or classifiers for short, keep in mind the possible values their target attribute can take and only predict among those values. Thus, when deciding which machine learning model(s) you should train on your dataset to predict categorical data, make sure to only use classifiers.

The last big difference between categorical data and numerical data is in visualization techniques. A number of visualization techniques were discussed in the previous chapter that are applicable for categorical data, two of the most common of which are bar graphs (including stacked and grouped bar graphs) and pie charts.

These types of visualization focus on the portion of the whole dataset each unique value takes up.

For example, with the preceding weather dataset, we can create a pie chart using the following code:

```
weather_df['weather'].value_counts().plot.pie(autopct='%1.1f%%')
plt.ylabel('')
plt.show()
```

This will create the following visualization:

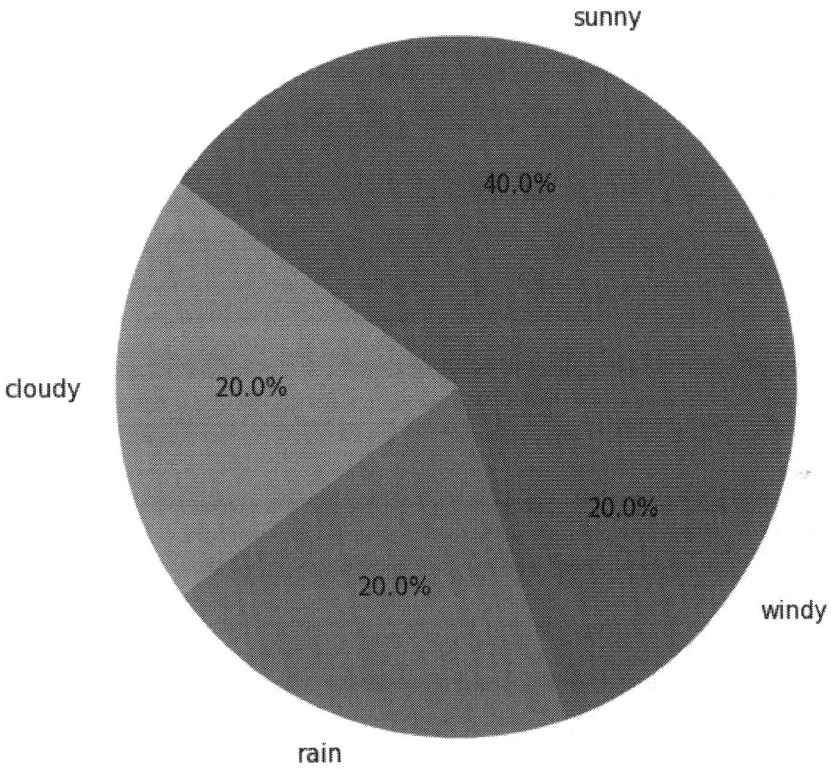

Figure 3.2: Pie chart for weather data

We can see that in the whole dataset, the value **`'sunny'`** occurs 40 percent of the time, while each of the other values occurs 20 percent of the time.

We have so far covered most of the biggest theoretical differences between a categorical attribute and a numerical attribute, which we will discuss in the next section. However, before moving on, there is another subtype of the categorical data type that should be mentioned: binary data.

A binary attribute, whose values can only be **True** and **False**, is a categorical attribute whose set of possible values contains the two Boolean values mentioned. Since Boolean values can be easily interpreted by machine learning and mathematical models, there is usually not a need to convert a binary attribute into any other form.

In fact, binary attributes that are not originally in the Boolean form should be converted into **True** and **False** values. We encountered an example of this in the sample student dataset in the previous chapter:

```
student_df
```

The output is as follows:

	name	sex	class	gpa	num_classes
0	Alice	female	FY	90	4
1	Bob	male	SO	93	3
2	Carol	female	SR	97	4
3	Dan	male	SO	89	4
4	Eli	male	JR	95	3
5	Fran	female	SR	92	2

Here, the column **'sex'** is a categorical attribute whose values can either be **'female'** or **'male'**. So instead, what we can do to make this data more machine-friendly (while ensuring no information will be lost or added in) is to *binarize* the attribute, which we have done via the following code:

```
student_df['female_flag'] = student_df['sex'] == 'female'
student_df = student_df.drop('sex', axis=1)
student_df
```

The output is as follows:

	name	class	gpa	num_classes	female_flag
0	Alice	FY	90	4	True
1	Bob	SO	93	3	False
2	Carol	SR	97	4	True
3	Dan	SO	89	4	False
4	Eli	JR	95	3	False
5	Fran	SR	92	2	True

> **NOTE**
>
> Since the newly created column `'female_flag'` contains all the information from the column `'sex'` and only that, we can simply drop the latter from our dataset.

Aside from that, binary attributes can be treated as categorical data in any other way (processing, making predictions, and visualization).

Let's now apply what we have discussed so far in the following exercise.

EXERCISE 3.01: VISUALIZING WEATHER PERCENTAGES

In this exercise, we are given a sample dataset that includes the weather in a specific city across five days. This dataset can be downloaded from https://packt.live/2Ar29RG. We aim to visualize the categorical information in this dataset to examine the percentages of different types of weather using the visualization techniques for categorical data that we have discussed so far:

1. In a new Jupyter notebook, import pandas, Matplotlib, and seaborn and use pandas to read in the aforementioned dataset:

```
import pandas as pd
import matplotlib.pyplot as plt
import seaborn as sns

weather_df = pd.read_csv('weather_data.csv')
weather_df.head()
```

When the first five rows of this dataset are printed out, you should see the following output:

Out[46]:

	day	city	weather
0	0	St Louis	sunny
1	0	New York	cloudy
2	0	San Francisco	sunny
3	1	New York	rain
4	1	St Louis	cloudy

Figure 3.3: The weather dataset

As you can see, each row of this dataset tells us what the weather was on a given day in a given city. For example, on day **0**, it was sunny in **St Louis** while it was **cloudy** in **New York**.

2. In the next code cell in the notebook, compute the counts (the numbers of occurrences) for all the weather types in our dataset and visualize that information using the **plot.bar()** method:

```
weather_df['weather'].value_counts().plot.bar()
plt.show()
```

This code will produce the following output:

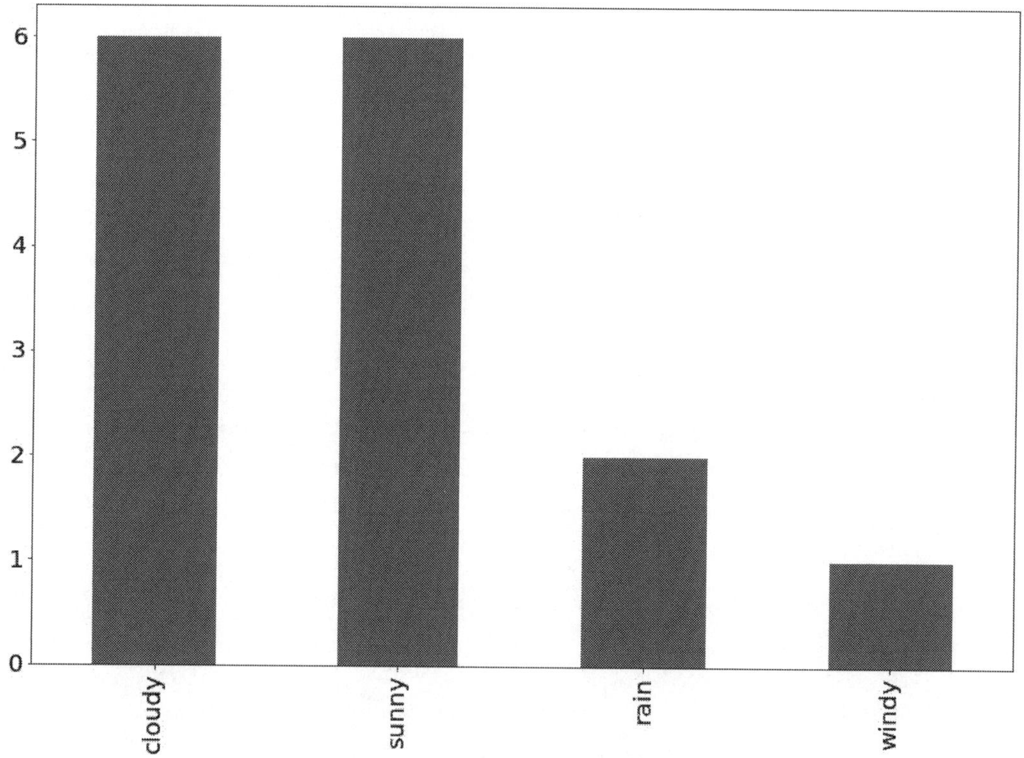

Figure 3.4: Counts of weather types

3. Visualize the same information we have in the previous step as a pie chart using the **plot.pie(autopct='%1.1f%%')** method:

```
weather_df['weather'].value_counts().plot.pie(autopct='%1.1f%%')
plt.ylabel('')
plt.show()
```

This code will produce the following output:

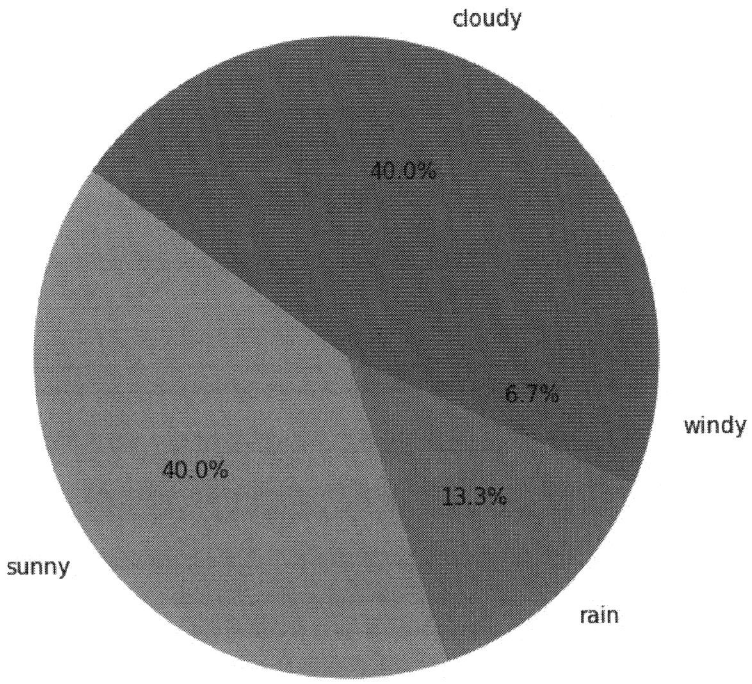

Figure 3.5: Counts of weather types

4. Now, we would like to visualize these counts of weather types, together with the information on what percentage each weather type accounts for in each city. First, this information can be computed using the **groupby()** method, as follows:

```
weather_df.groupby(['weather', 'city'])['weather'].count()\
                                        .unstack('city')
```

The output is as follows:

```
city       New York    San Francisco    St Louis
weather
cloudy     3.0         NaN              3.0
rain       1.0         NaN              1.0
sunny      1.0         4.0              1.0
windy      NaN         1.0              NaN
```

We see that this object contains the information that we wanted. For example, looking at the **cloudy** row in the table, we see that the weather type **cloudy** occurs three times in New York and three times in St Louis. There are multiple places where we have **NaN** values, which denote non-occurrences.

5. We finally visualize the table we have in the previous step as a stacked bar plot:

```
weather_df.groupby(['weather', 'city'])\
                   ['weather'].count().unstack('city')\
                   .fillna(0).plot(kind='bar', stacked=True)
plt.show()
```

This will produce the following plot:

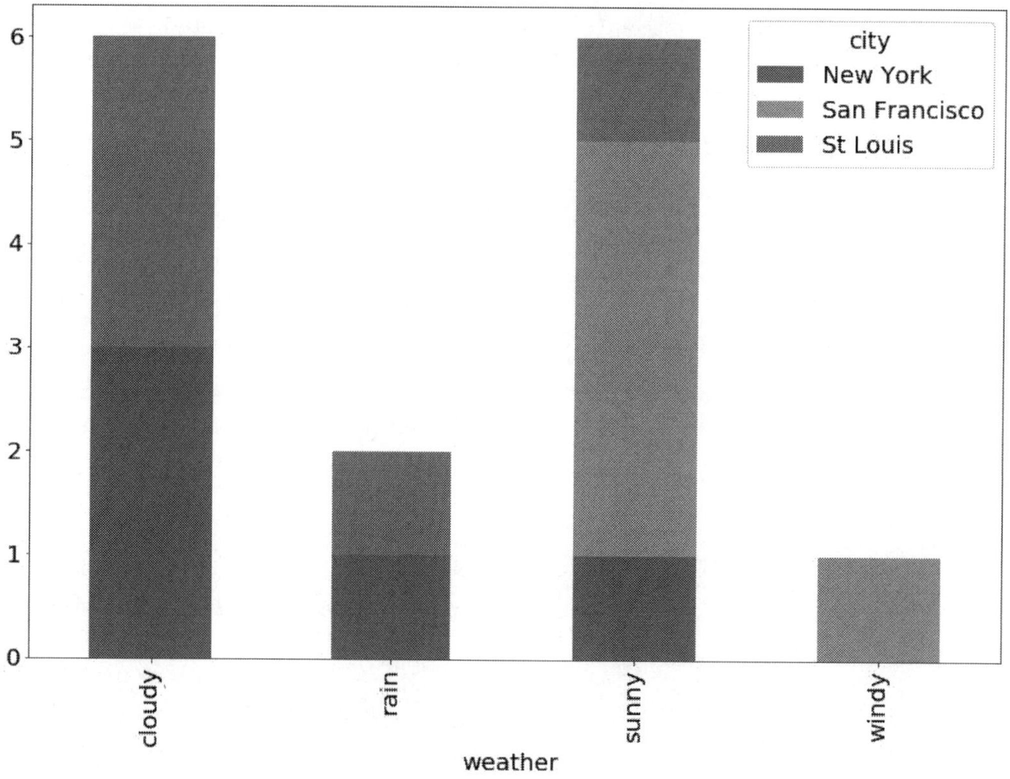

Figure 3.6: Counts of weather types with respect to cities

Throughout this exercise, we have put our knowledge regarding categorical data into practice to visualize various types of counts computed from a sample weather dataset.

> **NOTE**
>
> To access the source code for this specific section, please refer to https://packt.live/2ArQAtw.
>
> You can also run this example online at https://packt.live/3gklWAw.

With that, let's move on to the second main type of data: numerical data.

NUMERICAL DATA

The term proves to be intuitive in helping us understand what type of data this is. A numerical attribute should contain numerical and continuous values or real numbers. The values belonging to a numerical attribute can have a specific range; for example, they can be positive, negative, or between 0 and 1. However, an attribute being numerical implies that its data can take any value within its given range. This is notably different from values in a categorical attribute, which only belong to a given discrete set of values.

There are many examples of numerical data: the height of the members of a population, the weight of the students in a school, the price of houses that are for sale in certain areas, the average speed of track-and-field athletes, and so on. As long as the data can be represented as real-valued numbers, it is most likely numerical data.

Given its nature, numerical data is vastly different from categorical data. In the following text, we will lay out some of the most important differences with respect to statistics and machine learning that we should keep in mind.

As opposed to a few probability distributions that can be used to model categorical data, there are numerous probability distributions for numerical data. These include the normal distribution (also known as the bell curve distribution), the uniform distribution, the exponential distribution, the Student's t distribution, and many more. Each of these probability distributions is designed to model specific types of data. For example, the normal distribution is typically used to model quantities with linear growth such as age, height, or students' test scores, while the exponential distribution models the amount of time between the occurrences of a given event.

It is important, therefore, to research what specific probability distribution is suitable for the numerical attribute that you are attempting to model. An appropriate distribution will allow for coherent analysis as well as accurate predictions; on the other hand, an unsuitable choice of probability distribution might lead to unintuitive and incorrect conclusions.

On another topic, many processing techniques can be applied to numerical data. Two of the most common of these include scaling and normalization.

Scaling involves adding and/or multiplying all the values in a numerical attribute by a fixed quantity to scale the range of the original data to another range. This method is used when statistical and machine learning models can only handle values within a given range (for example, positive numbers or numbers between 0 and 1 can be processed and analyzed more easily).

One of the most commonly used scaling techniques is the min-max scaling method, which is explained by the following formula, where *a* and *b* are positive numbers:

$$X' = a + (b - a)\frac{X - X_{min}}{X_{max} - X_{min}}$$

Figure 3.7: Formula for min-max scaling

X' and X denote the data after and before the transformation, while X_{max} and X_{min} denote the maximum and minimum values within the data, respectively. It can be mathematically proven that the output of the formula is always greater than *a* and less than *b*, but we don't need to go over that here. We will come back to this scaling method again in our next exercise.

As for normalization, even though this term is sometimes used interchangeably with *scaling*, it denotes the process of specifically scaling a numerical attribute to the normalized form with respect to its probability distribution. The goal is for us to obtain a transformed dataset that nicely follows the shape of the probability distribution we have chosen.

For example, say the data we have in a numerical attribute follows a normal distribution with a mean of **4** and a standard deviation of **10**. The following code randomly generates that data synthetically and visualizes it:

```
samples = np.random.normal(4, 10, size=1000)


plt.hist(samples, bins=20)
plt.show()
```

This produces the following plot:

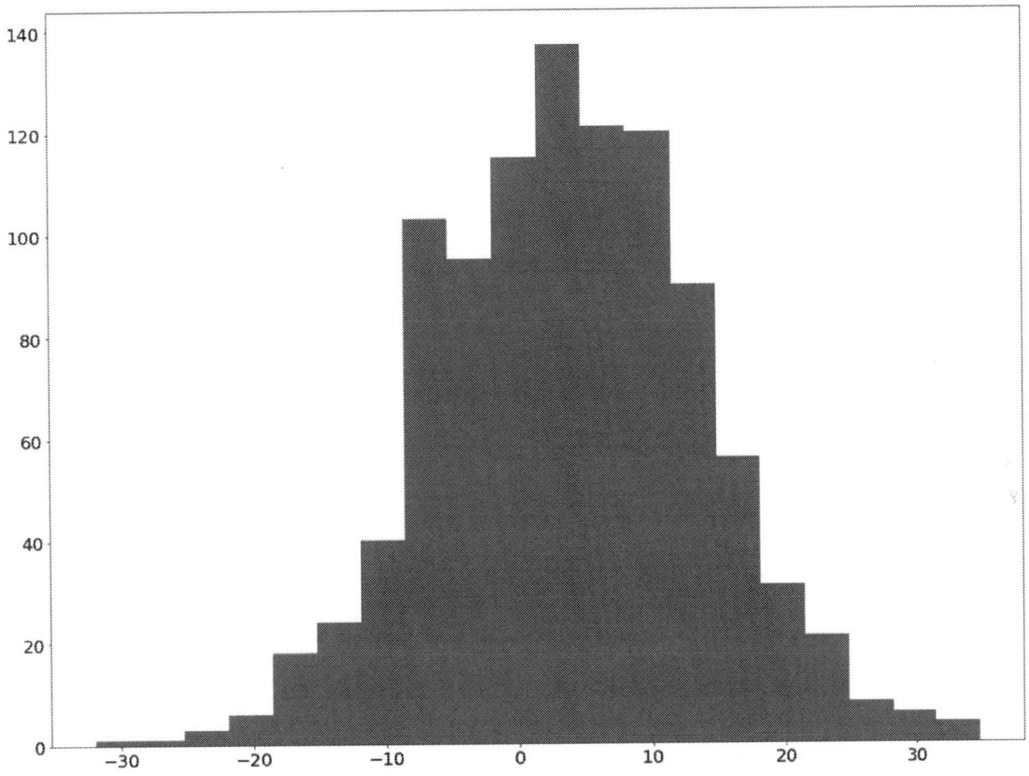

Figure 3.8: Histogram for normally distributed data

Now, say you have a model that assumes the standard form of the normal distribution for this data, where the mean is **0** and the standard deviation is **1**, and if the input data is not in this form, the model will have difficulty learning from it. Therefore, you'd like to somehow transform the preceding data into this standard form, without sacrificing the true pattern (specifically the general shape) of the data.

Here, we can apply the normalization technique for normally distributed data, in which we subtract the true mean from the data points and divide the result by the true standard deviation. This scaling process is more generally known as a standard scaler. Since the preceding data is already a NumPy array, we can take advantage of vectorization and perform the normalization as follows:

```
normalized_samples = (samples - 4) / 10

plt.hist(normalized_samples, bins=20)
plt.show()
```

This code will generate the histogram for our newly transformed data, which is shown here:

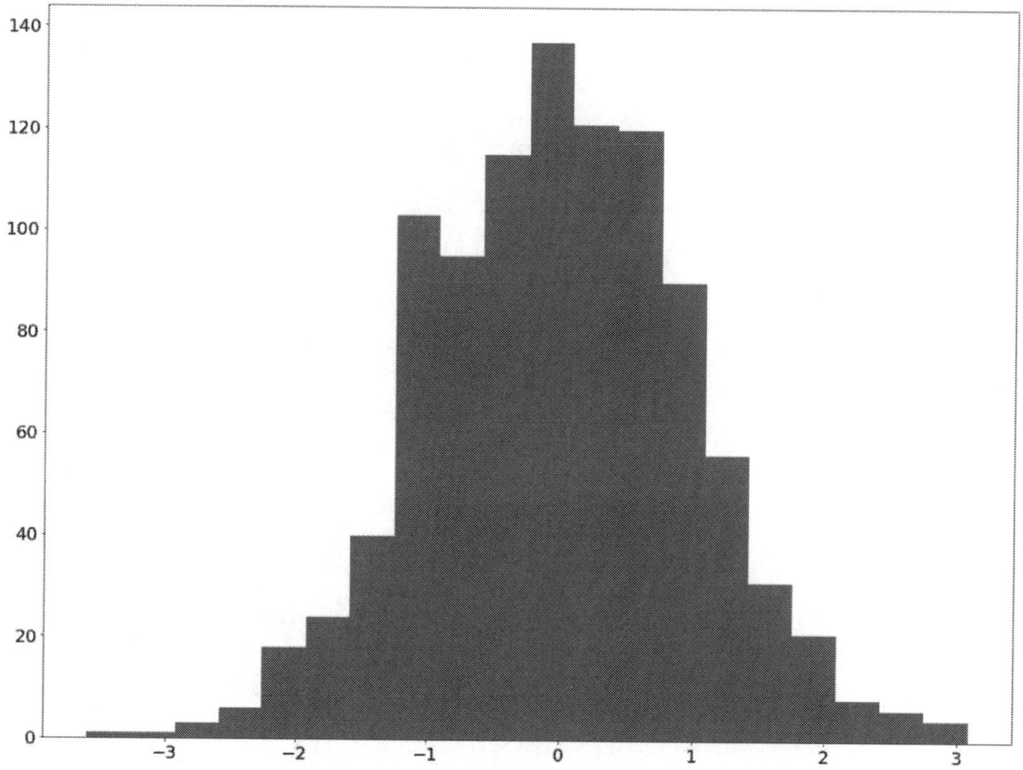

Figure 3.9: Histogram for normalized data

We see that while the data has been successfully shifted to the range we want, now it centers around **0** and most of the data lies between **−3** and **3**, which is the standard form of the normal distribution, but the general shape of the data has not been altered. In other words, the relative differences between the data points have not been changed.

On an additional note, in practice, when the true mean and/or the true standard deviation are not available, we can approximate those statistics with the sample mean and standard deviation as follows:

```
sample_mean = np.mean(samples)
sample_sd = np.std(samples)
```

With a large number of samples, these two statistics offer a good approximation that can be further used for this type of transformation. With that, we can now feed this normalized data to our statistical and machine learning models for further analysis.

Speaking of the mean and the standard deviation, those two statistics are usually used to describe numerical data. To fill in missing values in a numerical attribute, central tendency measures such as the mean and the median are typically used. In some special cases such as a time-series dataset, you can use more complex missing value imputation techniques such as interpolation, where we estimate the missing value to be somewhere *in between* the ones immediately before and after it in a sequence.

When we'd like to train a predictive model to target a numerical attribute, regression models are used. Instead of making predictions on which possible categorical values an entry can take like a classifier, a regression model looks for a reasonable prediction across a continuous numerical range. As such, similar to what we have discussed, we must take care to only apply regression models on datasets whose target values are numerical attributes.

Finally, in terms of visualizing numerical data, we have seen a wide range of visualization techniques that we can use. Immediately before this, we saw histograms being used to describe the distribution of a numerical attribute, which tells us how the data is dispersed along its range.

In addition, line graphs and scatter plots are generally good tools to visualize patterns of an attribute with respect to other attributes. (For example, we plotted the PDF of various probability distributions as line graphs.) Lastly, we also saw a heatmap being used to visualize a two-dimensional structure, which can be applied to represent correlations between numerical attributes in a dataset.

Before we move on with our next topic of discussion, let's performa quick exercise on the concept of scaling/normalization. Again, one of the most popular scaling/normalization methods is called *Min-Max scaling*, which allows us to transform all values in a numerical attribute into any arbitrary range *[a, b]*. We will explore this method next.

EXERCISE 3.02: MIN-MAX SCALING

In this exercise, we will write a function that facilitates the process of applying Min-Max scaling to a numerical attribute. The function should take in three parameters: **data**, **a**, and **b**. While **data** should be a NumPy array or a pandas **Series** object, **a** and **b** should be real-valued positive numbers denoting the endpoints of the numerical range that **data** should be transformed into.

Referring back to the formula included in the *Numerical Data* section, Min-Max scaling is given by the following:

$$X' = a + (b - a)\frac{X - X_{min}}{X_{max} - X_{min}}$$

Figure 3.10: Formula for min-max scaling

Let's have a look at the steps that need to be followed to meet our goal:

1. Create a new Jupyter notebook and in its first code cell, import the libraries that we will be using for this exercise, as follows:

```
import pandas as pd
import numpy as np

import matplotlib.pyplot as plt
```

   In the dataset that we will be using, the first column is named **'Column 1'** and contains 1,000 samples from a normal distribution with a mean of 4 and a standard deviation of 10. The second column is named **'Column 2'** and contains 1,000 samples from a uniform distribution from 1 to 2. The third column is named **'Column 3'** and contains 1,000 samples from a Beta distribution with parameters 2 and 5. In the next code cell, read in the **'data.csv'** file, which we generated for you beforehand (and which can be found at https://packt.live/2YTrdKt), as a **DataFrame** object using pandas and print out the first five rows:

```
df = pd.read_csv('data.csv')
df.head()
```

You should see the following numbers:

	Column 1	Column 2	Column 3
0	-1.231356	1.305917	0.511994
1	7.874195	1.291636	0.155032
2	13.169984	1.274973	0.183988
3	13.442203	1.549126	0.391825
4	-8.032985	1.895236	0.398122

2. In the next cell, write a function named **`min_max_scale()`** that takes in three parameters: **`data`**, **`a`**, and **`b`**. As mentioned, **`data`** should be an array of values in an attribute of a dataset, while **`a`** and **`b`** specify the range that the input data is to be transformed into.

3. Given the (implicit) requirement we have about **`data`** (a NumPy array or a pandas **`Series`** object—both of which can utilize vectorization), implement the scaling function with vectorized operations:

```
def min_max_scale(data, a, b):
    data_max = np.max(data)
    data_min = np.min(data)

    return a + (b - a) * (data - data_min) / (data_max \
                                              - data_min)
```

4. We will consider the data in the **`'Column 1'`** attribute first. To observe the effect that this function will have on our data, let's first visualize the distribution of what we currently have:

```
plt.hist(df['Column 1'], bins=20)
plt.show()
```

This code will generate a plot that is similar to the following:

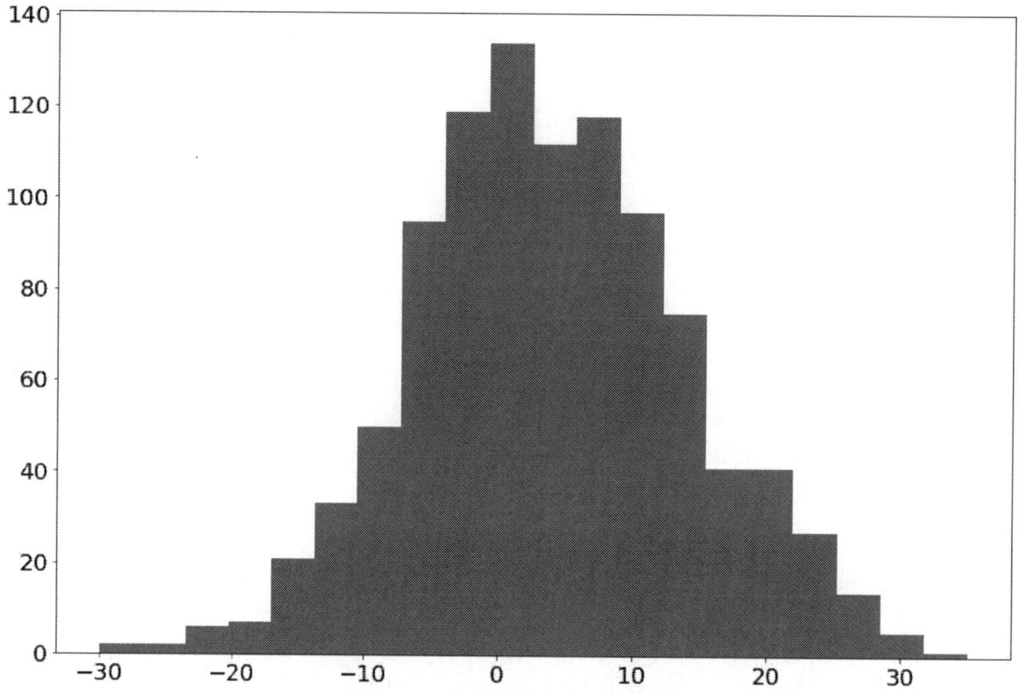

Figure 3.11: Histogram of unscaled data

5. Now, use the same **`plt.hist()`** function to visualize the returned value of the **`min_max_scale()`** function when called on **`df['Column 1']`** to scale that data to the range **`[-3, 3]`**:

```
plt.hist(min_max_scale(df['Column 1'], -3, 3), bins=20)
plt.show()
```

This will produce the following:

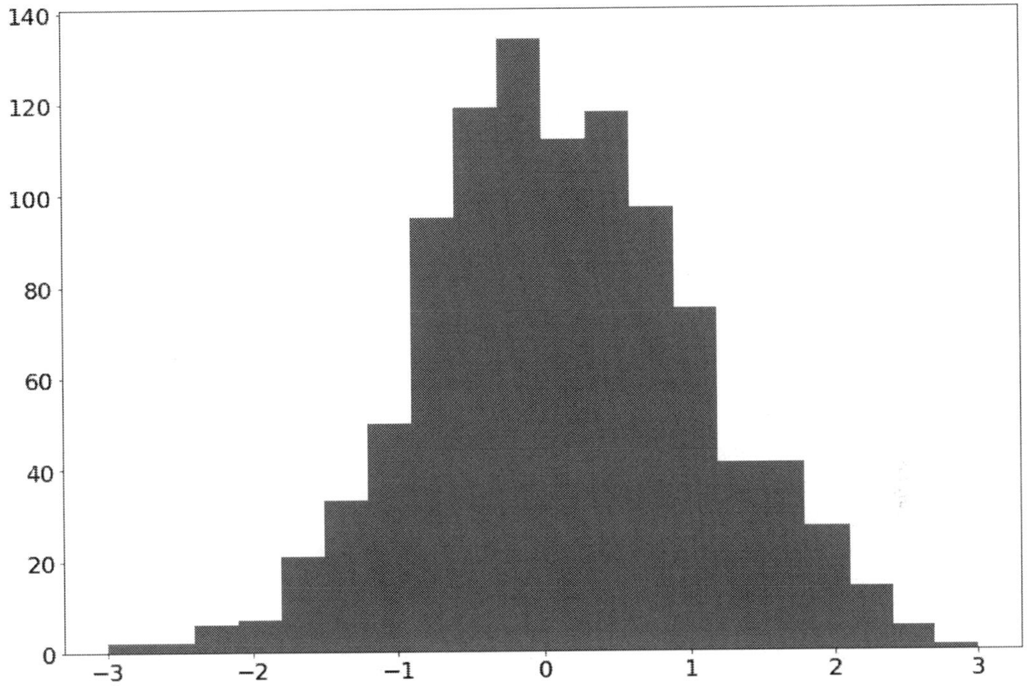

Figure 3.12: Histogram of scaled data

We see that while the general shape of the data distribution remains the same, the range of the data has been effectively changed to be from **-3** to **3**.

6. Go through the same process (visualizing the data before and after scaling with histograms) for the **'Column 2'** attribute. First, we visualize the original data:

```
plt.hist(df['Column 2'], bins=20)
plt.show()
```

7. Now we visualize the scaled data, which should be scaled to the range **`[0, 1]`**:

```
plt.hist(min_max_scale(df['Column 2'], 0, 1), bins=20)
plt.show()
```

8. The second block of code should produce a graph similar to the following:

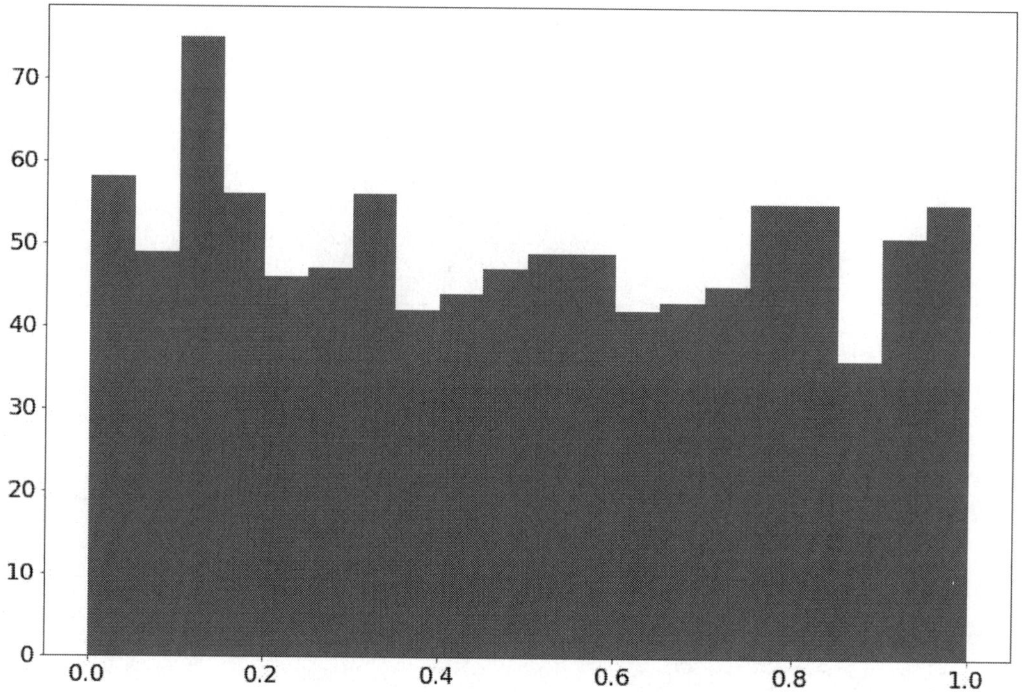

Figure 3.13: Histogram of scaled data

9. Go through the same process (visualizing the data before and after the scaling with histograms) for the **`'Column 3'`** attribute. First, we visualize the original data:

```
plt.hist(df['Column 3'], bins=20)
plt.show()
```

10. Now we visualize the scaled data, which should be scaled to the range **[10, 20]**:

```
plt.hist(min_max_scale(df['Column 3'], 10, 20), \
                                     bins=20)
plt.show()
```

11. The second block of code should produce a graph similar to the following:

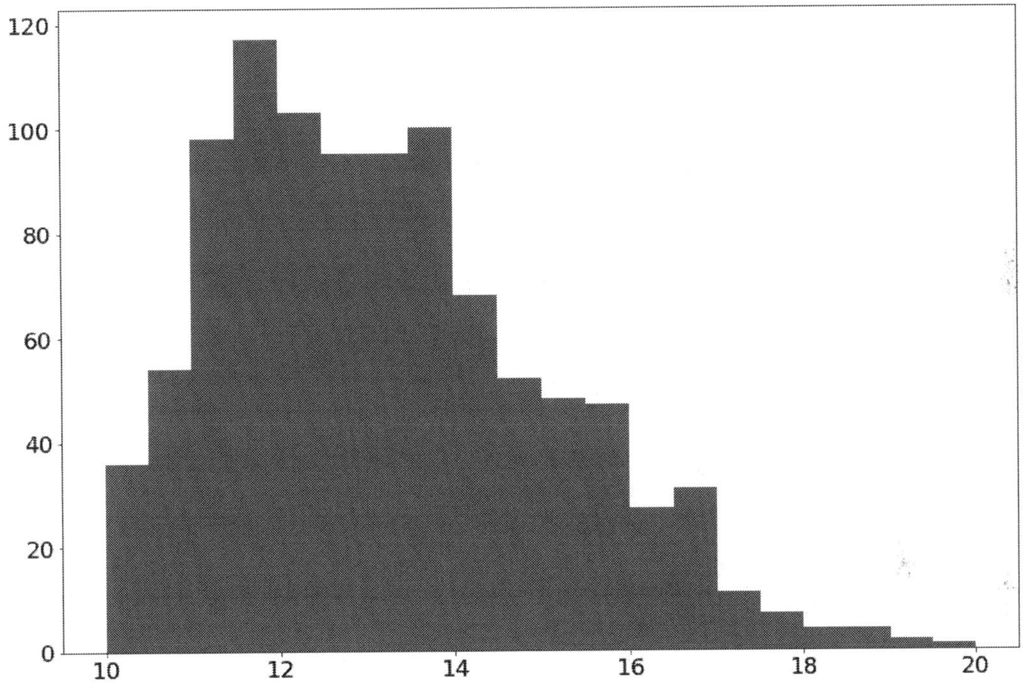

Figure 3.14: Histogram of scaled data

In this exercise, we have considered the concept of scaling/normalization for numerical data in more detail. We have also revisited the **plt.hist()** function as a method to visualize the distribution of numerical data.

> **NOTE**
>
> To access the source code for this specific section, please refer to https://packt.live/2VDw3JP.
>
> You can also run this example online at https://packt.live/3ggiPdO.

The exercise concludes the topic of numerical data in this chapter. Together with categorical data, it makes up most of the data types that you might see in a given dataset. However, there is actually another data type in addition to these two, which is less common, as we will discuss in the next section.

ORDINAL DATA

Ordinal data is somewhat of a combination of categorical data (values in an ordinal attribute belonging to a specific given set) and numerical data (where the values are numbers—this fact implies an ordered relationship between them). The most common examples of ordinal data are letter scores (`"A"`, `"B"`, `"C"`, `"D"`, and `"E"`), integer ratings (for example, on a scale of 1 to 10), or quality ranking (for example, `"excellent"`, `"okay"`, and `"bad"`, where `"excellent"` implies a higher level of quality than `"okay"`, which in itself is better than `"bad"`).

Since entries in an ordinal attribute can only take on one out of a specific set of values, *categorical probability distributions* should be used to model this type of data. For the same reason, missing values in an ordinal attribute can be filled out using the mode of the attribute, and visualization techniques for categorical data can be applied to ordinal data as well.

However, other processes might prove different from what we have discussed for categorical data. In terms of data processing, you could potentially assign a one-to-one mapping between each ordinal value and a numerical value/range.

In the letter score example, it is commonly the case that the grade `"A"` corresponds to the range `[90, 100]` in the raw score, and other letter grades have their own continuous ranges as well. In the quality ranking example, `"excellent"`, `"okay"`, and `"bad"` can be mapped to 10, 5, and 0, respectively, as an example; however, this type of transformation is undesirable unless the degree of difference in quality between the values can be quantified.

In terms of fitting a machine learning model to the data and having it predict unseen values of an ordinal attribute, classifiers should be used for this task. Furthermore, since ranking is a unique task that constitutes many different learning structures, considerable effort has been dedicated to *machine-learning ranking*, where models are designed and trained specifically to predict ranking data.

This discussion concludes the topic of data types in statistics and machine learning. Overall, we have learned that there are two main data types commonly seen in datasets: categorical and numerical data. Depending on which type your data belongs to, you will need to employ different data processing, machine learning, and visualization techniques.

In the next section, we will talk about descriptive statistics and how they can be computed in Python.

DESCRIPTIVE STATISTICS

As mentioned before, descriptive statistics and inferential statistics are the two main categories in the field of statistics. With descriptive statistics, our goal is to compute specific quantities that can convey important information about—or in other words, describe—our data.

From within descriptive statistics, there are two main subcategories: central tendency statistics and dispersion statistics. The actual terms are suggestive of their respective meaning: **central tendency statistics** are responsible for describing the *center* of the distribution of the given data, while **dispersion statistics** convey information about the spread or range of the data away from its center.

One of the clearest examples of this distinction is from the familiar normal distribution, whose statistics include a mean and a standard deviation. The mean, which is calculated to be the average of all the values from the probability distribution, is suitable for estimating the center of the distribution. In its standard form, as we have seen, the normal distribution has a mean of 0, indicating that its data revolves around point 0 on the axis.

The standard deviation, on the other hand, represents how much the data points vary from the mean. Without going into much detail, in a normal distribution, it is calculated to be the mean distance from the mean of the distribution. A low-valued standard deviation indicates that the data does not deviate too much from the mean, while a high-valued standard deviation implies that the individual data points are quite different from the mean.

Overall, these types of statistics and their characteristics can be summarized in the following table:

Characteristics	Statistic	Description
Central tendency	Mean	Average of all values
	Median	The middlemost value in the sorted version of the datapoints
	Mode	The most frequently occurring value
Dispersion	Standard deviation	The average distance from each point to the mean
	Range	The distance between the minimum and the maximum
	Quartile	The value that is greater than a specific portion of the data points
	Interquartile range	The distance between the 25- and the 75-percent quartiles

Figure 3.15: Types of descriptive statistics

There are also other, more specialized descriptive statistics, such as skewness, which measures the asymmetry of the data distribution, or kurtosis, which measures the sharpness of the distribution peak. However, these are not as commonly used as the ones we listed previously, and therefore will not be covered in this chapter.

In the next subsection, we will start discussing each of the preceding statistics in more depth, starting with central tendency measures.

CENTRAL TENDENCY

Formally, the three commonly used central tendency statistics are the mean, the median, and the mode. The **median** is defined as the middlemost value when all the data points are ordered along the axis. The **mode**, as we have mentioned before, is the value that occurs the most. Due to their characteristics, the mean and the median are only applicable for numerical data, while the mode is often used on categorical data.

All three of these statistics capture the concept of central tendency well by representing the center of a dataset in different ways. This is also why they are often used as replacements for missing values in an attribute. As such, with a missing numerical value, you can choose either the mean or the median as a potential replacement, while the mode could be used if a categorical attribute contains missing values.

In particular, it is actually not arbitrary that the mean is often used to fill in missing values in a numerical attribute. If we were to fit a probability distribution to the given numerical attribute, the mean of that attribute would actually be the sample mean, an estimation of the true population mean. Another term for the population mean is the expected value of an unknown value within that population, which, in other words, is what we should expect an arbitrary value from that population to be.

This is why the mean, or the expectation of a value from the corresponding distribution, should be used to fill in missing values in certain cases. While it is not exactly the case for the median, a somewhat similar argument can be made for its role in replacing missing numerical values. The mode, on the other hand, is a good estimation for missing categorical values, being the most commonly occurring value in an attribute.

DISPERSION

Different from central tendency statistics, dispersion statistics, again, attempt to quantify how much variation there is in a dataset. Some common dispersion statistics are the standard deviation, the range (the difference between the maximum and the minimum), and quartiles.

The standard deviation, as we have mentioned, calculates the difference between each data point and the mean of a numerical attribute, squares them, takes their average, and finally takes the square root of the result. The further away the individual data points are from the mean, the larger this quantity gets, and vice versa. This is why it is a good indicator of how dispersed a dataset is.

The range—the distance between the maximum and the minimum, or the 0- and 100-percent quartiles—is another, simpler way to describe the level of dispersion of a dataset. However, because of its simplicity, sometimes this statistic does not convey as much information as the standard deviation or the quartiles.

A quartile is defined to be a threshold below which a specific portion of a given dataset falls. For example, the median, the middlemost value of a numerical dataset, is the 50-percent quartile for that dataset, as (roughly) half of the dataset is less than that number. Similarly, we can compute common quartile quantities such as the 5-, 25-, 75-, and 95-percent quartiles. These quartiles are arguably more informative in terms of quantifying how dispersed our data is than the range, as they can account for different distributions of the data.

In addition, the *interquartile range*, another common dispersion statistic, is defined to be the difference between the 25- and 75-percent quartiles of a dataset.

So far, we have discussed the concepts of central tendency statistics and dispersion statistics. Let's go through a quick exercise to reinforce some of these important ideas.

EXERCISE 3.03: VISUALIZING PROBABILITY DENSITY FUNCTIONS

In *Exercise 2.04, Visualization of Probability Distributions* of *Chapter 2, Python's Main Tools for Statistics*, we considered the task of comparing the PDF of a probability distribution against the histogram of its sampled data. Here, we will implement an extension of that program, where we also visualize various descriptive statistics for each of these distributions:

1. In the first cell of a new Jupyter notebook, import NumPy and Matplotlib:

```
import numpy as np
import matplotlib.pyplot as plt
```

2. In a new cell, randomly generate 1,000 samples from the normal distribution using **`np.random.normal()`**. Compute the mean, median, and the 25- and 75-percent quartiles descriptive statistics as follows:

```
samples = np.random.normal(size=1000)
mean = np.mean(samples)
median = np.median(samples)

q1 = np.percentile(samples, 25)
q2 = np.percentile(samples, 75)
```

3. In the next cell, visualize the samples using a histogram. We will also indicate where the various descriptive statistics are by drawing vertical lines—a red vertical line at the mean point, a black one at the median, a blue line at each of the quartiles:

```
plt.hist(samples, bins=20)

plt.axvline(x=mean, c='red', label='Mean')
plt.axvline(x=median, c='black', label='Median')
plt.axvline(x=q1, c='blue', label='Interquartile')
plt.axvline(x=q2, c='blue')

plt.legend()
plt.show()
```

Note here that we are combining the specification of the **`label`** argument in various plotting function calls and the **`plt.legend()`** function. This will help us create a legend with appropriate labels, as can be seen here:

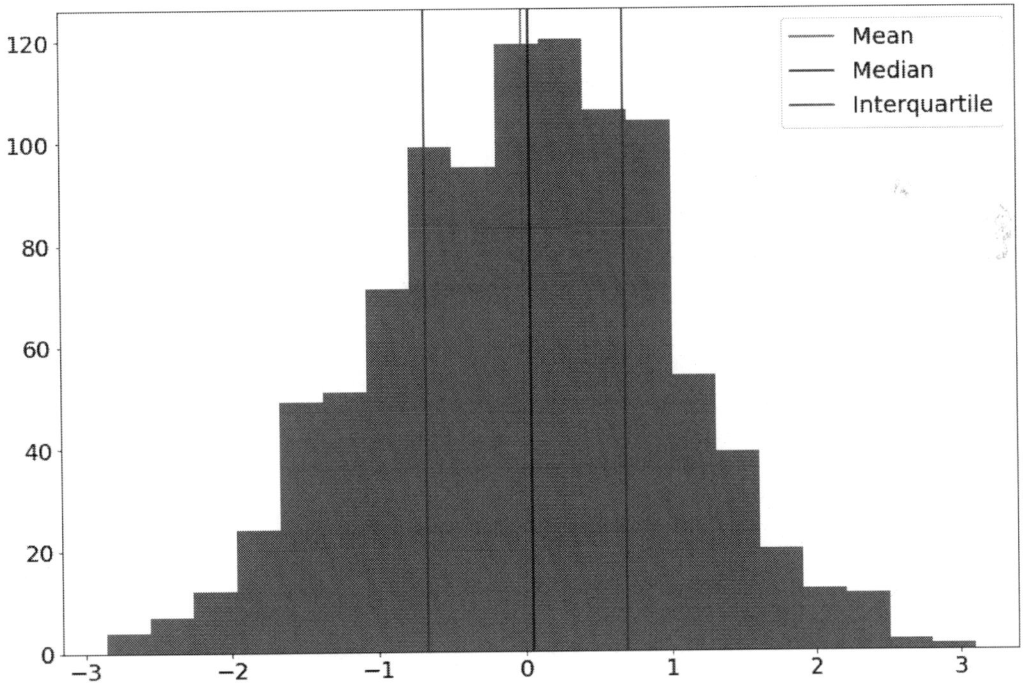

Figure 3.16: Descriptive statistics for a normal distribution

One thing is of interest here: the mean and the median almost coincide on the x axis. This is one of the many mathematically convenient features of a normal distribution that is not found in many other distributions: its mean is equal to both its median and its mode.

4. Apply the same process to a Beta distribution with parameters **2** and **5**, as follows:

```
samples = np.random.beta(2, 5, size=1000)
mean = np.mean(samples)
median = np.median(samples)

q1 = np.percentile(samples, 25)
q2 = np.percentile(samples, 75)

plt.hist(samples, bins=20)

plt.axvline(x=mean, c='red', label='Mean')
plt.axvline(x=median, c='black', label='Median')
plt.axvline(x=q1, c='blue', label='Interquartile')
plt.axvline(x=q2, c='blue')

plt.legend()
plt.show()
```

This should generate a graph similar to the following:

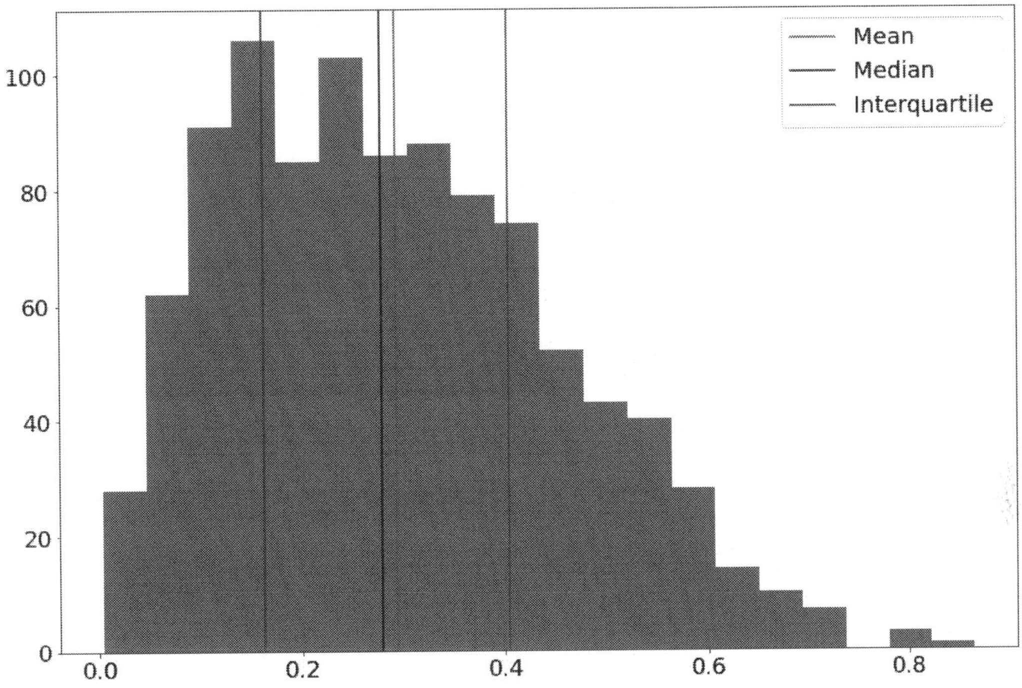

Figure 3.17: Descriptive statistics for a Beta distribution

5. Apply the same process to a Gamma distribution with parameter **5**, as follows:

```
samples = np.random.gamma(5, size=1000)
mean = np.mean(samples)
median = np.median(samples)

q1 = np.percentile(samples, 25)
q2 = np.percentile(samples, 75)

plt.hist(samples, bins=20)

plt.axvline(x=mean, c='red', label='Mean')
plt.axvline(x=median, c='black', label='Median')
plt.axvline(x=q1, c='blue', label='Interquartile')
plt.axvline(x=q2, c='blue')

plt.legend()
plt.show()
```

This should generate a graph similar to the following:

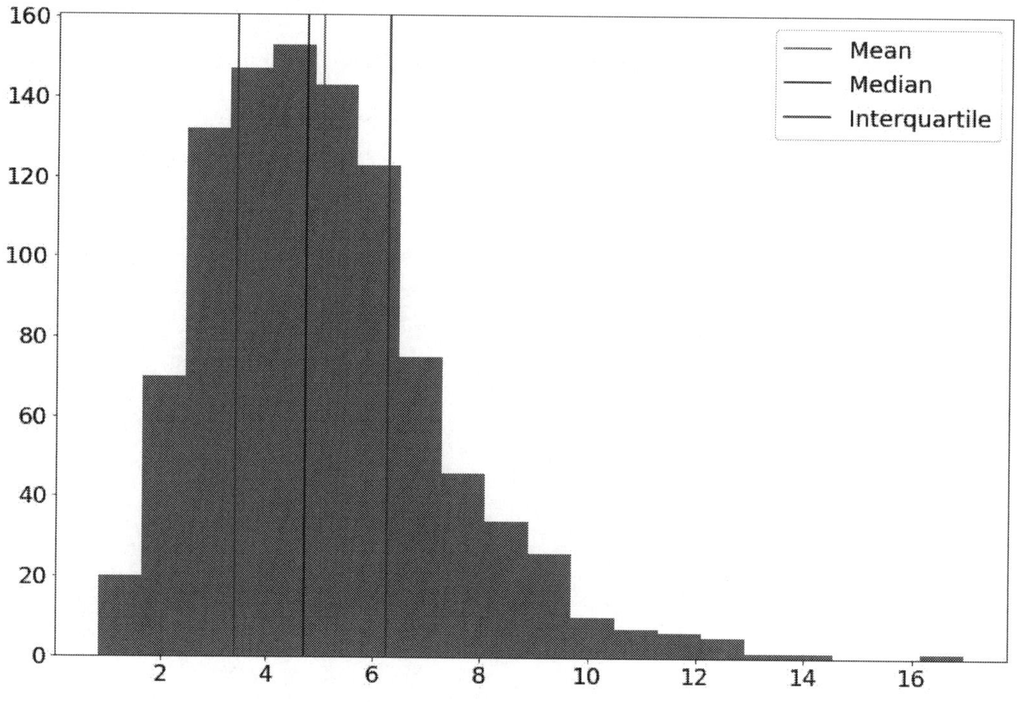

Figure 3.18: Descriptive statistics for a Gamma distribution

With this exercise, we have learned how to compute various descriptive statistics of a dataset using NumPy and visualize them in a histogram.

> **NOTE**
>
> To access the source code for this specific section, please refer to https://packt.live/2YTobpm.
>
> You can also run this example online at https://packt.live/2CZf26h.

In addition to computing descriptive statistics, Python also offers other additional methods to describe data, which we will discuss in the next section.

PYTHON-RELATED DESCRIPTIVE STATISTICS

Here, we will examine two intermediate methods for describing data. The first is the **describe()** method, to be called on a **DataFrame** object. From the official documentation (which can be found at https://pandas.pydata.org/pandas-docs/stable/reference/api/pandas.DataFrame.describe.html), the function "generate(s) descriptive statistics that summarize the central tendency, dispersion, and shape of a dataset's distribution, excluding **NaN** values."

Let's see the effect of this method in action. First, we will create a sample dataset with a numerical attribute, a categorical attribute, and an ordinal one, as follows:

```
df = pd.DataFrame({'numerical': np.random.normal(size=5),\
                   'categorical': ['a', 'b', 'a', 'c', 'b'],\
                   'ordinal': [1, 2, 3, 5, 4]})
```

Now, if we were to call the **describe()** method on the **df** variable, a tabular summary would be generated:

```
df.describe()
```

The output is as follows:

	numerical	ordinal
count	5.000000	5.000000
mean	-0.251261	3.000000
std	0.899420	1.581139
min	-1.027348	1.000000
25%	-0.824727	2.000000
50%	-0.462354	3.000000
75%	-0.192838	4.000000
max	1.250964	5.000000

As you can see, each row in the printed output denotes a different descriptive statistic about each attribute in our dataset: the number of values (**count**), mean, standard deviation, and various quartiles. Since both the **numerical** and **ordinal** attributes were interpreted as numerical data (given the data they contain), **describe()** only generates these reports for them by default. The **categorical** column, on the other hand, was excluded. To force the reports to apply to all columns, we can specify the **include** argument as follows:

```
df.describe(include='all')
```

The output is as follows:

	numerical	categorical	ordinal
count	5.000000	5	5.000000
unique	NaN	3	NaN
top	NaN	a	NaN
freq	NaN	2	NaN
mean	-0.251261	NaN	3.000000
std	0.899420	NaN	1.581139
min	-1.027348	NaN	1.000000
25%	-0.824727	NaN	2.000000
50%	-0.462354	NaN	3.000000
75%	-0.192838	NaN	4.000000
max	1.250964	NaN	5.000000

This forces the method to compute other statistics that apply for categorical data, such as the number of unique values (**unique**), the mode (**top**), and the count/frequency of the mode (**freq**). As we have discussed, most of the descriptive statistics for numerical data do not apply for categorical data and vice versa, which is why **NaN** values are used in the preceding reports to indicate such a non-application.

Overall, the **describe()** method from pandas offers a quick way to summarize and obtain an overview of a dataset and its attributes. This especially comes in handy during exploratory data analysis tasks, where we'd like to broadly explore a new dataset that we are not familiar with yet.

The second descriptive statistics-related method that is supported by Python is the visualization of boxplots. Obviously, a boxplot is a visualization technique that is not unique to the language itself, but Python, specifically its seaborn library, provides a rather convenient API, the **sns.boxplot()** function, to facilitate the process.

Theoretically, a boxplot is another method to visualize the distribution of a numerical dataset. It, again, can be generated with the **sns.boxplot()** function:

```
sns.boxplot(np.random.normal(2, 5, size=1000))
plt.show()
```

This code will produce a graph roughly similar to the following:

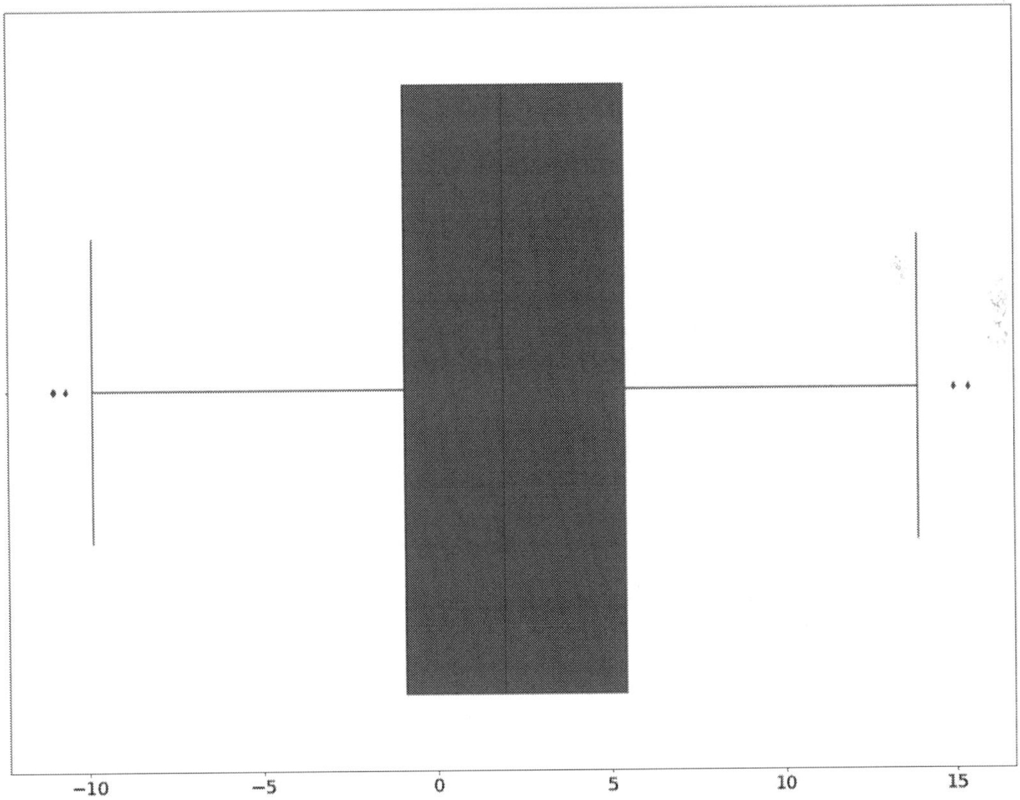

Figure 3.19: Boxplot using seaborn

In the preceding boxplot, the blue box in the middle denotes the interquartile range of the input data (from the 25- to 75-percent quartile). The vertical line in the middle of the box is the median, while the two thresholds on the left and right but outside of the box denote the minimum and maximum of the input data, respectively.

It is important to note that the minimum is calculated to be the 25-percent quartile *minus* the interquartile range multiplied by 1.5, and the maximum the 75-percent quartile *plus* the interquartile range also multiplied by 1.5. It is common practice to consider any number outside of this range between the minimum and the maximum to be outliers, visualized as black dots in the preceding graph.

In essence, a boxplot can represent the statistics computed by the **describe()** function from pandas visually. What sets this function from seaborn apart from other visualization tools is the ease in creating multiple boxplots given a criterion provided by seaborn.

Let's see this in this next example, where we extend the sample dataset to **1000** rows with random data generation:

```
df = pd.DataFrame({'numerical': np.random.normal(size=1000),\
                   'categorical': np.random.choice\
                                  (['a', 'b', 'c'], size=1000),\
                   'ordinal': np.random.choice\
                              ([1, 2, 3, 4, 5], size=1000)})
```

Here, the **'numerical'** attribute contains random draws from the standard normal distribution, the **'categorical'** attribute contains values randomly chosen from the list **['a', 'b', 'c']**, while **'ordinal'** also contains values randomly chosen from a list, **[1, 2, 3, 4, 5]**.

Our goal with this dataset is to generate a slightly more complex boxplot visualization—a boxplot representing the distribution of the data in **'numerical'** for the different values in **'categorical'**. The general process is to split the dataset into different groups, each corresponding to the unique value in **'categorical'**, and for each group, we'd like to generate a boxplot using the respective data in the **'numerical'** attribute.

However, with seaborn, we can streamline this process by specifying the **x** and **y** arguments for the **sns.boxplot()** function. Specifically, we will have our *x* axis contain the different unique values in **'categorical'** and the *y* axis represent the data in **'numerical'** with the following code:

```
sns.boxplot(y='numerical', x='categorical', data=df)
plt.show()
```

This will generate the following plot:

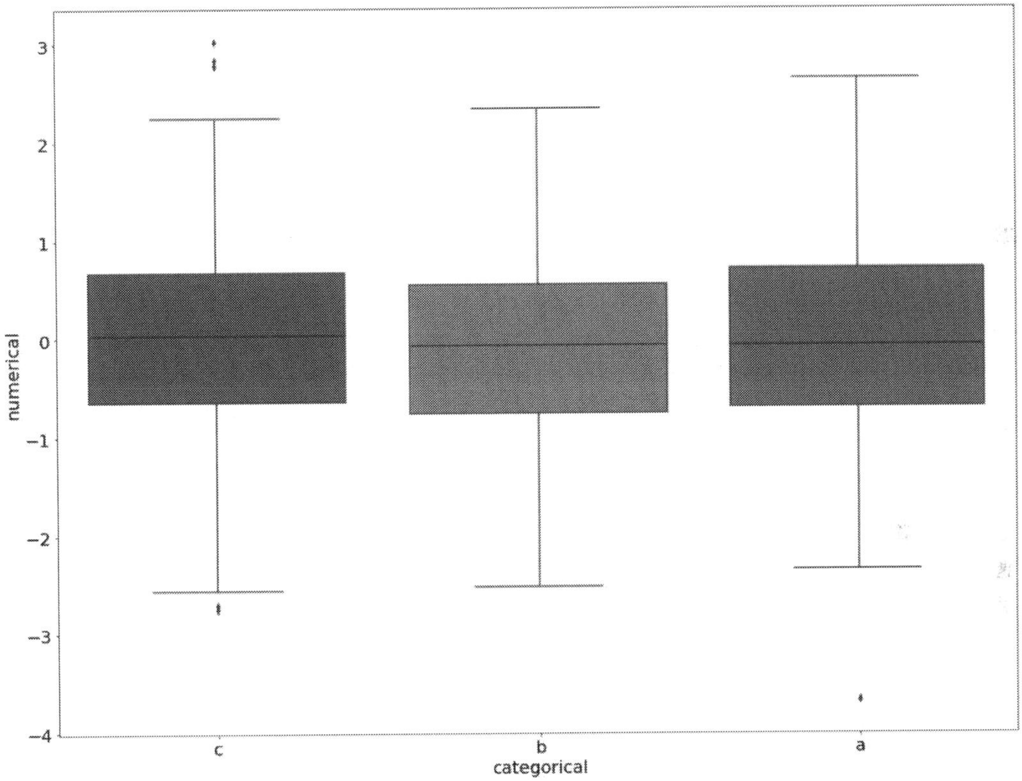

Figure 3.20: Multi-boxplot using seaborn

The visualization contains what we wanted to display: the distribution of the data in the **'numerical'** attribute, represented as boxplots and separated by the unique values in the **'categorical'** attribute. Considering the unique values in **'ordinal'**, we can apply the same process as follows:

```
sns.boxplot(y='numerical', x='ordinal', data=df)
plt.show()
```

This will generate the following graph:

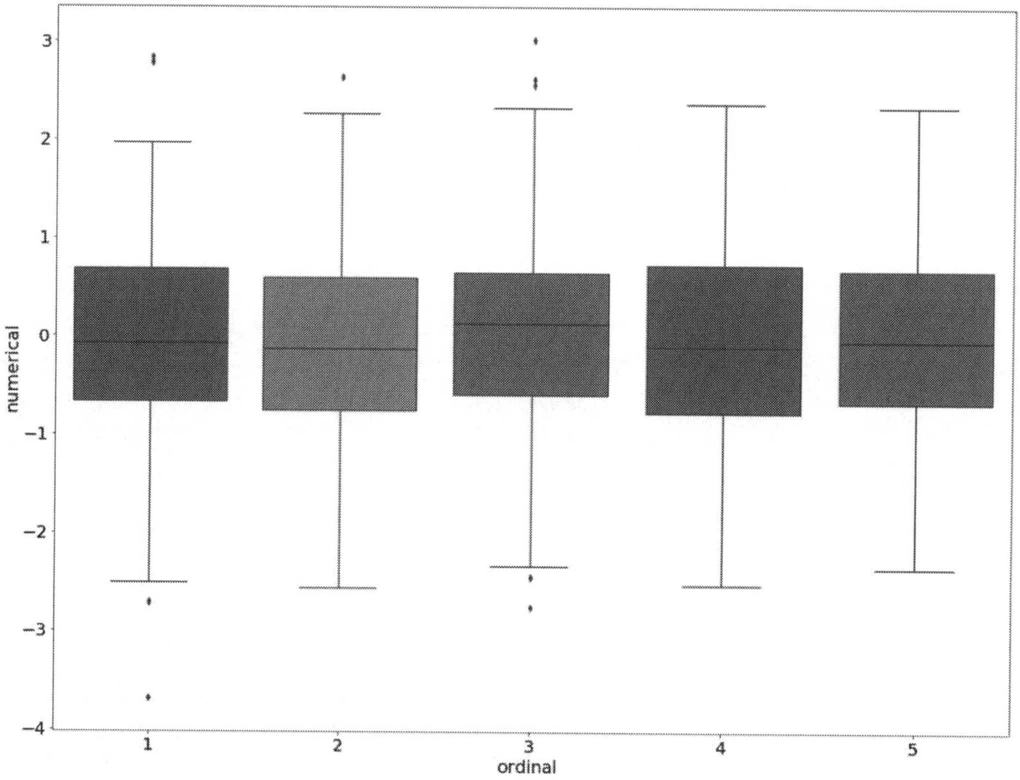

Figure 3.21: Multi-boxplot using seaborn

As you can imagine, this method of visualization is ideal when we'd like to analyze the differences in the distribution of a numerical attribute with respect to categorical or ordinal data.

And that concludes the topic of descriptive statistics in this chapter. In the next section, we will talk about the other category of statistics: inferential statistics.

INFERENTIAL STATISTICS

Unlike descriptive statistics, where our goal is to describe various characteristics of a dataset using specific quantities, with inferential statistics, we'd like to perform a particular statistical modeling process on our dataset so that we can *infer* further information, either about the dataset itself or even about unseen data points that are from the same population.

In this section, we will go through a number of different methods of inferential statistics. From these discussions, we will see that each method is designed for specific data and situations, and it is the responsibility of the statistician or machine learning engineer to appropriately apply them.

The first method that we will discuss is one of the most fundamental in classical statistics: t-tests.

T-TESTS

In general, t-tests (also known as Student's t-tests) are used to compare two mean (average) statistics and conclude whether they are different enough from each other. The main application of a t-test is comparing the effect of an event (for example, an experimental drug, an exercise routine, and so on) on a population against a controlled group. If the means are different enough (we call this statistically significant), then we have good reason to believe in the effect of the given event.

There are three main types of t-tests in statistics: independent samples t-tests (used to compare the means of two independent samples), paired sample t-tests (used to compare the means of the same group at different times), and one-sample t-tests (used to compare the mean of one group with a predetermined mean).

The general workflow of a t-test is to first declare the null hypothesis that the two means are indeed equal and then consider the output of the t-test, which is the corresponding p-value. If the p-value is larger than a fixed threshold (usually, 0.05 is chosen), then we cannot reject the null hypothesis. If, on the other hand, the p-value is lower than the threshold, we can reject the null hypothesis, implying that the two means are different. We see that this is an inferential statistics method as, from it, we can *infer* a fact about our data; in this case, it is whether the two means we are interested in are different from each other.

We will not go into the theoretical details of these tests; instead, we will see how we can simply take advantage of the API offered in Python, or specifically the SciPy library. We used this library in the last chapter, so if you are not yet familiar with the tool, be sure to head back to *Chapter 2, Python's Main Tools for Statistics* to see how it can be installed in your environment.

Let's design our sample experiment. Say we have two arrays of numbers, each was drawn from an unknown distribution, and we'd like to find out whether their respective means are equal to each other. Thus, we have our null hypothesis that the means of these two arrays are equal, which can be rejected if the p-value of our t-test is less than 0.05.

To generate the synthetic data for this example, we will use **20** samples from the standard form of the normal distribution (a mean of **0**, and a standard deviation of **1**) for the first array, and another **20** samples from a normal distribution with a mean of **0.2** and a standard deviation of **1** for the second array:

```
samples_a = np.random.normal(size=20)
samples_b = np.random.normal(0.2, 1, size=20)
```

To quickly visualize this dataset, we can use the **plt.hist()** function as follows:

```
plt.hist(samples_a, alpha=0.2)
plt.hist(samples_b, alpha=0.2)
plt.show()
```

This generates the following plot (note that your own output might be different):

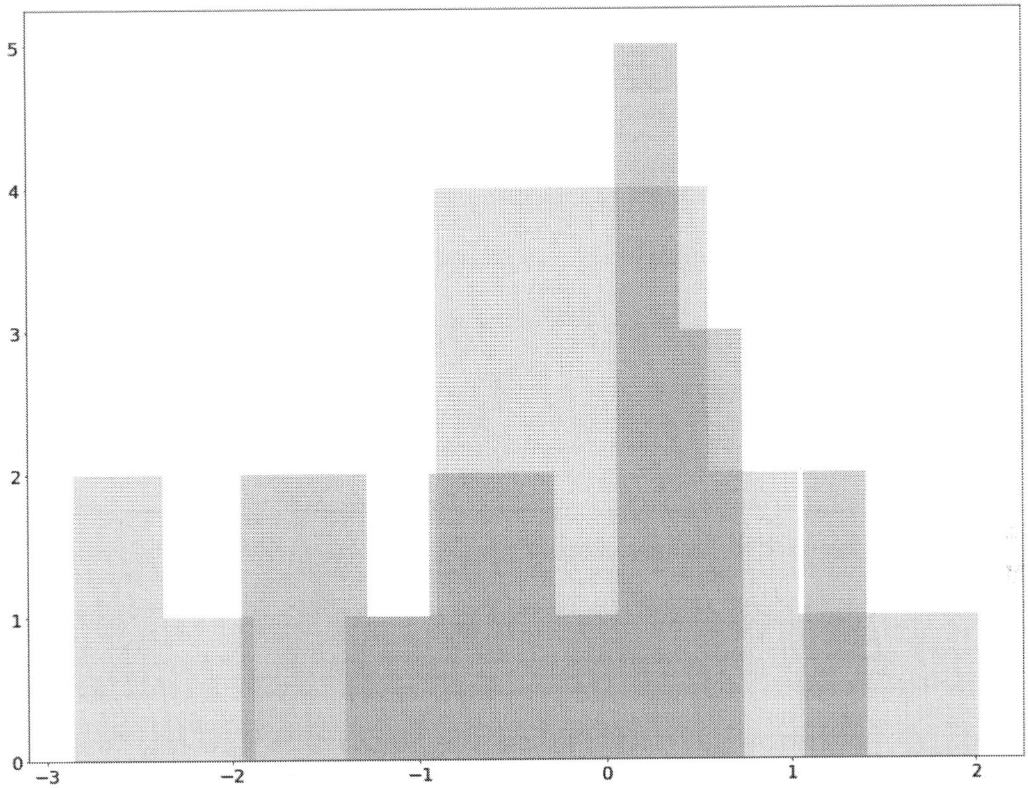

Figure 3.22: Histogram of sample data for a t-test

Now, we will call the **`ttest_ind()`** function from the **`scipy.stats`** package. This function facilitates an independent samples t-test and will return an object having an attribute named **`pvalue`**; this attribute contains the p-value that will help us decide whether to reject our null hypothesis or not:

```
scipy.stats.ttest_ind(samples_a, samples_b).pvalue
```

The output is as follows:

```
0.8616483548091348
```

With this result, we do not reject our null hypothesis. Again, your p-value might be different from the preceding output, but chances are it is not lower than 0.05 either. Our final conclusion here is that we don't have enough evidence to say that the means of our two arrays are different (even though they were actually generated from two normal distributions with different means).

Let's repeat this experiment, but this time we have significantly more data—each array now contains 1,000 numbers:

```
samples_a = np.random.normal(size=1000)
samples_b = np.random.normal(0.2, 1, size=1000)

plt.hist(samples_a, alpha=0.2)
plt.hist(samples_b, alpha=0.2)
plt.show()
```

The histogram now looks like the following:

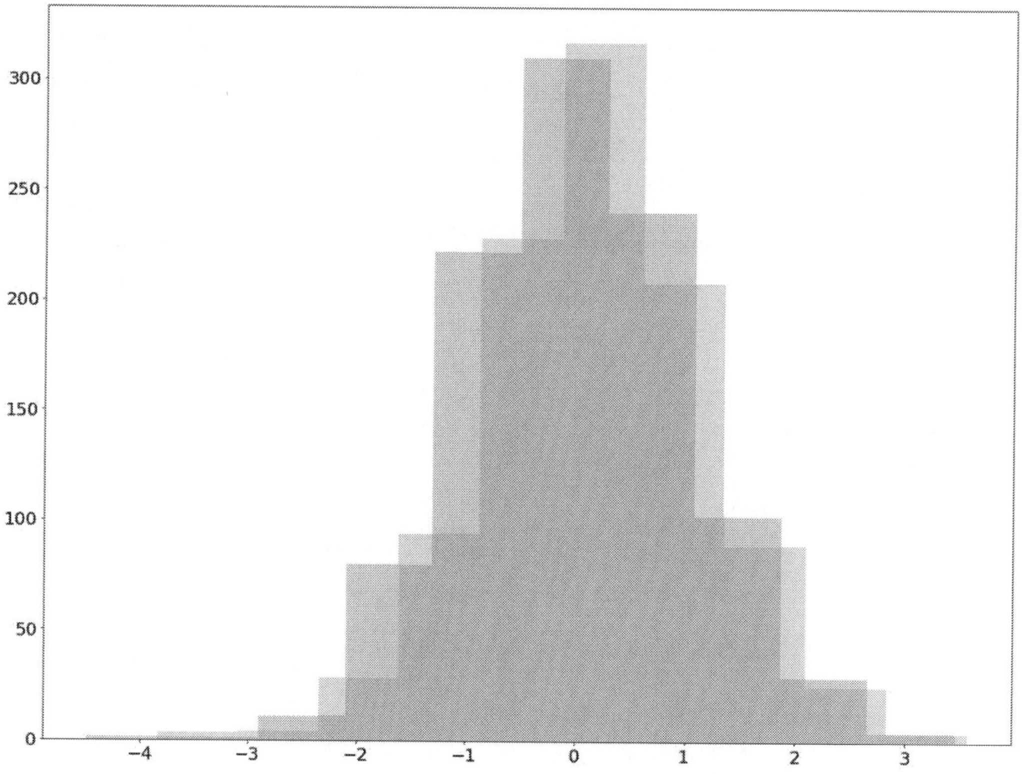

Figure 3.23: Histogram of sample data for a t-test

Running the t-test again, we see that this time, we obtain a different result:

```
scipy.stats.ttest_ind(samples_a, samples_b).pvalue
```

The output is as follows:

```
3.1445050317071093e-06
```

This p-value is a lot lower than 0.05, thus rejecting the null hypothesis and giving us enough evidence to say that the two arrays have different means.

These two experiments demonstrated a phenomenon we should keep in mind. In the first experiment, our p-value wasn't low enough for us to reject the null hypothesis, even though our data was indeed generated from two distributions with different means. In the second experiment, with more data, the t-test was more conclusive in terms of differentiating the two means.

In essence, with only 20 samples in each array, the first t-test didn't have a high enough level of confidence to output a lower p-value, even if the two means were indeed different. With 1,000 samples, this difference was more consistent and robust so that the second t-test was able to positively output a lower p-value. In general, many other statistical methods will similarly prove to be more conclusive as more data is used as input.

We have looked at an example of the independent samples t-test as a method of inferential statistics to test for the degree of difference between the averages of two given populations. Overall, the **scipy.stats** package offers a wide range of statistical tests that take care of all of the computation in the background and only return the final test output. This follows the general philosophy of the Python language, keeping the API at a high level so that users can take advantage of complex methodologies in a flexible and convenient manner.

> **NOTE**
>
> More details on what is available in the **scipy.stats** package can be found in its official documentation at https://docs.scipy.org/doc/scipy-0.15.1/reference/tutorial/stats.html.
>
> Some of the most commonly used tests that can be called from the package include: t-tests or ANOVAs for differences in means; normality testing to ascertain whether samples have been drawn from a normal distribution; and computation of the Bayesian credible intervals for the mean and standard deviation of a sample population.

Moving away from the **scipy.stats** package, we have seen that the pandas library also supports a wide range of statistical functionalities, especially with its convenient **describe()** method. In the next section, we will look into the second inferential statistics method: the correlation matrix of a dataset.

CORRELATION MATRIX

A correlation matrix is a two-dimensional table containing correlation coefficients between each pair of attributes of a given dataset. A correlation coefficient between two attributes quantifies their level of linear correlation, or in other words, how similarly they behave in a linear fashion. A correlation coefficient lies in the range between -1 and +1, where +1 denotes perfect linear correlation, 0 denotes no correlation, and -1 denotes perfect negative correlation.

If two attributes have a high linear correlation, then when one increases, the other tends to increase by the same amount multiplied by a constant. In other words, if we were to plot the data in the two attributes on a scatter plot, the individual points would tend to follow a line with a positive slope. For two attributes having no correlation, the best-fit line tends to be horizontal, and two attributes having a negative correlation are represented by a line with a negative slope.

The correlation between two attributes can, in a way, tell us how much information is shared among the attributes. We can infer from two correlated attributes, either positively or negatively, that there is some underlying relationship between them. This is the idea behind the correlation matrix as an inferential statistics tool.

In some machine learning models, it is recommended that if we have highly correlated features, we should only leave one in the dataset before feeding it to the models. In most cases, having another attribute that is highly correlated to one that a model has been trained on does not improve its performance; what's more, in some situations, correlated features can even mislead our models and steer their predictions in the wrong direction.

This is to say that the correlation coefficient between two data attributes, and thus the correlation matrix of the dataset, is an important statistical object for us to consider. Let's see this in a quick example.

Say we have a dataset of three attributes, **'x'**, **'y'**, and **'z'**. The data in **'x'** and **'z'** is randomly generated in an independent way, so there should be no correlation between them. On the other hand, we will generate **'y'** as the data in **'x'** multiplied by 2 and add in some random noise. This can be done with the following code, which creates a dataset with 500 entries:

```
x = np.random.rand(500,)
y = x * 2 + np.random.normal(0, 0.3, 500)
z = np.random.rand(500,)

df = pd.DataFrame({'x': x, 'y': y, 'z': z})
```

From here, the correlation matrix (which, again, contains correlation coefficients of every pair of attributes in our dataset) can be easily computed with the **`corr()`** method:

```
df.corr()
```

The output is as follows:

	x	y	z
x	1.000000	0.8899950.869522	0.019747 -0.017913
y	0.8899950.869522	1.000000	0.045332 -0.023455
z	0.019747 -0.017913	0.045332 -0.023455	1.000000

We see that this is a 3 x 3 matrix, as there are three attributes in the calling **`DataFrame`** object. Each number denotes the correlation between the row and the column attributes. One effect of this representation is that we have all of the diagonal values in the matrix as 1, as each attribute is perfectly correlated to itself.

What's more interesting to us is the correlation between different attributes: as **`'z'`** was generated independently of **`'x'`** (and therefore **`'y'`**), the values in the **`'z'`** row and column are relatively close to 0. In contrast to this, the correlation between **`'x'`** and **`'y'`** is quite close to 1, as one was generated to be roughly two times the other.

Additionally, it is common to visually represent the correlation matrix with a heatmap. This is because when we have a large number of attributes in our dataset, a heatmap will help us identify the regions that correspond to highly correlated attributes more efficiently. The visualization of a heatmap can be done using the **`sns.heatmap()`** function from the seaborn library:

```
sns.heatmap(df.corr(), center=0, annot=True)
bottom, top = plt.ylim()
plt.ylim(bottom + 0.5, top - 0.5)

plt.show()
```

The **annot=True** argument specifies that the values in the matrix should be printed out in each cell of the heatmap.

The code will produce the following:

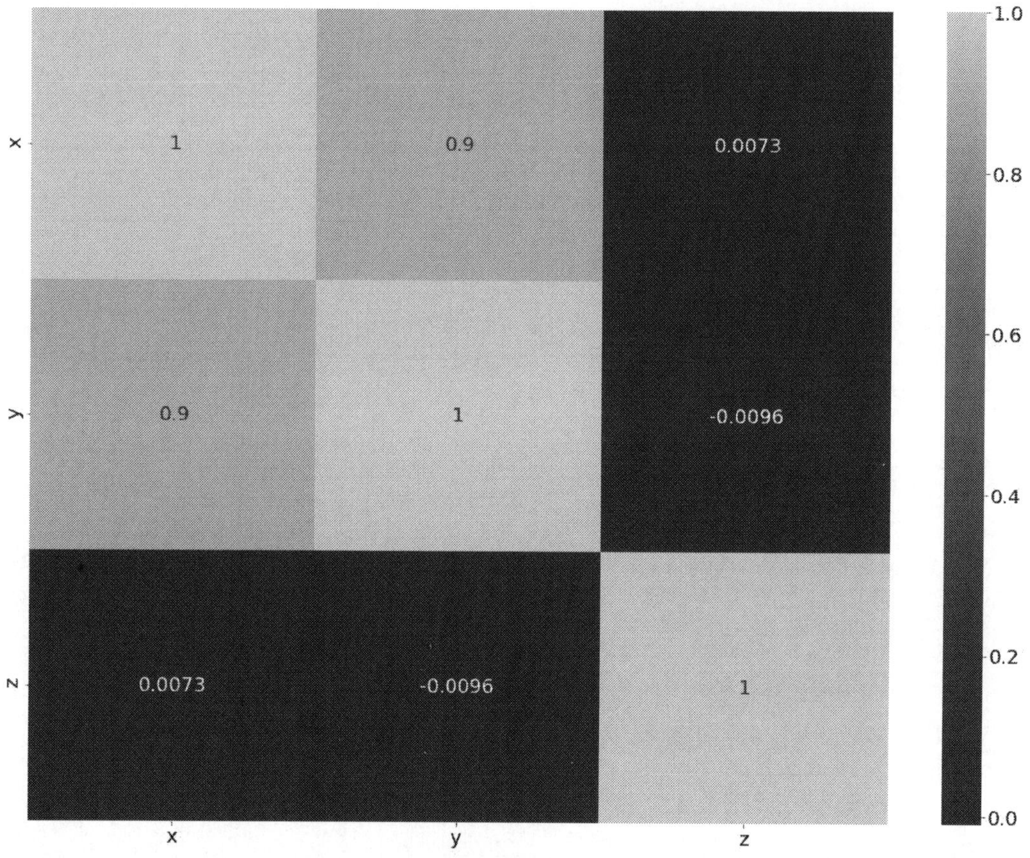

Figure 3.24: Heatmap representing a correlation matrix

In this case, while visually inspecting a correlation matrix heatmap, we can focus on the bright regions, aside from the diagonal cells, to identify highly correlated attributes. If there were negatively correlated attributes in a dataset (which we don't have in our current example), those could be detected with dark regions as well.

Overall, the correlation matrix of a given dataset can be a useful tool for us to understand the relationship between the different attributes of that dataset. We will see an example of this in the upcoming exercise.

EXERCISE 3.04: IDENTIFYING AND TESTING EQUALITY OF MEANS

In this exercise, we will practice the two inferential statistics methods to analyze a synthetic dataset that we have generated for you. The dataset can be downloaded from the GitHub repository at https://packt.live/3ghKkDS.

Here, our goal is to first identify which attributes in this dataset are correlated with each other and then apply a t-test to determine whether any pair of attributes have the same mean.

With that said, let's get started:

1. In a new Jupyter notebook, import **pandas**, **matplotlib**, **seaborn**, and the **ttest_ind()** method from the **stats** module from SciPy:

```
import pandas as pd
from scipy.stats import ttest_ind

import matplotlib.pyplot as plt
import seaborn as sns
```

2. Read in the dataset that you have downloaded. The first five rows should look like the following:

```
In [4]: df = pd.read_csv('data.csv')

        df.head()

Out[4]:
```

	x	y	z	t
0	0.108610	0.901637	3.495175	5.548247
1	1.441267	1.666423	3.554596	-3.839294
2	-0.492374	0.112673	3.902964	13.713320
3	1.106691	0.754194	3.447355	8.432243
4	1.553509	3.087109	3.756501	-1.373107

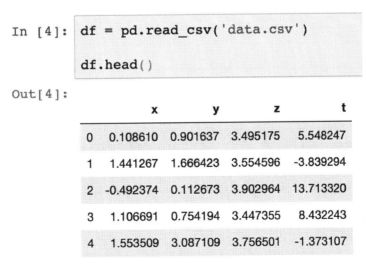

Figure 3.25: Reading the first five rows of the dataset

3. In the next code cell, use seaborn to generate the heatmap that represents the correlation matrix for this dataset. From the visualization, identify the pair of attributes that are correlated with each other the most:

```
sns.heatmap(df.corr(), center=0, annot=True)
bottom, top = plt.ylim()
plt.ylim(bottom + 0.5, top - 0.5)
plt.show()
```

This code should produce the following visualization:

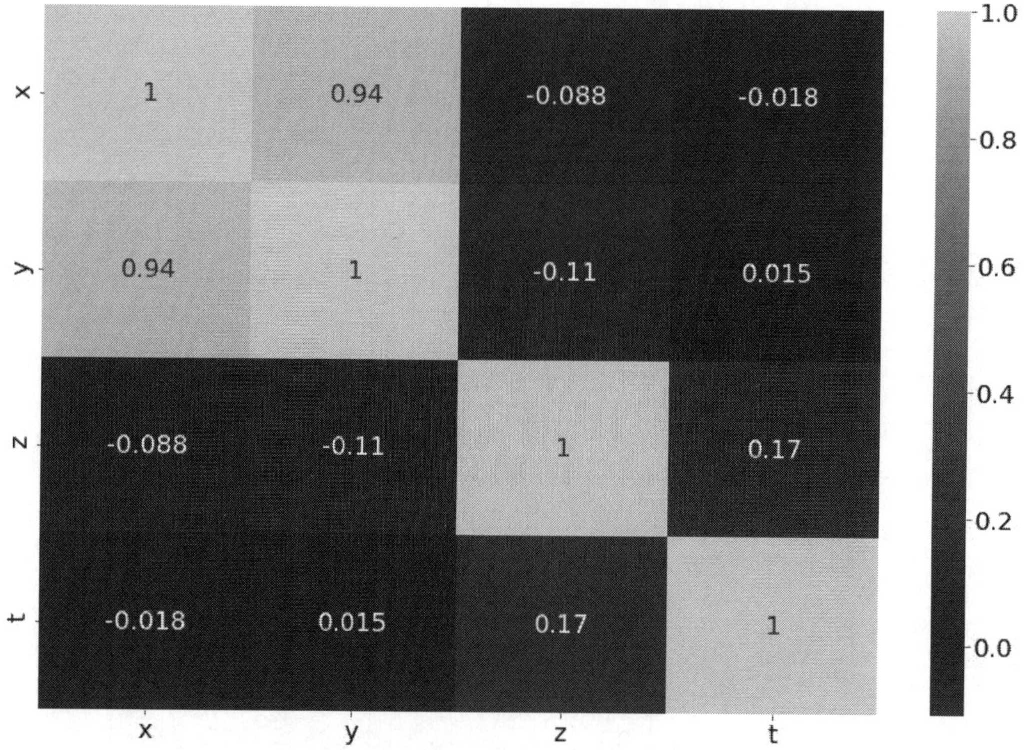

Figure 3.26: Correlation matrix for the dataset

From this output, we see that attributes `'x'` and `'y'` have a correlation coefficient that is quite high: `0.94`.

4. Using this **`jointplot()`** method in seaborn, create a combined plot with two elements: a scatter plot on a two-dimensional plane where the coordinates of the points correspond to the individual values in **`'x'`** and **`'y'`** respectively, and two histograms representing the distributions of those values. Observe the output and decide whether the two distributions have the same mean:

```
sns.jointplot(x='x', y='y', data=df)
plt.show()
```

This will produce the following output:

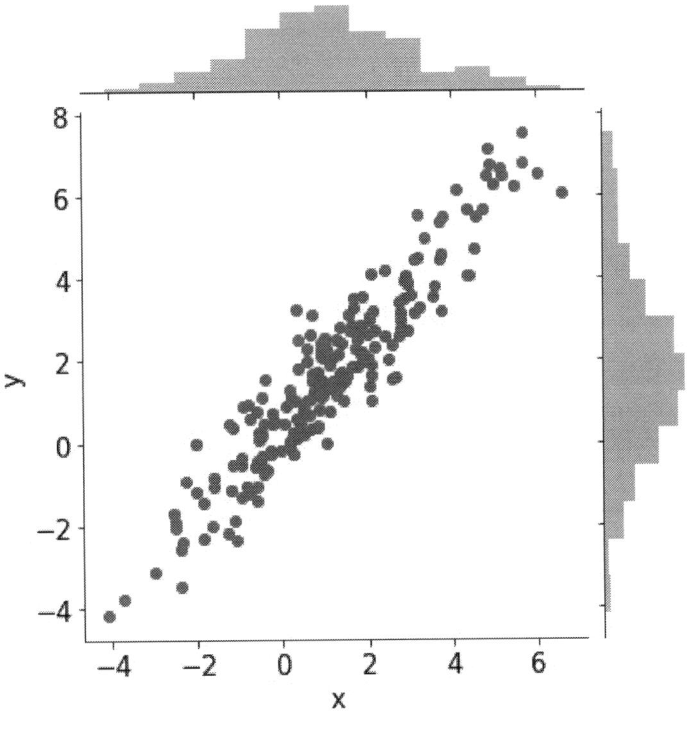

Figure 3.27: Combined plot of correlated attributes

From this visualization, it is not clear whether the two attributes have the same mean or not.

5. Instead of using a visualization, run a t-test with 0.05 level of significance to decide whether the two attributes have the same mean:

```
ttest_ind(df['x'], df['y']).pvalue
```

This command will have the following output:

```
0.011436482008949079
```

This p-value is indeed lower than 0.05, allowing us to reject the null hypothesis that the two distributions have the same mean, even though they are highly correlated.

In this exercise, we applied the two inferential statistics methods that we have learned in this section to analyze a pair of correlated attributes in a dataset.

> **NOTE**
>
> To access the source code for this specific section, please refer to https://packt.live/31Au1hc.
>
> You can also run this example online at https://packt.live/2YTt7L7.

In the next and final section on the topic of inferential statistics, we will discuss the process of using statistical and machine learning models as a method of making inferences using statistics.

STATISTICAL AND MACHINE LEARNING MODELS

Modeling a given dataset using a mathematical or machine learning model, which in itself is capable of generalizing any potential patterns and trends in the dataset to unseen data points, is another form of inferential statistics. Machine learning itself is arguably one of the fastest-growing fields in computer science. However, most machine learning models actually leverage mathematical and statistical theories, which is why the two fields are heavily connected. In this section, we will consider the process of training a model on a given dataset and how Python can help facilitate that process.

It is important to note that a machine learning model does not actually learn in the same sense that humans do. Most of the time, a model attempts to solve an optimization problem that minimizes its training error, which represents how well it can process the pattern within the training data, with the hope that the model can generalize well on unseen data that is drawn from the same distributions as the training data.

For example, a linear regression model generates the line of best fit that passes through all the data points in a given dataset. In the model definition, this line corresponds to the line that has the minimal sum of distances to the individual data points, and by solving the optimization problem of minimizing the sum of distances, a linear regression model is able to output that best-fitted line.

Overall, each machine learning algorithm models the data and therefore the optimization problem in a different way, each suitable for specific settings. However, different levels of abstraction built into the Python language allow us to skip through these details and apply different machine learning models at a high level. All we need to keep in mind is that statistical and machine learning models are another method of inferential statistics where we are able to make predictions on unseen data, given the pattern represented in a training dataset.

Let's say we are given the task of training a model on the sample dataset we have in the previous section, where the learning features are **`'x'`** and **`'z'`**, and our prediction target is **`'y'`**. That is, our model should learn any potential relationship between **`'x'`** or **`'z'`** and **`'y'`**, and from there know how to predict unseen values of **`'y'`** from the data in **`'x'`** and **`'z'`**.

Since **`'y'`** is a numerical attribute, we will need a regression model, as opposed to a classifier, to train on our data. Here, we will use one of the most commonly used regressors in statistics and machine learning: linear regression. For that, we will require the scikit-learn library, one of the most—if not the most—popular predictive data analysis tools in Python.

To install scikit-learn, run the following **`pip`** command:

```
$ pip install scikit-learn
```

You can also use the **`conda`** command to install it:

```
$ conda install scikit-learn
```

Now, we import the linear regression model and fit it to our training data:

```
from sklearn import linear_model

model = linear_model.LinearRegression()
model.fit(df[['x', 'z']], df['y'])
```

In general, the **`fit()`** method, called by a machine learning model object, takes in two arguments: the independent features (that is, the features that will be used to make predictions), which in this case are **`'x'`** and **`'z'`**, and the dependent feature or the prediction target (that is, the attribute that we'd like to make predictions on), which in this case is **`'y'`**.

This **`fit()`** method will initiate the training process of the model on the given data. Depending on the complexity of the model as well as the size of the training data, this process might take a significant amount of time. For a linear regression, however, the training process should be relatively fast.

Once our model has finished training, we can look at its various statistics. What statistics are available depends on the specific model being used; for a linear regression, it is common for us to consider the coefficients. A regression coefficient is an estimate of the linear relationship between an independent feature and the prediction target. In essence, the regression coefficients are what the linear regression model estimates for the slope of the best-fit line for a specific predictor variable, **`'x'`** or **`'z'`** in our case, and the feature we'd like to predict—**`'y'`**.

These statistics can be accessed as follows:

```
model.coef_
```

This will give us the following output:

```
array([1.98861194, 0.05436268])
```

Again, the output from your own experiment might not be exactly the same as the preceding. However, there is a clear trend to these coefficients: the first coefficient (denoting the estimated linear relationship between **`'x'`** and **`'y'`**) is approximately 2, while the second (denoting the estimated linear relationship between **`'z'`** and **`'y'`**) is close to 0.

This result is quite consistent with what we did to generate this dataset: **'y'** was generated to be roughly equal to the elements in **'x'** multiplied by 2, while **'z'** was independently generated. By looking at these regression coefficients, we can obtain information about which features are the best (linear) predictors for our prediction target. Some consider these types of statistics to be explainability/interpretability statistics, as they give us insights regarding how the prediction process was done.

What's more interesting to us is the process of making predictions on unseen data. This can be done by calling the **predict()** method on the model object like so:

```
model.predict([[1, 2], [2, 3]])
```

The output will be as follows:

```
array([2.10790143, 4.15087605])
```

Here, we pass to the **predict()** method any data structure that can represent a two-dimensional table (in the preceding code, we used a nested list, but in theory, you could also use a two-dimensional NumPy array or a pandas **DataFrame** object). This table needs to have its number of columns equal to the number of independent features in the training data; in this case, we have two (**'x'** and **'z'**), so each sub-list in **[[1, 2], [2, 3]]** has two elements.

From the predictions produced by the model, we see that when **'x'** is equal to 1 and **'z'** is equal to 2 (our first test case), the corresponding prediction is roughly 2. This is consistent with the fact that the coefficient for **'x'** is approximately 2 and the one for **'z'** is close to 0. The same goes for the second test case.

And that is an example of how a machine learning model can be used to make predictions on data. Overall, the scikit-learn library offers a wide range of models for different types of problems: classification, regression, clustering, dimensionality reduction, and so on. The API among the models is consistent with the **fit()** and **predict()** methods, as we have seen. This allows a greater degree of flexibility and streamlining.

An important concept in machine learning is model selection. Not all models are created equal; some models, due to their design or characteristics, are better suited to a given dataset than others. This is why model selection is an important phase in the whole machine learning pipeline. After collecting and preparing a training dataset, machine learning engineers typically feed the dataset to a number of different models, and some models might be excluded from the process due to poor performance.

We will see a demonstration of this in the following exercise, where we are introduced to the process of model selection.

EXERCISE 3.05: MODEL SELECTION

In this exercise, we will go through a sample model selection procedure, where we attempt to fit three different models to a synthetic dataset and consider their performance:

1. In the first code cell of a new Jupyter notebook, import the following tools:

```
import numpy as np

from sklearn.datasets import make_blobs
from sklearn.model_selection import train_test_split
from sklearn.metrics import accuracy_score

from sklearn.neighbors import KNeighborsClassifier
from sklearn.svm import SVC
from sklearn.ensemble import GradientBoostingClassifier

import matplotlib.pyplot as plt
```

> **NOTE**
>
> We are not yet familiar with some of the tools, but they will be explained to us as we go through this exercise.

Now, we'd like to create a synthetic dataset of points lying on a two-dimensional plane. Each of these points belongs to a specific group, and points belonging to the same group should revolve around a common center point.

2. This synthetic data can be generated using the **make_blobs** function that we have imported from the **sklearn.datasets** package:

```
n_samples = 10000
centers = [(-2, 2), (0, 0), (2, 2)]

X, y = make_blobs(n_samples=n_samples, centers=centers, \
                  shuffle=False, random_state=0)
```

As we can see, this function takes in an argument named **n_samples**, which specifies the number of data points that should be produced. The **centers** argument, on the other hand, specifies the total number of groups that the individual points belong to and their respective coordinates. In this case, we have three groups of points centering around **(-2, 2)**, **(0, 0)**, and **(2, 2)** respectively.

3. Lastly, by specifying the **random_state** argument as **0**, we ensure that the same data is generated every time we rerun this notebook. As we mentioned in *Chapter 1*, *Fundamentals of Python*, this is good practice in terms of reproducibility.

   Our goal here is to train various models on this data so that when fed a new list of points, the model can decide which group each point should belong to with high accuracy.

   This function returns a tuple of two objects that we are assigning to the variables **X** and **y**, respectively. The first element in the tuple contains the independent features of the dataset; in this case, they are the *x* and *y* coordinates of the points. The second tuple element is our prediction target, the index of the group each point belongs to. The convention is to store the independent features in a matrix named **X**, and the prediction targets in a vector named **y**, as we are doing.

4. Print out these variables to see what we are dealing with. Type **X** as the input:

```
X
```

This will give the following output:

```
array([[-0.23594765,  2.40015721],
       [-1.02126202,  4.2408932 ],
       [-0.13244201,  1.02272212],
       ...,
       [ 0.98700332,  2.27166174],
       [ 1.89100272,  1.94274075],
       [ 0.94106874,  1.67347156]])
```

Now, type **y** as the input:

```
y
```

This will give the following output:

```
array([0, 0, 0, ..., 2, 2, 2])
```

5. Now, in a new code cell, we'd like to visualize this dataset using a scatter plot:

```
plt.scatter(X[:, 0], X[:, 1], c=y)
plt.show()
```

We use the first attribute in our dataset as the *x* coordinates and the second as the *y* coordinates for the points in the scatter plot. We can also quickly specify that points belonging to the same group should have the same color by passing our prediction target **y** to argument **c**.

This code cell will produce the following scatter plot:

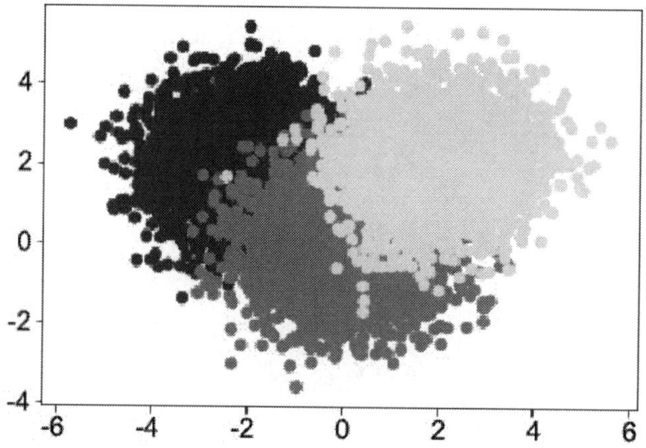

Figure 3.28: Scatter plot for a machine learning problem

The most common strategy of a model selection process is to first split our data into a training dataset and a test/validation dataset. The training dataset is used to train the machine learning models we'd like to use, and the test dataset is used to validate the performance of those models.

6. The **train_test_split()** function from the **sklearn.model_selection** package facilitates the process of splitting our dataset into the training and test datasets. In the next code cell, enter the following code:

```
X_train, X_test, \
y_train, y_test = train_test_split(X, y, shuffle=True, \
                                   random_state=0)
```

As we can see, this function returns a tuple of four objects, which we are assigning to the four preceding variables: **X_train** contains the data in the independent features for the training dataset, while **X_test** contains the data of the same features for the test dataset, and the equivalent goes for **y_train** and **y_test**.

7. We can inspect how the split was done by considering the shape of our training dataset:

```
X_train.shape
(7500, 2)
```

By default, the training dataset is randomly selected from 75 percent of the input data, and the test dataset is the remaining data, randomly shuffled. This is demonstrated by the preceding output, where we have 7,500 entries in our training dataset from the original data with 10,000 entries.

8. In the next code cell, we will initialize the machine learning models that we have imported without specifying any hyperparameters (more on this later):

```
models = [KNeighborsClassifier(), SVC(),\
          GradientBoostingClassifier()]
```

9. Next, we will loop through each of them, train them on our training dataset, and finally compute their accuracy on the test dataset using the **accuracy_score** function, which compares the values stored in **y_test** and the predictions generated by our models in **y_pred**:

```
for model in models:
    model.fit(X_train, y_train)
    y_pred = model.predict(X_test)

    print(f'{type(model).__name__}: {accuracy_score(y_pred, y_
test)}')
```

Again, the **fit()** method is used to train each model on **X_train** and **y_train**, while **predict()** is used to have the models make predictions on **X_test**. This will produce an output similar to the following:

```
KNeighborsClassifier: 0.8792
SVC: 0.8956
GradientBoostingClassifier: 0.8876
```

From here, we see that the **SVC** model performed the best, which is somewhat expected as it is the most complex model out of the three used. In an actual model selection process, you might incorporate more tasks, such as cross-validation, to ensure that the model you select in the end is the best option.

And that is the end of our model selection exercise. Through the exercise, we have familiarized ourselves with the general procedure of working with a scikit-learn model. As we have seen, the fit/predict API is consistent across all models implemented in the library, which leads to a high level of flexibility and convenience for Python programmers.

This exercise also concludes the general topic of inferential statistics.

> **NOTE**
>
> To access the source code for this specific section, please refer to https://packt.live/2BowiBl.
>
> You can also run this example online at https://packt.live/3dQdZ5h.

In the next and final section of this chapter, we will iterate a number of other libraries that can support various specific statistical procedures.

PYTHON'S OTHER STATISTICS TOOLS

In the previous chapter, we considered Python's three main libraries, which make up the majority of a common data science/scientific computing pipeline: NumPy for multi-dimensional matrix computation, pandas for tabular data manipulation, and Matplotlib for data visualization.

Along the way, we have also discussed a number of supporting tools that complement those three libraries well; they are seaborn for the implementation of complex visualizations, SciPy for statistical and scientific computing capability, and scikit-learn for advanced data analysis needs.

Needless to say, there are also other tools and libraries that, even though they did not fit into our discussions well, offer unique and powerful capabilities for particular tasks in scientific computing. In this section, we will briefly consider some of them so that we can gain a comprehensive understanding of what Python tools are available for which specific tasks.

These tools include:

- **statsmodels**: This library was originally part of SciPy's overarching ecosystem but ultimately split off into its own project. The library offers a wide range of statistical tests and analysis techniques, models, and plotting functionalities, all grouped into one comprehensive tool with a consistent API, including time-series analysis capabilities, which its predecessor SciPy somewhat lacks.

  The main website for statsmodels can be found here: http://www.statsmodels.org/stable/index.html.

- **PyMC3**: In a subfield of statistics called Bayesian statistics, there are many unique concepts and procedures that can offer powerful capabilities in modeling and making predictions that are not well supported by the libraries that we have considered.

  In PyMC3, Bayesian statistical modeling and probabilistic programming techniques are implemented to make up its own ecosystem with plotting, testing, and diagnostic capabilities, making it arguably the most popular probabilistic programming tool, not just for Python users but for all scientific computing engineers.

  More information on how to get started with PyMC3 can be found on its home page, at https://docs.pymc.io/.

- **SymPy**: Moving away from statistics and machine learning, if you are looking for a Python library that supports symbolic mathematics, SymPy is most likely your best bet. The library covers a wide range of core mathematical subfields such as algebra, calculus, discrete math, geometry, and physics-related applications. SymPy is also known to have quite a simple API and extensible source code, making it a popular choice for users looking for a symbolic math library in Python.

  You can learn more about SymPy from its website at https://www.sympy.org/en/index.html.

- **Bokeh**: Our last entry on this list is a visualization library. Unlike Matplotlib or seaborn, Bokeh is a visualization tool specifically designed for interactivity and web browsing. Bokeh is typically the go-to tool for visualization engineers who need to process a large amount of data in Python but would like to generate interactive reports/dashboards as web applications.

  To read the official documentation and see the gallery of some of its examples, you can visit the main website at https://docs.bokeh.org/en/latest/index.html.

These libraries offer great support to their respective subfields of statistics and mathematics. Again, it is also always possible to find other tools that fit your specific needs. One of the biggest advantages of using a programming language as popular as Python is the fact that many developers are working to develop new tools and libraries every day for all purposes and needs. The libraries we have discussed so far will help us achieve most of the basic tasks in statistical computing and modeling, and from there we can incorporate other more advanced tools to extend our projects further.

Before we close out this chapter, we will go through an activity as a way to reinforce some of the important concepts that we have learned so far.

ACTIVITY 3.01: REVISITING THE COMMUNITIES AND CRIMES DATASET

In this activity, we will once again consider the *Communities and Crimes* dataset that we analyzed in the previous chapter. This time, we will apply the concepts we have learned in this chapter to gain additional insights from this dataset:

1. In the same directory that you stored the dataset in, create a new Jupyter notebook. Alternatively, you can download the dataset again at https://packt.live/2CWXPdD.
2. In the first code cell, import the libraries that we will be using: **`numpy`**, **`pandas`**, **`matplotlib`**, and **`seaborn`**.
3. As we did in the previous chapter, read in the dataset and print out its first five rows.
4. Replace every `'?'` character with a **`nan`** object from NumPy.
5. Focus on the following columns: **`'population'`** (which includes the total population count of a given region), **`'agePct12t21'`**, **`'agePct12t29'`**, **`'agePct16t24'`**, and **`'agePct65up'`**, each of which includes the percentage of different age groups in that population.
6. Write the code that creates new columns in our dataset that contain the actual number of people in these age groups. These should be the product of the data in the column **`'population'`** and each of the age percentage columns.
7. Use the **`groupby()`** method from pandas to compute the total number of people in different age groups for each state.
8. Call the **`describe()`** method on our dataset to print out its various descriptive statistics.

9. Focus on the `'burglPerPop'`, `'larcPerPop'`, `'autoTheftPerPop'`, `'arsonsPerPop'`, and `'nonViolPerPop'` columns, each of which describes the number of various crimes (burglary, larceny, auto theft, arson, and non-violent crimes) committed per 100,000 people.
10. Visualize the distribution of the data in each of these columns in a boxplot while having all the boxplots in a single visualization. From the plot, identify which type of crime out of the five is the most common and which is the least common.
11. Focus on the `'PctPopUnderPov'`, `'PctLess9thGrade'`, `'PctUnemployed'`, `'ViolentCrimesPerPop'`, and `'nonViolPerPop'` columns. The first three describe the percentage of the population in a given region that falls into the corresponding categories (percentages of people living under the poverty level, over 25 years old with less than a ninth-grade education, and in the labor force but unemployed). The last two give us the number of violent and non-violent crimes per 100,000 people.
12. Compute the appropriate statistical object and visualize it accordingly to answer this question. Identify the pair of columns that correlate with each other the most.

> **NOTE**
>
> The solution for this activity can be found on page 659.

SUMMARY

This chapter formalized various introductory concepts in statistics and machine learning, including different types of data (categorical, numerical, and ordinal), and the different sub-categories of statistics (descriptive statistics and inferential statistics). During our discussions, we also introduced relevant Python libraries and tools that can help facilitate procedures corresponding to the topics covered. Finally, we briefly touched on a number of other Python libraries, such as statsmodels, PyMC3, and Bokeh, that can serve more complex and advanced purposes in statistics and data analysis.

In the next chapter, we will begin a new part of the book looking at mathematics-heavy topics such as sequences, vectors, complex numbers, and matrices. Specifically, in the next chapter, we will take a deep dive into functions and algebraic equations.

4

FUNCTIONS AND ALGEBRA WITH PYTHON

OVERVIEW

Throughout the previous chapter, we discussed a plethora of statistics-related topics, including variables, descriptive statistics, and inference. In this chapter, we come back to the general topic of mathematics and examine two of its most fundamental components: functions and algebra. These topics will be introduced and theoretically discussed in parallel with their respective implementations in Python. Knowledge of these topics will allow you to tackle some of the most common real-life problems that can be solved using mathematics and programming, which we will see an example of in the final activity of this chapter.

By the end of this chapter, you will have a firm grasp on the concept of mathematical functions and relevant notions such as domain, range, and graphing. Additionally, you will learn how to solve algebraic equations or systems of equations by hand as well as via Python programming.

INTRODUCTION

While mathematics can be divided into multiple subfields, such as calculus, number theory, and geometry, there are certain fundamental concepts that every mathematics student must be familiar with. Two of these concepts are functions and algebra, which are the main topics of this chapter.

A function is a general mathematical process that describes a certain mapping from one object to another. A function can take in one number and produce another number. It can also take in an array or vector of numbers and return a single output, or even multiple outputs. Functions are so important that they are also widely used in other scientific fields, including physics, economics, and, as we have seen throughout this book, programming.

Our goal in this chapter is to establish a concrete foundational discussion on the concept of functions in a mathematical context. This discussion will be coupled with other related topics, such as the domain, the range, and the plot of a function. A solid understanding of these topics will allow you to explore more complex mathematical analyses in later chapters.

In addition to functions, we will also consider algebra, one of the most important parts of mathematics. While the term generally denotes the analysis and manipulation of mathematical objects in the broadest sense, we will consider it in the context of algebraic equations and systems of equations. This will allow us to study its important role in mathematics while learning how to apply that knowledge to practical problems.

FUNCTIONS

As previously explained, functions are mathematical objects that generally take in some input and produce a desired output. A function is therefore often considered as a mapping of one mathematical object to another. When a function receives an input and subsequently produces an output, the concept of *relation* can also be used, which emphasizes the relationship between the set of possible inputs and that of possible outputs that is established by the function itself.

A function is typically denoted by the lowercase letter f with parentheses, which surround an input that f takes in. This symbol, $f(x)$, also denotes the output that f produces when taking in x as input. For example, let's say the function f that outputs the square of its input; f can be denoted as $f(x) = x^2$.

We see that the syntax for declaring a function in Python also follows this convention. For example, to declare the same squaring function in Python, the code would look like the following:

```
def f(x):
    return x ** 2
```

And when we would like to obtain the value of *f* with a number as its input, we simply say that we call *f* on the input. For example:

```
print(f(2))
print(f(-3))
```

This code will print out **4** and **9**, respectively. As we also know, the value returned from a function can also be stored in a variable via assignment.

One of the most important characteristics of a function is the fact that no input can be mapped to different outputs. Once an input *x* has been associated with a corresponding output *f(x)*, that output is deterministic and cannot have more than one possible value. On the other hand, it is entirely possible that multiple inputs can be mapped to the same output. In other words, multiple values of *x* can cause *f(x)* to be a common value.

It is also possible that a function does not have to take in any input, nor does it necessarily need to produce any output. For instance, in the context of programming, a function whose job is to read and return the data included in a specific file does not need to take in any input. Another example would be a function that updates the value of a global variable, in which case it is not required to return anything. That said, these functions can be considered to belong to a specific subset of general functions, so our discussions will still revolve around functions with inputs and outputs.

In this upcoming subsection, let's consider a number of common types of functions in mathematics and programming.

COMMON FUNCTIONS

While each function is unique in its own way, there are a number of special classifications, or *families*, of functions that we need to be aware of. These are constant, linear, polynomial, logarithmic, and exponential functions, which are summarized in the following table:

Type	**Form**	**Graph example**
Constant	$f(x) = c$, with c being a constant	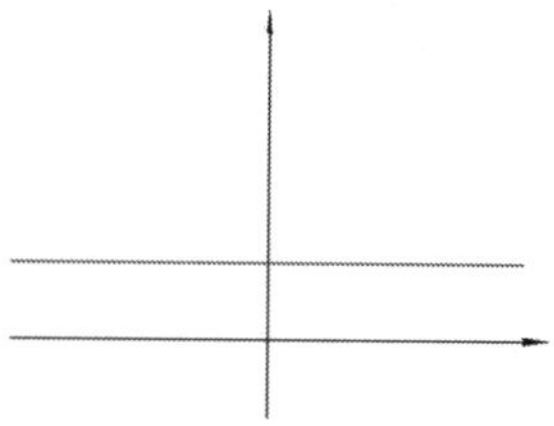
Linear	$f(x) = mx + c$, with m and c being constants	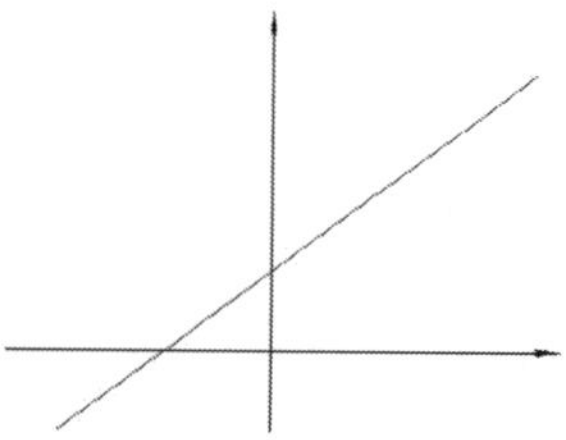
Polynomial	$f(x) = a_0 + a_1x + a_2x^2 + ... + a_nx^n$, with a_i being constant coefficients and n being the degree of the polynomial	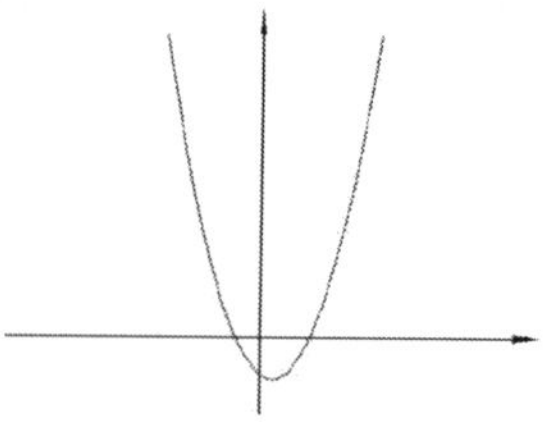
Logarithmic	$f(x) = c\ log_ax$, with log_a being the logarithmic function in base a, and a and c being constants	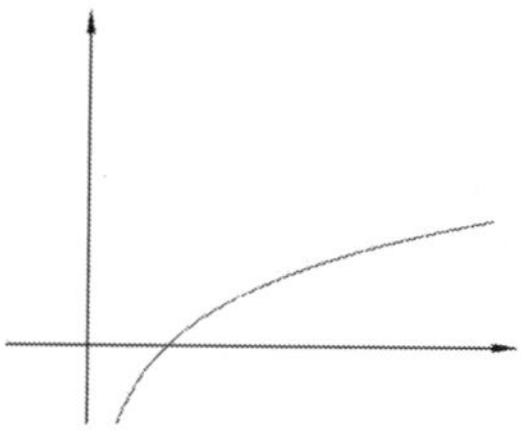
Exponential	$f(x) = ab^x$, with a and b being constants	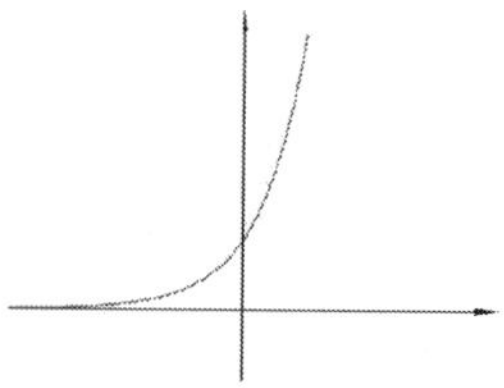

Figure 4.1: Table of special families of functions

Take a moment to consider the third column of our table, which contains the plots of sample functions belonging to each of the function families that are listed. We will go further into the theoretical details of the plot of a function later on in this section, but for now, we see that each family of functions gives us a unique style of graph; in fact, the identification of functions from their plots is the topic of our upcoming exercise.

Note that constant and linear functions are actually subsets of the polynomial function family (when the coefficients for larger powers of x are all zeros). Another interesting fact you may have already noticed is that the input of a logarithmic function has to be positive, which is why its plot does not extend past the left side of the y axis. Conversely, the output of an exponential function (given that the constant is positive) is always positive; correspondingly, its graph stays above the x axis. These points directly transition us to our next topic: the domain and range of a function.

DOMAIN AND RANGE

The domain and the range are two essential concepts in the context of functions. The domain of a function denotes the set of all possible inputs that the function takes in, while the range specifies the set of all possible outputs.

Most of the time, the domain and range of a given function can be identified by considering its formulaic expression. For example, a linear function, $f(x) = mx + c$, takes in any real-valued x to produce a real-valued $mx + c$, so both its domain and range are the set of real numbers, R. The quadratic function $f(x) = x^2$, on the other hand, only produces non-negative outputs, so its range is the set of non-negative real numbers.

The domain and range of a function can also be examined using its plot. Consider the plot of a function with a single input and a single output: its domain corresponds to the projection of the plot onto the x axis; similarly, the range is obtained when the plot is projected onto the y axis. This is why we can claim that the domain of the logarithmic function $f(x) = ln(x)$, whose plot is included in the table from the previous section, is the set of positive numbers. Conversely, the range of the exponential function $f(x) = e^x$ is the set of positive numbers as well.

Overall, the domain and range of a function are dependent on the form of the function itself and can be highly informative regarding various behaviors of the function. One of these behaviors that is often of interest is the root of a function, which we will discuss in the next subsection.

FUNCTION ROOTS AND EQUATIONS

A root of a function is a value belonging to its domain that makes the output equal to zero. Again, which value the root of a function takes is highly dependent on the function itself. Still using the examples that are included in the preceding table, *Figure 4.1*, we see that $f(x) = mx + c$ accepts the unique root of $x = - c / m$ if m is non-zero, while $f(x) = ln(x)$ has the unique root of $x = 1$. Some functions might have more than one root: $f(x) = x^2 - 3x + 2$ has $x = 1$ and $x = 2$ as its roots, while $f(x) = 0$ (whose plot corresponds to the x axis) accepts all values of x as its roots. Finally, if the range of a function does not include 0, then the function itself does not have any root; examples of this include $f(x) = e^x$, $f(x) = x^2 + 1$, and $f(x) = 3$.

The process of finding all roots of a function $f(x)$ is equivalent to solving the equation $f(x) = 0$. The term *equation* here denotes the fact that we have two separate quantities, $f(x)$ and 0, that are equal to each other in the mathematical expression. Solving equations is arguably one of the most central tasks in mathematics, and there are multiple techniques for doing so that apply to specific equation types.

We are only introducing the concept of equations here as part of the topic of functions, and we will come back to it later in this chapter. For now, we will move on to the last important component of a function: plots.

THE PLOT OF A FUNCTION

In the earlier examples, the plot of a function is a visual representation of the behavior of the output, with respect to the input of the function. Specifically, with a function plot, we aim to examine how the output changes across the function range as the input of the function changes across its domain.

In the context of programming, the plot of a function can be produced by connecting the scatter points corresponding to the individual values of a function over a set of fine-grained evenly spaced values on the x axis. For example, say we would like to visualize the plot of the function $f(x) = x + 1$ between **-10** and **10**, we would first declare the corresponding evenly spaced values of **x** using NumPy:

```
x = np.linspace(-10, 10, 1000)
```

This NumPy function generates an array of 1,000 evenly spaced numbers between **-10** and **10**, which is illustrated by the output of **x**:

```
Out[3]: array([-10.        , -9.97997998, -9.95995996, -9.93993994,
               -9.91991992, -9.8998999 , -9.87987988, -9.85985986,
               -9.83983984, -9.81981982, -9.7997998 , -9.77977978,
               -9.75975976, -9.73973974, -9.71971972, -9.6996997 ,
               -9.67967968, -9.65965966, -9.63963964, -9.61961962,
               -9.5995996 , -9.57957958, -9.55955956, -9.53953954,
               -9.51951952, -9.4994995 , -9.47947948, -9.45945946,
               -9.43943944, -9.41941942, -9.3993994 , -9.37937938,
               -9.35935936, -9.33933934, -9.31931932, -9.2992993 ,
               -9.27927928, -9.25925926, -9.23923924, -9.21921922,
               -9.1991992 , -9.17917918, -9.15915916, -9.13913914,
               -9.11911912, -9.0990991 , -9.07907908, -9.05905906,
               -9.03903904, -9.01901902, -8.998999  , -8.97897898,
               -8.95895896, -8.93893894, -8.91891892, -8.8988989 ,
               -8.87887888, -8.85885886, -8.83883884, -8.81881882,
               -8.7987988 , -8.77877878, -8.75875876, -8.73873874,
               -8.71871872, -8.6986987 , -8.67867868, -8.65865866,
               -8.63863864, -8.61861862, -8.5985986 , -8.57857858,
               -8.55855856, -8.53853854, -8.51851852, -8.4984985 ,
               -8.47847848, -8.45845846, -8.43843844, -8.41841842,
```

Figure 4.2: Evenly spaced numbers from NumPy

The plot can then be generated using the **plot()** function from Matplotlib:

```
plt.plot(x, x + 1)
plt.show()
```

Remember that due to vectorization, the expression **x + 1** will compute an array of the same size as **x**, whose elements are the elements of **x** with 1 added to each. This is a great feature of the Python language, or more specifically, the NumPy library, that allows us to quickly generate the points that make up the graph of a function.

This code should produce the following visualization:

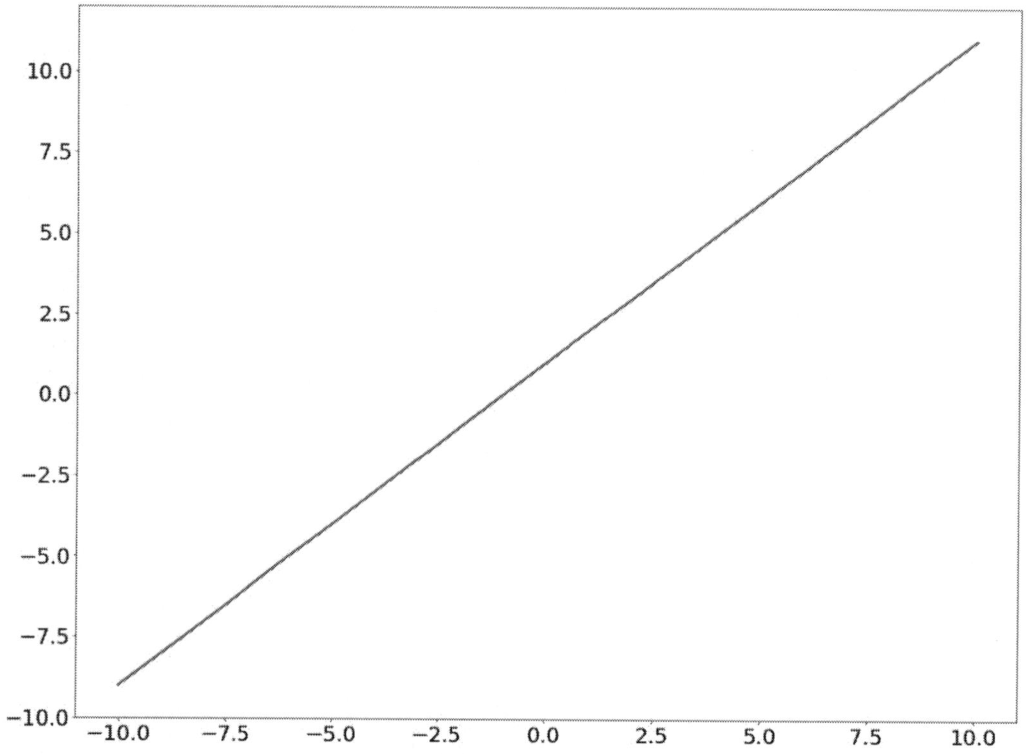

Figure 4.3: Plot of f(x) = x + 1 in Python

The same logic can be applied to different forms of functions. We will come back to this process during our next exercise. For now, let's return to our theoretical discussion.

The plot of a function is a direct visualization of its formulaic expression and contains all of the information we need to know about that function. In particular, we have already argued that a function plot can help us identify the domain and range of the function. Furthermore, given a graph, we can even determine whether that graph is a plot of a valid function. This is done with the vertical line test, which dictates the following.

Given a graph on a two-dimensional plane, if, for every vertical line (every line that is parallel to the *y* axis), the graph has more than one intersection, then it is not the plot of a valid function. This is a direct corollary of the requirement of a function that we stated earlier: one single input cannot be mapped to more than one output. If a graph did have at least two intersections with a vertical line, that would mean a point on the *x* axis could be mapped to at least two points on the *y* axis, which would necessarily mean that this is not a plot of a function.

For example, consider the following graph of the unit circle (whose center is *O(0, 0)* and radius is equal to *1*), which fails the vertical line test, illustrated by the red line:

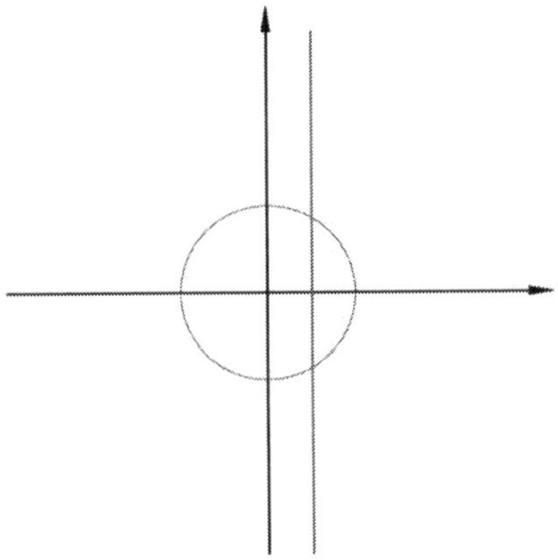

Figure 4.4: The vertical line test for the unit circle

This is to say that the unit circle is, in fact, not the plot of a function with respect to the two-dimensional plane that we are considering.

This topic also marks the end of our introduction to the definition of functions. Before we move on to the next section, let's go through an exercise that aims to solidify all the concepts that we have learned so far.

EXERCISE 4.01: FUNCTION IDENTIFICATION FROM PLOTS

In this exercise, we will practice the skill of analyzing the behavior of a function given its plot. This process will allow us to combine various topics that we have mentioned previously, as well as understand the connection between the behavior of a function and its plot.

For each of the following graphs:

- Determine whether it corresponds to a function and if so, go on to the next step.
- Identify the domain, the range, and the formula of the function (hint: use the labeled ticks).
- Determine whether the function has at least one root.
- Reproduce the plot using Python (the axes and their arrows are not necessary).

1. **Horizontal line**:

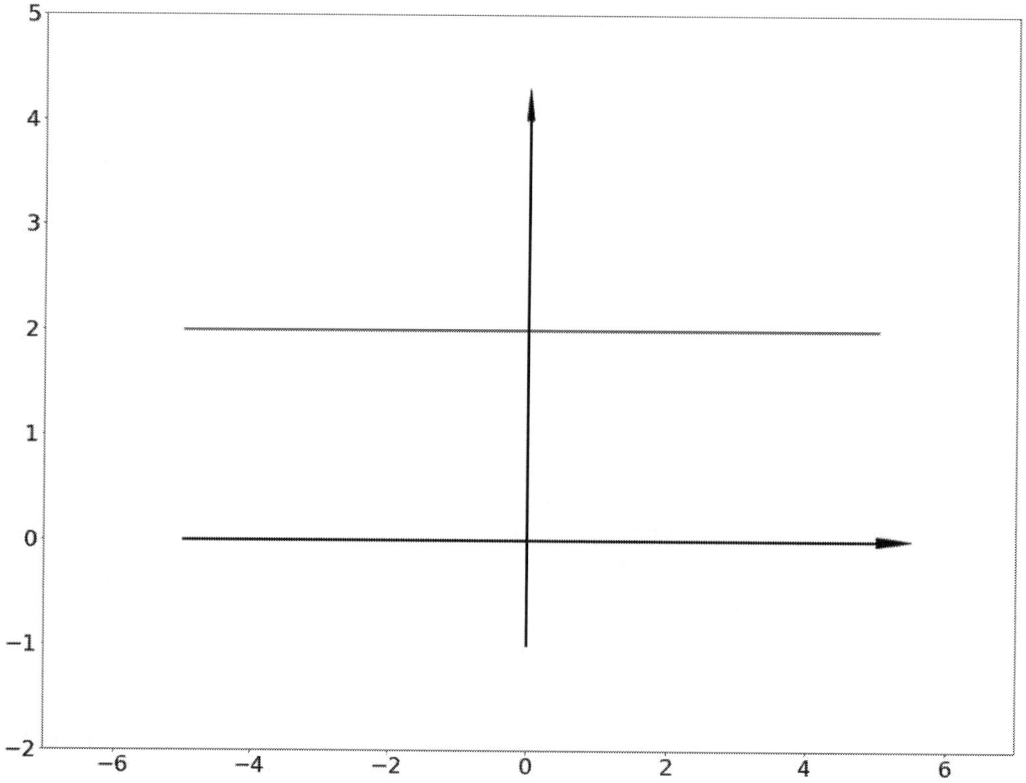

Figure 4.5: Horizontal line

The graph does correspond to a function. The function is *f(x) = 2*, the domain is the set of real numbers, and the range is *{2}*. The function does not have any root.

The following code can be used to reproduce the plot:

```
import numpy as np
import matplotlib.pyplot as plt
x = np.linspace(-5, 5, 1000)
plt.plot(
    x,  # evenly spaced numbers in the x-axis
    np.ones(1000) * 2  # all 2s in the y-axis
)

plt.show()
```

2. **Rotated quadratic curve**:

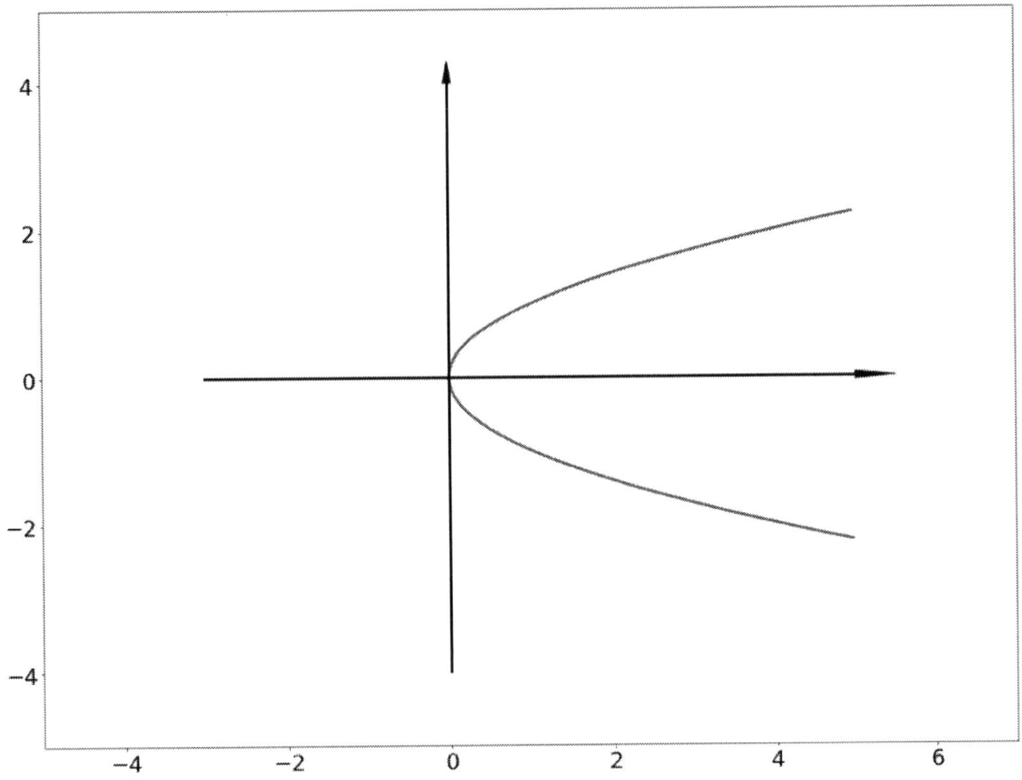

Figure 4.6: Rotated quadratic curve

The graph does not correspond to a function since it fails the vertical line test.

3. **Straight line**:

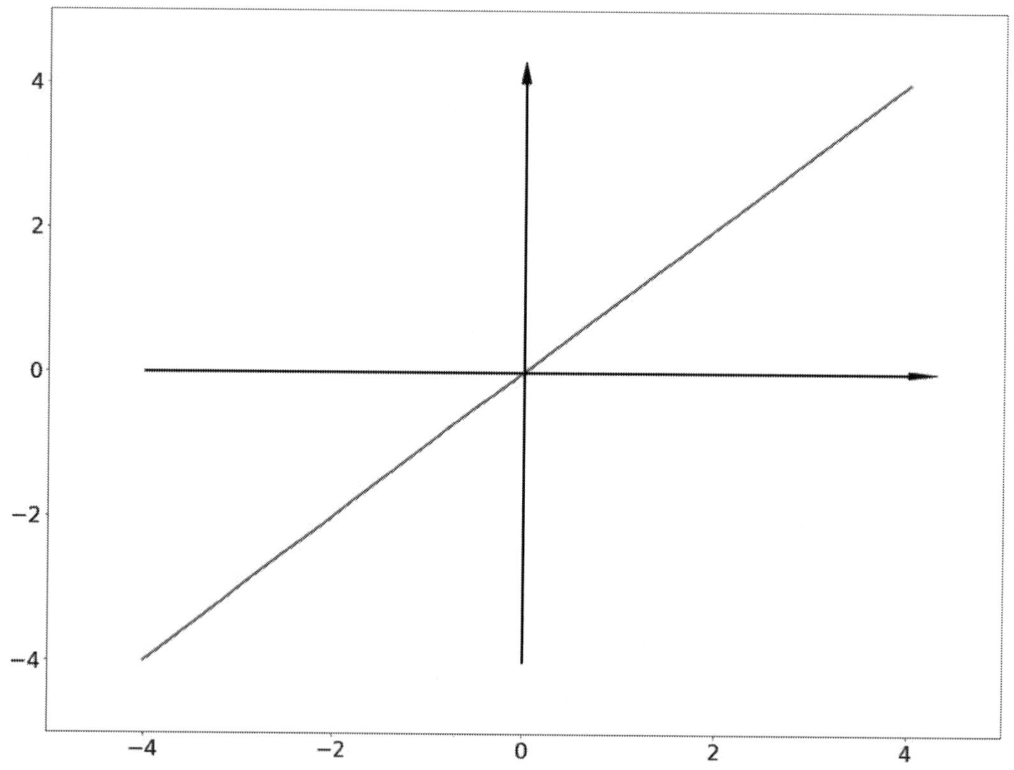

Figure 4.7: Straight line

The graph corresponds to the plot of the function *f(x) = x*. Both the domain and the range of this function are a set of real-valued numbers. The function has one root: *x = 0*.

The following code can be used to reproduce the plot (using the same **x** variable as in the solution to *Horizontal line*):

```
plt.plot(x, x)
plt.show()
```

4. **Quadratic curve**:

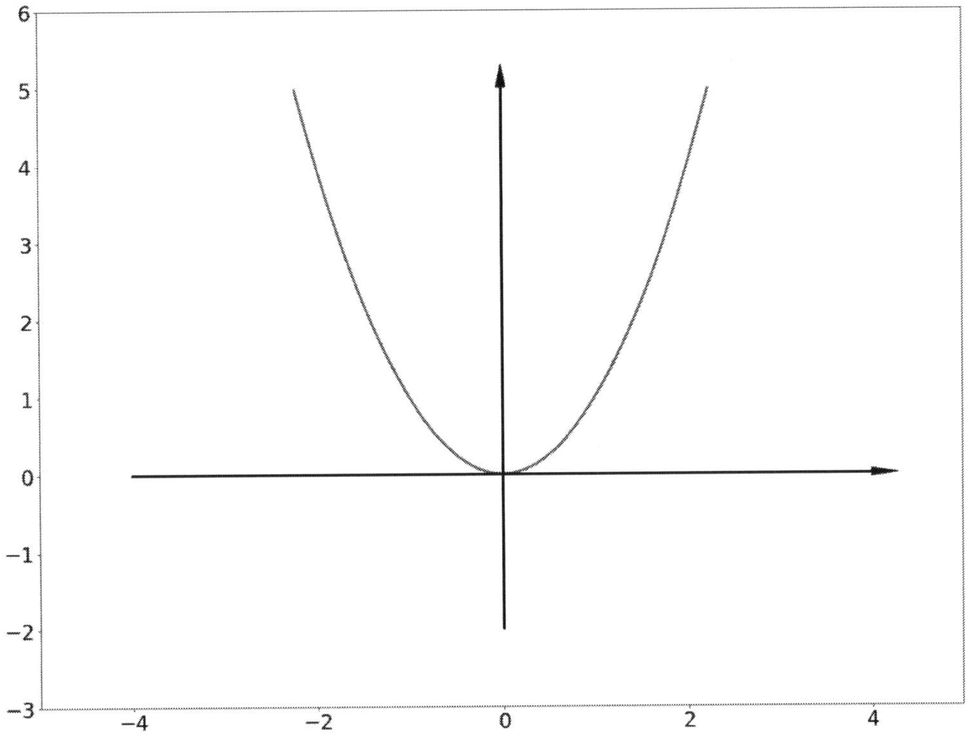

Figure 4.8: Quadratic curve

The graph corresponds to the plot of the function $f(x) = x^2$. The domain of the function is the set of all real numbers, while the range is the set of non-negative numbers. The function also has one root: $x = 0$.

The following code can be used to reproduce the plot (thanks to vectorization for NumPy arrays):

```
plt.plot(x, x ** 2)
plt.show()
```

Through this quick exercise, we have solidified our understanding of functions and a number of relevant concepts, including the domain, the range, the vertical line test, and the process of plotting a graph using Python.

> **NOTE**
>
> To access the source code for this specific section, please refer to https://packt.live/2YRMZhL.
>
> You can also run this example online at https://packt.live/2YSBgj2.

In the next section, we will discuss the transformation of functions.

FUNCTION TRANSFORMATIONS

Transformation is one of the most important concepts for mathematical functions. As suggested by the name of the term, a transformation of a function is the output we obtain after putting the returned value of a function through a specific transformation technique such as a shift or a scaling. In the most general sense, we can think of this process as a *composite function*: putting the output of one function through another function. However, there are specific types of functions that are commonly used as transformations due to their particular characteristics and usefulness, and we will go through them in the following subsections, starting with shifting.

Since a transformation is most easily understood in the context of the changes that it applies to the plot of a function, we will also frame our following discussions accordingly.

SHIFTS

A shift of a function happens when the plot of a function is shifted by a specific amount along the *x* axis and/or the *y* axis. For example, in the following visualization, the blue curve is the graph of the function $f(x) = x^2$, while the red curve is the same graph shifted vertically by *1*:

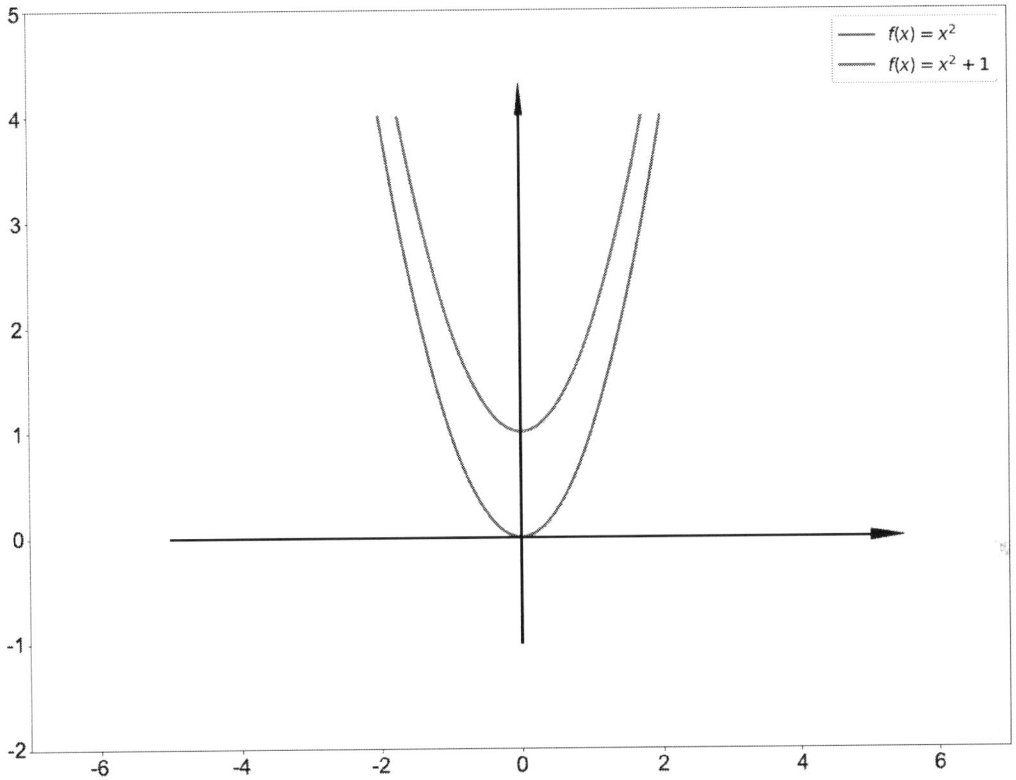

Figure 4.9: Vertical shift of a function

We see that every point *(x, y)* belonging to the graph of $f(x) = x^2$ has been effectively translated to $(x, y + 1)$. Since $y = x^2$ if *(x, y)* belongs to the graph of *f(x)*, the output of the shift is essentially the graph of the function $f(x) = x^2 + 1$.

This example allows us to generalize every case of a vertical shift: the output of the vertical shift of any given function *f(x)* by a constant *c* is the new function $f(x) + c$. In our example this is $c = 1$, corresponding to a horizontal shift up by *1*. However, *c* can also be a negative number, in which case the function is shifted down, or even zero, in which case the transformation is the identity transformation where the graph of the function does not change.

We see that a vertical shift is done when a change is added to (or subtracted from) the output values of a function, or, in other words, the *y* coordinates of the points lying on the graph. In the same manner, a horizontal shift can be applied to a function by implementing a change in the input values of a function (when a number is added to the *x* coordinates of the points).

In general, when the graph of a function $f(x)$ is shifted to the left of a two-dimensional plane by an amount c, the resulting graph is the plot of the function $f(x + c)$. Conversely, the graph of the function $f(x - c)$ corresponds to a horizontal shift to the right by c of the function $f(x)$.

Still using the example of the function $f(x) = x^2$, the following graph visualizes the shift of the function to the right by *2*, or, in other words, the graph of the function $f(x) = (x - 2)^2$:

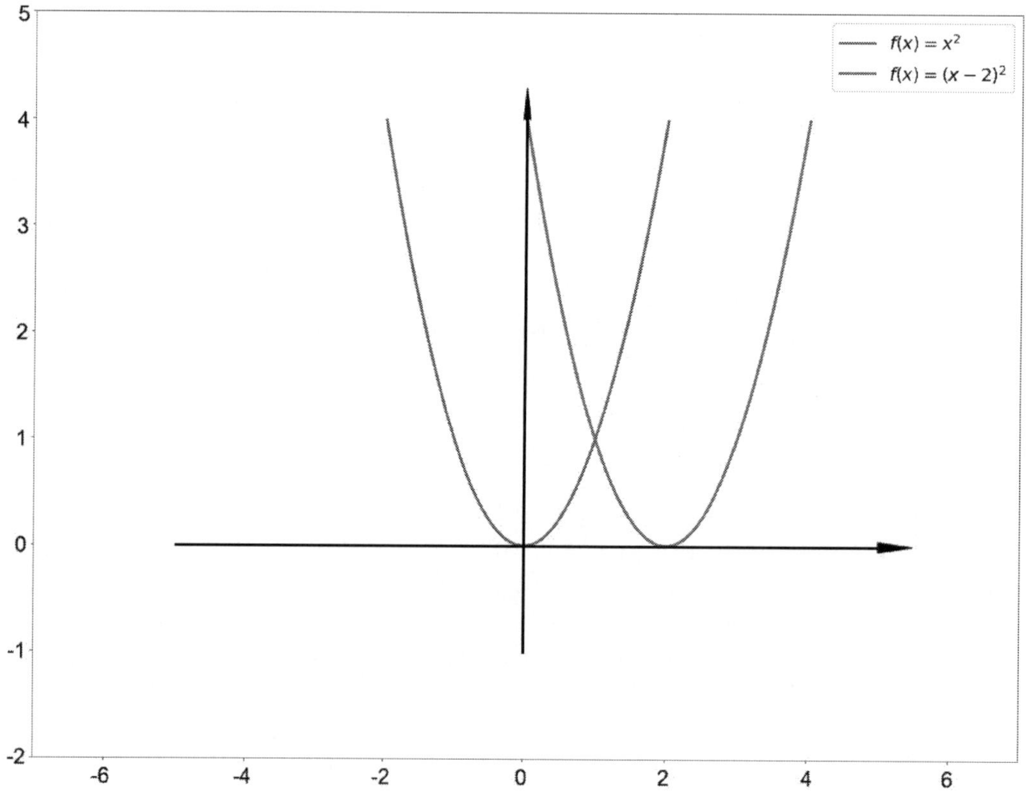

Figure 4.10: Horizontal shift of a function

It is also possible to combine both a vertical shift and a horizontal shift to transform a function so that the entire graph is moved in any given direction. For example, say we would like to shift the function $f(x) = x^2$ in the North-East direction (up and right) by the amount vector *(2, 1)*, then the transformed function will, as you can guess by now, be $f(x) = (x - 2)^2 + 1$.

Overall, a shift as a transformation *moves* the graph of a function by a specific amount vertically and/or horizontally. For this reason, a shift is also an *affine transformation*, which is defined to be a transformation that moves all the points of a graph in the same direction and by a constant distance. However, a shift cannot change the size and scale of a graph. In the next section, we will discuss another method of transformation that can: scaling.

SCALING

A scaling transformation stretches or shrinks the graph of a function by a specific amount, depending on the scaling factor. Consider in the following visualization the output of a scaling transformation when applied to our familiar function, $f(x) = x^2$:

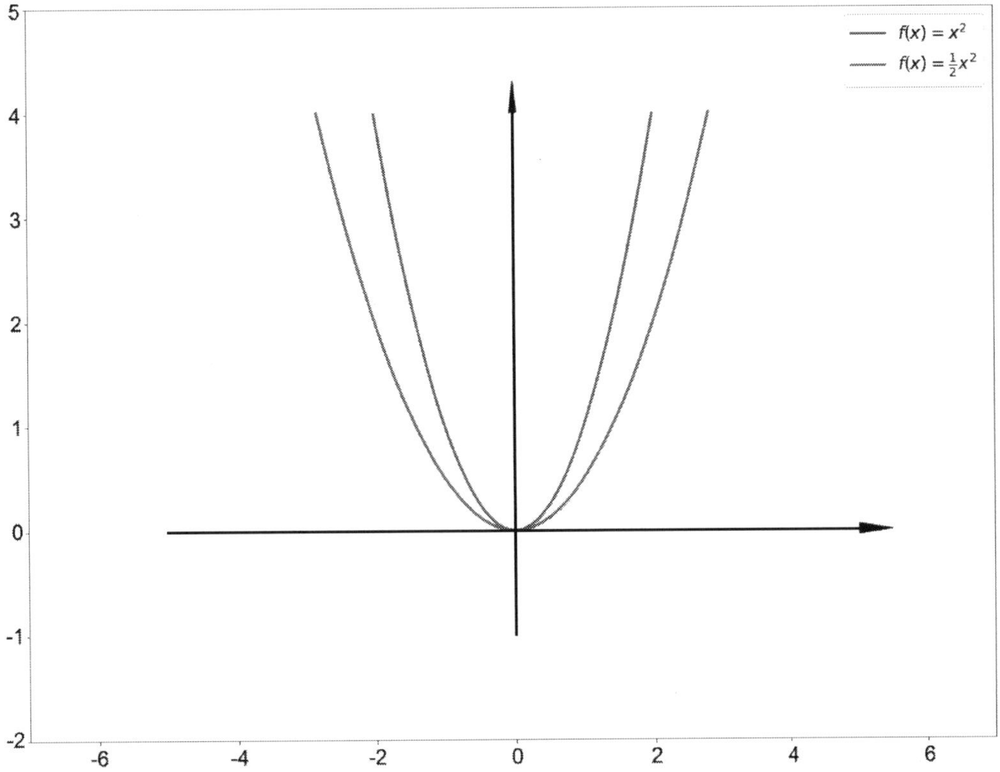

Figure 4.11: Scaling of a function

Through the preceding scaling transformation, every point *(x, y)* lying on the graph of the function is transformed to *(x, y / 2)*, effectively scaling the graph horizontally to be closer to the *x* axis. The transformed graph, which corresponds to the function $f(x) = x^2 / 2$, is wider than the original graph, due to the fact that the curve is scaled to be closer to the *x* axis. To be more exact, aside from the origin *(0, 0)*, any point from the original graph has been *pulled down* to be closer to the *x* axis. This would also make the overall slope of the graph less steep. Conversely, scaling transformations that would bring the transformed graph further away from the *x* axis might be $f(x) = 2x^2$, or $f(x) = 3x^2$, thereby making the slope of the transformed graph steeper.

In these transformations, we are multiplying the *y* coordinates of the graph by a constant, which gives us control of the scaling with respect to the *x* axis. In a similar manner, when a scaling is applied by multiplying the *x* coordinates of the graph of a function, a graph will be stretched or shrunk with respect to the *y* axis.

In general, the effect of a scaling transformation is controlled by the *scaling factor*—the constant that the *x*- or *y*-coordinates of a graph are multiplied by. A positive scaling factor does not change the relative location of the graph with respect to the axes.

When it is a vertical scaling (when the *y*-coordinates are scaled), a positive factor that is smaller than 1 will *pull* the graph to be closer to the *x* axis, while a large factor will *push* the graph away from the axis. The opposite is true for a horizontal scaling (when the *x* coordinates are scaled); a positive factor that is smaller than 1 will *push* the graph away from the *y* axis, and a large factor will *pull*.

While this *pulling/pushing* effect is also the same for negative scaling factors, when a function is scaled by a negative constant, its graph will be *flipped* along the corresponding axis:

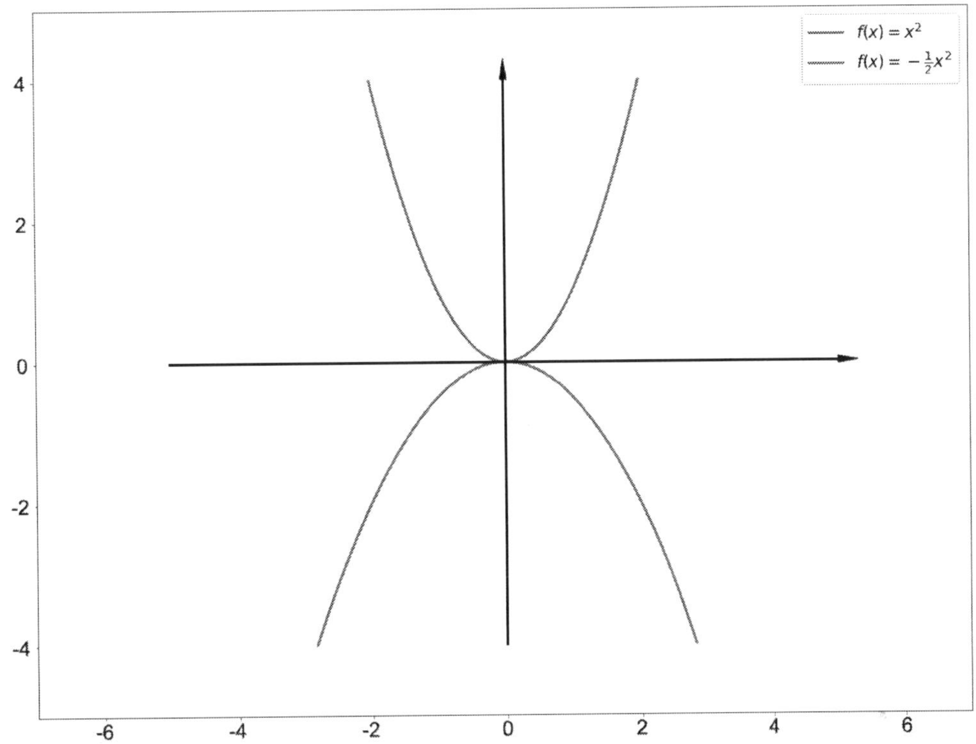

Figure 4.12: Negative scaling of a function

Just as we have seen in the case of shifts, multiple scaling transformations can be applied to a function at the same time to obtain a combined effect.

In general, shifts and scaling constitute two of the most common methods of function transformation. In the next exercise, we will practice the skill of identifying these two transformations from their respective effect on function graphs.

EXERCISE 4.02: FUNCTION TRANSFORMATION IDENTIFICATION

Here, we aim to analyze the effect a specific transformation has on the graph of a function and identify the type as well as the characteristics of the transformation. This exercise will help us familiarize ourselves with how transformations can manipulate the behavior of functions.

The following graph includes the plot of a cubic function, $f(x) = x^3 - x$, and the plot of the sine function, $f(x) = sin(x)$, also commonly known as the sine wave due to its periodicity:

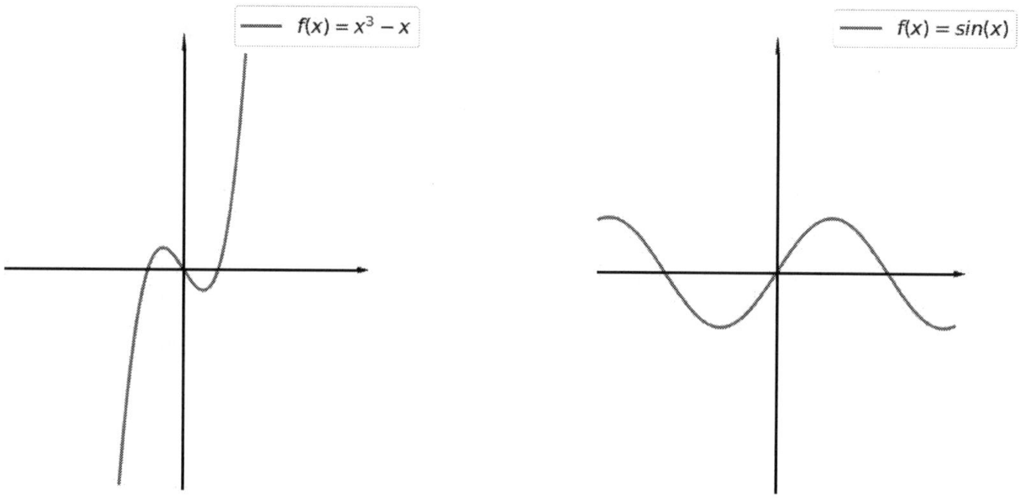

Figure 4.13: Graph of a cubic function and a sine wave

Each of the following graphs includes one of these two function plots as a blue curve and the result of a specific transformation from it as a red curve. For each of the graphs:

1. Identify which transformation could have produced the effect.
2. If it is a shift, identify the value of the shift vector (that is, up/down by how much, left/right by how much).
3. If it is a scaling, identify whether the scaling factor is positive or negative and estimate its value (using the tick marks as a hint).
4. Verify your estimations by producing the same graph using Python (not including the axes and arrows).

Let's now have a look at the graphs:

5. **First transformation of a cubic curve**:

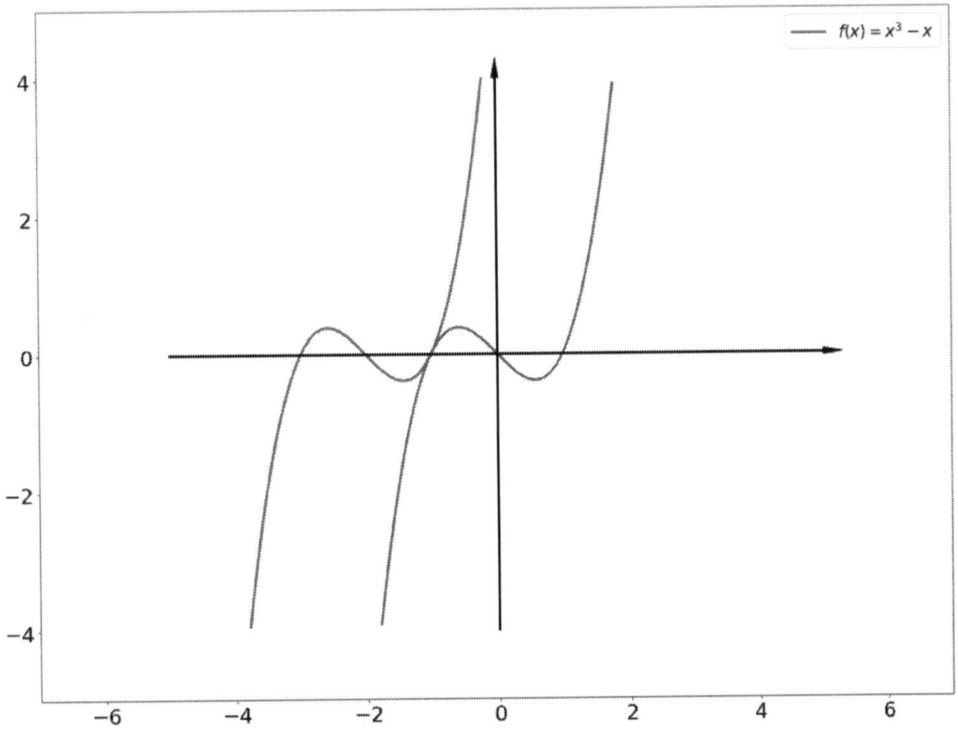

Figure 4.14: First transformation of a cubic curve

The red curve is the result of a shift of the original sine wave. It is a horizontal shift to the left by **2**, so the shift is **−2**.

The following code can be used to reproduce the plot:

```
import numpy as np
import matplotlib.pyplot as plt
x = np.linspace(-5, 5, 1000)
plt.plot(x, x ** 3 - x, c='blue')
plt.plot(x, (x + 2) ** 3 - (x + 2), c='red')

plt.ylim(-5, 5)

plt.show()
```

6. **Second transformation of a cubic curve**:

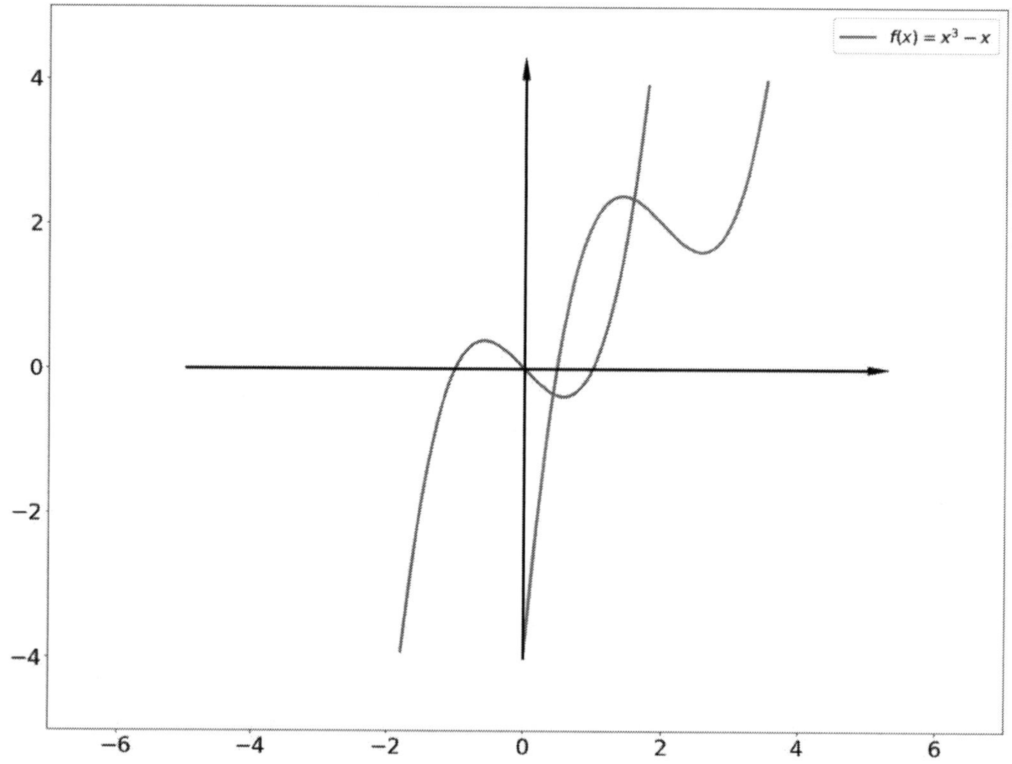

Figure 4.15: Second transformation of a cubic curve

The red curve results from a composite shift. It is a horizontal shift to the right by **2** combined with a vertical shift up by **2**.

The following code can be used to reproduce the plot (using the same variable, **x**):

```
plt.plot(x, x ** 3 - x, c='blue')  # original func
plt.plot(x, (x - 2) ** 3 - (x - 2) + 2, c='red')  # transformed func

plt.ylim(-5, 5)

plt.show()
```

7. **First transformation of a sine wave**:

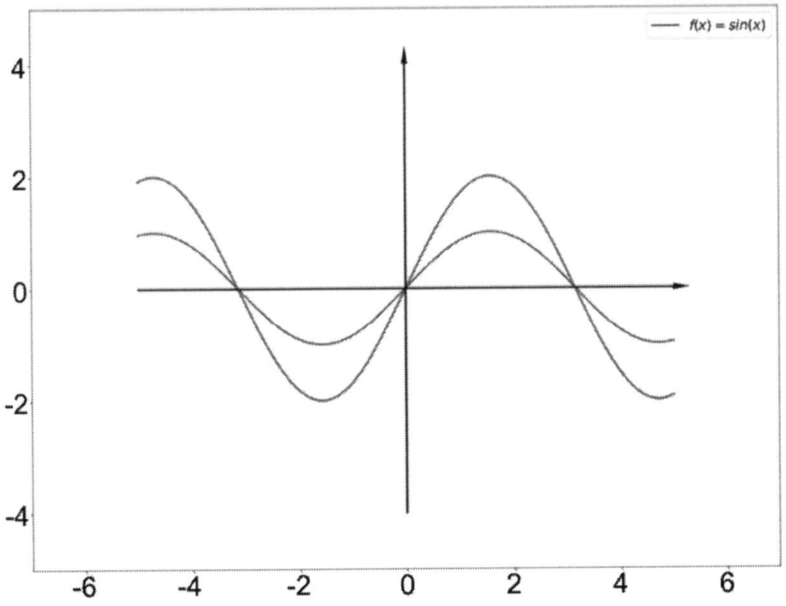

Figure 4.16: First transformation of a sine wave

The red curve results from a scaling. It is a vertical scaling away from the *x* axis by a factor of **2**, so the scaling factor is **2**.

The following code can be used to reproduce the plot (using the same variable, **x**):

```
plt.plot(x, np.sin(x), c='blue')  # original func
plt.plot(x, np.sin(x) * 2, c='red')  # transformed func


plt.ylim(-5, 5)


plt.show()
```

8. **Second transformation of a sine wave**:

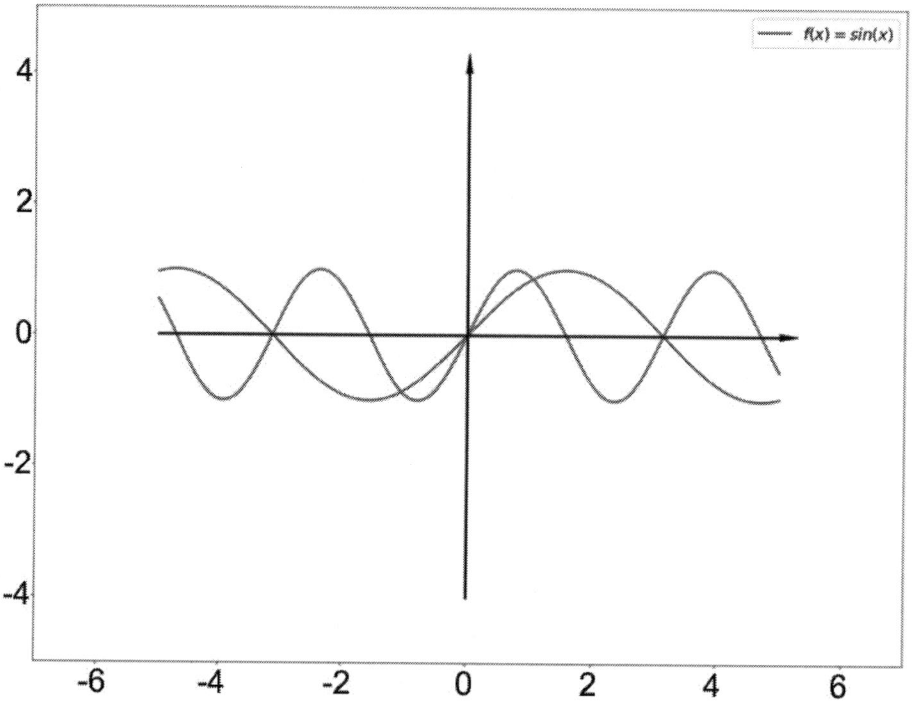

Figure 4.17: Second transformation of a sine wave

The red curve results from a scaling. It is a horizontal scaling that pulls the curve closer to the *y* axis by a factor of **2**, so the scaling factor is **2**.

The following code can be used to reproduce the plot (using the same variable, **x**):

```
plt.plot(x, np.sin(x), c='blue')  # original func
plt.plot(x, np.sin(x * 2), c='red')  # transformed func


plt.ylim(-5, 5)


plt.show()
```

We have thus learned how to identify the transformation type and its degree of change by examining the effect a transformation has on the graph of a function. This exercise also concludes the topic of functions in this chapter.

> **NOTE**
>
> To access the source code for this specific section, please refer to https://packt.live/2D2U7iR.
>
> You can also run this example online at https://packt.live/2YPtHcJ.

In the next section, we will dive into a relevant concept that was briefly mentioned earlier: equations.

EQUATIONS

Again, an equation is formed when a function is assigned the value 0 and we are asked to find the values of the function input, normally *x*, that satisfy the equation. These values are called the roots of the original function. The process of finding these values is called solving an equation, which is a rich topic in mathematics and, specifically, algebra.

In this section, we will discuss two fundamental methods of solving equations by hand as well as examine the available computational tools in Python to facilitate the process of automatically solving equations. We will start with the first method, algebraic manipulations.

ALGEBRAIC MANIPULATIONS

While we are classifying this as a method, algebra is, in general, a technique to *translate* an equation to a simpler form so that solutions can be found easily. Some typical ways to translate an equation are adding/subtracting a constant to both sides of the equation, multiplying/dividing both sides by a non-zero constant, or moving all the terms of the equation to one side.

A simple example of this would be the $3x - 5 = 6$ equation.

To solve for *x*, we first move the number *5* on the left-hand side to the right by adding *5* to both sides of the equation. This gives us $3x = 11$.

Finally, we multiply both sides by *1/3* so that we obtain the value of the variable *x*, which is $x = 11/3$.

This simple example illustrates the idea behind the whole process of manipulating an equation algebraically so that we can isolate the value of *x*. Let's go through another example to nail down the point. Say we have an equation: $3x - 7 - 2(19x - 7) = (5x + 9) / 3 + 12$.

While this equation seems significantly more complicated than the first, the process is actually the same. We first expand the terms inside the parentheses and gather the terms involving *x* into one group, and then gather the remaining terms into another.

This will give us the following algebraic transformations:

$$3x - 7 - (38x - 14) = (5x/3 + 3) + 12$$

$$-35x + 7 = 5x/3 + 15$$

$$110x/3 = -8$$

$$x = -12/55$$

Figure 4.18: Substituting the values to find the value of x

We see that this process is, in general, quite simple, especially when we are only dealing with *linear* terms of *x*. The term *linear* denotes the quantities that are the variable *x* multiplied by a constant. Overall, the general term for the two equations seen here is **linear equations**, which only contain linear terms of *x*. Solving linear equations, as we have seen, is a straightforward process, even when we do it by hand.

In contrast, polynomial equations are equations with terms containing the variable *x* with degrees larger than *1*. Polynomial equations can be effectively solved using a specific technique, which will be discussed in the next subsection. For now, let's consider an example of a non-linear equation, $3e^{x+2} + 3 = 2(e^x + 100)$, that can be solved simply using algebraic manipulations.

Note that *e* is the mathematical constant that is the base of the natural logarithmic function; it is approximately *2.71828*.

> **NOTE**
>
> You can find more information on this constant at https://mathworld.wolfram.com/e.html.

To solve this equation, we first expand the terms in this equation like so: $3e^xe^2 + 3 = 2e^x + 200$

The transformation on the left-hand side is possible because of the identity $a^{x+y} = a^x a^y$ for all positive numbers of *a*, and real numbers *x* and *y*. Now, we see that even though there is no linear term of *x* in this equation, we can still employ our strategy of isolating the terms involving *x* and group them together:

$$\left(3e^2-2\right)e^x=197$$
$$e^x=197/\left(3e^2-2\right)$$

Figure 4.19: Substituting the values in the equation to find e^x

Now, having the value for e^x, we would like to extract out the *x* term. To do this, we will apply the natural logarithmic function, $f(x) = ln(x)$, to both sides of the equation. Since $ln(e^x) = x$ for all real values of *x*, this step will transform the left-hand side of the equation to simply *x*:

$$x=In\left(197/\left(3e^2-2\right)\right)$$

Figure 4.20: Substituting the values in the equation to find x

Overall, the general idea behind using algebraic transformation to solve an equation is to group all the terms involving *x* together and manipulate them into a single term. Again, this strategy alone does not always work for any equation, as sometimes it is not possible to simplify all the *x* terms into one single term. This is the case for polynomial equations, which we will be discussing in the context of the next method of solving equations: factoring.

FACTORING

While it technically belongs to the umbrella term of algebra, **factoring** specifically denotes the process of manipulating a given equation into the following form:

$$f_1(x)f_2(x)\ldots f_n(x)=0$$

Figure 4.21: Formula for factoring

If the product of these terms is equal to zero, at least one of the terms must be equal to zero to satisfy the equation. In other words, solving the original equation is equivalent to solving each of the equations $f_1(x) = 0$, $f_2(x) = 0$, ..., and $f_n(x) = 0$. Ideally, we would want each of these $f_i(x) = 0$ equations to be easier to solve than the original.

Let's consider a starting example: $x^2 = 100$

Using the identity $x^2 - y^2 = (x - y)(x + y)$ for all real x and y values, the equation is equivalent to $(x - 10)(x + 10) = 0$.

Since their product is zero, either $x - 10$ or $x + 10$ must also be zero. Solving these two equations gives us the solution for the original equation: $x = 10$ or $x = -10$.

While this is a fairly simple example, it is able to illustrate a number of points. First, by factoring the equation into different terms multiplied together being equal to 0, the problem was converted into a set of simpler sub-problems. Additionally, with factoring, we can achieve something that the simple addition/multiplication of manipulations cannot: solving polynomial equations.

Let's consider our next example of an equation: $x^3 - 7x^2 + 15x = 9$

We see that even when all the terms involving x have already been grouped together, it is not clear how we should proceed with simple algebra.

Here, an insightful mathematics student may notice that this equation accepts $x = 1$ or $x = 3$ as solutions (since plugging in these values makes the left-hand side of the equation evaluate to 0). The fact that a polynomial equation accepts $x = c$ as a solution not only means that by replacing x with c in the equation it will evaluate to zero, but it also means that the equation itself can be factored into the form $(x - c)\,g(x) = 0$, where $g(x)$ is the other factored term of the equation. This technique also has another name, Ruffini's rule, about which you can find more information at https://mathworld.wolfram.com/RuffinisRule.html. With that in mind, we attempt to factor the given equation with respect to the term $(x - 1)$ as follows:

$$
\begin{aligned}
&x^3 - 7x^2 + 15x = 9 \\
&\left(x^3 - x^2\right) - \left(6x^2 - 6x\right) + (9x - 9) = 0 \\
&x^2(x - 1) - 6x(x - 1) + 9(x - 1) = 0 \\
&(x - 1)\left(x^2 - 6x + 9\right) = 0
\end{aligned}
$$

Figure 4.22: Factoring the given equation

Keeping in mind that the equation also accepts $x = 3$ as a solution, we continue to factor $(x^2 - 6x + 9)$ into $(x - 3)$ multiplied by another term. If you are familiar with the quadratic formula, you might already be able to tell that the equation can be factored into $(x - 1)(x - 3)^2 = 0$.

In the end, we have proven that the given equation does accept two solutions: $x = 1$ and $x = 3$.

A polynomial equation of degree *n* is one where the largest degree that *x* has is *n*. Overall, we would like to factor such an equation to *n* different factors. This is because it can be mathematically proven that a polynomial equation of degree *n* can only have, at most, *n* unique solutions.

In other words, if we can successfully transform an equation into *n* different factors, each of those factors is a linear term of *x*, which can be easily solved using the first method that we discussed above. For example, the equation $2x^3 - 7x^2 + 7x - 2 = 0$ can be factored into $(x - 1)(x - 2)(2x - 1) = 0$, which gives us three solutions: $x = 1$, $x = 2$, and $x = 1 / 2$.

Of course, there are situations in which a polynomial equation of degree *n* cannot be factored into *n* different linear terms of *x*. Consider the following example equation $x^3 + 4x - 5 = 0$.

This accepts a solution $x = 1$, and therefore has a factor of $(x - 1)$:

$$\left(x^3 - x^2\right) + \left(x^2 - x\right) + (5x - 5) = 0$$
$$(x - 1)\left(x^2 + x + 5\right) = 0$$

Figure 4.23: Factor for x = 1

Now, consider the term $x^2 + x + 5$. If we try plugging various values of *x* into the equation, we will see that none of the values can satisfy the equation. This suggests that this equation has no solution or, more specifically, $x^2 + x + 5$ is greater than 0 for all values of *x*, and we will prove that statement.

When we'd like to prove that a quadratic function of a variable is always greater than 0, we can utilize the fact that $(g(x))^2$ is always non-negative, for all real values of *x* and for all functions *g* (this is because the square of any real number is non-negative). If we could then rewrite the term $x^2 + x + 5$ into the form $(g(x))^2 + c$, where *c* is a positive constant, we can prove that the term is always positive.

Here, we use the **completing the square technique** to group the *x* terms into a square. This technique involves using the identity $(a + b)^2 = a^2 + 2ab + b^2$ for all values of *a* and *b* to construct $(g(x))^2$. Specifically, the term *x* can be rewritten as $2 x (1/2)$, since we need it to be in the form of 2 multiplied by *x* multiplied by another number. So, we have x^2 and $2 x (1/2)$; we therefore need $(1/2)^2 = 1/4$ to *complete* the sum of the three numbers as a square: $x^2 + x + 1/4 = x^2 + 2 x (1/2) + (1/2)^2 = (x + 1/2)^2$.

The whole term can therefore be transformed as $x^2 + x + 5 = (x^2 + x + 1/4) + 19/4 = (x + 1/2)^2 + 19/4$.

$(x + 1/2)^2$ is non-negative for any real value of *x*, so the whole term $(x + 1/2)^2 + 19/4$ is greater than or equal to *19/4*. This is to say that there is no real value of *x* that makes the term $x^2 + x + 5$ equal to *0*; in other words, the equation $x^2 + x + 5 = 0$ does not have any solution.

And that is an overview of the factoring technique to solve polynomial equations. By way of a final point on the topic of equations, we will discuss the use of Python to automate the process of solving equations.

USING PYTHON

In addition to the two methods of solving equations by hand, we also have the option of leveraging the computational power of Python to automatically solve any equation. In this section, we will look into this process in the context of the **`SymPy`** library.

Broadly speaking, SymPy is one of the best libraries in Python for symbolic mathematics, which is an umbrella term for algebraic computations involving symbols (such as *x*, *y*, and *f(x)*). While SymPy offers an extensive API that includes support for different mathematical subfields, including calculus, geometry, logic, and number theory, we will only be exploring its options for solving equations and (in the next section) systems of equations in this chapter.

> **NOTE**
>
> You can find more information on the library on its official website at https://docs.sympy.org/latest/index.html.

First, we need to install the library for our Python environment. This process, as always, can be done via **pip** and **conda**. Run either of the following commands:

```
$ pip install sympy
$ conda install sympy
```

Following a successful installation of the library, let's explore the options that it offers using a specific example, an equation that we considered in the last section: $x^3 - 7x^2 + 15x = 9$.

Being a tool for symbolic mathematics, SymPy offers an easy API to declare variables and functions. To do this, we first import the **Symbol** class from the SymPy library and declare a variable named **x**:

```
from sympy import Symbol
x = Symbol('x')
```

When **x** is printed out in a Jupyter notebook, we will see that the letter is actually formatted as a mathematical symbol:

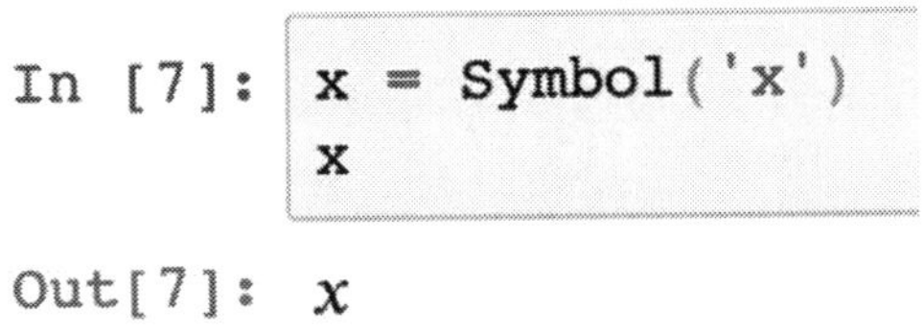

Figure 4.24: SymPy symbols in Jupyter notebook

Now, to solve the given equation, we import the **solve()** function from the **sympy.solvers** package. This **solve()** function takes in an expression containing a SymPy symbol (in this case, it is our variable **x**) and finds the values of **x** that make the expression evaluate to 0. In other words, to solve for $x^3 - 7x^2 + 15x = 9$, we enter the following code:

```
from sympy.solvers import solve
solve(x ** 3 - 7 * x ** 2 + 15 * x - 9, x)
```

This code snippet returns a list of solutions for **x**, which, in this case, is **[1, 3]**. We see that this corresponds to the solution that we found earlier via factoring.

Let's examine another example that we have solved earlier: $3e^{x+2} + 3 = 2(e^x + 100)$. Remember that this equation has a root, $x = ln(197 / (3e^2 - 2))$, which is approximately 2.279. Now, we enter this equation into the **`solve()`** function like so (after importing the constant **`e`** from the built-in **`math`** library):

```
from math import e
solve(3 * e ** (x + 2) + 3 - 2 * (e ** x + 100), x)
```

This will give us the following output:

```
[2.279147778845756]
```

This, as we can see, is the same solution obtained from our algebraic analysis. Overall, with the ability to declare variables and have a function of any form as input for the **`solve()`** function, SymPy offers us a flexible and convenient way to computationally solve equations in Python.

This topic also concludes our discussion on equations and methods of finding their solutions. Before we move on to the next topic in this chapter, let's go through an exercise to practice what we have learned in this section.

EXERCISE 4.03: INTRODUCTION TO BREAK-EVEN ANALYSIS

Break-even analysis is a common practice in economics and financial engineering. The goal of a break-even analysis is to find the specific points in time where the revenue of a business balances its costs. Finding these points in time is therefore very important to business owners and stakeholders, who are interested in knowing if, and when, they will make a profit.

This scenario can be modeled fairly easily using mathematical variables and functions, which we will be doing in this exercise. Specifically, we aim to model a simple business and conduct a break-even analysis by solving for the break-even points. By the end, you will become more familiar with the process of representing real-life situations using mathematical models, functions, and variables.

Scenario: A burger restaurant incurs a cost of \$6.56 for the ingredients of every burger that it sells. It also incurs a fixed cost of \$1,312.13 every month, which goes into the cooks' wages, rent, utilities, and so on. The owner of the restaurant would like to perform a break-even analysis to determine if and when the revenue will cover the cost.

1. Create a new Jupyter notebook and import NumPy, Matplotlib, and SymPy in the first code cell:

```
import numpy as np
import matplotlib.pyplot as plt

from sympy.solvers import solve
from sympy import Symbol
```

2. Say the restaurant sets the price of each of the burgers it sells at \$8.99 and let *x* be a variable that represents the number of burgers that need to be sold each month so that the revenue made is equal to the cost. Write down the equation for *x* in this situation.

   With *x* being the number of burgers sold, $8.99x$ is the revenue that the restaurant will make, while $6.56x + 1312.13$ is the cost that the restaurant will incur. The equation for *x* will therefore be:

   $8.99x = 6.56x + 1312.13$

3. Solve for *x* by hand and verify the result using Python in the next cell of the Jupyter notebook. For testing purposes, store the list of solutions returned by SymPy to a variable named **`sols`**.

   Using simple algebraic transformation, we can solve for *x* to be $x = 1312.13 / (8.99 - 6.56) = 539.97$. So, the restaurant needs to sell roughly 540 burgers to break even.

   The following code can be used to solve for *x* using SymPy:

```
x = Symbol('x')
sols = solve(8.99 * x - 6.56 * x - 1312.13, x)
```

   The **`sols`** variable should have the value **`[539.971193415638]`**, which corresponds to our solution.

4. Instead of solving for *x* to be the break-even point, construct a function of *x* that represents the total profit (revenue minus cost) of the restaurant every month.

   The function should be $f(x) = 8.99x - 6.56x - 1312.13 = 2.43x - 1312.13$.

5. In the next code cell of the Jupyter notebook, plot this function for the *x* values between 0 and 1000 using NumPy and Matplotlib, along with a horizontal line at 0, which should be colored black:

```
xs = np.linspace(0, 1000, 1000)
plt.plot(xs, 2.43 * xs - 1312.13)
plt.axhline(0, c='k')

plt.show()
```

This should produce the following plot:

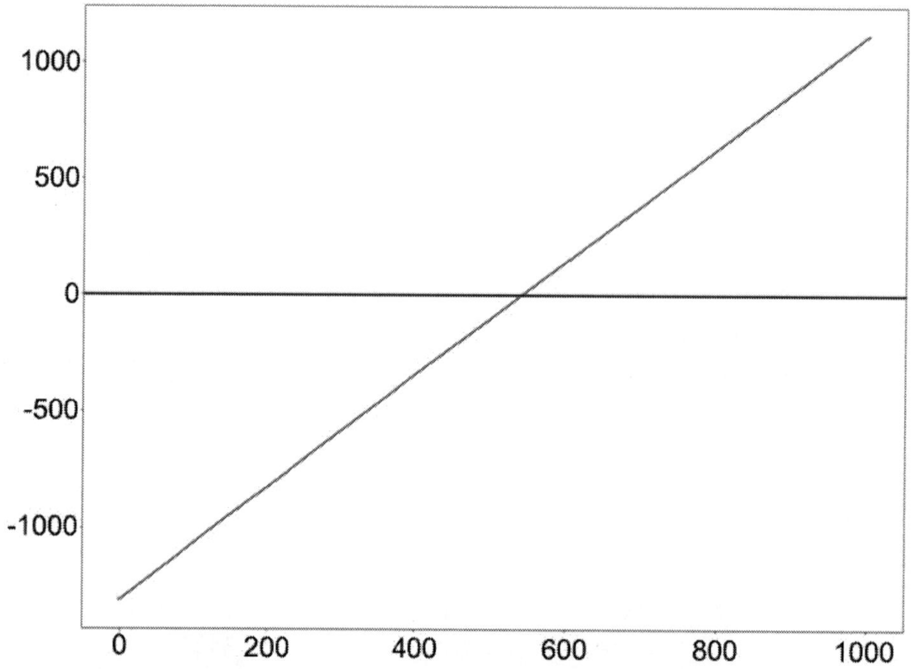

Figure 4.25: Visualization of a break-even analysis

The intersection of our profit curve and the horizontal line represents the break-even point. In this case, we see that it is roughly at the *x*-coordinate of **540**, which corresponds to the actual break-even point.

6. Say the restaurant on average sells 400 burgers every month and now let *x* be the price of a burger that the restaurant can set so that they can break even. Write down the equation for *x* in this situation.

   With *x* being the price of a burger, $400x$ is the profit that the restaurant will make, while $(400)\ 6.56 + 1312.13 = 3936.13$ (*$6.56* for each burger and a fixed amount of *$1312.13*) is the cost the restaurant will incur. The equation for *x* will therefore be $400x = 3936.13$.

7. Solve for *x* by hand and verify the result with SymPy in the Jupyter notebook. Store the list of solutions returned by SymPy in a variable named **sols1**.

   The equation can be simply solved by dividing both sides by 400, which gives us $x = 9.84$. The Python code that solves the same equation is the following, which also produces the same result:

```
sols1 = solve(400 * x - 3936.13, x)
sols1
```

8. In the next code cell, plot the function that represents the difference between profit and cost for the *x* values between **0** and **10**, together with the horizontal line at **0**:

```
xs = np.linspace(0, 10, 1000)
plt.plot(xs, 400 * xs - 3936.13)
plt.axhline(0, c='k')

plt.show()
```

This should produce the following plot:

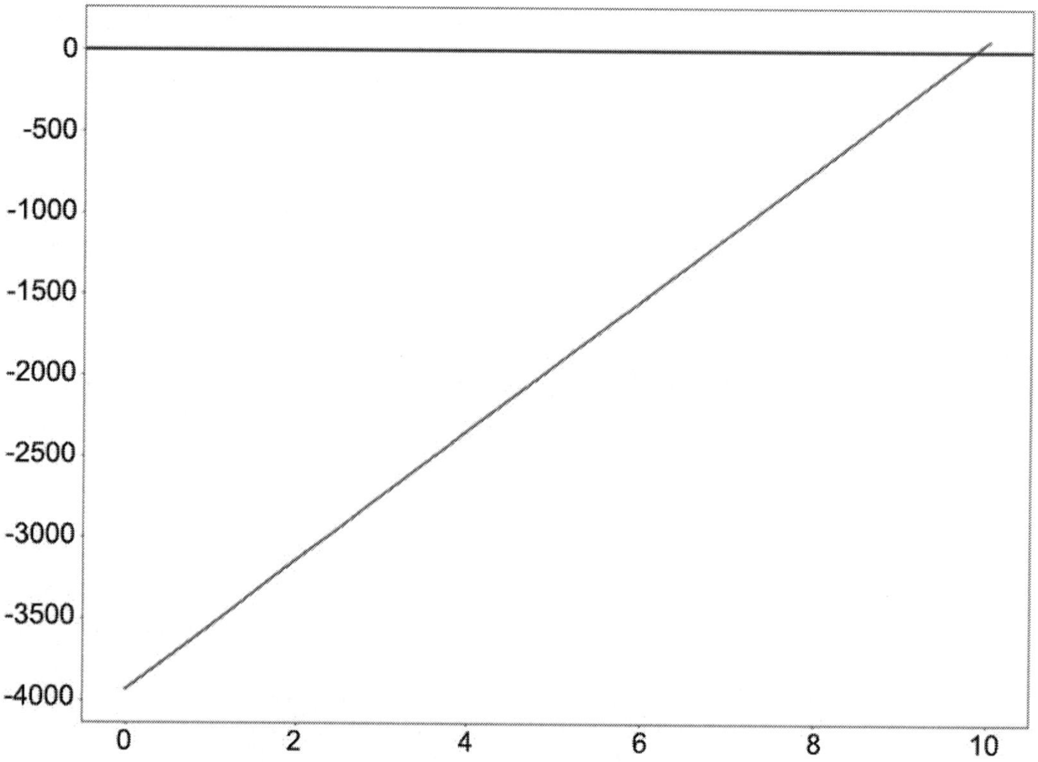

Figure 4.26: Visualization of a break-even analysis

Once again, the intersection of the two lines (which represents the break-even point) coincides with the actual solution that we have derived.

And that is the end of our exercise. In it, we have been introduced to the concept of break-even analysis by modeling a sample real-life business with mathematical functions and variables. We have learned how to find the number of products to be produced as well as the correct price to set to break even.

> **NOTE**
>
> To access the source code for this specific section, please refer to https://packt.live/3gn3JU3.
>
> You can also run this example online at https://packt.live/3gkeA0V.

Of course, a real-life business scenario is more complicated and has many more factors involved. We will come back to the task of break-even analysis in the activity at the end of the chapter, but before that, we need to discuss this chapter's final section: systems of equations.

SYSTEMS OF EQUATIONS

An equation is an equality that we need to satisfy by solving for the values of a specific variable. In a system of equations, we have multiple equations involving multiple variables, and the goal is still the same: solving for the values of these variables so that each and every equation in the system is satisfied.

Overall, there is no limit to the number of equations a system can have. However, it can be rigorously proven that when the number of equations a system has is not equal to the number of its variables, the system has either infinitely many solutions or no solutions. In this section, we will only be considering the case where these two numbers match.

Additionally, we will consider two different types of systems of equations: systems of linear equations and those of non-linear equations. We will consider the methods of solving each of these two types of systems of equations, both by hand and by using Python. First, let's discuss the concept of systems of linear equations.

SYSTEMS OF LINEAR EQUATIONS

Similar to linear equations, which only contain constants and linear terms of their variables, a system of linear equations consists of linear equations, which also only contain linear combinations of its variables and constants.

A simple example of such a system is the following:

$$\begin{cases} x + y = 5 \\ 2y - x = 3 \end{cases}$$

Figure 4.27: An example of a linear equation system

As we can see, this system of equations has two variables: *x* and *y*. Each of the two equations contains those variables multiplied by constants (linear terms) as well as constants themselves.

To solve this system of equations, you may have already noticed that if we were to add respective sides of the two equations together, we would obtain an extra equation, $3y = 8$, which we can then solve for $y = 8/3$ and subsequently solve for $x = 5 - 8/3 = 7/3$.

Overall, this method involves multiplying the equations provided to us by different constants and adding them together to sequentially eliminate variables. The goal is to obtain an equation that only has linear terms of a single variable left (and potentially constants), from which we can solve for that one variable. The solution value for this variable will then be plugged into the original equations, and the process continues for the rest of the variables.

While this process is straightforward when the number of variables/equations we have is relatively small, it can get quite messy as this number grows. In this subsection, we will consider a method called *row reduction*, or *Gaussian elimination*, that will help us formalize and then automate the process of solving the system of equations.

Say we are asked to solve the following general system of linear equations with *n* variables and *n* equations:

$$\begin{cases} c_{11}x_1 + \cdots + c_{1n}x_n = c_1 \\ \cdots \\ c_{n1}x_1 + \cdots + c_{nn}x_n = c_n \end{cases}$$

Figure 4.28: System of linear equations with n variables and n equations

Here, c_{ij} is the constant coefficient for variable x_j in the ith equation. Again, these c_{ij} values can take on any constant value, and this system of equation is the most general form of any system of linear equations.

To apply the row reduction method, we construct what is called an augmented matrix, which is the following:

$$\left[\begin{array}{ccc|c} c_{11} & \cdots & c_{1n} & c_1 \\ \cdots & \cdots & \cdots & \cdots \\ c_{n1} & \cdots & c_{nn} & c_n \end{array}\right]$$

Figure 4.29: An augmented matrix

The left section of the matrix is an *n*-by-*n* submatrix whose elements correspond to the constant coefficients in the original system of equations; the right section of the matrix is a column with *n* values, which correspond to the constant values on the right-hand side of the equations in the original system.

Now, from this augmented matrix, we can perform three types of transformation:

- Swap the locations of any given two rows.
- Multiply a row by a non-zero constant.
- Add a row to any other row (potentially multiplied by a non-zero constant as well).

The goal of the method is to transform the augmented matrix into *reduced row echelon form*, or, since we have a system of *n* equations and *n* variables, an identity matrix, where the ith element in the ith row is 1 and every other element in that row is *0*. Essentially, we would like to transform the augmented matrix into this matrix:

$$\left[\begin{array}{cccc|c} 1 & 0 & \dots & 0 & c_1' \\ 0 & 1 & \dots & 0 & c_2' \\ \dots & \dots & \dots & \dots & \dots \\ 0 & 0 & \dots & 1 & c_n' \end{array}\right]$$

Figure 4.30: Matrix transformation

Once this is done, the c_i' values correspond to the values that make up the solution for the original system of equations. In other words, the solution would be $x_1 = c_1'$, $x_2 = c_2'$, and so on.

While this mathematical generalization can seem intimidating, let's demystify the process by considering a specific example. Let's say we are to solve the following system of linear equations:

$$\begin{cases} x + 3y - 2z = 1 \\ 3x + 5y + 6z = 31 \\ 2x + 4y + 3z = 19 \end{cases}$$

Figure 4.31: System of linear equations

We first construct the corresponding augmented matrix:

$$\left[\begin{array}{ccc|c} 1 & 3 & -2 & 1 \\ 3 & 5 & 6 & 31 \\ 2 & 4 & 3 & 19 \end{array}\right]$$

Figure 4.32: Corresponding augmented matrix

Now, we aim to transform this matrix into the identity form by using the three mentioned methods of transformation. We first subtract the second row by three times the first row and subsequently divide it by 4 to obtain:

$$\left[\begin{array}{ccc|c} 1 & 3 & -2 & 1 \\ 0 & -1 & 3 & 7 \\ 2 & 4 & 3 & 19 \end{array}\right]$$

Figure 4.33: Step 1 to transform the matrix into an identity matrix

Again, the goal is to create the structure of an identity matrix on the left-hand side, which can be done by forcing the non-diagonal elements to be zero. We have done this for the first element on the second row, so let's now try to do the same for the third row by subtracting it by two times the first row:

$$\left[\begin{array}{ccc|c} 1 & 3 & -2 & 1 \\ 0 & -1 & 3 & 7 \\ 0 & -2 & 7 & 17 \end{array}\right]$$

Figure 4.34: Step 2 to transform the matrix into an identity matrix

The second element on the third row is to be transformed to 0, which can be done by subtracting the third row by two times the second row:

$$\left[\begin{array}{ccc|c} 1 & 3 & -2 & 1 \\ 0 & -1 & 3 & 7 \\ 0 & 0 & 1 & 3 \end{array}\right]$$

Figure 4.35: Step 3 to transform the matrix into an identity matrix

Once the last row is in the correct form, transforming the other rows is relatively easy as well. We now subtract the second row by three times the third row and multiply it by -1, which gives us:

$$\left[\begin{array}{ccc|c} 1 & 3 & -2 & 1 \\ 0 & 1 & 0 & 2 \\ 0 & 0 & 1 & 3 \end{array}\right]$$

Figure 4.36: Step 4 to transform the matrix into an identity matrix

As for the first row, we first add two times the third row to it to eliminate the last element:

$$\left[\begin{array}{ccc|c} 1 & 3 & 0 & 7 \\ 0 & 1 & 0 & 2 \\ 0 & 0 & 1 & 3 \end{array}\right]$$

Figure 4.37: Step 5 to transform the matrix into an identity matrix

Finally, we subtract it by three times the second row, which allows us to obtain the reduced row echelon form of our augmented matrix (with the identity matrix on the left):

$$\left[\begin{array}{ccc|c} 1 & 0 & 0 & 1 \\ 0 & 1 & 0 & 2 \\ 0 & 0 & 1 & 3 \end{array}\right]$$

Figure 4.38: Identity matrix

This corresponds to the solution where $x = 1$, $y = 2$, and $z = 3$. We can ensure that our solution is indeed correct by plugging these values into the original system of equations, which shows that they do satisfy the system.

And that is the process of using the row reduction method. As mentioned earlier, another method to solve a system of linear equations is the matrix solution. This involves representing a given system as a matrix equation. Specifically, from the general form of any system of linear equations:

$$\begin{cases} c_{11}x_1 + \ldots + c_{1n}x_n = c_1 \\ \ldots \\ c_{n1}x_1 + \ldots + c_{nn}x_n = c_n \end{cases}$$

Figure 4.39: System of linear equation

We can rewrite it in matrix notation as $Ax = c$, where A is the n-by-n matrix containing the constant coefficients, x is the vector containing the variables that we have to solve for: x_1, x_2, ..., x_n, and c is similarly the vector containing the constant coefficients c_1, c_2, ..., c_n. Due to the definition of a product of a matrix and a vector, the equation $Ax = c$ is indeed equivalent to the original system of equations.

In this matrix notation, the vector x can be solved quite easily as $x = A^{-1} c$, where A^{-1} is the *inverse matrix* of A. An inverse matrix, M^{-1}, of any given matrix, M, is the matrix that satisfies the equation $A A^{-1} = I$, where I is the identity matrix.

This product between a matrix and a vector is called a **dot product**, which outputs another vector whose elements equal the sums of products of corresponding elements in the original matrix and vector. In our case, the dot product between A^{-1} and c will give us a vector that makes up the solution of the system.

There are matrices that do not have their corresponding inverse matrices; these matrices are called singular matrices. One of the signs we can use to tell that a matrix is singular is if one row of the matrix is exactly another row multiplied by a constant.

Theoretically speaking, this is analogous to the situation where the coefficients in one equation of a system are exact multiplications of the coefficients in another equation by a constant. If this is the case, we either have duplicate information (when the two equations have the same information, then the system has infinitely many solutions) or conflicting information (when the constants on the right-hand side of the two equations do not match up, then the system has no solution).

The theory behind this is not within the scope of this book. For now, we just need to know that if the corresponding coefficient matrix of a system of linear equations does not have an inverse matrix, the system does not have a definite solution.

So, not every matrix has its own inverse matrix, and even if a given matrix does, the process of computing the inverse matrix can be quite involved. Luckily, this can be done relatively easily in Python with NumPy, which we will see in the upcoming exercise. Specifically, the **linalg** (which stands for linear algebra) package in NumPy offers efficient implementation of many linear algebra-related algorithms. Here, we are interested in the **inv()** function, which takes in a two-dimensional NumPy array representing a matrix and returns the corresponding inverse matrix. We will see the effect of this function first-hand in the next exercise; more information about the package can also be found at https://docs.scipy.org/doc/numpy/reference/routines.linalg.html.

EXERCISE 4.04: MATRIX SOLUTION WITH NUMPY

In this exercise, we will write a program that takes in a system of linear equations and produces its solution using the matrix solution method. Again, this will be done by the computation of the inverse of the coefficient matrix using NumPy:

1. Create a Jupyter notebook. In its first cell, import NumPy and the **inv()** function from its **linalg** package:

```
import numpy as np
from numpy.linalg import inv
```

2. In the next code cell, declare a function named **solve_eq_sys()** (for testing purposes) that takes in two arguments: **coeff_matrix**, which stores the matrix of constant coefficients in a system of linear equations, and **c**, which stores a vector of the constant values on the right-hand side of the equations:

```
def solve_eq_sys(coeff_matrix, c):
```

   These two arguments completely define an instance of a system of linear equations, and the job of the **solve_eq_sys()** function is to compute its solution. We further assume that the arguments are both stored as NumPy arrays.

3. Recalling that the solution for the system is $x = A^{-1} c$, we simply return the product of the inverse matrix of **coeff_matrix** and **c**.

The inverse matrix can be computed using the **inv()** function from NumPy:

```
inv_matrix = inv(coeff_matrix)
```

Finally, the solution can be computed using the **dot()** method, which calculates the dot product of a matrix and a vector:

```
return inv_matrix.dot(c)
```

Our function should look like the following:

```
def solve_eq_sys(coeff_matrix, c):
    inv_matrix = inv(coeff_matrix)
    return inv_matrix.dot(c)
```

4. In the next code cell, declare the corresponding coefficient matrix and **c** vector for the system of equations that we considered earlier and call the **solve_eq_sys()** function on them:

$$\begin{cases} x + 3y - 2z = 1 \\ 3x + 5y + 6z = 31 \\ 2x + 4y + 3z = 19 \end{cases}$$

Figure 4.40: System of linear equations

The code for this should be:

```
coeff_matrix = np.array([[1, 3, -2],\
                         [3, 5, 6],\
                         [2, 4, 3]])

c = np.array([1, 31, 19])

solve_eq_sys(coeff_matrix, c)
```

This code should produce the following output:

```
array([1., 2., 3.])
```

We see that this output exactly corresponds to the actual solution to the system of equations that we have derived using the row reduction method: *x = 1*, *y = 2*, and *z = 3*.

5. Now, we would like to take into account the case where our coefficient matrix is singular. We do this by testing our code on the following sample system of linear equations that has no solution:

$$\begin{cases} x+3y-2z=1 \\ 3x+5y+6z=31 \\ 2x+6y-4z=19 \end{cases}$$

Figure 4.41: Sample system of linear equations

We see that if we multiply the first equation by **2**, the equation we obtain contradicts the third equation. In other words, there is no combination of values for variables *x*, *y*, and *z* that can satisfy the system.

In the next code cell, call the **inv()** function on this coefficient matrix:

```
inv(np.array([[1, 3, -2],\
              [3, 5, 6],\
               [2, 6, -4]]))
```

We will see that this code produces a **LinAlgError: Singular matrix** error, which we will fix in the next step.

For testing purposes, uncomment out this cell.

6. Come back to our code and modify our current **solve_eq_sys()** function with a **try...except** block to handle this error, which will need to be imported from NumPy first:

```
from numpy.linalg import inv, LinAlgError
```

Now, the function should return **False** if the input matrix is singular. It should look like the following:

```
def solve_eq_sys(coeff_matrix, c):
    try:
        inv_matrix = inv(coeff_matrix)
        return inv_matrix.dot(c)
    except LinAlgError:
        return False
```

7. In the next code cell, call this function on the sample system of equations we used in *step 5*:

```
coeff_matrix = np.array([[1, 3, -2],\
                          [3, 5, 6],\
                          [2, 6, -4]])

c = np.array([1, 31, 19])

solve_eq_sys(coeff_matrix, c)
```

This time, the function returns the value **False**, which is the behavior we desire.

Through this exercise, we have learned how to implement the matrix solution method to solve a system of linear equations using NumPy. This also concludes the topic of linear equation systems.

> **NOTE**
>
> To access the source code for this specific section, please refer to https://packt.live/2NPpQpK.
>
> You can also run this example online at https://packt.live/2VBNg6w.

In the next and final section of this chapter, we will consider systems of equations that are not completely linear.

SYSTEMS OF NON-LINEAR EQUATIONS

When a system contains an equation that contains some non-linear terms of its variables, the methods that we discussed in the previous section do not apply. For example, consider the following system:

$$\begin{cases} x + y = 5 \\ x^2 - x + 2y = 8 \end{cases}$$

Figure 4.42: An example system of non-linear equations

The problem arises with the non-linear term, x^2, which complicates whatever transformations we want to apply to the system.

However, we can still have a systematic approach to solving these types of systems. Specifically, notice that from either equation, we can solve for a variable in terms of the other variable. To do this, we algebraically transform each equation so that one variable can be represented purely in terms of the other. In particular, *y* can be represented as a function of *x* as follows:

$$\begin{cases} y = 5 - x \\ y = \dfrac{8 - x^2 + x}{2} \end{cases}$$

Figure 4.43: Substituting the equations to find the values of y

So, in order for the system to have a valid solution, the two values of *y* need to match up. In other words, we have the following equation that just contains *x*:

$$5 - x = \frac{8 - x^2 + x}{2}$$

Figure 4.44: Substituting the value of y on both sides

This is simply a polynomial equation for *x*, which, as we know, can be solved via factoring. Specifically, the equation can be factored to $(x - 2)(x - 1) = 0$, which obviously accepts $x = 1$ and $x = 2$ as solutions. Each of these values for *x* corresponds to a value for *y*, which can be found by plugging in 1 and 2 into the original system of equations. In the end, the system has two solutions: $(x = 1, y = 4)$ and $(x = 2, y = 3)$.

Overall, this method is called **substitution**, denoting the fact that we are able to solve for a variable in terms of another variable by transforming an equation. This solution is then substituted into another equation so that we obtain an equation of a single variable.

Let's see another example of the application of this method with the following system of equations:

$$\begin{cases} x^2 - 2x - y^2 = -1 \\ x^2 - 2y = 1 \end{cases}$$

Figure 4.45: Example system of equations

While there are multiple ways of solving this, one clear way is to solve for *y* in the second equation, which leads to $y = (x^2 - 1) / 2$, which can then be plugged into the first equation like $x^2 - 2x - (x^2 - 1)^2 / 4 = -1$.

With some algebra, we can simplify the equation as $x^4 - 6x^2 + 8x - 3 = 0$.

We now have an equation that only contains one variable, so we can apply the techniques that we have learned in the last section to solve for *x*. Once we have the solution for *x*, we can also solve for *y* using the preceding $y = (x^2 - 1) / 2$ substitution.

Here, factoring can be applied to find the values of *x* that satisfy this equation. Let's try plugging in a few values of *x* such as *-1*, *0*, *1*, or *2* to see which would evaluate the function to 0. Noticing that $x = 1$ is a valid solution, we first factor the equation with respect to $(x - 1)$, which leads to $(x - 1)(x^3 + x^2 - 5x + 3) = 0$.

Once again, we notice that $x = 1$ still satisfies the equation $x^3 + x^2 - 5x + 3 = 0$, thus taking another factoring step to $(x - 1)^2 (x^2 + 2x - 3) = 0$.

The quadratic function $x^2 + 2x - 3$ can then be factored into $(x - 1)(x + 3)$. In the end, we have the following equation $(x - 1)^3 (x + 3) = 0$.

Two values of *x* satisfy the equation: $x = 1$ and $x = -3$. By plugging them into the original system, we can then solve for *y* and obtain two solutions for the system: $(x = 1, y = 0)$ and $(x = -3, y = 4)$.

Unfortunately, not all systems of non-linear equations allow us to employ the substitution method in such a straightforward manner. In many cases, subtle and ingenious techniques have to be used to solve complex systems of equations.

What if, then, we would like to automate the process of finding the solutions for such systems? This is where the symbolic computation ability offered by the **sympy** library comes in handy once again. We have seen that with SymPy, we can solve for any one-variable equation. The same idea can also apply to systems of non-linear equations, only in this case, we pass a list of symbolic functions to the **solve()** function.

Say we want to use SymPy to solve the two systems of equations we have in this section; firstly:

$$\begin{cases} x+y=5 \\ x^2-x+2y=8 \end{cases}$$

Figure 4.46: The first system of equation

And secondly:

$$\begin{cases} x^2-2x-y^2=-1 \\ x^2-2y=1 \end{cases}$$

Figure 4.47: The second system of equation

To do this, we first declare our variables as instances of the **Symbol** class from SymPy:

```
x = Symbol('x')
y = Symbol('y')
```

We can then call the **solve()** function from SymPy to find solutions for the systems of equations we have. For the first:

```
solve([x + y - 5, x ** 2 - x + 2 * y - 8],\
      x, y)
```

This code will return `[(1, 4), (2, 3)]`, which is the list of valid solutions for *x* and *y*, as we derived earlier. As for the second system:

```
solve([x ** 2 - 2 * x - y ** 2 + 1, x ** 2 - 2 * y - 1],\
      x, y)
```

This code returns `[(-3, 4), (1, 0)]`, which also corresponds to the solution we have derived. As we can see, SymPy offers a straightforward syntax for us to solve both equations and systems of equations effortlessly.

This example also marks the end of the material for this section. To end this chapter, we will consider an extension of the break-even analysis exercise that we worked on earlier.

ACTIVITY 4.01: MULTI-VARIABLE BREAK-EVEN ANALYSIS

As we have mentioned at the end of the first break-even analysis exercise, a break-even analysis can become quite complex as the number of variables in our model grows. When there is more than one variable in a model, a system of equations needs to be used to find break-even points, which is what we will do in this activity.

Recall that in our example business model of a burger restaurant, we have a cost of $6.56 for each burger we produce as well as a fixed cost of $1,312.13 each month for utilities, rent, and other expenses. In this activity, we will explore how the total profit of the business changes as a function of both the number of burgers we sell and the price of each burger.

One additional piece of information we need for this model is the demand for burgers from the people living in the area of the restaurant. Let's say, on average, the restaurant observes that their revenue is around $4,000 every month, so the demand for burgers is roughly 4,000 divided by the price of a burger.

To complete this activity, perform the following steps:

1. Consider the number of burgers that the restaurant produces every month and the price of each burger as two variables for our model. Represent the monthly revenue, cost, and total profit of the restaurant in terms of these two variables.

2. Construct a system of equations that corresponds to the break-even point: when the number of burgers the restaurant makes satisfies demand and revenue equals costs.

3. Solve this system of equations by hand and verify the result using SymPy in a Jupyter notebook.
4. In the same Jupyter notebook, write a Python function that takes in any given combination of the number of burgers produced and the price of each burger. The function is to return the total profit of the restaurant.
5. In the next code cell, create a list of potential values for the number of burgers to be produced, ranging from 300 to 500 every month. Generate the list of corresponding profits using a fixed price of $9.76 per burger and store it in a variable named **`profits_976`** (for testing purposes). Plot this list of profits as a function of the number of burgers produced.
6. In the next code cell, generate the same list of profits, this time with a fixed price of $9.99 per burger, and store it in a variable named **`profits_999`**. Create the same plot and interpret it in the context of break-even points.
7. In the next cell, create a list of potential values for the number of burgers to be produced; it should be every even number between 300 and 500 (for example, 300, 302, 304, ..., 500). Additionally, create a NumPy array of 100 evenly spaced numbers between 5 and 10 as potential prices for each burger.
8. Finally, generate a two-dimensional list where the item in the row indexed at *i* and the column indexed at *j* is the profit the restaurant will make, with the ith number in the first list as the number of burgers it will produce and the jth number in the second list (the NumPy array) as the price of each burger. Store this list in the variable named **`profits`** for testing purposes.
9. Create a heatmap using Matplotlib to visualize the two-dimensional list of profits generated in the previous step as a function of the number of burgers produced (as the *y* axis) and the price of each burger (as the *x* axis).

> **NOTE**
>
> The solution to this activity can be found on page 665.

SUMMARY

This chapter formally introduced the definition of functions and variables in the context of mathematics. Various topics relevant to functions, such as the domain, the range, and the plot of a function, were also discussed. In the second part of the chapter, we talked about the concept of equations and systems of equations, as well as special methods to find their solutions. During these discussions, the SymPy library and the function to compute the inverse of a matrix from NumPy were also examined. We concluded the chapter by completing a task that used algebra and functions to construct a multi-variable break-even analysis for a business.

In the next chapter, we will continue with another important topic in mathematics: sequences and series.

5

MORE MATHEMATICS WITH PYTHON

OVERVIEW

By the end of this chapter, you will be able to grasp the basic concepts of sequences and series and write Python functions that implement these concepts. You will understand the relationships between basic trigonometric functions and their applications, such as the famous Pythagorean theorem. You will practice vector calculus and know where it is applicable by performing vector algebra in Python. Finally, you will feel happy knowing that complex numbers are not any less a type of number; they are intimately connected to trigonometry and are useful for real-world applications.

INTRODUCTION

In the previous chapter, we covered functions and algebra with Python, starting with basic functions before working through transformations and solving equations. In this chapter, we'll introduce sequences and series, which have many applications in the real world, such as finance, and also form the basis for an understanding of calculus. Additionally, we will explore trigonometry, vectors, and complex numbers to give us a better understanding of the mathematical world.

The core skills of any exceptional Python programmer include a solid understanding of the background mathematics and an effective application of them. Think of vectors and complex numbers as valuable extensions to our *mathematical toolbox* that, later on, will contribute to efficiently describing, quantifying, and tackling real-world problems from the finance, science, or business and social domains.

Sequences and series, among others, appear in situations where profits, losses, dividends, or other payments occur on a regular basis. Trigonometry and trigonometric functions are necessary to solve geospatial problems, while vectors are applied widely in physics and engineering, machine learning, and more, where several different values are grouped together and the notion of direction is pivotal. Complex numbers are some of the most fundamental concepts that enjoy wide applications in electromagnetism, optics, quantum mechanics, and computer science.

SEQUENCES AND SERIES

If you were to participate in a TV show where the $10,000 question was *"Given the numbers 2, 4, 8, 16, and 32, what comes next in the sequence?"*, what would your best guess be? If your response is 64, then congratulations—you just came closer to understanding one of the key concepts in mathematical abstraction: that of a sequence. A **sequence** is, pretty much like in the ordinary sense of the word, a particular order in which things follow each other. Here, *things* are (in most cases) integers or real numbers that are related. The order of the elements matters. The elements are also called the members or terms of the sequence.

For example, in the preceding sequence of the TV show you participated in, every term stems from the number prior being multiplied by 2; there is no end in this sequence as there is no end in the number of terms (integer numbers) you can come up with. In other instances, elements in a sequence can appear more than once. Think of the number of days in the months of a year, or just the sequence of the outcomes of a random event, say, the toss of a coin. A well-known sequence that has been known since the ancient Indian times is the Fibonacci sequence—1, 1, 2, 3, 5, 8, 13.... This is the sequence where each *new* term is the sum of the two previous terms.

That is, we need to know at least two terms before we can derive any other. In other words, we need to read the two first numbers (in the preceding sequence, 1 and 1, but generally any two numbers) before we are capable of deriving and predicting the third number. We know that some sequences, such as the Fibonacci sequence, include some logic inside them; a basic rule that we can follow and derive any term of the sequence.

In this chapter, we will be focusing on basic sequences, also known as **progressions**, that are repeatedly found across many fields in applied mathematics and programming that fall in either of the three basic categories: arithmetic, geometric, and recursive. These are not the only possibilities; they are, nonetheless, the most popular families of sequences and illustrate the logic that they entail.

A **sequence** of numbers $\{a_n\} = \{a_1, a_2, a_3, \ldots, a_N, \ldots\}$ is an ordered collection of terms (elements or members) for which there is a rule that associates each natural number n = 1, 2, 3, ..., N with just one of the terms in the sequence. The length of the sequence (that is, the number of its terms) can be finite or infinite, and the sequence is hence called finite or infinite, accordingly.

A **series** is a mathematical sequence that is summed as follows:

$$a_1 + a_2 + a_3 + \ldots$$

Figure 5.1: Equation of series

This can also be summed using the summation sign, as follows:

$$\sum_{i=1}^{\infty} a_i$$

Figure 5.2: Equation of an infinite series

In the preceding case, our series is infinite (that is, it is the sum of all the terms of an infinite sequence). However, a series, such as a sequence, can also be finite. Why would a sum have infinite terms? Because it turns out that, in many cases, the summation is carried out computationally more efficiently by applying known formulas. Moreover, the summation can converge to a number (not infinite) or some function, even when the sequence is infinite. Due to this, series can be considered the *building blocks* of known functions, and their terms can be used to represent functions of increasing complexity, thus making the study of their properties intuitive. Series and sequences are ubiquitous in mathematics, physics, engineering, finance, and beyond and have been known since ancient times. They appear and are particularly useful as infinite sums in the definition of derivates and other functions as well.

ARITHMETIC SEQUENCES

Like most mathematical concepts, sequences can be found everywhere in our daily lives. You might not have thought about it before, but every time you ride a cab, a sequence is *running* in the background to calculate the total cost of your ride. There is an initial charge that increments, by a fixed amount, for every kilometer (or mile) you ride. So, at any given moment, there's a real, corresponding number (the price of the ride so far). The ordered set of all these subtotals forms a sequence. Similarly, your body height as you grow up is a sequence of real numbers (your height expressed in centimeters or inches) in time (days or months). Both these examples constitute sequences that are non-decreasing in time—in other words, every term is either larger than or equal to any previous term, but never smaller. However, there is a subtle difference between the two examples: while the rate at which we gain height as we grow differs (growth is fast for kids, slow for teenagers, and zero for adults), the rate at which the taxi fare increases is constant. This leads us to need to introduce a special class of sequences—arithmetic sequences—which are defined as follows.

Sequences where the difference between any two consecutive terms is constant are called **arithmetic**. Hence, the formula for arithmetic sequences is as follows:

$$a_{n+1} - a_n = d$$

Here, d is constant and must hold for all n. Of course, it becomes clear that, if you know the parameter d and some (any) term a_n, then the term a_{n+1} can be found by a straightforward application of the preceding relation. By repetition, all the terms, a_{n+2}, a_{n+3} …, as well as the terms a_{n-1}, a_{n-2} can be found. In other words, all of the terms of our sequence are known (that is, uniquely determined) if you know the parameter d, and the first term of the sequence a_1. The general formula that gives us the nth term of the sequence becomes the following:

$$a_n = a_1 + (n - 1)d$$

Here, d is known as the common difference.

Inversely, to test whether a generic sequence is an arithmetic one, it suffices to check all of the pairwise differences, $a_{n+1} - a_n$, of its terms and see whether these are the same constant number. In the corresponding arithmetic series, the sum of the preceding sequence becomes the following:

$$\Sigma^n_j a_j = \Sigma^n_j [a_1 + (j - 1)d] = n(a_1 + a_n)/2$$

This means that by knowing the length, n, the first, and the last term of the sequence, we can determine the sum of all terms from a_1 to a_n. Note that the sum $(a_1 + a_n)$ gives twice the arithmetic mean of the whole sequence, so the series is nothing more than n times the arithmetic mean.

Now, we know what the main logic and constituents of the arithmetic sequence are. Now, let's look at some concrete examples. For now, we do not need to import any particular libraries in Python as we will be creating our own functions. Let's remind ourselves that these always need to begin with **def**, followed by a space, the function name (anything that we like), and a list of arguments that the function takes inside brackets, followed by a semi-colon. The following lines are indented (four places to the right) and are where the logic, that is, the algorithm or method of the function, is written. For instance, consider the following example:

```
def my_function(arg1, arg2):
    '''Write a function that adds two numbers
       and returns their sum'''
    result = arg1 + arg2
    return result
```

What follows the final statement, **`result`**, is what is being returned from the function. So, for instance, if we are programming the preceding **`my_function`** definition, which receives two input numbers, **`arg1`** and **`arg2`**, then we can pass it to a new variable, say, the following one:

```
summed = my_function(2,9)
print(summed)
```

The output will be as follows:

```
11
```

Here, **`summed`** is a new variable that is exactly what is being returned (produced) by **`my_function`**. Note that if the **`return`** statement within the definition of a function is missing, then the syntax is still correct and the function can still be called. However, the **`summed`** variable will be equal to **`None`**.

Now, if we want to create a (any) sequence of numbers, we should include an iteration inside our function. This is achieved in Python with either a **`for`** or a **`while`** loop. Let's look at an example, where a function gives a sequence of **`n`** sums as the output:

```
def my_sequence(arg1, arg2, n):
    '''Write a function that adds two numbers n times and
       prints their sum'''
    result = 0
    for i in range(n):
        result = result + arg1 + arg2
        print(result)
```

Here, we initiate the variable result (to zero) and then iteratively add to it the sum, **`arg1 + arg2`**. This iteration happens **`n`** times, where **`n`** is also an argument of our new function, **`my_sequence`**. Every time the loop (what follows the **`for`** statement) is executed, the **`result`** increases by **`arg1 + arg2`** and is then printed on-screen. We have omitted the **`return`** statement here for simplicity. Here, we used Python's built-in **`range()`** method, which generates a sequence of integer numbers that starts at 0 and ends at one number before the given stop integer (the number that we provide as input). Let's call our function:

```
my_sequence(2,9,4)
```

We will obtain the following output:

```
11
22
33
44
```

Had we used a **while** loop, we would have arrived at the same result:

```
def my_sequence(arg1, arg2, n):
    '''Write a function that adds two numbers n times
       and prints their sum'''
    i = 0
    result = 0
    while i < n:
        result = result + arg1 + arg2
        i += 1
        print(result)
```

If we were to call the **my_sequence** function, we would obtain the same output that we received previously for the same input.

GENERATORS

One more interesting option for sequential operations in Python is the use of generators. **Generators** are objects, similar to functions, that return an iterable set of items, one value at a time. Simply speaking, if a function contains at least one **yield** statement, it becomes a generator function. The benefit of using generators as opposed to functions is that we can call the generator as many times as desired (here, an infinite amount) without cramming our system's memory. In some situations, they can be invaluable tools. To obtain one term of a sequence of terms, we use the **next()** method. First, let's define our function:

```
def my_generator(arg1, arg2, n):
    '''Write a generator function that adds
       two numbers n times and prints their sum'''
    i = 0
    result = 0
    while i < n:
        result = result + arg1 + arg2
        i += 1
        yield result
```

Now, let's call the **next()** method multiple times:

```
my_gen = my_generator(2,9,4)
next(my_gen)
```

The following is the output:

```
11
```

Call the method for the second time:

```
next(my_gen)
```

The following is the output:

```
22
```

Call it for the third time:

```
next(my_gen)
```

The following is the output:

```
33
```

Call the method for the fourth time:

```
next(my_gen)
```

The following is the output:

```
44
```

So, we obtained the same results as in the previous example, but one at a time. If we call the **next()** method repetitively, we will get an error message since we have *exhausted* our generator:

```
next(my_gen)
Traceback (most recent call last):
    File "<stdin>", line 1, in <module>
StopIteration
```

Now, we are ready to implement the relations of sequences we learned in Python code.

EXERCISE 5.01: DETERMINING THE NTH TERM OF AN ARITHMETIC SEQUENCE AND ARITHMETIC SERIES

In this exercise, we will create a finite and infinite arithmetic sequence using a simple Python function. As inputs, we want to provide the first term of the sequence, **a1**, the common difference, **d**, and the length of the sequence, **n**. Our goal is to obtain the following:

- Just one term (the nth term) of the sequence.
- The full sequence of numbers.
- The sum of n terms of the arithmetic sequence, in order to compare it to our result of the arithmetic series given previously.

To calculate the preceding goals, we need to provide the first term of the sequence, **a1**, the common difference, **d**, and the length of the sequence, **n**, as inputs. Let's implement this exercise:

1. First, we want to write a function that returns just the nth term, according to the general formula $a_n = a_1 + (n - 1)d$:

```
def a_n(a1, d, n):
    '''Return the n-th term of the arithmetic sequence.
    :a1: first term of the sequence. Integer or real.

    :n: the n-th term in sequence
    returns: n-th term. Integer or real.'''
    an = a1 + (n - 1)*d
    return an
```

By doing this, we obtain the nth term of the sequence without needing to know any other preceding terms. For example, let's call our function with arguments **(4, 3, 10)**:

```
a_n(4, 3, 10)
```

We will get the following output:

```
31
```

2. Now, let's write a function that increments the initial term, **a1**, by **d**, **n** times and stores all terms in a list:

```
def a_seq(a1, d, n):
    '''Obtain the whole arithmetic sequence up to n.
    :a1: first term of the sequence. Integer or real.
    :d: common difference of the sequence. Integer or real.
    :n: length of sequence
    returns: sequence as a list.'''
    sequence = []
    for _ in range(n):
        sequence.append(a1)
        a1 = a1 + d
    return sequence
```

3. To check the resulting list, add the following code:

```
a_seq(4, 3, 10)
```

The output will be as follows:

```
[4, 7, 10, 13, 16, 19, 22, 25, 28, 31]
```

Here, we obtained the arithmetic sequence, which has a length of 10, starts at **4**, and increases by 3.

4. Now, let's generate the infinite sequence. We can achieve this using Python generators, which we introduced earlier:

```
def infinite_a_sequence(a1, d):
    while True:
        yield a1
        a1 = a1 + d

for i in infinite_a_sequence(4,3):
    print(i, end=" ")
```

If you run the preceding code, you will notice that we have to abort the execution manually; otherwise, the **for** loop will print out the elements of the sequence eternally. An alternative way of using Python generators is, as explained previously, to call the **next()** method directly on the generator object (here, this is **infinite_a_sequence()**).

5. Let's calculate the sum of the terms of our sequence by calling the **sum()** Python method:

```
sum(a_seq(4, 3, 10))
```

The output will be as follows:

```
175
```

6. Finally, implement the $a_n = a_1 + (n - 1)d$ formula, which gives us the arithmetic series so that we can compare it with our result for the sum:

```
def a_series(a1, d, n):
    result = n * (a1 + a_n(a1, d, n)) / 2
    return result
```

7. Run the function, as follows:

```
a_series(4, 3, 10)
```

The output is as follows:

```
175.0
```

> **NOTE**
>
> To access the source code for this specific section, please refer to https://packt.live/2D2S52c.
>
> You can also run this example online at https://packt.live/31DjRfO.

With that, we have arrived at the same result for the summation of elements of an arithmetic sequence by using either a sequence or series. The ability to cross-validate a given result with two independent mathematical methods is extremely useful for programmers at all levels and lies at the heart of scientific validation. Moreover, knowing different methods (here, the two methods that we used to arrive at the series result) that can solve the same problem, and the advantages (as well as the disadvantages) of each method can be vital for writing code at an advanced level.

We will study a different, but also fundamental, category of sequences: geometric ones.

GEOMETRIC SEQUENCES

An infectious disease spreads from one person to another or more, depending on the density of the population in a given community. In a situation such as a pandemic, for a moderately contagious disease, it is realistic that, on average, each person who has the disease infects two people per day. So, if on day 1 there is just one person that's infected, on day 2 there will be two newly infected, and on day 3, another two people will have contracted the disease for each of the two previously infected people, bringing the number of the newly infected to four. Similarly, on day 4, eight new cases appear, and so on. We can see that the rate that a disease expands at is not constant since the number of new cases depends on the number of existing cases at a given moment—and this explains how pandemics arise and spread exponentially.

The preceding numbers (1, 2, 4, 8...) form a sequence. Note that now, the requirement of the arithmetic sequence hasn't been met: the difference between two successive terms is not constant. The ratio, nonetheless, is constant. This exemplifies the preceding sequence as a special type of sequence, known as **geometric**, and is defined as a sequence or a collection of ordered numbers where the ratio of any two successive terms is constant.

In the compact language of mathematics, we can write the preceding behavior as $a_{n+1} = r\, a_n$.

Here, a_n is the number of *cases* on day *n*, a_{n+1} is the number of new cases on day *n+1*, and $r>0$ is a coefficient that defines how fast (or slow) the increase happens. This is known as the common ratio. The preceding formula is universal, meaning that it holds for all members, *n*. So, if it holds true for *n*, it does so for *n-1*, *n-2*, and so on. By working with the preceding relationship recursively, we can easily arrive at $a_n = r^{n-1}a$ equation.

Here, we give the nth term of the geometric sequence once the first term, $a=a_1$, and the common ratio, *r*, have been given. The term *a* is known as the **scale factor**.

Note that *r* can have any non-zero value. If $r>1$, every generation, a_{n+1}, is larger than the one prior and so the sequence is ever-increasing, while the opposite is true if $r<1$: a_{n+1} tends towards zero as *n* increases. So, in the initial example of an infectious disease, $r>1$ means that the transmission is increasing, while $r<1$ yields a decreasing transmission.

Let's write a Python function that calculates the nth term of a geometric function, based on the $a_n = r^{n-1}a$ formula:

```
def n_geom_seq(r, a, n):
    an = r**(n-1) * a
    return an
```

The inputs in that function are **r**, the common ratio, **a**, the scale factor, and **n**, the nth term that we want to find. Let's call this function with some arguments, **(2, 3, 10)**:

```
n_geom_seq(2, 3, 10)
```

The output is as follows:

```
1536
```

Similarly, for the case of the arithmetic sequence, we define a geometric series as the sum of the terms of the sequence of length *n*:

$$\sum_{k=1}^{n} ar^{k-1} = ar^0 + ar^1 + ar^2 + ar^3 + \ldots + ar^{n-1}$$

Figure 5.3: A geometric sequence

Alternatively, we can express this as follows:

$$\sum_{k=1}^{n} ar^{k-1} = \frac{a(1-r^n)}{1-r}$$

Figure 5.4: Alternative expression for a geometric sequence

To get a better understanding of the geometric series, let's check out how it works in Python and visualize it. We need to define a function that admits **r**, **a**, and **n** (as we did previously) as input and calculate the second formula, that is, the series up to term *n*:

```
def sum_n(r, a, n):
    sum_n = a*(1 - r**n) / (1 - r)
    return sum_n
```

Now, call the function for arguments **(2, 3, 10)**, as we did previously:

```
sum_n(2, 3, 10)
```

The output is as follows:

```
3069.0
```

Have a look at the following example plot of geometric sequences, where the value increases for *r>1*:

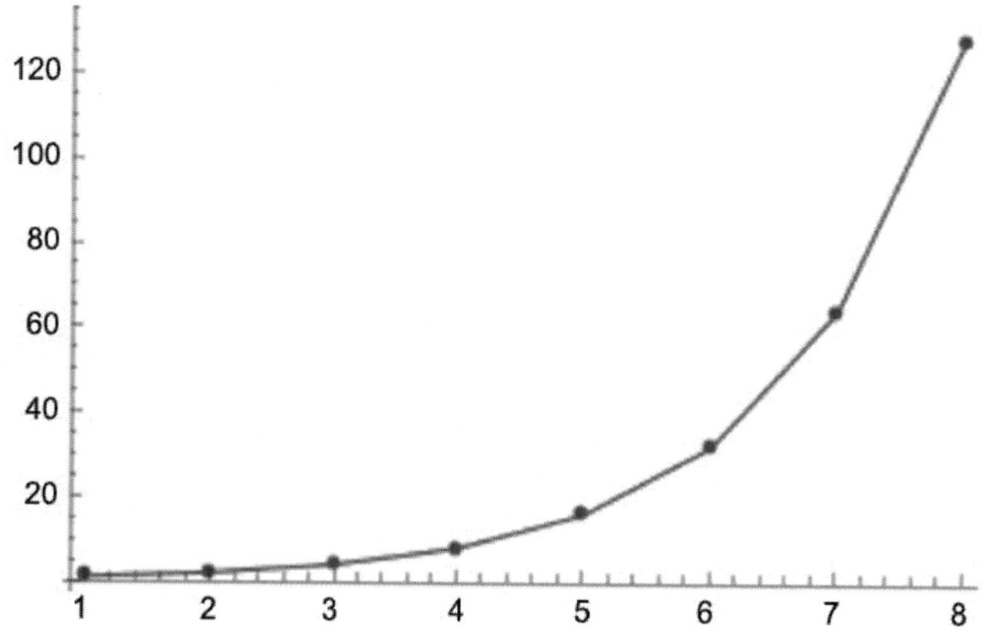

Figure 5.5: Geometric sequences increasing for r>1

Have a look at the following example plot of geometric sequences, where the value decreases for *r<1*:

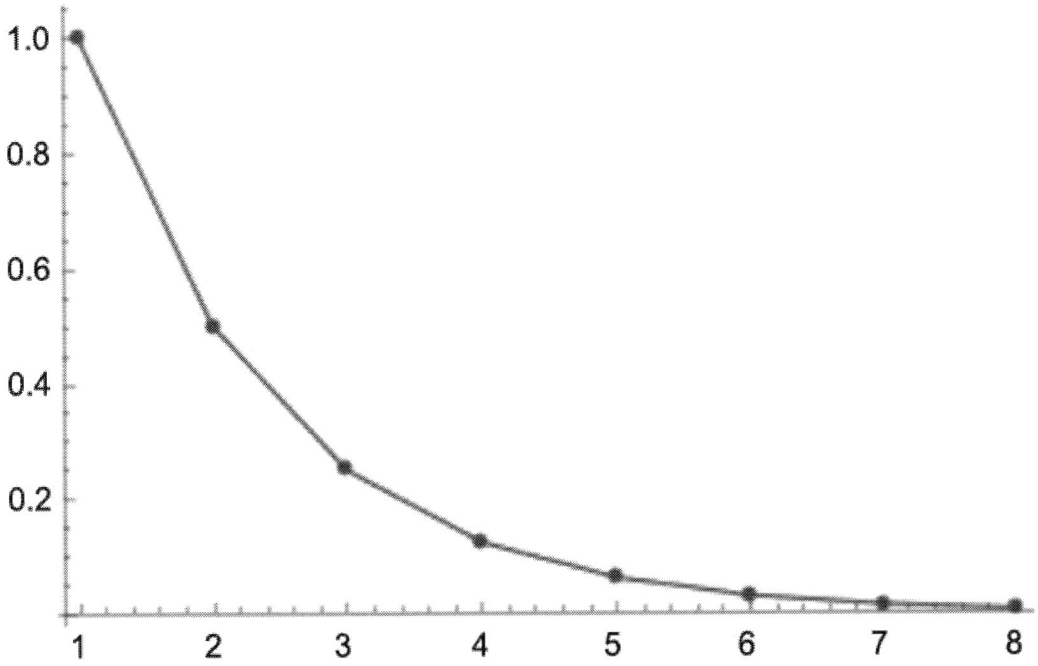

Figure 5.6: Geometric sequences decreasing for r<1

In this section, we have seen how a geometric sequence progresses and how we can easily find the terms of it in Python, as well as the geometric series. We are now ready to implement what we've learned in an exercise in order to obtain a better understanding of sequences and their applications.

EXERCISE 5.02: WRITING A FUNCTION TO FIND THE NEXT TERM OF THE SEQUENCE

The number of bacteria in a Petri dish increases as a geometric sequence. Given the population (number) of bacteria per day, across a number of days, *n*, write a function that calculates the population on day *n+1*. Follow these steps to complete this exercise:

1. Write a function that admits a variable number of arguments (**`*args`**) and calculates the ratio between any element and its preceding element (starting from the second element). Then, check whether all the ratios found are identical and return their unique value. Otherwise, the function returns **`-1`** (the sequence does not possess a unique common ratio):

```
def find_ratio(*args):
    arg0=args[0]
    ratios = []
    for arg in args[1:]:
        ratio = round(arg/arg0,8)
        arg0=arg
        ratios.append(ratio)
    if len(set(ratios)) == 1:
        return ratio
    else:
        return -1
```

2. Now, check the **`find_ratio`** function for two distinct cases. First, let's use the following sequence:

```
find_ratio(1,2,4,8,16,32,64,128,256,512)
```

   The output is as follows:

```
2.0
```

3. Now, let's use the following sequence:

```
find_ratio(1,2,3)
```

   The output is as follows:

```
-1
```

   As shown in the preceding outputs, the **`find_ratio`** function prints out the ratio, if it exists, or prints **`-1`** if the sequence is not geometric.

4. Now, write a second function that reads in a sequence and prints out what the next term will be. To do so, read in a (comma-separated) list of numbers, find their ratio, and from that, predict the next term:

```
def find_next(*args):
    if find_ratio(*args) == -1:
        raise ValueError('The sequence you entered' \
                         'is not a geometric sequence. '\
                         'Please check input.')
    else:
        return args[-1]*find_ratio(*args)
```

   Note that we want to check whether the sequence possesses a common ratio by calling the **find_ratio()** function we wrote previously. If it doesn't, raise an error; if it does, find the next term and return it.

5. Check if it works by using the following sequence:

```
find_next(1,2,4)
```

   The following is the output of the preceding code:

```
8.0
```

6. Now, try this with a different sequence:

```
find_next(1.36,0.85680,0.539784,0.34006392)
```

   The output is as follows:

```
0.2142402696
```

It does work. In the first case, the obvious result, **8.0**, was printed. In the second case, the less obvious result of the decreasing geometric sequence was found and printed out. To summarize, we are able to write a function that detects a geometric sequence, finds its ratio, and uses that to predict the next-in-sequence term. This is extremely useful in real-life scenarios, such as in cases where the compound interest rate needs to be verified.

> **NOTE**
>
> To access the source code for this specific section, please refer to https://packt.live/2NUyT8N.
>
> You can also run this example online at https://packt.live/3dRMwQV.

In the previous sections, we saw that sequences, either arithmetic or geometric, can be defined in two equivalent ways. We saw that the nth term of the sequence is determined by knowing a given term of the sequence (commonly the first, but not necessarily) and the common difference, or common ratio. More interestingly, we saw that the nth term of a sequence can be found by knowing the $(n-1)^{th}$ term, which, in turn, can be found by knowing the $(n-2)^{th}$ term, and so on. So, there is an interesting pattern here that dictates both sequence types that we studied and which, in fact, extends beyond them. It turns out that we can generalize this behavior and define sequences in a purely recursive manner that isn't necessarily arithmetic or geometric. Now, let's move on to the next section, where we will understand recursive sequences.

RECURSIVE SEQUENCES

A **recursive sequence** is a sequence of elements, u_n, that are produced via a recursive relation, that is, each element uniquely stems from the preceding ones.

u_n can depend on one or more elements preceding it. For example, the Fibonacci series that we saw earlier in this chapter is a recursive sequence where knowledge of the nth term requires knowing both the $(n-1)^{th}$ and $(n-2)^{th}$ terms. On the other hand, the factorial only needs the element that precedes it. Specifically, it is defined by the recurrence relation, $n! = n(n-1)!$, $n > 0$, and the initial condition, $0! = 1$.

Let's convert the preceding formulas into Python code:

```
def factorial(n):
    if n == 0 or n ==1:
        return 1
    elif n == 2:
        return 2
    else:
        return n*factorial(n - 1)
```

The preceding code is a recursive implementation of the factorial function: to calculate the result for *n*, we call the function for *n-1*, which, in turn, calls the function for *n-2* and so on until *n=2* is reached.

If we execute the preceding function for the case *n=11*, we obtain the following:

```
factorial(11)
```

The output is as follows:

```
39916800
```

Note that while the first two categories of sequences that we've seen so far (arithmetic and geometric) are mutually exclusive, the recursive family of sequences is not, meaning that sequences can be both recursive and arithmetic or recursive and geometric. Conventionally, we use the term *recursive* for these types of sequences that, unlike geometric and arithmetic, cannot be expressed in a non-recursive manner.

Now that we have explored the basic concepts of recursive sequences, we can implement this in Python and write code that calculates any number of elements of any sequence that is recursively defined.

EXERCISE 5.03: CREATING A CUSTOM RECURSIVE SEQUENCE

In this exercise, we will create a custom recursive sequence using the concepts we explained in the previous section. Given the first three elements of the sequence, P_n, that is, $P_1=1$, $P_2=7$, and $P_3=2$, find the next seven terms of the sequence that is recursively defined via the relation: $P_{n+3}= (3*P_{n+1} - P_{n+2})/(P_n - 1)$. Follow these steps to complete this exercise:

1. Define a Python function that is recursive and implements the relation given previously for the nth element of the sequence:

```
def p_n(n):
    if n < 1:
        return -1
    elif n == 1:
        return 1
    elif n == 2:
        return 7
    elif n == 3:
        return 2
    else:
        pn = (3*p_n(n-2) - p_n(n-1) )/ (p_n(n-3) + 1)
        return pn
```

Here, we started by defining the base cases, that is, the known result as given in the brief: if *n=1*, then *P=1*, if *n=2*, then *P=7*, and if *n=3*, then *P=2*. We also included the case where *n<1*. This is invalid input and, as is customary, our function returns the value **-1**. This makes our function *bounded* and protected from entering infinite loops and invalid input. Once these cases have been taken care of, then we have defined the recursive relation.

2. Now, let's test our function and print out the first 10 values of the sequence (three that correspond to the base cases and seven of them that are for our task):

```
for i in range(1,11):
    print(p_n(i))
```

The output is as follows:

```
1
7
2
9.5
-0.4375
9.645833333333334
-1.0436507936507937
53.29982363315697
-5.30073825572847
-3784.586609737289
```

As you can see from the preceding output, our function works and gives back both the known values (P_1 = *1*, P_2 = *7*, and P_3 = *2*) of the sequence and the next terms (*P_1* to *P_10*) that we were looking for.

3. As a bonus, let's plot our findings by using the **matplotlib** module. We will create a list that holds the first nine values of the sequence and then plot it with **pyplot**:

```
from matplotlib import pyplot as plt
plist = []
for i in range(1,40):
    plist.append(p_n(i))

plt.plot(plist, linestyle='--', marker='o', color='b')
plt.show()
```

The output is as follows:

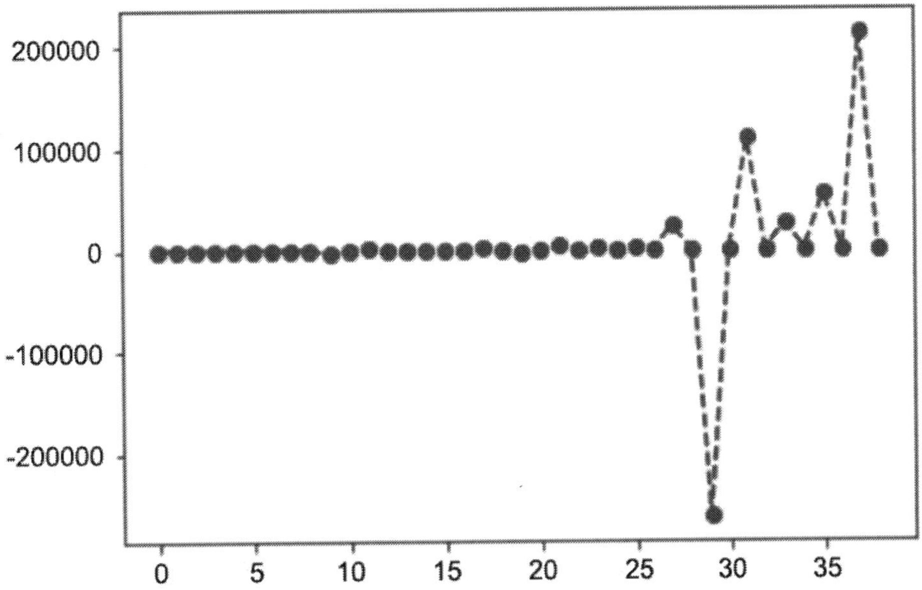

Figure 5.7: Plot created using the matplotlib library

> **NOTE**
>
> To access the source code for this specific section, please refer to https://packt.live/2D3vlPF.
>
> You can also run this example online at https://packt.live/3eY05Q4.

We can see that a simple and well-defined recursive relation can lead to apparently random or chaotic results. Indeed, if you continue plotting the terms of the preceding sequence, you will soon notice that there is no apparent regularity in the pattern of the terms as they widely and asymmetrically oscillate around 0. This prompts us to arrive at the conclusion that even though defining a recursive sequence and predicting its nth term is straightforward, the opposite is not always true. As we saw, given a sequence (a list of numbers), it is quite simple to check whether it forms an arithmetic sequence, a geometric sequence, or neither. However, to answer whether a given sequence has been derived by a recursive relation—let alone what this recursion is—is a non-trivial task that, in most cases, cannot be answered.

In this section, we have presented what sequences are, why they are important, and how they are connected to another important concept in mathematics: series. We studied three general types of sequences, namely arithmetic, geometric, and recursive, and saw how they can be implemented in Python in a few simple steps. In the next section, we'll delve into trigonometry and learn how trigonometric problems can be easily solved using Python.

TRIGONOMETRY

Trigonometry is about studying triangles and, in particular, the relation of their angles to their edges. The ratio of two of the three edges (sides) of a triangle gives information about a particular angle, and to such a pair of sides, we give it a certain name and call it a function. The beauty of trigonometry and mathematics in general is that these functions, which are born inside a triangle, make (abstract) sense in any other situation where triangles are not present and operate as independent mathematical objects. Hence, functions such as the tangent, cosine, and sine are found across most fields of mathematics, physics, and engineering without any reference to the triangle.

Let's look at the most fundamental trigonometric functions and their usage.

BASIC TRIGONOMETRIC FUNCTIONS

We will start by defining a right-angled triangle (or simply a right triangle), triangle ABC. One of its angles (the angle BCA in the following diagram) is a **right angle**, that is, a 90-degree angle. The side opposite the right angle is called the **hypotenuse** (side *h* in the following diagram), while the other sides (*a* and *b*) are known as legs. They are also referred to as *opposite* and *adjacent* to the respective angle. For instance, side *b* is adjacent to the lower right angle in the following diagram (angle CAB or θ), while it is opposite when we refer to the top angle (angle CBA):

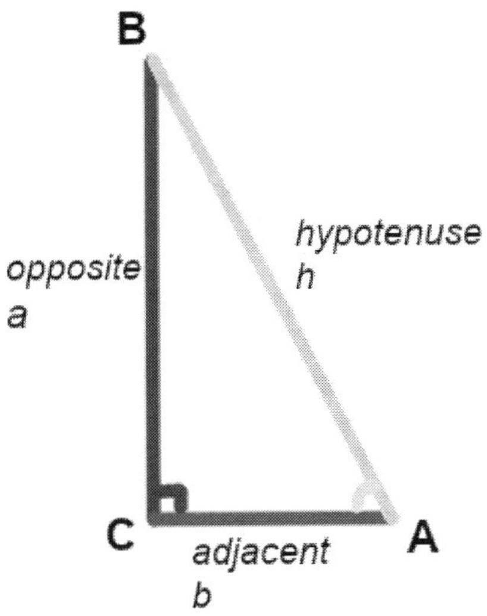

Figure 5.8: A right-angled triangle

The most common trigonometric functions are defined with the help of the preceding diagram and are defined as follows:

sine

$$\sin\theta = \frac{a}{h} = \frac{opposite}{hypotenuse}$$

cosine

$$\cos\theta = \frac{a}{h} = \frac{adjacent}{hypotenuse}$$

tangent

$$\tan\theta = \frac{a}{b} = \frac{opposite}{adjacent}$$

Figure 5.9: Trigonometric functions

For the tangent function, it also holds that $tan\theta = sin\theta/cos\theta$.

Also, for any angle, θ, the following identity always holds true: $sin\theta^2 + cos\theta^2 = 1$.

By construction, the trigonometric functions are periodic. This means that, regardless of the sizes of the edges of a triangle, the preceding functions take on values that repeat themselves every 2π. This will become apparent in the next exercise, where we will be plotting them. The range of the sine and cosine functions is the interval [-1,1]. This means that the smallest value they can obtain is -1, and the largest is 1, no matter what the input θ is.

Last but not least, the edges of the right-angled triangle are connected via the famous Pythagorean theorem: $h^2 = a^2 + b^2$

In Python code, a simple implementation of the Pythagorean theorem would be to write a function that calculates *h*, given *a* and *b*, with the help of the square root (**sqrt**) method of the **math** module; for instance:

```
from math import sqrt
def hypotenuse(a,b):
    h = sqrt(a**2 + b**2)
    return h
```

Calling this function for *a=3* and *b=4* gives us the following:

```
hypotenuse(a = 3, b = 4)
```

The output is as follows:

```
5.0
```

Now, let's look at some concrete examples so that we can grasp these ideas.

EXERCISE 5.04: PLOTTING A RIGHT-ANGLED TRIANGLE

In this exercise, we will write Python functions that will plot a right triangle for the given points, p_1 and p_2. The right-angled triangle will correspond to the endpoints of the legs of the triangle. We will also calculate the three trigonometric functions for either of the non-right angles. Let's plot the basic trigonometry functions:

1. Import the **numpy** and **pyplot** libraries:

```
import numpy as np
from matplotlib import pyplot as plt
```

Now, write a function that returns the hypotenuse by using the Pythagorean theorem when given the two sides, p_1 and p_2, as inputs:

```
def find_hypotenuse(p1, p2):
    p3 = round( (p1**2 + p2**2)**0.5, 8)
    return p3
```

2. Now, let's write another function that implements the relations for the **sin**, **cos**, and **tan** functions. The inputs are the lengths of the adjacent, opposite, and hypotenuse of a given angle, and the result is a tuple of the trigonometric values:

```
def find_trig(adjacent, opposite, hypotenuse):
    '''Returns the tuple (sin, cos, tan)'''
    return opposite/hypotenuse, adjacent/hypotenuse, \
           opposite/adjacent
```

3. Now, write the function that plots the triangle. For simplicity, place the right angle at the origin of the axes at (0,0), the first input point along the *x* axis at (p_1, 0), and the second input point along the *y* axis at (0, p_2):

```
def plot_triangle(p1, p2, lw=5):
    x = [0, p1, 0]
    y = [0, 0, p2]
    n = ['0', 'p1', 'p2']

    fig, ax = plt.subplots(figsize=(p1,p2))
    # plot points
    ax.scatter(x, y,  s=400, c="#8C4799", alpha=0.4)
    ax.annotate(find_hypotenuse(p1,p2),(p1/2,p2/2))

    # plot edges
    ax.plot([0, p1], [0, 0], lw=lw, color='r')
    ax.plot([0, 0], [0, p2], lw=lw, color='b')
    ax.plot([0, p1], [p2, 0], lw=lw, color='y')

    for i, txt in enumerate(n):
        ax.annotate(txt, (x[i], y[i]), va='center')
```

Here, we created the lists, **x** and **y**, that hold the points and one more list, **n**, for the labels. Then, we created a **pyplot** object that plots the points first, and then the edges. The last two lines are used to annotate our plot; that is, add the labels (from the list, **n**) next to our points.

4. We need to choose two points in order to define a triangle. Then, we need to call our functions to display the plot:

```
p01 = 4
p02 = 4

print(find_trig(p01,p02,find_hypotenuse(p01,p02)))
plot_triangle(p01,p02)
```

The first line prints the values of the three trigonometric functions, **`sin`**, **`cos`**, and **`tan`**, respectively. Then, we plot our triangle, which in this case is isosceles since it has two sides that are of equal length.

The output will be as follows:

```
(0.707106781123095, 0.707106781123095, 1.0)
```

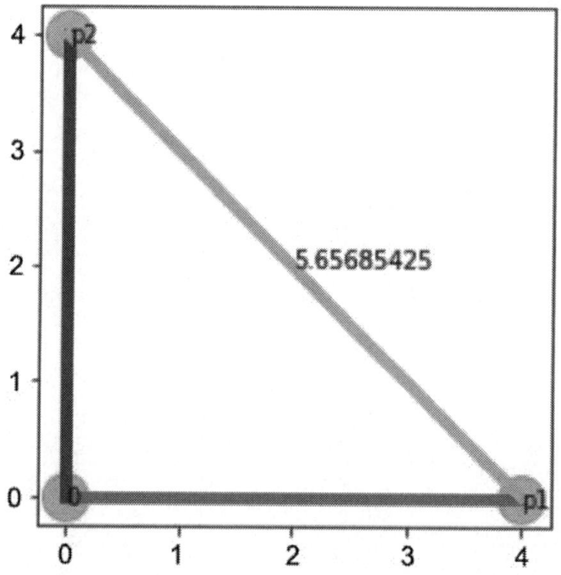

Figure 5.10: Plotting the isosceles triangle

The results are expected and correct—upon rounding the error—since the geometry of this particular shape is simple (an isosceles orthogonal triangle that has two angles equal to π/4). Then, we checked the result (note that in NumPy, the value of pi can be directly called **`np.pi`**).

5. Finally, to get a general overview of the **sin** and **cos** trigonometric functions, let's plot them:

```
x = np.linspace(0, 10, 200)

sin = np.sin(x)
cos = np.cos(x)

plt.xticks([0, np.pi/2, np.pi, 3*np.pi/2, 2*np.pi, \
            5*np.pi/2, 3*np.pi], \
           ['0','','\u03C0','','2\u03C0','','3\u03C0'])


plt.plot(x, sin, marker='o', label='sin')
plt.plot(x, cos, marker='x', label='cos')

plt.legend(loc="upper left")
plt.ylim(-1.1, 1.6)
plt.show()
```

The output will be as follows:

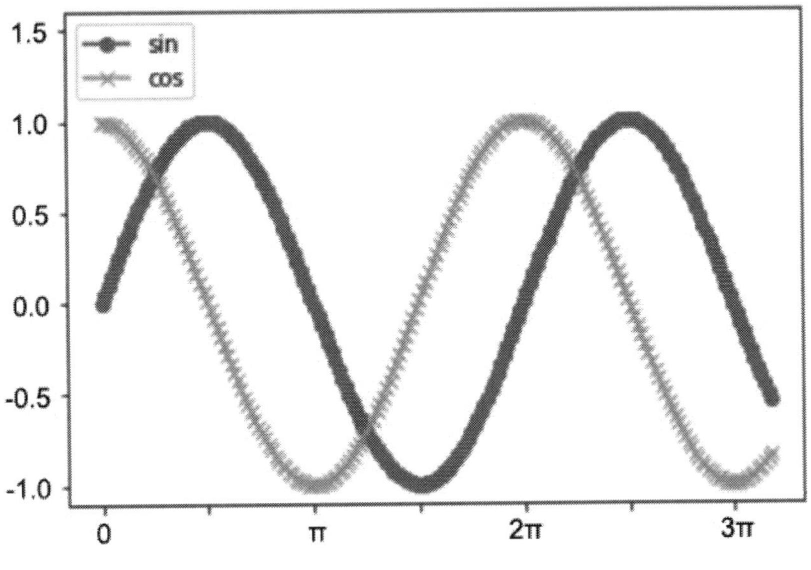

Figure 5.11: Plot of the sin and cos trigonometric functions

In this exercise, we kick-started our explorations of the sphere of trigonometry and saw how to arrive at useful visualizations in Python.

> **NOTE**
>
> To access the source code for this specific section, please refer to https://packt.live/2Zz0TnU.
>
> You can also run this example online at https://packt.live/2AoxS63.

With that, we have established the main trigonometric functions and saw how these provide an operation between an angle and an associated trigonometric value, given by either the sin, cos, or tan function. Moreover, we saw that these three functions are periodic, that is, repeated every 2π, while the first two are bounded, that is, the values they can take never exceed the interval, [-1,1]. These values are directly found in Python or in a scientific pocket calculator. In many situations, however, the inverse process is desired: can I find the angle if I give the value of sin, cos, or tan to some function? Does such a function exist? We'll answer these questions in the next section.

INVERSE TRIGONOMETRIC FUNCTIONS

Inverse trigonometric functions are the inverse functions of the trigonometric functions and are just as useful as their counterparts. An inverse function is a function that *reverses* the operation or result of the original function. Recall that trigonometric functions admit angles as input values and output pure numbers (ratios). Inverse trigonometric functions do the opposite: they admit a pure number as input and give an angle as output. So, if, for instance, a point, π, is mapped to point -1 (as the cos function does), then its inverse needs to do exactly the opposite. This mapping needs to hold for every point where the inverse function is defined.

The inverse function of the *sin(x)* function is called *arcsin(x)*: if *y=sin(x)*, then *x=arcsin(y)*. Recall that *sin* is a periodic function, so many different *x*'s are mapped to the same *y*. So, the inverse function would map one point to several different ones. This cannot be allowed since it clashes with the very definition of a function. To avoid this drawback, we need to restrict our domain of *arcsin* (and similarly for *arccos*) to the interval [-1,1], while the images, *y=arcsin(x)* and *y=arccos(x)*, are restricted to the ranges [-π/2,π/2] and [0, π] respectively.

We can define the three basic inverse trigonometric functions as follows:

- *arcsin(x) = y such that arcsin(sin(x)) = x*
- *arccos(x) = y such that arccos(cos(x)) = x*
- *arctan(x) = y such that arctan(tan(x)) = x*

In Python, these functions can be called either from the **math** module or from within the **numpy** library. Since most Python implementations of trigonometric inverse functions return radians, we may want to convert the outcome into degrees. We can do this by multiplying the radians by 180 and then dividing by π.

Let's see how this can be written in code. Note that the input, **x**, is expressed as a pure number between -1 and 1, while the output is expressed in radians. Let's import the required libraries and declare the value of **x**:

```
from math import acos, asin, atan, cos
x = 0.5
```

Now, to print the inverse of cosine, add the following code:

```
print(acos(x))
```

The output is as follows:

```
1.0471975511965979
```

To print the inverse of sine, add the following code:

```
print(asin(x))
```

The output is as follows:

```
0.5235987755982989
```

To print the inverse of tan, add the following code:

```
print(atan(x))
```

The output is as follows:

```
0.4636476090008061
```

Let's try adding an input to the **acos** function that's outside the range [-1,1]:

```
x = -1.2
print(acos(x))
```

We will get an error, as follows:

```
Traceback (most recent call last):
    File "<stdin>", line 1, in <module>
```

Something similar will happen for **asin**. This is to be expected since no angle, φ, exists that can return **-1.2** as cos (or sin). However, this input is permitted in the **atan** function:

```
x = -1.2
print(atan(x))
```

The output is as follows:

```
-0.8760580505981934
```

Last, let's check what the inverse of the inverse **arccos(cos(x))** function gives us:

```
print(acos(cos(0.2)))
```

The output is as follows:

```
0.2
```

As expected, we retrieve the value of the input of the **cos** function.

The inverse trigonometric functions have a variety of applications across mathematics, physics, and engineering. For example, calculating integrals can be done by using inverse trigonometric functions. The indefinite integrals are as follows:

$$\int \frac{dx}{\sqrt{a^2 - x^2}} = \arcsin\frac{x}{a} + c$$

$$\int \frac{dx}{a^2 + x^2} = \frac{1}{a}\arctan\frac{x}{a} + c$$

$$\int \frac{dx}{x\sqrt{x^2 + a^2}} = \frac{1}{a}\operatorname{arcsec}\left|\frac{x}{a}\right| + c$$

Figure 5.12: Inverse trigonometric functions

Here, *a* is a parameter and *C* is a constant, and the integrals become immediately solvable with the help of inverse trigonometric functions.

EXERCISE 5.05: FINDING THE SHORTEST WAY TO THE TREASURE USING INVERSE TRIGONOMETRIC FUNCTIONS

In this exercise, you will be given a secret map that points to **B**, where some precious treasure has been lying for centuries. You are at point **A** and the instructions are clear: you have to navigate 20 km south then 33 km west so that you arrive at the treasure. However, the straight-line segment, **AB**, is the shortest. You need to find the angle **θ** on the map so that your navigation is correctly oriented:

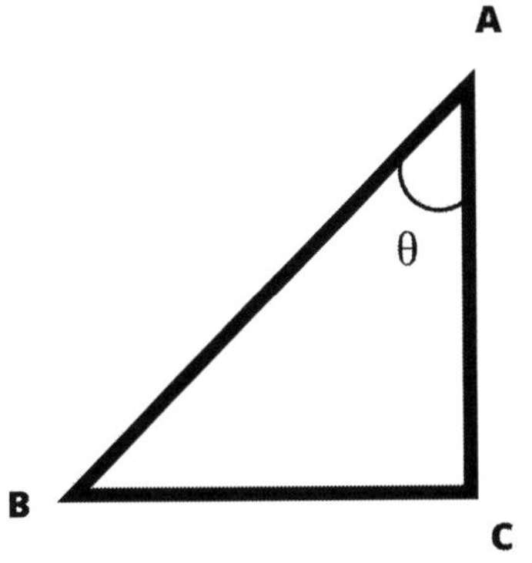

Figure 5.13: Graphical representation of the points A, B, and C

We need to find the angle **θ**, which is the angle between the segments **AB** and **AC**. Follow these steps:

1. Import the **`atan`** (arctan or inverse tangent) function:

```
from math import atan, pi
```

2. Find the tangent of θ using **`BC`** and **`AC`**:

```
AC = 33
BC = 20
tan_th = BC/AC
print(tan_th)
```

   The output is as follows:

```
0.6060606060606061
```

3. Next, find the angle by taking the inverse tangent function. Its argument is the tangent of θ:

```
theta = atan(tan_th)
```

4. Convert that into degrees and print the value:

```
theta_degrees = theta*180/pi
print(theta_degrees)
```

The output is as follows:

```
31.218402764346372
```

So, the answer is that we need to turn 31.22 degrees in order to navigate correctly.

5. As a bonus point, calculate the distance that we will travel along the path **AB**. This is simply given by the Pythagorean theorem as follows:

$AB^2 = AC^2 + BC^2$

In Python, use the following code:

```
AB = (AC**2 + BC**2)**0.5
print(AB)
```

The output is as follows:

```
38.58756276314948
```

The course will be 38.59 km.

It is straightforward to calculate this in Python by calling the **find_hypotenuse()** function. As expected, this is much shorter than the path $AC + BC = 53$ km.

> **NOTE**
>
> To access the source code for this specific section, please refer to https://packt.live/31CF4qr.
>
> You can also run this example online at https://packt.live/38jfVll.

EXERCISE 5.06: FINDING THE OPTIMAL DISTANCE FROM AN OBJECT

You are visiting your local arena to watch your favorite show, and you are standing in the middle of the arena. Besides the main stage, there is also a viewing screen so that people can watch and not miss the details of the show. The bottom of the screen stands 3 m above your eye level, and the screen itself is 7 m high. The angle of vision is formed by looking at both the bottom and top of the screen. Find the optimal distance, *x*, between yourself and the screen so that the angle of vision is maximized:

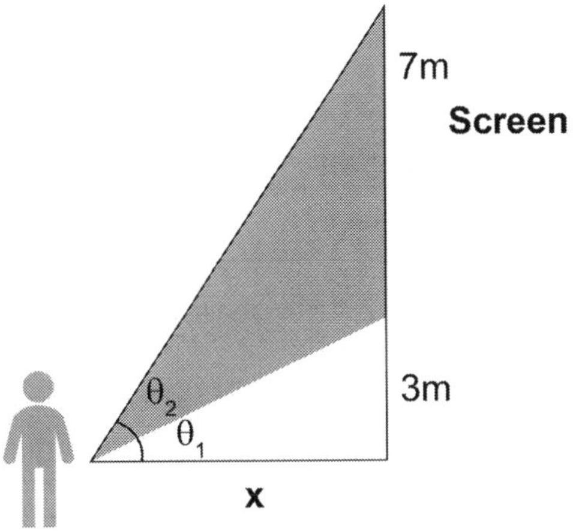

Figure 5.14: Angle of vision formed between the eyes and the screen

This is a slightly involved problem that requires a bit of algebra, but we will break it down into simple steps and explain the logic. First, note how much the plot of the problem guides us and helps us arrive at a solution. This apparently complex real-world problem translates into a much more abstract and simple geometric picture. Follow these steps to complete this exercise:

1. Calculate *x*. This is the lower side of the triangle and also the adjacent side to the angle, θ_1 (and also $\theta=\theta_1+\theta_2$). The answer, *x*, will be given by the condition that the viewing angle, θ_2 or equivalently, $tan(\theta_2)$), is maximized. From the preceding plot of the *screen*, we can immediately draw the following relations for the three angles: θ_1 (the inner angle), θ_2 (the outer angle), and $\theta=\theta_1+\theta_2$:

   $tan(\theta_1) = opposite/adjacent = 3/x$

   $tan(\theta) = tan(\theta_1+\theta_2) = opposite/adjacent = (7+3)/x$.

   Now, use algebra to work around these two relations and obtain a condition for θ_2.

2. A known identity for the tangent of a sum of two angles is as follows:

$$\tan\left(\theta_1+\theta_2\right)=\frac{\tan\left(\theta_1\right)+\tan\left(\theta_2\right)}{1-\tan\left(\theta_1\right)\tan\left(\theta_2\right)}$$

Figure 5.15: Formula for tangent of a sum of two angles

By substituting what we have found for *tan(θ)* and $tan(\theta_1)$ in the latter relation and after working out the algebra, we arrive at the following:

$tan(\theta_2) = 7x/(30+x^2)$ *or*

$\theta_2 = arctan(7x/(30+x^2))$.

In other words, we have combined the elements of the problem and found that the angle, θ_1, ought to change with the distance, *x*, as a function of *x*, which was given in the preceding line.

3. Let's plot this function to see how it changes. First, load the necessary libraries:

```
from matplotlib import pyplot as plt
import numpy as np
```

4. Then, plot the function by defining the domain, **x**, and the values, **y**, by using the **arctan** method of **numpy**. These are easily plotted with the **plot()** method of **pyplot**, as follows:

```
x = np.linspace(0.1, 50, 2000)
y = np.arctan(7*x / (30+x**2) )
plt.plot(x,y)

plt.show()
```

The output will be as follows:

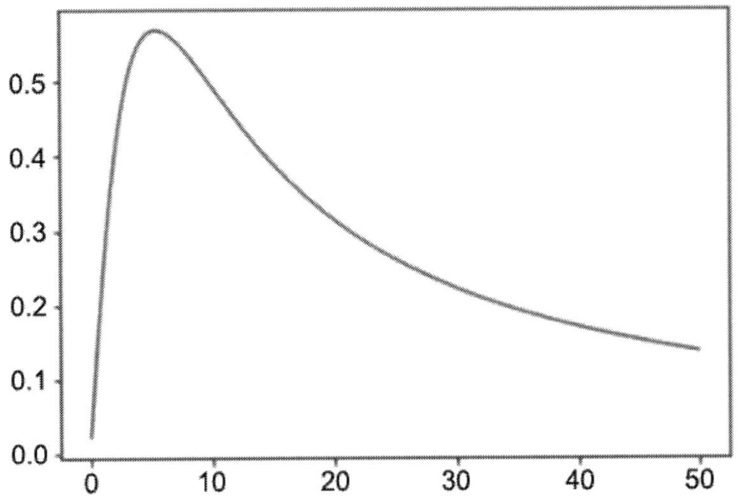

Figure 5.16: Plot of the function using the arctan method

From the preceding graph, we can see that the functions obtain a maximum.

5. Determine the function's maximum value, **y**, and the position, **x**, where this occurs:

```
ymax = max(y)
xmax = x[list(y).index(ymax)]

print(round(xmax,2), round(ymax,2))
```

The output is as follows:

```
5.47 0.57
```

6. Lastly, convert the found angle into degrees:

```
ymax_degrees = round(ymax * 180 / np.pi, 2)
print(ymax_degrees)
```

The output is as follows:

```
32.58
```

So, the viewing angle, θ_2, is at its maximum at 32.58 degrees and occurs when we stand 5.47 m away from the screen. We used the trigonometric and inverse trigonometric functions, implemented them in Python, and found the answer to a problem that arises from a *geometric* setup in a real-life situation. This sheds more light on how concepts from geometry and trigonometry can be usefully and easily coded to provide the expected results.

> **NOTE**
>
> To access the source code for this specific section, please refer to https://packt.live/2VB3Oez.
>
> You can also run this example online at https://packt.live/2VG9x2T.

Now, we will move on and study another central concept in mathematics with a wide range of applications in algebra, physics, computer science, and applied data science: vectors.

VECTORS

Vectors are abstract mathematical objects with a magnitude (size) and direction (orientation). A vector is represented by an arrow that has a base (tail) and a head. The head shows the direction of the vector, while the length of the arrow's body shows its magnitude.

A **scalar**, in contrast to a vector, is a sole number. It's a non-vector, that is, a pure integer, real or complex (as we shall see later), that has no elements and hence no direction.

Vectors are symbolized by either a bold-faced letter **A**, a letter with an arrow on top, or simply by a regular letter, if there is no ambiguity regarding the notation in the discussion. The magnitude of the vector, **A**, is stylized as $|A|$ or simply *A*. Now, let's have a look at the various vector operations.

VECTOR OPERATIONS

Simply put, a vector is a collection (think of a list or array) of two, three, or more numbers that form a mathematical object. This object lives in a particular geometrical space called a vector space that has some properties, such as metric properties, and dimensionality. A vector space can be two-dimensional (think of the plane of a sheet of your book), three-dimensional (the ordinary Euclidean space around us), or higher, in many abstract situations in mathematics and physics. The elements or numbers that are needed to identify a vector equals the dimensionality of the space. Now that we have defined a vector space—the playground for vectors—we can equip it with a system of axes (the usual *x*, *y*, and *z* axes) that mark the origin and measure the space. In such a well-defined space, we need to determine a set of numbers (two, three, or more) in order to uniquely define a vector, since vectors are assumed to begin at the origin of axes. The elements of a vector can be integers, rational, real, or (rarely) complex numbers. In Python, they are, most commonly, represented by lists or NumPy arrays.

Similar to real numbers, a set of linear operations is defined on vectors. Between two vectors, $A = (a_1, a_2, a_3)$ and $B = (b_1, b_2, b_3)$, we can define the following:

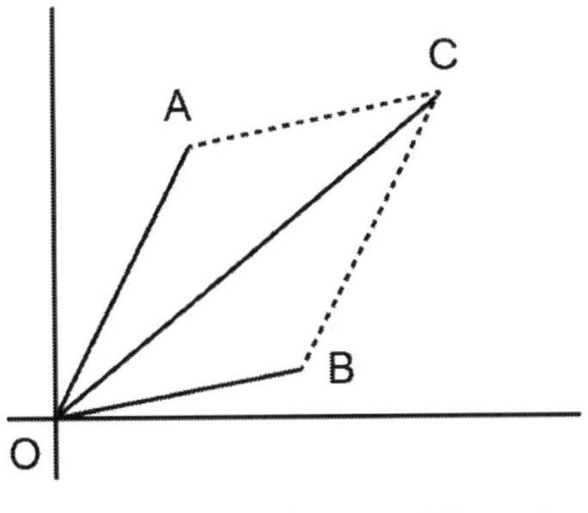

Figure 5.17: Points A, B, and C and their relations while performing vector operations

Now let us see the various operations that can be performed on these vectors:

- **Addition** as the operation that results in vector $C = A + B = (a_1 + b_1, a_2 + b_2, a_3 + b_3)$.
- **Subtraction** as the operation that results in vector $C = A - B = (a_1 - b_1, a_2 - b_2, a_3 - b_3)$.
- **Dot** (or inner or scalar) *product* of the *scalar* $C = b.\ b = a_1 b_1 + a_2 b_2 + a_3 b_3$.

- **Cross** (or exterior) *product* of the vector $C = A \times B$, which is perpendicular to the plane define by A and B and has elements $(a_2b_3 - a_3b_2, a_3b_1 - a_1b_3, a_1b_2 - a_2b_1)$.
- **Element-wise** or Hadamard *product* of two vectors, A and B, is the vector, C, whose elements are the pairwise product of elements of A and B; that is, $C = (a_1 b_1, a_2 b_2, a_3 b_3)$.

We can define and use the preceding formulas in Python code as follows:

```
import numpy as np
A = np.array([1,2,3]) # create vector A
B = np.array([4,5,6]) # create vector B
```

Then, to find the sum of **A** and **B**, enter the following code:

```
A + B
```

The output is as follows:

```
array([5, 7, 9])
```

To calculate the difference, enter the following code:

```
A - B
```

The output is as follows:

```
array([-3, -3, -3])
```

To find the element-wise product, enter the following code:

```
A*B
```

The output is as follows:

```
array([ 4, 10, 18])
```

To find the dot product, use the following code:

```
A.dot(B)
```

The output is as follows:

```
32
```

Finally, the cross product can be calculated as follows:

```
np.cross(A,B)
```

The output is as follows:

```
array([-3,  6, -3])
```

Note that vector addition, subtraction, and the dot product are associative and commutative operations, whereas the cross product is associative but not commutative. In other words, a x b does not equal b x a, but rather b x a, which is why it is called **anticommutative**.

Also, a vector, *A*, can be multiplied by a scalar, λ. In that case, you simply have to multiply each vector element by the same number, that is, the scalar:
$\lambda A = \lambda (a_1, a_2, a_3) = (\lambda a_1, \lambda a_2, \lambda a_3)$

Another important operation between vectors is the dot product, since it is arguably the most common operation to appear in mathematics, computer science, and its applications. The dot product is a funny type of operation that has no analog in the realm of real numbers. Indeed, it needs two vectors as input to produce a single scalar as output. This means that the result of the operation (scalar) is of a different type than its ingredients (vectors), and thus an inverse operation (a *dot division*) cannot generally exist.

By definition, it is given as follows:

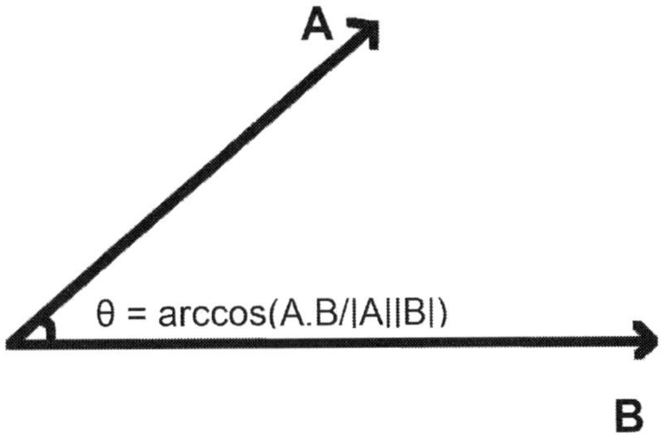

Figure 5.18: Graphical representation of the θ angle

This can be represented by the following equation:

$A.B = |A|\ |B|\ cos(\theta)$

Here, θ is the angle between *A* and *B*.

Let's have a look at some typical cases:

- If *A* and *B* are orthogonal, then the dot product vanishes:

  $A.B = 0$ if and only if $\theta = angle(A,B) = \pi/2$, since $|A|$ and $|B|$ are not zero.

- If *A* and *B* are co-linear and co-directional, then $\theta = 0$, $cos(\theta)=1$ and $A.B = |A|\ |B|$. If they are co-linear and have opposite directions, then $\theta = \pi$, $cos(\theta)=-1$, and $A.B = -|A|\ |B|$.

- It follows on from the definition for the dot product of a vector with itself:
  $A.A = |A|\ |A| \quad or \quad |A| = \sqrt{(A.A)}$

- It follows directly from $A.B = |A|\ |B|\ cos(\theta)$, where the angle between the two vectors is given as follows:
  $\theta = arccos(A.B / |A|\ |B|)$

  Here, *arccos* is the inverse *cos* function that we saw in the previous section.

For example, we can write a Python program that calculates the angle between any two given vectors with the help of **numpy** and the preceding relation that gives us the angle, θ:

```
import numpy as np
from math import acos
A = np.array([2,10,0])
B = np.array([9,1,-1])
```

To find the norm (magnitude) of each vector, we can use the following code:

```
Amagn = np.sqrt(A.dot(A))
Bmagn = np.sqrt(B.dot(B))
```

As an alternative, you can also use the following code:

```
Amagn = np.linalg.norm(A)
Bmagn = np.linalg.norm(B)
```

Print their values:

```
print(Amagn, Bmagn)
```

You will get the following output:

```
10.198039027185569
9.1104335791443
```

Both alternatives lead to the same result, which you can immediately check by printing **Amagn** and **Bmagn** once more.

Finally, we can find the angle, θ, as follows:

```
theta = acos(A.dot(B) / (Amagn * Bmagn))
print(theta)
```

The output is as follows:

```
1.2646655256233297
```

Now, let's have a look at exercise where will perform the various vector operations that we just learned about.

EXERCISE 5.07: VISUALIZING VECTORS

In this exercise, we will write a function that plots two vectors in a 2D space. We'll have to find their sum and the angle between them.

Perform the following steps to complete this exercise:

1. Import the necessary libraries, that is, **numpy** and **matplotlib**:

```
import numpy as np
import matplotlib.pyplot as plt
```

2. Create a function that admits two vectors as inputs, each as a list, plots them, and, optionally, plots their sum vector:

```
def plot_vectors(vec1, vec2, isSum = False):

    label1 = "A"; label2 = "B"; label3 = "A+B"
    orig = [0.0, 0.0]  # position of origin of axes
```

The **vec1** and **vec2** lists hold two real numbers each. Each pair denotes the endpoint (head) coordinates of the corresponding vector, while the origin is set at (0,0). The labels are set to **"A"**, **"B"**, and **"A+B"**, but you could change them or even set them as variables of the **plot_vectors** function with (or without) default values. The Boolean variable, **isSum**, is, by default, set to **False** and the sum, **vec1+vec2**, will not be plotted unless it's explicitly set to **True**.

3. Next, we put the coordinates on a **matplotlib.pyplot** object:

```
ax = plt.axes()
ax.annotate(label1, [vec1[0]+0.5,vec1[1]+0.5] )
# shift position of label for better visibility
ax.annotate(label2, [vec2[0]+0.5,vec2[1]+0.5] )
if isSum:
    vec3 = [vec1[0]+vec2[0], vec1[1]+vec2[1]]
    # if isSum=True calculate the sum of the two vectors
    ax.annotate(label3, [vec3[0]+0.5,vec3[1]+0.5] )

ax.arrow(*orig, *vec1, head_width=0.4, head_length=0.65)
ax.arrow(*orig, *vec2, head_width=0.4, head_length=0.65, \
         ec='blue')
if isSum:
    ax.arrow(*orig, *vec3, head_width=0.2, \
             head_length=0.25, ec='yellow')
    # plot the vector sum as well

plt.grid()
e=3
# shift limits by e for better visibility
plt.xlim(min(vec1[0],vec2[0],0)-e, max(vec1[0],\
             vec2[0],0)+e)
# set plot limits to the min/max of coordinates
plt.ylim(min(vec1[1],vec2[1],0)-e, max(vec1[1],\
             vec2[1],0)+e)
# so that all vectors are inside the plot area
```

Here, we used the annotate method to add labels to our vectors, as well as the arrow method, in order to create our vectors. The star operator, *, is used to unpack the arguments within the list's **orig** and **vec1**, **vec2** so that they are read correctly from the **arrow()** method. **plt.grid()** creates a grid on the plot's background to guide the eye and is optional. The **e** parameter is added so that the plot limits are wide enough and the plot is readable.

4. Next, we give our graph a title and plot it:

```
    plt.title('Vector sum',fontsize=14)

    plt.show()
    plt.close()
```

5. Now, we will write a function that calculates the angle between the two input vectors, as explained previously, with the help of the dot (inner) product:

```
def find_angle(vec1, vec2, isRadians = True, isSum = False):
    vec1 = np.array(vec1)
    vec2 = np.array(vec2)

    product12 = np.dot(vec1,vec2)
    cos_theta = product12/(np.dot(vec1,vec1)**0.5 * \
                           np.dot(vec2,vec2)**0.5 )
    cos_theta = round(cos_theta, 12)
    theta = np.arccos(cos_theta)

    plot_vectors(vec1, vec2, isSum=isSum)
    if isRadians:
        return theta
    else:
        return 180*theta/np.pi
```

First, we map our input lists to **numpy** arrays so that we can use the methods of this module. We calculate the dot product (named **product12**) and then divide that by the product of the magnitude of **vec1** with the magnitude of **vec2**. Recall that the magnitude of a vector is given by the square root (or ****0.5**) of the dot product with itself. As given by the definition of the dot product, we know that this quantity is the cos of the angle theta between the two vectors. Lastly, after rounding cos to avoid input errors in the next line, calculate theta by making use of the **arccos** method of **numpy**.

6. We want to combine the two functions that we wrote—**find_angle** and **plot_vectors**—and call the former inside the latter. We also want to give the user the option to print the result for the angle either in radians (**isRadians=True**) or degrees (**isRadians=False**). We are now ready to try our function. First, let's try this with two perpendicular vectors:

```
ve1 = [1,5]
ve2 = [5,-1]

find_angle(ve1, ve2, isRadians = False, isSum = True)
```

The output is as follows:

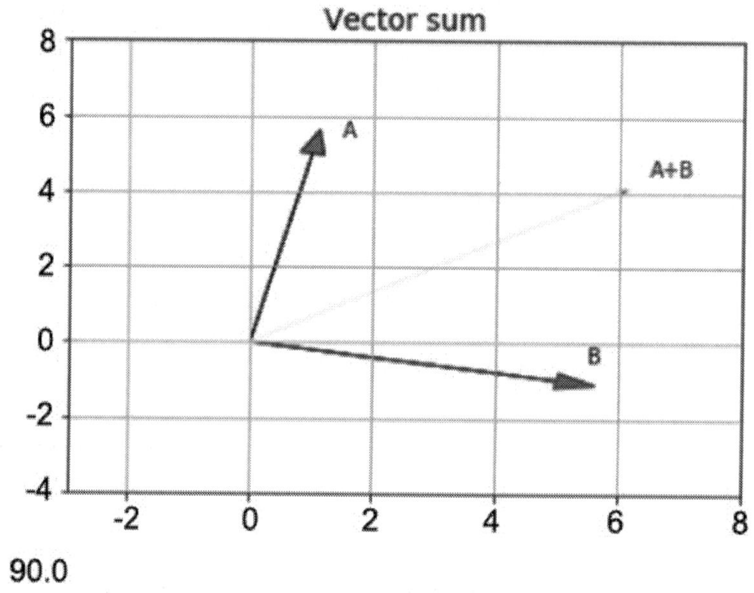

Figure 5.19: Plot of two perpendicular vectors

The plot looks good and the result is 90 degrees, as expected.

7. Now, let's try using the same function to create two co-linear vectors:

```
ve1 = [1,5]
ve2 = [0.5,2.5]

find_angle(ve1, ve2, isRadians = False, isSum = True)
```

The output is as follows:

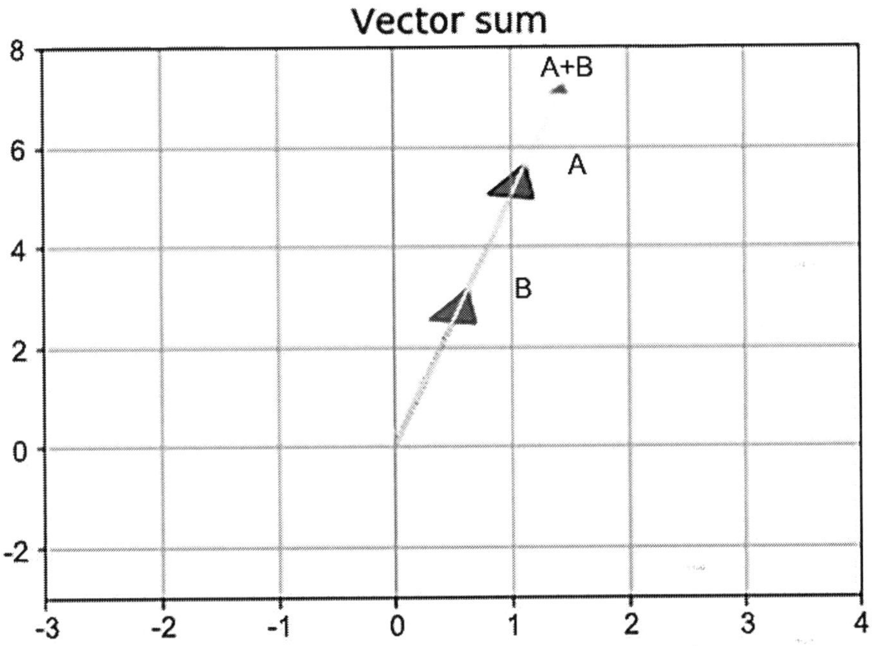

0.0

Figure 5.20: Plot of two co-linear vectors

The output is 0 degrees, as expected.

8. Lastly, again, using the same function, let's create two generic vectors:

```
ve1 = [1,5]
ve2 = [-3,-5]

find_angle(ve1, ve2, isRadians = False, isSum = True)
```

The output is as follows:

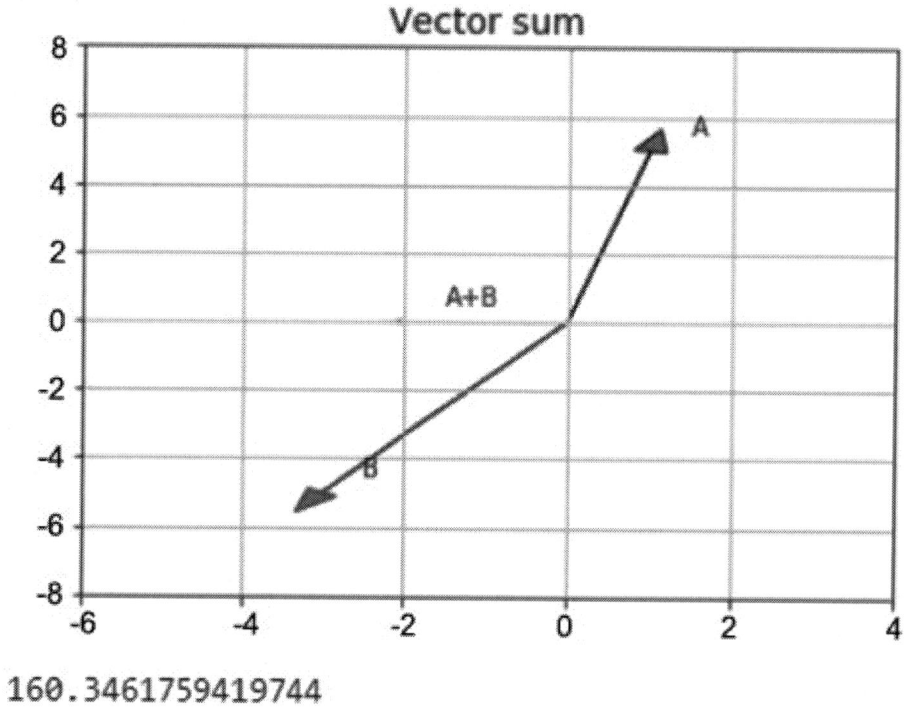

Figure 5.21: Plot of two generic vectors

In summary, we have studied vectors as mathematical objects that live in a vector space. We have learned how to construct and represent vectors in Python and how to visualize them. Vectors follow some simple rules, and performing operations with them is possible. Addition and subtraction follow exactly the same logic when dealing with real numbers. Multiplication is somewhat more involved and different types of products are defined. The most common product is the inner or dot product, which enjoys wide *popularity* in the mathematical and physics communities due to its simple geometric representation. We learned how to calculate the dot product of any two vectors in Python and, moreover, found the angle between the duet by using our knowledge (and some NumPy methods) of the dot product. In simple terms, a vector, in two dimensions, is a pair of numbers that form a geometric object with interesting properties.

> **NOTE**
>
> To access the source code for this specific section, please refer to https://packt.live/2Zxu7n5.
>
> You can also run this example online at https://packt.live/2YPntJQ.

Next, we will learn how a pair of two numbers can be combined into an even more exciting object, that of a complex number.

COMPLEX NUMBERS

Mathematical ideas have been evolving regarding numbers and their relationships since ancient numerical systems. Historically, mathematical ideas have evolved from concrete to abstract ones. For instance, a set of natural numbers was created so that all physical objects in the world around us directly correspond to some number within this set. Since arithmetic and algebra have developed, it has become clear that numbers beyond the naturals or integers are necessary, so decimal and rational numbers were introduced. Similarly, around the times of Pythagoras, it was found that rational numbers cannot solve all numerical problems that we could construct with the geometry that was known at that time. This happened when irrational numbers—numbers that result from taking the square root of other numbers and that have no representation as ratios—were introduced.

Complex numbers are an extension of real numbers and include some special numbers that can provide a solution to some equations that real numbers cannot.

Such a number does, in fact, exist and has the symbol *i*. It is called an imaginary number or imaginary unit, even though there is nothing imaginary about it; it is as real as all the other numbers that we have seen and has, as we shall see, some very beautiful properties.

BASIC DEFINITIONS OF COMPLEX NUMBERS

We define the imaginary number *i* as follows:

$i^2 = -1$

Any number that consists of a real and an imaginary number (part) is called a **complex number**. For example, consider the following numbers:

$z = 3 - i$

$z = 14/11 + i\,3$

$z = -\sqrt{5} - i\,2.1$

All the preceding numbers are all complex numbers. Their real part is symbolized as *Re(z)* and their imaginary part is symbolized as *Im(z)*. For the preceding examples, we get the following:

$Re(z) = 3\,,\ Im(z) = -1$

$Re(z) = 14/11\,,\ Im(z) = 3$

$Re(z) = -\sqrt{5}\,,\ Im(z) = -2.1$

Let's look at some examples using code. In Python, the imaginary unit is symbolized with the letter *j* and a complex number is written as follows:

```
c = <real> + <imag>*1j,
```

Here, **`<real>`** and **`<imag>`** are real numbers. Equivalently, a complex number can be defined as follows:

```
c = complex(<real>, <imag>).
```

In code, it becomes as follows:

```
a = 1
b = -3
z = complex(a, b)
print(z)
```

The output is as follows:

```
(1-3j)
```

We can also use the **real** and **imag** functions to separate the real and imaginary parts of any complex number, **z**. First, let's use the **real** function:

```
print(z.real)
```

The output is as follows:

```
1.0
```

Now, use the **imag** function:

```
print(z.imag)
```

The output is as follows:

```
-3.0
```

In other words, any complex number can be decomposed and written as $z=Re(z) + i\,Im(z)$. As such, a complex number is a pair of two real numbers and can be visualized as a vector that lives in two dimensions. Hence, the geometry and algebra of vectors, as discussed in the previous section, can be applied here as well.

Methods and functions that admit complex numbers as inputs are found in the **cmath** module. This module contains mathematical functions for complex numbers. The functions there accept integers, floating-point numbers, or complex numbers as input arguments.

A *complex conjugate* is defined as the complex number, z^* (also $\bar{z}$), that has the same real part as the complex number, z, and the opposite imaginary part; that is, if $z = x+iy$, then $z^* = x - iy$. Note that the product, zz^*, is the real number, x^2+y^2, which gives us the square of the *modulus* of z:

$$zz^* = z^*z = |z|^2$$

A complex number is plotted, similar to a vector, on the complex plane (as shown in the following diagram). This is the plane that's formed by the real part on the *x* axis and the imaginary part on the *y* axis. The complex conjugate is simply a reflection of the vector with respect to the real axis:

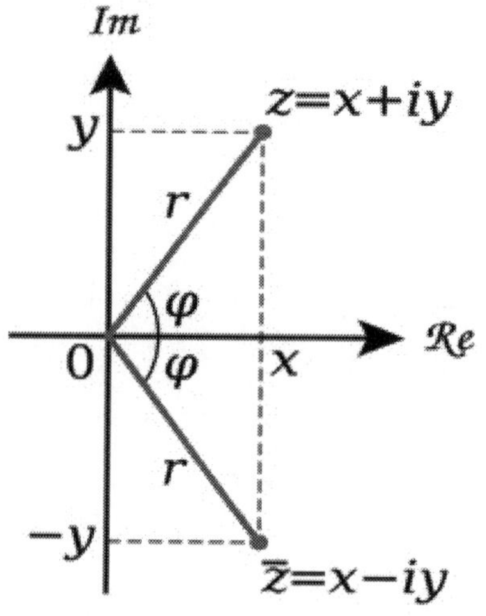

Figure 5.22: A plot of a complex number

A complex number, *z*, can be visualized as a vector with coordinates (x, y). Alternatively, we can write it as a vector with polar coordinates (r, φ). The complex conjugate, z^* or $\bar{z}$, is a vector the same as *z* but reflected with respect to the *x* axis.

A complex number is zero if both its real and complex parts are zero. The following operations can be performed on two complex numbers, *z = x+iy* and *w = u+iv*:

- **Addition**: *z+w = (x+u) + i(y+v)*
- **Subtraction**: *z-w = (x-u) + i(y-v)*
- **Multiplication**: *z w = (x+iy)(u+iv) = (xu-yv) + i(xv + yu)*
- **Division**: *z/w = (x+iy)/(u+iv) = (ux+vy)+i(uy-xv) / (u2+v2)*

POLAR REPRESENTATION AND EULER'S FORMULA

A complex number is easily visualized as a vector on the complex plane. As such, it has a magnitude, which is determined by the vector's size, and an orientation, which is determined by the angle, φ, that is formed with the *x* (real) axis. To determine these two numbers, we need to find the absolute value (or modulus), *r*, of $z=x+iy$:

$r = |z| = \sqrt{x^2+y^2}$

Its angle (also, called the argument, *arg*, or *phase*), φ, is as follows:

$\varphi = arg(z) = arctan(x+iy) = arctan(y/x)$

Both of these relations stem from the geometry of the complex vector. The first relation is simply the application of the Pythagorean theorem, while the second comes from applying the tangent relation to the angle, φ.

By examining the graphical representation of the vector (see the preceding diagram), we can see the following:

$cos(\varphi) = x/r$ *and*

$sin(\varphi) = y/r$

Or

$x = r\ cos(\varphi)$ *and*

$y = r\ sin(\varphi)$

By substituting these with $z = x+iy$, we get the following:

$z = r\ (cos(\varphi) + i\ sin(\varphi))$

We can write some code in Python to find (r, φ) (the polar coordinates) once (x, y) (the cartesian coordinates) are given and vice versa:

```
def find_polar(z):
    from math import asin
    x = z.real
    y = z.imag
    r = (x**2 + y**2)**0.5
    phi = asin(y/r)
    return r, phi
find_polar(1-3j)
```

The output is as follows:

```
(3.1622776601683795, -1.2490457723982544)
```

Equivalently, we can use the **polar** method from the **cmath** module:

```
import cmath
z = 1-3j
cmath.polar(z)
```

The output is as follows:

```
(3.1622776601683795, -1.2490457723982544)
```

> **NOTE**
>
> The input (0,0) is not allowed since it leads to division by zero.

Therefore, a complex number can be represented by its modulus, *r*, and phase, *φ*, instead of its abscissa (*x*, the real part) and ordinate (*y*, the imaginary part). The modulus, *r*, is a real, non-negative number and the phase, *φ*, lies in the interval [-π,π]: it is *0* and *π* for purely real numbers and *π/2* or *-π/2* for purely imaginary numbers. The latter representation is called polar, while the former is known as rectangular or Cartesian; they are equivalent. The following representation is also possible:

$$z = r\, e^{i\varphi} = r\, (\cos(\varphi) + i \sin(\varphi))$$

Here is the base of the natural logarithm. This is known as Euler's formula. The special case, *φ=π*, gives us the following:

$$e^{i\pi} + 1 = 0$$

This is known as Euler's identity.

The benefit of using Euler's formula is that complex number multiplication and division obtain a simple geometric representation. To multiply (divide) two complex numbers, z_1 and z_2, we simply multiply (divide) their respective moduli and add (subtract) their arguments:

$$z_1 * z_2 = r\, e^{i\varphi} = r_1 * r_2\, e^{i(\varphi 1+\varphi 2)}$$

Now, let's implement some mathematical operations with complex numbers in Python. We will code the addition, subtraction, multiplication, and division of two complex numbers:

```
def complex_operations2(c1, c2):
    print('Addition =', c1 + c2)
    print('Subtraction =', c1 - c2)
    print('Multiplication =', c1 * c2)
    print('Division =', c1 / c2)
```

Now, let's try these functions for a generic pair of complex numbers, *c1=10+2j/3* and *c2=2.9+1j/3*:

```
complex_operations2(10+2j/3, 2.9+1j/3)
```

The output is as follows:

```
Addition = (12.9+1j)
Subtraction = (7.1+0.3333333333333333j)
Multiplication = (28.77777777777778+5.266666666666666j)
Division = (3.429391054896336-0.16429782240187768j)
```

We can do the same for a purely real number with a purely imaginary number:

```
complex_operations2(1, 1j)
```

The output is as follows:

```
Addition = (1+1j)
Subtraction = (1-1j)
Multiplication = 1j
Division = -1j
```

From the last line, we can easily see that *1/i* = *-i*, which is consistent with the definition of the imaginary unit. The **cmath** library also provides useful functions for complex numbers, such as **phase** and **polar**, as well as trigonometric functions for complex arguments:

```
import cmath
def complex_operations1(c):
    modulus = abs(c)
    phase = cmath.phase(c)
    polar = cmath.polar(c)
```

```
    print('Modulus =', modulus)
    print('Phase =', phase)
    print('Polar Coordinates =', polar)
    print('Conjugate =',c.conjugate())
    print('Rectangular Coordinates =', \
          cmath.rect(modulus, phase))

complex_operations1(3+4j)
```

The output is as follows:

```
Modulus = 5.0
Phase = 0.9272952180016122
Polar Coordinates = (5.0, 0.9272952180016122)
Conjugate = (3-4j)
Rectangular Coordinates = (3.0000000000000004+3.9999999999999996j)
```

Hence, calculating the modulus, phase, or conjugate of a given complex number becomes extremely simple. Note that the last line gives us back the rectangular (or Cartesian) form of a complex number, given its modulus and phase.

Now that we learned how the arithmetic and representation of complex numbers work, let's move on and look at an exercise that involves logic and combines what we have used and learned about in the previous sections.

EXERCISE 5.08: CONDITIONAL MULTIPLICATION OF COMPLEX NUMBERS

In this exercise, you will write a function that reads a complex number, **c**, and multiplies it by itself if the argument of the complex number is larger than zero, takes the square root of **c** if its argument is less than zero, and does nothing if the argument equals zero. Plot and discuss your findings:

1. Import the necessary libraries and, optionally, suppress any warnings (this isn't necessary but is helpful if you wish to keep the output tidy from warnings that depend on the versions of the libraries you're using):

```
import cmath
from matplotlib import pyplot as plt
import warnings
warnings.filterwarnings("ignore")
```

2. Now, define a function that uses Matplotlib's **`pyplot`** function to plot the vector of the input complex number, **`c`**:

```
def plot_complex(c, color='b', label=None):

    ax = plt.axes()
    ax.arrow(0, 0, c.real, c.imag, head_width=0.2, \
             head_length=0.3, color=color)
    ax.annotate(label, xy=(0.6*c.real, 1.15*c.imag))

    plt.xlim(-3,3)
    plt.ylim(-3,3)

    plt.grid(b=True, which='major') #<-- plot grid lines
```

3. Now, create a function that reads the input complex number, **`c`**, plots it by calling the function defined previously, and then investigates the different cases, depending on the phase of the input. Plot the phases before and after the operation, as well as the result, in order to compare the resulting vector with the input vector:

```
def mult_complex(c, label1='old', label2='new'):

    phase = cmath.phase(c)
    plot_complex(c, label=label1)

    if phase == 0:
        result = -1
    elif phase < 0:
        print('old phase:', phase)
        result = cmath.sqrt(c)
        print('new phase:', cmath.phase(result))
        plot_complex(result, 'red', label=label2)
    elif phase > 0:
        print('old phase:', phase)
        result = c*c
        print('new phase:', cmath.phase(result))
        plot_complex(result, 'red', label=label2)
    return result
```

Note that for negative phases, we take the square root of **c** (using the **math.sqrt()** method), whereas for positive phases, we take the square of **c**.

4. Now, transform a number that lies on the upper half of the complex plane:

```
mult_complex(1 + 1.2j)
```

The output is as follows:

```
old phase: 0.8760580505981934
new phase: 1.7521161011963868
(-0.43999999999999995+2.4j)
```

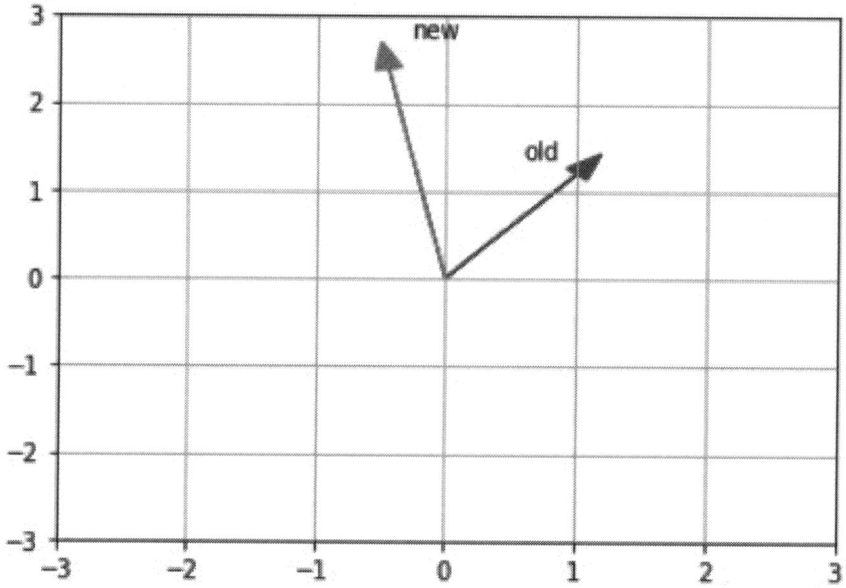

Figure 5.23: The plot of a number that lies on the upper half of the complex plane

Here, a complex number with a positive argument, φ (blue vector), is being transformed (or mapped) to a new complex number (red vector) with a larger modulus and a new argument that is twice the previous value. This is expected: remember Euler's formula for the polar representation of $c=r\ e^{i\varphi}$? It becomes obvious that the square, c^2, is a number with double the original argument, φ, and modulus, r^2.

5. Next, transform a number that lies on the lower half of the complex plane:

```
mult_complex(1-1.2j)
```

The output is as follows:

```
old phase:  -0.8760580505981934
new phase:  -0.43802902529909676
(1.1318237352126281-0.5301178808441246j)
```

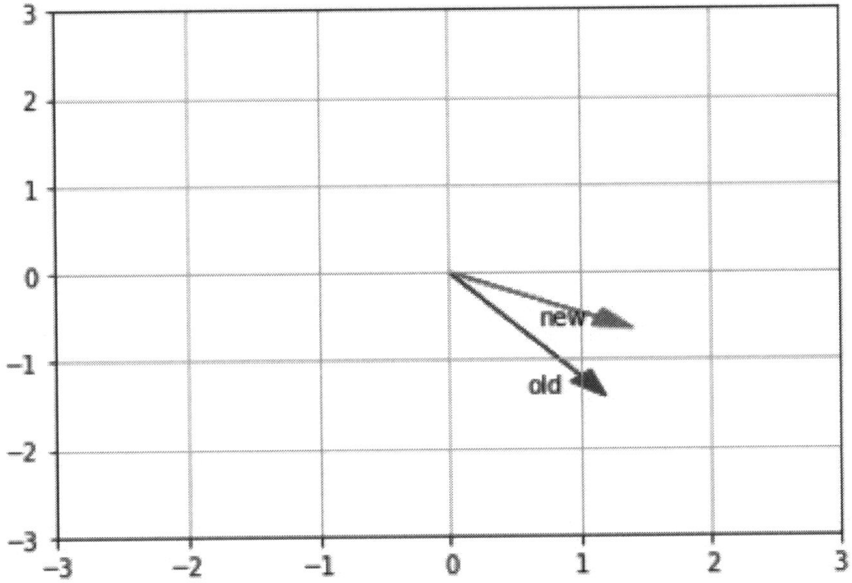

Figure 5.24: Plot of a number that lies on the lower half of the complex plane

In this case, the square root is calculated. Similar to the first example, the newly transformed vector has a modulus that is the square root of the modulus of the original vector and an argument that is half of the original one.

> **NOTE**
>
> Fun fact: In both cases, the vector has been rotated anti-clockwise.

6. Write a **`while`** iteration that calls the **`mult_complex()`** function *n* times to check what happens if we keep the vectors rotating:

```
c0 = 1+1.2j
n = 0
while n < 6:
    c0 = mult_complex(c0, None, str(n))
    n+=1
```

The output is as follows:

```
old phase:  0.8760580505981934
new phase:  1.7521161011963868
old phase:  1.7521161011963868
new phase:  -2.778953104786813
old phase:  -2.778953104786813
new phase:  -1.3894765523934065
old phase:  -1.3894765523934065
new phase:  -0.6947382761967033
old phase:  -0.6947382761967033
new phase:  -0.3473691380983516
old phase:  -0.3473691380983516
new phase:  -0.1736845690491758
```

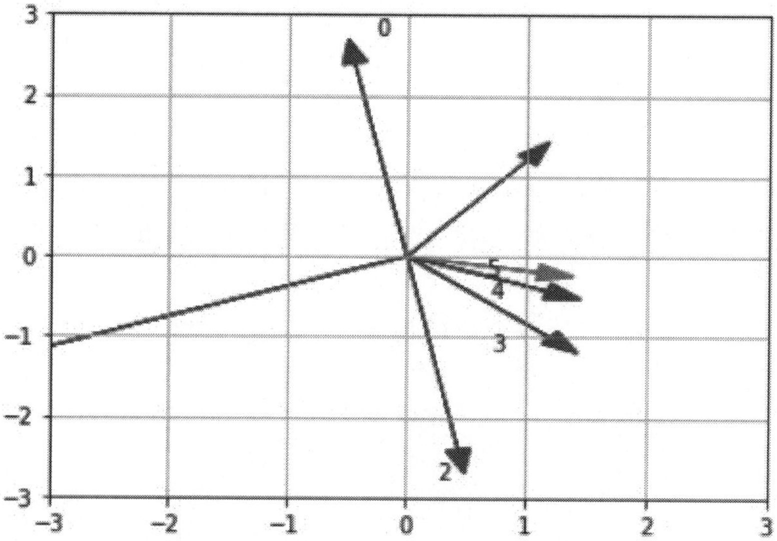

Figure 5.25: Plot of rotating vectors

With that, we've seen how vectors and vector algebra can be used to visualize geometric operations. In particular, dividing and multiplying complex numbers results in acquiring a geometric representation that can be helpful when dealing with large sets of data and visualizations.

> **NOTE**
>
> To access the source code for this specific section, please refer to https://packt.live/31yU8W1.
>
> You can also run this example online at https://packt.live/2BXWJOw.

ACTIVITY 5.01: CALCULATING YOUR RETIREMENT PLAN USING SERIES

In many countries, a retirement plan (also known as 401(k)) is offered by some employers. Such plans allow you to contribute directly from your paycheck, so they are an easy and effective way to save and invest for retirement. You have been tasked with writing some code that calculates and plots your monthly return based on the amount and duration of contributions.

A retirement plan accumulates in time, exactly like a geometric series does. It is an investment: you save money on a monthly basis in order to collect it later, on a monthly basis, with added value or interest. The main *ingredients* to calculate the retirement return are your current balance, a monthly contribution, the employer match (employer's contribution), the retirement age, the rate of return (the average annual return you expect from your 401(k) investment), life expectancy, and any other fees. In a realistic case, *caps* are introduced: the employer match (typically between 50% and 100%) cannot be raised by more than 6% of your annual salary. Similarly, the employee's contribution cannot be larger than a given amount in a year (typically, this is 18 K), regardless of how high the salary is.

Perform the following steps to complete this activity:

1. Identify the variables of our problem. These will be the variables of our functions. Make sure you read through the activity description carefully and *internalize* what is known and what is to be calculated.

2. Identify the sequence and write one function that calculates the value of the retirement plan at some year, *n*. The function should admit the current balance, annual salary, year, *n*, and more as inputs and return a tuple of contribution, employer's match, and total retirement value at year *n*.

3. Identify the series and write one function that calculates the accumulated value of the retirement plan *after n* years. The present function should read the input, call the previous function that calculates the value of the plan at each year, and sum all the (per year) savings. For visualization purposes, the contributions (per year), employer match (per year), and total value (per year) should be returned as lists in a tuple.
4. Run the function for a variety of chosen values and ensure it runs properly.
5. Plot the results with Matplotlib.

> **NOTE**
>
> The solution for this activity can be found on page 672.

SUMMARY

In this chapter, you have been provided with a general and helpful exposition of the most central mathematical concepts in sequences, series, trigonometry, vectors, and complex numbers and, more importantly, their implementation in Python using concrete and short examples. As a real-life example, we examined a retirement plan and the progression of our savings in time. However, numerous other situations can be modeled after sequences or series and be studied by applying vectors or complex numbers. These concepts and methods are widely used in physics, engineering, data science, and more. Linear algebra, that is, the study of vectors, matrices, and tensors, heavily relies on understanding the concept of geometry and vectors and appears almost everywhere in data science and when studying neural networks. Geometry and trigonometry, on the other hand, are explicitly used to model physical motion (in video games, for instance) and more advanced concepts in geospatial applications. However, having background knowledge of these concepts makes using and applying data science methods more concrete and understandable.

In the next chapter, we will discuss matrices and how to apply them to solve real-world problems. We'll also examine Markov chains, which are used to tie concepts regarding probability, matrices, and limits together.

6

MATRICES AND MARKOV CHAINS WITH PYTHON

OVERVIEW

In this chapter, we intend to foray into matrices and their applications using Python. We will look at different matrix manipulation techniques that will help us use them efficiently to build useful tools in real-world applications.

By the end of this chapter, you will understand matrices and be able to perform operations on them. You will implement one of the applications of matrices, known as Markov chains, using transition matrices and then use Markov chains and the Markov property to solve real-world problems.

INTRODUCTION

A matrix is a rectangular array of numbers or expressions arranged in rows and columns and considered as a single entity. As we are considering a matrix as a single object, if we perform an operation on it, it will apply to each of the elements within it:

$$A(m,n) = \begin{bmatrix} a_{11} & a_{12} & \cdot & a_{1n} \\ a_{21} & a_{22} & \cdot & a_{2n} \\ \cdot & \cdot & \cdot & \cdot \\ a_{m1} & a_{m2} & \cdot & a_{mn} \end{bmatrix}$$

Figure 6.1: A simple m × n matrix with m rows and n columns

A simple linear single-dimension array rarely suffices for the physical world we live in, and almost all attributes related to space and time require more than one dimension. Compactness is one of the main reasons for the use of matrices. A matrix is compact when it is closed and bounded or simply has its points within a fixed distance of one another. Primarily for these two reasons, matrices find applications in practically every field, including fundamental mathematical concepts, ranging from graph theory, linear transformations, and probability theory, to different branches of physics, such as quantum mechanics and electromagnetism.

The Markov chain model and its variations are one such application, tying concepts of matrices, limits, and probability together to produce results in real-world problems where uncertainty is predominant. In a mathematical space, whenever there is uncertainty, decisions are based on probability; this forms the basis of Markov chains. These use a specific type of matrix, called a transition matrix, to build state diagrams. A Markov chain is effectively a memoryless process that is primarily based on the current state to decide the outcome of the next state. We find their application in some very important use cases, including page-rank algorithms, autocomplete applications, and text generators. We will be studying these concepts in more detail later in the chapter, and for that, we need to first understand matrices.

MATRIX OPERATIONS ON A SINGLE MATRIX

In this chapter, we will study the different ways of manipulating matrices and how to implement them in Python. Understanding how a matrix works broadly means understanding the fundamentals of how 2D or multidimensional arrays work. Once we have a good understanding of the basics of 2D matrices, those interested can delve into advanced studies of matrices, which includes special types of matrices such as sparse matrices, vector spaces, eigenvalues, and eigenvectors, which can involve more than two dimensions.

Matrices in Python can be implemented using either lists or arrays. Nested lists in Python work perfectly fine, but Python has a powerful package that makes matrix implementation much easier called NumPy. SciPy is another package that helps in matrix manipulation, but it is usually more suitable for larger matrix computations. We will be using both of these modules throughout this chapter.

BASIC OPERATIONS ON A MATRIX

It is assumed at this point that you have the Python and its default libraries installed for running a basic Python program.

Once you have the package in place, let's define our first matrix:

```
# Importing Numpy package
import numpy as np

# Initializing and printing matrix z
x = np.array([[1, 2], [3, 4]])
print(x)
```

This matrix is the same as the following matrix, **z**, which is simply better represented and, as a good practice, is advisable whenever possible:

```
# Initializing and printing matrix z
z = np.array([[1, 2],\
              [3, 4]])
print(type(z))
```

Note that in the preceding code, we have printed the type of the variable **z**. Can you guess the output? The output should be as follows:

```
<type 'numpy.ndarray'>
```

The **ndarray** is the standard array format used by NumPy. The array object is homogenous, multidimensional, and has a data type object that is associated with it internally depending on its assignment.

For example, let's take an element in matrix **z**, which we defined previously:

```
# Printing the data types for matrix-z
print(z)
print(type(z))
print(z[0][1])
print(type(z[0][1]))
```

This produces the following output:

```
[[1 2]
 [3 4]]
[[5 6]
 [7 8]]
<type 'numpy.ndarray'>
2
<type 'numpy.int64'>
[Finished in 0.221s]
```

We find that the elements of the given matrix are of the **int64** type, that is, the 64-bit integer type. Other data types include **np.float32**, **np.complex**, **np.bool**, **np.object**, **np.string_**, and **np.unicode_**.

For now, it is enough to know that pretty much every data structure that we build uses Python version 3.8 and NumPy version 1.17. As of the date of publication, NumPy has a special class called a **matrix** class that does pretty much the same things that **ndarray** does. The only difference is that the **matrix** class maintains its 2D nature and has some operators built in, such as ***** for multiplication and ****** for power. Although the **matrix** class might come in handy and can be explored, the official NumPy documentation advises using a regular **ndarray** instead of **np.matrix** as it may be removed in the future. So, it is good to note here that the term **ndarray** in this context can be considered synonymous with the term **matrix** and will be used interchangeably in this chapter.

Let's continue working with **ndarray**. Assuming we have a single matrix, we will see some of the simple operations that we can do with it. We can use the same matrix, **z**, that we defined previously.

Let's print the sum of the elements:

```
# Sum of all elements of the matrix
print(z)
print(np.sum(z))
```

This produces the following output:

```
[[1 2]
 [3 4]]
10
[Finished in 0.237s]
```

This is pretty straightforward. Let's now look at some other things that we can do.

Let's find the maximum, minimum, mean, and standard deviation of the **z** matrix:

```
# Value of the largest integer in the matrix
print("Max ", np.max(z))

# Value of the smallest integer in the matrix
print("Min ", np.min(z))

# Mean of elements in the matrix
print("Mean ", np.mean(z))

# Standard deviation
print("Standard deviation ", np.std(z))
```

This produces the following output:

```
('Max ', 4)
('Min ', 1)
('Mean ', 2.5)
('Standard deviation ', 1.1180339887498949)
[Finished in 0.207s]
```

There are a number of other operations that can be performed on an **ndarray**, including common mathematical functions such as sin, cos, log, and square root, and statistical functions, such as finding correlation coefficients and the cumulative sum, some of which we will be using shortly.

INSPECTING A MATRIX

Now, we will deal with some useful functions that can help us learn more about any array that we are working with. Let's continue to use the same matrix/**`ndarray`**, **`z`**, that we have been using so far:

1. Let's print the information of a matrix:

```
# 1. Information about a matrix
print("Information: ")
print(np.info(z))
```

The output will be as follows:

```
Information:
class:  ndarray
shape:  (2, 2)
strides:  (16, 8)
itemsize:  8
aligned:  True
contiguous:  True
fortran:  False
data pointer: 0x7ff57665fef0
byteorder:  little
byteswap:  False
type: int64
None
```

2. Now, to ascertain the shape of the matrix, write the following code:

```
# 2. Gives the shape of the matrix
print("Shape: ")
print(np.shape(z))
```

The output will be as follows:

```
Shape:
(2, 2)
```

3. To check whether the matrix is a 2D or 3D matrix, write the following code:

```
# 3. Dimensions of the matrix
print("Dimensions: ")
print(np.ndim(z))
```

The output will be as follows:

```
Dimensions:
2
```

4. To print the data type of the matrix, use the following code:

```
# 4. Data type of the matrix
print("Data type of elements")
print(z.dtype.name)
```

The output will be as follows:

```
Data type of elements
int64
```

5. To print the length of the matrix, use the following code:

```
print("Length of the ndarray: ")
print(len(z))
```

The output will be as follows:

```
Length of the ndarray:
2
```

As we can see, the **`info`** function already displays the values of the other two functions we have called, namely, shape and type. Nevertheless, these functions serve a limited purpose, and that is all that is required sometimes. The multidimensional **`ndarray`**, as we know, is an array of arrays, and the **`len`** function of the NumPy array will always be the length of the first dimension. If **`z`** is a 2D matrix, then **`len(z)`** will be the number of rows in **`z`**.

In the following exercise, we will create a matrix. We can pretty much create a matrix with a nested list, but this problem will elaborate on how matrices are packaged and utilized in the real world.

EXERCISE 6.01: CALCULATING THE TIME TAKEN FOR SUNLIGHT TO REACH EARTH EACH DAY

In this exercise, we will calculate the time it takes for sunlight to reach the Earth each day of the year.

As we know, the Earth revolves around the Sun in an elliptical orbit. As such, the distance between the Earth and the Sun changes, which will change the amount of time it takes for light to reach the Earth. There are three main equations that we can use to deal with this.

The mathematical formula to calculate time is as follows:

$$Time = \frac{Distance}{Speed}$$

Figure 6.2: Formula to calculate time

We need to calculate the distance, *r*, between the Earth and the Sun:

$$r = \frac{a\left(1 - e^2\right)}{1 - e\cos\theta}$$

Figure 6.3: Formula to calculate distance

In the preceding equation, the value of *a* is 149,600,000 km, which is the semi-major axis distance, *e* is 0.0167, which is the eccentricity of Earth's orbit, and θ is the angle from perihelion.

The dependent variable θ that will be required in the preceding equation is calculated as follows:

$$\theta = \frac{2\pi n}{365.256}$$

Figure 6.4: Formula for calculating the dependent variable

Note here that *n* is the number of days from the perihelion that occurs on January 3rd. To keep things simple, we will take this to be the beginning of the year.

Do not get bogged down by these equations as they are nothing but simple mathematical multiplications of constants and can be easily solved by a nifty Python library called **`math`**.

Let's now get started with the exercise:

1. First, import the **`math`** and **`numpy`** libraries:

```
import math
import numpy as np
```

   We will be using these libraries later.

2. Next, define the two constants and use capitalization, which is the standard Python practice for naming these constants:

```
def earth_sun_distance():
    # Semi-major axis between earth and sun
    A = 149600000
    # Eccentricity of earth
    E = 0.0167
    l = []
```

   A here is the semi-major axis distance between the Earth and the Sun.

   E is known as the eccentricity of the Earth.

   l is a list that we have initialized for storing the values later.

3. Let's jump into the main part of the code. For each of the **365** days, calculate **theta**, as it is different for each day of the year. Then, calculate the distance of the Earth from the Sun, and finally append that distance to a list:

```
    # Calculating the distance between earth and sun
    for i in range(365):
        theta = (2 * math.pi * i) / 365.25
        r = A*(1 - E**2) / (1 - (E * math.cos(theta)))
        l.append(r)
    return l
```

   Note the use of the **math.pi** and **math.cos** functions from the **math** library that we imported previously.

4. Calculate the time required in seconds, assuming the speed of light to be a constant value of 299,792 km/s:

```
# Calculating the time taken
S = 299792
t = np.divide(l, S)
```

   Here, we first harness the power of NumPy arrays by using the **divide** function, which applies the values to all members of the list without having to use a loop. We store its values in **t**, which is type-casted automatically into a NumPy array.

5. Finally, we do two things here. First, we use another useful Python function called **zip()**, which binds the respective elements of two lists together, and then we use the **np.asarray()** function, which converts the list of tuples into a NumPy array:

```
sunny = np.asarray(list(zip(l, t)))
print("Earth sun distance: \n", sunny)
```

Run the program to see the output:

```
Earth sun distance:
[[  1.52098320e+08   5.07346160e+02]
 [  1.52097938e+08   5.07344885e+02]
 [  1.52096791e+08   5.07341061e+02]
 [  1.52094881e+08   5.07334688e+02]
 [  1.52092207e+08   5.07325770e+02]
 [  1.52088771e+08   5.07314309e+02]
 ...
 [  1.52072354e+08   5.07259546e+02]
 [  1.52078259e+08   5.07279242e+02]
 [  1.52083406e+08   5.07296411e+02]
 [  1.52087793e+08   5.07311046e+02]
 [  1.52091420e+08   5.07323143e+02]
 [  1.52094284e+08   5.07332697e+02]
 [  1.52096385e+08   5.07339707e+02]
 [  1.52097723e+08   5.07344168e+02]]
[Finished in 0.197s]
```

We now have in systematic tabular format the values of distance between the Earth and the Sun and the time taken for light to reach the Earth. We can go on adding other parameters to our matrix, and that is the flexibility that comes with using matrices and NumPy arrays.

Please note here that these values are by no means accurate, and we have made a few safe assumptions for simplicity, but it is nevertheless a good illustration of how matrices can be utilized for practically anything. Also, note that the values reflected here are in scientific notation format used in Python and can easily be converted to float or any other type as required. The values on the left are in km, and the ones on the right are in the form 507.346... seconds.

6. Append the results as follows:

```
d = []
for i in range(1,len(l) - 1):
    d.append(l[i]-l[i-1])
print(d)
```

A section of the output is as follows:

```
[-382.2014582455158, -1146.4797523021698, -1910.3842301666737,
 -2673.6658524870872, -3436.075836390257, -4197.365758448839,
 -4957.287656396627, -5715.5941315591335, -6472.038449823856,
 -7226.374643236399, -7978.357610076666, -8727.743215203285,
 -9474.288]
```

> **NOTE**
>
> To access the source code for this specific section, please refer to https://packt.live/3irS3Bk.
>
> You can also run this example online at https://packt.live/3abV9pe.

OPERATIONS AND MULTIPLICATION IN MATRICES

Now that we understand how to perform simple operations, let's perform a number of operations, such as resize, reshape, and transpose, over a matrix that results in the formation of a new matrix.

When indices of rows and columns in a matrix are exchanged, flipping them along the diagonal, this is known as the transpose of a matrix. Let's now examine how to transpose a matrix. This can be done in three different ways, as follows:

```
print("matrix z: ")
print(z)

# Transpose matrix
# Method 1
print("new matrix: ")
print(np.transpose(z))

# Method 2
```

```
print(z.transpose())

# Method 3
t = z.transpose()
print(t)
```

If you run this code, the output will be as follows:

```
matrix z:
[[1 2]
 [3 4]]

new matrix:
[[1 3]
 [2 4]]

[[1 3]
 [2 4]]

[[1 3]
 [2 4]]
[Finished in 0.207s]
```

In method 3, we assign the value of the transpose matrix to a new variable that will hold the value.

The functions that we will now see are among the most widely used while you are performing matrix manipulation.

The first function we will be dealing with is flattening. The process of converting a matrix into a single row is known as the **flattening of a matrix**:

```
# Flatten the array
y = z.ravel()
print(y)
```

This produces the following output:

```
[1 2 3 4]
```

Let's now have a look at the various comparison operators:

```
# Comparison operators on matrix
print(z == 3)
```

In this case, all the values inside a matrix are compared to a base value (in this case, **3**) and Boolean results are displayed against the corresponding indices in a matrix. The output is as follows:

```
[[False False]
 [ True False]]
```

To check whether the value of **z** is less than **3**, use the following code:

```
print(z < 3 )
```

The output is as follows:

```
[[ True  True]
 [False False]]
```

reshape is a function used to change the dimensions of a matrix according to the values passed for row and column inside the function. To reshape the matrix, use the following code:

```
# Reshaping the matrix
r = z.reshape(4,1)
print(r)
```

This produces the following output:

```
[[1]
 [2]
 [3]
 [4]]
```

To resize the matrix, use the following code:

```
# Resizing the matrix
resize = np.resize(z, (3,3))
print(resize)
```

This produces the following output:

```
 [[1 2 3]
 [4 1 2]
 [3 4 1]]
[Finished in 0.205s]
```

Note here how, when we use the **resize** function, the values are iteratively repeated until the size is met, even though all values from the original matrix may not be added. Also, note that the **reshape** function is often used instead of the **ravel** function to flatten the matrix.

AXES IN A MATRIX

This relatively simple topic is easy to understand and equally easy to misunderstand and, hence, we need to deal with it independently. For arrays in Python, axes are defined for any matrix or array that has more than one dimension. When dealing with complex data science and data manipulation problems, oftentimes, we will need to deal with more than two dimensions, which is difficult to visualize and can be confusing. To simplify this, the dimensions in matrices are represented by axes.

Simply speaking, a 2D matrix will have two axes, horizontal and vertical, but in this case, they will be represented or named numerically. The first axis, called *axis 0*, runs vertically downward across rows, and the second, called *axis 1*, runs horizontally across columns.

The same set of functions that we used earlier can be used to run along a single axis, which, in the case of large datasets, reduces the overhead of calculations. Let's deal with some examples. For clarity, we will be creating a slightly larger matrix:

```
import numpy as np
z = np.array([[1, 5, 9, 4],\
              [8, 3, 7, 6]])
print(z.max(axis = 0))
print(z.max(axis = 1))
```

This produces the following output:

```
[8 5 9 6]
[9 8]
[Finished in 0.198s]
```

What happened here is that the maximum value is calculated along *each* of the axes. In the first array that is returned, the comparison is between **1** and **8**, **5** and **3**, **9** and **7**, and **4** and **6**, as those are the only two elements along axis 0. Similarly, in the case of axis 1, the comparison is between the four elements along the subarrays and the maximum element is returned.

Let's take another example:

```
print(z.sum(axis = 1))
```

Can you guess the result? Let's have a look at the output:

```
[19 24]
[Finished in 0.255s]
```

Let's now look at one last, more complex, example:

```
print(np.concatenate((z[1], z[0]), axis=0))
```

This produces the following output:

```
[8 3 7 6 1 5 9 4]
[Finished in 0.252s]
```

What we have done is firstly use a concatenation function that accepts two arrays. The two arrays taken are simply the first and second elements of the array **`z`**, which are **`[8 3 7 6]`** and **`[1 5 9 4]`**, respectively. Since the two arrays each have a single dimension, we have taken them along axis 0. If we had entered axis 1 here, NumPy would throw **`AxisError`**, as shown here:

```
print(np.concatenate((z[1], z[0]), axis=1))
```

This produces the following output:

```
Traceback (most recent call last):
  File "/matrix.py", line 9, in <module>
    print(np.concatenate((z[1], z[0]), axis=1))
numpy.core._internal.AxisError: axis 1 is out of bounds for array of
dimension 1
```

EXERCISE 6.02: MATRIX SEARCH

In this exercise, we will be searching for a given input value in a matrix that is sorted in ascending order, both row- and column-wise. This will help us understand the general rules of traversal inside a matrix, especially if we are not using a NumPy array.

To give a spoiler, we will be implementing a binary search over a matrix. Even if you have not dealt with a binary search before, this will be easy enough to follow.

The aim is to return a **True** or **False** value, depending on whether the value is present inside the matrix:

1. Let's define the input matrix that we are going to search:

```
matrix = [[7, 10, 15, 18],\
          [25, 29, 35, 47],\
           [56, 78, 85, 104]]
```

2. Now, let's define and write a function, **matrixsearch()**, that will take this matrix as an input along with the value we have to search. We will first be covering the edge cases, which, in this instance, means where a matrix is empty or the target value is non-zero:

```
def matrixsearch(matrix, value):
    # Check for edge cases
    if value is None or not matrix:
         return False
```

3. Next, we will be defining four variables:

```
# Initialize the variables
    row = len(matrix)
    col = len(matrix[0])
    start = 0
    end   = row * col - 1
```

   Please note here how **row** and **column** variables are initialized. In any matrix, this is exactly how they will be initialized, and it is worth understanding. The **start** and **end** variables are initialized as the first and last values in a matrix as the matrix is already sorted and can be treated as a single list, from starting to the diagonally opposite end.

4. Now comes the actual logic of the program that we will be breaking down into a couple of steps to aid understanding. While looping from start to end, first we find the midpoint of the matrix (treating the matrix as a list):

```
    while start <= end:
        mid = int((start + end) / 2)
```

5. Then, we define a variable named **pointer**, which is initialized by the value of this middle value that we have found:

```
        pointer = matrix[int(mid/col)][int(mid%col)]
        print(int(mid/col), int(mid%col))
```

   Please note that **/** is used for division, and **%** is used as a modulus here. Hence, in the first iteration, their values will be (1,1), respectively.

6. Now, we go to the heart of the binary search, where we increment or decrement our pointer by comparison with the value that we have. If we find the value, we return **True**, or else we keep looping until we can find or return **False** at the end if we cannot find anything:

```
        if pointer == value:
            return True
        elif pointer < value:
            start = mid + 1
        else:
            end = mid - 1
    return False
sol = matrixsearch(matrix, 78)
print(sol)
```

   The output will be as follows:

```
1 1
2 0
2 2
2 1
True
```

In this exercise, we implemented a binary search over a matrix using NumPy and, as per the values of the matrix, our code has returned **True**.

> **NOTE**
>
> To access the source code for this specific section, please refer to https://packt.live/3eVd0Ch.
>
> You can also run this example online at https://packt.live/2ZusZkj.

MULTIPLE MATRICES

So far, we have learned how to perform operations and manipulations when we have a single matrix. Next, we will be dealing with multiple matrices. The combination of matrices with Python is most commonly used today in data science as it requires the storage and processing of large arrays. Let's start with a simple example. We will take two matrices, **z** and **x**, and multiply the values as follows:

```
import numpy as np
z = np.array([[1, 2],\
              [3, 4]])
x = np.array([[4, 5],\
              [7, 8]])
print(np.multiply(x,z))
print(np.multiply(z,x))
```

If you run the preceding code, you'll see the following output:

```
[[ 4 10]
 [21 32]]
[[ 4 10]
 [21 32]]
[Finished in 0.206s]
```

The output shows that intuitively, the respective elements of the two matrices multiply to give a product value. This is simply the element-wise multiplication or, as it is known in mathematics, the Hadamard product.

Let's now change matrix **x** slightly:

```
import numpy as np
z = np.array([[1, 2],\
              [3, 4]])
x = np.array([[4, 5, 6],\
              [7, 8, 9]])

print("Multiplying with a number: ")
print(np.multiply(3,x))
print(np.multiply(x,3))

print("Multiplication between matrices of different sizes: ")
print(np.multiply(x,z))
print(np.multiply(z,x))
```

Now, the output will be as follows:

```
Multiplying with a number:
[[12 15 18]
 [21 24 27]]
[[12 15 18]
 [21 24 27]]
Multiplication between matrices of different sizes:
Traceback (most recent call last):
    File "/Users/.../matrix operations.py", line 52, in <module>
    print(np.multiply(x,z))
ValueError: operands could not be broadcast together with shapes (2,3)
(2,2)
[Finished in 0.204s]
```

What we get here is **`ValueError`**, due to the property of arrays in NumPy known as broadcasting.

BROADCASTING

It is important to understand the concept of broadcasting so that we know what is allowed and not allowed while using arrays for matrix operations.

In simple terms, broadcasting is the NumPy way of handling two arrays that have different shapes. As a general rule, the array that is smaller among the two will be broadcasted across the larger array in a certain way to make them compatible. The general rules for broadcasting as per the official documentation are as follows:

- It starts with trailing dimensions working their way forward.
- The two dimensions of comparison are equal when one of them is 1, or when they both are equal.

> **NOTE**
>
> You can also refer to the official documentation at https://docs.scipy.org/doc/numpy/user/basics.broadcasting.html.

So, as we saw in the earlier examples, when multiplied by matrices of equal dimensions and by a scalar variable, multiplication works perfectly. On the other hand, if the dimensions of the two matrices are different, **`ValueError`** will be thrown as NumPy was not efficiently able to broadcast the values of a smaller matrix across the larger matrix. This broadcasting is primarily done internally to make the arrays faster and more memory efficient. It provides a way to vectorize the array to implement the looping in C instead of Python, which effectively makes it faster. An important thing to remember here is in the case of a pair of NumPy arrays, the operations are done on an element-by-element basis. To help overcome the problem with the dimensions, the two main methods employed are **`reshape`** and **`newaxis`**. Before we wrap this up, let's look at one more variation to the concept of broadcasting:

```
import numpy as np
z = np.array([[1,2],\
              [3]])
x = np.array([[4,5]])
print(np.multiply(x,z))
```

Any guesses what the output will look like? Let's have a look:

```
[[list([1, 2, 1, 2, 1, 2, 1, 2]) list([3, 3, 3, 3, 3])]]
[Finished in 0.244s]
```

Since the array **`z`** here is not a regular square-shaped array, NumPy internally does not interpret it as a matrix, treating it as a regular row of objects and performing element-by-element multiplication on it. So, **`z[0]`** is multiplied by **`x[0]`**, and **`z[1]`** is multiplied by **`x[1]`** to produce objects that happen to be a list in this case.

OPERATIONS ON MULTIPLE MATRICES

We will now be performing operations between two or more matrices and see the functions that will help us to achieve that. We will be covering how to write an inverse of a matrix, logical operators, dot products, eigenvalues and eigenvectors, outer products, and the determinates of a matrix.

It should be noted that there are plenty of other things you can do with matrices, and the official NumPy documentation is a really good resource for referencing information according to the requirements of the user. Most of the topics that we are going to cover are part of the linear algebra package of the NumPy library. There are far wider applications in physics and mathematics that are beyond the scope of this chapter for each of the topics we are going to cover, but it should suffice to know that they all play a very important role in understanding matrices.

> **NOTE**
>
> For more information about the NumPy library, refer to https://docs.scipy.org/doc/numpy/reference/.

IDENTITY MATRIX

Identity matrices have ones along the diagonal, and zeros everywhere else. We will be creating identity matrices using the **linalg** function of NumPy:

```
import numpy as np
from numpy.linalg import inv

def identity():
    print(np.identity(3))
```

The output will be as follows:

```
[[ 1.  0.  0.]
 [ 0.  1.  0.]
 [ 0.  0.  1.]]
[Finished in 0.206s]
```

THE EYE FUNCTION

An **eye** function is similar to an identity matrix, except for one difference, which is that you can offset the value of the matrix. This means that it will create an identity matrix starting from the kth row, as you can see here:

```
def eye():
    print(np.eye(3, k = 1))
```

The output will be as follows:

```
[[ 0.  1.  0.]
 [ 0.  0.  1.]
 [ 0.  0.  0.]]
[Finished in 0.277s]
```

INVERSE OF A MATRIX

Inverse or multiplicative inverse is the matrix that produces an identity matrix when you multiply it by the original matrix. The inverse of a matrix is most commonly used when applied in 3D geometry and graphics:

```
def inverse():
    z = np.array([[1,2],\
                  [3,4]])
    z_inv = inv(z)
    product = np.dot(z, z_inv)
    print(z_inv)
    print(product)
```

This produces the following output:

```
# Output of print(z_inv)
[[-2.   1. ]
 [ 1.5 -0.5]]
# Output of print(product)
 [[  1.00000000e+00   0.00000000e+00]
 [  8.88178420e-16   1.00000000e+00]]
[Finished in 0.202s]
```

We have two outputs here. The first one is what is called the inverse of the matrix, and the second one is where we have multiplied the inverse by the original matrix using the **dot** function to produce the identity matrix. The values displayed are floats and should not be a point of concern.

LOGICAL OPERATORS

We will be creating two lists here, containing binary **True** (1) or **False** (0) values. We will see the output of using the **AND** operation on them by using the built-in **logical_and()** function of NumPy:

```
def and_op():
    m1 = [True, False, False]
    m2 = [True, False, True]
    print(np.logical_and(m1, m2))
```

The output will be as follows:

```
[ True False False]
[Finished in 0.253s]
```

Pretty straightforward. You can similarly use 1s and 0s instead of **True** and **False** and it still gives the results. In fact, as long as it is not 0, it is considered to be **True**. Let's see an example with 1s and 0s:

```
def and_op():
    m1 = [0, 1, 0]
    m2 = [1, 1, 0]
    print(np.logical_and(m1, m2))
```

This output will be as follows:

```
[False  True False]
[Finished in 0.192s]
```

The same thing can be done for other logical functions using the **logical_or**, **logical_not**, and **logical_xor** functions.

OUTER FUNCTION OR VECTOR PRODUCT

np.outer is the function that is used to produce a vector or the cross product of two matrices:

```
def vector():
    horizontal = np.array([[1,3,2]])

    vertical = np.array([[2],\
                         [0],\
                         [1]])
```

```
    print("Output for dimension 1 x 1: ")
    print(horizontal.dot(vertical))

    print("Output for dimension 3 x 3: ")
    print(vertical.dot(horizontal))

    print("Output using outer for getting cross product: ")
    print(np.outer(vertical.ravel(), horizontal.ravel()))
    print(np.outer(horizontal.ravel(), vertical.ravel()))
```

This produces the following output:

```
Output for dimension 1 x 1:
[[4]]

Output for dimension 3 x 3:
[[2 6 4]
 [0 0 0]
 [1 3 2]]

Output using outer for getting cross product:
[[2 6 4]
 [0 0 0]
 [1 3 2]]
[[2 0 1]
 [6 0 3]
 [4 0 2]]
[Finished in 0.289s]
```

So far, we have learned all the different ways in which we can use matrices. By no means can the list of methods we use be considered restrictive, and it is always a good practice to explore the libraries in detail as and when a certain manipulation needs to be done. It is also worth mentioning again that there are several specific types of matrices that have a limited use case depending on the requirements of the field in which the work is done.

SOLVING LINEAR EQUATIONS USING MATRICES

Linear equations are the foundational blocks of algebra, and anyone who has studied basic elementary mathematics knows how they work. Let's cover them briefly, and we can then see how easily they can be solved using matrices in Python.

Linear equations are typically in the form:

$$a_1 x_1 + \ldots + a_n x_n + b = 0,$$

Figure 6.5: Formula for calculating linear equations

Here, $a_1, a_2,.., a_n$ are the coefficients, and $x_1, x_2,.. x_n$ are variables.

These linear equations with two variables can be represented in a two-dimensional space graph where *x* is the horizontal dimension and *y* is the vertical dimension.

Let's take a quick example of a linear equation with two variables. Suppose the equation is *y = 2x + 6*. This representation is known as the **slope-intercept** form and has the format *y = mx + c*, where *m* is the slope and *c* is the *y* intercept of the equation.

Here, *m=2* and *c=6*, and the line can be drawn on a graph by plotting different values of *x* and *y*:

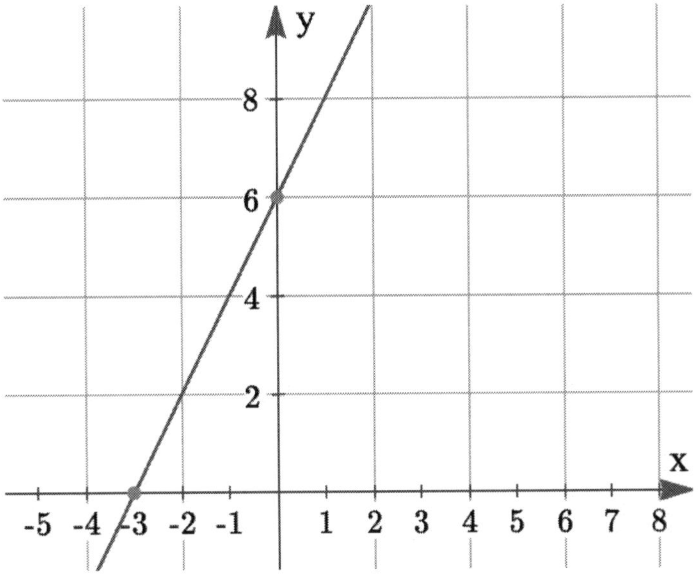

Figure 6.6: Representation of y = 2x + 6 in a 2D space

Without getting into much detail, we can imagine that there may be another line in the plane that will either be parallel to the line or will intersect this line. The linear equations intend to find the intersecting point of these lines and, based on the value of the intersecting common point, find the values of the variables *x* and *y*. As the number of dimensions increase, it becomes difficult to visualize, but fundamentally, the concept remains the same. Matrices greatly simplify the process of solving these equations. There are typically two matrices, one that contains the coefficient of *x* and *y*, and the other containing the variables *x* and *y*. Their dot product yields the resultant matrix, which is the constant or the *y* intercept mentioned previously. It is fairly easy to understand once we look at a quick exercise.

EXERCISE 6.03: USE OF MATRICES IN PERFORMING LINEAR EQUATIONS

We will now solve a linear equation problem using matrices.

John is out of town for three days and in a mood to spend until he exhausts his resources. He has three denominations of currency with him. On the first day, John spends $435 on the latest electronic tablet that he likes, on which he spends `37` of type *a* denomination, `20` of type *b*, and `12` of type *c*. On the second day, he goes skydiving and spends `15`, `32`, and `4` of denominations *a*, *b*, and *c*, respectively, a total of $178. On the third day, with whatever amount he is left with, he decides to go to the theatre, which costs $70, and he shells out `5`, `40`, and `2` of the *a*, *b*, and *c* denominations, respectively. Can you tell what the values of the respective denominations are?

Looking at the problem, we can tell that there are three equations and three unknown variables that we need to calculate.

1. Let's put the values we know for three days in a matrix using NumPy arrays:

```
import numpy as np

# Input
z = np.array([[37, 20, 12],\
              [15, 32, 4],\
              [5,  40, 2]])
```

   We now have the matrix that we need to work with. There are a few ways to solve this. In essence, this is what we need to do:

   $Ax = b$

   Where *A* is the matrix whose values we know, *x* is the matrix with unknown variables, and *b* is the resultant matrix.

2. The resultant *b* matrix will be as follows. These are the amounts that John spent on the three given days:

```
r = np.array([[435],[178],[70]])
```

There are a couple of ways to solve this problem in Python:

Method 1: Finding *x* by doing x = A^{-1}b:

3. Let's first calculate the inverse of matrix A with the help of the function we learned earlier:

```
print(np.linalg.inv(z))
```

> **NOTE**
>
> We will be using a dot product of the matrix and not pure multiplication, as these are not scalar variables.

The output is as follows:

```
[[-0.06282723  0.28795812 -0.19895288]
 [-0.0065445   0.0091623   0.02094241]
 [ 0.28795812 -0.90314136  0.57853403]]
```

It is not necessary here to understand this matrix as it is just an intermediary step.

4. Then, we take the dot product of the two matrices to produce a matrix, **X**, which is our output:

```
X = np.linalg.inv(z).dot(r)
print(X)
```

The output will be as follows:

```
[[10.  ]
 [ 0.25]
 [ 5.  ]]
```

Method 2: Using in-built methods in the **`linalg`** package:

5. This same thing can be done even more easily with the help of another NumPy function called **solve()**. Let's name the output variable here as **y**.

```
y = np.linalg.solve(z,r)
print(y)
```

This produces the following output:

```
[[10.  ]
 [ 0.25]
 [ 5.  ]]
```

And in a single line, we were able to solve the linear equation in Python. We can extrapolate and comprehend how similar equations with a large number of unknown variables can be easily solved using Python.

Thus, we can see that the output after using both methods 1 and 2 is the same, which is $10, 25 cents, and $5, which are the respective denominations that we were trying to establish.

What if we were receiving the information about John's expenses iteratively instead of in one go?

6. Let's first add the information that we received about John's expenses:

```
a = np.array([[37, 20, 12]])
```

7. Then, let's also add the information received relating to John's other two expenses:

```
b = np.array([[15, 32, 4]])
c = np.array([[5,  40, 2]])
```

8. We can easily bind these arrays together to form a matrix using the **concat()** function:

```
u = np.concatenate((a, b, c), axis=0)
print(u)
```

This produces the following output:

```
[[37 20 12]
 [15 32  4]
 [ 5 40  2]]
[Finished in 0.188s]
```

This was the same input that we used for the preceding program.

Again, if we have a lot more of these, we might apply loops to form a larger matrix, which we can then use to solve the problem.

> **NOTE**
>
> To access the source code for this specific section, please refer to https://packt.live/3eStF9N.
>
> You can also run this example online at https://packt.live/38rZ6Fl.

TRANSITION MATRIX AND MARKOV CHAINS

Now, we will be looking at one of the applications of matrices, which is a field of study all by itself. Markov chains make use of transition matrices, probability, and limits to solve real-world problems. The real world is rarely as perfect as the mathematical models we create to solve them. A car may want to travel from point A to B, but distance and speed prove insufficient parameters in reality. A cat crossing the street may completely alter all the calculations that were made to calculate the time traveled by the car. A stock market may seem to be following a predictable pattern for a few days, but overnight, an event occurs that completely crashes it. That event may be some global event, a political statement, or the release of company reports. Of course, our development in mathematical and computational models has still not reached the place where we can predict the outcome of each of these events, but we can try and determine the probability of some event happening more than others. Taking one of the previous examples, if the company reports are to be released on a particular date, then we can expect that a particular stock will be affected, and we can model this according to market analysis done on the company.

Markov chains are one such model, in which the variable depending on the Markov property takes into account only the *current state* to predict the outcome of the next state. So, in essence, Markov chains are a memoryless process. They make use of transition state diagrams and transition matrices for their representations, which are used to map the probability of a certain event occurring given the current event. When we call it a memoryless process, it is easy to confuse it with something that has no relation to past events, but that is not actually the case. Things are much easier to understand when we take an example to illustrate how they work. Before we jump into using Markov chains, let's first take a deeper look at how transition states and matrices work and why exactly they are used.

FUNDAMENTALS OF MARKOV CHAINS

To keep things simple, let's break the concepts down into pieces and learn about them iteratively from the information that we have before we can put them together to understand the concepts.

STOCHASTIC VERSUS DETERMINISTIC MODELS

When we are trying to solve real-world problems, we often encounter situations that are beyond our control and that are hard to formulate. Models are designed to emulate the way a given system functions. While we can factor in most of the elements of the system in our model, many aspects cannot be *determined* and are then emulated based on their likelihood of happening. This is where probability comes into the picture. We try and find the probability of a particular event happening given a set of circumstances. There are two main types of models that we use, deterministic and stochastic. Deterministic models are those that have a set of parameter values and functions and can form a predictable mathematical equation and will provide a predictable output. Stochastic models are inclusive of randomness, and even though they have initial values and equations, they provide quantitative values of outcomes possible with some probability. In stochastic models, there will not be a fixed answer, but the likelihood of some event happening more than others. Linear programming is a good example of deterministic models, while weather prediction is a stochastic model.

TRANSITION STATE DIAGRAMS

Broadly, these form the basis for object-oriented programming, where you can describe all possible states that object can have based on given events and conditions. The *state* is that of the object at a given moment in time when a certain previous condition is met. Let's illustrate this with an example:

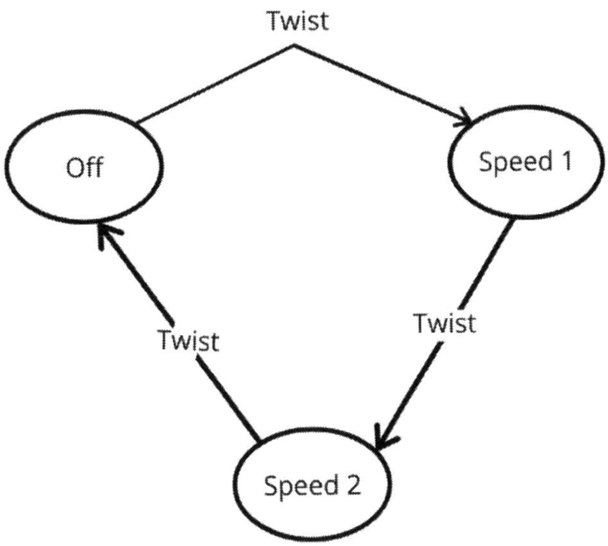

Figure 6.7: State transition diagram for a fan

This is the state transition diagram for the regulator of a table fan, which usually changes state every time we turn it clockwise until it turns back to the `Off` position.

Here, the state of the table fan is changing in terms of the speed, while the action is that of twisting. In this case, it is based on events, while in some other cases it will be based on a condition being met.

Let's take an example in text generation using the Markov chain that is in line with what we are going to implement. We will recall the first two lines of a nursery rhyme:

Humpty Dumpty sat on a wall,

Humpty Dumpty had a great fall.

First, let's prepare a frequency table of all the words present in the sentence:

Word	Frequency
Humpty	2
Dumpty	2
sat	1
on	1
a	2
wall	1
had	1
great	1
fall	1

Figure 6.8: Frequency table of words in the rhyme

Tokens are the number of words present, while keys are unique words. Hence, the values will be as follows:

Tokens = 12

Keys = 9

We may not even require everything we learn here, but it will be important once you decide to implement more complicated problems. Every transition diagram has a start and end state, and so we will add these two states here as keys:

Word	Frequency
start	1
end	1

Figure 6.9: Frequency table of start and end states

We then prepare a state chart to show the transition from one state to the next. In this case, it requires showing which word will follow the current word. So, we will be forming pairs as follows:

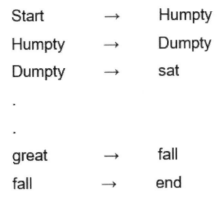

Start	→	Humpty
Humpty	→	Dumpty
Dumpty	→	sat
.		
.		
great	→	fall
fall	→	end

Figure 6.10: Word pairs

If we condense this according to keys instead of tokens, we will see that there is more than one transition for some keywords, as follows:

Dumpty	→	sat, had
a	→	wall, great

Figure 6.11: More than one transition for some keywords

This is done not only to reduce the state transitions, but also to add meaning to what we are doing, which we will see shortly. The whole purpose of this is to determine words that can pair with other words. We are now ready to draw our state transition diagram.

We add all the unique keys as states, and show which states these words can transition to:

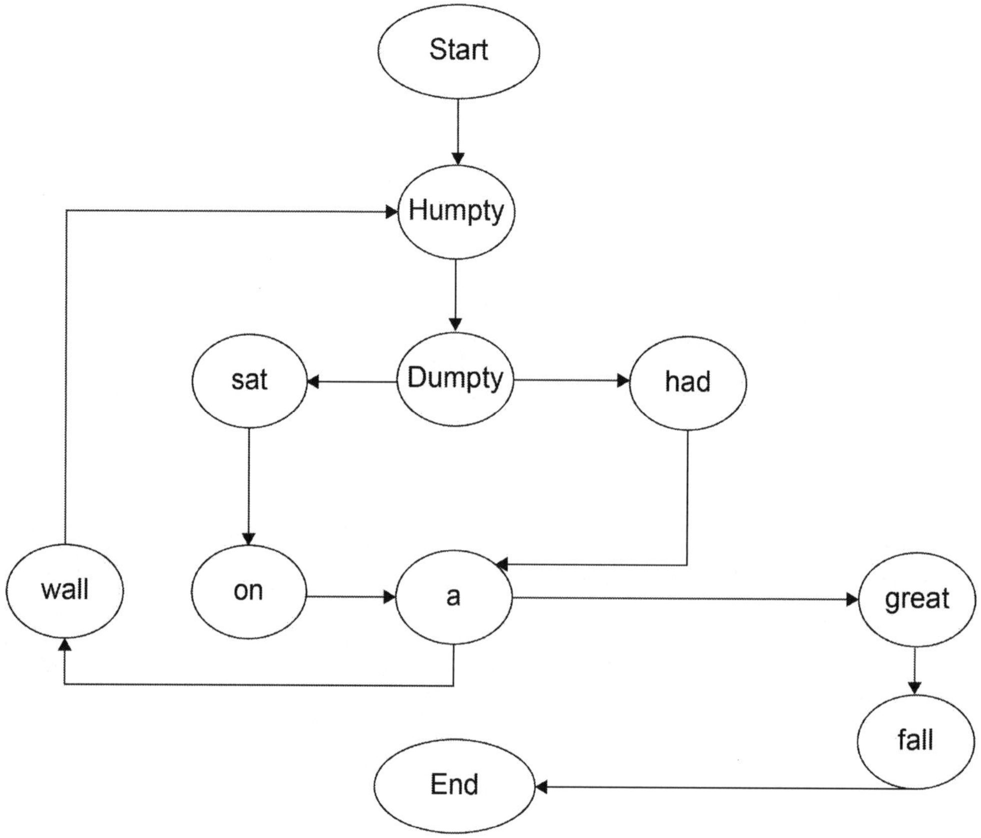

Figure 6.12: State transition diagram

If we look at the preceding diagram, we can follow any word to complete the rhyme from the set of conditions given. What remains is the probability of the keywords occurring after the given word. For that, look at the following diagram, and we can see in a fairly straightforward manner how the probability is divided between keywords according to their frequency. Note that Humpty is always followed by Dumpty, and so will have a probability of **1**:

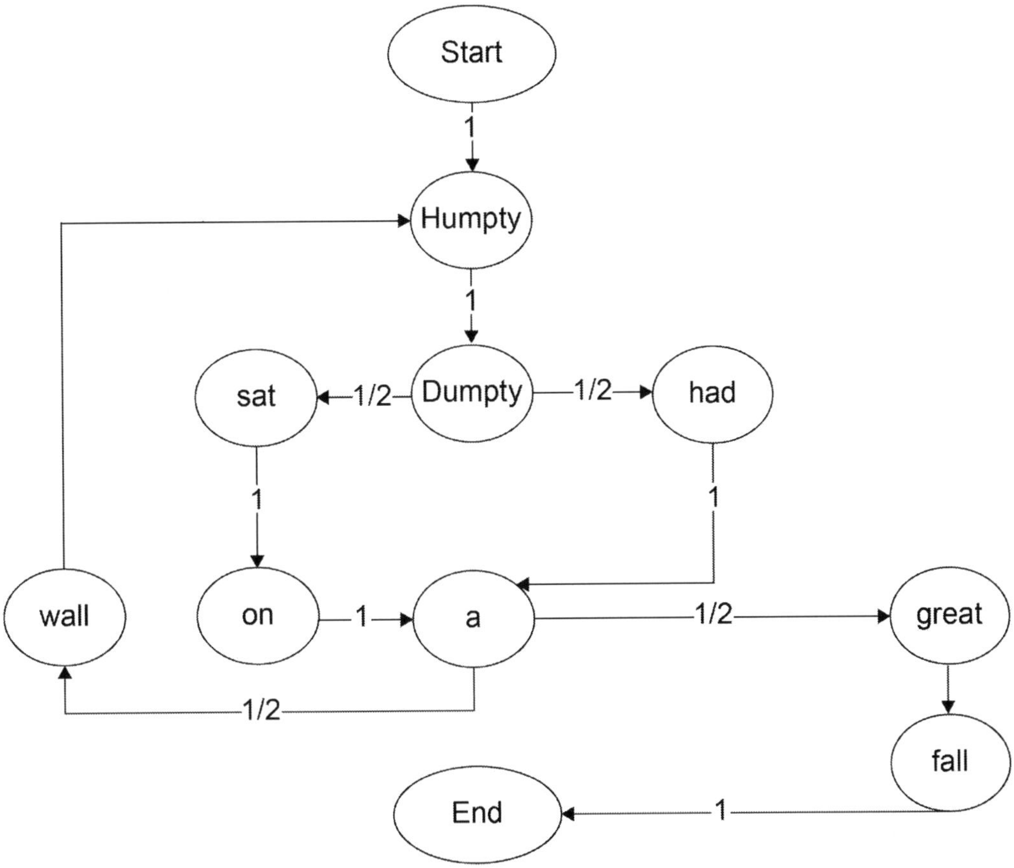

Figure 6.13: State transition diagram with probability

Now that we have discussed the state transition diagrams, we will move on to drawing transition matrices.

TRANSITION MATRICES

In the Markov process, we need to show the probability of state transitions in mathematical format for which transition matrices are used. The rows and columns are simply the states of the transition diagram. Each value in the transition matrix shows the probability of transition from one state to another. As you can imagine, many of the values in such matrices will be 0. For the problem discussed earlier, the transition matrix will have 9 states and lots of 0s. We will take a simpler example of a transition diagram and find its corresponding matrix:

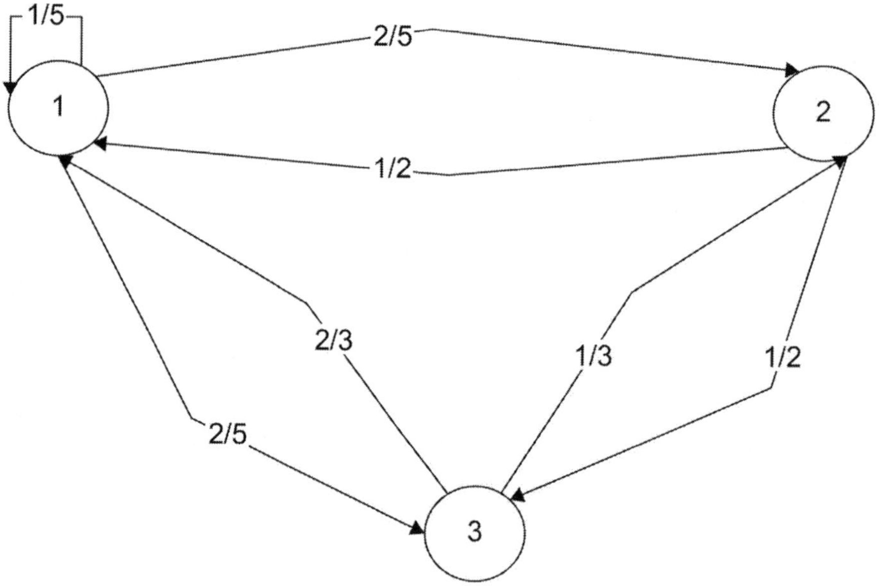

Figure 6.14: State diagram with states 1, 2, and 3

When we look at this diagram, we see the three transition states. Note that we have not included the start and end states explicitly here, but they can be necessary in certain cases. The outward arrows represent the transition from one state to the next. Once we have the diagram, it is easy to draw the matrix. Write rows and columns equal to the states of the diagram. In this case, it will be 3. Then, the 0th row will show the transition for the 1st state, the 1st row will show the second state, and so on. To generalize, each row in the matrix represents the transition probabilities of one state.

Let's first look at the matrix, and we can then discuss a couple more things:

$$\begin{bmatrix} 1/5 & 2/5 & 2/5 \\ 1/2 & 0 & 1/2 \\ 2/3 & 1/3 & 0 \end{bmatrix}$$

Figure 6.15: Transition matrix

In addition to the property of rows, we can observe one more thing. The sum of all probabilities in a given row will always be equal to 1. In the first row here, the sum will be *1/5 + 2/5 + 2/5 = 5/5 = 1*. This is because these states are exhaustive.

If there is no transition between two given states, the value of the states in that matrix will be 0. We can verify this by comparing the number of values present in the matrix with the number of state transitions we can see in the diagram. In this case, they are both equal to 7.

EXERCISE 6.04: FINDING THE PROBABILITY OF STATE TRANSITIONS

Given an array containing four states, **A**, **B**, **C**, and **D**, that are randomly generated, let's find the probability of transition between these four states. We will be finding the probability of each state transition and form a transition matrix from it.

Let's generate a transition matrix in Python from a given array of inputs. We will extrapolate the same concept in the future while creating Markov chains.

1. Generate an array of random states out of the characters **A**, **B**, **C**, and **D** using the **random** package in Python. We will then define how many elements we want by creating a constant, **LEN_STR**, which, in this case, we will set to **50**:

```
# Generate random letters from 4 states A B C D
import random
tokens = []
LEN_STR = 50
for i in range(LEN_STR):
    tokens.append(random.choice("ABCD"))
print(tokens)
LEN_TOKENS = len("ABCD")
```

This produces the following output:

```
['C', 'A', 'A', 'B', 'A', 'A', 'D', 'C', 'B', 'A', 'B',
 'A', 'A', 'D', 'A', 'A', 'C', 'B', 'C', 'D', 'D', 'C',
 'C', 'B', 'A', 'D', 'D', 'C', 'A', 'A', 'D', 'C', 'A',
 'D', 'A', 'A', 'A', 'C', 'B', 'D', 'D', 'C', 'A', 'A',
 'B', 'A', 'C', 'A', 'D', 'D']
```

> **NOTE**
>
> The use of another constant, **LEN_TOKENS**, which we created from the length of the string, will indicate the number of states that will be present in the problem.

2. Next, we will be finding the relative values of letters and converting them into integers, primarily because integers are easier for calculations:

```
# Finding the relative values with ordinal values of
# ASCII characters
relative_value = [(ord(t) - ord('A')) for t in tokens]
print(relative_value)
```

This produces the following output:

```
[2, 0, 0, 1, 0, 0, 3, 2, 1, 0, 1, 0, 0, 3, 0, 0, 2, 1,
 2, 3, 3, 2, 2, 1, 0, 3, 3, 2, 0, 0, 3, 2, 0, 3, 0, 0,
 0, 2, 1, 3, 3, 2, 0, 0, 1, 0, 2, 0, 3, 3]
```

We have used cardinal values here for convenience, but we could have also done this by using a dictionary or some other method. If you are not aware, the **ord()** function here returns the ASCII value of characters in the string. For example, the ASCII values for **A** and **D** are **65** and **68**, respectively.

3. Now, find the difference between these ASCII values and put them in a list, **ti**. We could have also updated the token list in situ, but we are keeping them separate simply for clarity:

```
#create Matrix of zeros
m = [[0]*LEN_TOKENS for j in range(LEN_TOKENS)]
print(m)

# Building the frequency table(matrix) from the given data
for (i,j) in zip(relative_value, relative_value [1:]):
    m[i][j] += 1
```

```
print(list(zip(relative_value, relative_value [1:])))

print(m)
```

This produces the following output:

```
[[0, 0, 0, 0], [0, 0, 0, 0], [0, 0, 0, 0], [0, 0, 0, 0]]

[(2, 0), (0, 0), (0, 1), (1, 0), (0, 0), (0, 3), (3, 2),
 (2, 1), (1, 0), (0, 1), (1, 0), (0, 0), (0, 3), (3, 0),
 (0, 0), (0, 2), (2, 1), (1, 2), (2, 3), (3, 3), (3, 2),
 (2, 2), (2, 1), (1, 0), (0, 3), (3, 3), (3, 2), (2, 0),
 (0, 0), (0, 3), (3, 2), (2, 0), (0, 3), (3, 0), (0, 0),
 (0, 0), (0, 2), (2, 1), (1, 3), (3, 3), (3, 2), (2, 0),
 (0, 0), (0, 1), (1, 0), (0, 2), (2, 0), (0, 3), (3, 3)]

[[8, 3, 3, 6], [5, 0, 1, 1], [5, 4, 1, 1], [2, 0, 5, 4]]
```

We have now initialized a matrix of zeros depending on the size of the **LEN_TOKENS** constant we generated earlier and used that to build a zero matrix.

In the second part, we are creating tuples of pairs, as we did in the earlier problem, and updating the frequency of the transition matrix according to the number of transitions between two states. The output of this is the last line in the preceding code.

> **NOTE**
>
> We are iteratively choosing to update the value of matrix *m* in each step instead of creating new matrices.

4. We will now be generating the probability, which is merely the relative frequency in a given row. As in the first row, the transition from A to A is 8, and the total transitions from A to any state are 20. So, in this case, the probability will be *8/20 = 0.4*:

```
# Finding the Probability
for state in m:
    total = sum(state)
    if total > 0:
        state[:] = [float(f)/sum(state) for f in state]
```

The code goes like that for every row and, if the **sum** function is greater than **0**, we find the probability. Note here that the **float** function is used to avoid type conversion to **int** in some versions of Python. Also, note the use of **state[:]**, which creates a shallow copy and thereby prevents conflicts of type conversions internally.

5. Now, let's print the **state** object by adding the following code:

```
for state in m:
        print(state)
```

Here, we iterate through the rows in a matrix and print out the values, and this is our transition matrix.

This produces the following output:

```
[0.4, 0.15, 0.15, 0.3]
[0.7142857142857143, 0.0, 0.14285714285714285,
 0.14285714285714285]
[0.45454545454545453, 0.36363636363636365,
 0.09090909090909091, 0.09090909090909091]
[0.18181818181818182, 0.0, 0.45454545454545453,
 0.36363636363636365]
```

Thus, we are able to construct a transition matrix for describing state transitions, which shows us the probability of transition from one state to the next. Hence, the likelihood of **A** finding **A** as the next letter is **0.4**, **A** going to **B** will be **0.15**, and so on.

> **NOTE**
>
> To access the source code for this specific section, please refer to https://packt.live/31Ejr9c.
>
> You can also run this example online at https://packt.live/3imNsAb.

MARKOV CHAINS AND MARKOV PROPERTY

Transition states and matrices essentially cover the majority of Markov chains. Additionally, there are a few more things worth understanding. As mentioned earlier, the Markov property applies when variables are dependent on just the current state for their next state. The probabilistic model formed may determine the likelihood of the outcome from the current state, but the past state is seen as independent and will not affect the result. Take a coin toss; we may create a chart of probabilities of heads or tails, but that will not determine the outcome.

The Markov property should essentially meet two criteria:

- It should only be dependent on the current state.
- It should be specific for a discrete time.

Without getting too confused, the time considered in models is either discrete or continuous. The flipping of a coin can be considered a discrete-time event because it has a definite outcome, such as heads or tails. On the other hand, weather patterns or stock markets are continuous-time events; weather, for example, is variable throughout the day and does not have a start and end time to measure when it changes. To deal with such continuous events, we require techniques such as binning to make them discrete. Binning, in simple terms, means grouping data in fixed amounts based on quantity or time. As a Markov chain is memoryless, it essentially becomes a discrete-time and state-space process.

There are special matrices that are built for specific purposes. For example, sparse matrices are extensively used in data science as they are memory- and computationally-efficient. We did not deal too much with the manipulation of elements within the matrix as that is essentially like dealing with a list of lists, but it is worthwhile spending some time on this in the future.

Other than Markov chains, there are a few more models for random processes. These include autoregressive models, Poisson models, Gaussian models, moving-average models, and so on. Each deals with the aspect of randomness differently, and there are supporting libraries in Python for almost all of them. Even within Markov chains, there are complicated topics involving multidimensional matrices or second-order matrices, Hidden Markov models, MCMC or Markov chain Monte Carlo methods, and so on. You have to make your own choice of how deep you want to go down the rabbit hole.

ACTIVITY 6.01: BUILDING A TEXT PREDICTOR USING A MARKOV CHAIN

The aim of this activity is to build our very own text predictor based on what we have learned. We will take the transcripts of a speech from a famous leader and build a text predictor based on the content of the speech using a Markov chain model and state transitions. Perform these steps to achieve the goal:

1. First, find a suitable, sufficiently large transcript of a speech given by a famous person, such as a scientist or a political or spiritual leader of your choice. To get you started, a sample text with the filename **`churchill.txt`** is added to the GitHub repository at https://packt.live/38rZy6v.

2. Generate a list that describes state transition by showing a correlation between a given word and the words that follow it.

3. Sort through the list you have made and make a hash table by grouping the words that follow a given word in different positions. For example, these follow-up words will group to form *John: [cannot, completely, thought, ...]*:

   John cannot..., John completely..., and John thought ..,

4. Use a random word generator to generate and assign a value to the first word.

5. Finally, create a random generator that will create a sentence based on the transition states that we have declared.

> **HINTS**
>
> This activity requires a few Python methods that you should be familiar with.
>
> To get you started, you can read in the transcript from a text file using **`open('churchill.txt').read()`**, and then split it into a list of words using **`split()`**.
>
> You can then iterate through the list and append the elements to a new list, which will store the keyword and the word following it.
>
> Then, use a dictionary to form a key-value pair for each tuple in your new list.
>
> A random word corpus can be generated using the **`np.random()`** function.
>
> The sentence formation comes from joining together the elements of the list that we generated.

> **NOTE**
>
> The solution to this activity can be found on page 677.

This way, we have made our own text predictor. Such a text predictor can be considered a foundational step in terms of the vast and fast-growing field of text generators. It is far from perfect; there are several reasons for this, some of which are as follows:

- The text sample that we have chosen is usually many times larger than the one we have chosen. Our text contains about 22,000 words while, in practice, millions of words are fed as data.
- There is a lot better moderation in terms of the stop words, punctuation, and beginning/ending of sentence formations using the proper rules of NLP that is not applied here.
- We have used a simple random generator to select our words, while actual models use probability and statistical models to generate significantly more accurate outputs.

Having said that, we have completed our first text predictor, and more complicated text predictors are fundamentally based on the way we have described them.

Though by no means can this be considered smooth, we have still written our first text predictor with just a few lines of code, and that is a great start.

SUMMARY

In this chapter, we were able to cover the topic of matrices, which is fundamental to a number of topics, both in mathematics and in using Python. Data science today is primarily based on the efficient use of matrices. We studied their application in the form of Markov chains and, although an important topic, there is no dearth of topics to explore that come under the umbrella of applications using matrices.

Next, we will delve into the world of statistics. We will use a more formal and systematic approach in first understanding the building blocks of statistics, then understanding the role of probability and variables, and finally tying these concepts together to implement statistical modeling.

7

DOING BASIC STATISTICS WITH PYTHON

OVERVIEW

In this chapter, we'll learn how to use the main descriptive statistics metrics and also produce and understand the main visualizations used in Exploratory Data Analysis.

By the end of this chapter, you will be able to load and prepare a dataset for basic statistical analysis, calculate and use the main descriptive statistics metrics, use descriptive statistics to understand numerical and categorical variables, and use visualizations to study relationships between variables.

INTRODUCTION

Python and its analytical libraries, such as pandas and Matplotlib, make it very easy to perform both simple and complex statistical calculations on many types of datasets. This chapter introduces the first steps for any statistical analysis: defining and understanding the problem, loading and preparing the dataset, and after that, understanding the variables individually and exploring some relationships between them.

This chapter consists of three sections: in the first section, we introduce the dataset we will be using in this chapter along with a hypothetical (yet very realistic) business problem. Then we load the dataset and perform many of the common tasks of data preparation, including changing variable types and filtering for useful observations. With the dataset ready, the second section presents a brief conceptual introduction to the main metrics of descriptive statistics, then this knowledge is immediately applied to the dataset we are working with. As part of this, we will produce an example of how to translate the information of descriptive statistics into knowledge. The third section introduces the learner to the practice of **Exploratory Data Analysis** (**EDA**). Beginning with some questions and basic calculations, we complement our understanding of basic statistics with some of the most useful statistical visualizations, such as histograms, boxplots, and scatterplots.

This chapter will take a different approach from that traditionally taken in other treatments of the subject; rather than just presenting the statistical concepts, we will be more practical and use them as tools for doing data analysis, which means transforming data into information and information into knowledge.

DATA PREPARATION

All applied statistics starts with a dataset and a problem to solve. In the real world, we never do statistical analysis in a vacuum; there is always a business problem to solve, a topic that needs to be quantitatively understood, or a scientific question to ask. Understanding the problem is always the very first step of any statistical analysis. The second step is to collect and prepare the data. Data collection is not a topic of this book, so we will go directly into data preparation. Therefore, before diving into doing some statistical calculations, we need to make sure we understand our business problem and that we have prepared our dataset.

INTRODUCING THE DATASET

In this subsection, we will introduce the dataset we will use in this chapter and perform some basic data preparation tasks. Knowing the dataset will give you a bit more context when we define the business problem.

We are going to use the **strategy games** dataset, which contains real-world information about strategy games from the Apple App Store (available at https://www.kaggle.com/tristan581/17k-apple-app-store-strategy-games, under the following license: Attribution 4.0 International (CC BY 4.0)). It was collected in August 2019 and it contains 18 columns from about 17,000 strategy games. The description of the columns the file contains is as follows:

- **URL**: The URL of the game
- **ID**: The assigned ID
- **Name**: The name of the game
- **Subtitle**: The secondary text under the name
- **Icon URL**: 512 px x 512 px JPG
- **Average User Rating**: Rounded to the nearest 0.5
- **User Rating Count**: Number of ratings internationally; null means it is below 5
- **Price**: Price in USD
- **In-app Purchases**: Prices of available in-app purchases
- **Description**: App description
- **Developer**: App developer
- **Age Rating**: Either 4+, 9+, 12+, or 17+
- **Languages**: ISO2A language codes
- **Size**: Size of the app in bytes
- **Primary Genre**: The main genre
- **Genres**: Genres of the app
- **Original Release Date**: When it was released

- **Current Version Release Date**: When it was last updated

> **NOTE**
>
> You can also download the dataset from the GitHub repository at https://packt.live/2O1hv2B.

INTRODUCING THE BUSINESS PROBLEM

We will use this dataset along with a fictional business problem to learn how to turn data into information and information into useful recommendations. Imagine it is a glorious Monday morning and you are enjoying an excellent cup of a premium Guatemalan coffee. As part of a talented analytics team, you receive the following news:

The CEO of the game development company you work for has come up with a plan to strengthen the position of the company in the gaming market. From his industry knowledge and other business reports, he knows that a very effective way to attract new customers is to develop a great reputation in the mobile game space. Given this fact, he has the following plan: develop a strategy game for the iOS platform that will get a lot of positive attention, which in turn will bring a large number of new customers to the company. He is sure his plan will work if and only if the game gets great ratings from users. Since he is new in the mobile game space, he asks you for your help to answer the following question: What types of strategy games have great user ratings?

Now, you are the owner of this business problem. Before you get dirty with your data, you must be sure you understand the problem, and that at least in principle the problem is solvable (partially or completely) with the dataset that you have. We will use the dataset we introduced earlier to perform some statistical analysis and draw some recommendations about what makes a strategy game receive good ratings in this sub-market of the gaming industry.

PREPARING THE DATASET

Let's begin by loading the dataset and the libraries we will be using in this chapter. First, let's load the libraries we'll use for now, which are NumPy, Seaborn, pandas, and Matplotlib:

```
import pandas as pd
import numpy as np
import matplotlib.pyplot as plt
import seaborn as sns

# line to allow the plots to be shown in the Jupyter Notebook
%matplotlib inline
```

Now let's read the dataset. This can be done by using a single line of code, thanks to the power of pandas. The dataset contains 18 columns of 17,007 strategy games. This line will read the CSV file and create a DataFrame ready to be used:

```
games = pd.read_csv('data/appstore_games.csv')
```

It is always a good idea to check if we've loaded the correct/expected number of rows and columns from the file:

```
games.shape
```

This gives us the following output:

```
(17007, 18)
```

Good, now we know we have read all the rows and columns from the file.

Now let's take a quick look at the first five rows of our newly created DataFrame to see what it looks like:

```
games.head()
```

This gives the following output:

	URL	ID	Name	Subtitle	Icon URL	Average User Rating	User Rating Count	Price	In-app Purchases
0	https://apps.apple.com/us/app/sudoku/id284921427	284921427	Sudoku	NaN	https://is2-ssl.mzstatic.com/image/thumb/Purpl...	4.0	3553.0	2.99	NaN
1	https://apps.apple.com/us/app/reversi/id284926400	284926400	Reversi	NaN	https://is4-ssl.mzstatic.com/image/thumb/Purpl...	3.5	284.0	1.99	NaN
2	https://apps.apple.com/us/app/morocco/id284946595	284946595	Morocco	NaN	https://is5-ssl.mzstatic.com/image/thumb/Purpl...	3.0	8376.0	0.00	NaN
3	https://apps.apple.com/us/app/sudoku-free/id28...	285755462	Sudoku (Free)	NaN	https://is3-ssl.mzstatic.com/image/thumb/Purpl...	3.5	190394.0	0.00	NaN
4	https://apps.apple.com/us/app/senet-deluxe/id2...	285831220	Senet Deluxe	NaN	https://is1-ssl.mzstatic.com/image/thumb/Purpl...	3.5	28.0	2.99	NaN

Figure 7.1: First five rows and nine columns of the DataFrame

A couple of things to notice here:

- Column names were read correctly (URL, Name, ID, and so on); however, the names from the file are not that friendly if we want easy typing, since they contain uppercase and lowercase letters, and some contain blank spaces between words.
- The DataFrame was loaded using the automatically produced integer index. We can see this by looking at the left-most column and looking at the integers printed there in bold (**0**, **1**, **2**, ...).

Let's address these two issues separately.

First, it is useful to have a single standard format for the names of your DataFrame columns. This is of course a personal choice, and there are no strict guidelines regarding this. However, I recommend the following format:

- Lowercase names
- No blank spaces – instead of blank spaces, use underscores to separate words

Using this format will allow you to type faster by achieving the following:

- Avoiding confusion when typing ("Was this letter upper or lowercase?").
- Taking advantage of the autocomplete features in your favorite IDE and/or Jupyter Notebook (using the *Tab* key in Jupyter).

To make the change, let's create a dictionary (using the dictionary comprehension Python feature) that contains both the original column name and the transformed version:

```
original_colums_dict = {x: x.lower().replace(' ','_') \
                        for x in games.columns}
original_colums_dict
```

The resulting dictionary is this one:

```
{'URL': 'url',
 'ID': 'id',
 'Name': 'name',
 'Subtitle': 'subtitle',
 'Icon URL': 'icon_url',
 'Average User Rating': 'average_user_rating',
 'User Rating Count': 'user_rating_count',
 'Price': 'price',
 'In-app Purchases': 'in-app_purchases',
 'Description': 'description',
 'Developer': 'developer',
 'Age Rating': 'age_rating',
 'Languages': 'languages',
 'Size': 'size',
 'Primary Genre': 'primary_genre',
 'Genres': 'genres',
 'Original Release Date': 'original_release_date',
 'Current Version Release Date': 'current_version_release_date'}
```

Figure 7.2: Dictionary with original and transformed column names

Now we can use this dictionary to change the column names using the **rename** function:

```
games.rename(columns = original_colums_dict,\
             inplace = True)
```

The second issue was related to the index of the DataFrame. It is always recommended to use a meaningful DataFrame index, as it will make our data processing easier, particularly the issue of merging with other tables. In this case, we have a column that includes a unique ID (**id**) for each row of our dataset, so let's use this column as the index for our DataFrame:

```
games.set_index(keys = 'id', inplace = True)
```

Now we can again use the following line of code to look at the first rows and columns of our modified DataFrame:

```
games.head()
```

The result looks like this:

id	url	name	subtitle	icon_url	average_user_rating	user_rating_count	price
284921427	https://apps.apple.com/us/app/sudoku/id284921427	Sudoku	NaN	https://is2-ssl.mzstatic.com/image/thumb/Purpl...	4.0	3553.0	2.99
284926400	https://apps.apple.com/us/app/reversi/id284926400	Reversi	NaN	https://is4-ssl.mzstatic.com/image/thumb/Purpl...	3.5	284.0	1.99
284946595	https://apps.apple.com/us/app/morocco/id284946595	Morocco	NaN	https://is5-ssl.mzstatic.com/image/thumb/Purpl...	3.0	8376.0	0.00
285755462	https://apps.apple.com/us/app/sudoku-free/id28...	Sudoku (Free)	NaN	https://is3-ssl.mzstatic.com/image/thumb/Purpl...	3.5	190394.0	0.00
285831220	https://apps.apple.com/us/app/senet-deluxe/id2...	Senet Deluxe	NaN	https://is1-ssl.mzstatic.com/image/thumb/Purpl...	3.5	28.0	2.99

Figure 7.3: First rows and columns of the modified DataFrame

Now it looks better; however, it still needs a bit more preparation.

We know there are 18 columns in this dataset; however, there are some columns that we can anticipate won't provide useful information. How can we know whether a column will provide useful information? Everything depends on the context: remember that in this case, our goal is to understand what makes a strategy game receive great ratings. In this context, it can be safely assumed that the URL of the game and the URL of the game's icon won't provide any useful information about this problem. Therefore, there is no reason to keep these columns. To drop the columns, run the following code:

```
games.drop(columns = ['url', 'icon_url'], inplace = True)
```

Another important processing step is to make sure that the columns in our DataFrame are correctly typed, which will make everything else easier: calculations, visualizations, and the creation of new features. We can use the **info()** method to check the type of our columns along with other useful information:

```
games.info()
```

This gives the following output:

```
<class 'pandas.core.frame.DataFrame'>
Int64Index: 17007 entries, 284921427 to 1475076711
Data columns (total 15 columns):
name                            17007 non-null object
subtitle                        5261 non-null object
average_user_rating             7561 non-null float64
user_rating_count               7561 non-null float64
price                           16983 non-null float64
in-app_purchases                7683 non-null object
description                     17007 non-null object
developer                       17007 non-null object
age_rating                      17007 non-null object
languages                       16947 non-null object
size                            17006 non-null float64
primary_genre                   17007 non-null object
genres                          17007 non-null object
original_release_date           17007 non-null object
current_version_release_date    17007 non-null object
dtypes: float64(4), object(11)
memory usage: 2.1+ MB
```

Figure 7.4: Output of the info method

As you can see, the columns that are conceptually numerical and categorical variables seem to have the correct types: **float64** and **object** respectively. However, we have two columns that refer to dates, and they have the **object** type. Let's transform those two columns to a **datetime** type using the following code:

```
games['original_release_date'] = pd.to_datetime\
                                 (games['original_release_date'])

games['current_version_release_date'] =\
pd.to_datetime(games['current_version_release_date'])
```

After running the previous lines of code, we can again check the column types by using the **info** method:

```
games.info()
```

This gives the following output:

```
<class 'pandas.core.frame.DataFrame'>
Int64Index: 17007 entries, 284921427 to 1475076711
Data columns (total 15 columns):
name                          17007 non-null object
subtitle                      5261 non-null object
average_user_rating           7561 non-null float64
user_rating_count             7561 non-null float64
price                         16983 non-null float64
in-app_purchases              7683 non-null object
description                   17007 non-null object
developer                     17007 non-null object
age_rating                    17007 non-null object
languages                     16947 non-null object
size                          17006 non-null float64
primary_genre                 17007 non-null object
genres                        17007 non-null object
original_release_date         17007 non-null datetime64[ns]
current_version_release_date  17007 non-null datetime64[ns]
dtypes: datetime64[ns](2), float64(4), object(9)
memory usage: 2.1+ MB
```

Figure 7.5: Output of the info method after changing the two date column types

Notice that the two columns that contain dates (**original_release_date** and **current_version_release_date**) have the correct **datetime64** type.

Our dataset now seems to be ready for us to start working on analyzing some data. The usage of the term *seems* is because as we analyze our dataset, we may find some additional preparation/cleaning is needed.

You can take a final look at the processed DataFrame using the **head()** method again:

```
games.head()
```

The output looks like this:

id	name	subtitle	average_user_rating	user_rating_count	price	in-app_purchases	description	developer	age_rating	languages	size
284921427	Sudoku	NaN	4.0	3553.0	2.99	NaN	Join over 21,000,000 of our fans and download ...	Mighty Mighty Good Games	4+	DA, NL, EN, FI, FR, DE, IT, JA, KO, NB, PL, PT...	15853568.0
284926400	Reversi	NaN	3.5	284.0	1.99	NaN	The classic game of Reversi, also known as Oth...	Kiss The Machine	4+	EN	12328960.0
284946595	Morocco	NaN	3.0	8376.0	0.00	NaN	Play the classic strategy game Othello (also k...	Bayou Games	4+	EN	674816.0
285755462	Sudoku (Free)	NaN	3.5	190394.0	0.00	NaN	Top 100 free app for over a year.\nRated "Best...	Mighty Mighty Good Games	4+	DA, NL, EN, FI, FR, DE, IT, JA, KO, NB, PL, PT...	21552128.0
285831220	Senet Deluxe	NaN	3.5	28.0	2.99	NaN	"Senet Deluxe - The Ancient Game of Life and A...	RoGame Software	4+	DA, NL, EN, FR, DE, EL, IT, JA, KO, NO, PT, RU...	34689024.0

Figure 7.6: First rows and columns of the processed DataFrame

When working with a real-world dataset, it is almost certain that you will find missing values in some of the columns, therefore it is a good idea to check for how many missing values you have in each column of the dataset. We can do this with the following line of code:

```
games.isnull().sum()
```

The preceding line of code shows us the following output:

```
name                                0
subtitle                        11746
average_user_rating              9446
user_rating_count                9446
price                              24
in-app_purchases                 9324
description                         0
developer                           0
age_rating                          0
languages                          60
size                                1
primary_genre                       0
genres                              0
original_release_date               0
current_version_release_date        0
dtype: int64
```

Figure 7.7: Number of nulls by columns

We see that there are more than 11,000 missing values in the **subtitle** column, although for the analysis we will do in this chapter, perhaps that column is not that important (perhaps we should eliminate it? What do you think?). On the other hand, **average_user_rating** and **user_rating_count** have the same number of missing values: 9,446. That suggests that those missing values might be related. Let's verify this hunch using the **np.array_equal** NumPy function. This function evaluates whether two arrays are equal element-wise and returns **True** if that is the case. We will use this function to check whether these columns have missing values in the same corresponding places. By doing this, we will confirm that the missing values happen on the same rows. The following lines of code accomplish what we just explained:

```
np.array_equal(games['average_user_rating'].isnull(),\
               games['user_rating_count'].isnull())
```

This gives the result **True**.

From the result, we can conclude that whenever we have a missing value in one of the columns, the other column also shows a missing value. Therefore, our guess was correct: if we don't have a **user_rating_count**, we don't have an **average_user_rating** either (if it was the case, then we would have to deal with the missing values those two columns separately). Going back to the columns' description (the *Introducing the Dataset* section) for user rating count, we find that "null means it is below 5", therefore if we have fewer than 5 people rating a game, then we don't have a rating at all.

Continuing with our exploration of missing values, for the in-app purchases column, we have 9,324, a relatively high value. Finally, for price, languages, and size, we have 24, 60, and 1 missing values respectively, which is not a big deal for our purposes, given the dimensions of our data.

Now we know that we have missing values in some of the columns of our dataset, there are many ways to deal with them. *Imputation* basically means replacing missing values with reasonable values. There are very complex methods for doing that, which are beyond the scope of this book. We will use very simple approaches to deal with some missing values; however, we will wait until we finish our preparation to decide what to do about these missing values. Imputation is usually the last step in the data preparation process.

Now it is time for us to decide which observations (games) are relevant for our analysis; in other words, we have to answer the question: Should we keep all the games we have?

From the context of our analysis, there is one thing that is clear: games that have no ratings are of no use for our goal, since we want to understand the ratings. Therefore, we should exclude them from our analysis. The following line of code will keep only the rows in which the **average_user_rating** is not null:

```
games = games.loc[games['average_user_rating'].notnull()]
```

Remember that the number of nulls in **average_user_rating** was **9446**, so the last line of code will remove those rows.

There is another fact we should be aware of: the number of people rating the game. From the dataset description, we know that at least five users must rate the game for the game to have a rating. For reasons that we will explain in *Chapter 9, Intermediate Stats with Python*, we will keep only those games that have at least 30 user ratings (basically, a size of **30**, for technical reasons, guarantees that the mean rating is usable for analysis). The following line of code will perform the operation we just described:

```
games = games.loc[games['user_rating_count'] >= 30]
```

Let's see how many observations we have left by using the **shape** method:

```
games.shape
```

The result is as follows:

```
(4311, 15)
```

Now, it is a good idea to check again how many missing values we have in each of the columns. We will use the same code we used before for this task:

```
games.isnull().sum()
```

This shows us the following output:

```
name                              0
subtitle                       2523
average_user_rating               0
user_rating_count                 0
price                             0
in-app_purchases               1313
description                       0
developer                         0
age_rating                        0
languages                        14
size                              0
primary_genre                     0
genres                            0
original_release_date             0
current_version_release_date      0
dtype: int64
```

Figure 7.8: Number of nulls by column

Now we see that from the potentially relevant columns, there are only two with missing values: **in-app_purchases** (**1,313**) and **languages** (**14**).

> **NOTE**
>
> A quick note on all the exercises and related tests scripts: If you are using a **command-line interface** (**CLI**) (such as Windows' Command Prompt or Mac's Terminal) to run the tests scripts, it will throw an error as **Implement enable_gui in a subclass**, which is to do with some of the commands used in the notebooks (such as **%matplotlib inline**). So, if you want to run the test scripts, then please use the IPython shell. It is best to run the code of the exercises on Jupyter Notebooks.

EXERCISE 7.01: USING A STRING COLUMN TO PRODUCE A NUMERICAL COLUMN

In this exercise, we will create a new numerical variable in our DataFrame that will have information about the number of languages in which the game is available. This will be an example of how to transform text data into numerical information.

1. Create a copy of the DataFrame we have been using so far and name it **games2**, so we have another object to work with:

```
games2 = games.copy()
```

2. Take a look at the first five values of the **languages** column using the **head** method:

```
games2['languages'].head()
```

The result looks like this:

```
id
284921427    DA, NL, EN, FI, FR, DE, IT, JA, KO, NB, PL, PT...
284926400                                                   EN
284946595                                                   EN
285755462    DA, NL, EN, FI, FR, DE, IT, JA, KO, NB, PL, PT...
286210009                                                   EN
Name: languages, dtype: object
```

Figure 7.9: First five values of the languages column

3. As you can see, it consists of a string of language abbreviations separated commas. Use the **fillna()** method to replace the missing values in that column with **EN**, which is the most common value:

```
games2['languages'] = games2['languages'].fillna('EN')
```

4. Use the **split** (which works in the same way as the **split** method for strings) method from the **str** accessor method to get a list of the different languages, and save the resulting series in an object named **list_of_languages**:

```
list_of_languages = games2['languages'].str.split(',')
```

5. Finally, let's create a column in the DataFrame called **n_languages** that has the count of how many elements we have in each of the resulting lists. For this, use a **lambda** function with the **apply** method that returns the length of the list:

```
games2['n_languages'] = list_of_languages.apply(lambda x: len(x))
```

6. The first 10 elements of the new column should look like this:

```
id
284921427    17
284926400     1
284946595     1
285755462    17
286210009     1
286313771     1
286363959     1
286566987     1
286682679     1
288096268     1
Name: n_languages, dtype: int64
```

In this exercise, we have used a text column and produced a numerical column from a text-based one, by using the **str.split** method of pandas and a lambda function.

> **NOTE**
>
> To access the source code for this specific section, please refer to https://packt.live/31xEnyy.
>
> You can also run this example online at https://packt.live/38lpuk2.

In this section, we talked about the importance of defining the business problem, and we also introduced the dataset we will use in the rest of the chapter. After all the work we have done, the dataset is at a point where we can start making sense of the values. For this, we will use descriptive statistics, which is the topic of the next section.

CALCULATING AND USING DESCRIPTIVE STATISTICS

Descriptive statistics is a set of methods that we use to summarize the information of a set of measurements (data), which helps us to make sense of it. In this section, we will first explain the need for descriptive statistics. After that, we will introduce the most common metrics of descriptive statistics, including mean, median, and standard deviation. First, we will understand them at a conceptual level using a simple set of measurements, and then we will apply what we have learned about them to the dataset we prepared in the previous section.

THE NEED FOR DESCRIPTIVE STATISTICS

Why do we need descriptive statistics? Here is an example that will show you why we need these types of analytical tools: our brains are very good at a wide variety of tasks, such as recognizing the emotion expressed in a human face. Try to notice how much effort your brain puts into reading the emotion of the following face:

Figure 7.10: A facial expression

Answer: practically nothing, and certainly you can say something meaningful about what is going on in the picture.

Now, in contrast, let's give our brain a different task: we will use the games dataset from the previous section, randomly choose 300 observations from the average user ratings column, and then print them. The following lines of code do just that:

```
random_ratings = games['average_user_rating'].sample(n=300)
for r in random_ratings:
    print(r, end=', ')
```

The output is the following:

```
3.0, 4.5, 4.5, 4.0, 4.5, 4.0, 4.0, 3.0, 4.5, 4.0, 4.5, 4.0, 4.5, 4.5, 4.5, 2.5, 4.0, 4.5, 4.5, 4.5,
3.0, 4.0, 4.5, 4.0, 4.0, 5.0, 4.0, 3.5, 4.5, 4.5, 4.5, 4.5, 4.0, 4.0, 4.5, 4.5, 4.5, 4.0, 5.0, 4.5,
4.0, 5.0, 4.5, 4.5, 4.5, 4.5, 4.5, 5.0, 3.5, 3.5, 4.5, 4.5, 4.5, 4.5, 4.5, 4.0, 4.5, 4.5, 4.5, 4.0,
4.5, 4.0, 4.0, 5.0, 4.5, 4.0, 4.5, 5.0, 4.5, 4.0, 4.0, 4.5, 4.0, 4.5, 4.0, 1.5, 4.5, 4.5, 4.5, 4.5,
4.5, 4.5, 3.5, 3.5, 4.0, 4.0, 3.0, 4.5, 3.5, 4.0, 4.5, 4.0, 4.0, 3.0, 4.5, 4.5, 4.0, 4.0, 3.5, 4.0,
4.0, 3.5, 4.0, 4.5, 4.5, 4.5, 3.0, 3.5, 4.5, 4.5, 4.0, 4.0, 3.5, 3.0, 5.0, 4.5, 4.0, 4.0, 4.5, 4.5,
4.0, 5.0, 4.5, 3.5, 4.5, 3.0, 4.5, 4.5, 3.0, 4.5, 4.5, 3.5, 4.5, 4.5, 4.0, 4.5, 3.0, 4.5, 4.5, 4.5,
4.5, 4.0, 4.5, 3.5, 4.5, 3.5, 4.5, 4.5, 4.5, 4.5, 4.5, 4.5, 3.5, 3.5, 4.0, 4.5, 4.5, 4.5, 4.5, 4.5,
4.5, 4.5, 4.0, 4.5, 4.5, 4.5, 4.5, 4.5, 4.0, 3.0, 4.0, 4.5, 3.5, 4.5, 3.5, 4.5, 4.5, 4.5, 4.5, 4.5,
3.0, 3.0, 4.5, 4.0, 4.5, 4.5, 4.0, 5.0, 4.5, 3.0, 4.5, 4.0, 4.5, 4.5, 4.0, 4.0, 4.5, 4.5, 4.5, 4.5,
3.5, 4.5, 2.5, 3.5, 5.0, 4.5, 4.5, 4.5, 4.5, 4.5, 4.5, 4.5, 4.5, 4.5, 4.5, 5.0, 2.5, 4.5, 4.0, 3.5,
4.0, 3.0, 4.5, 4.5, 4.5, 4.5, 3.5, 5.0, 4.0, 4.5, 4.5, 4.0, 4.0, 4.0, 3.5, 3.5, 4.5, 3.5, 4.5, 4.0,
4.0, 4.5, 4.5, 4.0, 4.5, 4.0, 3.5, 5.0, 4.5, 4.5, 4.5, 4.5, 4.5, 4.5, 4.5, 4.5, 5.0, 4.5, 4.5, 4.5,
4.5, 5.0, 4.5, 4.5, 5.0, 4.5, 4.5, 4.5, 4.5, 4.0, 5.0, 5.0, 4.5, 5.0, 4.0, 3.0, 5.0, 4.5, 4.5, 4.5,
4.5, 4.5, 4.5, 4.5, 3.5, 4.5, 3.0, 3.5, 4.0, 4.5, 4.0, 4.5, 5.0, 5.0, 4.5, 4.0, 3.0, 4.5, 4.0, 4.5,
```

Figure 7.11: Random sample of 300 average user ratings

Look at the output, try to analyze it, and answer the following questions:

- How much mental effort does it take to say something meaningful?
- What can you say about average ratings just by looking at the numbers?

Your answers to these questions will most probably be something like:

- How much mental effort does it take to say something meaningful? *"I had to spend some time looking at the numbers."*
- What can you say about average ratings just by looking at the numbers? *"Not much, the numbers end in either .0 or .5."*

Just by looking at *Figure 7.10*, we can automatically *summarize* and understand the information contained in thousands of pixels by saying *woman laughing*. However, in the case of *Figure 7.11*, there is no way we can understand something about them in an automatically. This is why we need descriptive statistics: it allows us to summarize and understand numerical information by performing relatively simple calculations.

A BRIEF REFRESHER OF STATISTICAL CONCEPTS

If you are reading this book, it is very likely that you have already learned or used some of the most common descriptive statistics, and it is very hard for me to provide an original definition of the concepts that have been presented in literally hundreds of books on statistics. Therefore, you can view the following pages just as a refresher of the most important concepts regarding descriptive statistics measures.

In this subsection, just to make the conceptual explanations a bit easier to understand, we will divert a bit from our strategy game dataset, and we will use a small set of 24 observations. Suppose we have the heights (in meters) of 24 men. Here we have the original observations:

```
1.68, 1.83, 1.75, 1.80, 1.88, 1.80, 1.89, 1.84,
1.90, 1.65, 1.67, 1.62, 1.81, 1.73, 1.84, 1.78,
1.76, 1.97, 1.81, 1.75, 1.65, 1.87, 1.85, 1.64.
```

We will use this small set of observations for our conceptual introduction to the most important descriptive statistics. To make our calculations easy, let´s create a pandas series containing these values:

```
mens_heights = pd.Series\
               ([1.68, 1.83, 1.75, 1.8, 1.88, 1.8, 1.89, 1.84,\
                 1.9, 1.65, 1.67,1.62, 1.81, 1.73, 1.84, 1.78,\
                 1.76, 1.97, 1.81, 1.75, 1.65, 1.87, 1.85, 1.64])
```

Now we are ready for our review of the most commonly used descriptive statistics.

Arithmetic mean: Also known simply as **mean**, this is a measure of the *center of the distribution* or the center of the set of numbers. Given a set of observations, the mean is calculated by summing the observations and dividing that sum by the number of observations. The formula is as follows, where *x bar* ($\bar{x}$) is the mean and *n* is the number of observations:

$$\bar{x} = \frac{1}{n}\left(\sum_{i=1}^{n} x_i\right) = \frac{x_1 + x_2 + \ldots + x_n}{n}$$

Figure 7.12: Formula for arithmetic mean

The mean is especially useful and informative when most of the values are clustered around a single *center*, because in that case the mean will be close to that center, and thus will be close to many values, making it a *representative* number of the set of observations. Many (perhaps most) of the numerical variables you will encounter in real-world data will have values that will cluster around the mean, therefore the mean is usually a good indicator of the *typical* value of a set of measurements.

Let's calculate the mean for the set of men's heights by using the built-in pandas method:

```
mens_heights.mean()
```

The result is the following:

```
1.7820833
```

This number tells us that 1.78 meters is a value that is *representative* of the set of the heights of the 24 men. After performing this calculation, we know that a typical man (from the population from which we got that sample) will have a height of around `1.78` meters.

Something to be aware of about the mean is that it gets affected by extreme values. This is especially troublesome when analyzing variables in which the extreme values could potentially be orders of magnitude greater than the most common values.

Finally, it is worth mentioning that the arithmetic mean is often what most people have in mind when they say the word *average*, although there are other averages, such as the median, which we will define later.

Standard deviation: This is a measure of the spread of the data. It measures how different or *dispersed* the observations in a set of measurements are. The mathematical formula is based on the arithmetic mean, and for your reference, it is as follows:

$$s = \sqrt{\frac{1}{N-1}\sum_{i=1}^{N}\left(x_i - \bar{x}\right)^2}$$

Figure 7.13: Formula for standard deviation

In the preceding formula, *s* refers to the standard deviation, *x bar* ($\bar{x}$) is the mean, and *N* is the number of observations. Because of a technical detail (beyond our scope) the formula has *N – 1* instead of just *N* as a denominator, but let's pretend for a moment that we have an *N* in the denominator: if you look at the formula closely you will see that what we have inside the square root symbol is *the mean of the squared deviations with respect to the mean*. So, the standard deviation is a kind of arithmetic mean of how distant the observations are to its mean. The square root is in the formula, so the resulting number is in the same units as the original measurements.

Let's calculate the standard deviation of our small set of measurements of men's heights, again using pandas' built-in methods:

```
mens_heights.std()
```

This gives the following result:

```
0.0940850
```

Our answer is **`0.094`** meters, or 9.4 centimeters. The interpretation of this number is that, *on average*, a man's height differs by 9.4 centimeters from the mean (which was in this case 1.78 meters). Notice that we say *on average*, meaning that we can expect individual men's heights to be closer or farther apart than 9.4 centimeters from the average, but 9.4 is an informative number of how far apart we expect a typical observation will be from the mean.

To better understand the concept of standard deviation, it would be useful to contrast the former calculation with another hypothetical set of measurements. Let's say we have the heights of another 24 men with a similar average:

```
mens_heights_2 = pd.Series\
                 ([1.77, 1.75, 1.75, 1.75, 1.73, 1.75, 1.73, 1.75,\
                   1.74, 1.76, 1.75, 1.75, 1.74, 1.76, 1.75, 1.76,\
                   1.76, 1.76, 1.75, 1.73, 1.74, 1.76, 1.76, 1.76])
```

Let's calculate the average, to see how these 24 men compare with the average of our first group:

```
mens_heights_2.mean()
```

The result is the following:

```
1.750416
```

This is around 3 centimeters below the average of the first group. Now let's calculate the standard deviation of the second group:

```
mens_heights_2.std()
```

The result is the following:

```
0.01082
```

This is only 1 centimeter, which means that the heights of the second group are much more homogeneous. In other words, the heights of the second group are closer to each other (that is, they have less dispersion) than the heights in the first group. Since we have very few observations, we can tell this by looking closely at the measurements of the second group: notice that all the measurements are between 1.73 and 1.77, so the variability is less compared with the first group.

On the extreme end, if all observations are exactly the same, that is, there is no variation among them, then the standard deviation will be zero. The more different the measurements, the larger the standard deviation will be.

There are other measures of the spread of the data, but the standard deviation is maybe the most important. You should make sure you know how to interpret it.

Quartiles: Quartiles are *measures of location*. They indicate that the value is in a certain relative position when the observations have been ordered from the smallest (minimum) to the largest (maximum) values. The first, second, and third quartiles are usually denoted as **Q1**, **Q2**, and **Q3**:

- **Q1**: Divides the data in such a way that 25% of the observations are below this value.
- **Q2**: Also called *the median*, this is the number that divides the set of numbers in two halves, meaning that 50% of the observations are below this value, and the other 50% are above this value. The median is another type of average.
- **Q3**: Divides the data in such a way that 75% of the observations are below this value.

Again using our first 24 heights, we can order them and split this little dataset into four parts, each consisting of 6 observations. This is visually shown in the following figure:

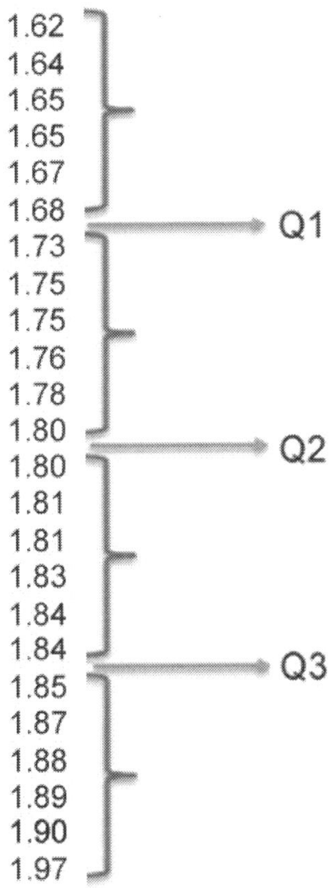

Figure 7.14: Illustration of quartiles

In this example, we can split the dataset into *exactly* four parts. The first one consists of the smallest six observations; the sixth observation is **`1.68`**, and the next one (which belongs to the second quartile) is **`1.73`**. Technically any number between **`1.68`** and **`1.73`** (**`1.68`** < **`Q1`** < **`1.73`**) could be called the *first quartile*, for instance, **`1.70`**, because the statement *25% of observations are below 1.70* would be true. We could also pick **`1.71`** because the statement *25% of observations are below 1.71* would also be true.

The median (**Q2**) splits the observations into two halves. **`1.80`** is the 12th and 13th observation in this case, so the median is **`1.80`**. (If there was a number between the 12th and 13th observation, the median would be the number in between.)

Finally, for the third quartile (**Q3**), we see from the figure that any number between **`1.84`** and **`1.85`** (say 1.845) would be a value that splits the bottom 75% observations from the top 25%.

Notice that I have not given any formula to calculate quartiles, so how exactly are the quartiles calculated? There are a few methods that we won't be going into in this book. The exact method is not important – what is really important is that you understand the concept. Now let's see how to calculate these values. In the following line of code, we will use the **`quantile`** method from pandas (quartiles are a special case of the more general concept of **quantile**, a concept close to that of **percentile**):

```
mens_heights.quantile([0.25, 0.5, 0.75])
```

The result is the following:

```
0.25    1.7175
0.50    1.8000
0.75    1.8425
dtype:  float64
```

We had to pass a list to this method indicating the percentage (proportion) of observations where we wanted the splits—these are 25%, 50%, and 75%, that correspond to **Q1**, **Q2**, and **Q3** respectively. As you can see, the first quartile (**`1.7175`**) is a number between 1.68 and 1.73, the median is **`1.80`**, and the third quartile (**`1.8425`**) is a number between 1.84 and 1.85.

To calculate quantiles, as opposed to quartiles, we use any proportion to split the observations into two parts: for example, let's say that we what to divide the observations between the bottom 80% and the top 20%, the 80th percentile is equivalent to the 0.8 quantile, and would be the number below which there are 80% of observations. Similarly, the 33rd percentile would be equivalent to the 0.33 quantile and would be the number below which there are 33% of observations. This explains why we have to pass a list of quantiles to the quantile function in pandas; for instance, the following code calculates the 0.33 and 0.8 quantiles (which correspond to the 33rd and 80th percentiles):

```
mens_heights.quantile([0.33, 0.80])
```

The result is:

```
0.33    1.750
0.80    1.858
dtype: float64
```

According to this result, 80% of our observations are below **1.858**. As a mini-exercise, check if the 33rd percentile is what you would expect by comparing its value to the range illustrated in *Figure 7.14*.

Descriptive statistics is not only about the standard set of metrics such as mean, median, and so on. Any simple, *descriptive* calculation done on the data is also considered to be descriptive statistics, including sums, proportions, percentages, and so on. For instance, let's calculate the proportion of men above 1.80 meters. There are many ways to do it, but we will use a two-step approach. First, let's run the following line of code, which gives the value **True** if the observation satisfies the condition and **False** otherwise:

```
mens_heights >= 1.8
```

The result looks like this:

```
0      False
1       True
2      False
3       True
4       True
5       True
6       True
7       True
8       True
9      False
10     False
11     False
12      True
13     False
14      True
15     False
16     False
17      True
18      True
19     False
20     False
21      True
22      True
23     False
dtype: bool
```

Figure 7.15: Boolean series

The second step is to count how many **True** values we have. We can do this with the **sum** method, which will transform **True** to 1s and **False** to 0s. Then we could simply divide by the number of observations in our series by the **shape** method. The whole line of code will look like this:

```
(mens_heights >= 1.8).sum()/mens_heights.shape[0]
```

The result is the following:

```
0.54166
```

Or 54% of our 24 heights are equal to or greater than 1.8 meters. This proportion is also considered descriptive statistics, since it is a number that is also describing what is going on with our data.

The preceding calculation could have been done more succinctly like so:

```
(mens_heights >= 1.8).mean()
```

As a mini-exercise, you can use the mean formula given in *Figure 7.12* to deduce why the **mean** method will give you the proportion of true values in a Boolean series.

USING DESCRIPTIVE STATISTICS

Now that we have refreshed our understanding of the most important measures of descriptive statistics, it is time for us to go back to our original dataset and start using those concepts in the context of the business problem given to us.

The descriptive statistics we reviewed in the preceding section are so important that the pandas **describe** method (which belongs to both series and DataFrames) calculates all of them. In addition, we will find the following:

- **Count**: Number of non-null values in the column
- **Minimum**: Smallest value
- **Maximum**: Largest value

When the **describe** method is used on a DataFrame, it takes all the columns with numerical types and calculates their descriptive statistics:

```
games.describe()
```

This gives the following output:

	average_user_rating	user_rating_count	price	size
count	4311.000000	4.311000e+03	4311.000000	4.311000e+03
mean	4.163535	5.789754e+03	0.677878	1.759569e+08
std	0.596239	5.592425e+04	2.910916	2.866278e+08
min	1.500000	3.000000e+01	0.000000	2.158400e+05
25%	4.000000	7.000000e+01	0.000000	4.073626e+07
50%	4.500000	2.210000e+02	0.000000	9.730048e+07
75%	4.500000	1.192000e+03	0.000000	2.085176e+08
max	5.000000	3.032734e+06	139.990000	4.005591e+09

Figure 7.16: Descriptive statistics for numerical columns of the DataFrame

Before interpreting the results, you need to be aware that by default, pandas shows the output in scientific notation: for example, **`4.311000e+03`** means 4.311 x 10^3 = 4,311. The notation **`"e+k"`** means (x 10^k) and **`"e-k"`** means (x 10^{-k}).

To put these concepts into practice, let's read and interpret the statistics from the **`user_rating_count`** variable:

- **`count`**: The value in the output for count is 4,311. This is the amount of not-null observations in our variable.
- **`mean`**: The value in the output for mean is 5,789.75. Now we know that on average we have about 5,800 users rating a game in our dataset. To extract more information about this number (and whether it is useful or not), let's read the other statistics.
- **`std`**: The standard deviation value is 5,592.43. On average, the number of users rating a game in our dataset varies from the mean by almost 5,600 users: think about it, the average number of ratings was roughly 5,800, and the *typical* deviation from that number is almost ~5,600. This tells us that the variability is very large in this variable (dispersion is high), or in other words: we have some games with only a few user ratings, and we have some games with a very large number of user ratings.

- **min**, **25%**, **50%**, **75%**, **max**: These numbers tell us important information about how the observations in our variable are distributed. We see that the minimum is 30 (remember that we explicitly selected games with at least 30 ratings), and the maximum value is more than 3 million! The first quartile tells us that 25% of the games in our dataset have less than 70 user ratings; this is very few, considering that the mean was 5,789.75. The median is 221 user ratings, so half of our games have less than 221 ratings! Finally, the third quartile indicates that 75% of the observations are below 1,192.

So far, we have more or less only read the results, so now let's discuss a bit more to be able to transform this data into useful information.

Knowing the maximum (more than 3 million), we can be sure that the *mean* of this variable has been highly affected by the extreme values, namely hugely popular games. So perhaps the mean is not that informative for this variable. Maybe it is not meaningful to talk about *the typical number of user ratings for a game*, because the data suggests there is no *typical* number. In fact, we know that more than 75% of the observations have fewer than 1,200 user ratings. This would imply that we should observe a few popular games. Let's test this hunch and dive a bit into the games with the most ratings, using the **sort_values** method from the series to see the first 10 values of **user_rating_count** in descending order:

```
games['user_rating_count'].sort_values(ascending=False).head(10)
```

The result is the following:

```
id
529479190     3032734.0
1053012308    1277095.0
1330123889     711409.0
597986893      469562.0
1094591345     439776.0
672150402      400787.0
1270598321     374772.0
1116645064     283035.0
297558390      273687.0
847985808      259030.0
Name: user_rating_count, dtype: float64
```

Figure 7.17: First 10 values of user rating count

Notice that only two games have more than one million user ratings, which explains the high variability we observed from the standard deviation (5,592.43). Let's check how many games have at least 100,000 user ratings. First, we will filter our column by the condition **>= 100000** and then we will use the **sum** method, which will count how many values satisfy that condition:

```
(games['user_rating_count'] >= 100000).sum()
```

The result is as follows:

```
40
```

So only 40 games have more than 100,000 ratings, which is less than 1% of the current dataset (of 4,311 games) and 0.23% of the original dataset (of 17,007 games).

In summary, the number of user ratings that a game has is highly variable. In addition, 25% of the games in our sample have less than 70 user ratings, and half of the games have less than 221. Moreover, we have only **40** games with more than 100,000 user ratings, with the first and second most popular games having more than 3.0 million and more than 1.2 million respectively.

Here is the way we might present the information to the CEO:

The data from the user rating count, which is a proxy for the popularity of the game, suggests that it is very hard for a strategy game to become hugely popular. The data tells us that less than 1% of the strategy games can be considered hugely popular (in terms of the number of user ratings), while more than 75% of the games have less than 1,200 user ratings, indicating a relatively low user base. Keep in mind that for this exercise we have excluded those games that have less than 30 user ratings, therefore the odds for a strategy game to become hugely popular is way below 1%.

The preceding paragraph is an example of how to extract valuable information from descriptive statistics. Notice that we had no need to mention any statistical terminology, such as mean, median, or standard deviation, nor the terms quantile, percentile, and so on. Notice also that the fact that the mean was 5,789.75 was not used, because that fact was not necessary for the message we were trying to convey. That is the kind of information that someone like a CEO would like to hear, since it is clear, informative, and actionable.

We finish this section with a very important piece of advice: don't make the mistake of presenting a list of the descriptive statistics calculations as your *analysis*. Another common mistake is to include a paragraph containing analysis such as *the mean is x, the standard deviation is y, the maximum is 88*, basically just re-writing the information contained in the statistical table. Keep in mind that it is your job not only to perform the calculations, but also to explain what these numbers mean and their implications regarding the problem you are trying to solve.

EXERCISE 7.02: CALCULATING DESCRIPTIVE STATISTICS

In this exercise, we will use descriptive statistics to calculate the value of the average user rating variable. For this, we will use the descriptive statistics metrics that we discussed in the previous section. In addition, we will also perform other descriptive calculations, including counts and proportions.

1. Calculate the descriptive statistics of the **average_user_rating** column:

```
games['average_user_rating'].describe()
```

The result is as follows:

```
count    4311.000000
mean        4.163535
std         0.596239
min         1.500000
25%         4.000000
50%         4.500000
75%         4.500000
max         5.000000
Name: average_user_rating, dtype: float64
```

As you can see, the median and the third quartile have the same value, **4.5**, which means that at least 25% of the games have an average rating of **4.5**.

2. Calculate the number and the proportion of games with a rating of exactly **4.5**. The **mean** method can be used for this goal:

```
ratings_of_4_5 = (games['average_user_rating'] == 4.5).sum()

proportion_of_ratings_4_5 = (games['average_user_rating'] == 4.5)\
                            .mean()

print(f'''The number of games with an average rating of 4.5 is \
{ratings_of_4_5}, \
which represents a proportion of {proportion_of_ratings_4_5:.3f} or \
{100*proportion_of_ratings_4_5:.1f}%''')
```

The output we get is the following:

```
The number of games with an average rating of 4.5 is 2062, which
represents a proportion of 0.478 or 47.8%
```

3. Use the **unique** method to see the unique values for this variable. What do you notice?

```
games['average_user_rating'].unique()
```

In this exercise, we have used descriptive statistics to understand another key variable of our business problem.

> **NOTE**
>
> To access the source code for this specific section, please refer to https://packt.live/2VUWhI3.
>
> You can also run this example online at https://packt.live/2Zp0Z1u.

Here are some questions that might come to mind:

- Is the mean of this variable a statistic you would use to understand this variable? Would you choose it as a *typical* value of the variable, or would you choose another value?
- Based on the standard deviation, would you consider that this variable has high or low variability?
- How could the information you obtained by using the descriptive statistics be summarized in a paragraph?

In this section, we learned why we need and use descriptive statistics. From the first example we introduced, we learned that our brains don't have the capacity to automatically make sense of numerical information. It is therefore necessary to have these types of analytical tools if we want to understand numerical data.

Then we presented a brief refresher on (or introduction to) some of the most commonly used metrics of descriptive statistics, including mean, standard deviation, and quantiles. Then we immediately applied that knowledge using the strategy games dataset and calculated the descriptive statistics for the numerical variables. We analyzed the results for the user rating count variable and produced a summary that contained relevant information that a non-technical audience can understand.

Finally, we did all the calculations using pandas built-in methods such as **`mean`**, **`std`**, **`describe`**, and **`quantile`**, among others.

Now that we know the basics of descriptive statistics, we can expand our statistical toolkit and complement our analysis using visualizations, which we will cover in the following section.

EXPLORATORY DATA ANALYSIS

In this section, we will be referring back to the business problem that we performed some initial analysis on in the first section of this chapter, which is as follows:

The CEO of the game development company you work for has come up with a plan to strengthen the position of the company in the gaming market. From his industry knowledge and other business reports, he knows that a very effective way to attract new customers is to develop a great reputation in the mobile game space. Given this fact, he has the following plan: develop a strategy game for the iOS platform that will get a lot of positive attention, which in turn will bring a large number of new customers to the company. He is sure his plan will work if and only if the game gets great ratings from users. Since he is new in the mobile game space, he asks you for your help to answer the following question: What types of strategy games have great user ratings?

In this section, we will do some exploratory data analysis. You can think of this section as a continuation of the last section, as we will continue using descriptive statistics, and in addition to that, we will expand our analytical toolkit with one of the most powerful analytical devices: visualizations.

The field of **Exploratory Data Analysis** (**EDA**) (like any other field related to data) has been growing rapidly, and the content of this section covers only some of the very basic concepts and visualizations. Despite that, it is very likely that you will use the visualizations presented in this section in every data analysis project you will encounter.

WHAT IS EDA?

Now that we have refreshed our basic statistical definitions, we are ready to put them to use and complement the information we get from them with visualizations. In simple terms, EDA is the process of analyzing data by combining descriptive statistics with visualizations. The reasons and objectives of doing EDA include the following:

- Understanding the distributions of the variables
- Understanding the relationships between two or more variables
- Detecting patterns that can't be found using numerical calculations
- Spotting anomalies or outliers in the data
- Formulating a hypothesis about causal relationships
- Informing us about how to engineer new variables (feature engineering)
- Informing us about possible formal inferential statistical tests

By definition, while doing EDA we are exploring the data, so there are no recipes or sets of fixed steps to follow, and a lot of creativity is involved. However, it is also very important to provide some structure to the process, otherwise we could be producing plots and calculations with no clear end point. In data analytics (as in life), without a clear purpose, it is very easy to get lost, since there are countless ways to look at any regularly-sized dataset. Before starting to perform EDA, we need to define what is that we are trying to find, which is where the understanding of the business problem is key.

I would recommend performing EDA in two steps:

1. **Univariate step**: Understand each of the most important variables in the dataset: distributions, key characteristics, extreme values, and so on.
2. **Look for relationships**: With the business/scientific problem in mind, *formulate a list of questions* whose answers will give you useful information about the problem you are trying to solve, and then let these questions guide the EDA process.

The first step is what is usually called *univariate analysis*, and is relatively straightforward. For the second step, we use *bi-variate* or *multivariate* techniques since we need to look for relationships between variables. In the next section, we will do univariate EDA.

UNIVARIATE EDA

As the name implies, univariate EDA is about analyzing a single variable at the time. In the previous section, we saw how easy it is to calculate the main descriptive statistics with pandas. Now we will complement the information we get from descriptive statistics using appropriate visualizations.

Before performing EDA, it is absolutely necessary to know which type of variables we are working with. As a refresher, here we have the main types of variables we can encounter:

1. **Numerical variables**: Those variables that can take numerical values:

   a. **Continuous**: These are variables that can take a whole range of real values between a certain interval, such as height, weight, and mass.

   b. **Discrete**: These are variables that take only a specific, limited number of values, frequently integers. Examples include the number of children in a family or the number of employees.

2. **Categorical variables**: Those that can take only a specified number of categories as values:

   a. **Ordinal**: Variables where the categories have some natural order. For instance, the variable **`age group`** could have the categories 20-29, 30-39, 40-49, and 50+. Notice that there is an order in those categories: 20-29 is lower than 40-49.

   b. **Nominal**: These are categorical variables where there are no ordered relationships. For example, the colors blue, green, and red are categories without any sort of order.

3. **Time-related variables**: Variables that relate to dates or datetimes.

Let's begin by identifying the numerical variables in our dataset. As we did previously while preparing the dataset, we realized that the variables that are *conceptually* numerical have an appropriate corresponding Python numerical data type. Let's use the **info** method in our (modified) games DataFrame to check this again:

```
games.info()
```

The output is this:

```
<class 'pandas.core.frame.DataFrame'>
Int64Index: 4311 entries, 284921427 to 1474461379
Data columns (total 15 columns):
name                            4311 non-null object
subtitle                        1788 non-null object
average_user_rating             4311 non-null float64
user_rating_count               4311 non-null float64
price                           4311 non-null float64
in-app_purchases                2998 non-null object
description                     4311 non-null object
developer                       4311 non-null object
age_rating                      4311 non-null object
languages                       4297 non-null object
size                            4311 non-null float64
primary_genre                   4311 non-null object
genres                          4311 non-null object
original_release_date           4311 non-null datetime64[ns]
current_version_release_date    4311 non-null datetime64[ns]
dtypes: datetime64[ns](2), float64(4), object(9)
memory usage: 538.9+ KB
```

Figure 7.18: Numerical variables in the dataset

As we can see, the columns that are conceptually numerical: **average_user_rating**, **user_rating_count**, **price**, and **size** have datatypes of **float64**.

The most commonly used useful visualization for a single numerical variable is the histogram. Let's see how it looks and then describe how it's constructed. For this, we will use the **size** variable. Since this variable is in bytes, before visualizing it we will transform it to megabytes:

```
games['size'] = games['size']/1e6
```

Now we can use pandas' built-in **hist** method:

```
games['size'].hist(bins=30, ec='black');
```

We have included two additional parameters: **`bins`**, which is (roughly) the number of bars we see, and **`ec`** (edge color), which is the color of the bar edges. The resulting figure is the following:

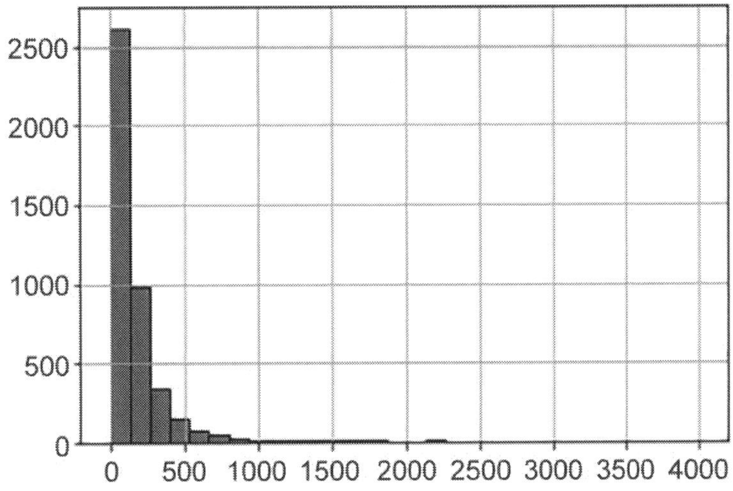

Figure 7.19: Histogram of size

The histogram is built by dividing the *range* of the variable, which is defined as the maximum minus the minimum into equally sized intervals called bins. In this case, the maximum and the minimum are 4,005.6 and 0.2 respectively, so the range is about 4,005. Since we indicated 30 as the number of bins, each bin will have a size of about 133 ~ 4,005 / 30. So, the first bin goes from roughly the minimum (about 0) to 133, the second bin goes from 133 to 266 = 133 + 133, and so on. The height of the bar corresponds to the number of observations that fall in the interval of a particular bin. For instance, we see that the first bar goes a bit beyond 2,500 observations, which is the number of observations that fall in the first bin (which goes from 0 to ~133). As with quartiles, the exact algorithm to build the histogram varies with the software used. Pandas uses the Matplotlib implementation, so please check out Matplotlib's documentation if you want to know the details.

You should get used to seeing histograms and try reading them. For instance, the histogram of the *size* shows the following:

- An important proportion of the games fall in the first bin (the tallest bar).
- Most of the values are below 500 MB.
- The number (frequency) of observations goes down as the variable increases: we observe fewer and fewer games as the size grows.

- The *x* axis of the plot goes until about 4,000 MB; however, we don't even see a bar there, the reason being that we have so few observations and that bar is so tiny that it's indistinguishable from zero. This means that we must have at least one extreme value (a game of a very large size).
- The height of the bars above 1,000 MB is very low, so there are very few games above 1,000 MB.

The histogram is a perfect complement for the numerical information we get from the descriptive statistics:

```
games['size'].describe()
```

The output is the following:

```
count          4311.000000
mean           175.956867
std            286.627800
min            0.215840
25%            40.736256
50%            97.300480
75%            208.517632
max            4005.591040
NameL size,    dtype: float64
```

The median tells us that more than half of the games have a size of less than 97.3 MB, and the game with the largest size is more than 40 times the median, which we could consider an *outlier* or an observation that is much more extreme than most of the values in our variable. As we did with user rating count, we could examine the largest games by sorting the series in descending order and then showing the first 12 values:

```
games['size'].sort_values(ascending=False).head(12)
```

The output is the following:

```
id
1245565445    4005.591040
1106831630    3916.692480
633625517     3747.742720
1235863443    3716.897792
1183898700    3599.435776
881270303     3518.277632
1107741196    3321.082880
909472985     2996.021248
1321791212    2897.696768
1298734617    2581.730304
1264531625    2547.534848
1257031979    2512.028672
Name: size, dtype: float64
```

Figure 7.20: Largest values of size

We see that there are actually a few outliers, which are not just the maximum. There is actually no standard definition of *outlier*—it depends on the context. We are calling these observations outliers because they can be considered large sizes for a set of games in which 75% of them have sizes of less than 208 MB.

OK, back to histograms. One very cool feature of pandas is its ability to produce histograms for many numerical variables at the same time using the **hist** method of the **DataFrame** class. This feature will be useful when you have a lot of numerical variables in your dataset and you want to take a quick look at them:

```
games.hist(figsize = (10, 4), bins = 30, ec = 'black');
# This line prints the four plots without overlap
plt.tight_layout()
```

Pandas automatically takes all the numerical variables and produces a grid (which is adjustable) of rows and columns with the plots. In our case, we have four numerical variables, and the result is the following:

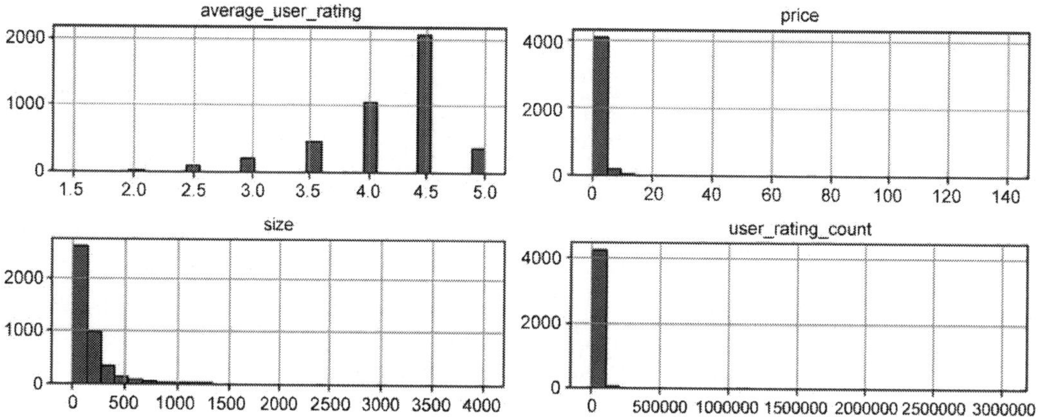

Figure 7.21: Example of histograms of a DataFrame

The fact that we have a few extreme values (outliers) in **`price`**, **`size`**, and **`user_rating_count`** has the effect of not letting us see how the values of these variables are truly distributed.

With our knowledge of quantiles (and percentiles), let's create a filter that will exclude the 1% of largest values in each of these three variables, which will hopefully allow us to understand the distributions better:

```
filter_price = games['price'] <= games['price'].quantile(0.99)

filter_user_rating_count = games['user_rating_count'] \
                           <= games['user_rating_count'].quantile(0.99)

filter_size = games['size'] <= games['size'].quantile(0.99)

filter_exclude_top_1_percent = filter_price \
                               & filter_user_rating_count \
                               & filter_size

games[filter_exclude_top_1_percent].hist(figsize = (10, 4),\
                                         bins = 30, ec = 'black');
# This line prints the four plots without overlap
plt.tight_layout()
```

The result is the following:

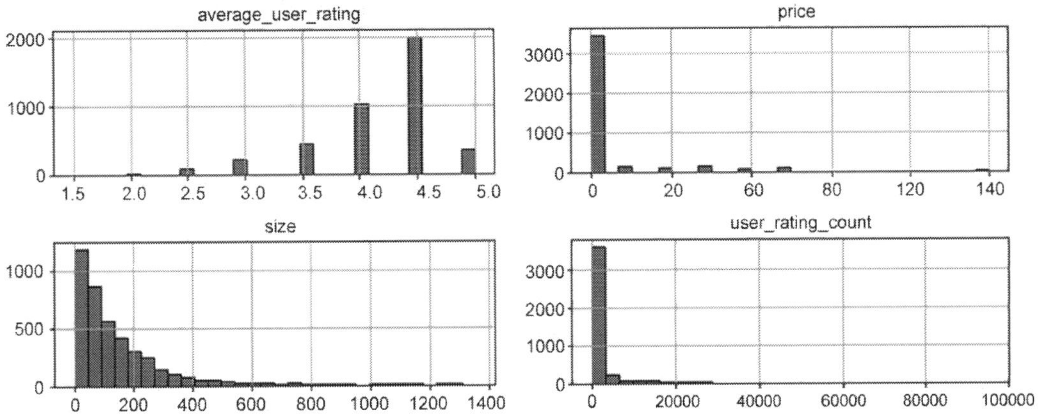

Figure 7.22: Example of histograms of a DataFrame

Now that the histograms have revealed more information, here are a few of the things we can read from the histograms:

- Most games are free, and of the very few that are not free, the vast majority cost less than 10 dollars.
- 4.5 is the most common average user rating; in fact, we observe very few games with low average ratings (3 or below).
- Larger-sized games are rare.
- Most games have very few user ratings.

As an exercise, try to extract more information from these graphs and complement it with the descriptive statistics for these variables: for instance, comment on the decaying pattern of the size variable, or the highly concentrated pattern we see in the user rating count: what could explain those shapes?

Now let's talk about another useful plot to see the distribution of a continuous variable: the boxplot. A boxplot is a graphical representation of the position statistics **Q1**, median, and **Q3**, and usually also shows the minimum and maximum. The boxplot for the sample dataset of 24 observations can be generated using the following line of code:

```
mens_heights.plot(kind='box');
```

The result is as follows (annotations of the descriptive statistics have been added to the figure):

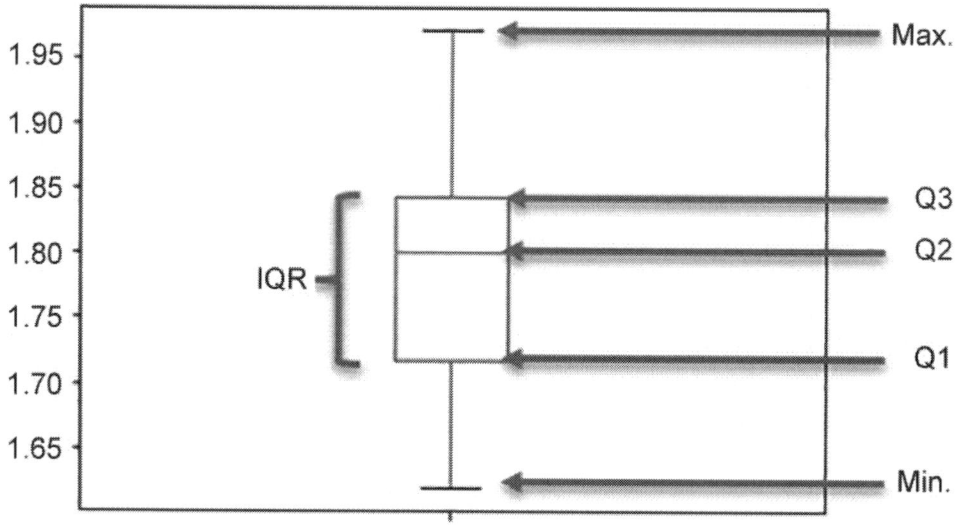

Figure 7.23: Example of a boxplot

The boxplot consists of two *whiskers* and a box. The first whisker (usually) starts at the minimum value, then it goes until **Q1**, which marks the beginning of the box, therefore the first whisker covers the bottom 25% of observations. The box goes from **Q1** to **Q3**, covering the *middle half* of the observations. The height of the box is called the **Inter Quartile Range** (**IQR**) and is a measure of dispersion, which tells us how *packed* the middle 50% of observations are: a larger IQR implies more dispersion. The line in the middle of the box corresponds to the median, and finally, the upper whisker (usually) finishes at the maximum value.

Notice I have added a couple of *usually* in parenthesis for the maximum and minimum. When an observation is above *Q3 + 1.5 x IQR* (or below *Q1 - 1.5 x IQR*), it is often considered a candidate for an outlier and is plotted as a dot. If we have such observations, then the upper (lower) whisker ends at *Q3 + 1.5 x IQR* (or *Q1 - 1.5 x IQR*). Here is, for example, the boxplot for the **`size`** variable:

```
games['size'].plot(kind='box');
```

The result is the following:

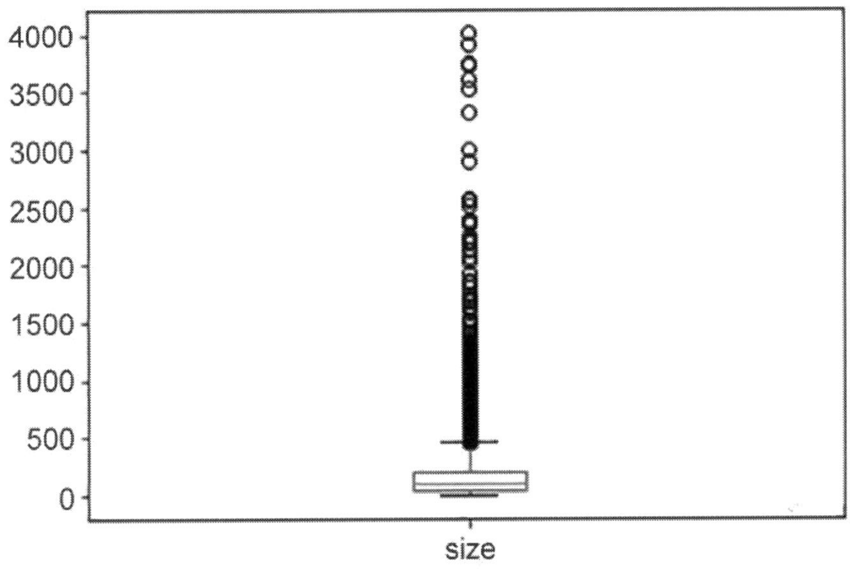

Figure 7.24: Boxplot of size

In this case, the upper whisker does not finish on the maximum value, but it goes until *Q3 + 1.5 x IQR*. From this plot, we can say that the variable has many extreme values. Although the boxplots might sometimes be useful for univariate EDA, the histogram is preferable. The best use for boxplots is when analyzing the relation of a numerical variable versus a categorical one. We will return to the boxplots in the next subsection.

To finish this subsection, let's see how to produce a bar plot, which is used to show either counts, proportions, or percentages of a categorical variable. Let's take a look at the **age_rating** column, which is a categorical variable. The following line will count the number of games for each of the values of the variable:

```
games['age_rating'].value_counts()
```

The result is the following:

```
4+     2287
9+     948
12+    925
17+    151
Name: age_rating,  dtype: int64
```

Since the result is also a pandas series, we can chain the methods and use the **`plot`** method with the argument **`kind = 'bar'`** to get our bar plot:

```
games['age_rating'].value_counts().plot(kind = 'bar');
```

The result looks like this:

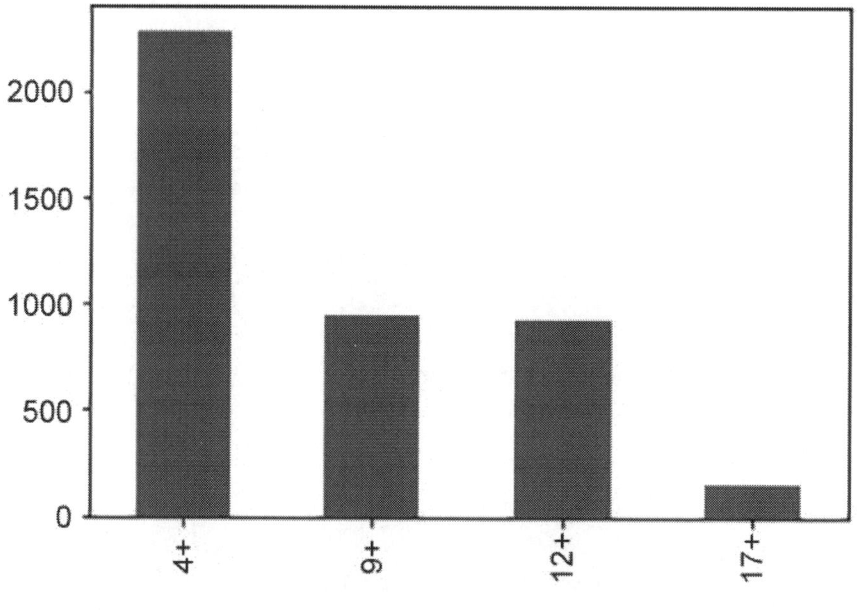

Figure 7.25: Bar plot for absolute counts of age_rating

If we wanted to visualize the proportions, we could have modified the preceding line of code by adding the **normalize=True** argument to the **value_counts** method:

```
games['age_rating'].value_counts(normalize=True).plot(kind='bar');
```

The figure looks almost identical, the only change being in the *y* axis labels, which now show the proportions:

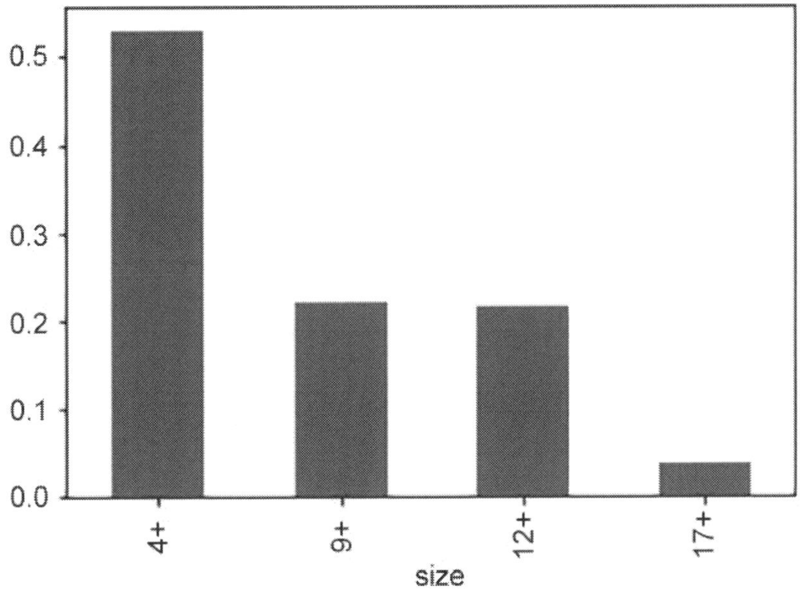

Figure 7.26: Bar plot for proportions of age ratings

Finally, another alternative to visualize proportions is using a pie chart. Pie charts are known to have some problems, among them the fact that they are not a good way to convey information, which is why I never use them. However, they are useful for presenting business information, so if your boss asks you for a pie chart, here is how to produce one:

```
games['age_rating'].value_counts().plot(kind = 'pie');
```

This is the result:

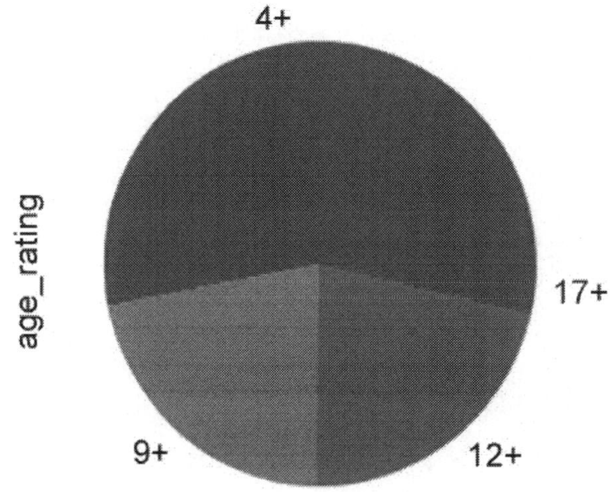

Figure 7.27: Pie chart of age ratings

The problem with pie charts is that they are just a way to beautify documents, not a good way to communicate quantitative information; visualizations are meant to be used when we want to complement and go beyond what numerical calculations can communicate. If we want to communicate proportions (or percentages), it is simply better to show the actual values, like so:

```
percentages = 100*games['age_rating'].value_counts(normalize=True)

for k, x in percentages.items():
    print(f'{k}: {x:0.1f}%')
```

This gives the following output:

```
4+: 53.1%
9+: 22.0%
12+: 21.5%
17+: 3.5%
```

BI-VARIATE EDA: EXPLORING RELATIONSHIPS BETWEEN VARIABLES

Exploring relationships between variables is one of the most interesting aspects of statistical analysis. When exploring relations between pairs of variables, and considering only the broadest division of numerical and categorical variables, we have three cases:

- Numerical versus numerical
- Numerical versus categorical
- Categorical versus categorical

For the first case, the scatter plot is the visualization of choice. For the second case, depending on what we are trying to find, we have some choices, but often boxplots are most useful. Finally, for the third case, the most common choice is to present what is called a contingency table: although some visualizations options exist for comparing categorical data, they are not so common.

As we said back in *Exploratory Data Analysis*, when doing this type of analysis, it is often a good idea to formulate a list of questions we want to answer before we start producing visualizations. Keeping in mind our business problem, we will try to shed some light on the following three questions:

- What is the relationship between the size and average user rating?
- What is the relationship between the age rating and average user rating?
- What is the relationship between having in-app purchases and the game rating?

We will try answering the first question using a scatter plot. In its most simple version, the scatter plots show each point of a pair of variables using a Cartesian plane. Each pair of points is represented by a dot, and the pattern of the dots indicate if there is some kind of relationship between the two plotted variables. The following table shows illustrations of some of the patterns you can detect using a scatter plot:

		Strength of the relationship		
		Weak or null	**Medium**	**Strong**
Nature of relation	**Positive**	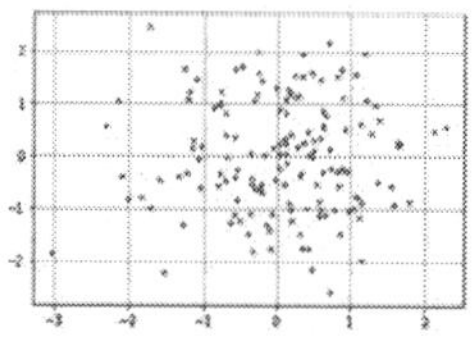	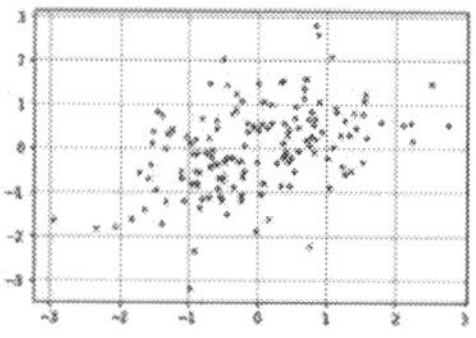	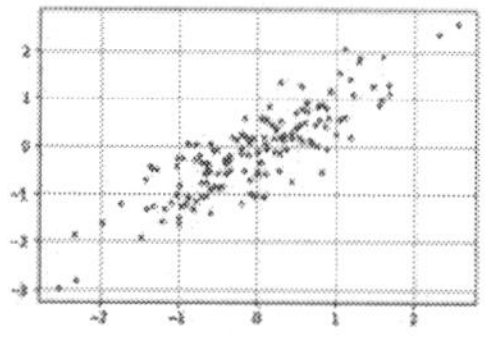
	Negative	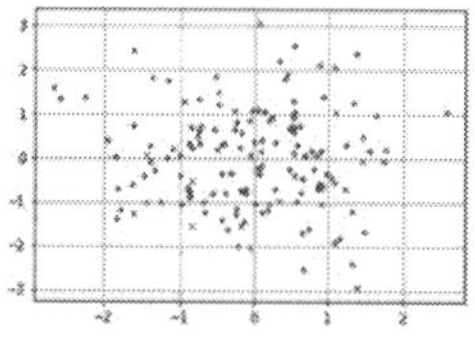	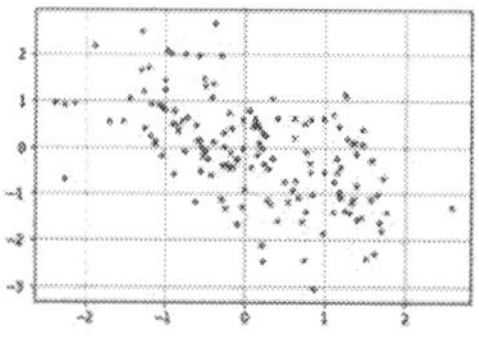	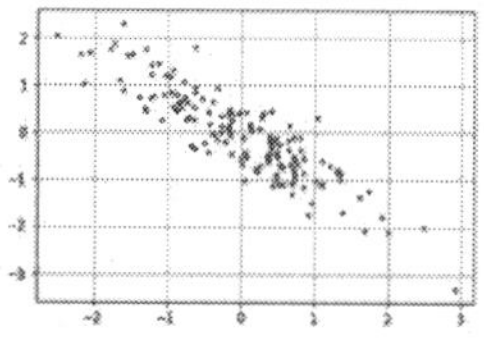

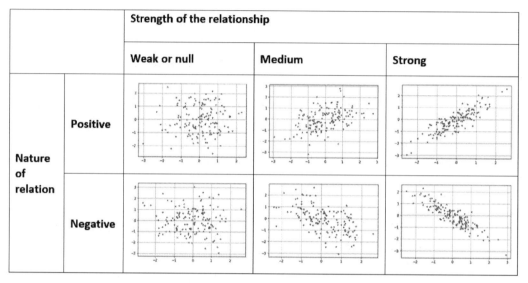

Figure 7.28: Examples of patterns in scatter plots

Keep in mind that the examples from the table are just for reference: usually, real-world datasets do not offer such easily identifiable patterns.

Although we can create plots using pandas, we will use Seaborn, a very popular statistical visualization that is capable of producing beautiful and complex plots with just a few lines of code. We will use the **`scatterplot`** function, which takes the names of the variables that will go on each axis and the name of the DataFrame:

```
sns.scatterplot(x='size', y='average_user_rating',\
                data=games, \
                # this is for controlling the size of the points
                s=20);
```

Here we have the output:

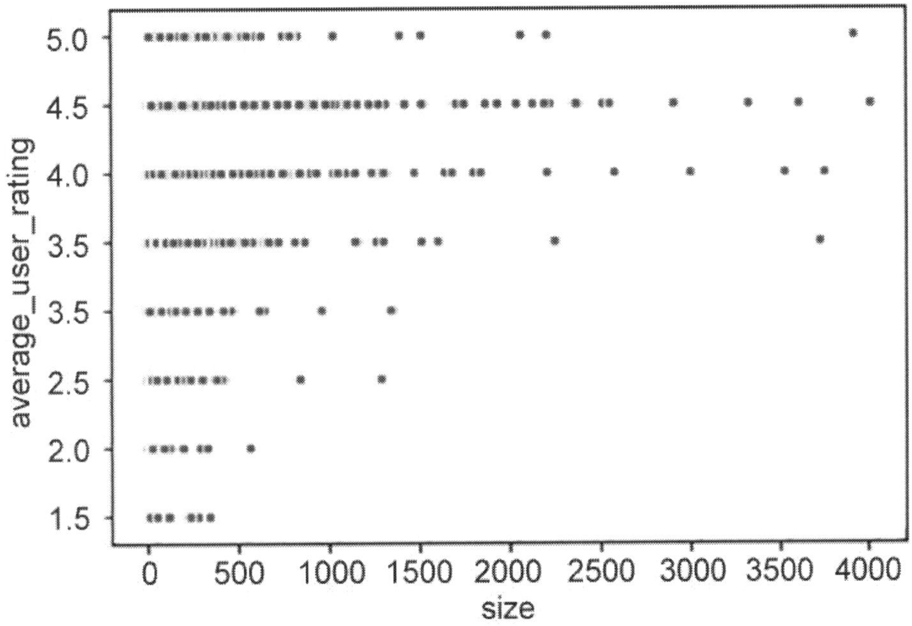

Figure 7.29: Scatter plot of size versus average user ratings

If we take a look at the upper-right quarter of the plot, it looks like games of a certain size, say above 1,500 MB, tend to have ratings of 3.5 and above. Since size is a proxy for the quality of the graphics and the complexity of the game, this plot seems to suggest that a way to improve the chances of getting a decent average rating is by producing games of a certain complexity and visual quality. However, the plot also shows relatively small games getting average ratings of 5.

Now let's explore the relationship between a numerical and a categorical variable. Maybe we can get more insights into the ratings if we treat the average rating as a categorical variable; after all, due to some quirks of the dataset, this variable is discrete instead of continuous; it takes values only on whole and half points. The following code categorizes the variable using the mapping defined in a dictionary:

```
ratings_mapping = {1.5: '1_poor', 2.: '1_poor',\
                   2.5: '1_poor', 3: '1_poor',\
                   3.5: '2_fair', 4. : '2_fair',\
                   4.5: '3_good',5. : '4_excellent'}

games['cat_rating'] = games['average_user_rating']\
                      .map(ratings_mapping)
```

We have created a new average user rating scale that uses categorical variables. We can now use a boxplot to see if the distribution of size values changes for the different types of ratings:

```
sns.boxplot(x='cat_rating', y='size', \
            data=games[games['size'] <= 600], \
            order=['1_poor', '2_fair', '3_good', '4_excellent']);
```

The result is the following:

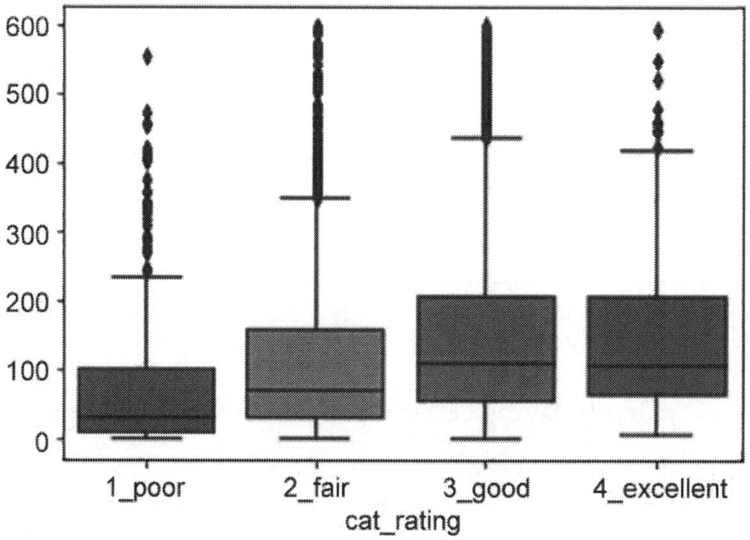

Figure 7.30: Boxplot of size versus categorical user ratings

We have restricted the dataset to games below 600 MB to see if the relationship of size-rating holds for games that are not too large. We see that the distributions are in fact different, with poorly-rated games having smaller sizes in general than the other categories (the boxplot is lower than the rest). Notice that the distributions of good and excellently-rated games are almost identical, perhaps suggesting that, for games below 600 MB, complexity and quality graphics influence ratings up to a point.

Finally, let's review the third case: how to explore the relationship between two categorical variables. To do this, let's explore age ratings versus the categorical rating that we just created. We can produce a table that counts how many observations we have in each combination of the values of our two variables. This is often called a contingency table. Pandas has the handy **crosstab** function for this purpose:

```
pd.crosstab(games['age_rating'], games['cat_rating'])
```

The result is this:

cat_rating	1_poor	2_fair	3_good	4_excellent
age_rating				
12+	57	327	466	75
17+	11	59	68	13
4+	238	821	1029	199
9+	57	309	499	83

Figure 7.31: Contingency table of age ratings versus categorical user ratings

It is good to have the counts; however, it is still a bit tricky to make sense of this data. What we need in order to find out if these two variables are related is to find out whether the proportion of age ratings changes according to how good or bad the game has been rated. For instance, if we find that 90% of 4+ games are poorly rated, and at the same time, only 15% of 17+ games are poorly rated, then it is reasonable to assume that these variables have some sort of relationship. To perform this calculation, we have to normalize the rows of the former table. We do this by adding the **`normalize='index'`** parameter:

```
100*pd.crosstab(games['age_rating'],\
                games['cat_rating'], \
                normalize='index')
```

We have multiplied the whole table by 100, so it is easier to read as percentages:

cat_rating	1_poor	2_fair	3_good	4_excellent
age_rating				
12+	6.162162	35.351351	50.378378	8.108108
17+	7.284768	39.072848	45.033113	8.609272
4+	10.406646	35.898557	44.993441	8.701355
9+	6.012658	32.594937	52.637131	8.755274

Figure 7.32: Row-normalized contingency table of age ratings versus categorical user ratings

Since the rows have been normalized, every row should add up to 100. Now we can easily compare the distribution of the different user ratings across the different age ratings. For instance, we observe that the proportion of excellently rated games is almost the same, regardless of the age rating, and that the same happens (more or less) for the other columns. This suggests that perhaps the age rating of the game is not a big factor for the ratings of the games.

Here is where statistical analysis becomes an art. The findings of the initial exploration produce new questions and hypotheses that we would further explore using more numerical and visual analysis, and hopefully, after a few iterations, we will produce useful information we can turn into knowledge about the problem at hand.

I will close this section by stating that while the scope of this book focuses on visualizing the relationships between two variables, it is possible to visually explore relationships between three or more variables. However, keep in mind that having more than two variables in a visualization often exponentially increases the complexity of the analysis.

EXERCISE 7.03: PRACTICING EDA

In this exercise, we will use a boxplot to visualize whether free games have different ratings than paid games.

1. First, let's take a look at the different prices we have in our dataset. For this, take a look at the unique values of price:

```
games['price'].unique()
```

   The output looks like this:

```
array([  2.99,   1.99,   0.  ,   0.99,   5.99,   7.99,   4.99,
         3.99,  9.99,  19.99,   6.99,  11.99,   8.99, 139.99,
        14.99,  59.99])
```

2. It looks like all the games are sold for some number of dollars plus **99** cents. We know that in practice **2.99** means **3** dollars. Transform this variable to integer values using the built-in **round** method, so the values are nice round numbers:

```
games['price'] = games['price'].round()
```

3. Since this is a discrete numerical variable, use a bar plot to visualize the distribution of the games for each of the prices:

```
games['price'].value_counts().sort_index().plot(kind='bar');
```

The output is as follows:

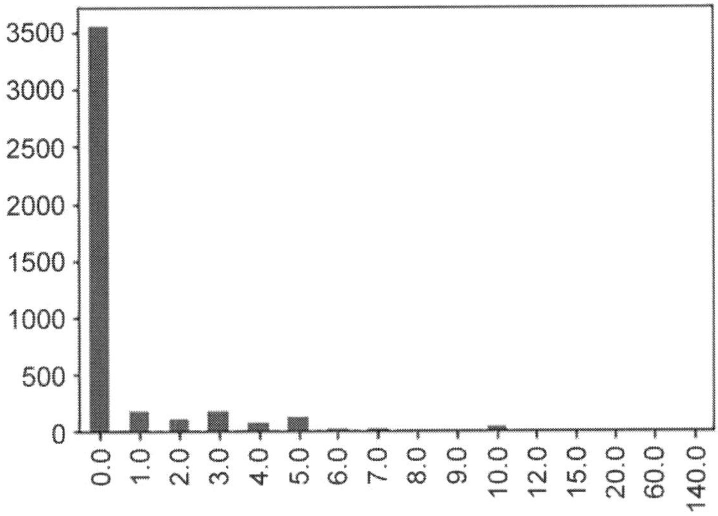

Figure 7.33: Bar plot of the number of observations by price

4. It looks like the majority of the games are free. To simplify the analysis, create a categorical variable named **`cat_price`** that indicates whether a games is free or paid:

```
games['cat_price'] = (games['price'] == 0).astype(int)\
                     .map({0:'paid', 1:'free'})
```

5. Use a boxplot to visualize the relationship between the variable created in the previous point:

```
sns.boxplot(x='cat_price', y='average_user_rating', \
            data=games);
```

The output is as follows:

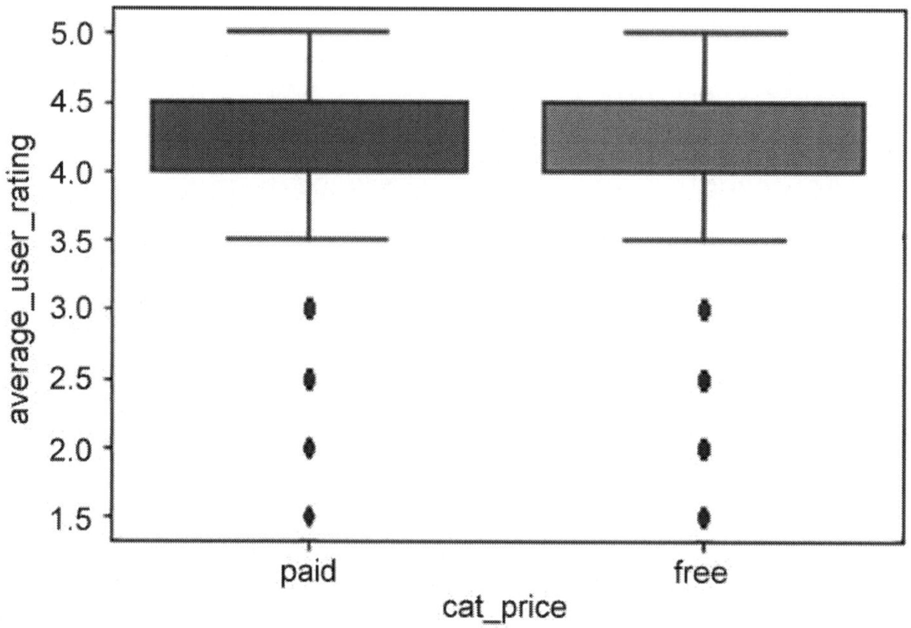

Figure 7.34: Boxplot: cat_price versus average user ratings

From the plot, we can see that the distributions of average user ratings look almost identical for free and paid games. This suggests that the status of free versus paid games does not affect the rating of the game.

In this exercise, we have used a boxplot to explore the distribution of the variable price and see if there is some relationship between this variable and the average user rating.

> **NOTE**
>
> To access the source code for this specific section, please refer to https://packt.live/2VBV2gI.
>
> You can also run this example online at https://packt.live/2YUGv1I.

In this section, we have learned about EDA, which is the process of complementing descriptive statistics with visualizations. We learned about some of the most useful types of visualizations that are used in virtually every type of statistical analysis. You have become familiar with histograms, boxplots, bar plots, and scatter plots, which are all powerful tools to complement the numerical analysis and reveal useful information about a dataset.

EDA is an essential step in every statistical analysis since it allows us, among other things, to get to know the variables in a dataset, recognize potential relationships between them, and generate a hypothesis that can be formally tested using formal inferential methods. Now that we have learned the basics of descriptive statistics, we can move on to learn about inferential statistics, but first, we must learn about some fundamentals of probability theory, which is the topic of the next chapter.

ACTIVITY 7.01: FINDING OUT HIGHLY RATED STRATEGY GAMES

The game development company you work for has come up with a plan to strengthen its position in the gaming market. From industry knowledge and other business reports, it is evident that a very effective way to attract new customers is to develop a great reputation in the mobile game space. Given this fact, your company has the following plan: develop a strategy game for the iOS platform that will get a lot of positive attention, which in turn will bring a large number of new customers to the company. The company believes that this plan will work if and only if the game gets great ratings from users. Since you are an experienced individual in the mobile game space, you are asked to answer the following question: what types of strategy games have great user ratings?

The goal of this activity is two-fold: first is to create a new variable based on the combination of two categorical variables. Then, use the **groupby** method to calculate descriptive statistics on the user ratings to see whether there is a relationship between the average user ratings and the newly created variable.

Steps for completion:

1. Load the **numpy** and **pandas** libraries.
2. Load the strategy games dataset (in the **data** folder of the chapter).

3. Perform all the transformations we did in the first section of the chapter:

   a. Change the names of the variables.

   b. Set the column **id** to **index**.

   c. Drop the **url** and **icon_url** columns.

   d. Change **original_release_date** and **current_version_release_date** to **datetime**.

   e. Eliminate the rows where **average_user_rating** is null from the DataFrame.

   f. Keep in the DataFrame only the rows where **user_rating_count** is equal or greater than 30.

4. Print the dimensions of the dataset. You must have a DataFrame with 4,311 rows and 15 columns.
5. Impute the missing values in the **languages** column with the string **EN** to indicate that those games are available only in English.
6. Create a variable called **free_game** that has the value of **free** if the game has a price of zero and **paid** if the price is above zero.
7. Create a variable called **multilingual** that has the values of **monolingual** if the language column has only one language string, and **multilingual** if the language column has at least two language strings.
8. Create one variable that contains the four combinations from the two variables created in the previous step (**free-monolingual**, **free-multilingual**, **paid-monolingual**, and **paid-multilingual**).
9. Calculate how many observations we have of each type in the **price_language** variable.
10. Use the **groupby** method on the games DataFrame, group by the newly created variable, then select the **average_user_rating** variables and calculate the descriptive statistics.

> **NOTE**
>
> The solution for this activity can be found on page 681.

In this activity, we have shown one approach to create a new categorical variable that results from the possible combinations of two other categorical variables. Then we have used the `groupby` method to calculate the descriptive statistics across the possible values of the newly created variable.

SUMMARY

In this chapter, we learned about the first steps toward performing any kind of statistical analysis: first, we defined our business problem and introduced the dataset. Based on the problem we wanted to solve, we prepared the dataset accordingly: we deleted some records, imputed missing values, transformed the types of some variables, and created new ones. Then we learned about the need for descriptive statistics; we learned how easy it is to calculate them using pandas and how to use and interpret those calculations. In the final section, we learned about how we can combine visualizations with descriptive statistics to get a deeper understanding of the relationships between variables in our datasets. What we learned in this chapter are concepts and techniques that you will be able to put in practice in any data analysis you perform. However, to get more sophisticated in your analysis, you need to have a good grasp of the basics of probability theory, which is the subject of our next chapter.

8

FOUNDATIONAL PROBABILITY CONCEPTS AND THEIR APPLICATIONS

OVERVIEW

By the end of this chapter, you will be familiar with basic and foundational concepts in probability theory. You'll learn how to use NumPy and SciPy modules to perform simulations and solve problems by calculating probabilities using simulations. This chapter also covers how to calculate the probabilities of events using simulations and theoretical probability distributions. Along with this, we'll conceptually define and use random variables included in the scipy.stats module. We will also understand the main characteristics of the normal distribution and calculate probabilities by computing the area under the curve of the probability distribution.

INTRODUCTION

In the previous chapter, we learned how to perform the first steps in any statistical analysis. Given a business or scientific problem and a related dataset, we learned how to load the dataset and prepare it for analysis. Then, we learned how to calculate and use descriptive statistics to make sense of the variables. Finally, we performed EDA to complement the information we gathered from the descriptive statistics and gained a better understanding of the variables and their possible relationships. After getting a basic understanding of an analytical problem, you may need to go one step further and use more sophisticated quantitative tools, some of which are used in the following fields:

- Inferential statistics
- Machine learning
- Prescriptive analytics
- Optimization

What do all of these domains have in common? Many things: for example, they have a mathematical nature, they make heavy use of computational tools, and in one way or another they use **probability theory**, which is one of the most useful branches of applied mathematics and provides the foundation and tools for other disciplines, such as the ones mentioned previously.

In this chapter, we'll give a very brief introduction to probability theory. Unlike traditional statistical books, in this chapter, we'll make heavy use of simulations to put the theoretical concepts into practice and make them more concrete. For this, we will make extensive use of NumPy's and SciPy's random number generation capabilities and we will learn how to use simulations to solve problems. After introducing the mandatory foundational concepts, we'll show you how to produce random numbers using NumPy and use these capabilities to calculate probabilities. After doing that, we'll define the concept of random variables.

Later in this chapter, we'll delve deeper into the two types of random variables: discrete and continuous, and for each type, we will learn how to create random variables with SciPy, as well as how to calculate exact probabilities with these distributions.

RANDOMNESS, PROBABILITY, AND RANDOM VARIABLES

This is a dense section, with many theoretical concepts to learn. Although it is heavy, you will finish this section with a very good grasp of some of the most basic and foundational concepts in probability theory. We will also introduce very useful methods you can use to perform simulations using NumPy so that you get to play around with some code. By using simulations, we hope to show you how the theoretical concepts translate into actual numbers and problems that can be solved with these tools. Finally, we will define **random variables** and **probability distribution**, two of the most important concepts to know about when using statistics to solve problems in the real world.

RANDOMNESS AND PROBABILITY

We all have an intuitive idea of the concept of randomness and use the term in everyday life. Randomness means that certain events happen unpredictably or without a pattern.

One paradoxical fact about random events is that although individual random events are, by definition, unpredictable, when considering many such events, it is possible to predict certain results with very high confidence. For instance, when flipping a coin *once*, we cannot know which of the two possible outcomes we will see (heads or tails). On the other hand, when flipping a coin *1,000* times, we can be almost sure that we will get between 450 and 550 heads.

How do we go from individually unpredictable events to being able to predict something meaningful about a collection of them? The key is probability theory, the branch of mathematics that formalizes the study of randomness and the calculation of the likelihood of certain outcomes. Probability can be understood as a measure of uncertainty, and probability theory gives us the mathematical tools to understand and analyze uncertain events. That's why probability theory is so useful as a decision-making tool: by rigorously and logically analyzing uncertain events, we can reach better decisions, despite the uncertainty.

Uncertainty can come from either ignorance or pure randomness, in such a way that flipping a coin is not a truly random process if you know the mass of the coin, the exact position of your fingers, the exact force applied when throwing it, the exact gravitational pull, and so on. With this information, you could, in principle, predict the outcome, but in practice, we don't know all these variables or the equations to actually make an exact prediction. Another example could be the outcome of a football (soccer) game, the results of a presidential election, or if it's going to rain one week from now.

Given our ignorance about what will happen in the future, assigning a probability is what we can do to come up with a *best guess*.

Probability theory is also a big business. Entire industries, such as lotteries, gambling, and insurance, have been built around the laws of probability and how to monetize the predictions we can make from them. The casino does not know if the person playing roulette will win in the next game, but because of probability laws, the casino owner is completely sure that roulette is a profitable game. The insurance company does not know if a customer will have a car crash tomorrow, but they're sure that having enough car insurance costumers paying their premiums is a profitable business.

Although the following section will feel a bit theoretical, it is necessary to get to know the most important concepts before we can use them to solve analytical problems.

Foundational Probability Concepts

We will start with the basic terminology that you will find on most treatments of this subject. We must learn these concepts in order to be able to solve problems rigorously and to communicate our results in a technically correct fashion.

We will start with the notion of an **experiment**: a situation that happens under controlled conditions and from which we get an observation. The result we observe is called the **outcome** of the experiment. The following table presents some examples of experiments, along with some possible outcomes:

Experiment	Outcome
Tossing a die	5
Team A plays a football game against B	Team A wins
Recording the number of transactions on an ATM	244
Recording the closing price of the stock of company X	USD 34.5

Figure 8.1: Example experiments and outcomes

The **sample space** of the experiment consists of the *mathematical set* of all possible outcomes. Finally, an **event** is any subset of the sample space. Each element of the sample space is called a **simple event** because it consists of a single element. We now have four terms that are related to each other and that are essential to probability theory: experiment, sample space, event, and outcome. To continue with our examples from the previous table, the following table presents the sample space and examples of events for the experiments:

Experiment	**Sample space**	**Example events**
Tossing a die	S = {1, 2, 3, 4, 5, 6}	{ 1 } Odd number (or {1, 3, 5}) A number below 5 (or {1, 2, 3, 4})
Team A plays a football game against B	S = {A wins, B wins, draw}	Team A wins Draw
Recording the number of transactions on an ATM*	S = {0, 1, 2, 3, ... 1,440}	{330, 331, 332} {12, 1000} Less than 500
Recording the closing price of the stock of company X	S = {all non-negative numbers below USD 1,000}	The price was greater than yesterday's The price is in the range [30.4, 32.6]

Figure 8.2: Example experiments, sample spaces, and events

> **NOTE**
>
> Please note that the details in the preceding table are assuming a maximum of 1 transaction per minute is happening.

It is worth noting that we defined the sample space as a *set* in the mathematical sense. Therefore, we can use all the mathematical operations we know from set theory, including getting subsets (which are events). As events are subsets of a larger set, they are sets themselves, and we can use unions, intersections, and so on. The conventional notation for events is to use uppercase letters such as A, B, and C.

We say that an event has happened when the outcome of the experiment belongs to the event. For example, in the experiment *tossing a die*, if we are interested in the event *getting an odd number* and we observe any of the outcomes, that is, 1, 3, or 5, then we can say that the event has happened.

When performing a random experiment, we don't know which outcome we are going to get. What we do in probability theory is assign a number to all the possible events related to an experiment. This number is what we know as the *probability* of an event.

How do we assign probabilities to events? There are a couple of alternatives. However, regardless of the method we use to assign probabilities to events, the theory of probability and its results hold if our way of assigning probabilities to events fulfills the following four conditions. Given events *A* and *B* and their probabilities, denoted as *P(A)* and *P(B)*:

1. $0 \leq P(A) \leq 1$: The probability of an event is always a number between 0 and 1. The closer to 1, the more likely the event will occur. The extremes are 0 for an event that can't occur and 1 for an event that will certainly occur.
2. $P(\varnothing) = 0$: If A is the empty set, then the probability must be 0. For instance, for the experiment *tossing a die*, the event *getting a number greater than 10* does not exist, hence this is the empty set and its probability is 0.
3. $P(S) = 1$: This basically says that when performing an experiment, some outcome must occur for sure.
4. $P(A \cup B) = P(A) + P(B)$ for disjoint events A and B: If we have a collection of non-overlapping events, A and B, then the probability the event (A U B), also known as *A or B*, can be obtained by adding the individual probabilities. These rules also apply for more than two events.

This subsection has been heavy in terms of concepts and theory, but it is important to understand these now, in order to avoid mistakes later. Fortunately, we have Python and NumPy with their great numerical capabilities that will help us put this theory into practice.

> **NOTE**
>
> A quick note on all the exercises and related test scripts: If you are using a CLI (such as Windows' Command Prompt or Mac's Terminal) to run the test scripts, it will throw an error, such as **Implement enable_gui in a subclass**. This is something to do with some of the commands being used in the notebooks (such as **%matplotlib** inline). So, if you want to run the test scripts, please use the IPython shell. The code for the exercises in this book is best run on Jupyter Notebooks.

INTRODUCTION TO SIMULATIONS WITH NUMPY

To start putting all this theory into practice, let's begin by loading the libraries we will use in this chapter:

```
import pandas as pd
import numpy as np
import matplotlib.pyplot as plt
import seaborn as sns

# line to allow the plots to be shown in the Jupyter Notebook
%matplotlib inline
```

We will make extensive use of NumPy's random number generation capabilities. We will use the random module (**np.random**), which is able to generate random numbers that follow many of the most important probability distributions (more on probability distributions later).

Let's begin by simulating a random experiment: *tossing a regular die*.

Let's learn how to perform this experiment using NumPy. There are different ways to do this. We'll use the function **randint** from the **random** module, which generates random integers between **low** (inclusive) and **high** (exclusive) arguments. Since we want to generate numbers between 1 and 6, our function will look like this:

```
def toss_die():
    outcome = np.random.randint(1, 7)
    return outcome
```

Let's use our function ten times in a row to observe how it works:

```
for x in range(10):
    print(toss_die())
```

The following is an example output:

```
6, 2, 6, 5, 1, 3, 3, 6, 6, 5
```

Since these numbers are randomly generated, you will most likely get different values.

For this function and almost every other function that produces random numbers (or some other random result), it is sometimes necessary to generate random numbers in such a way that anyone running the code at any moment obtains the same results. For that, we need to use a **seed**.

Let's add a line that creates the seed and then use our function ten times in a row to observe how it works:

```
np.random.seed(123)

for x in range(10):
    print(toss_die(), end=', ')
```

The result is as follows:

```
6, 3, 5, 3, 2, 4, 3, 4, 2, 2
```

As long as you run the first line containing the number 123 inside the seed function, anyone running this code (with the same NumPy version) will get the same output numbers.

Another useful function from the **numpy.random** module is **np.random.choice**, which can sample elements from a vector. Say we have a class of 30 students, and we would like to randomly chose four of them. First, we generate the fictional student list:

```
students = ['student_' + str(i) for i in range(1,31)]
```

Now, can use **np.random.choice** to randomly select four of them:

```
sample_students = np.random.choice(a=students, size=4,\
                                   replace=False)
sample_students
```

The following is the output:

```
array(['student_16', 'student_11', 'student_19', \
       'student_26'], dtype='<U10')
```

The **`replace=False`** argument ensures that once an element has been chosen, it can't be selected again. This is called **sampling without replacement**.

In contrast, **sampling with replacement** means that all the elements of the vector are considered when producing each sample. Imagine that all the elements of the vector are in a bag. We randomly pick one element for each sample and then put the element we got in the bag before drawing the next sample. An application of this could be as follows: say that we will give a surprise quiz to one student of the group, every week for 12 weeks. All the students are subjects who may be given the quiz, even if that student was selected in a previous week. For this, we could use **`replace=True`**, like so:

```
sample_students2 = np.random.choice(a=students, \
                                    size=12, replace=True)


for i, s in enumerate(sample_students2):
    print(f'Week {i+1}: {s}')
```

The result is as follows:

```
Week 1: student_6
Week 2: student_23
Week 3: student_4
Week 4: student_26
Week 5: student_5
Week 6: student_30
Week 7: student_23
Week 8: student_30
Week 9: student_11
Week 10: student_6
Week 11: student_13
Week 12: student_5
```

As you can see, poor student 6 was chosen on weeks 1 and 10, and student 30 on 6 and 8.

Now that we know how to use NumPy to generate dice outcomes and get samples (with or without replacement), we can use it to practice probability.

EXERCISE 8.01: SAMPLING WITH AND WITHOUT REPLACEMENT

In this exercise, we will use **random.choice** to produce random samples with and without replacement. Follow these steps to complete this exercise:

1. Import the NumPy library:

```
import numpy as np
```

2. Create two lists containing four different suits and 13 different ranks in the set of standard cards:

```
suits = ['hearts', 'diamonds', 'spades', 'clubs']
ranks = ['Ace', '2', '3', '4', '5', '6', '7', '8', \
         '9', '10', 'Jack', 'Queen', 'King']
```

3. Create a list, named **cards**, containing the 52 cards of the standard deck:

```
cards = [rank + '-' + suit for rank in ranks for suit in suits]
```

4. Use the **np.random.choice** function to draw a hand (five cards) from the deck. Use **replace=False** so that each card gets selected only once:

```
print(np.random.choice(cards, size=5, replace=False))
```

The result should look something like this (you might get different cards):

```
['Ace-clubs' '5-clubs' '7-clubs' '9-clubs' '6-clubs']
```

5. Now, create a function named **deal_hands** that returns two lists, each with five cards drawn from the same deck. Use **replace=False** in the **np.random.choice** function. This function will perform sampling *without* replacement:

```
def deal_hands():
    drawn_cards = np.random.choice(cards, size=10, \
                                   replace=False)
    hand_1 = drawn_cards[:5].tolist()
    hand_2 = drawn_cards[5:].tolist()
    return hand_1, hand_2
```

To print the output, run the function like so:

```
deal_hands()
```

You should get something like this:

```
(['9-spades', 'Ace-clubs', 'Queen-diamonds', '2-diamonds',
  '9-diamonds'],
 ['Jack-hearts', '8-clubs', '10-clubs', '4-spades',
  'Queen-hearts'])
```

6. Create a second function called **deal_hands2** that's identical to the last one, but with the **replace=True** argument in the **np.random.choice** function. This function will perform sampling *with* replacement:

```
def deal_hands2():
    drawn_cards = np.random.choice(cards, size=10, \
                                   replace=True)
    hand_1 = drawn_cards[:5].tolist()
    hand_2 = drawn_cards[5:].tolist()
    return hand_1, hand_2
```

7. Finally, run the following code:

```
np.random.seed(2)
deal_hands2()
```

The result is as follows:

```
(['Jack-hearts', '4-clubs', 'Queen-diamonds', '3-hearts',
  '6-spades'],
 ['Jack-clubs', '5-spades', '3-clubs', 'Jack-hearts', '2-clubs'])
```

As you can see, by allowing sampling *with replacement*, the **Jack-hearts** card was drawn in both hands, meaning that when each card was sampled, all 52 were considered.

In this exercise, we practiced the concept of sampling with and without replacement and learned how to apply it using the **np.random.choice** function.

> **NOTE**
>
> To access the source code for this specific section, please refer to https://packt.live/2Zs7RuY.
>
> You can also run this example online at https://packt.live/2Bm7A4Y.

PROBABILITY AS A RELATIVE FREQUENCY

Let's return to the question of the conceptual section: how do we assign probabilities to events? Under the *relative frequency* approach, what we do is repeat an experiment a large number of times and then define the probability of an event as the *relative frequency it has occurred*, that is, how many times we observed the event happening, divided by the number of times we performed the experiment:

$$P(A) = \frac{\#\ times\ A\ occurred}{\#\ of\ \ experiments}$$

Figure 8.3: Formula to calculate the probability

Let's look into this concept with a practical example. First, we will perform the experiment of tossing a die 1 million times:

```
np.random.seed(81)

one_million_tosses = np.random.randint(low=1, \
                                       high=7, size=int(1e6))
```

We can get the first 10 values from the array:

```
one_million_tosses[:10]
```

This look like this:

```
array([4, 2, 1, 4, 4, 4, 2, 2, 6, 3])
```

Remember that the sample space of this experiment is S = {1, 2, 3, 4, 5, 6}. Let's define some events and assign them probabilities using the relative frequency method. First, let's use a couple of simple events:

- **A**: Observing the number 2
- **B**: Observing the number 6

We can use the vectorization capabilities of NumPy and count the number of *simple events* happening by summing the Boolean vector we get from performing the comparison operation:

```
N_A_occurs = (one_million_tosses == 2).sum()

Prob_A = N_A_occurs/one_million_tosses.shape[0]

print(f'P(A)={Prob_A}')
```

The result is as follows:

```
P(A)=0.16595
```

Following the exact same procedure, we can calculate the probability for event **B**:

```
N_B_occurs = (one_million_tosses == 6).sum()

Prob_B = N_B_occurs/one_million_tosses.shape[0]

print(f'P(B)={Prob_B}')
```

The result is as follows:

```
P(B)=0.166809
```

Now, we will try with a couple of compounded events (they have more than one possible outcome):

- **C**: Observing an odd number (or {1, 3, 5})
- **D**: Observing a number less than 5 (or {1, 2, 3, 4})

Because the event *observing an odd number* will occur if we get a 1 *or* 3 *or* 5, we can translate the *or* that we use in our spoken language into the mathematical **OR** operator. In Python, this is the **|** operator:

```
N_odd_number = (
    (one_million_tosses == 1) |
    (one_million_tosses == 3) |
    (one_million_tosses == 5)).sum()

Prob_C = N_odd_number/one_million_tosses.shape[0]

print(f'P(C)={Prob_C}')
```

The result is as follows:

```
P(C)=0.501162
```

Finally, let's calculate the probability of **D**:

```
N_D_occurs = (one_million_tosses < 5).sum()

Prob_D = N_D_occurs/one_million_tosses.shape[0]

print(f'P(D)={Prob_D}')
```

We get the following value:

```
P(D)=0.666004
```

Here, we have used the relative frequency approach to calculate the probability of the following events:

- **A**: Observing the number 2: 0.16595
- **B**: Observing the number 6: 0.166809
- **C**: Observing an odd number: 0.501162
- **D**: Observing a number less than 5: 0.666004

In summary, under the relative frequency approach, when we have a set of outcomes from repeated experiments, what we do to calculate the probability of an event is count how many times the event has happened and divide that count by the total number of experiments. As simple as that.

In other cases, the assignments of probabilities can arise based on a definition. This is what we may call **theoretical probability**. For instance, a *fair* coin, *by definition*, has an equal probability of showing either of the two outcomes, say, heads or tails. Since there are only two outcomes for this experiment {heads, tails} and the probabilities must add up to 1, each simple event must have a 0.5 probability of occurring.

Another example is as follows: a *fair* die is one where the six numbers have the same probability of occurring, so the probability of tossing any number must be equal to *1/6 = 0.1666666*. In fact, the default behavior of the **numpy.randint** function is to simulate the chosen integer numbers, each with the same probability of coming out.

Using the theoretical definition, and knowing that we have simulated a *fair* die with NumPy, we can arrive at the probabilities for the events we presented previously:

- **A**: Observing the number 2, P(A) = 1/6 = 0.1666666
- **B**: Observing the number 6, P(B) = 1/6 = 0.1666666

- **C**: Observing an odd number: P(observing 1 *or* observing 3 *or* observing 5) = P(observing 1) + or P(observing 3) + P(observing 5) = 1/6 + 1/6 + 1/6 = 3/6 = 0.5
- **D**: Observing a number less than 5: P(observing 1 *or* observing 2 *or* observing 3 *or* observing 4) = P(observing 1) + or P(observing 2) + P(observing 3) + P(observing 4) = 1/6 + 1/6 + 1/6 + 1/6 = 4/6 = 0.666666

Notice two things here:

- These numbers are surprisingly (or unsurprisingly, if you already knew this) close to the results we obtained by using the relative frequency approach.
- We could decompose the sum of **C** and **D** because of rule 4 of the *Foundational Probability Concepts* section.

DEFINING RANDOM VARIABLES

Often, you will find quantities whose values are (or seem to be) the result of a random process. Here are some examples:

- The sum of the outcome of two dice
- The number of heads when throwing ten coins
- The price of the stock of IBM one week from now
- The number of visitors to a website
- The number of calories ingested in a day by a person

All of these are examples of quantities that can vary, which means they are *variables*. In addition, since the value they take depends partially or entirely on randomness, we call them *random variables*: quantities whose values are determined by a random process. The typical notation for random variables is uppercase letters at the end of the alphabet, such as X, Y, and Z. The corresponding lowercase letter is used to refer to the values they take. For instance, if X is *the sum of the outcomes of two dice*, here are some examples of how to read the notation:

- $P(X = 10)$: Probability of X taking the number 10
- $P(X > 5)$: Probability of X taking a value greater than 5
- $P(X = x)$: Probability of X taking the value x (when we are making a general statement)

Since *X* is the sum of two numbers from two dice, *X* can take the following values: {2, 3, 4, 5, 6, 7, 8, 9, 10, 11, 12}. Using what we learned in the previous section, we can simulate a large number of values for our random variable, *X*, like this:

```
np.random.seed(55)

number_of_tosses = int(1e5)

die_1 = np.random.randint(1,7, size=number_of_tosses)
die_2 = np.random.randint(1,7, size=number_of_tosses)

X = die_1 + die_2
```

We have simulated 100,000 die tosses for two dice and got the respective values for *X*. These are the first values for our vectors:

```
print(die_1[:10])
print(die_2[:10])
print(X[:10])
```

The result is as follows:

```
[6 3 1 6 6 6 6 6 4 2]
[1 2 3 5 1 3 3 6 3 1]
[7  5  4 11  7  9  9 12  7  3]
```

So, in the first simulated roll, we got **6** on the first die and **1** on the second, so the first value of *X* is **7**.

Just as with experiments, we can define events over random variables and calculate the respective probabilities of those events. For instance, we can use the relative frequency definition to calculate the probability of the following events:

- $X = 10$: Probability of *X* taking the number 10
- $X > 5$: Probability of *X* taking a value greater than 5

The calculations to get the probabilities of those events are essentially the same as the ones we did previously:

```
Prob_X_is_10 = (X == 10).sum()/X.shape[0]

print(f'P(X = 10) = {Prob_X_is_10}')
```

The result is as follows:

```
P(X = 10) = 0.08329
```

And for the second event, we have the following:

```
Prob_X_is_gt_5 = (X > 5).sum()/X.shape[0]

print(f'P(X > 5) = {Prob_X_is_gt_5}')
```

The result is as follows:

```
P(X > 5) = 0.72197
```

We can use a bar plot to visualize the number of times each of the possible values has appeared in our simulation. This will allow us to get to know our random variable better:

```
X = pd.Series(X)

# counts the occurrences of each value
freq_of_X_values = X.value_counts()

freq_of_X_values.sort_index().plot(kind='bar')
plt.grid();
```

The plot that's generated is as follows:

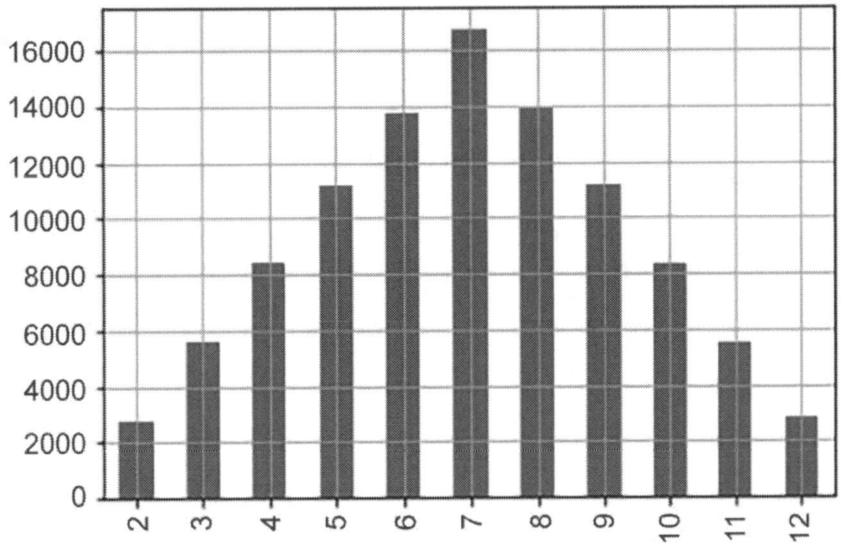

Figure 8.4: Frequencies of the values of X

We can see out of the 100,000 of *X*, it took the value 3 around 5,800 times and the value 6 a little less than 14,000 times, which is also very close to the number of times the value 8 appeared. We can also observe that the most common outcome was the number 7.

Following the relative frequency definition of probability, if we divide the frequencies by the number of values of *X*, we can get the probability of observing each of the values of *X*:

```
Prob_of_X_values = freq_of_X_values/X.shape[0]

Prob_of_X_values.sort_index().plot(kind='bar')
plt.grid();
```

This gives us the following plot:

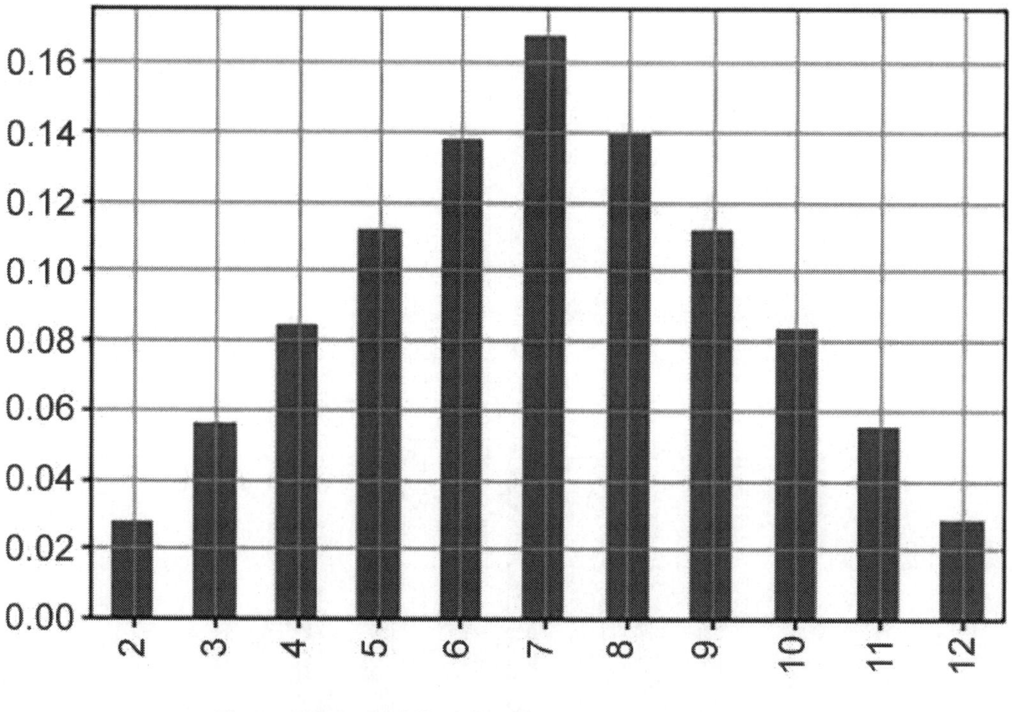

Figure 8.5: Probability distribution of the values of X

The plot looks almost exactly like the last one, but in this case, we can see the probabilities of observing all the possible values of *X*. This is what we call the *probability distribution* (or simply the distribution) of a random variable: the probabilities of observing each of the values the random variable can take.

Let's illustrate both concepts, random variables and probability distribution, with another example. First, we'll define the random variable:

Y: Number of heads when tossing 10 fair coins.

Now, our task is to estimate the probability distribution. We know that this random variable can take 11 possible values: {0, 1, 2, 3, 4, 5, 6, 7, 8, 9, 10}. For each of these values, there is a corresponding probability that the *Y* variable will take that value. Intuitively, we know that it is very unlikely to observe extreme values of the variable: getting 10 heads (*Y=10*) or 10 tails (*Y=0*) is very unlikely. We also expect the *Y* variable to take values such as 4, 5, and 6 most of the time. We can calculate the probability distribution to validate our intuition.

Once again, let's simulate the experiment of tossing 10 coins. From there, we can observe the values of this random variable. Let's begin by simulating tossing 10 fair coins 1 million times:

```
np.random.seed(97)

ten_coins_a_million_times = np.random.randint(0, 2, \
                                              size=int(10e6))\
                                              .reshape(-1,10)
```

The preceding code will produce a matrix of 1,000,000 x 10, with each row representing the experiment of tossing 10 coins. We can consider 0s as tails and 1s as heads. Here, we have the first 12 rows:

```
ten_coins_a_million_times[:12, :]
```

The result is as follows:

```
array([[0, 1, 1, 1, 1, 1, 0, 1, 1, 0],
       [0, 0, 1, 1, 1, 0, 1, 0, 0, 0],
       [0, 1, 0, 1, 1, 0, 0, 0, 0, 1],
       [1, 0, 1, 1, 0, 1, 0, 0, 1, 1],
       [1, 0, 1, 0, 1, 0, 1, 0, 0, 0],
       [0, 1, 1, 1, 0, 1, 1, 1, 1, 0],
       [1, 1, 1, 1, 0, 1, 0, 1, 0, 1],
       [0, 1, 0, 0, 1, 1, 1, 0, 0, 0],
       [1, 0, 0, 1, 1, 1, 0, 0, 0, 0],
       [0, 1, 0, 1, 0, 1, 0, 1, 0, 1],
       [1, 0, 1, 1, 1, 0, 0, 0, 1, 0],
       [0, 0, 0, 0, 1, 1, 1, 0, 1, 1]])
```

To produce the different values of *Y*, we need to add every row, like so:

```
Y = ten_coins_a_million_times.sum(axis=1)
```

Now, we can use the former calculated object (**Y**) to calculate probabilities of certain events, for instance, the probability of obtaining zero heads:

```
Prob_Y_is_0 = (Y == 0).sum() / Y.shape[0]

print(f'P(Y = 0) = {Prob_Y_is_0}')
```

The output is as follows:

```
P(Y = 0) = 0.000986
```

This is a very small number and is consistent with our intuition: it is very unlikely to get 10 tails. In fact, that only happened 986 times in 1 million experiments.

Just as we did previously, we can plot the probability distribution of *Y*:

```
Y = pd.Series(Y)

# counts the occurrences of each value
freq_of_Y_values = Y.value_counts()

Prob_of_Y_values = freq_of_Y_values/Y.shape[0]

Prob_of_Y_values.sort_index().plot(kind='bar')
plt.grid();
```

This is the output:

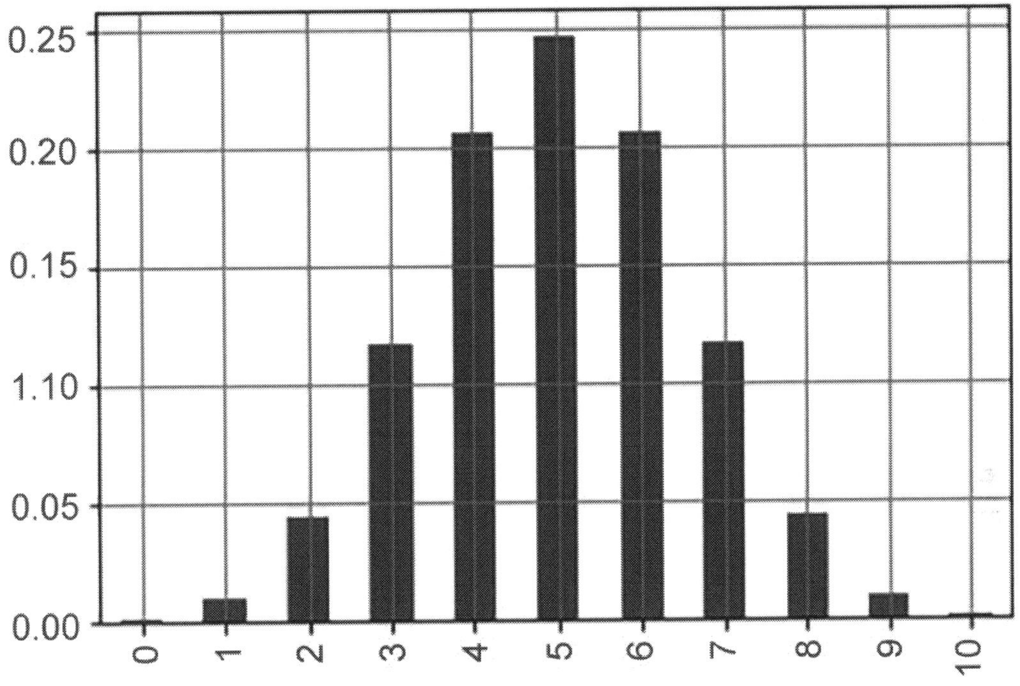

Figure 8.6: Probability distribution of Y

The probability of getting 5 heads is around 0.25, so around 25% of the time, we could expect to get 5 heads. The chance of getting 4 or 6 heads is also relatively high. What is the probability of getting 4, 5, or 6 heads? We can easily calculate this using **`Prob_of_Y_values`** by adding the respective probabilities of getting 4, 5, or 6 heads:

```
print(Prob_of_Y_values.loc[[4,5,6]])

print(f'P(4<=Y<=6) = {Prob_of_Y_values.loc[[4,5,6]].sum()}')
```

The result is as follows:

```
4      0.205283
5      0.246114
6      0.205761
dtype: float64

P(4<=Y<=6) = 0.657158
```

So, around 2/3 (~66%) of the time, we will observe 4, 5, or 6 heads when tossing 10 fair coins. Going back to the definition of probability as a measure of uncertainty, we could say that we are 66% confident that, when tossing 10 fair coins, we will see between 4 and 6 heads.

EXERCISE 8.02: CALCULATING THE AVERAGE WINS IN ROULETTE

In this exercise, we will learn how to use **`np.random.choice`** to simulate a real-world random process. Then, we will take this simulation and calculate how much money we will gain/lose on average if we play a large number of times.

We will simulate going to a casino to play roulette. European roulette consists of a ball falling on any of the integer numbers from 0 to 36 randomly with an equal chance of falling on any number. Many modalities of betting are allowed, but we will play it in just one way (which is equivalent to the famous way of betting on red or black colors). The rules are as follows:

- Bet *m* units (of your favorite currency) on the numbers from 19 to 36.
- If the outcome of the roulette is any of the selected numbers, then you win *m* units.
- If the outcome of the roulette is any number between 0 and 18 (inclusive), then you lose *m* units.

To simplify this, let's say the bets are of 1 unit. Let's get started:

1. Import the NumPy library:

```
import numpy as np
```

2. Use the **np.random.choice** function to write a function named **roulette** that simulates any number of games from European roulette:

```
def roulette(number_of_games=1):

    # generate the Roulette numbers
    roulette_numbers = np.arange(0, 37)

    outcome = np.random.choice(a = roulette_numbers, \
                               size = number_of_games,\
                               replace = True)
    return outcome
```

3. Write a function named **payoff** that encodes the preceding payoff logic. It receives two arguments: **outcome**, a number from the roulette wheel (an integer from 0 to 36); and **units** to bet with a default value of 1:

```
def payoff(outcome, units=1):
    # 1. Bet m units on the numbers from 19 to 36
    # 2. If the outcome of the roulette is any of the
    #    selected numbers, then you win m units
    if outcome > 18:
        pay = units
    else:
    # 3. If the outcome of the roulette is any number
    #    between 0 and 18 (inclusive) then you lose m units
        pay = -units
    return pay
```

4. Use **np.vectorize** to vectorize the function so it can also accept a vector of roulette outcomes. This will allow you to pass a vector of outcomes and get the respective payoffs:

```
payoff = np.vectorize(payoff)
```

5. Now, simulate playing roulette 20 times (betting one unit). Use the **payoff** function to get the vector of outcomes:

```
outcomes = roulette(20)
payoffs = payoff(outcomes)

print(outcomes)
print(payoffs)
```

The output is as follows:

```
[29 36 11  6 11  6  1 24 30 13  0 35  7 34 30  7 36 32 12 10]
[ 1  1 -1 -1 -1 -1 -1  1  1 -1 -1  1 -1  1  1 -1  1  1 -1 -1]
```

6. Simulate 1 million roulette games and use the outcomes to get the respective payoffs. Save the payoffs in a vector named **payoffs**:

```
number_of_games = int(1e6)
outcomes = roulette(number_of_games)
payoffs = payoff(outcomes)
```

7. Use the **np.mean** function to calculate the mean of the payoffs vector. The value you will get should be close to -0.027027:

```
np.mean(payoffs)
```

The negative means that, on average, you lose -0.027027 for every unit you bet. Remember that your loss is the casino's profit. That is their business.

In this exercise, we learned how to simulate a real-world process using the capabilities of NumPy for random number generation. We also simulated a large number of events to get a long-term average.

> **NOTE**
>
> To access the source code for this specific section, please refer to https://packt.live/2AoiyGp.
>
> You can also run this example online at https://packt.live/3irX6Si.

With that, we learned how we can make sense of random events by assigning probabilities to quantify uncertainty. Then, we defined some of the most important concepts in probability theory. We also learned how to assign probabilities to events using the relative frequency definition. In addition, we introduced the important concept of random variables. Computationally, we learned how to simulate values and samples with NumPy and how to use simulations to answer questions about the probabilities of certain events.

Depending on the types of values random variables can take, we can have two types:

- Discrete random variables
- Continuous random variables

We will provide some examples of both in the following two sections.

DISCRETE RANDOM VARIABLES

In this section, we'll continue learning about and working with random variables. We will study a particular type of random variable: **discrete random variables**. These types of variables arise in every kind of applied domain, such as medicine, education, manufacturing, and so on, and therefore it is extremely useful to know how to work with them. We will learn about perhaps the most important, and certainly one of the most commonly occurring, discrete distributions: the binomial distribution.

DEFINING DISCRETE RANDOM VARIABLES

Discrete random variables are those that can take only a specific number of values (technically, a *countable* number of values). Often, the values they can take are specific integer values, although this is not necessary. For instance, if a random variable can take the set of values {1.25, 3.75, 9.15}, it would also be considered a discrete random variable. The two random variables we introduced in the previous section are examples of discrete random variables.

Consider an example in which you are the manager of a factory that produces auto parts. The machine producing the parts will produce, on average, defective parts 4% of the time. We can interpret this 4% as the probability of producing defective parts. These auto parts are packaged in boxes containing 12 units, so, in principle, every box can contain anywhere from 0 to 12 defective pieces. Suppose we don't know which piece is defective (until it is used), nor do we know when a defective piece will be produced. Hence, we have a random variable. First, let's formally define it:

Z: number of defective auto parts in a 12-box pack.

As the manager of the plant, one of your largest clients asks you the following questions:

- What percentage of boxes have 12 non-defective pieces (zero defective pieces)?
- What percentage of boxes have 3 or more defective pieces?

You can answer both questions if you know the probability distribution for your variable, so you ask yourself the following:

What does the probability distribution of Z look like?

To answer this question, we can again use simulations. To simulate a single box, we can use **np.random.choice** and provide the probabilities via the **p** parameter:

```
np.random.seed(977)

np.random.choice(['defective', 'good'], \
                 size=12, p=(0.04, 0.96))
```

The result is as follows:

```
array(['good', 'good', 'good', 'good', 'good', 'good', 'good', \
       'defective', 'good', 'good', 'good', 'good'], dtype='<U9')
```

We can see that this particular box contains one defective piece. Notice that the probability vector that was used in the function must add up to one: since the probability of observing a defective piece is 4% (0.04), the probability of observing a good piece is *100% - 4% = 96%* (0.96), which are the values that are passed to the p argument.

Now that we know how to simulate a single box, to estimate the distribution of our random variable, let's simulate a large number of boxes; 1 million is more than enough. To make our calculations easier and faster, let's use 1s and 0s to denote defective and good parts, respectively. To simulate 1 million boxes, it is enough to change the size parameter to a tuple that will be of size *12 x 1,000,000*:

```
np.random.seed(10)

n_boxes = int(1e6)
parts_per_box = 12

one_million_boxes = np.random.choice\
                    ([1, 0], \
                     size=(n_boxes, parts_per_box), \
                     p=(0.04, 0.96))
```

The first five boxes can be found using the following formula:

```
one_million_boxes[:5,:]
```

The output will be as follows:

```
array([[0, 1, 0, 0, 0, 0, 0, 0, 0, 0, 0, 0],
       [1, 0, 0, 0, 0, 0, 0, 0, 0, 0, 0, 0],
       [0, 0, 0, 0, 0, 0, 0, 0, 0, 0, 0, 0],
       [0, 0, 0, 0, 0, 0, 0, 0, 0, 0, 0, 0],
       [0, 0, 0, 0, 0, 0, 0, 0, 0, 0, 0, 0]])
```

Each of the zeros in the output represents a non-defective piece, and one represents a defective piece. Now, we count how many defective pieces we have per box, and then we can count how many times we observed 0, 1, 2, ..., 12 defective pieces, and with that, we can plot the probability distribution of Z:

```
# count defective pieces per box
defective_pieces_per_box = one_million_boxes.sum(axis=1)

# count how many times we observed 0, 1,…, 12 defective pieces
defective_pieces_per_box = pd.Series(defective_pieces_per_box)
frequencies = defective_pieces_per_box.value_counts()

# probability distribution
probs_Z = frequencies/n_boxes
```

Finally, let's visualize this:

```
print(probs_Z.sort_index())
probs_Z.sort_index().plot(kind='bar')
plt.grid()
```

The output will be as follows:

```
0    0.612402
1    0.306383
2    0.070584
3    0.009630
4    0.000940
5    0.000056
6    0.000004
7    0.000001
```

Here's what the probability distribution will look like:

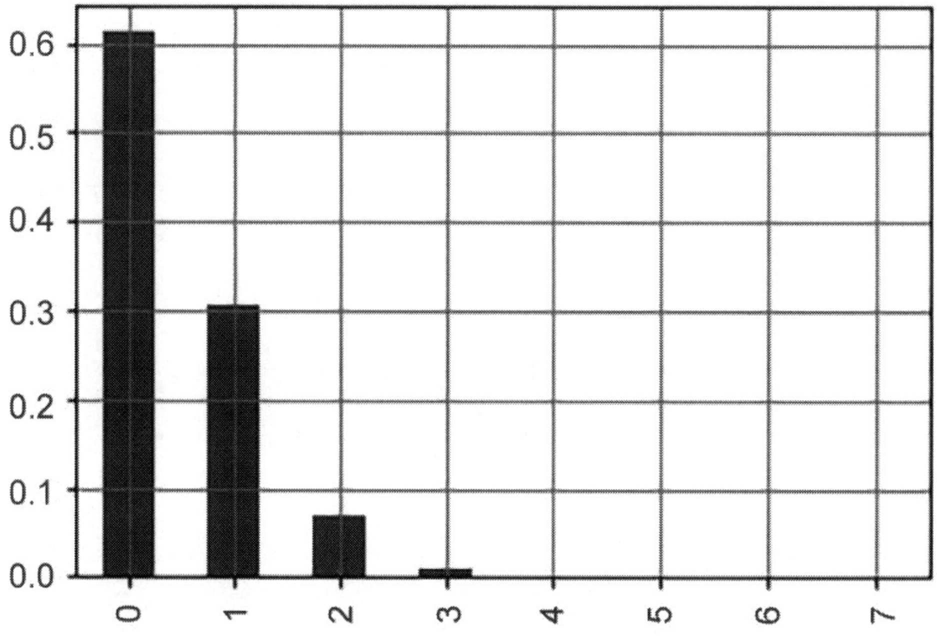

Figure 8.7: Probability distribution of Z

From this simulation, we can conclude that around 61% of boxes will be shipped with zero defective parts, and around 30% of the boxes will contain one defective part. We can also see that it is very, very unlikely to observe three or more defective parts in a box. Now, you can answer the questions your client had:

- What percentage of boxes have 12 non-defective parts? *Answer: 61% of the boxes will contain 12 non-defective parts.*
- What percentage of boxes have 3 or more defective pieces? *Answer: Only about 1% of the boxes will contain 3 or more defective parts.*

THE BINOMIAL DISTRIBUTION

It turns out that, under certain conditions, we can find out the exact probability distribution of certain discrete random variables. The *binomial distribution* is a theoretical distribution that applies to random variables and fulfills the following three characteristics:

- **Condition 1**: For an individual observation, there are *only two possible outcomes*, usually denoted as *success* and *failure*. If the probability of success is *p*, then the probability of failure must be *1 – p*.
- **Condition 2**: The experiment is performed a *fixed number of times*, usually denoted by *n*.
- **Condition 3**: All the experiments are *independent*, meaning that knowing the outcome of an experiment does not change the probability of the next. Therefore, the probability of success (and failure) remains the same.

If these conditions are met, then we say that the random variable follows a binomial distribution, or that the random variable is a *binomial random variable*. We can get the exact probability distribution of a binomial random variable, *X*, using the following formula:

$$P(X=x) = \frac{n!}{x!(n-x)!}p^x(1-p)^{n-x}$$

Figure 8.8: Formula to calculate the probability distribution of X

Technically, the *mathematical function* that takes a possible value of a discrete random variable (*x*) and returns the respective probability is called the **probability mass function**. Notice that once we know the values of *n* and *p* from the previous equation, the probability depends only on the *x* value, so the former equation defines the probability mass function for a binomial random variable.

OK, this sounds and looks very theoretical and abstract (because it is). However, we have already introduced two random variables that follow the binomial distribution. Let's verify the conditions for the following:

Y: Number of heads when tossing 10 fair coins.

- **Condition 1**: For each individual coin, there are only two possible outcomes, *head* or *tails*, each with a fixed probability of 0.5. Since we were interested in the *number of heads*, *heads* can be considered our *success* and *tails* our *failure*.
- **Condition 2**: The number of coins was fixed at 10 coins.
- **Condition 3**: Each coin toss is independent: we implicitly (and logically) assumed that the outcome of one coin does not influence the outcome of any other coin.

So, we have the numbers we need to use in the preceding formula:

- $p = 0.5$
- $n = 10$

If we want to get the probability of getting five heads, then we only need to replace $x = 5$ in the formula with the known p and n:

$$P(Y=5) = \frac{10!}{5!(10-5)!}0.5^5(1-0.5)^{10-5}=0.24609375$$

Figure 8.9: Substituting the values of x, p and n in the probability distribution formula

Now, let's do these theoretical calculations with Python. It is time to introduce another Python module that we will be using heavily in this and the following chapter. The **`scipy.stats`** module contains many statistical functions. Among those, there are many that can be used to create random variables that follow many of the most commonly used probability distributions. Let's use this module to create a random variable that follows the theoretical binomial distribution. First, we instantiate the random variable with the appropriate parameters:

```
import scipy.stats as stats

Y_rv = stats.binom(
    n = 10, # number of coins
    p = 0.5 # probability of heads (success)
)
```

Once created, we can use the **pmf** method of this object to calculate the exact theoretical probabilities for each of the possible values *Y* can take. First, let's create a vector containing all the values *Y* can take (integers from 0 to 10):

```
y_values = np.arange(0, 11)
```

Now, we can simply use the **pmf** (which stands for **probability mass function**) method to get the respective probabilities for each of the former values:

```
Y_probs = Y_rv.pmf(y_values)
```

We can visualize the **pmf** we got like so:

```
fig, ax = plt.subplots()

ax.bar(y_values, Y_probs)

ax.set_xticks(y_values)

ax.grid()
```

The output we get is as follows:

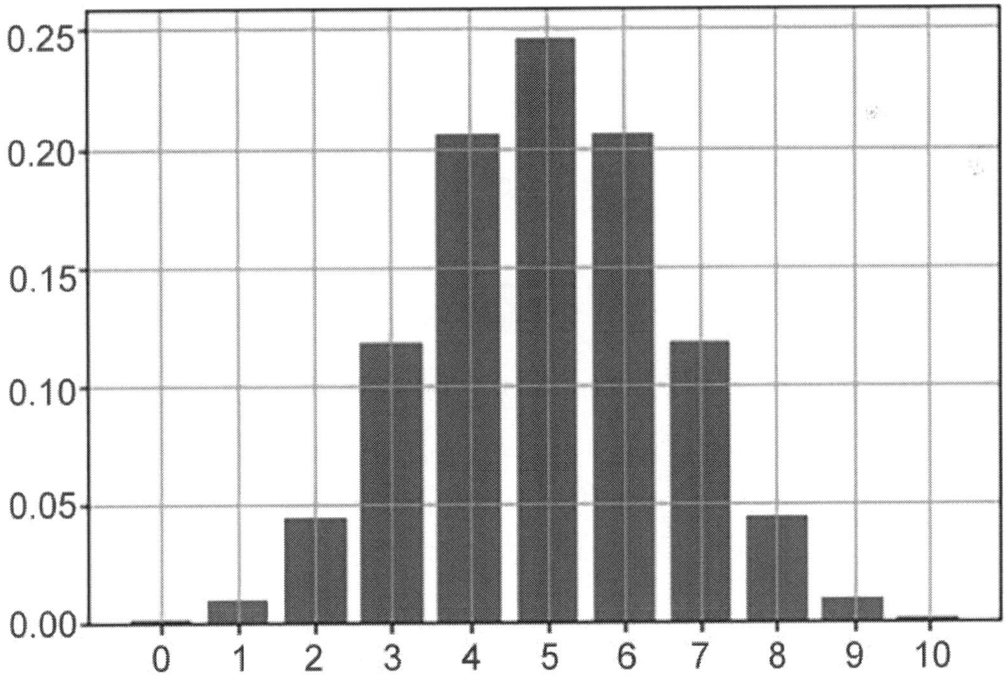

Figure 8.10: pmf of Y

This looks very similar to what we got using the simulations. Now, let's compare both plots. We will create a DataFrame to make the plotting process easier:

```
Y_rv_df = pd.DataFrame({'Y_simulated_pmf': Prob_of_Y_values,\
                        'Y_theoretical_pmf':  Y_probs},\
                        index=y_values)

Y_rv_df.plot(kind='bar')
plt.grid();
```

The output is as follows:

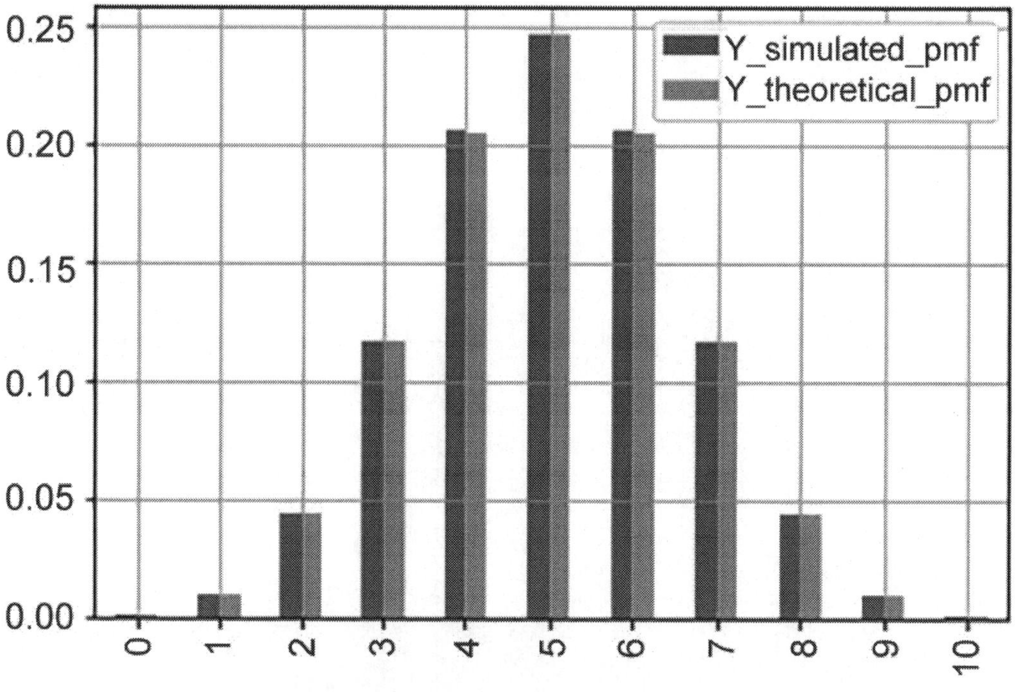

Figure 8.11: pmf of Y versus simulated results

The two sets of bars are practically identical; the probabilities we got from our simulation are very close to the theoretical values. This shows the power of simulations.

EXERCISE 8.03: CHECKING IF A RANDOM VARIABLE FOLLOWS A BINOMIAL DISTRIBUTION

In this exercise, we will practice how to verify if a random variable follows a binomial distribution. We will also create a random variable using **scipy.stats** and plot the distribution. This will be a mostly conceptual exercise.

Here, we will check if the random variable, *Z: number of defective auto parts in a 12-box pack*, follows a binomial distribution (remember that we consider 4% of the auto parts are defective). Follow these steps to complete this exercise:

1. Import NumPy, Matplotlib, and **scipy.stats** following the usual conventions:

```
import numpy as np
import scipy.stats as stats
import matplotlib.pyplot as plt
%matplotlib inline
```

2. Just as we did in the *Defining Discrete Random Variables* section, try to conceptually check if *Z* fulfills the three characteristics given for a binomial random variable:

   a. **Condition 1**: For each individual auto part, there are only two possible outcomes, *defective* or *good*. Since we were interested in the *defective* parts, then that outcome can be considered the *success*, with a fixed probability of 0.04 (4%).

   b. **Condition 2**: The number of parts per box was fixed at 12, so the experiment was performed a fixed number of times per box.

   c. **Condition 3**: We assumed that the defective parts had no relationship between one another because the machine randomly produces an average of 4% defective parts.

3. Determine the *p* and *n* parameters for the distributions of this variable, that is, $p = 0.04$ and $n = 12$.

4. Use the theoretical formula with the former parameters to get the exact theoretical probability of getting exactly one defective piece per box (using $x = 1$):

$$P(Z=1) = \frac{12!}{1!(12-1)!}0.04^{1}(1-0.04)^{12-1}=0.3063549$$

Figure 8.12: Substituting the values of x, p and n in the probability distribution formula

5. Use the **scipy.stats** module to produce an instance of the *Z* random variable. Name it **Z_rv**:

```
# number of parts per box
parts_per_box = 12

Z_rv = stats.binom\
        (n = parts_per_box,\
         p = 0.04 # probability of defective piece (success)
         )
```

6. Plot the probability mass function of *Z*:

```
z_possible_values = np.arange(0, parts_per_box + 1)

Z_probs = Z_rv.pmf(z_possible_values)

fig, ax = plt.subplots()
ax.bar(z_possible_values, Z_probs)
ax.set_xticks(z_possible_values)
ax.grid();
```

The result looks like this:

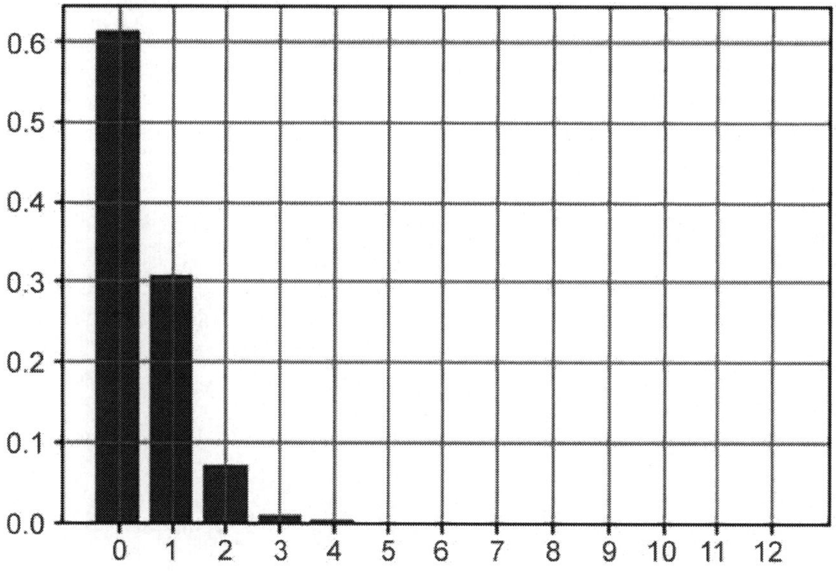

Figure 8.13: pmf of Z

In this exercise, we learned how to check for the three conditions that are needed for a discrete random variable to have a binomial distribution. We concluded that the variable we analyzed indeed has a binomial distribution. We were also able to calculate its parameters and use them to create a binomial random variable using **`scipy.stats`** and plotted the distribution.

> **NOTE**
>
> To access the source code for this specific section, please refer to https://packt.live/3gbTm5k.
>
> You can also run this example online at https://packt.live/2Anhx1k.

In this section, we focused on discrete random variables. Now, we know they are the kind of random variables that can take on a specific number of values. Typically, these are integer values. Often, these types of variables are related to counts: the number of students that will pass a test, the number of cars crossing a bridge, and so on. We also learned about the most important distribution of discrete random variables, known as the binomial distribution, and how we can get the exact theoretical probabilities of a binomial random variable using Python.

In the next section, we'll focus on continuous random variables.

CONTINUOUS RANDOM VARIABLES

In this section, we'll continue working with random variables. Here, we'll discuss continuous random variables. We will learn the key distinction between continuous and discrete probability distributions. In addition, we will introduce the mother of all distributions: the famous **normal distribution**. We will learn how to work with this distribution using **`scipy.stats`** and review its most important characteristics.

DEFINING CONTINUOUS RANDOM VARIABLES

There are certain random quantities that, in principle, can take any real value in an interval. Some examples are as follows:

- The price of the IBM stocks one week from now
- The number of calories ingested by a person in a day
- The closing exchange rate between the British pound and the Euro
- The height of a randomly chosen male from a specific group

Because of their nature, these variables are known as *continuous* random variables. As with discrete random variables, there are many theoretical distributions that can be used to model real-world phenomena.

To introduce this type of random variable, let's look at an example we are already familiar with. Once again, let's load the games dataset we introduced in *Chapter 7, Doing Basic Statistics with Python*:

```
games = pd.read_csv('./data/appstore_games.csv')

original_colums_dict = {x: x.lower().replace(' ','_') \
                        for x in games.columns}

# renaming columns
games.rename(columns = original_colums_dict, inplace = True)
```

One of the variables we have in the dataset is *size of the game* in bytes. Before visualizing the distribution of this variable, we will transform it into megabytes:

```
games['size'] = games['size']/(1e6)

# replacing the one missing value with the median
games['size'] = games['size'].fillna(games['size'].median())

games['size'].hist(bins = 50, ec='k');
```

The output is as follows:

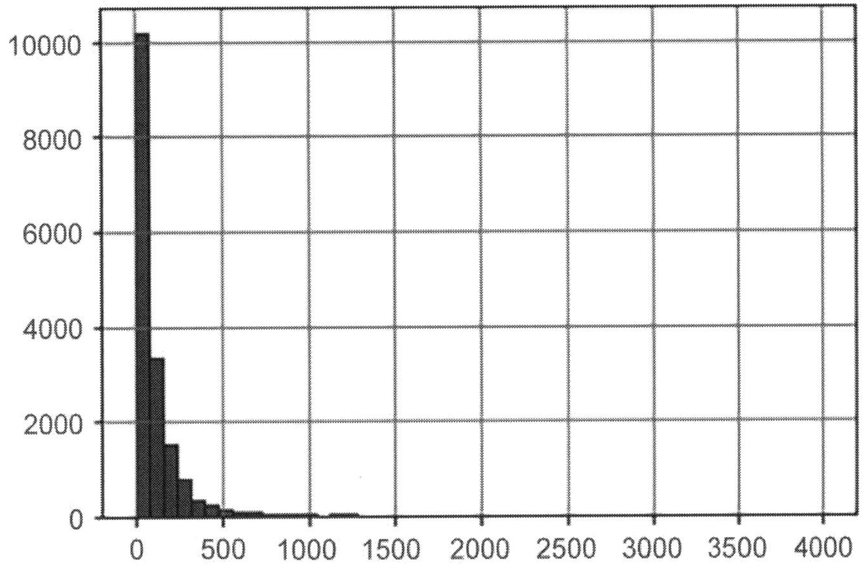

Figure 8.14: Distribution of the size of the game

Let's define our random variable, *X*, as follows:

X: Size of a randomly chosen strategy game from the app store.

Having defined this random variable, we can start asking questions about the probabilities of certain events:

- $P(X > 100)$: Probability that *X* is strictly greater than 100 MB
- $P(100 \leq X \leq 400)$: Probability that *X* is between 100 and 400 MB
- $P(X = 152.53)$: Probability of *X* being exactly 152.53 MB

By now, you know how you can estimate these probabilities by using the relative frequency definition of probability: count the number of times an event happens and divide this by the total number of events (games, in this case):

```
# get the number of games to use as denominator
number_of_games = games['size'].size

# calculate probabilities
prob_X_gt_100 = (games['size'] > 100).sum()/number_of_games

prob_X_bt_100_and_400 = ((games['size'] >= 100) & \
                         (games['size'] <= 400))\
                         .sum()/number_of_games

prob_X_eq_152_53 = (games['size'] == 152.53).sum()/number_of_games

# print the results
print(f'P(X > 100) = {prob_X_gt_100:0.5f}')
print(f'P(100 <= X <= 400) = {prob_X_bt_100_and_400:0.5f}')
print(f'P(X = 152.53) = {prob_X_eq_152_53:0.5f}')
```

The results are as follows:

```
P(X > 100) = 0.33098
P(100 <= X <= 400) = 0.28306
P(X = 152.53) = 0.00000
```

Notice the last probability we calculated, *P(X = 152.53)*. The estimated probability that a random variable takes a *specific* value (such as 152.53) is zero. This is always the case for any continuous random variable. Since these types of variables can, in principle, take an infinite number of values, then the probability of taking *exactly* a specific value must be zero.

The preceding example shows that when we have enough data points about a continuous random variable, we can use the data to estimate the probability of the random variable taking values within certain intervals. However, having lots of observations about one variable might not always be the case. Given this fact, let's consider the following questions:

- What if we have no data at all?
- What if we don't have enough data?
- Can we perform simulations to get an estimation of the probabilities of certain events (as we did with discrete random variables)?

These are sensible questions, and we can answer them by knowing more about **theoretical continuous probability distributions**:

- What if we have no data at all? *We can make some reasonable assumptions about the variable, and then model it using one of the many theoretical continuous probability distributions.*
- What if we don't have enough data? *We can make some reasonable assumptions about the variable, support these assumptions with the data, and use estimation techniques (the subject of the next chapter) to estimate the parameters of the chosen theoretical continuous probability distribution.*
- Can we perform simulations to get an estimation of the probabilities of certain events (as we did with discrete random variables)? *Yes. Once we have chosen the probability distribution, along with its parameters, we can use simulations to answer complicated questions.*

To make the previous answers clear, in the following subsections, we'll introduce the most important continuous probability distribution: the normal distribution.

It is worth noting that for continuous random variables, the probability distribution is also known as the **probability density function** or **pdf**.

THE NORMAL DISTRIBUTION

Let's introduce the most famous and important distribution in probability theory: the normal distribution. The pdf of the normal distribution is defined by the following equation:

$$f(x) = \frac{1}{\sigma\sqrt{2\pi}} e^{-\frac{1}{2}\left(\frac{x-\mu}{\sigma}\right)^2}$$

Figure 8.15: The pdf of the normal distribution

Here, π and e are the well-known mathematical constants. Don't try to understand the equation; all you need to know is two things: first, that the distribution is completely determined when we have two parameters:

- μ: The mean of the distribution
- σ: The standard deviation of the distribution

Second, if X is a random variable that follows a normal distribution, then for a possible value x, the preceding formula will give you a value that is *directly related* to the probability of the variable *taking values near* x. Unlike the formula of the binomial distribution, where we got the probability by directly plugging the value, x, into the formula, in the case of continuous random variables, it is different: there is no direct interpretation of the values given by the formula. The following example will clarify this.

We will create a random variable that follows a normal distribution using the **scipy.stats** module. Let's suppose that the heights of a certain population of males is described by a normal distribution with a mean of 170 cm and a standard deviation of 10 cm. To create this random variable using **scipy.stats**, we need to use the following code:

```
# set the mu and sigma parameters of the distribution
heights_mean = 170
heights_sd = 10

# instantiate the random variable object
heights_rv = stats.norm(
        loc = heights_mean, # mean of the distribution
        scale = heights_sd  # standard deviation
)
```

The preceding code creates the normally distributed random variable, whose pdf looks like this:

$$f(x) = \frac{1}{10\sqrt{2\pi}} e^{-\frac{1}{2}\left(\frac{x-170}{10}\right)^2}$$

Figure 8.16: The pdf of a normally distributed random variable

For every value, *x*, say, **`175`**, we can get the value of the pdf by using the **`pdf`** method, like so:

```
heights_rv.pdf(175)
```

The result is as follows:

```
0.03520653267642
```

This number is what you would get if you replaced *x* with **`175`** in the preceding formula:

$$f(175) = \frac{1}{10\sqrt{2\pi}} e^{-\frac{1}{2}\left(\frac{175-170}{10}\right)^2} = 0.03520653267642$$

Figure 8.17 Substituting the vale of x=175

To be clear, this *is not* the probability of observing a male whose height is 175 cm (remember that the probability of this variable taking a specific value should be zero) as this number does not have a simple direct interpretation. However, if we plot the whole density curve, then we can start understanding the distribution of our random variable. To plot the whole probability density function, we must create a vector that contains a collection of possible values that this variable can take. According to the context of male heights, let's say that we want to plot the pdf for values between 130 cm and 210 cm, which are the likely values for healthy male adults. First, we create the vector of values using **`np.linspace`**, which in this case will create 200 equally spaced numbers between 120 and 210 (inclusive):

```
values = np.linspace(130, 210, num=200)
```

Now, we can produce the pdf and plot against the created values:

```
heights_rv_pdf = heights_rv.pdf(values)

plt.plot(values, heights_rv_pdf)
plt.grid();
```

The curve looks like this:

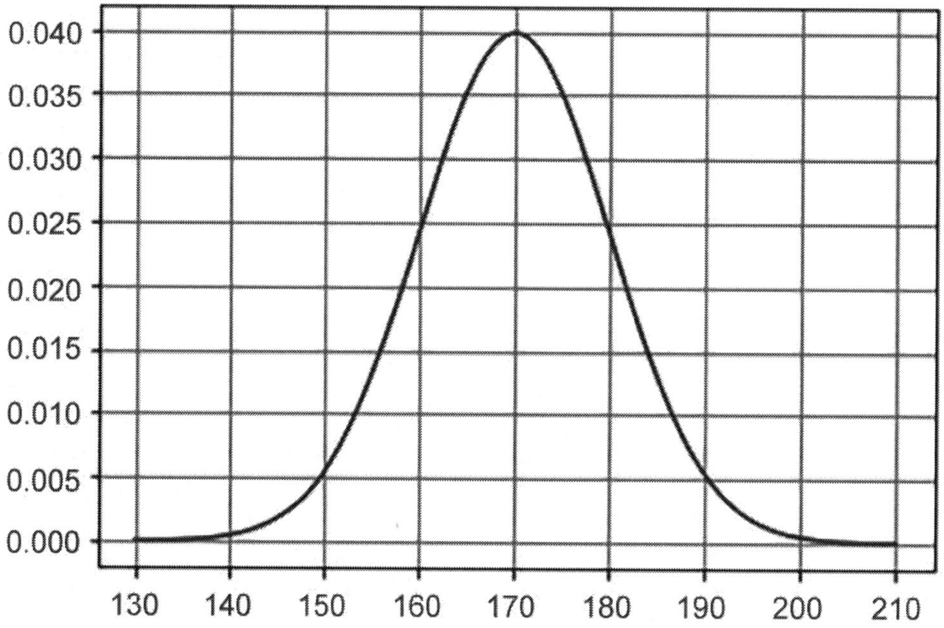

Figure 8.18: Example of a normal distribution with mean=170 and sd=10

The higher the curve, the more likely it is to observe those values around the corresponding *x* axis value. For instance, we can see that we are more likely to observe male heights between 160 cm and 170 cm than those between 140 cm and 150 cm.

Now that we have defined this normally distributed random variable, can we use simulations to answer certain questions about it? Absolutely. In fact, now, we will learn how to use the already defined random variable to simulate sample values. We can use the **rvs** method for this, which generates random samples from the probability distribution:

```
sample_heighs = heights_rv.rvs\
                (size = 5, \
                 random_state = 998 # similar to np.seed)

for i, h in enumerate(sample_heighs):
    print(f'Men {i + 1} height: {h:0.1f}')
```

The result is as follows:

```
Men 1 height: 171.2
Men 2 height: 173.3
Men 3 height: 157.1
Men 4 height: 164.9
Men 5 height: 179.1
```

Here, we are simulating taking five random males from the population and measuring their heights. Notice that we used the **random_state** parameter, which plays a similar role to the **numpy.seed**: it ensures anyone running the same code will get the same random values.

As we did previously, we can use the simulations to answer questions about the probability of events related to this random variable. For instance, what is the probability of finding a male taller than 190 cm? The following code calculates this simulation using our previously defined random variable:

```
# size of the simulation
sim_size = int(1e5)

# simulate the random samples
sample_heights = heights_rv.rvs\
                 (size = sim_size,\
                  random_state = 88 # similar to np.seed)

Prob_event = (sample_heights > 190).sum()/sim_size

print(f'Probability of a male > 190 cm: {Prob_event:0.5f} \
 (or {100*Prob_event:0.2f}%)')
```

The result is:

```
Probability of a male > 190 cm: 0.02303 (or 2.30%)
```

As we will see in the following section, there is a way to get the exact probabilities from the **density** function without the need to simulate values, which can sometimes be computationally expensive and unnecessary.

SOME PROPERTIES OF THE NORMAL DISTRIBUTION

One impressive fact about the universe and mathematics is that many variables in the real world follow a normal distribution:

- Human heights
- Weights of members of most species of mammals
- Scores of standardized tests
- Deviations from product specifications in manufacturing processes
- Medical measurements such as diastolic pressure, cholesterol, and sleep times
- Financial variables such as the returns of some securities

The normal distribution describes so many phenomena and is so extensively used in probability and statistics that it is worth knowing two key properties:

- The normal distribution is completely determined by its two parameters: mean and standard deviation.
- The *empirical rule* of a normally distributed random variable tells us what proportion of observations that we will find, depending on the number of standard deviations away from the mean.

Let's understand these two key properties. First, we will illustrate how the parameters of the distribution determine its shape:

- The mean determines the center of the distribution.
- The standard deviation determines how wide (or spread out) the distribution is.

To illustrate this property, let's say that we have the following three populations of male heights. Each population correspond to a different country:

- **Country A**: Mean = 170 cm, standard deviation = 10 cm

- **Country B**: Mean = 170 cm, standard deviation = 5 cm
- **Country C**: Mean = 175 cm, standard deviation = 10 cm

With these parameters, we can visualize and contrast the distributions of the three different countries. Before visualizing, let's create the random variables:

```
# parameters of distributions
heights_means = [170, 170, 175]
heights_sds = [10, 5, 10]
countries = ['Country A', 'Country B', 'Country C']

heights_rvs = {}
plotting_values = {}

# creating the random variables
for i, country in enumerate(countries):
    heights_rvs[country] = stats.norm(
        loc = heights_means[i], # mean of the distribution
        scale = heights_sds[i]  # standard deviation
    )
```

With these objects created, we can proceed with the visualizations:

```
# getting x and y values for plotting the distributions
for i, country in enumerate(countries):
    x_values = np.linspace(heights_means[i] - 4*heights_sds[i], \
                           heights_means[i] + 4*heights_sds[i])
    y_values = heights_rvs[country].pdf(x_values)
    plotting_values[country] = (x_values, y_values)


# plotting the three distributions
fig, ax = plt.subplots(figsize = (8, 4))
for i, country in enumerate(countries):
    ax.plot(plotting_values[country][0], \
            plotting_values[country][1], \
            label=country, lw = 2)

ax.set_xticks(np.arange(130, 220, 5))
plt.legend()
plt.grid();
```

The plot looks like this:

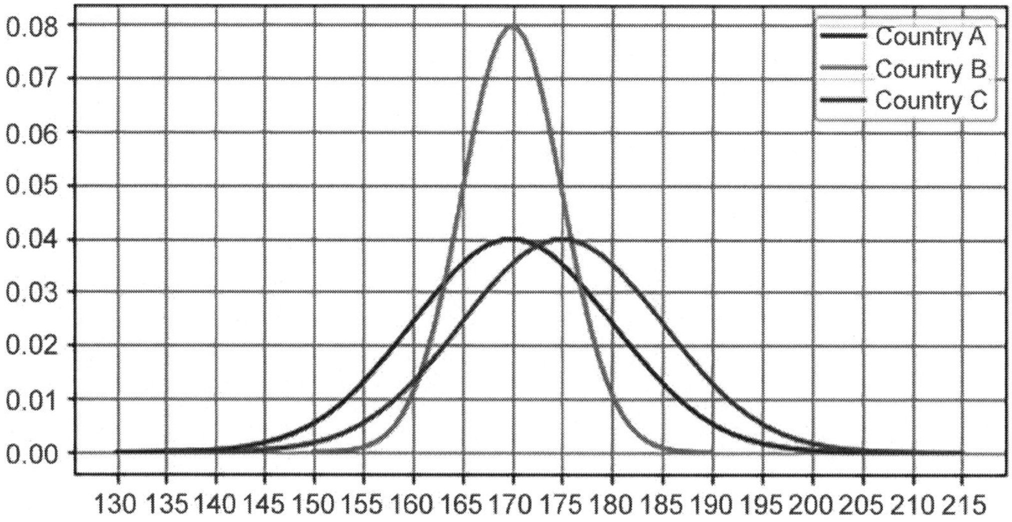

Figure 8.19: Comparison of normal distributions with different parameters

Although the populations for **Country A** and **Country B** have the same mean (170 cm), the difference in standard deviations implies that the distribution for **Country B** is much more concentrated around 170 cm. We could say that the males in this country tend to have more homogenous heights. The curves for **Country A** and **Country C** are basically the same; the only difference is that the curve for **Country C** is *shifted* to the right by 5 cm, which implies that it would be more likely to find males around 190 cm in height and above in **Country C** than in **Country A** or **Country B** (the green curve has a greater *y* axis value than the other two at *x=190* and above).

The second important characteristic of the normal distribution is known as the **empirical rule**. Let's take our example of the population of male heights that are normally distributed with a mean of 170 cm and a standard deviation of 10 cm:

- *~68% of observations will lie in the interval: mean ± 1 sd*. For the height of males, we will find that around 68% of males are between 160 cm and 180 cm (170 ± 10) in height.
- *~95% of observations will lie in the interval: mean ± 2 sd*. For the height of males, we will find that around 95% of males are between 150 cm and 190 cm (170 ± 20) in height.

- *More than 99% of observations will lie in the interval: mean ± 3 sd*. Virtually all observations will be at a distance that is less than three standard deviations from the mean. For the height of males, we will find that around 99.7% of males will be between 150 cm and 200 cm (170 ± 30) in height.

The empirical rule can be used to quickly give us a sense of the proportion of observations we expect to see when we consider some number of standard deviations from the mean.

To finish this section and this chapter, one very important fact you should know about any continuous random variable is that the **area under the probability distribution** will give the probability of the variable being in a certain range. Let's illustrate this with the normal distribution, and also connect this with the empirical rule. Say we have a normally distributed random variable with *mean = 170* and *standard deviation = 10*. What is the area under the probability distribution between *x = 160* and *x = 180* (one standard deviation away from the mean)? The empirical rule tells us that 68% of the observations will lie in this interval, so we would expect that $P(160 \leq X \leq 180) \cong 0.68$, which will correspond with the area below the curve in the interval [160, 180]. We can visualize this plot with matplotlib. The code to produce the plot is somewhat long, so we will split it into two parts. First, we will create the function to plot, establish the limits of the plots in the *x* axis, and define the vectors to plot:

```
from matplotlib.patches import Polygon

def func(x):
    return heights_rv.pdf(x)


lower_lim = 160
upper_lim = 180

x = np.linspace(130, 210)
y = func(x)
```

Now, we will create the figure with a shaded region:

```
fig, ax = plt.subplots(figsize=(8,4))
ax.plot(x, y, 'blue', linewidth=2)
ax.set_ylim(bottom=0)

# Make the shaded region
ix = np.linspace(lower_lim, upper_lim)
```

```
iy = func(ix)
verts = [(lower_lim, 0), *zip(ix, iy), (upper_lim, 0)]
poly = Polygon(verts, facecolor='0.9', edgecolor='0.5')
ax.add_patch(poly)

ax.text(0.5 * (lower_lim + upper_lim), 0.01, \
        r"$\int_{160}^{180} f(x)\mathrm{d}x$", \
        horizontalalignment='center', fontsize=15)

fig.text(0.85, 0.05, '$height$')
fig.text(0.08, 0.85, '$f(x)$')

ax.spines['right'].set_visible(False)
ax.spines['top'].set_visible(False)
ax.xaxis.set_ticks_position('bottom')

ax.set_xticks((lower_lim, upper_lim))
ax.set_xticklabels(('$160$', '$180$'))
ax.set_yticks([]);
```

The output will be as follows:

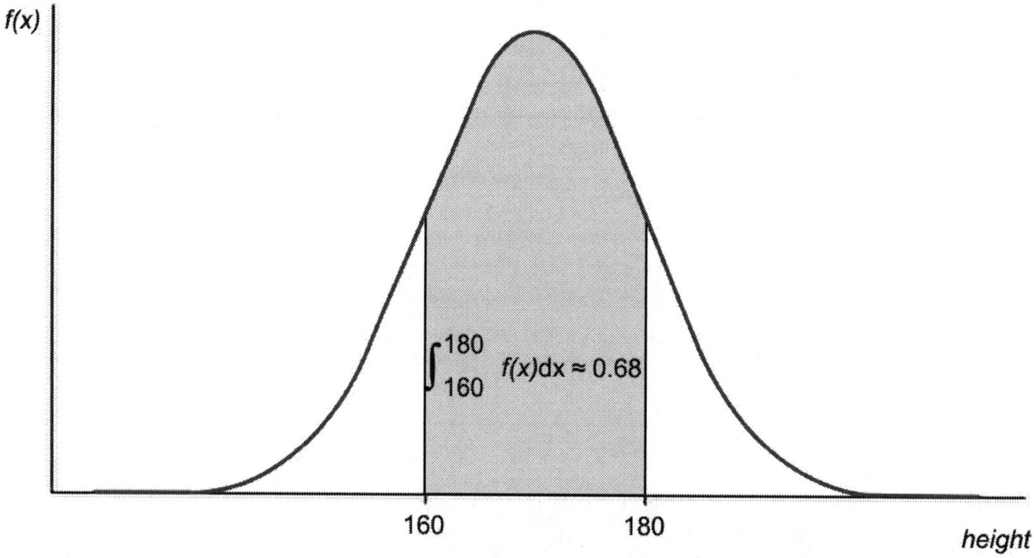

Figure 8.20: Area under the pdf as the probability of an event

How do we calculate the integral that will give us the area under the curve? The **`scipy.stats`** module will make this very easy. Using the **`cdf`** (**cumulative distribution function**) method of the random variable, which is essentially the integral of the pdf, we can easily evaluate the integral by subtracting the lower and upper limits (remember the fundamental theorem of calculus):

```
# limits of the integral
lower_lim = 160
upper_lim = 180

# calculating the area under the curve
Prob_X_in_160_180 = heights_rv.cdf(upper_lim) - \
                    heights_rv.cdf(lower_lim)

# print the result
print(f'Prob(160 <= X <= 180) = {Prob_X_in_160_180:0.4f}')
```

The result is as follows:

```
Prob(160 <= X <= 180) = 0.6827
```

And this is how we get probabilities from the **`pdf`** without the need to perform simulations. Let's look at one last example to make this clear by connecting it with an earlier result. A few pages earlier, for the same population, we asked, *What is the probability of finding a male taller than 190 cm?* We got the answer by performing simulations. Now, we can get the exact probability like so:

```
# limits of the integral
lower_lim = 190
upper_lim = np.Inf # since we are asking X > 190

# calculating the area under the curve
Prob_X_gt_190 = heights_rv.cdf(upper_lim) - \
                heights_rv.cdf(lower_lim)

# print the result
print(f'Probability of a male > 190 cm: {Prob_X_gt_190:0.5f} \
      (or {100*Prob_X_gt_190:0.2f}%)')
```

The result is as follows:

```
Probability of a male > 190 cm: 0.02275 (or 2.28%)
```

If you compare this with the result we got earlier, you will see it is virtually the same. However, this approach is better since it's exact and does not require us to perform any computationally heavy or memory-consuming simulations.

EXERCISE 8.04: USING THE NORMAL DISTRIBUTION IN EDUCATION

In this exercise, we'll use a normal distribution object from **scipy.stats** and the **cdf** and its inverse, **ppf**, to answer questions about education.

In psychometrics and education, it is a well-known fact that many variables relevant to education policy are normally distributed. For instance, scores in standardized mathematics tests follow a normal distribution. In this exercise, we'll explore this phenomenon: in a certain country, high school students take a standardized mathematics test whose scores follow a normal distribution with the following parameters: *mean = 100, standard deviation = 15*. Follow these steps to complete this exercise:

1. Import NumPy, Matplotlib, and **scipy.stats** following the usual conventions:

```
import numpy as np
import scipy.stats as stats
import matplotlib.pyplot as plt
%matplotlib inline
```

2. Use the **scipy.stats** module to produce an instance of a normally distributed random variable, named **X_rv**, with *mean = 100* and *standard deviation = 15*:

```
# producing the normal distribution
X_mean = 100
X_sd = 15

# create the random variable
X_rv = stats.norm(loc = X_mean, scale = X_sd)
```

3. Plot the probability distribution of X:

```
x_values = np.linspace(X_mean - 4 * X_sd, X_mean + 4 * X_sd)
y_values = X_rv.pdf(x_values)

plt.plot(x_values, y_values, lw=2)
plt.grid();
```

The output will be as follows:

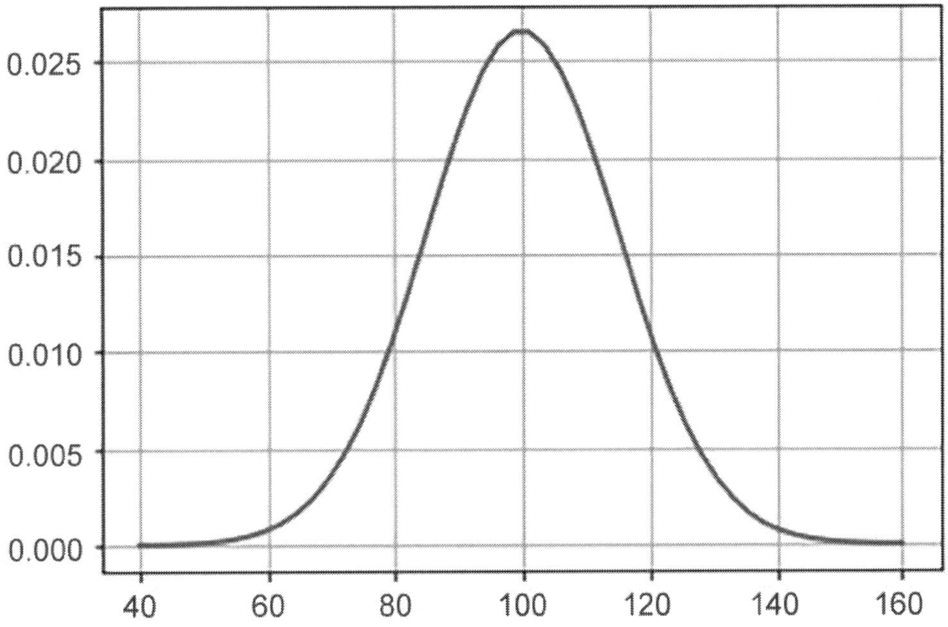

Figure 8.21: Probability distribution of tests scores

4. The Ministry of Education has decided that the minimum score for someone to be considered *competent* in mathematics is 80. Use the **cdf** method to calculate the proportion of students that will get a score above that score:

```
Prob_X_gt_80 = X_rv.cdf(np.Inf) - X_rv.cdf(80)

print(f'Prob(X >= 80): {Prob_X_gt_80:0.5f} \
(or {100*Prob_X_gt_80:0.2f}%)')
```

The result is as follows:

```
Prob(X >= 80): 0.90879 (or 90.88%)
```

Around 91% of the students are considered *competent* in mathematics.

5. A very selective university wants to set very high standards for high school students that are admitted to their programs. The policy of the university is to only admit students with mathematics scores in the top 2% of the population. Use the **ppf** method (which is essentially the inverse function of the **cdf** method) with an argument of *1 - 0.02 = 0.98* to get the cut-off score for admission:

```
proportion_of_admitted = 0.02

cut_off = X_rv.ppf(1-proportion_of_admitted)

print(f'To admit the top {100*proportion_of_admitted:0.0f}%, \
the cut-off score should be {cut_off:0.1f}')
top_percents = np.arange(0.9, 1, 0.01)
```

The result should be as follows:

```
To admit the top 2%, the cut-off score should be 130.8
```

In this exercise, we used a normal distribution and the **cdf** and **ppf** methods to answer real-world questions about education policy.

> **NOTE**
>
> To access the source code for this specific section, please refer to https://packt.live/3eUizB4.
>
> You can also run this example online at https://packt.live/2VFyF9X.

In this section, we learned about continuous random variables, as well as the most important distribution of these types of variables: the normal distribution. The key takeaway from this section is that a continuous random variable is determined by its probability density function, which is, in turn, determined by its parameters. In the case of the normal distribution, its two parameters are the mean and the standard deviation. We used an example to demonstrate how these parameters influence the shape of the distribution.

Another important takeaway is that you can use the area below the pdf to calculate the probability of certain events. This is true for any continuous random variable, including, of course, those that follow a normal distribution.

Finally, we also learned about the empirical rule for the normal distribution, which is a good-to-know *rule of thumb* if you want to quickly get a sense of the proportion of values that will lie *k* standard deviations away from the mean of the distribution.

Now that you are familiar with this important distribution, we will continue using it in the next chapter when we encounter it again in the context of the **central limit theorem**.

ACTIVITY 8.01: USING THE NORMAL DISTRIBUTION IN FINANCE

In this activity, we'll explore the possibility of using the normal distribution to understand the daily returns of the stock price. By the end of this activity, you should have an opinion regarding whether the normal distribution is an appropriate model for the daily returns of stocks.

In this example, we will use daily information about Microsoft stock provided by Yahoo! Finance. Follow these steps to complete this activity:

> **NOTE**
>
> The dataset that's required to complete this activity can be found at https://packt.live/3imSZqr.

1. Using pandas, read the CSV file named **`MSFT.csv`** from the **`data`** folder.
2. Optionally, rename the columns so they are easy to work with.
3. Transform the **`date`** column into a proper **`datetime`** column.
4. Set the **`date`** column as the index of the DataFrame.
5. In finance, the daily returns of a stock are defined as the percentage change of the daily closing price. Create the **`returns`** column in the MSFT DataFrame by calculating the percent change of the **`adj close`** column. Use the **`pct_change`** series pandas method to do so.
6. Restrict the analysis period to the dates between **`2014-01-01`** and **`2018-12-31`** (inclusive).

7. Use a histogram to visualize the distribution of the returns column, using 40 bins. Does it look like a normal distribution?

   The output should look like this:

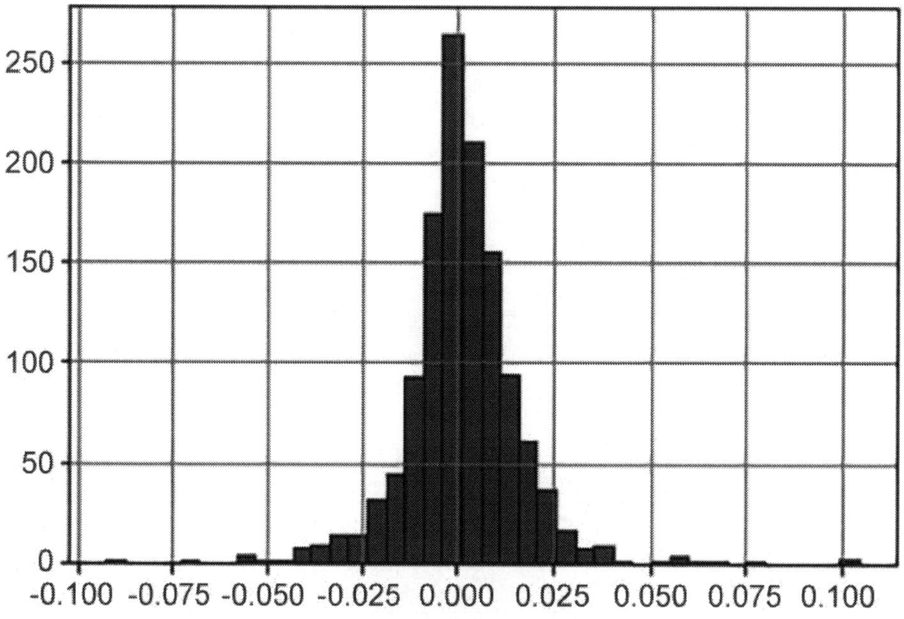

Figure 8.22: Histogram of returns of the MSFT stock

8. Calculate the descriptive statistics of the **returns** column:

```
count    1258.000000
mean        0.000996
std         0.014591
min        -0.092534
25%        -0.005956
50%         0.000651
75%         0.007830
max         0.104522
Name: returns, dtype: float64
```

9. Create a random variable named **R_rv** that will represent *The daily returns of the MSFT stock*. Use the mean and standard deviation of the return column as the parameters for this distribution.

10. Plot the distribution of **`R_rv`** and the histogram of the actual data. Then, use the **`plt.hist()`** function with the **`density=True`** parameter so that both the real data and the theoretical distribution appear in the same scale:

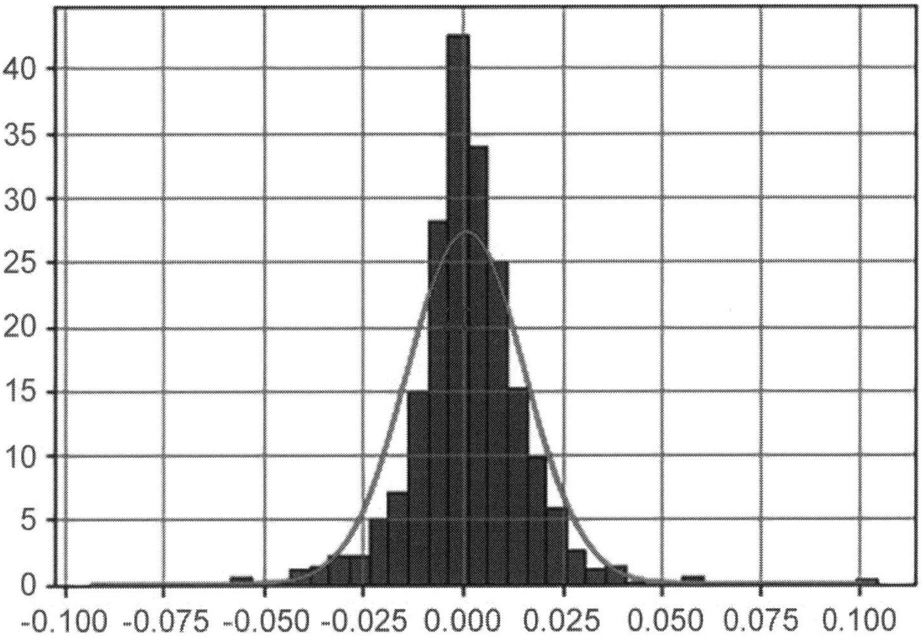

Figure 8.23: Histogram of returns of the MSFT stock

11. After looking at the preceding plot, *would you say that the normal distribution provides an accurate model for the daily returns of Microsoft stock?*

12. Additional activity: Repeat the preceding steps with the **`PG.csv`** file, which contains information about the Procter and Gamble stock.

This activity was about observing real-world data and trying to use a theoretical distribution to describe it. This is important because by having a theoretical model, we can use its known properties to arrive at real-world conclusions and implications. For instance, you could use the *empirical rule* to say something about the daily returns of a company, or you could calculate the probability of losing a determined amount of money in a day.

> **NOTE**
>
> The solution for this activity can be found on page 684.

SUMMARY

This chapter gave you a brief introduction to the branch of mathematics regarding probability theory.

We defined the concept of probability, as well as some of its most important rules and associated concepts such as experiment, sample space, and events. We also defined the very important concept of random variables and provided examples of the two main discrete and continuous random variables. Later in this chapter, we learned how to create random variables using the **`scipy.stats`** module, which we also used to generate the probability mass function and the probability density function. We also talked about two of the most important random variables in the (literal) universe: the normal distribution and the binomial distribution. These are used in many applied fields to solve real-world problems.

This was, of course, a brief introduction to the topic, and the goal was to present and make you familiar with some of the basic and foundational concepts in probability theory, especially those that are crucial and necessary to understand and use inferential statistics, which is the topic of the next chapter.

9

INTERMEDIATE STATISTICS WITH PYTHON

OVERVIEW

In this chapter, we will progress through to some intermediate statistical concepts. We will learn what the law of large numbers tells us about the value of the sample mean as a sample gets larger.

By the end of this chapter, you will be able to apply the central limit theorem to describe the distribution of the sample mean, create confidence intervals to describe the possible value of the average with some degree of confidence, use hypothesis testing to evaluate conclusions based on the evidence that our sample provides, and use regression equations to analyze data.

INTRODUCTION

In previous chapters, we have described and explored data using descriptive statistics and visual techniques. We have also looked at probability, randomness, and using simulations of random variables to solve problems. The idea of distributions was also examined, which plays a much bigger role later in this chapter.

When looking at applying statistical ideas, there are some important questions to answer concerning methodology. Some examples of these questions could include "how large should I make my sample?" or "how confident can we be in the results?". For this chapter, we will look at how we can apply two of the most important theorems in statistics, starting with their practical implications before moving onto solving common problems using the more useful techniques that are derived from these important ideas.

In this chapter, we will explain what the law of large numbers is and clarify how sample size affects the sample mean. The central limit theorem will be discussed, along with its application in confidence intervals and hypothesis testing. Using Python, we will construct functions to calculate our confidence intervals to describe sample statistics and margin of error in a poll. Hypothesis tests will be conducted in Python to evaluate the evidence of a collected sample against a set of contradictory hypotheses. Finally, using the linear regression capabilities of Python, we will create a linear model to predict new data values.

LAW OF LARGE NUMBERS

There are many schemes and systems that people claim can make you a big winner at the casino. But what these people fail to see is the reason why casinos are lucrative money-makers; the odds are always on the casino's side, ensuring that the casino will come out ahead and always win (in the long run). What the casinos have come to depend on is something called the law of large numbers.

Before we figure out how the casinos always make themselves winners in the long run, we need to define several terms. The first is **sample average**, or **sample mean**. The sample mean is what everybody thinks of when they think of the average. You calculate the sample mean by adding up the results and dividing by the number of results. Let's say we flip a coin 10 times and it comes up heads 7 times. We calculate the sample mean, or the average number of heads per flip, like so:

$$\bar{x} = \frac{7}{10} = 0.7$$

Figure 9.1: Formula for sample mean

The sample average is typically denoted as $\bar{x}$, pronounced *x bar*.

The second term we need to understand is **expected value**. Expected value is the theoretical value we can expect our average to be, based on probability. For the discrete examples, like our coin flipping experiment, we calculate it by taking the sum of each result multiplied by the probability of it occurring. For our coin flipping example, we take the number of heads on each side of the coin, 1 for heads and 0 for tails, and multiply it by the probability of each side occurring, 0.5 for each side in this instance. To write it out mathematically:

$$E(X) = 1 * 0.5 + 0 * 0.5 = 0.5$$

Figure 9.2: Formula for expected value

We can expect 0.5 heads per coin flip, which makes sense since we have a 50% chance of obtaining heads in any given coin flip.

Another term is **sample**, which is a collection of results. In this instance, the collection of coin flip results is our sample. One important characteristic of a sample is its size, or the number of results you have. We have 10 coin flips, so our sample size is 10. The final term is the idea of **independence**, which is the notion that one result in no way impacts another result. Our coin flips are independent; getting heads on the first coin flip is in no way going to impact the result of the 10th coin flip.

Notice that our sample average and expected value are not the same. While getting 7 heads out of a sample of 10 coin flips may seem unlikely, it is not an impossible result. Yet we know that about half of our sample should be heads. What happens if we keep flipping our coin 10 more times? Or even 100 or 1,000 more times? The answer to this is provided by the law of large numbers. **The law of large numbers** states that the value of the sample mean will converge to our expected value as the size of the sample grows. In other words, as we flip our coin more and more, the sample average should get closer and closer to 0.5.

PYTHON AND RANDOM NUMBERS

In this chapter, we will use the random library several times, but it is not truly random at all—it is what we call pseudo-random. A **pseudo-random** number is a number that is typically generated from an algorithm. We initialize the algorithm using a number called a **seed**. A lot of the time, the seed is based on the time or date the program is executed. However, Python (and most other languages) allows you to set the seed equal to whatever number you want. If you initialize your algorithm with the same seed, then the same pseudo-random numbers will be generated every time. This is useful when you are working with random numbers and want to produce the same results every time.

EXERCISE 9.01: THE LAW OF LARGE NUMBERS IN ACTION

Let's expand upon our coin flipping experiment in Python. First, let's create a coin flipping simulator. Open up your Jupyter notebook and type the following code:

1. We first need to import the **random** Python package and set the **seed** method:

```
# coin_flip_scenario.py
# import the random module
import random
random.seed(54321)
```

2. Let's define a variable for our sample size and, for this instance, set it equal to **10**:

```
# set the sample size or coin flips you what to run
sample_size = 10
```

3. We create an empty list so that we can collect the results of our coin flip experiment:

```
# create a for loop and collect the results in a list
# 1 = heads and 0 = tails
result_list = []
for i in range(sample_size):
    result = random.randint(0, 1)
    result_list.append(result)
```

4. Define two variables to compile the results (the number of heads and the average number of heads per flip, respectively):

```
# compile results
num_of_heads = sum(result_list)
avg_of_heads = float(num_of_heads) / sample_size
```

5. Finally, we print the results to the console:

```
# print the results
print(f'Results: {num_of_heads} heads out of {sample_size} \
flips.')
print(f'Average number of heads per flip is {avg_of_heads}.')
```

6. Running your notebook should get you results that look like the following:

```
Results: 4 heads out of 10 flips. Average number of
heads per flip is 0.4.
```

7. Since we are generating random numbers in this simulation, the results that you get may vary. Getting 4 heads out of 10 coin tosses (a sample mean of 0.4 heads per flip) is something that seems plausible, but is different than our expected value of 0.5. But notice what happens when we change the sample size from 10 to 100:

```
# set the sample size or coin flips you what to run
sample_size = 100
```

8. Rerun the entire program again (make sure to include the line with **`random.seed(54321)`**) and this time, the result will be as follows:

```
Results: 51 heads out of 100 flips. Average number
    of heads per flip is 0.51.
```

Notice that the sample average (`0.51`) is now a lot closer to the expected value (`0.50`) with a sample size of 100 rather than 10. This is a prime example of the law of large numbers.

> **NOTE**
>
> To access the source code for this specific section, please refer to https://packt.live/2VCT9An.
>
> You can also run this example online at https://packt.live/2NOMGhk.

EXERCISE 9.02: COIN FLIPPING AVERAGE OVER TIME

Let's go back to our coin flipping simulator code and build it out to keep a running sample average as we flip our coin. We are going to flip a coin 20,000 times and graph the sample mean using a line graph to show how it changes over time and compares to our expected value.

1. Import the **random** and **matplotlib** Python packages and set the random seed:

```
# coin_clip_scenario_2.py
# import the module
import random
import matplotlib.pyplot as plt
random.seed(54321)
```

2. Define the sample size or the number of coin flips:

```
# set the sample size or coin flips you what to run
sample_size = 20000
```

3. Initialize the variables that we are going to use to collect the results of our simulation:

```
# initialize the variables required for our loop
# 1 = heads and 0 = tails
num_of_heads = 0
heads_list = []
trials_list = []
freq_list = []
```

4. Run the simulation and collect the results:

```
# create a for loop and collect the results in a list
for i in range(1,sample_size+1):
    result = random.randint(0, 1)
    if result == 1:
        num_of_heads += 1
    avg_of_heads = float(num_of_heads) / i
    heads_list.append(num_of_heads)
    trials_list.append(i)
    freq_list.append(avg_of_heads)
```

5. Print the results to the console:

```
# print the results
print(f'Results: {num_of_heads} heads out of {sample_size} flips.')

print(f'Average number of heads is {avg_of_heads}')
```

6. Create a line graph that shows the sample mean over time, along with marking our expected value using a dashed line:

```
#create a simple line graph to show our results over time
plt.plot(trials_list, freq_list)
plt.ylabel('Sample Average')
plt.xlabel('Sample Size')
plt.hlines(0.50,0,sample_size,linestyles='dashed')
plt.show()
```

7. Running our notebook will yield the following results:

```
Results: 10008 heads out of 20000 flips. Average number of
heads is 0.5004
```

The code will generate the following graph, which shows how the average number of heads per coin flip changes as our sample size gets bigger (denoted by the solid line). Notice that after approximately 2,000 coin flips, the sample mean matches the expected value (about 0.5 heads per coin flip):

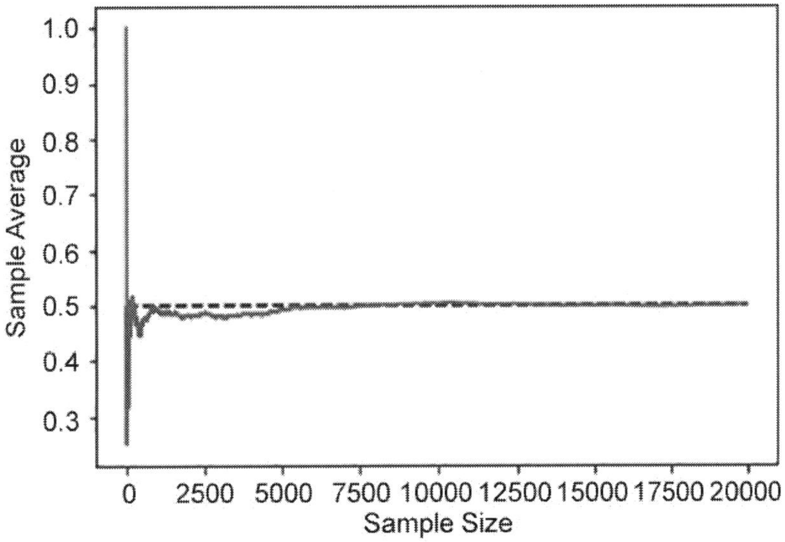

Figure 9.3: Average number of heads per coin flip over a sample size

> **NOTE**
>
> To access the source code for this specific section, please refer to https://packt.live/2BZcR2h.
>
> You can also run this example online at https://packt.live/31Alxpc.

A PRACTICAL APPLICATION OF THE LAW OF LARGE NUMBERS SEEN IN THE REAL WORLD

One of the best casino games to analyze through the lens of probability is roulette. Playing the game is relatively simple. The centerpiece of the game is a giant wheel with spaces and labels 1 through 36, 0, and 00 (double zero). The odd numbers are colored red, the even numbers are colored black, and both zero spaces are colored green. The wheel is spun and a ball is dropped into the wheel space moving the opposite direction to which the wheel is spinning. Eventually, the ball drops down into one of the 38 spots on the wheel. The result of where the ball lands is what people are betting on. They can place many different types of bets, ranging from landing on one specific number or which color space the ball will land on. The casino pays out according to the type of bet you have placed. When most people see roulette for the first time, a lot of them ask the question, "What's the deal with the two green spaces?" We will see clearly in a couple of pages why the green spaces are very important to casinos, but first let's talk about what we can expect from playing Roulette.

To add a little simplicity to the game, we are going to bet on the ball landing on a red number every single time. The payout on winning such a bet is 1:1, so if we bet $5 and win, we get to keep our $5 and win $5 more. If we lose the bet, we win nothing and lose the $5 bet. If we bet on red, here are the following probabilities of what can happen:

- Bet on red and if the ball lands on red, we win: $\frac{18}{38} \approx 0.474$
- Bet on red and if the ball lands on black, we lose: $\frac{18}{38} \approx 0.474$
- Bet on red and if the ball lands on green, we lose: $\frac{2}{38} \approx 0.053$

Let's look at the outcomes in terms of the money we can win or lose when placing a $1 bet:

- Bet on red and if the ball lands on red, we win $1
- Bet on red and if the ball lands on black, we lose $1
- Bet on red and if the ball lands on green, we lose $1

This is an example of a discrete distribution. To calculate the expected value of a discrete distribution, you multiply the value of the outcome by the probability with which it occurs. If you look at the preceding two lists, we have the probability and the value of each outcome in our game of roulette, so now we can calculate the expected amount of money we can win or lose for a typical game of roulette:

*(probability of landing on red * winnings or losses when we land on red) +*
*(probability of landing on black * winnings or losses when we land on black) +*
*(probability of landing on green * winnings or losses when we land on green)*

Now, if we calculate the expected amount we can win based on the probabilities we've calculated, we'll get the *(0.474*1)+(0.474*-1)+(0.053*-1) ≈ -0.05* value:

The preceding calculation tells us that we can expect to lose about 5 cents for every $1 bet on red. If we increase our bet, we can expect to lose more money.

Exercise 9.03: Calculating the Average Winnings for a Game of Roulette if We Constantly Bet on Red

Let's rework our simulation code to simulate playing games of roulette and track the overall average amount of money we win or lose per game. Then, we will graph the results like we did for the coin flipping scenario:

1. Import the **`random`** and **`matplotlib`** packages:

```
# roulette simulation.py
# import the module
import random
import matplotlib.pyplot as plt
random.seed(54321)
```

2. Create a variable for the sample size and set it to **10**. Create a variable called **bet** and set it to $1:

```
# set the number of games of roulette you want to play
sample_size = 10

#set the amount of money you want to bet
bet = 1
```

3. Initialize the variables that we will use to collect the results of our simulation:

```
# initialize the variables required for our loop
# 1 to 36 represent numbers on roulette wheel, 37 represents 0, 38
represents 00
net_money = 0
wins = 0
money_track = []
trials_track = []
```

4. Run the simulation and collect the results:

```
# create a for loop and collect the results in a list
for i in range(1,sample_size+1):
    result = random.randint(1,38)
    if result % 2 == 1 and result != 37:
        net_money += bet
        wins += 1
    else:
        net_money -= bet
    money_track.append(net_money/i)
    trials_track.append(i)
```

5. Print the results of the simulation and the expected value of the average:

```
# print the results
print(f'Results: You won {wins} games out of\
{sample_size} and won an average of\
{net_money/sample_size} dollars per game')
print(f'Results: You are expected to win\
{((18/38)*bet+(20/38)*(-bet))} per game')
```

6. Graph the expected value of the net change in money per game and the sample average of the net change in money per game:

```
#create a simple line graph to show our results over time
plt.plot(trials_track, money_track)
plt.ylabel('Net Money')
plt.xlabel('Number of games')
plt.hlines(((18/38)*bet+(20/38)*(-bet)), 0,
           sample_size, linestyles='dashed')
plt.show()
```

7. Run your notebook and you will get the following results:

```
Results: You won 4 games out of 10 and won an average of -0.2 dollars
per game
Results: You are expected to win -0.05263157894736842 per game
```

The preceding code will generate the following graph:

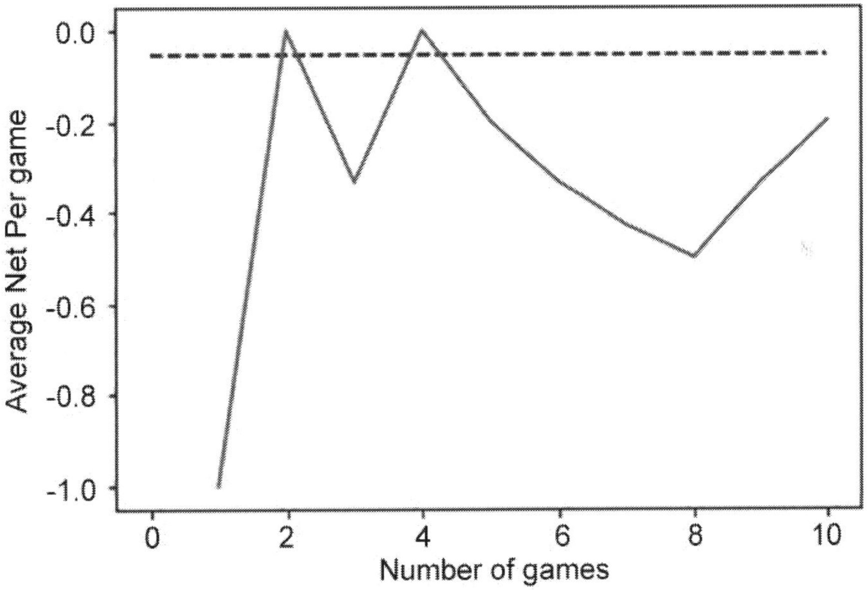

Figure 9.4: Running average net per game of roulette over 10 games played

In the preceding diagram, the solid line represents the average winnings per game during the 10 games we played. The dashed line represents how much money we can expect to win or lose per game. We should be losing about 5 cents per game but, in this specific scenario, we ended up losing 20 cents in total, much less than losing 5 cents per game. If you remove **random.seed(54321)** from the code and rerun the simulation, the results will be different. Feel free to experiment and change the amount you bet each time and see what happens.

> **NOTE**
>
> To access the source code for this specific section, please refer to https://packt.live/3dTdlEb.
>
> You can also run this example online at https://packt.live/2ZtkOEV.

But this isn't reflective of what happens in a casino. No casino only opens for 10 games of roulette a day. So, what happens to our graph if we change the number of games from 10 to 100,000? Setting the sample size variable to 100,000 and rerunning the code yields a graph that looks like this:

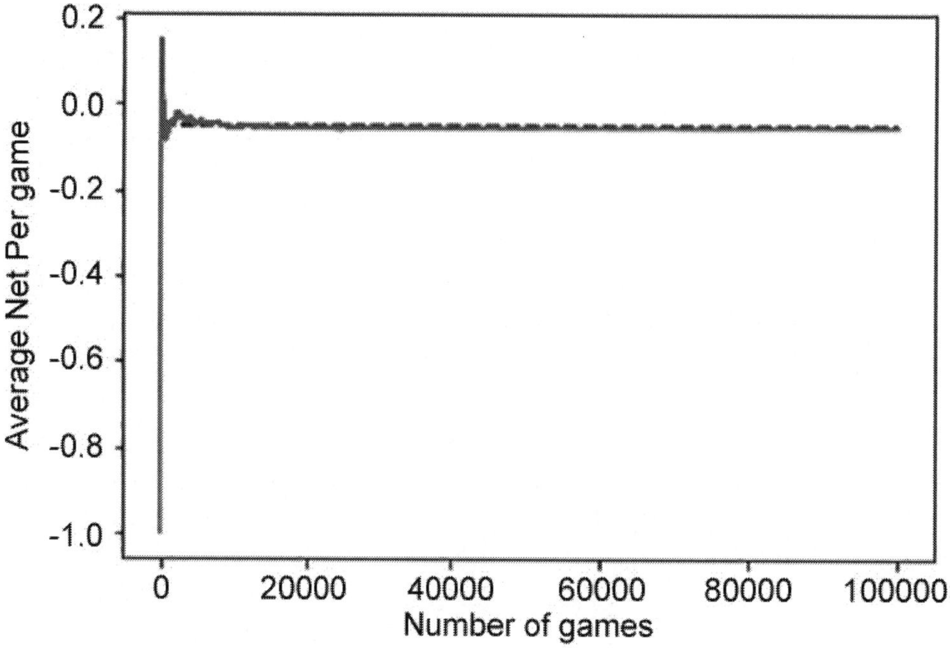

Figure 9.5: Running average net per game of roulette over 100,000 games played

Notice that the blue line quickly converges to the average dollar net per game of -0.05. Specifically, this simulation yielded a -0.054 dollar net, not too far off our expected value. In practical terms, the casino will gain money and gamblers will lose money on a per game basis in the long run. Now, back to the question of the green spaces. If we removed them from the game, there would be 18 red and 18 black spaces. Let's recalculate our expected value under these conditions:

*(probability of landing on red * winnings or losses when we land on red) +*

*(probability of landing on black * winnings or losses when we land on black)*

$$\left(\frac{18}{36} * 1\right) + \left(\frac{18}{36} * -1\right) = 0$$

Figure 9.6: Formula to calculate the expected value

What this means is that without the green spaces, neither the casino nor the gamblers will win or lose any money in the long run; both parties will walk away with the same amount of money they started with.

CENTRAL LIMIT THEOREM

By way of a quick review of the previous section, the law of large numbers tells us that as our sample gets larger, the closer our sample mean matches up with the population average. While this tells us what we should expect the value of the sample mean to be, it does not tell us anything at all about the distribution. For that, we need the central limit theorem. The **central limit theorem** (**CLT**) states that if we have a large enough sample size, the distribution of the sample mean is approximately normal, with a mean of the population mean and a standard deviation of the population standard deviation divided by the square root of *n*. This is important because not only do we know the typical value that our population mean can take, but we know the shape and variance of the distribution as well.

NORMAL DISTRIBUTION AND THE CLT

In *Chapter 8, Foundational Probability Concepts and Their Applications*, we looked at a type of continuous distribution known as *normal distribution*, also known as a bell curve or a Gaussian curve (all three of these names mean the same thing). While there are many instances of normal distribution that appear, that's not the main reason why it is special. The reason that normal distribution is special is because the distribution of many statistics follows a normal distribution, including the sample mean.

Knowing the distribution of the sample mean turns out to be vital in many of the typical statistical problems that we end up solving day to day. We take the mean and the variance information and put it together to have some idea of how our sample mean will vary from sample to sample. This tells us whether a sample mean is something we expect to show up or something that we are not expecting and need to study closer. We can take two different samples from supposedly identical populations and prove that they are, in fact, significantly different to one another.

RANDOM SAMPLING FROM A UNIFORM DISTRIBUTION

We can illustrate and verify the CLT by constructing a couple of simulations in Python, which is what we will do in the following exercises. The first simulation we are going to run is to take a random sample from a uniform distribution. A **uniform distribution** is one where every outcome is equally likely to be picked. If we were to graph a uniform distribution, it would look like a straight horizontal line going across the page. Some examples of uniform distributions are a dice roll, flipping a coin, or typical random number generators.

EXERCISE 9.04: SHOWING THE SAMPLE MEAN FOR A UNIFORM DISTRIBUTION

Let's draw a random sample from a random number generator that generates random numbers between 0 and 100 and calculates the sample average:

1. Import the following Python packages that we will be using and set the **seed**:

```
# sample_from_uniform_dist.py
# import the module
import random
import matplotlib.pyplot as plt
import math
import numpy as np
import scipy.stats as stats
random.seed(54312)
```

2. Create a variable for the size of each sample and the total number of samples that you want to take. Since the CLT states that we need a sufficiently large sample, we have selected a sample size of 30. Next, we are going to need a lot of sample means to graph and have set that value equal to 10,000:

```
# select the sample size you want to take
sample_size = 30
# select the number of sample mean you want to simulate
calc_means = 10000
```

3. Initialize the list we will use to collect our sample means and run through our simulation the specified number of times, collecting the sample mean of each sample:

```
mean_list = []
# run our loop and collect a sample
for j in range(calc_means):
    # initialize the variables to track our results
    sample_list = []
    for i in range(sample_size):
        sample_list.append(random.randint(0, 100))
    sample_mean = sum(sample_list) / sample_size
    mean_list.append(sample_mean)
```

4. Create a histogram of the sample means that we collected. Over the top of the histogram, we will overlay what the CLT says the distribution of the sample mean should look like:

```
"""
create a histogram of our sample and compare it
to what the CLT says it should be
"""
n, bins, patches = plt.hist(mean_list, \
                            math.floor(math.sqrt(calc_means)),\
                            density=True, facecolor='g', alpha=0.75)
plt.grid(True)
mu = 50
sigma = math.sqrt(((100 ** 2) / 12)) / (math.sqrt(sample_size))
x = np.linspace(mu - 3 * sigma, mu + 3 * sigma, 100)
plt.plot(x, stats.norm.pdf(x, mu, sigma))
plt.show()
```

Running this code in our notebook will give us the following result:

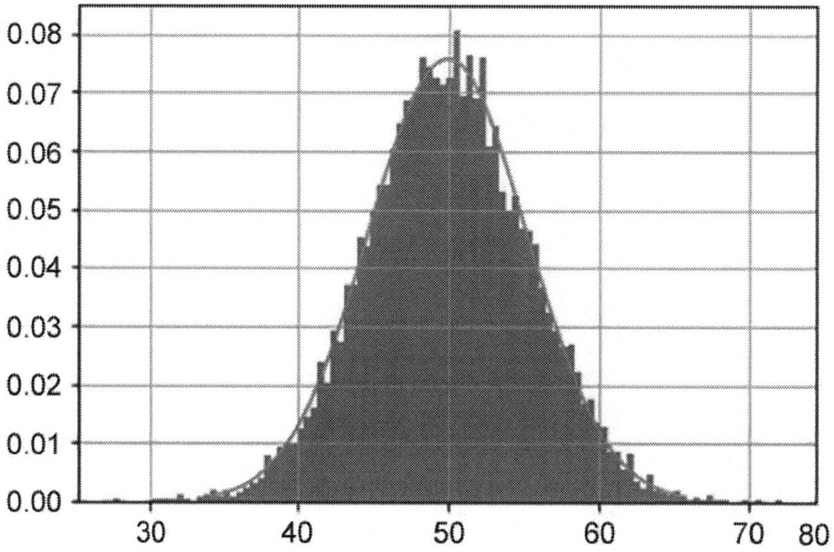

Figure 9.7: Distribution of sample average from 10,000 samples from a uniform distribution with a sample size of 30

The expected distribution given to us by the CLT almost perfectly overlays the histogram of the results of our simulation. Feel free to experiment and change the sample size and the number of sample means used to generate the graph.

> **NOTE**
>
> To access the source code for this specific section, please refer to https://packt.live/31JG77I.
>
> You can also run this example online at https://packt.live/3ggAq5m.

RANDOM SAMPLING FROM AN EXPONENTIAL DISTRIBUTION

We know that the CLT worked for the sample mean taken from a uniform distribution, but what about something that looks nothing like a uniform distribution? The CLT does not restrict the distribution of the sample we are drawing from, so would it work for something that looks nothing like a normal distribution? Let's look at the exponential distribution. The **exponential distribution** is a distribution that falls very quickly as it goes left to right before leveling off and approaching, but not quite touching, zero. The following graph is of a typical exponential distribution:

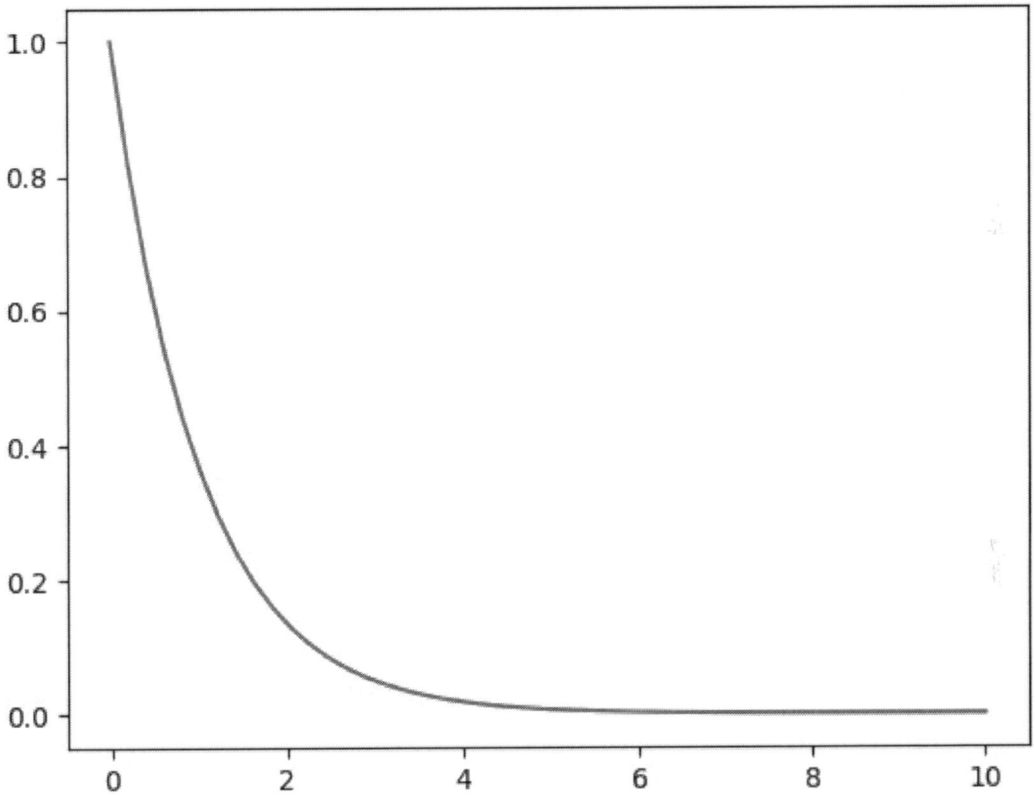

Figure 9.8: Example of exponential distribution

There a lot of examples of exponential distributions in the real world. Examples include how fast hot liquids cool, radioactive decay, and modeling the failure of mechanical parts.

EXERCISE 9.05: TAKING A SAMPLE FROM AN EXPONENTIAL DISTRIBUTION

In this exercise, we will randomly sample an exponential distribution. The following is the code that we can use to simulate drawing from an exponential distribution:

1. Import the Python packages that we will need. In order to see the effects of taking a smaller sample, we will set the sample size to **5** (refer to the following code), but keep the number of samples at **10000**:

```
# sample_from_exp_dist.py
# import the module
import random
import matplotlib.pyplot as plt
import math
import numpy as np
import scipy.stats as stats
# select the sample size you want to take
sample_size = 5
# select the number of sample mean you want to simulate
calc_means = 10000
```

2. Initialize the variable that we will use to collect the results of our simulation. Run the simulation, but this time sample from an exponential distribution rather than a uniform distribution:

```
mean_list = []
# run our loop and collect a sample
for j in range(calc_means):
    # initialize the variables to track our results
    sample_list = []
    for i in range(sample_size):
        draw = np.random.exponential(1)
        sample_list.append(draw)
    sample_mean = sum(sample_list) / sample_size
    mean_list.append(sample_mean)
```

3. Create a histogram of the sample means we collected and overlay what the CLT says we should expect from it:

```
""" create a histogram of our sample and compare it to what the CLT
says it should be """
n, bins, patches = plt.hist(mean_list, \
                            math.floor(math.sqrt(calc_means)), \
                            density=True, facecolor='g', \
                            alpha=0.75)
plt.grid(True)
mu = 1
sigma = 1 / (math.sqrt(sample_size))
x = np.linspace(mu - 3 * sigma, mu + 3 * sigma, 100)
plt.plot(x, stats.norm.pdf(x, mu, sigma))
plt.show()
```

4. Running the code that we typed in our Jupyter notebook will give us the following graph:

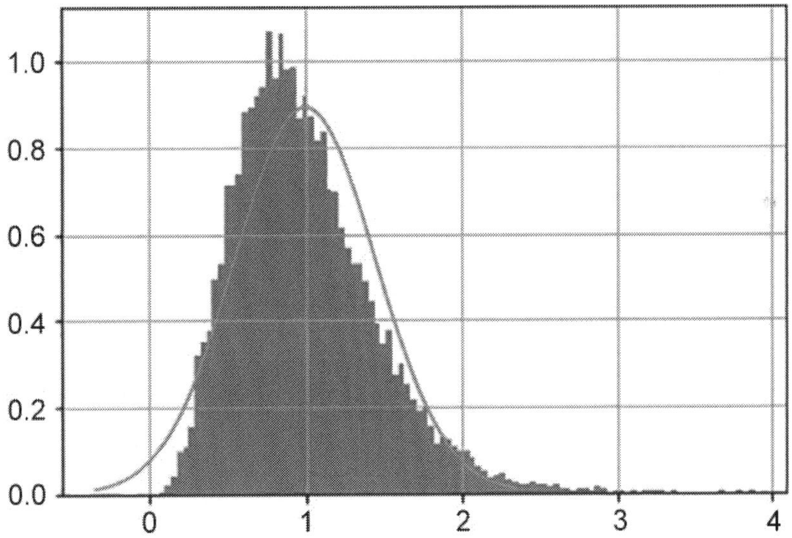

Figure 9.9: Distribution of sample average from 10,000 samples from an exponential distribution with a sample size of 5

As in the previous exercise entitled *Exercise 9.04, Showing the Sample Mean for a Uniform Distribution*, the orange line tells us what the CLT expects us to have. While our green histogram is similar to what we should expect, it is clearly skewed to the right and not a bell-shaped curve at all. But remember that the CLT requires us to take a large enough sample. Clearly, 5 is not large enough, so let's increase our sample size from 5 to 50 and rerun the code. Doing so should yield something like the following:

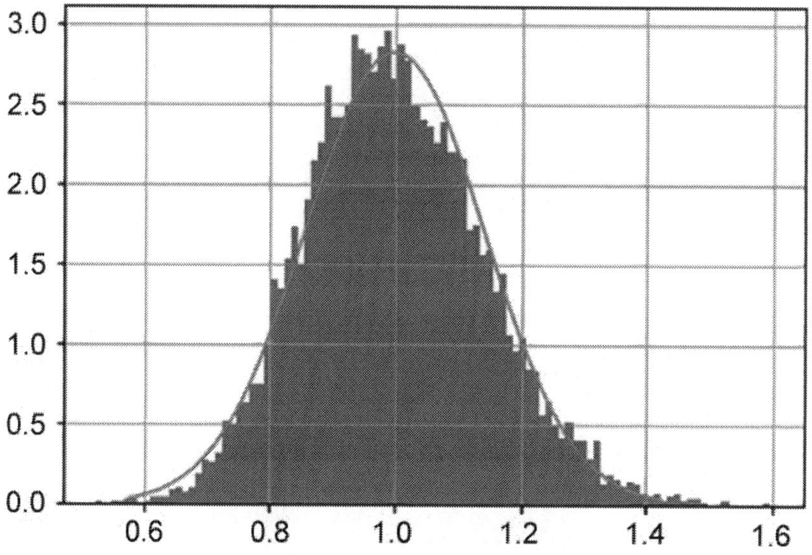

Figure 9.10: Distribution of sample average from 10,000 samples from an exponential distribution with a sample size of 50

This looks a lot closer to what we expected. Clearly, a sample size of 50 is big enough, while a sample size of 5 is not. But a question might be running through your head right now: "What sample size is large enough and how will we know?". The answer really depends on the underlying distributions; the more skewed the underlying distribution, the larger sample you must take to ensure a large enough sample for the CLT.

> **NOTE**
>
> To access the source code for this specific section, please refer to https://packt.live/2D2phXE.
>
> You can also run this example online at https://packt.live/2NRcvNP.

Later in the chapter, we will go through how to calculate the sample size you would need to take for a desired result, but we only consider the CLT to apply to samples of size 30 or more.

CONFIDENCE INTERVALS

As we saw with the previous simulations, our sample mean can vary from sample to sample. While, in a simulation, we have the luxury of taking 10,000 samples, we cannot do that in the real world; it would be far too expensive and time-consuming. Typically, we are given only enough resources to gather one sample. So how can we be confident in the results of our sample? Is there any way we can account for this variability when reporting our sample mean?

The good news is that the CLT gives us an idea of the variance in our sample mean. We can apply the CLT and take sampling variability into account by using a confidence interval. More generally, a **confidence interval** is a range of values for a statistic (an example of a statistic is a sample mean) based on a distribution that has some degree of confidence of how likely it is to contain the true value for the mean. We are not always going to be calculating confidence intervals for just the sample mean; the idea applies to any statistic that you calculate from a sample (the only difference is how you calculate it). Confidence intervals can be used to calculate how big a sample we need to take and what the margin of error is.

CALCULATING THE CONFIDENCE INTERVAL OF A SAMPLE MEAN

The first type of confidence interval we will calculate is a **z-confidence interval**, which will give us an interval (or range) of values for our sample mean based on the standard normal model (sometimes referred to as a z-distribution).

In order to calculate a z-confidence interval for our sample mean, we are going to need to know four things:

- The sample mean
- The sample size
- The population variance
- The critical value or some level of confidence

The sample mean and size are calculated from the sample that we collect. The population variance isn't something we calculate from our sample; the population variance is a value that is given to us. Typically, it is some accepted value for variance given from prior studies and research. The final piece of the puzzle is the critical value, or the confidence level; this is where the normal distribution and the CLT come in. To get an idea of what a critical value is, let's look at a standard normal distribution (which is a normal distribution that always has a mean of 0 and a variance of 1) and the area under its curve:

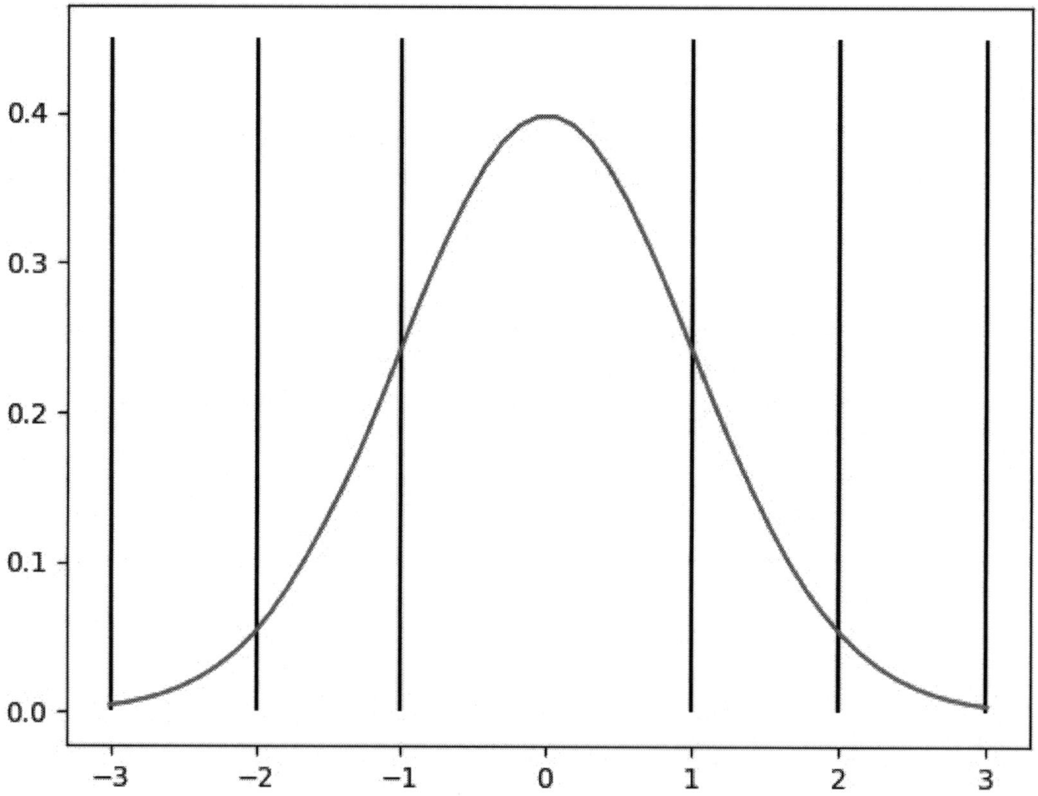

Figure 9.11: Example of a standard normal model

We know in our normal distribution that our mean is in the center (it is 0 in this case). The area underneath the curve from -1 to 1 accounts for 68% of the total area. Another way of putting this is that 68% of the values described by this distribution are between -1 and 1. About 95% of the values are between -2 and 2. Applying this to the distribution of the sample mean, we can find the range that 95% of our sample means will take. Referring back to *Figure 9.7*:

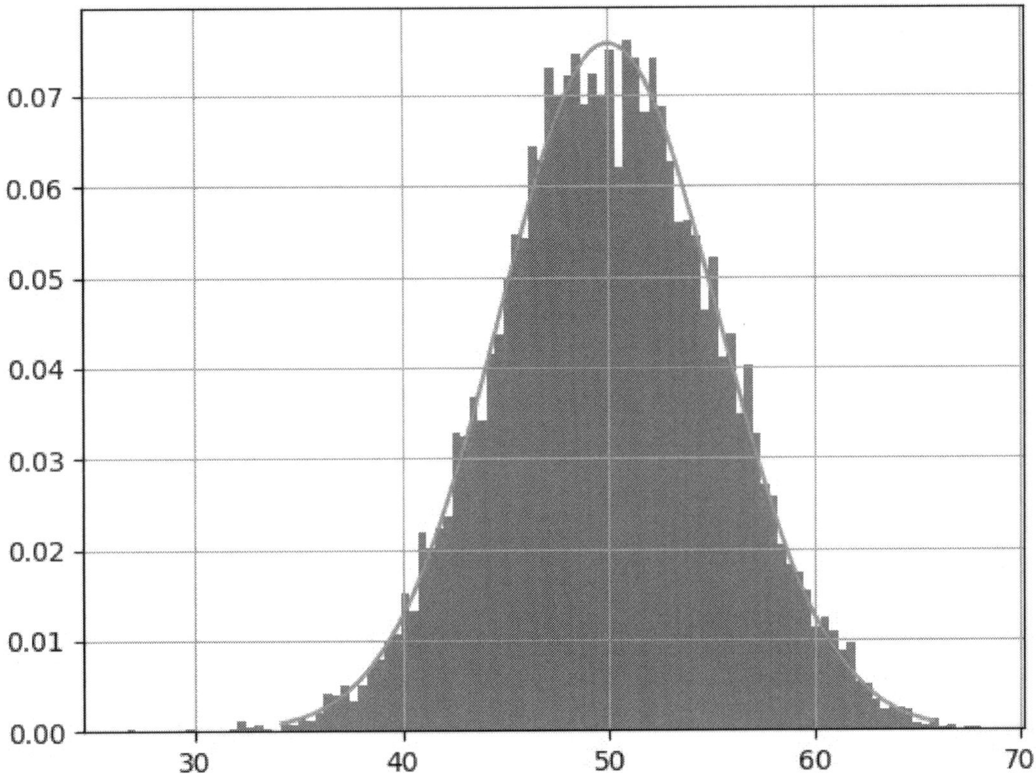

Figure 9.12: Distribution of sample average from 10,000 samples from a uniform distribution with a sample size of 30

If we look, the center of our bell curve is 50, which is the expected value of a uniform distribution that goes from 0 to 100. The expected standard deviation for a uniform distribution that goes from 0 to 100 would be about 5.27 ($\sqrt{\frac{(100-0)^2}{12}} \approx 5.27$). So, applying the same logic as before, about 68% of our values are between 45 and 55, and about 95% of our values are between 40 and 60. These ranges are our confidence intervals.

The more formal equation for calculating a z-confidence interval is given here:

$$\bar{x} \pm Z * \frac{\sigma}{\sqrt{n}}$$

Figure 9.13: Formula for calculating z-confidence interval

In this equation:

- $\bar{x}$ is the sample mean.
- n is the sample size.
- σ is the population standard deviation.
- Z is the critical value of our confidence level.

Our final confidence interval is going to be two numbers: an upper limit where we add the two terms together, and a lower limit where we subtract the two terms. Luckily, this is something we can write a function for in Python, as follows:

```
def z_confidence_interval(data, st_dev, con_lvl):
    import statistics as st
    import scipy.stats as sp
    import math
    sample_mean = st.mean(data)
    n = len(data)
    crit_value = sp.norm.ppf(((1 - con_lvl) / 2) + \
                             con_lvl)
    lower_limit = sample_mean - (crit_value * \
                                 (st_dev/math.sqrt(n)))
    higher_limit = sample_mean + (crit_value * \
                                  (st_dev / math.sqrt(n)))
    print (f'Your {con_lvl} z confidence interval
        is ({lower_limit}, {higher_limit})')
    return (lower_limit,higher_limit)
```

This function takes the following as input: the data we have gathered, along with the population standard deviation (given to us), and a level of confidence. It will print what the confidence level is to the console and return it as a tuple.

EXERCISE 9.06: FINDING THE CONFIDENCE INTERVAL OF POLLING FIGURES

You are running a political campaign and decide to run 30 focus groups with about 10 people in each group. You get the results and want to report to your candidate the number of people who would vote for them in a typical 10-person group. Since there is some variability in each focus group, you decide that the most accurate way is to give a 95% z-confidence interval. You assume from past experience that the standard deviation is 2.89. Let's model this using Python:

1. Import the **random** Python package and set the seed to **39809**. This will ensure that we get the same results every time we run the program:

```
import random
random.seed(39809)
```

2. Initialize our sample list and collect our samples from our focus groups. From there, we just enter the information into our function:

```
sample_list = []
for i in range(30):
    sample_list.append(random.randint(0, 10))

z_confidence_interval(sample_list,2.89,0.95)
```

3. If you did everything correctly, then the following should be printed when you run your notebook:

```
Your 0.95 z confidence interval is (3.965845784931483,
6.034154215068517)
```

This tells us that in a typical focus group, anywhere between 4 to 6 people in each group will vote for our candidate. This signals to you that the campaign should keep working harder to convince more people to vote for your candidate.

> **NOTE**
>
> To access the source code for this specific section, please refer to https://packt.live/2Zp6XiU.
>
> You can also run this example online at https://packt.live/3eUBL1B.

SMALL SAMPLE CONFIDENCE INTERVAL

The z-confidence interval works for when you have a large enough sample (remember our rule of thumb of a sample size of 30 or greater); but what if the sample you have is not large enough? Then you can use a **t-confidence interval**, which is basically the same as the z-confidence interval with two exceptions:

- The t-confidence interval does not assume that you know the population standard deviation, so we use the sample standard deviation.
- It uses the t-distribution to calculate the critical value rather than the z (standard normal) distribution. The difference between the two is that the t-distribution is less concentrated around the mean to account for not knowing the population standard deviation.

We need to know two things in order to calculate a t-confidence interval; the first is the degrees of freedom, which is calculated as the sample size minus 1 (*n-1*). The second is the confidence level. The formula for a t-confidence interval is given here:

$$\bar{x} \pm t_{n-1} * \frac{S}{\sqrt{n}}$$

Figure 9.14: Formula for calculating t-confidence interval

In this equation:

- $\bar{x}$ is the sample mean.
- t_{n-1} is the critical value with *n-1* degrees of freedom.
- *s* is the sample standard deviation.
- *n* is the sample size.

Just like with the z-interval, our final answer is going to be a lower and upper limit. We will write a function in Python to do all the calculation work for us:

```
def t_confidence_interval(data, con_lvl):
    import statistics as st
    import scipy.stats as sp
    import math
    sample_mean = st.mean(data)
    sample_st_dev = st.stdev(data)
    n = len(data)
    crit_value = sp.t.ppf(((1 - con_lvl) / 2) + \
```

```
                              con_lvl, n-1)
    lower_limit = sample_mean - (crit_value * \
                  (sample_st_dev/math.sqrt(n)))
    higher_limit = sample_mean + (crit_value * \
                   (sample_st_dev/math.sqrt(n)))
    print(f'Your {con_lvl} t confidence interval is \
({lower_limit},{higher_limit})')
    return (lower_limit,higher_limit)
```

Let's use the same sample list as the z-confidence interval. The **`t_confidence_interval`** function is used in the same way as our z-confidence interval function; we will enter a list of the data for which we want to calculate the t-confidence interval and specify our confidence level. There is no need to include a population standard deviation; the t-confidence interval uses the sample standard deviation and will calculate it for us automatically. The correct usage of the **`t_confidence_interval`** function is as follows:

```
t_confidence_interval(sample_list,0.95)
```

If you do everything correctly, the following should output in your notebook when you run the preceding code:

```
Your 0.95 t confidence interval is (3.827357936126168,6.172642063873832)
```

Notice that the t-confidence interval is wider than our z-confidence interval. This is because we have more uncertainty in using the sample standard deviation to estimate the standard deviation of the population than using the known value.

The nice thing about the t-confidence interval is that not only can it be used for small samples or situations where you do not know the population standard deviation; it can be used in any situation where you would use a z-confidence interval. In fact, as your sample size gets larger, the closer the t-distribution gets to the z (standard normal) distribution. So, if you are ever unsure of the value of the population standard deviation that you are given or find while looking at prior research, you can always play it safe and use the t-confidence interval.

CONFIDENCE INTERVAL FOR A PROPORTION

Let's go back to the example of the political campaign. After the different focus groups gave you results that were not definitive, a new poll came out that has your candidate winning the race, with 54% of the sample of 350 people saying they will vote for your candidate, while your opponent got the other 46%. You want to calculate a confidence interval for this proportion so you can consider sampling variability.

We know how to calculate the confidence interval of a sample mean, but how do we calculate a confidence interval for a proportion? The percentage of a sample is different than the mean value of a sample. Luckily for us, there is a formula for calculating a confidence interval for a proportion of a sample:

$$\hat{p} \pm Z * \sqrt{\frac{\hat{p} * (1 - \hat{p})}{n}}$$

Figure 9.15: Formula for calculating confidence interval

In this equation:

- $\hat{p}$ is the sample proportion. In this example, it is the 54% of people that voted for you.
- n is the sample size. For this example, it is the 350 people.
- Z is our critical value from the standard normal distribution. We calculate this the same way as the z-confidence interval.

There are some conditions that need to be met before we can apply this:

- The observations in our sample are independent—so, in our example, one person's answer did not influence another person's answer.
- We need at least 10 successes and 10 failures—so we need at least 10 people that vote for us and 10 people that would vote for your opponent.

Again, we can create a function in Python to do the calculations for us:

```
def prop_confidenct_interval(p_hat, n, con_lvl):
    import math
    import scipy.stats as sp
    crit_value = sp.norm.ppf(((1 - con_lvl) / 2) + \
                             con_lvl)
    lower_limit = p_hat - (crit_value * (math.sqrt(\
```

```
                (p_hat * (1-p_hat)) / n)))
    higher_limit = p_hat + (crit_value * (math.sqrt(\
                (p_hat * (1 - p_hat)) / n)))
    print(f'Your {con_lvl} proportional confidence \
interval is ({lower_limit},{higher_limit})')
    return (lower_limit,higher_limit)
```

Unlike the other functions we created, we do not feed in a list of our data values. Instead, we can enter our statistics directly and set a confidence level. To create a confidence interval for our poll, we enter the information like so:

```
prop_confidenct_interval(0.54,350, 0.95)
```

And the following results will be printed in the console:

```
Your 0.95 proportional confidence interval is (0.4877856513683282,0.592214
3486316719)
```

This tells us that we can be 95% confident that the true value of the proportion of the vote our candidate would get is between 48.8% and 59.2%. Hence, the results of the poll are inconclusive, and it shows us we still have more work to do to convince people to vote for our candidate. Note that this is where polls typically get the margin of error. The **margin of error** is the distance from our point estimator ($\hat{p}$ in this example) and either boundary (since the confidence interval is symmetrical; it does not matter whether we use the upper or lower bound). For this poll, our margin of error would be *0.592 - 0.54 = 0.052.*

So, the margin of error for the preceding poll would be about 5.2%. This is something to keep in mind when you are taking in the results of any poll, whether political or otherwise.

HYPOTHESIS TESTING

In the previous section, we ran simulations where the sample mean changed from sample to sample, despite sampling from the same population. But how will we know if a sample mean we calculate is significantly different from a preconceived value or even a different sample? How will we know if a difference is variability in action, or if the measures are different? The answer lies in conducting a hypothesis test.

A **hypothesis test** is a statistical test that is designed to determine whether a statistic is significantly different from what we expect. Examples of hypothesis tests include checking to see whether the sample mean is significantly different from a pre-established standard or compare two different samples to see whether they are statistically different or the same.

PARTS OF A HYPOTHESIS TEST

There are three main parts to any hypothesis test: the hypotheses, the test statistic, and the p-value. The *hypotheses* are what you are conducting the tests on to see whether they should be rejected or accepted. There are always two hypotheses for any test: a **null hypothesis** (typically referred to as using the symbol H_0) and an **alternative hypothesis** (typically referred to as using the symbol H_A). The null hypothesis is what we have always assumed or known to be true; in other words, it is what our pre-established standard is. The alternative hypothesis is the alternative we are going to compare to our null; in practical terms, it is the thing that we want to prove to be true.

Here are some examples of several hypotheses:

- You are the leader of a manufacturing company and you have a process that typically uses up 15 liters of fuel per hour. Your company is testing changes to this process to try and use less fuel. They took a sample of 24 hours and found that the new process used 13.7 liters of fuel per hour. The company needs to know if that reduction is significant or whether it can be attributed to variance in the process. Your null hypothesis would be what the process typically uses: $H_O: \mu = 15$. We want to try and prove that the new process uses less fuel, so our alternative hypothesis is: $H_A: \mu < 15$.
- Richard is a commercial baker in your city. He is wondering whether to invest in new equipment for the bread-making portion of his factory. Normally, his factory can make about 15,000 loaves of bread during one shift. Richard sent one of his shifts to try the new equipment for 5 shifts and they could make, on average, 17,500 loaves per shift. You tell Richard to test to see whether this is significantly different; the null hypothesis would be based on what he typically makes ($H_O: \mu=15000$), and the alternative hypothesis would be what he wants to try and prove ($H_A: \mu = 15000$).
- Linda is an analyst for a quality control department in her company. A part that the company makes needs to be 15 inches long. Since the company cannot measure every part that is made, Linda takes a sample of 100 parts and finds that the average length of this sample is 14.89 inches. She tells you that they expect each part to be 15 inches ($H_O: \mu = 15$), and they want to try and figure out whether the sample is evidence that the average part is not typically 15 inches ($H_A:\mu \neq 15$).

Each of the preceding situations depicts one of the three typical hypotheses tests that you will encounter: an upper-tailed test, a lower-tailed test, and a two-tailed test, respectively. Knowing the type of test you are conducting is necessary so that you can write your hypothesis and calculate your p-value correctly.

The **test statistic** is a number that describes how our observed sample compares to what we assume or know to be true about the mean we are testing. It is the part that is going to vary the most between the different tests that we conduct; it is based on the specific statistic we are testing and the test used. This is the most mathematical part of the statistics test, typically represented by a formula. The **p-value** is the last part of our hypothesis test; it is typically defined as the probability of seeing a sample like the one we collected if we assume the null hypothesis is true. We compare this value to some level of significance (0.05 is the most frequently used significance level); if our p-value is smaller than our level of significance, then we reject the null hypothesis and have evidence that the alternative hypothesis is true. Likewise, if our p-value is larger than our level of significance, we fail to reject the null hypothesis and do not have any evidence that the alternative hypothesis is true.

THE Z-TEST

Just like our z-confidence interval, there is a hypothesis test based on the standard normal model called the **z-test**. Just like the z-confidence interval, the z-test assumes that we know the population standard deviation and we have a large enough sample (again, the rule of thumb is a sample size of at least 30). The basic setup for a z-test is as follows:

- $H_0: \mu = \mu_0$ (don't worry; μ_0 is what we typically think the mean is and is just a number)
- $H_A: \mu < \mu_0$ or $H_A: \mu > \mu_0$ or $H_A: \mu \neq \mu_0$ (μ_0 will always match what we have for the null hypothesis)
- Test statistics: $Z = \frac{\bar{x} - \mu_0}{\frac{\sigma}{\sqrt{n}}}$

  Where:

  $\bar{x}$ is the sample average.

  σ is the known population standard deviation.

  n is the sample size.
- P value: $p = P(z < Z_\alpha)\ or\ p = P(z > Z_\alpha)\ or\ p = 2 * P(z < |Z_\alpha|)$

While none of this math is hard once you get the hang of it, we can use Python to make the calculations very simple.

EXERCISE 9.07: THE Z-TEST IN ACTION

Let's take a random sample from a distribution with a known population mean and see whether our z-test can select the correct hypothesis:

1. Let's start this exercise by importing all the libraries we are going to need in order to be able to run our code and set the **seed** value:

```
import scipy.stats as st
import numpy as np
import pandas as pd
import math as mt
import statistics as stat
import statsmodels.stats.weightstats as mod
import statsmodels.stats.proportion as prop
np.random.seed(12345)
```

2. We will write a function to do our z-test for us. The inputs will be a sample (in the form of a list), the population standard deviation (remember, specifying this is one of the requirements for the z-tests), the value of our hypothesis, the significance level of our test, and the test type (upper-, lower-, or two-tailed test). We will calculate the sample mean and sample size from the given list. Then, we will take the inputs and calculate our test statistic. Then, based on what hypothesis test we are deciding to do, we calculate a p-value accordingly. Finally, we compare our p-value to the level of significance, and if it is less than our level of significance, we reject the null hypothesis. Otherwise, we fail to reject the null hypothesis:

```
def z_test(sample, pop_st_dev, hypoth_value, \
           sig_level, test_type):
    sample_mean = stat.mean(sample)
    sample_size = len(sample)
    test_statistic = (sample_mean - hypoth_value) / \
                     (pop_st_dev / (mt.sqrt(sample_size)))
    if test_type == 'lower':
        p_value = st.norm.cdf(test_statistic)
    if test_type == 'upper':
        p_value = 1 - st.norm.cdf(test_statistic)
    if test_type == 'two':
```

```
        p_value = 2 * (1 - st.norm.cdf(abs(
            test_statistic)))
    print(f'P Value = {p_value}')
    if p_value < sig_level:
        print(f'Results are significant. Reject the Null')
    else:
        print(f'Results are insignificant. '\
               'Do Not Reject the Null')
```

3. We draw a random sample size of **50** from a normal distribution with a mean of **15** and a standard deviation of **1**. We will print the sample mean to the console so we know what it is (it will be different every time you run this code since we take a random sample every time). We use our z-test function to conduct a lower-tailed test since we want to see whether our mean is significantly less than **16**. We specify the list that contains our data (**data1**), the population standard deviation (we know this is **1**), the value of the hypothesis (we want to see whether it is significantly less than **16**), the level of significance (most of the time this will be **0.05**), and finally the type of test (since we want to see whether the mean is lower than **16**, this is a lower-tailed test):

```
# 1 - Lower Tailed Test
# Randomly Sample from Normal Distribution mu=
    and st_dev = 3
data1 = np.random.normal(15, 1, 50)

# Test to see if Mean is significantly less then 16
print(f'Sample mean: {stat.mean(data1)}')
z_test(data1,1,16,0.05,'lower')
# most of the time, the null should be rejected
```

When we run this code, we should get something that looks like this:

```
Sample mean: 14.94804802516884
P Value = 5.094688086201483e-14
Results are significant.  Reject the Null
(-7.43842374885694, 5.094688086201483e-14)
```

Since the p-value of our test statistic is less than 0.05 (written out from the scientific notation, it's 0.0000000000000509), we know that the sample mean of 15.06 is significantly less than 16, based on our sample size of 50. Since we took the sample from a population with a mean of 15, the test result was what we expected it to be. Again, since we are taking a random sample in the beginning, your results may vary, but, for most samples, this test should be rejecting the null hypothesis. In the tuple that is returned, the first value is the test statistic and the second is our p-value.

4. Next, let's test to see whether our mean is significantly larger than **14**. Following the same pattern as the lower-tailed test, our code will appear as follows:

```
#test to see if the mean is significantly more than 14
print(f'Sample mean: {stat.mean(data1)}')
z_test(data1,1,14,0.05,'upper')
#most of the time the null should reject
```

When we run the code, the following output is displayed in the console:

```
Sample mean: 14.94804802516884
P Value = 1.0159539876042345e-11
Results are significant.  Reject the Null
(6.703711874874011, 1.0159539876042345e-11)
```

5. For our final z-test, we will perform a two-tailed test and see whether our sample mean differs significantly from **15**. In this test, we really do not have a preference whether it is higher or lower than **15**; we just want to see whether it is different:

```
#test to see if the mean is significantly different than 15
print(f'Sample mean: {stat.mean(data1)}')
z_test(data1,1,15,0.05,'two')
#most of the type we should not reject the null
```

When we run this code, the result is as follows:

```
Sample mean: 14.94804802516884
P Value = 0.7133535345453159
Results are insignificant.  Do Not Reject the Null
(-0.3673559369914646, 0.7133535345453159)
```

This result makes sense because we sampled for a population where the mean was 15.

> **NOTE**
>
> To access the source code for this specific section, please refer to https://packt.live/2C24ItD.
>
> You can also run this example online at https://packt.live/2NNyntn.

PROPORTIONAL Z-TEST

The most common use of the z-test is not in testing the significance of a sample mean, but the significance of a percentage. The assumptions required for this are the same as the requirements for a proportional z-confidence interval: random sample, independence, and at least 10 successes and 10 failures. We would calculate the test statistics for this test as follows:

$$Z_p = \frac{\hat{p} - p_o}{\sqrt{\frac{\hat{p} * (1 - \hat{p})}{n}}}$$

Figure 9.16: Formula to calculate test statistics

We would calculate the p-value the same way as the z-test for a sample mean. We do not need to create a function for this test; one already exists in the **`statsmodels.stats.proportion`** Python package called **`proportions_ztest`**. The syntax for this function is as follows:

```
proportions_ztest(x,n,Po, alternative=['smaller',\
                                       'larger','two-sided'])
```

Here:

`x` is the number of successes in our sample.

`n` is the size of our sample.

`Po` is the hypothesized value we want to test against.

The alternative specifies a lower-tailed, upper-tailed, or two-tailed test.

The output of this function is a tuple; the first element is the test statistic, and the second element is the p-value. Let's go back to our polling example: your campaign conducted a poll of their own and sampled 350 people. Out of 350 people, 193 people said they would vote for you. We want to see whether this sample we collected is evidence that a majority of people are going to vote for you.

We will assign the results of our z-test to a variable called **`results`**. We call the function where **`193`** is the number of successes/people who will vote for us, and the sample size is **`350`**. Since we want to test to see whether our sample is evidence that we have the majority of the vote, we want to perform an upper-tailed test where the hypothesized value is **`0.50`**:

```
#z-test for proportion
results = prop.proportions_ztest(193,350,.50, \
                                 alternative='larger')
print(results)
```

When the code is run, the following is printed to the console:

```
(1.93454148164361, 0.026523293494118718)
```

Our p-value is about 0.027, which is a significant result at 0.05. This tells us that our sample is evidence that we have the majority of the vote.

THE T-TEST

While the z-test is useful for conducting a hypothesis test on a proportion, it is not very practical when testing a sample mean because we typically do not know the standard deviation of the population. There are other times where our sample size is very small. For this situation, we can use a t-test, which is analogous to our t-confidence interval. Just like with the t-confidence interval, you do not need to know the population standard deviation; you can use the sample to estimate it.

The formula for the t-test is given as follows:

$$T = \frac{\overline{x} - \mu_0}{\frac{s}{\sqrt{n}}}$$

Figure 9.17: Formula to calculate t-test

In this equation:

- $\bar{x}$ is the sample mean.
- μ_0 is the hypothesized value we are testing against.
- s is the sample standard deviation.
- n is the sample size.

We will calculate the p-value using a t-distribution instead of a standard normal distribution. However, we are not going to focus too much on the mechanics of this specific test, as it is like the other hypothesis tests we have covered. We are going to create a function to conduct our t-test, similar to our z-test:

```
def t_test(sample, hypoth_value, sig_level, test_type):
    sample_mean = stat.mean(sample)
    sample_st_dev = stat.stdev(sample)
    sample_size = len(sample)
    test_statistic = (sample_mean - hypoth_value) / \
                     (sample_st_dev/(mt.sqrt(sample_size)))
    if test_type == 'lower':
        p_value = st.t.cdf(test_statistic,df=sample_size-1)
    if test_type == 'upper':
        p_value = 1 - st.t.cdf(test_statistic,df=sample_size-1)
    if test_type == 'two':
        p_value = 2 * (1 - st.t.cdf(abs(test_statistic), \
                                   df=sample_size-1))
    print(f'P Value = {p_value}')
    if p_value < sig_level:
        print(f'Results are significant.  Reject the Null')
    else:
        print(f'Results are insignificant. '\
              'Do Not Reject the Null')
```

In the preceding code:

- **`sample`** is a list of the measures of your sample.
- **`hypoth_value`** is the value you are testing against.
- **`sig_level`** is the significance level.
- **`test_type`** is the type of test—lower, upper, or two.

EXERCISE 9.08: THE T-TEST

We will examine two different samples: one large sample and one small sample. Both samples will be randomly selected from a normal distribution from a mean of 50 and a standard deviation of 10. The only difference between the two samples is that the large sample will have a size of 100 and the smaller sample will have a size of 10:

1. First, let's import the libraries we will use, set the seed, and then randomly generate our large sample:

```
import scipy.stats as st
import numpy as np
import pandas as pd
import math as mt
import statistics as stat
import statsmodels.stats.weightstats as mod
import statsmodels.stats.proportion as prop
np.random.seed(1)

data1 = np.random.normal(50, 10, 100)
```

2. Create functions for our t-test:

```
def t_test(sample, hypoth_value, sig_level, test_type):
    sample_mean = stat.mean(sample)
    sample_st_dev = stat.stdev(sample)
    sample_size = len(sample)
    test_statistic = (sample_mean - hypoth_value) / \
                     (sample_st_dev/(mt.sqrt(sample_size)))
    if test_type == 'lower':
        p_value = st.t.cdf(test_statistic,df=sample_size-1)
    if test_type == 'upper':
        p_value = 1 - st.t.cdf(test_statistic,df=sample_size-1)
    if test_type == 'two':
        p_value = 2 * (1 - st.t.cdf(abs(test_statistic), \
                                    df=sample_size-1))
    print(f'P Value = {p_value}')
    if p_value < sig_level:
        print(f'Results are significant.  Reject the Null')
    else:
        print(f'Results are insignificant. '\
              'Do Not Reject the Null')
```

3. We will run three different tests: one to see whether the sample mean differs significantly from **50**, whether the sample mean is significantly lower than **51**, and whether the sample mean is significantly higher than **48**:

```
print('large sample')
print(f'Sample mean: {stat.mean(data1)}')
t_test(data1,50,0.05,'two')
t_test(data1,51,0.05,'lower')
t_test(data1,48,0.05,'upper')
```

Running this code will result in the following:

```
large sample
Sample mean: 50.60582852075699
P Value = 0.4974609984410545
Results are insignificant.  Do Not Reject the Null
P Value = 0.32933701868279674
Results are insignificant.  Do Not Reject the Null
P Value = 0.002109341573010237
Results are significant.  Reject the Null
```

The first test is insignificant, and we do not have evidence that the mean is significantly different to **50**. The second test is insignificant as well; the sample is not evidence that the mean is significantly greater than **51**. The last test is significant; the sample is evidence that the mean is significantly higher than **48**.

4. Now, we will run the same three tests, only this time we will use a sample with a size of **5** (we will use the first **5** elements from the large sample):

```
# select the first 5 elements of the data set
data2 = data1[:5]
print(data2)

#two-tailed test = Is the sample mean significantly
#different from 50?
print('small sample')
print(f'Sample mean: {stat.mean(data2)}')
t_test(data2,50,0.05,'two')
#lower tailed = Is the sample mean significantly
#lower than 51?
t_test(data2,51,0.05,'lower')
```

```
#upper tailed = is the sample mean significantly
#more than 48?
t_test(data2,48,0.05,'upper')
```

Running the preceding code produces the following:

```
[66.24345364 43.88243586 44.71828248 39.27031378 58.65407629]
small sample
Sample mean: 50.553712409836436
P Value = 0.918572770568147
Results are insignificant.  Do Not Reject the Null
P Value = 0.4671568669546634
Results are insignificant.  Do Not Reject the Null
P Value = 0.32103491333328793
Results are insignificant.  Do Not Reject the Null
```

The results for the first two tests do not change, while the third test did change despite the nearly identical sample mean. The reason for the difference is due to the small sample size; since there is less certainty due to the small sample, the test is more conservative and less likely to reject the null hypothesis. This can be shown in our equation for our test statistic:

$$T = \frac{\overline{x} - \mu_0}{\frac{s}{\sqrt{n}}}$$

Figure 9.18: Formula to calculate test statistics for t-test

Notice the denominator $\frac{s}{\sqrt{n}}$; if *n* is smaller, then the value of $\frac{s}{\sqrt{n}}$ will be larger (for a constant *s*). This causes the value of the denominator for the test statistic to be larger, leading to a smaller test statistic overall.

> **NOTE**
>
> To access the source code for this specific section, please refer to https://packt.live/38mMShg.
>
> You can also run this example online at https://packt.live/3gkBdlK.

2-SAMPLE T-TEST OR A/B TESTING

The final test we will be looking at is the 2-sample t-test. This is a hypothesis test that compares the means of two different samples and can tell you whether one mean is significantly higher, significantly lower, or significantly different than the other mean. One of the applications of this is something known as A/B testing. A/B testing is where you show two different groups two different versions of a website or app, and collect some sort of measure of performance. Examples of measures of performance could be something like the amount of money spent, the number of people that clicked on an ad, or the amount of money people spent on micro transactions inside your mobile game. Once you have collected the data, you test the two sample means and see whether the differences between the two different versions are significant.

The null and alternative hypotheses work a little bit differently for a two-sample test than they do for a one-sample test. Instead of comparing a sample mean to a value, you are comparing it to another mean. How we typically show this is by comparing the difference to zero. Using some algebra, you can figure out how the alternative hypotheses should be set up:

- Upper-tailed (mean 1 is greater than mean 2): $\mu_1 > \mu_2 \Rightarrow \mu_1 - \mu_2 > 0$
- Lower-tailed (mean 1 is less than mean 2): $\mu_1 < \mu_2 \Rightarrow \mu_1 - \mu_2 < 0$
- Two-tailed (mean 1 differs from mean 2): $\mu_1 \neq \mu_2 \Rightarrow \mu_1 - \mu_2 \neq 0$

For the 2-sample t-test, the null hypothesis will always be set to 0 ($\mu_1 - \mu_2 = 0$). In other words, the null hypothesis is saying that there is no difference between the two means, and the other is saying that there is a difference. The test statistic for the 2-sample t-test is given here:

$T = \frac{\bar{x}_1 - \bar{x}_2}{\sqrt{\frac{s_1^2}{n_1} - \frac{s_2^2}{n_2}}}$ with a degree of freedom $\frac{\left(\frac{s_1^2}{n_1} + \frac{s_2^2}{n_2}\right)^2}{\frac{\left(s_1^2/n_1\right)^2}{n_1 - 1} + \frac{\left(s_2^2/n_2\right)^2}{n_2 - 1}}$

The good news for this is that we do not have to calculate this by hand, nor do we have to go through the trouble of creating our own function to do this. There is a function in the **`scipy.stats`** package for this very test. The function is as follows:

```
scipy.stats.ttest_ind(x1,x2,equal_var=False)
```

Here:

- **x1** is a list of the data in the first sample.
- **x2** is a list of the data in the second sample.
- We set **equal_var** to **False** since we do not know whether the variance of the two samples is the same.

This function returns two values: the signed test statistic and the p-value. Some people may have noticed that there is no option to specify which test you are performing. That is because this function always assumes that you are conducting a two-tailed test. So how can you use this to get the results of your one-tailed test? Since the t-distribution is symmetrical, the p-value for a one-tailed test would be half of the p-value of a two-tailed test. The second thing to look at is the sign of the test statistic. For a lower-tailed test, you would only reject the null hypothesis if the test statistic is negative. Likewise, for an upper-tailed test, you would only reject the null hypothesis if the test statistic is positive. So, for single-tailed tests:

- **Lower**: Reject the null hypothesis if $\frac{p\ value}{2}$ is less than your significance level and your test statistic is negative.
- **Upper**: Reject the null hypothesis if $\frac{p\ value}{2}$ is less than your significance level and your test statistic is positive.

EXERCISE 9.09: A/B TESTING EXAMPLE

We have two samples, one drawn from a normal distribution with a mean of 50, and another drawn from a distribution with a mean of 100. Both samples have a size of 100. In this exercise, we are going to determine whether the sample mean of one sample is significantly different, lower, or higher than the other:

1. First, let's import the libraries we will use:

```
import scipy.stats as st
import numpy as np
```

2. Let's draw our random samples and print the sample means so we know what they are. Remember to set the seed:

```
# Randomly Sample from Normal Distributions
np.random.seed(16172)
sample1 = np.random.normal(50, 10, 100)
```

```
sample2 = np.random.normal(100,10,100)
print(f'Sample mean 1: {stat.mean(sample1)}')
print(f'Sample mean 2: {stat.mean(sample2)}')
```

The results are as follows:

```
Sample mean 1: 50.54824784997514
Sample mean 2: 97.95949096047315
```

3. We will perform a 2-sample t-test using the function from the **scipy** package and print the results:

```
two_tail_results = st.ttest_ind(sample1, sample2, \
                                equal_var=False)
print(two_tail_results)
```

The results are as follows:

```
Ttest_indResult(statistic=-33.72952277672986,
    pvalue=6.3445365508664585e-84)
```

Since, by default, the function does a two-tailed test, we know that the mean of sample 1 is significantly different to the mean of sample 2. If we wanted to do a lower-tailed test (where the mean of sample 1 is significantly less than sample 2), we would use the same code. The only difference is that we would divide the p-value by 2 and check to see whether our test statistic is negative. Since our p-value divided by 2 is less than 0.05 and our test statistic is negative, we know that the mean of sample 1 is significantly less than the mean of sample 2.

4. If we want to test whether the mean of sample 2 is significantly greater than the mean of sample 1, we just switch the position of sample 1 and sample 2 in the function:

```
upper_tail = st.ttest_ind(sample2, sample1, equal_var=False)
print(upper_tail)
```

The results are as follows:

```
Ttest_indResult(statistic=33.72952277672986,
pvalue=6.3445365508664585e-84)
```

Just like with the lower-tailed test, we would divide the p-value by 2. However, we would check to see that the test statistic is positive. Since the p-value divided by 2 is less than 0.05 and the test statistic is positive, we know that the mean of sample 2 is significantly more than the mean of sample 1.

> **NOTE**
>
> To access the source code for this specific section, please refer to https://packt.live/3iuHmOr.
>
> You can also run this example online at https://packt.live/3ghpdl4.

INTRODUCTION TO LINEAR REGRESSION

We have looked at describing and testing sample statistics, but what if we want to use characteristics of the data to describe one other characteristic? For example, how does the price of a mobile app impact the number of downloads? To do that, we would model the data using linear regression. **Linear regression** is where we use a linear equation of one or more independent variables to describe a single dependent variable. Typically, our regression equation is in slope-intercept form, shown here:

$$y = \beta_1 x + \beta_0$$

Figure 9.19: Formula for linear regression

Here:

- β_1 is the slope of our equation, typically called a coefficient.
- β_0 is the intercept of the equation.

How do we come up with the values for our coefficient and intercept? It starts with the **residuals**—which is the difference between the predicted y values and the actual y values. Another way to look at residuals is that this is the amount that our equation's prediction is off by. While we will not go into much detail here, we use calculus to figure out the values of β_1, β_0 that minimize the total sum of all the residuals. We are not necessarily restricted to one coefficient either; we can have multiple (two or more) coefficients, like so:

$$y = \beta_3 x_3 + \beta_2 x_2 + \beta_1 x_1 + \beta_0$$

Figure 9.20: Formula for linear regression with multiple coefficients

Luckily, we can use Python to do all the calculations for us, specifically the linear model function in the **sklearn** package.

EXERCISE 9.10: LINEAR REGRESSION

We are tasked with trying to predict the pH levels of red wine using the wine's other characteristics. The dataset can be downloaded from the GitHub repository at https://packt.live/3imVXv5.

> **NOTE**
>
> This is the wine quality dataset provided by the UCI Machine Learning Repository (http://archive.ics.uci.edu/ml). Irvine, CA: University of California, School of Information and Computer Science. *P. Cortez, A. Cerdeira, F. Almeida, T. Matos, and J. Reiss*. Modeling wine preferences by data mining from physicochemical properties. In Decision Support Systems, Elsevier, 47(4):547-553, 2009.

1. Import the packages we need and read in the data:

```
# import packages and read in data
import pandas as pd
import statistics as st
import scipy.stats as sp
import math
import sklearn.linear_model as lm
import matplotlib.pyplot as plt
from mpl_toolkits import mplot3d
import numpy as np

data = pd.read_csv("winequality-red.csv")
```

2. Subset the data to the two columns we need (we are going to try to use the amount of citric acid to predict the **pH** level). Set the **pH** level as our dependent variable and citric acid as the independent variable:

```
data1 = data[['pH','citric acid']]
plt.scatter(x=data1['citric acid'], y=data1['pH'])

y = data1['pH']
x = data1[['citric acid']]
```

3. Fit the linear model and graph the data as a scatter plot and our linear regression model:

```
model = lm.LinearRegression()
model.fit(x,y)

plt.scatter(x, y,color='g')
plt.plot(x, model.predict(x),color='k')

plt.show()
```

The output will be as follows:

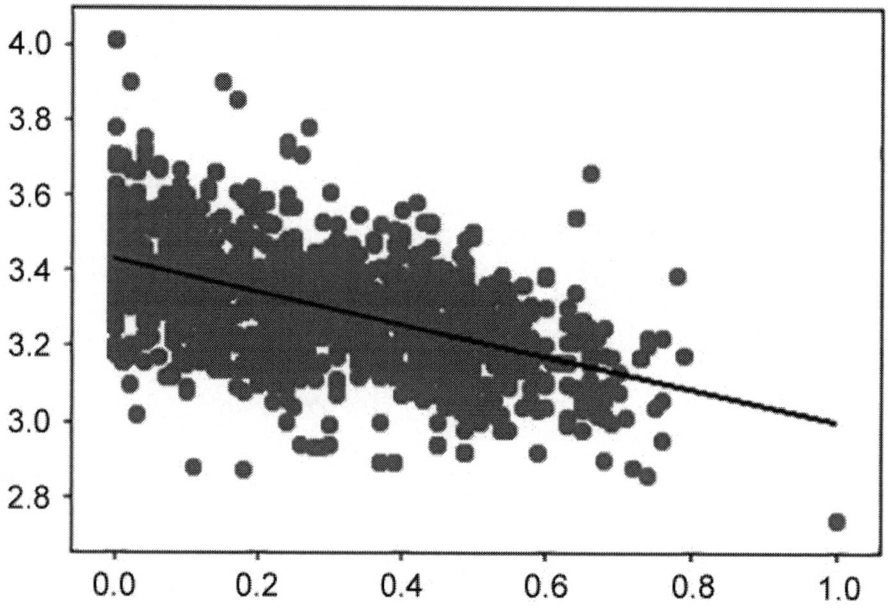

Figure 9.21: The linear equation seems to fit our data well

If you look at the picture, you notice that the line fits the data well. Let's add another independent variable; in this case, the amount of residual sugar, and see whether it improves the prediction.

4. This time, we set our independent variables as citric acid and residual sugar and fit the model:

```
#can we predict the pH of the wine using
#citric acid and residual sugar?
data2 = data[['pH','citric acid','residual sugar']]
y = data2['pH']
x = data2[['citric acid', 'residual sugar']]

model = lm.LinearRegression()

model.fit(x,y)

y_pred = model.predict(x)
```

5. Create a three-dimensional scatter plot and graph the line in the **`3d`** space to check to see whether it fits our data well:

```
threedee = plt.figure().gca(projection='3d')
threedee.scatter(data2['citric acid'],
    data2['residual sugar'],data2['pH'])
threedee.set_xlabel('citric acid')
threedee.set_ylabel('residual sugar')
threedee.set_zlabel('pH')

xline = np.linspace(0, 1, 100)
yline = np.linspace(0, 16, 100)
zline = xline*(-0.429) + yline*(-0.000877)+3.430
threedee.plot3D(xline, yline, zline, 'red')

plt.show()
```

The output will be as follows:

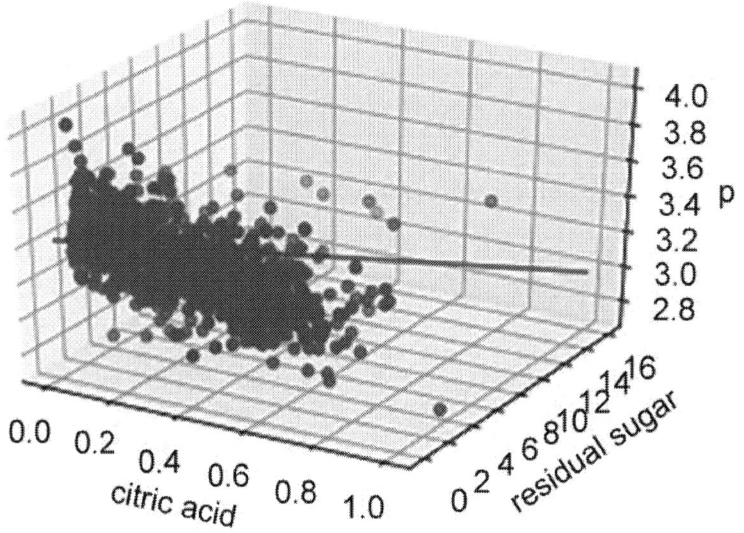

Figure 9.22: The linear equation doesn't seem to fit our data well

If you look at the picture, our linear model does not seem to fit the data as well as the first model we fitted. Based on this, residual sugar is probably not going to be involved in our final model.

> **NOTE**
>
> To access the source code for this specific section, please refer to https://packt.live/2Anl3ZA.
>
> You can also run this example online at https://packt.live/3eOmPlv.

ACTIVITY 9.01: STANDARDIZED TEST PERFORMANCE

You are given the task of describing the results of the 2015 PISA test and investigating possible effects of the prevalence of internet infrastructure on test scores.

To download the dataset, go to the GitHub repository at https://packt.live/3gi2hCg, download the **`pisa_test_scores.csv`** file, and save that file to your working directory.

> **NOTE**
>
> This PISA test scores dataset is based on data provided by the World Bank (https://datacatalog.worldbank.org/dataset/education-statistics). World Bank Edstats.

Once you have that file saved, do the following:

1. Describe the typical score of a student in reading, science, and mathematics using a confidence interval.
2. Using a hypothesis test, evaluate whether the prevalence of internet infrastructure can lead to higher test scores.
3. Construct a linear model that uses reading and writing scores to predict the mathematics score.

> **NOTE**
>
> The solution to this activity can be found on page 688.

SUMMARY

In this chapter, we examined the law of large numbers and how the stability of the sample mean statistic is affected by sample size. Through the CLT, the theoretical underpinnings of confidence intervals and hypothesis testing were examined. Confidence intervals were used to describe sample statistics, such as sample mean, sample proportion, and margin of error. Hypothesis testing was conducted to evaluate two opposing hypotheses using the evidence of a collected sample.

The next chapter begins your study of calculus, where you will examine such topics as the instantaneous rate of change and finding the slope of a curved line. After studying that, we will look at integration, which is finding the area underneath a curve. Finally, we will use derivatives to find optimal values of complicated equations and graphs.

10

FOUNDATIONAL CALCULUS WITH PYTHON

OVERVIEW

In this chapter, you will learn to calculate the derivatives of functions at a given value of x. You'll also learn to calculate the integrals of functions between given values and use derivation to solve optimization problems, such as maximizing profit or minimizing cost. By the end of this chapter, you will be able to use calculus to solve a range of mathematical problems.

INTRODUCTION

Calculus has been called the science of change, since its tools were developed to deal with constantly changing values such as the position and velocity of planets and projectiles. Previously, there was no way to express this kind of change in a variable.

The first important topic in calculus is the **derivative**. This is the rate of change of a function at a given point. Straight lines follow a simple pattern known as the slope. This is the change in the *y* value (the *rise*) over a given range of *x* values (the *run*):

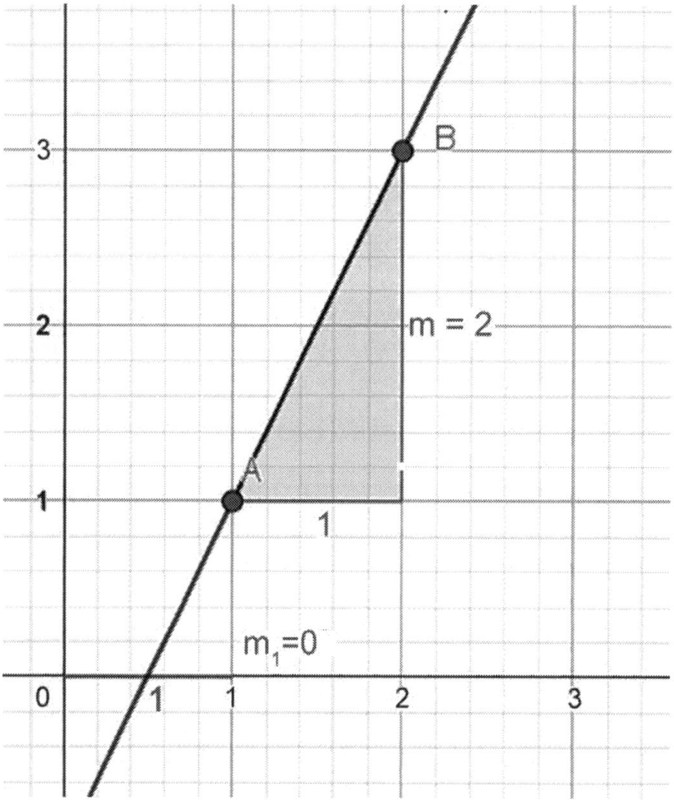

Figure 10.1: Slope of a line

In *Figure 10.1*, the *y* value in the line increases by 2 units for every 1-unit increase in the *x* value, so we divide 2 by 1 to get a slope of 2.

However, the slope of a curve isn't constant over the whole curve like it is in a line. So, as you can see in *Figure 10.2*, the rate of change of this function at point **A** is different from the rate of change at point **B**:

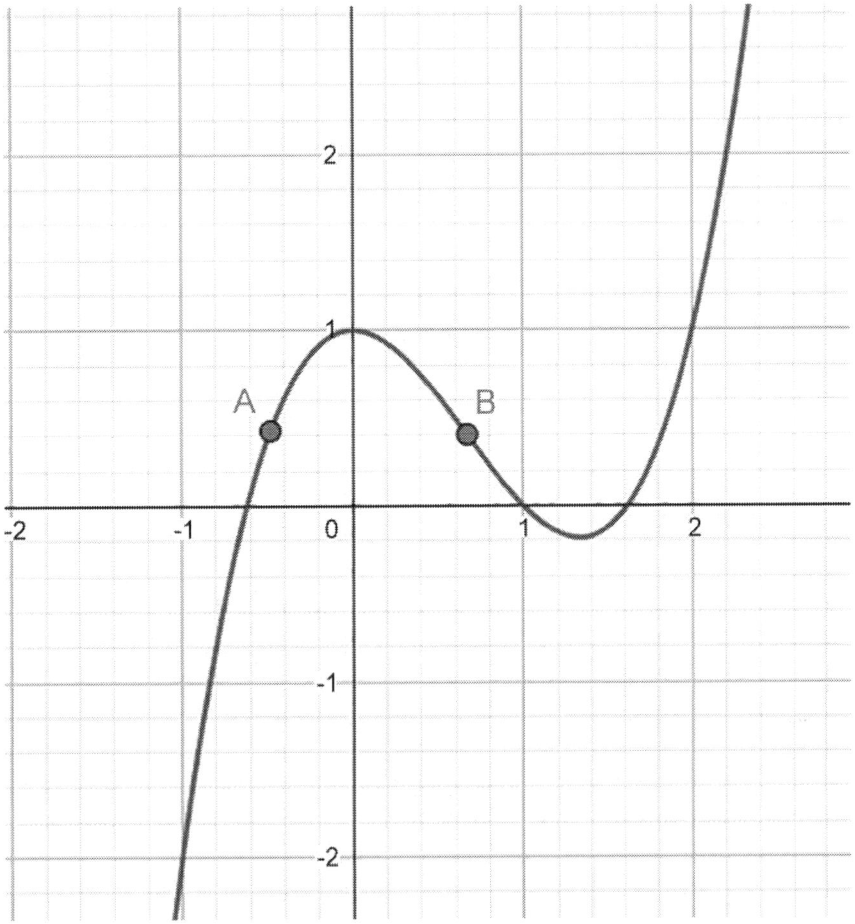

Figure 10.2: Finding the slope of a curve

However, if we zoom in closely enough on point **A**, we see the curve is pretty closely approximated by a straight line.

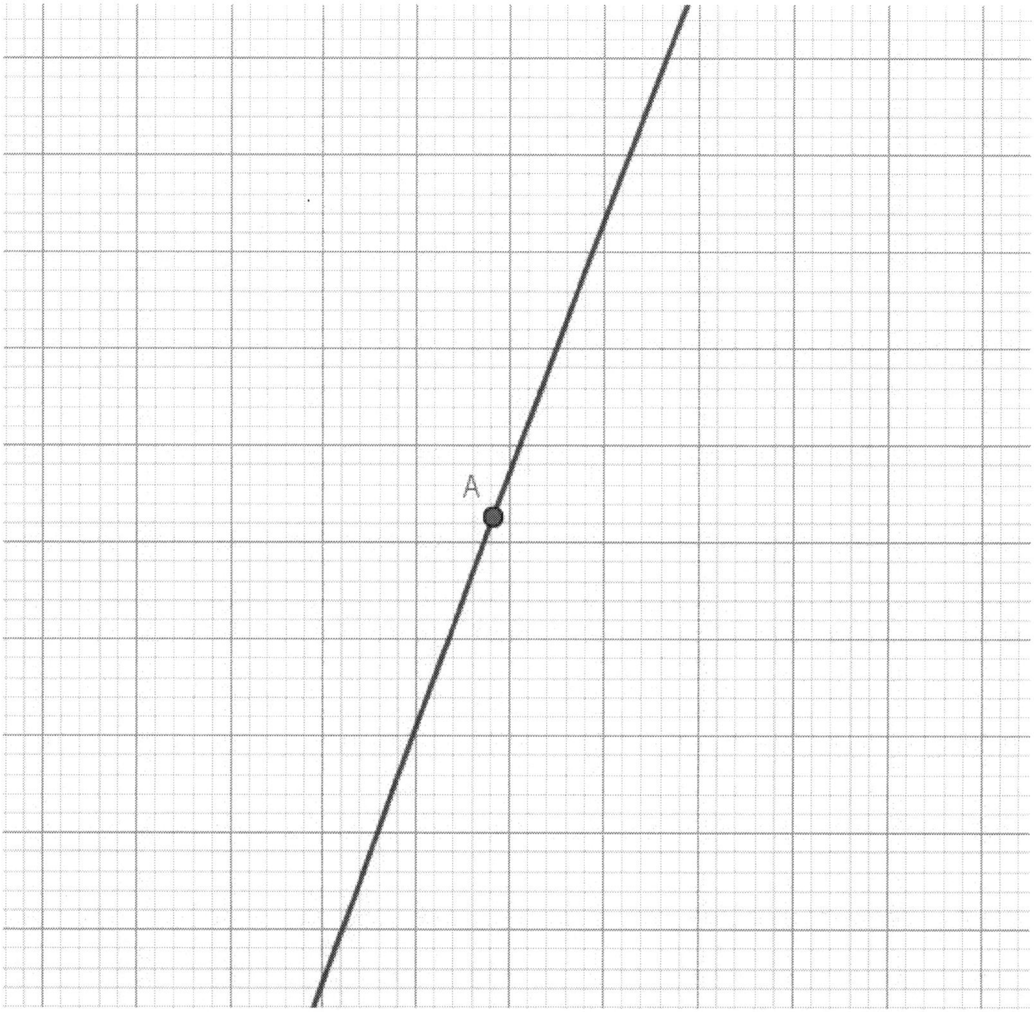

Figure 10.3: Zooming in on the curve

This is how derivatives work: we make the change in *x*, the *run*, small enough that the slope over that small part of the curve will closely approximate the rate of change of the curve at that point. Let's see what it looks like in Python.

WRITING THE DERIVATIVE FUNCTION

For all the fear whipped up about derivatives in calculus courses, the function for calculating a derivative numerically is surprisingly easy.

In a Jupyter notebook, we'll define a function, *f(x)*, to be the parabola $y = x^2$:

```
def f(x):
    return x**2
```

Now we can write a function to calculate the derivative at any point *(x, f(x))* using the classic formula:

$$\lim_{\Delta x \to 0} \frac{f(x+\Delta x) - f(x)}{\Delta x}$$

Figure 10.4: Formula for calculating derivatives

The numerator is the *rise* and the denominator is the *run*. *Δ x* means the *change in x*, and we're going to make that a really small decimal by dividing 1 by a million:

```
def f(x):
    return x**2

def derivative(f,x):
    """
    Returns the value of the derivative of
    the function at a given x-value.
    """
    delta_x = 1/1000000
    return (f(x+delta_x) - f(x))/delta_x
```

> **NOTE**
>
> The triple-quotes (""") shown in the code snippet below are used to denote the start and end points of a multi-line code comment. Comments are added into code to help explain specific bits of logic.

Now we can calculate the derivative of the function at any *x* value and we'll get a very accurate approximation:

```
for i in range(-3,4):
    print(i,derivative(f,i))
```

If you run the preceding code, you'll get the following output:

```
-3 -5.999999000749767
-2 -3.999998999582033
-1 -1.999999000079633
0 1e-06
1 2.0000009999243673
2 4.0000010006480125
3 6.000001000927568
```

These values are only a little off from their actual values (-5.999999 instead of -6). We can round up the printout to the nearest tenth and we'll see the values more clearly:

```
for i in range(-3,4):
    print(i,round(derivative(f,i),1))
```

The output will be:

```
-3 -6.0
-2 -4.0
-1 -2.0
0 0.0
1 2.0
2 4.0
3 6.0
```

We've calculated the derivative of the function $y = x^2$ at a number of points and we can see the pattern: the derivative is always twice the *x* value. This is the slope of the line that approximates the curve at that point. The awesome power of this method will become clear in this exercise.

EXERCISE 10.01: FINDING THE DERIVATIVES OF OTHER FUNCTIONS

We can use our derivative function to calculate the derivative of any function we can express. There's no need to go through tedious algebraic manipulations when we can simply use the *tiny run* method of calculating the slope. Here, our function will find the derivative of some complicated-looking functions. We reused *f*, but you can call other functions as well. In this exercise, you will find the derivatives of each function at the given *x* values:

$$f(x) = 6x^3 \ at \ x = -2$$

$$g(x) = \sqrt{2x+5} \ at \ x = 3$$

$$h(x) = \frac{1}{(x-3)^3} \ at \ x = 5$$

Figure 10.5: Function definitions at given x values

Perform the following steps:

1. First, we'll need to import the square root function from the **math** module:

```
from math import sqrt
```

2. Here are the preceding functions in the equations, translated into Python code:

```
def f(x):
    return 6*x**3

def g(x):
    return sqrt(2*x + 5)

def h(x):
    return 1/(x-3)**3
```

3. Define the derivative function if you haven't already:

```
def derivative(f,x):
    """Returns the value of the derivative of
    the function at a given x-value."""
    delta_x = 1/1000000
    return (f(x+delta_x) - f(x))/delta_x
```

4. Then print out the derivatives by calling each function and the desired *x* value:

```
print(derivative(f,-2),derivative(g,3),derivative(h,5))
```

The output will be as follows:

```
71.99996399265274 0.30151133101341543 -0.18749981253729509
```

You've just learned a very important skill: finding the derivative of a function (any function) at a specific *x* value. This is the reason calculus students do lots of hard algebra: to get the derivative as a function, and then they can plug in an *x* value. However, with Python, we just directly calculated the numerical derivative of a function without doing any algebra.

> **NOTE**
>
> To access the source code for this specific section, please refer to https://packt.live/2AnIJOC.
>
> You can also run this example online at https://packt.live/3gi4I7S.

FINDING THE EQUATION OF THE TANGENT LINE

A common question in calculus is to find the equation of the line tangent to the curve at a given point. Remember our points **A** and **B**? The tangent lines are the lines that closely approximate the curve at those points, as you can see in *Figure 10.6*:

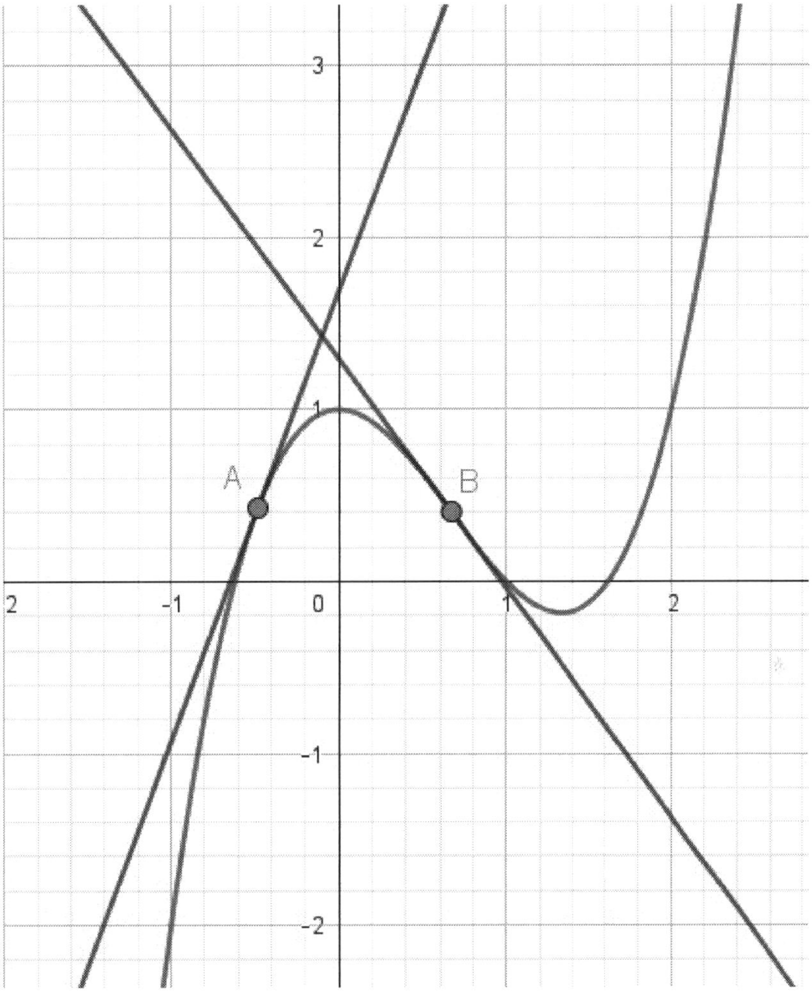

Figure 10.6: Two tangent lines to a curve

Let's use the information in *Figure 10.6*. The equation is as follows:

$$f(x) = x^3 - 2x + 1$$

Figure 10.7: Equation of f(x)

The *x* value at point **A** in *Figure 10.6* is -0.48 and the *x* value at **B** is 0.67. The great thing about using Python to do this is it won't matter if the given values are whole numbers, negatives, or decimals, the computer will easily process the number-crunching.

To find the equation of a line, all we need is a slope and a point. If you remember your algebra, you can use this formula:

$$y - y_0 = m\left(x - x_0\right)$$

Figure 10.8: Equation of a line

We're given the function and the point (x_0, y_0), so from that, we can find the slope *m* from the derivative of the function at the given *x* value. The equation of the tangent line will be in the form $y = mx + b$, and the only thing we don't know is *b*, the *y* intercept of the line. But if we rearrange the preceding equation, we can see it on the right side of the equation:

$$y = mx - mx_0 + y_0$$

Figure 10.9: Equation of line at the point

We need to find the slope *m* using the derivative function we already have, then plug it into $y_0 - m\,x_0$. To do this, perform the following steps:

5. First, we'll define our **f(x)** function:

```
def f(x):
    return x**3 - 2*x**2 + 1
```

6. Then we'll write a function to return the *y* intercept of a line given the slope and a point. Call it **point_slope**:

```
def point_slope(m,x,y):
    """Finds the y-intercept of a line
    given its slope m and a point (x,y)"""
    return y-m*x
```

7. Finally, we'll write a function that takes the function **f** and an **x** value and finds the derivative of **f** at **x**, puts that into the **point_slope** function, and prints out the equation of the line in $y = mx + b$ form. Call it **tangent_line**:

```
def tangent_line(f,x):
    """Finds the equation of the line
    tangent to f at x."""
```

8. We find the slope of the tangent line by taking the derivative of **f** at **x**:

```
    m = derivative(f,x)
```

9. Then we use the **point_slope** function to find the *y* intercept:

```
    y0 = f(x)
    b = point_slope(m,x,y0)
    print("y = ",round(m,2),"x + ",round(b,2))
```

10. Now, to get the equations of the lines tangent to **f** at $x = -0.48$ and $x = 0.67$, use the following code:

```
for x in [-0.48,0.67]:
    tangent_line(f,x)
```

The output is as follows:

```
y =  2.61 x +  1.68
y =  -1.33 x +  1.3
```

In this section, we learned how to find out the equations of tangent lines at specific values of **x**.

CALCULATING INTEGRALS

One major topic of calculus is differential calculus, which means taking derivatives, as we've been doing so far in this chapter. The other major topic is integral calculus, which involves adding up areas or volumes using many small *slices*.

When calculating integrals by hand, we're taught to reverse the algebra we would do to find a derivative. But that algebra gets messy and, in some cases, impossible. The *hard* version we learned in school was Riemann sums, which required us to cut the area under a curve into rectangular *slices* and add them up to get the area. But you could never work with more than 10 slices in a realistic amount of time, certainly not on a test.

However, using Python, we can work with as many slices as we want, and it saves us the drudgery of jumping through a lot of hoops to get an algebraic equation. The point of finding the algebraic equation is to obtain accurate number values, and if using a program will get us the most accurate numbers, then we should definitely take that route.

Figure 10.10 shows a function and the area under it. Most commonly the area is bounded by the function itself, a lower *x* value **a**, an upper *x* value **b**, and the *x* axis.

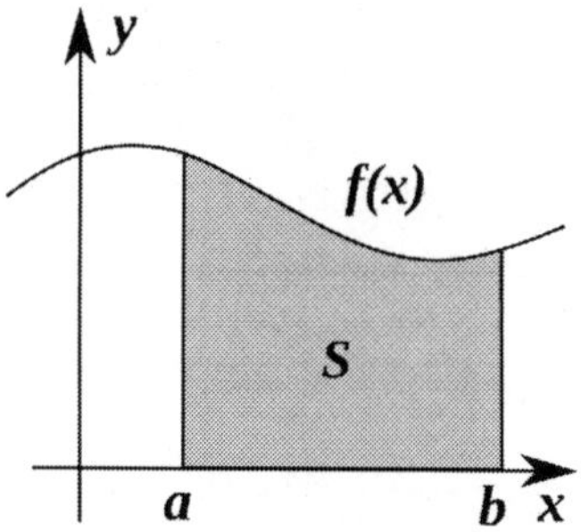

Figure 10.10: The area S under a curve defined by the function f(x) from a to b

What we're going to do is to slice the area **S** into rectangles of equal width, and since we know the height (*f(x)*), it'll be easy to add them all up using Python. *Figure 10.11* shows what the situation looks like for $f(x) = x^2$:

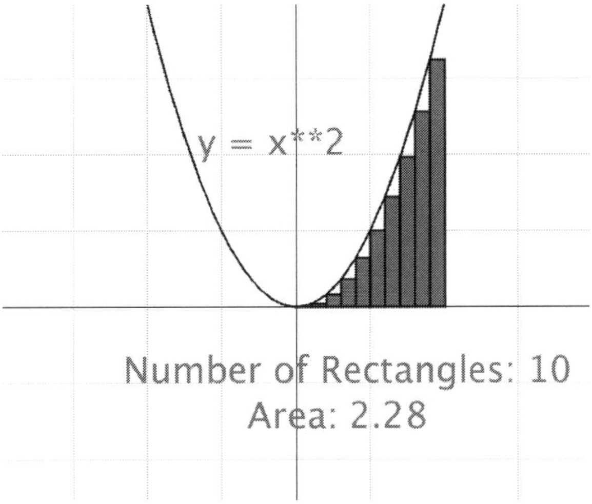

Figure 10.11: The area S sliced into 10 rectangles of equal width

First, we'll define the function and choose the number of rectangles (so that the value of both will be easy to change). In this instance, we will use 20 rectangles, which will give us a higher degree of accuracy than the 10 rectangles shown in *Figure 10.11*:

```
def f(x):
    return x**2

number_of_rectangles = 20
```

Then we define our integral function. First, divide the range **(b - a)** into equal widths by dividing by **num**, the number of rectangles:

```
def integral(f,a,b,num):
    """Returns the sum of num rectangles
    under f between a and b"""
    width = (b-a)/num
```

Then we'll loop over the range, adding the area of the rectangles as we go. We do this with a one-line list comprehension. For every **`n`**, we multiply the base of the rectangle (**`width`**) by the height (*f(x)*) to get the area of each rectangle. Finally, we return the sum of all the areas:

```
    area = sum([width*f(a+width*n) for n in range(num)])
    return area
```

This is how the function call looks:

```
for i in range(1,21):
    print(i,integral(f,0,1,i))
```

The output shows how, with more rectangles, we get closer and closer to the actual value of the area:

```
1 0.0
2 0.125
3 0.18518518518518517
4 0.21875
5 0.24000000000000005
6 0.2546296296296296
7 0.26530612244897955
8 0.2734375
9 0.279835390946502
10 0.2850000000000001
11 0.2892561983471075
12 0.292824074074074
13 0.2958579881656805
14 0.29846938775510196
15 0.30074074074074075
16 0.302734375
17 0.3044982698961938
18 0.3060699588477366
19 0.3074792243767312
20 0.3087500000000001
```

It seems to be growing slowly. What if we jump ahead to 100 rectangles? That would create the situation shown in *Figure 10.12*:

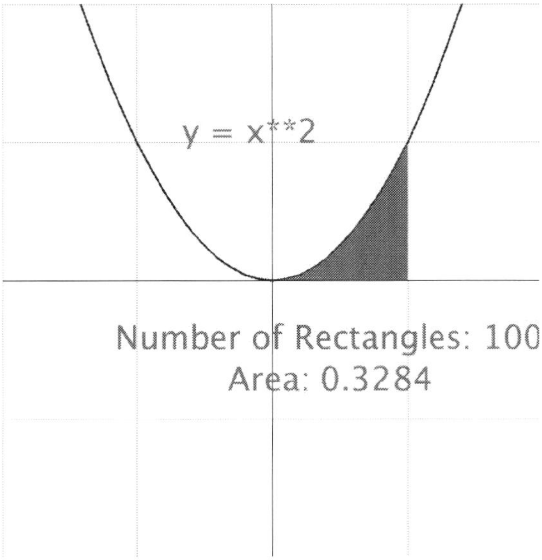

Figure 10.12: Smaller rectangles making a better approximation of the area

Here's how we change the **`print`** statement to give us the area of the 100 rectangles:

```
print(100,integral(f,0,1,100))
```

The output will be as follows:

```
100 0.32835000000000014
```

How about 1,000 rectangles, an integral that would be extremely difficult and time-consuming to calculate by hand? Using Python, we'll just change **`100`** to **`1000`** and get a much more accurate approximation:

```
print(1000,integral(f,0,1,1000))
```

The output will be as follows:

```
1000 0.33283350000000034
```

And summing up 100,000 rectangles gets us 0.3333283333. It seems like it's getting close to 0.333, or 1/3. But adding more zeroes doesn't cost us anything, so feel free to increase the number of rectangles as much as required to get a more accurate result.

USING TRAPEZOIDS

We can get better approximations sooner using trapezoids rather than rectangles. That way, we won't miss as much area, as you can see in *Figure 10.13*:

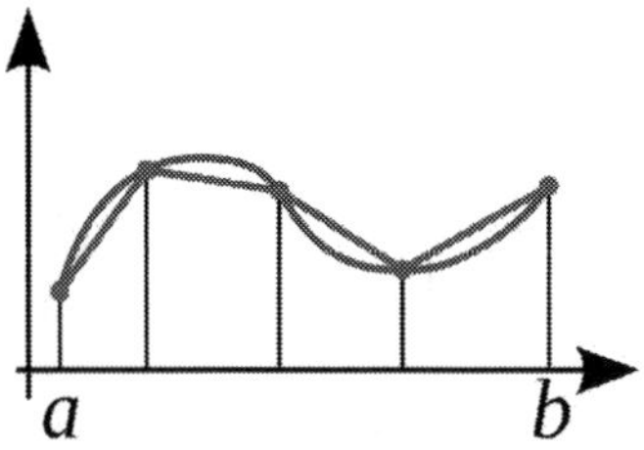

Figure 10.13: Using trapezoids for better approximations to the curve

The following is the formula for the trapezoidal rule:

$$Area\ of\ Trapezoids = \frac{\Delta x}{2}\left(f(x_0) + 2f(x_1) + 2f(x_2) + 2f(x_3) + \ldots. + 2f(x_{N-1}) + f(x_N)\right)$$

Figure 10.14: Formula for area of trapezoids

The heights of the segments at the endpoints $x = a$ and $x = b$ are counted once, while all the other heights are counted twice. That's because there are two *heights* in the formula for the area of a trapezoid. Can you guess how to adapt your integral function to be trapezoidal?

```
def trap_integral(f,a,b,num):
    """Returns the sum of num trapezoids
    under f between a and b"""
    width = (b-a)/num
    area = 0.5*width*(f(a) + f(b) + 2*sum([f(a+width*n) for n in
range(1,num)]))
    return area
```

Now we'll run the **`trap_integral`** function using **5** trapezoids:

```
print(trap_integral(f,0,1,5))
```

The output will be as follows:

```
0.3400000000000001
```

So, by using only 5 trapezoids, we have reduced the error to 3%. (Remember, we know the true value of the area for this function is 0.333...) Using 10 trapezoids, we get 0.335, which has an error of 0.6%.

EXERCISE 10.02: FINDING THE AREA UNDER A CURVE

In this exercise, we'll find the area under the following functions in the given intervals:

$$\int_{3}^{4} \left(x^3 + 3\right) dx$$

$$\int_{0}^{\pi/4} 3\cos x \, dx$$

$$\int_{2}^{4} \frac{\left(x^2 - 1\right)\left(x^2 + 1\right)}{x^2} dx$$

Figure 10.15: Formula for intervals

Perform the following steps to find the area. Having written the **`trap_integral`** function to use trapezoids to approximate the area under a curve, it's easy: just define the function (you may have to import a **`trig`** function and **`pi`**) and declare the endpoints. Have it use 100 trapezoids, because that'll be very accurate and quickl:

11. First, import the **math** functions you'll need and define **f**, **g**, and **h**:

```
from math import cos,pi

def f(x):
    return x**3 + 3

def g(x):
    return 3*cos(x)

def h(x):
    return ((x**2 - 1)*(x**2+1))/x**2
```

12. Then call the **trap_integral** function on each function between the specified *x* values:

```
print(trap_integral(f,3,4,100))
print(trap_integral(g,0,pi/4,100))
print(trap_integral(h,2,4,100))
```

The output is as follows:

```
46.75017499999999
2.1213094390731206
18.416792708494786
```

By now, you can probably see the power in this numerical method. If you can express a function in Python, you can get a very accurate approximation of its integral using the function for adding up all the rectangles under the curve, or even more accurately, the function for adding up all the trapezoids under the curve.

> **NOTE**
>
> To access the source code for this specific section, please refer to https://packt.live/3dTUVTG.
>
> You can also run this example online at https://packt.live/2Zsfxxi.

USING INTEGRALS TO SOLVE APPLIED PROBLEMS

If a curve is rotated about the *x* or *y* axis or a line parallel to one of the axes, to form a 3D object, we can calculate the volume of this solid by using the tools of integration. For example, let's say the parabola $y = x^2$ is rotated around its axis of symmetry to form a paraboloid, as in *Figure 10.16*:

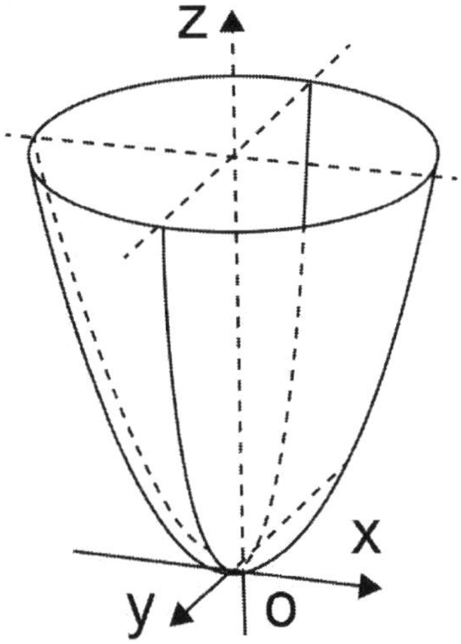

Figure 10.16: A parabola rotated about the z axis

We can find the volume by adding up all the *slices* of the paraboloid as you go up the solid. Just as before, when we were using rectangles in two dimensions, now we're using cylinders in three dimensions. In *Figure 10.16*, the slices are going up the figure and not to the right, so we can flip it in our heads and redefine the curve $y = x^2$ as $y = sqrt(x)$.

Now the radius of each cylinder is the *y* value, and let's say we're going from *x = 0* to *x = 1*:

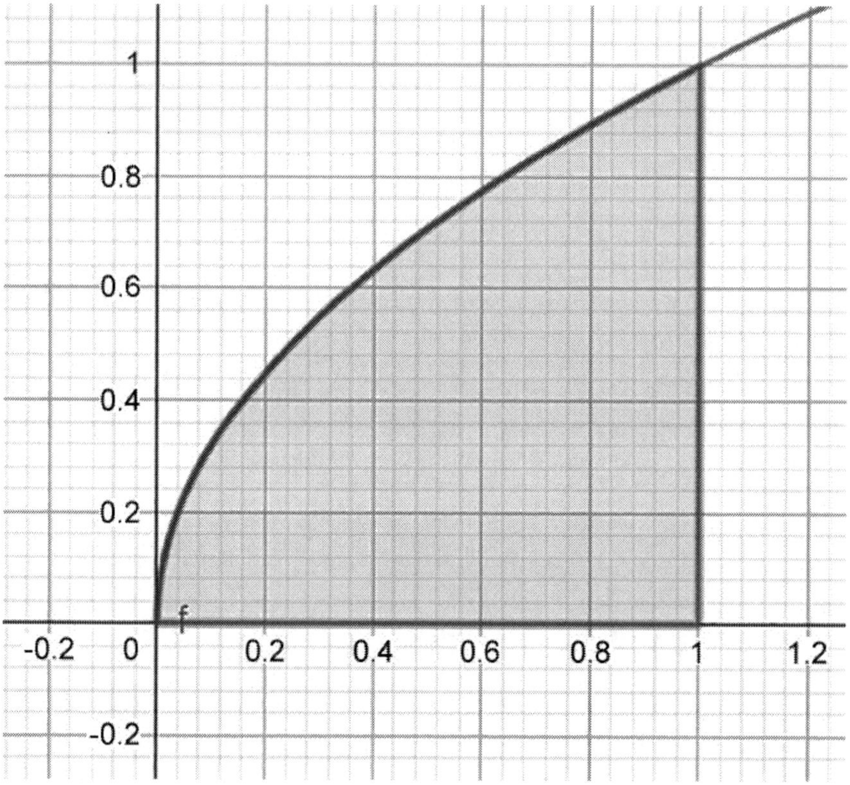

Figure 10.17: Flipping the paraboloid on its side

The endpoints are still *0* and *1*, but the radius of the curve is the *y* value, which is *sqrt(x)*. So the volume of each circular slice is the volume of a cylinder (*pi * radius² * height*), in this case *pi * r² * thickness*, or *pi * sqrt(x)² * width*.

First, we import **`sqrt`** and **`pi`** from the **`math`** module and define **`f(x)`**:

```
from math import sqrt, pi
def f(x):
    return sqrt(x)
```

Then we'll define a function that will take the function of the paraboloid and the beginning and ending values of **x**. It starts off by defining the running volume and the number of slices we're going to use:

```
def vol_solid(f,a,b):
    volume = 0
    num = 1000
```

Then we calculate the thickness of the slices by dividing the range of *x* values by the number of slices:

```
    width = (b-a)/num
```

Now we calculate the volume of each cylindrical slice, which is *pi* * r^2 * *width*. We add that to the running volume, and when the loop is done we return the final volume:

```
    for i in range(num):
    #      volume of cylindrical disk
        vol = pi*(f(a+i*width))**2*width
        volume += vol
    return volume
```

Let's add up all the volumes between **0** and **1**:

```
print(vol_solid(f,0,1))
```

The output will be as follows:

```
1.5692255304681022
```

This value is an approximation of the volume of the bounded paraboloid. Again, the more slices we split the function up into, the more accurate the approximation to the real volume.

EXERCISE 10.03: FINDING THE VOLUME OF A SOLID OF REVOLUTION

Here's another solid-of-revolution problem: find the volume of the solid formed when the following functions are rotated around the *x* axis on the given intervals.

In the following figure, the green curve is $f(x) = 4 - 4x^2$ and the red curve is $g(x) = 1\text{-}x^2$. Find the volume of the solid formed when the area between the functions is rotated about the *x* axis.

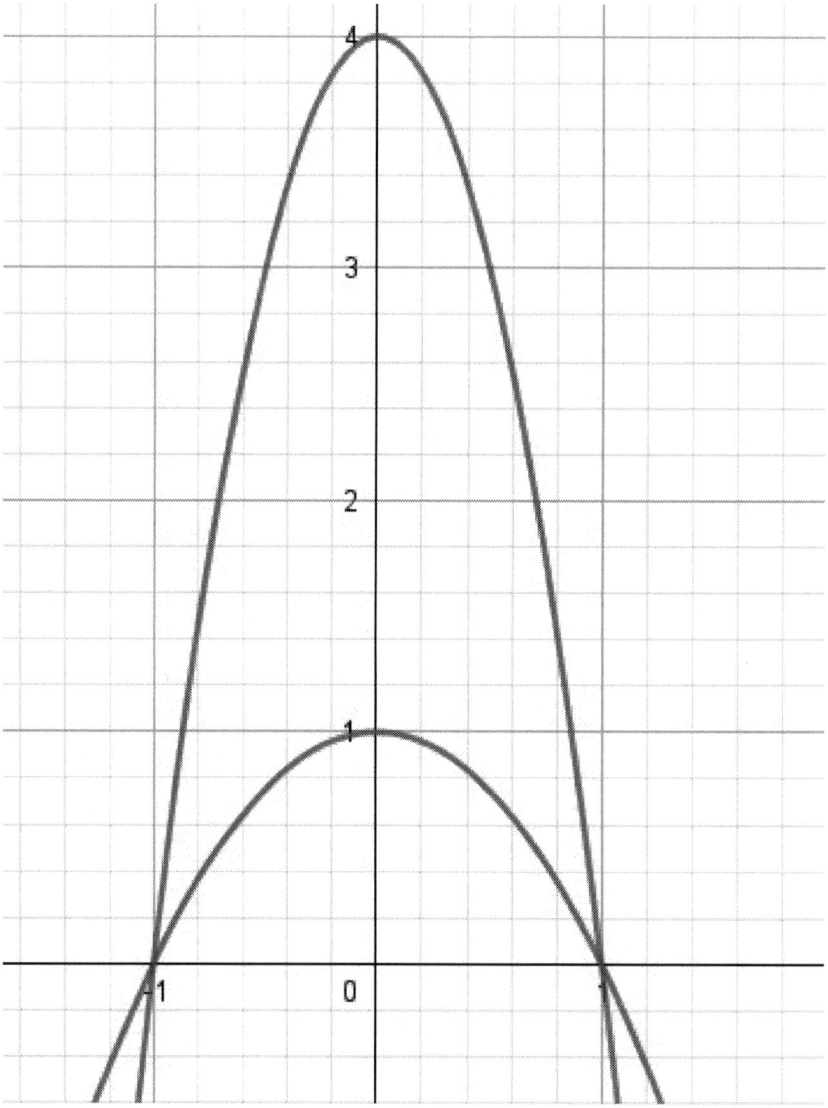

Figure 10.18: A two-dimensional look at the two functions

The resulting shape of the solid would be as follows:

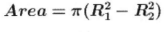

$$Area = \pi(R_1^2 - R_2^2)$$

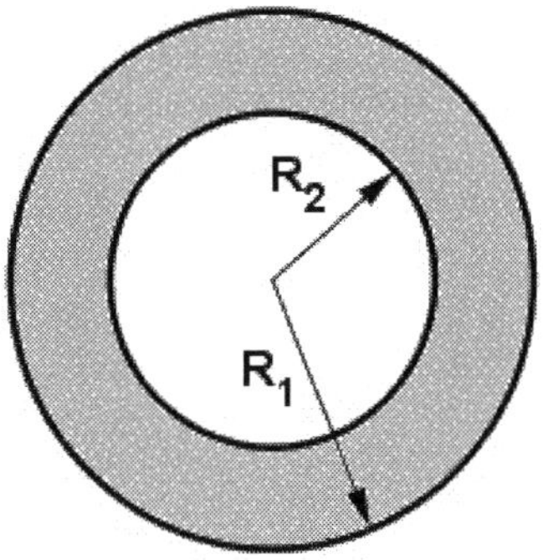

Figure 10.19: The resulting shape is like a ring

This is like a problem of finding the area of a ring, as shown in the preceding figure. The formula is as follows:

$$A = \pi R^2 - \pi r^2$$

$$A = \pi\left(R^2 - r^2\right)$$

Figure 10.20: Formula for area of a ring

Now to find the volume of the solid using Python, perform the following steps:

1. Create **f** and **g** as usual, and a third function (**h**) to be the difference of the squares of **f** and **g**, from the ring area formula:

```
def f(x):
    return 4 -4*x**2


def g(x):
    return 1-x**2


def h(x):
    return f(x)**2-g(x)**2
```

2. Now the volume of the solid will be the sum of a given number (**num**) of cylinders made between the functions. We do the same thing as in our integration function. The radius of the cylinder is the same as the height of our rectangle when we were integrating:

```
def vol_solid(f,a,b):
    volume = 0
    num = 10000
    width = (b-a)/num
    for i in range(num):
```

3. The volume of a cylinder is $pi*r^2*h$, and we'll add that to the running total volume:

```
        vol = pi*(f(a+i*width))*width
        volume += vol
    return volume
```

4. Here's where we call **vol_solid** on the **h** function for *x* between **-1** and **1**:

```
print(vol_solid(h,-1,1))
```

The output will be as follows:

```
50.26548245743666
```

Hence, the volume of the resulting solid is 50.3 cubic units. So, we have used our function to find the volumes of solids, and we have adapted it to find the volume of the solid between two curves.

> **NOTE**
>
> To access the source code for this specific section, please refer to https://packt.live/2NR9Svg.
>
> You can also run this example online at https://packt.live/3eWJaxs.

USING DERIVATIVES TO SOLVE OPTIMIZATION PROBLEMS

In many applied problems, we're looking for an optimal point, where the error is lowest, for example, or the profit is highest. The traditional way is to model the situation using a function, find the derivative of the function, and solve for the input that makes the derivative zero. This is because the derivative is zero at local minima and maxima, as shown in the following figure:

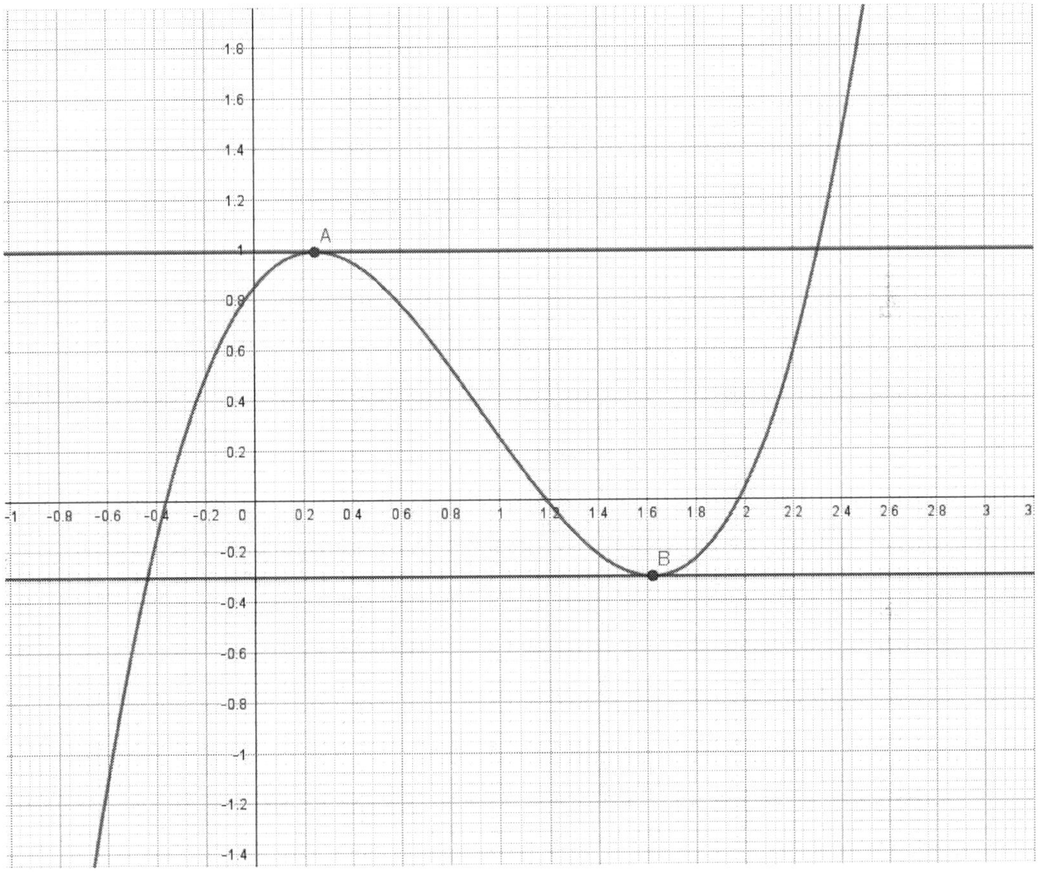

Figure 10.21: A cubic function and the points we want to find

The function we're given in the figure is $f(x) = x^3 - 2.8x^2 + 1.2x + 0.85$. We're interested in finding the local maximum, point **A**, and the local minimum, point **B**. We would have to differentiate the function and solve the resulting equation by hand. But using a computer, we can simply start at a value of *x* on the left of the grid and take small steps, checking *f(x)* until we get a change in direction. To do that, we can use our derivative function to check when the derivative changes sign.

First, we define **`f(x)`**:

```
def f(x):
    return x**3-2.8*x**2+1.2*x+0.85
```

Then we'll define a function called **`find_max_mins`** to start at a minimum *x* value and take tiny steps, checking if the derivative equals zero or if it changes sign, from positive to negative or vice versa. The most mathematical way to do that is to check whether the previous derivative times the new one is negative:

```
def find_max_mins(f,start,stop,step=0.001):
    x = start
    deriv = derivative(f,x)
    while x < stop:
        x += step
        #take derivative at new x:
        newderiv = derivative(f,x)
        #if derivative changes sign
        if newderiv == 0 or deriv*newderiv < 0:
            print("Max/Min at x=",x,"y=",f(x))
            #change deriv to newderiv
            deriv = newderiv
```

Finally, we call the function so it'll print out all the values at which the derivative changes sign:

```
find_max_mins(f,-100,100)
```

The output is as follows:

```
Max/Min at x= 0.247000000113438 y= 0.9906440229999803
Max/Min at x= 1.6200000001133703 y= -0.3027919999998646
```

These are the local maximum and local minimum of **`f`** in *Figure 10.21*.

EXERCISE 10.04: FIND THE QUICKEST ROUTE

We can use this procedure of finding maxima and minima to find the minimum value of a complicated function. In traditional calculus classes, students have to take the derivative algebraically, set it to zero, and then solve the resulting equation. We can model the situation in Python and use our derivative and the **`find_max_min`** functions to easily find the minimum value. Here's the situation: a lighthouse is located 6 kilometers offshore, and a cabin on the straight shoreline is 9 kilometers from the point on the shore nearest the lighthouse. If you row at a rate of 3 km/hr and walk at a rate of 5 km/hr, where should you land your boat in order to get from the lighthouse to the cabin as quickly as possible?

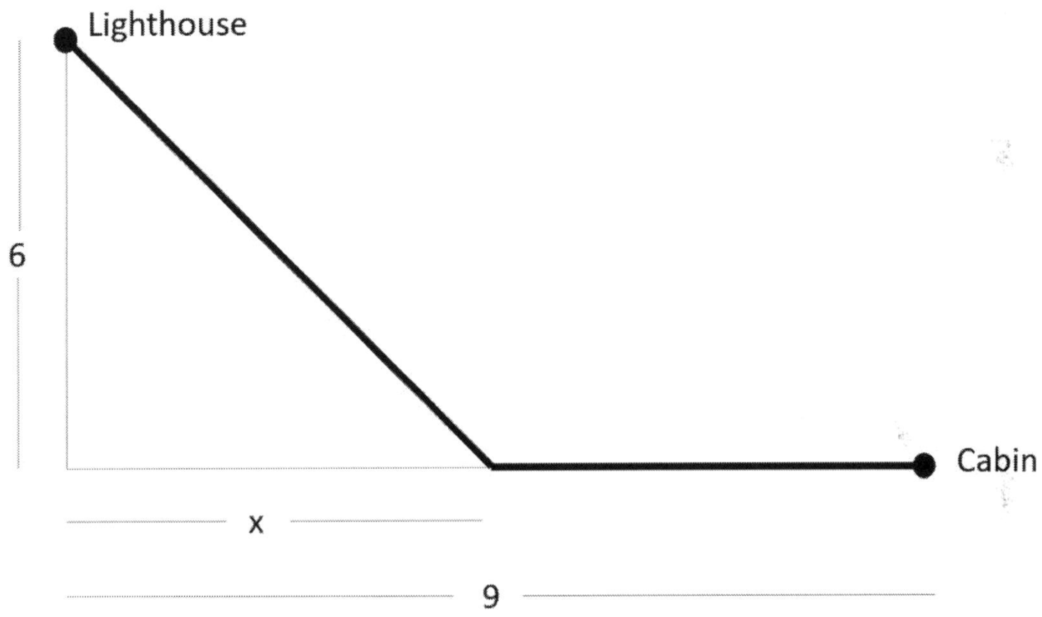

Figure 10.22: Distance of the lighthouse from the cabin

Perform the following steps to complete the exercise:

1. We're aiming to minimize the time it takes to make this trip, so let's make a formula for time. Remember, time is distance divided by rate:

$$t(x) = t_1 + t_2 = \frac{\sqrt{x^2 + 36}}{3} + \frac{9 - x}{5}$$

Figure 10.23: Formula for calculating time

2. And there's the function we need to minimize. The optimal *x* is going to be between 0 and 9 kilometers, so we'll set those as our start and end values when we call our **find_max_mins** function:

```
from math import sqrt

def t(x):
    return sqrt(x**2+36)/3 + (9-x)/5

find_max_mins(t,0,9)
```

The output will be as follows:

```
Max/Min at x= 4.4999999999998375 y= 3.4000000000000004
```

That's very close to 4.5 kilometers along the beach. This is a very useful calculation: we found the shortest distance between two points when other constraints have been put in place.

> **NOTE**
>
> To access the source code for this specific section, please refer to https://packt.live/31DwYxu.
>
> You can also run this example online at https://packt.live/38wNRM5.

EXERCISE 10.05: THE BOX PROBLEM

There's a classic problem given to all calculus students in which a manufacturer has a rectangular piece of material that they want to make into a box by cutting identical squares out of the corners, like in the following figure:

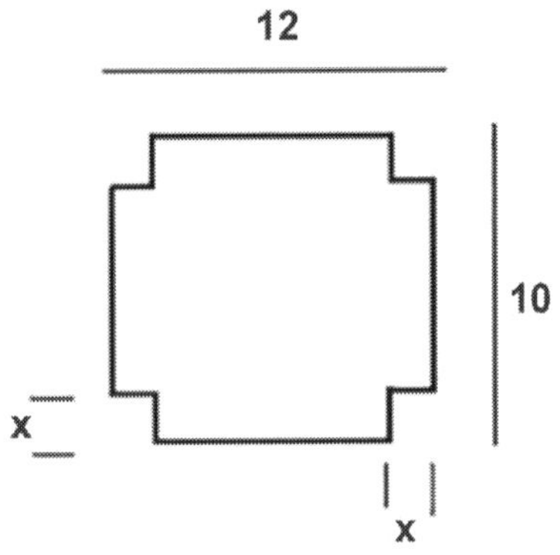

Figure 10.24: Cutting squares out of the corners of a rectangle

In this case, the piece of material is 10 inches by 12 inches. Here's the problem: find the size of the square to cut out in order to maximize the volume of the resulting box:

1. The formula for the volume of the box will be length multiplied by width multiplied by height. In terms of *x*, the length of the square cut from the corners, the length of the box is *12 - 2x*, since two corners are cut out of the 12-inch sides. Similarly, the width of the box will be *10 - 2x*. The height, once the "flaps" are bent upwards, will be *x*. So, the volume is:

$$V = x(10 - 2x)(12 - 2x)$$

Figure 10.25: Formula to calculate the volume

2. Here's how you define this function in Python:

```
def v(x):
    return x*(10-2*x)*(12-2*x)
```

3. By now, you know how to put this into your **find_max_mins** function. We only want to plug in values between 0 and 5 because more than 5 inches would mean we'd be left with no side (the width is 10 inches):

```
find_max_mins(v,0,5)
```

The output will be as follows:

```
Max/Min at x= 1.8109999999999113 y= 96.77057492400002
```

The maximum volume is achieved by cutting squares with side length 1.81 inches. Here's a plot of the volume:

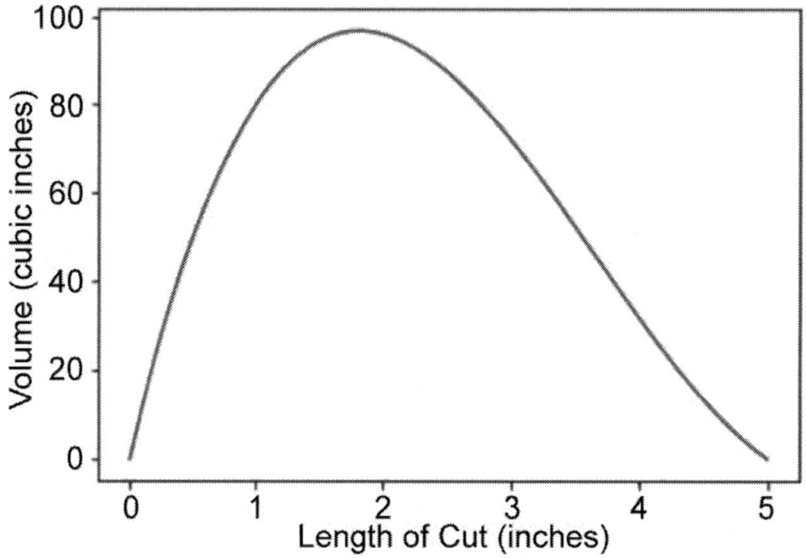

Figure 10.26: Plot of maximum value achieved

We can see that the maximum volume is achieved when a square of 1.81 inches is cut from each side, since this is where the maximum point of the plot lies.

> **NOTE**
>
> To access the source code for this specific section, please refer to https://packt.live/3gc11AC.
>
> You can also run this example online at https://packt.live/2NNSNmb.

EXERCISE 10.06: THE OPTIMAL CAN

A cylindrical can hold 355 cm^3 of soda. What dimensions (radius and height) will minimize the cost of metal to construct the can? You can neglect the top of the can:

1. The surface area of a cylinder is the area of the bottom (a circle, so πr^2) plus the area of its side, which is a rectangle of base $2\pi r$ and a height of h. The volume of a cylinder is $\pi r^2 h$, so we put it all together:

$$SA = \pi r^2 + 2\pi r h$$
$$V = \pi r^2 h$$

Figure 10.27: Formula to calculate the volume of a cylinder

2. The volume is already set to 355. From there, we can get an expression for h in terms of r and we'll have the surface area all in terms of one variable:

$$355 = \pi r^2 h$$
$$\frac{355}{\pi r^2} = h$$
$$SA = \pi r^2 + 2\pi r\left(\frac{355}{\pi r^2}\right)$$
$$SA = \pi r^2 + \frac{710}{r}$$

Figure 10.28: Substituting the values in the formula

3. Let's express it in Python and put it in our **find_max_mins** function:

```
from math import pi


def surf_area(r):
    return pi*r**2 + 710/r


find_max_mins(surf_area,0.1,10)
```

When you run the code, the output will be as follows:

```
Max/Min at x= 4.834999999999949 y= 220.28763352297025
```

So the solution is for the radius to be around 4.8 cm and the height to be 355/($\pi(4.8)^2$) = 4.9 cm. That means the can is about twice as wide as it is tall. Here's a plot of the **surf_area** function for cans between 2 and 6 cm. You can see the point that minimizes the material, between 4.5 and 5 cm. We calculated it to be exactly 4.9 cm:

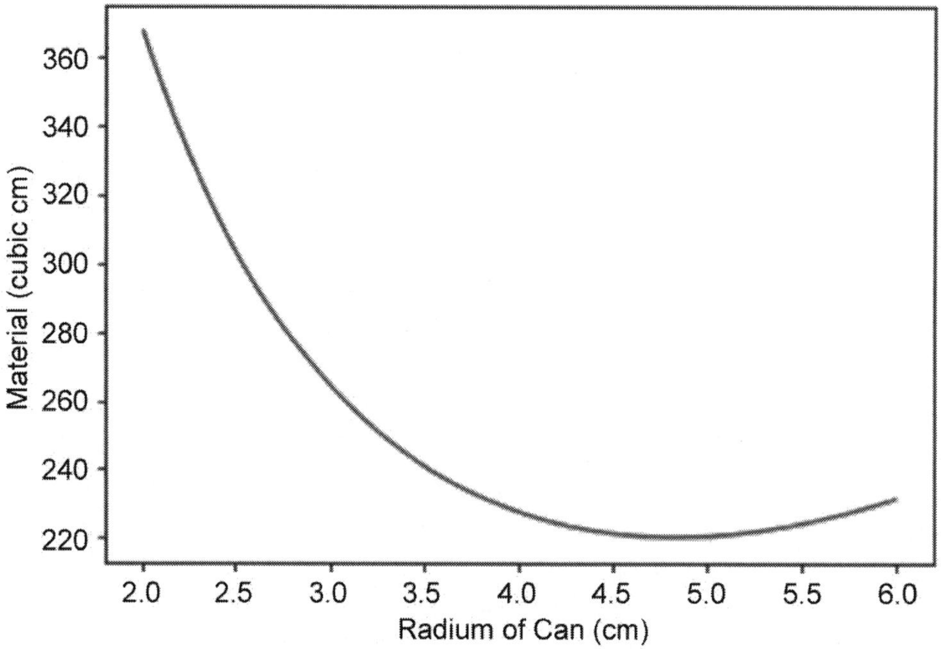

Figure 10.29: Finding the minimum material needed to make a can

> **NOTE**
>
> To access the source code for this specific section, please refer to https://packt.live/2Zu2bAK.
>
> You can also run this example online at https://packt.live/38lUNeE.

EXERCISE 10.07: CALCULATING THE DISTANCE BETWEEN TWO MOVING SHIPS

At noon, ship A is 20 km north of ship B. If ship A sails south at 6 km/hr and ship B sails east at 8 km/hr, find the time at which the distance between the two ships is smallest. The following figure shows the situation:

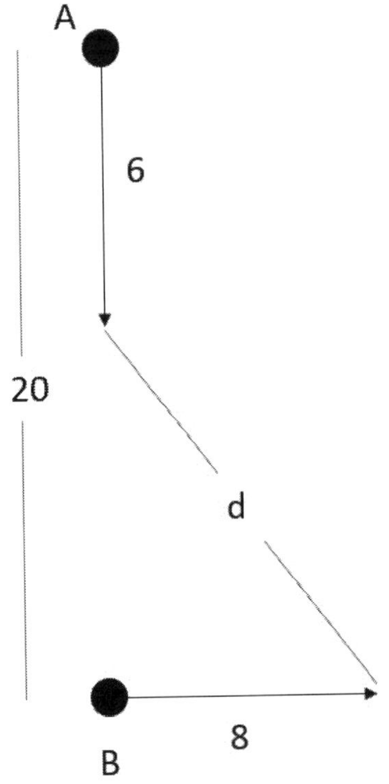

Figure 10.30: Ships A and B moving south and east

Perform the following steps to find the time:

1. The distance is velocity multiplied by time, so the distance between the two ships can be modeled by this equation:

$$d = \sqrt{(20 - 6t)^2 + (8t)^2}$$

Figure 10.31: Formula for calculating distance

2. Let's express that using Python and put it into our **`find_max_mins`** function:

```
from math import sqrt

def d(t):
    return sqrt((20-6*t)**2+(8*t)**2)
```

3. We assume the time will be between **0** and **4** hours:

```
find_max_mins(d,0,4)
```

The output will be as follows:

```
Max/Min at x= 1.1999999999999786 y= 16.0
```

The time is therefore 1.2 hours, illustrated by the minimum point on the following plot. Two tenths of an hour is 12 minutes, meaning the ships will be closest at 1:12 pm. Here's a plot of the distance versus time:

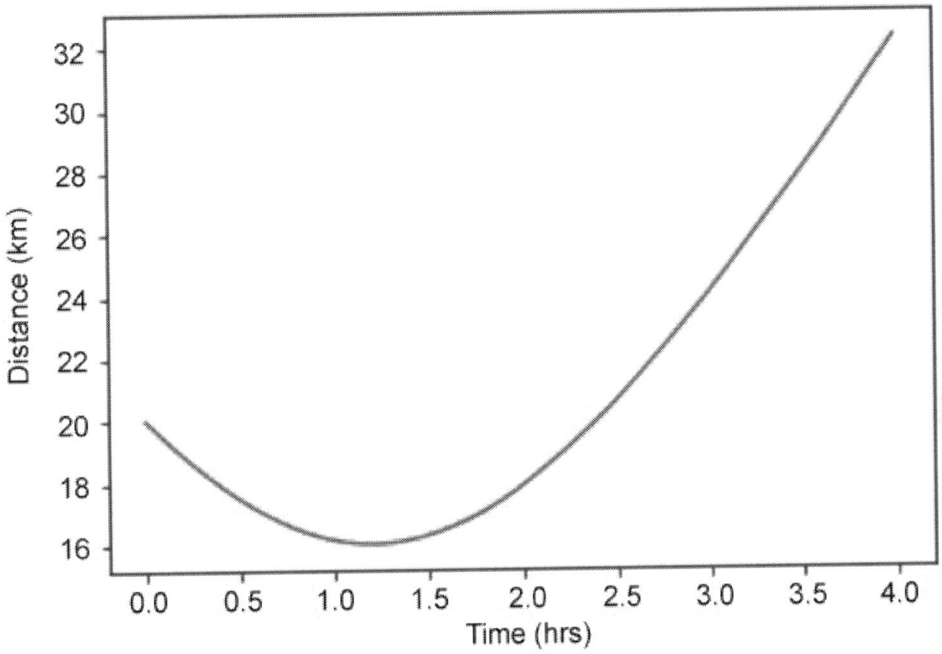

Figure 10.32: Plot of distance versus time

> **NOTE**
>
> To access the source code for this specific section, please refer to https://packt.live/38k2kuF.
>
> You can also run this example online at https://packt.live/31FK3GG.

ACTIVITY 10.01: MAXIMUM CIRCLE-TO-CONE VOLUME

This is a classic optimization problem, which results in some extremely complicated equations to differentiate and solve if you're doing it by hand. However, doing it with the help of Python will make the calculus part much easier. You start with a circle and cut out a sector of θ degrees. Then you attach points **A** and **B** in the following figure to make a cone:

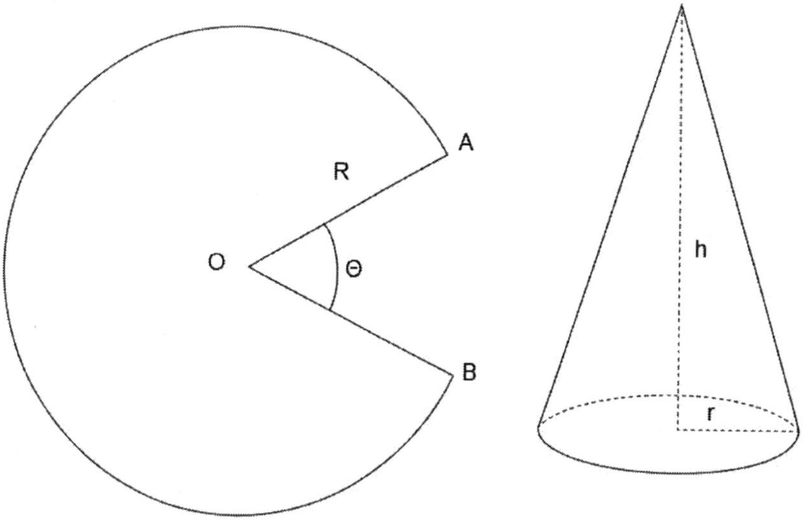

Figure 10.33: Circle to cone volume

The problem, like in the box problem, is to find the angle to cut out which maximizes the volume of the cone. It will require you to visualize cutting out the angle, attach the points to make a cone, and calculate the volume of the resulting cone.

Steps for completion:

1. Find the arc length of `AB`.
2. Find *h*, the height of the resulting cone.
3. Find *r*, the radius of the base of the cone.
4. Find an expression for the volume of the cone as a function of theta (θ), the angle cut out.

> **NOTE**
>
> The solution to this activity can be found on page 694.

SUMMARY

The tools of calculus allowed mathematicians and scientists to deal with constantly changing values, and those tools changed the way science is done. All of a sudden, we could use infinitely small steps to approximate the slope of a curve at a point, or infinitely small rectangles to approximate the area under a curve. These tools were developed hundreds of years before our modern world of computers and free programming software, but there's no reason to limit ourselves to the tools available to Newton, Leibniz, and the Bernoullis.

In this chapter, we learned to take derivatives of functions by simply dividing the *rise* of the function from one point to another by the infinitesimal *run* between those points. We simply told Python to divide 1 by a million to give us that small number. Without a computer, plugging those decimals into a function would be a daunting task, but Python plugs a decimal into a function as easily as a whole number.

We used the derivative idea to find the highest or lowest output of a function, where the derivative equals zero. This enabled us to find the optimal value of a function that would yield the shortest distance, or the greatest volume, for example.

The second most important topic in calculus is integration, and that allowed us to build up a complicated area or volume slice by slice using rectangles, trapezoids, or cylinders. Using Python, we could easily combine hundreds or thousands of slices to accurately approximate an area or volume.

We've only scratched the surface of the power that calculus and Python give us to work with changing values, infinitely small values, and infinitely large ones, too.

In the next chapter, we'll expand on these basic tools to find the lengths of curves, the areas of surfaces, and, most usefully for machine learning, the minimum point on a surface.

11

MORE CALCULUS WITH PYTHON

OVERVIEW

In this chapter, you will learn how to calculate the length of a curve, given its equation. You'll be introduced to partial derivatives in three dimensions and how to use them to calculate the area of a surface. Following in the footsteps of the mathematicians of the Middle Ages, you'll use an infinite series to calculate constants such as pi and determine the interval of convergence of a series. Like the mathematicians and machine learning engineers of the modern day, you'll learn how to find the minimum point on a surface using partial derivatives. By the end of this chapter, you will be able to use calculus to solve a variety of mathematical problems.

INTRODUCTION

In the previous chapter, we learned how to calculate derivatives and integrals. Now, we're going to use those tools to find the lengths of curves and spirals and extend this reasoning to three dimensions to find the area of a complicated surface. We'll also look at a common tool that's used in calculus, the infinite series, which is used to calculate important constants and approximate complicated functions. Finally, we'll look at an important idea in machine learning: finding the minimum point on a curve. When you use a neural network, you create a kind of "error function" and work hard to find the point on the surface that gives the minimum error. We'll create our own kind of gradient descent function to keep traveling downward until we're at the bottom of the surface.

LENGTH OF A CURVE

A major use of derivatives and integrals is finding the length of a curve. There's a formula for this:

$$L=\int_a^b \sqrt{1+[f'(x)]^2}\,dx$$

Figure 11.1: Formula to calculate the length of a curve

The preceding formula contains an integral *and* a derivative. To find the length of a curve, we'll need both our derivative and integral functions. Copy and paste them into your code if you don't have them yet:

```
from math import sqrt


def derivative(f,x):
    """Returns the value of the derivative of
    the function at a given x-value."""
    delta_x = 1/1000000
    return (f(x+delta_x) - f(x))/delta_x


def trap_integral(f,a,b,num):
    """Returns the sum of num trapezoids
    under f between a and b"""
    width = (b-a)/num
    area = 0.5*width*(f(a) + f(b) + 2*sum([f(a+width*n) \
                                          for n in range(num)]))
    return area
```

Here's the Python version of the formula:

```
def curve_length(f,a,b,num):
    def g(x):
        return sqrt(1+(derivative(f,x)**2))
    return trap_integral(g,a,b,num)
```

Notice we simply converted the math notation into Python code. We defined the **g** function inside the **f** function. The **g** function is everything under the square root in the formula. Then, we use our **trap_integral** function to find the accumulated value of the **g** function between **a** and **b**.

Let's check that using a curve we know the length of, such as the line $y = 2x$. We can calculate the distance of the curve's line between $x = (0,0)$ and $x = (2,4)$ using the Pythagorean theorem with $2\sqrt{5}$ or 4.47 units:

```
def f(x):
    return 2*x

print(curve_length(f,0,2,1000))
```

The preceding code prints out 4.47... as the output.

But when we try to check an actual curve that we know the length of, such as a semicircle, we run into a problem. We know the length of the curve of the following equation because it's half the circumference of a circle with radius 1. So, we should get π or 3.1415... as the output:

$$y=\sqrt{1-x^2}$$

Figure 11.2: Formula to calculate the length of a semicircle

Let's change **f(x)** to the equation for the preceding semicircle:

```
def f(x):
    return sqrt(1-x**2)

print(curve_length(f,-1,1,100))
```

When you execute the preceding code, you get an error. The last line of the error message (the first line I read) says the following:

```
ValueError: math domain error
```

This happens because the derivative of the semicircle at -1 and at 1, it is infinite. The tangent lines at those points are vertical, as shown in the following graph:

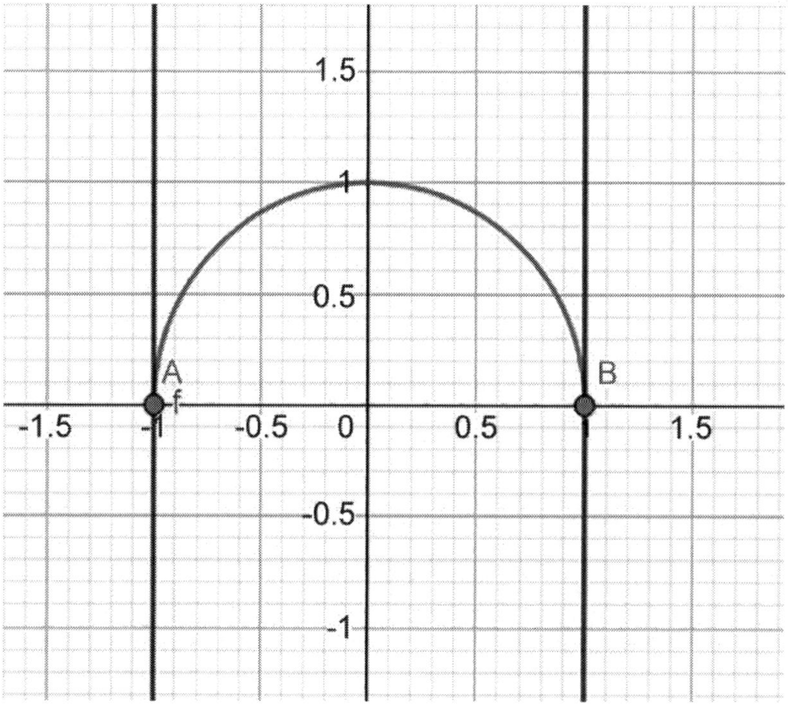

Figure 11.3: Vertical tangent lines, with an infinite slope

So, already, this method runs into a problem. Let's see if it'll find the length of a regular polynomial, such as the one shown in the following graph:

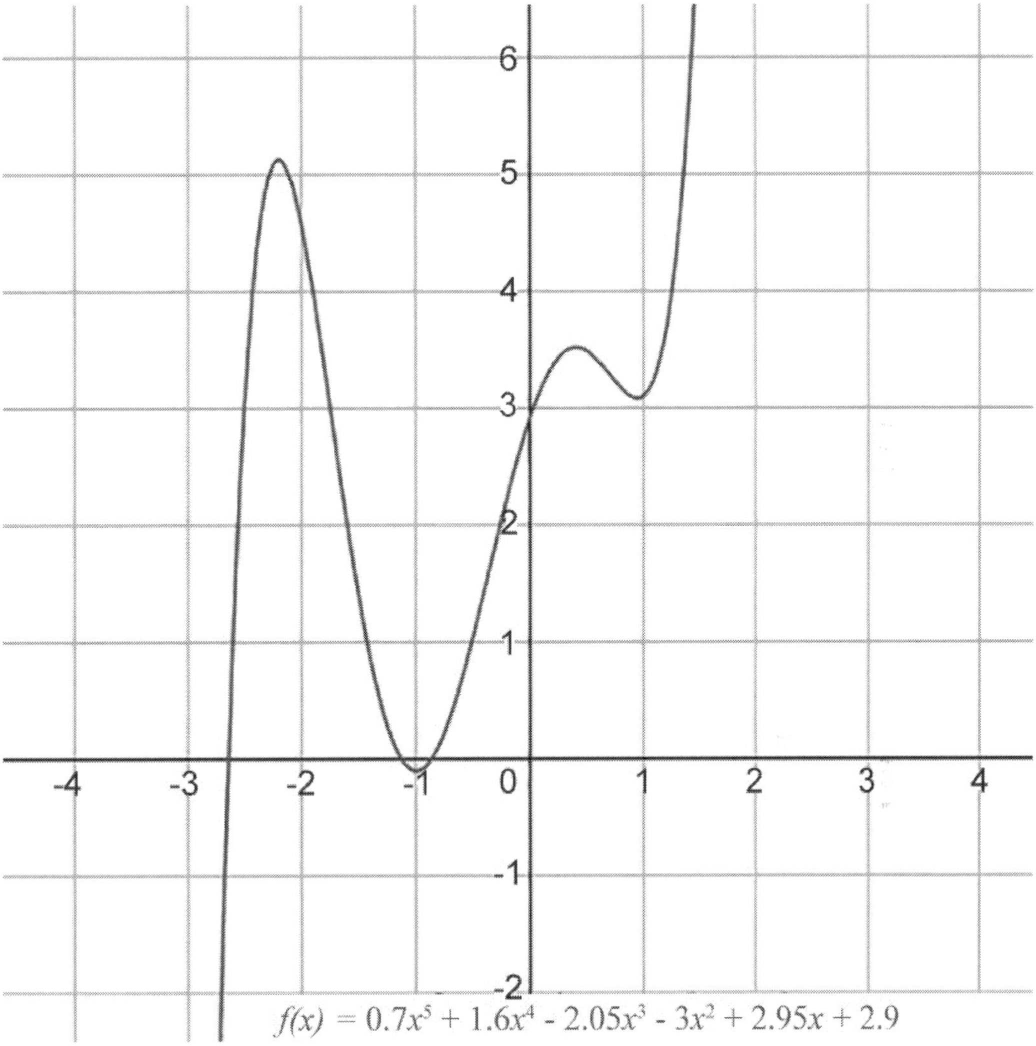

Figure 11.4: A complicated polynomial

This is a polynomial of degree 5, meaning the highest exponent of *x* is *5*. The equation for the curve is as follows:

$$y = 0.7x^5 + 1.6x^4 - 2.05x^3 - 3x^2 + 2.95x + 2.9$$

Figure 11.5: Equation of the curve

Complicated as it may seem, nowhere on the curve is the derivative infinite, as it was in *Figure 11.3*. That means we can use our curve length function on it.

Here's the code for the polynomial:

```
def f(x):
    return 0.7*x**5 + 1.6*x**4-2.05*x**3 -3*x**2+2.95*x+2.9

print(curve_length(f,-2,1,1000))
```

And the length of the curve is as follows:

```
9.628984854276812
```

We can use Wolfram Alpha to solve this by putting in *length of curve y = ... from -2 to 1* and checking whether it's a good approximation. But using Python, there's a more straightforward way of calculating the length of a curve that doesn't run into the problem we run into with derivatives. In fact, it doesn't even use derivatives or integrals. You can simply find the length of a tiny bit of the curve using the Pythagorean theorem and add up all those tiny bits, as shown in the following diagram. We know the width, and we're interested in the hypotenuse of the tiny right triangle. We can calculate the height, which is the difference between the function at *x* and the function at *x*, plus the width:

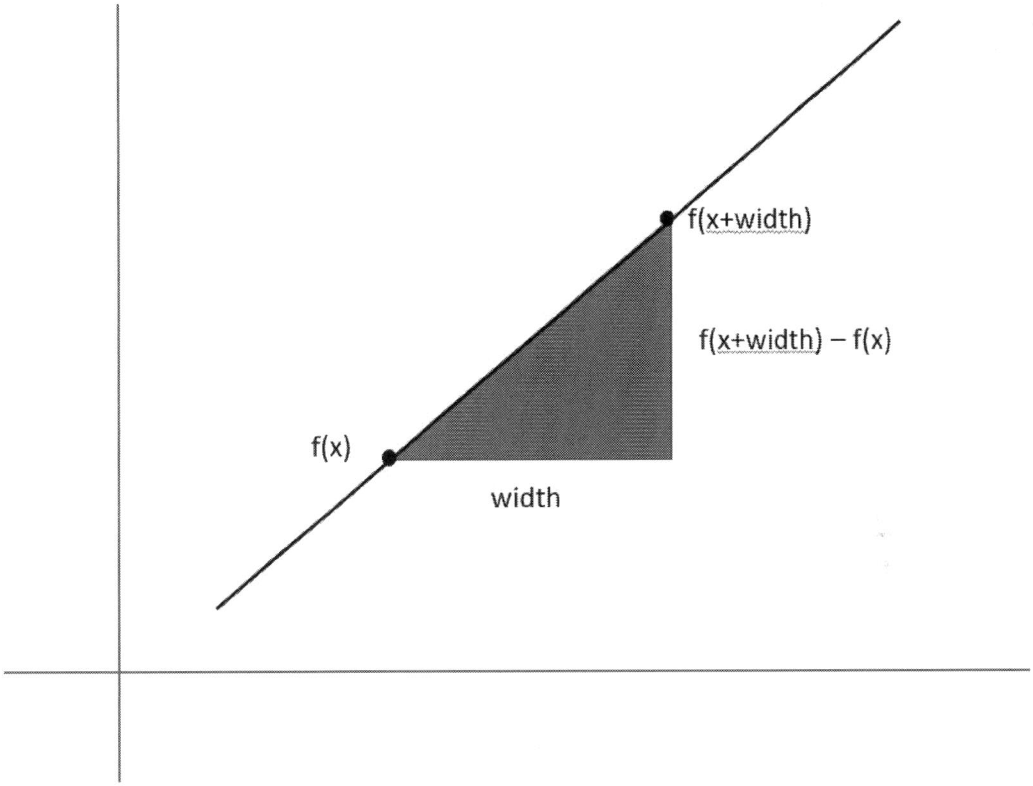

Figure 11.6: Finding the length of a tiny part of a curve

The hypotenuse of the right triangle shown in the preceding diagram is as follows:

$$\sqrt{(f(x+width)-f(x))^2+width^2}$$

Figure 11.7: Formula to calculate the hypotenuse of the right-angled triangle

All we have to do is go through the interval from **a** to **b**, counting up all those lengths. Here's how to do that in Python:

```
def f(x):
    return 0.7*x**5 + 1.6*x**4-2.05*x**3 -3*x**2+2.95*x+2.9

def curve_length2(f,a,b,num=1000):
    """Returns the length of f between\
    a and b using num slices"""
    output = 0
    width = (b-a)/num
    for i in range(num):
        output += sqrt((f(a+(i+1)*width)-f(a+i*width))**2 + width**2)
    return output
```

This should remind you of the integral program: create a running sum, then loop over each *slice* of the curve, adding the areas (in this case, the arc lengths) as you go. Finally, return the final value of the running sum.

Here is the curve length of the interval we're interested in:

```
print(curve_length2(f,-2,1))
```

This gives us the length of the curve as **9.614118659973549**. This is even closer than the previous version, and with much less fuss. Now, it's your turn to do the same in the following exercise.

EXERCISE 11.01: FINDING THE LENGTH OF A CURVE

In this exercise, you're provided with the following equation of a curve. Using this equation, determine the length of the curve between two given *x* values:

$$y = \sqrt{1-x^2}$$

Figure 11.8: Equation of the curve

These values will be from *x* = *-1* to *x* = *1*.

Perform the following steps:

1. First, we need to create a **circle** function with the preceding equation:

```
def circle(x):
    return sqrt(1-x**2)
```

> **NOTE**
>
> It's the semicircle again. This time, our **curve_length2** function will have no problem adding up the tiny slices of the arc.

2. Now, we'll run the **curve_length2** function (which we've already coded) on that curve to add up all the tiny segments, as we did previously:

```
def curve_length2(f,a,b,num=1000):
    """Returns the length of f between\
       a and b using num slices"""
    output = 0
    width = (b-a)/num
    for i in range(num):
        output += sqrt((f(a+(i+1)*width)-f(a+i*width))**2 \
                        + width**2)
    return output
```

3. Now, we print the output of the function, measuring from $x = -1$ to $x = 1$:

```
print(curve_length2 (circle,-1,1))
```

The output is as follows:

```
3.141566356216477З
```

There's no error message this time. We get a good approximation of half the circumference of a circle with radius 1, which we know is π.

> **NOTE**
>
> To access the source code for this specific section, please refer to https://packt.live/3gkI5Qi.
>
> You can also run this example online at https://packt.live/3eVpSbz.

EXERCISE 11.02: FINDING THE LENGTH OF A SINE WAVE

A very important and useful function in math and science is the sine wave. It makes one cycle between 0 and 2π, as shown in the following graph:

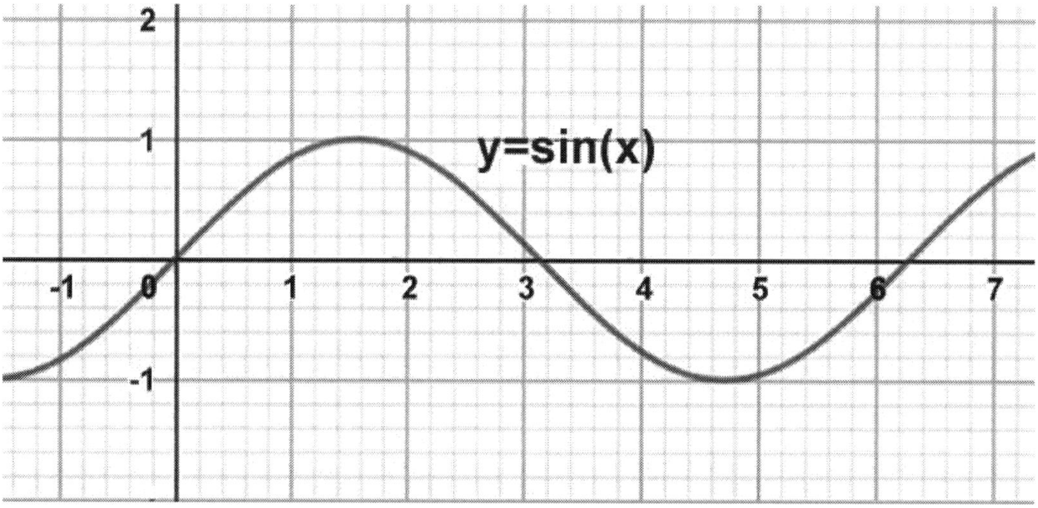

Figure 11.9: One cycle of the sine wave

It's easy to measure its wavelength (2π) and its amplitude (how far up and down it goes, that it, 1 unit), but how long is the actual curve? In this exercise, we'll find the length of the sine wave from 0 to 2π.

Perform the following steps:

1. We're going to use our **curve_length2** function again, but now we have to import our **sin** and **pi** functions from the **math** module:

```
from math import sin, pi
```

2. We've already written our **curve_length2** function, which will add up all the segments of the curve. We just need to tell it the function to use, and the beginning and ending *x* values:

```
print(curve_length2(sin,0,2*pi))
```

The output is as follows:

```
7.640391636335927
```

As you can see, using the **curve_length2** function, it becomes very easy to calculate the length of a sine wave.

> **NOTE**
>
> To access the source code for this specific section, please refer to https://packt.live/3dUy3nk.
>
> You can also run this example online at https://packt.live/2VFy2xd.

LENGTH OF A SPIRAL

What about spirals, which are expressed in polar coordinates, where *r*, the distance from the origin, is a function of the theta (θ) angle that's made with the *x* axis? We can't use our *x* and *y* functions to measure the spiral shown in the following diagram:

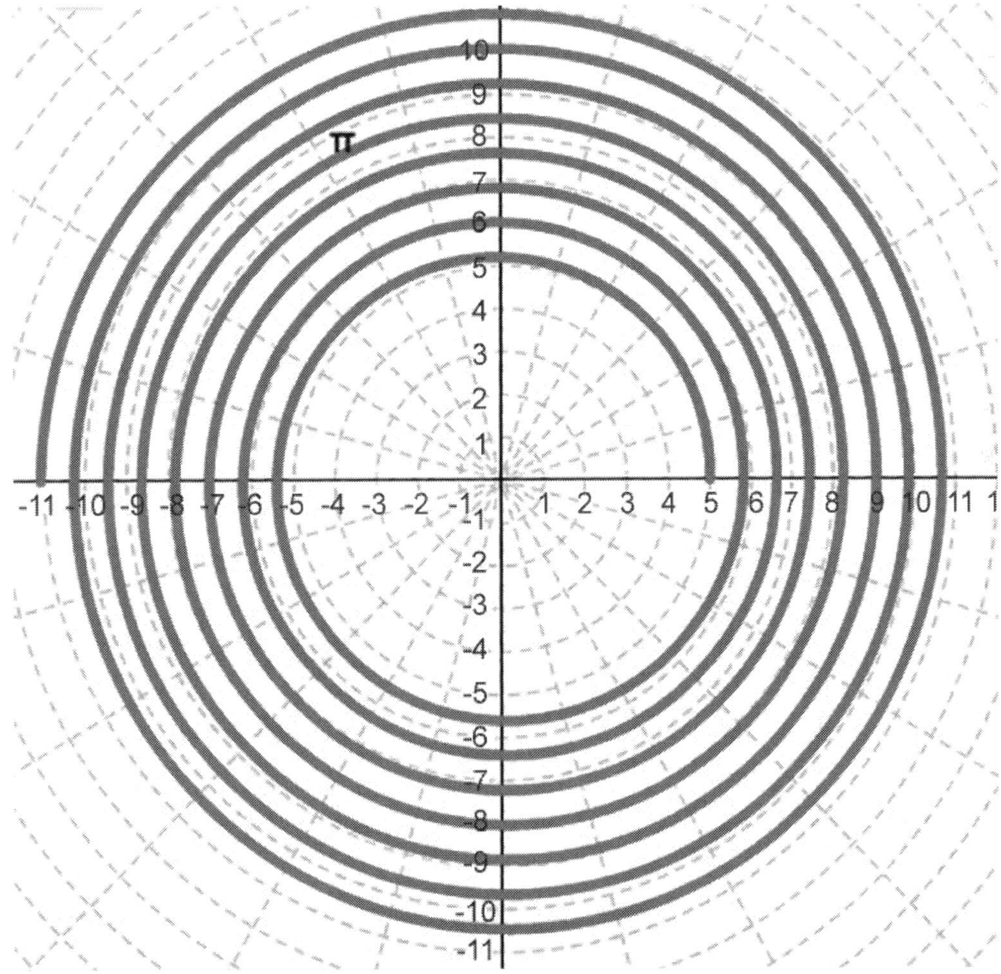

Figure 11.10: An Archimedean spiral

What we have in the preceding diagram is a spiral that starts at (5,0) and makes 7.5 turns, ending at (11,π). The formula for that curve is $r(\theta) = 5 + 0.12892\theta$. The number of radians turned is 7.5 times 2π, which is 15π. We're going to use the same idea as in the previous section: we're going to find the length of the straight line from $r(\theta)$ to $r(\theta+step)$ for some tiny step in the central angle, as shown in the following diagram:

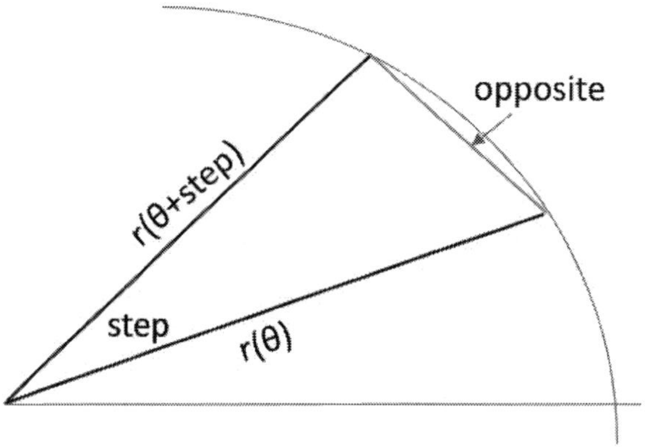

Figure 11.11: Approximating the length of a tiny part of the curve

The opposite side to the central angle of the triangle shown in the preceding diagram is just like the slice in our integration problems or the hypotenuse of the triangle in our previous length of curve program. This time, it isn't a right triangle, so we can't use the hypotenuse. But for this problem, there's a formula called the law of cosines. In triangle ABC, the length of the side opposite angle, C, is as follows:

$$c^2 = a^2 + b^2 - 2ab\cos C$$

Figure 11.12: Law of cosines

All we need to do is put that into a function, like this one:

```
def opposite(a,b,C):
    """Returns the side opposite the given angle in
       a triangle using the Law of Cosines
       Enter side, side, angle"""
    c = sqrt(a**2 + b**2 - 2*a*b*cos(C))
    return c
```

Then, we just need to write a function that will start at the starting angle and take tiny steps around the curve, measuring the sides opposite each tiny angle until it gets to the ending angle:

```
from math import sqrt,cos,pi
def spiral(r,a,b,step=0.0001):
    """Returns length of spiral r from
       a to b taking given step size"""
    length = 0
    theta = a
    while theta < b:
        length += opposite(r(theta),r(theta+step),step)
        theta += step
    return length
```

Our function is as follows:

```
def r(theta):
    return 5 + 0.12892*theta
```

So, all we have to do is execute our spiral function on that spiral, from 0 to 15π:

```
spiral(r,0,2*pi*7.5)
```

The output is as follows:

```
378.8146271783955
```

As you can see, the length of the spiral is **`378.8146271783955`**. In the next exercise, we'll look at how to find the length of a polar spiral curve.

EXERCISE 11.03: FINDING THE LENGTH OF THE POLAR SPIRAL CURVE

In this exercise, you will find the length of the polar spiral curve, which starts at (3,0), makes 12 complete revolutions around the center, and ends at (16,0).

Perform the following steps to find the required length:

1. We don't know the formula for this spiral, but we do know that the radius increases 13 units (from 3 to 16) in 12 revolutions. This means that for every increase of 2π in the angle, θ, the radius increases 13/12 units. So, we divide 13/12 by 2π. The increase in radius can be expressed as follows:

$$r(\theta) = 3 + \frac{13}{12(2\pi)}\theta$$

$$r(\theta) = 3 + 0.1724\theta$$

Figure 11.13: Formula to calculate the increase in radius

2. We can express that in Python this way:

```
def r(theta):
    return 3 + 0.1724*theta
```

3. We can check to make sure *r(0) = 3* and *r(24π) = 16* this way:

```
print(r(0),r(24*pi))
```

The output is as follows:

```
3.0 15.998653763493127
```

4. Now, we simply put that in our spiral function:

```
spiral(r,0,2*pi*12)
```

The output is as follows:

```
716.3778471288748
```

In this exercise, we easily found the length of this spiral curve, that is, **`716.3778471288748`**, just by knowing the start and end values of the curve and the number of revolutions it made around the center.

> **NOTE**
>
> To access the source code for this specific section, please refer to https://packt.live/2YT70EH.
>
> You can also run this example online at https://packt.live/2YV4wFT.

EXERCISE 11.04: FINDING THE LENGTH OF INSULATION IN A ROLL

You have been asked to find the (approximate) length of insulation that remains in the roll shown in the following picture:

Figure 11.14: Measuring rolled up materials using calculus

You measure the roll and find that the center is an empty circle whose diameter is 4 inches (so *r(0)* = *2*). The outer diameter of the roll is 26 inches. You count the layers from the center to the outside and estimate that the spiral takes 23 and a half turns, so *r(2π*23.5)= 26/2 = 13*.

Perform the following steps to calculate the length:

1. Calculate the equation using the preceding data:

$$r(\theta) = 2 + \frac{11}{23.5(2\pi)}\theta$$

$$r(\theta) = 2 + 0.745\theta$$

Figure 11.15: Formula to calculate radius

2. Here's what the graph of the spiral looks like:

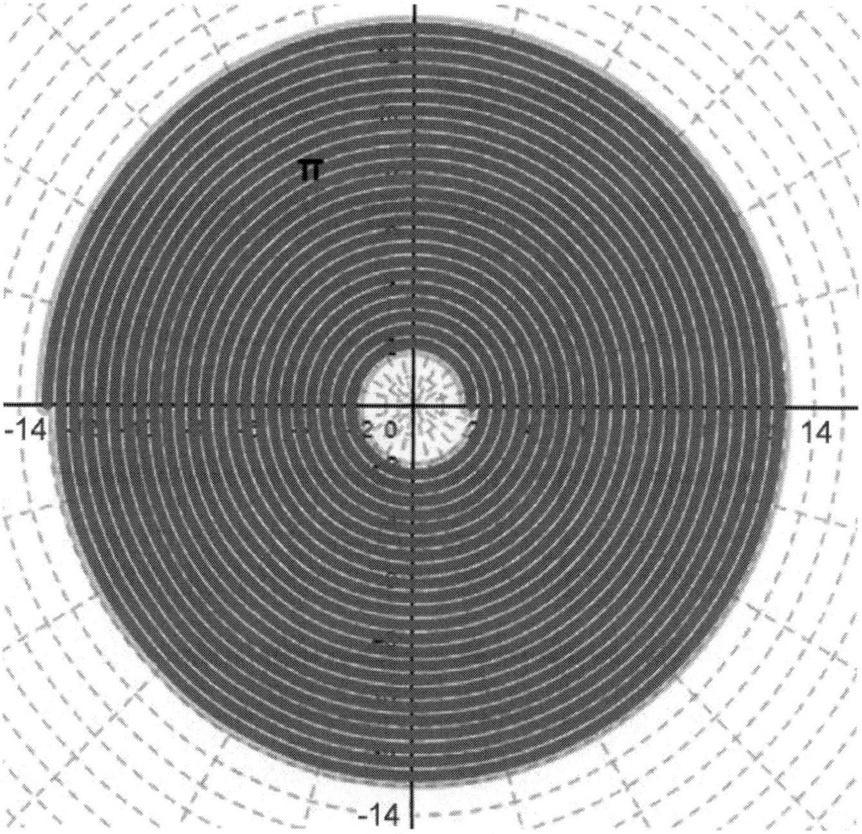

Figure 11.16: A graph of the roll of insulation

3. Now, it's not hard to change our **r** code to this spiral:

```
def r(theta):
    return 2 + 0.0745*theta
```

4. Now, we can run our spiral function on this function from *0* to *2*π*23.5*:

```
spiral(r,0,2*pi*23.5)
```

The output is as follows:

```
1107.502879450013
```

1,107 inches is just over 92 feet of insulation.

> **NOTE**
>
> To access the source code for this specific section, please refer to https://packt.live/2VE9YKZ.
>
> You can also run this example online at https://packt.live/31D43tG.

EXERCISE 11.05: FINDING THE LENGTH OF AN ARCHIMEDEAN SPIRAL

For this exercise, you have been given the equation of an Archimedean spiral. Find the length of the spiral from $\theta=0$ to $\theta=2\pi$:

$$\gamma(\theta) = 2e^{0.315\theta}$$

Figure 11.17: Equation of an Archimedean spiral

> **NOTE**
>
> This works on both logarithmic spirals as well as Archimedean spirals.

Perform the following steps to find the length:

1. We simply redefine **r** with the exponential function:

```
from math import e
def r(theta):
    return 2*e**(0.315*theta)
```

2. Then. we run the spiral function from *0* to *2π*:

```
spiral(r,0,2*pi)
```

The output is as follows:

```
41.518256747758976
```

The length of this spiral is **41.518256747758976**.

> **NOTE**
>
> To access the source code for this specific section, please refer to https://packt.live/2VEtjfo.
>
> You can also run this example online at https://packt.live/2VHasQN.

AREA OF A SURFACE

Let's learn how to take this from two to three dimensions and calculate the area of a 3D surface. In *Chapter 10, Foundational Calculus with Python*, we learned how to calculate the area of a surface of revolution, but this is a surface where the third dimension, *z*, is a function of the values of *x* and *y*.

THE FORMULAS

The traditional, algebraic way to solve this analytically is given by a double integral over a surface:

$$A = \iint_S \left\| \frac{\partial z}{\partial x} \times \frac{\partial z}{\partial y} \right\| dx\, dy$$

Figure 11.18: Formula to calculate area of a surface

Here, $z = f(x,y)$ or $(x,y,f(x,y))$. Those curly d's are deltas, meaning we'll be dealing with partial derivatives. Partial derivatives are derivatives but only with respect to one variable, even if the function is dependent on more than one variable. Here's a function that returns the partial derivative of a function, **f**, with respect to a variable, **u**, at a specific point (**v,w**). Depending on which variable we're interested in, *x* or *y*, the function will take a tiny step in that direction and calculate the derivative, as we've done already:

```
def partial_d(f,u,v,w,num=10000):
    """returns the partial derivative of f
    with respect to u at (v,w)"""
```

```
    delta_u = 1/num
    try:
        if u == 'x':
            return (f(v+delta_u,w) - f(v,w))/delta_u
        else:
            return (f(v,w+delta_u) - f(v,w))/delta_u
    except ValueError:
        pass
```

There is a **`try...except`** block in the code in case a **`ValueError`** is thrown. This happens if the slope gets too big, as in a vertical line. If that happens, it'll ignore it and keep going.

Now, we'll need a 3D vector and a **`cross`** function for the cross product in the area formula. The cross product gives the length of the vector perpendicular to both the given vectors, but also the area of the parallelogram that's formed by the given vectors:

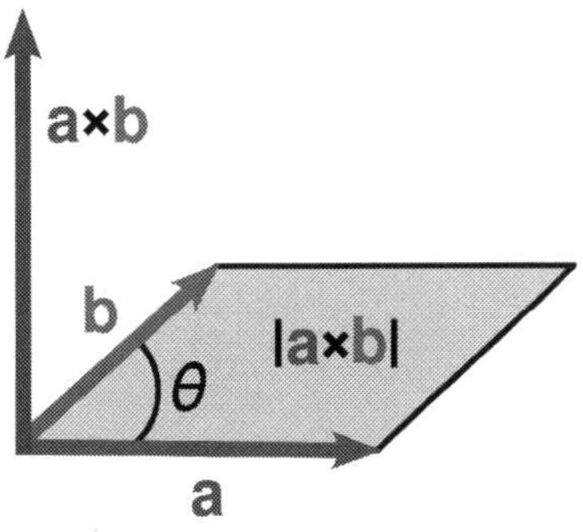

Figure 11.19: The cross product of two vectors

If you know the angle between the vectors, you can use that to find the cross product:

$$\left|a \times b\right| = |a||b|sin\theta$$

Figure 11.20: Formula to calculate cross product of two vectors

If you don't, as in our case, you can use 3D vectors to express the displacement of the vector in each direction, *x*, *y*, and *z*. For example, let's say we have two vectors, *u = 2i + 3j + 4k* and *v = 5i + 6j + 7k*. They're defined by their displacement in each of the three dimensions. The *i* part is the displacement in the *x* direction, the *j* part is the displacement in the *y* direction, and the *k* part is the displacement in the *z* direction. The good news is that there will be a few zeroes to simplify things. To cross two vectors, we can put them into a matrix and operate on them as the determinant of the following matrix:

$$\begin{vmatrix} \mathbf{i} & \mathbf{j} & \mathbf{k} \\ 2 & 3 & 4 \\ 5 & 6 & 7 \end{vmatrix} = (3*7-6*4)\mathbf{i} + (4*5-2*7)\mathbf{j} + (2*6-5*3)\mathbf{k} = -3\mathbf{i}+6\mathbf{j}-3\mathbf{k}$$

Figure 11.21: Calculating cross product of two vectors using matrix

We'll write a function to perform that operation on two 3D vectors. All we'll have to put in are the coefficients of *i*, *j*, and *k*. So, if *u = ai + bj + ck* and *v = di + ej + fk*, we'll get the following:

$$\begin{vmatrix} \mathbf{i} & \mathbf{j} & \mathbf{k} \\ a & b & c \\ d & e & f \end{vmatrix} = (bf-ce)\mathbf{i} + (cd-af)\mathbf{j} + (ae-bd)\mathbf{k}$$

Figure 11.22: Performing mathematical operations on 3D vectors

Let's use lists for the vectors, so *u = [a,b,c]* and *u[0] = a*, *u[1] = b* and *u[2] = c* for the coefficients:

```
def cross(u,v):
    """Returns the cross product of 2 3D vectors
    [[i,j,k],\
    [1,0,dz/dx],\
    [0,1,dz,dy]]
    cross([1,-1,2],[2,3,-5])
    >>> [-1, -9, 5]
    """
    return [u[1]*v[2]-v[1]*u[2],\
            -u[0]*v[2]+v[0]*u[2],\
            u[0]*v[1]-v[0]*u[1]]
```

We wrote a long docstring to make it clear what the function is used for, how to put values in, and what we'll get as the output. Let's check this to make sure we get the right output:

```
print(cross([2,3,4],[5,6,7]))
```

The output is as follows:

```
[-3, 6, -3]
```

That works. Now, we need to write a function to find the magnitude of a 3D vector, since that's going to give us the area of the parallelogram. It's just an extension of the Pythagorean theorem into three dimensions. So, the magnitude of vector *u* if $u = ai + bj + ck$ is $\sqrt{a^2+b^2+c^2}$:

```
def mag(vec):
    """Returns the magnitude of a 3D vector"""
    return sqrt(vec[0]**2+vec[1]**2+vec[2]**2)
```

Here's what the semicircle is going to look like, with its surface approximated by parallelograms. More parallelograms should mean a more accurate approximation:

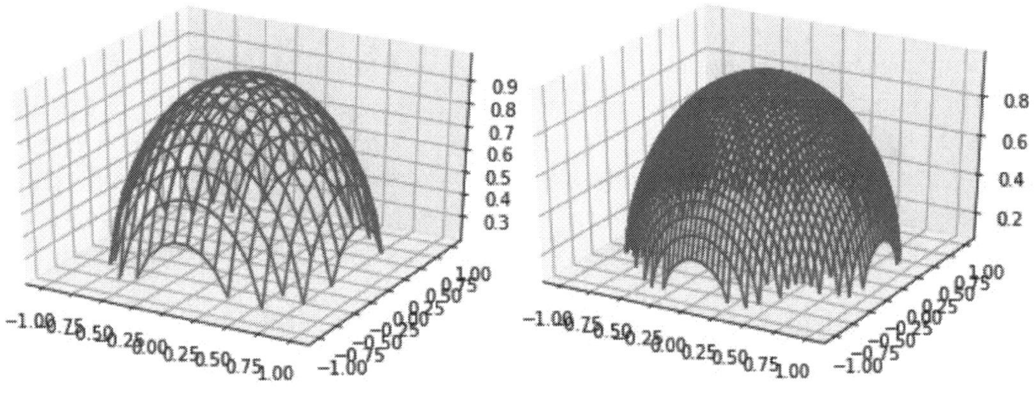

Figure 11.23: Using more parallelograms

Our area function is going to loop through all the *x* and *y* points in the grid, calculate the partial derivatives at each point, and use the cross product to find the area of the parallelogram at that point:

```
from math import sqrt

def sphere(x,y):
    """Sphere of radius 1"""
    return sqrt(1-x**2-y**2)
```

```
def area(f,ax,bx,ay,by,num=1000):
    """Returns area of parallelogram formed by
    vectors with given partial derives"""
    running_sum = 0
    dx = (bx-ax)/num
    dy = (by-ay)/num
    for i in range(num):
        for j in range(num):
            x = ax+i*dx
            y = ay+j*dy
            dz_dx=partial_d(f,'x',x,y)
            dz_dy=partial_d(f,'y',x,y)
            try:
                running_sum += mag(cross([1,0,dz_dx],[0,1,dz_dy]))*dx*dy
            except:
                pass
    return running_sum
```

First, we set the running sum of the areas to 0. Then, we calculate *dx* and *dy*, the tiny changes in *x* and *y*, as we divide the surface up into equal slices. The **`try...except`** block simply ignores (**`pass`**) the error that will arise if a partial derivative is infinite, when the slope of the line tangent to the sphere is vertical, as we saw in *Figure 11.3*. If there's no error, it adds the area of the parallelogram that has been formed at that point by the partial derivatives. Now, we run the area function on the hemisphere using 1,000 points in each direction and get a pretty accurate approximation. We know half the surface area of a sphere of radius 1 is 2π, or 6.28:

```
print("Area of hemisphere:",area(sphere,-1,1,-1,1))
```

The output is as follows:

```
Area of hemisphere: 6.210356913122
```

Now, let's quickly perform an exercise based on this concept.

EXERCISE 11.06: FINDING THE AREA OF A 3D SURFACE – PART 1

Now, let's find the area of a complicated surface, which would be difficult to find using algebraic methods. Consider the surface for the following equation:

$$f(x,y) = 10 \sin\left(\sqrt{x^2 + y^2}\right)$$

Figure 11.24: Equation of the surface

The surface is shown in the following image:

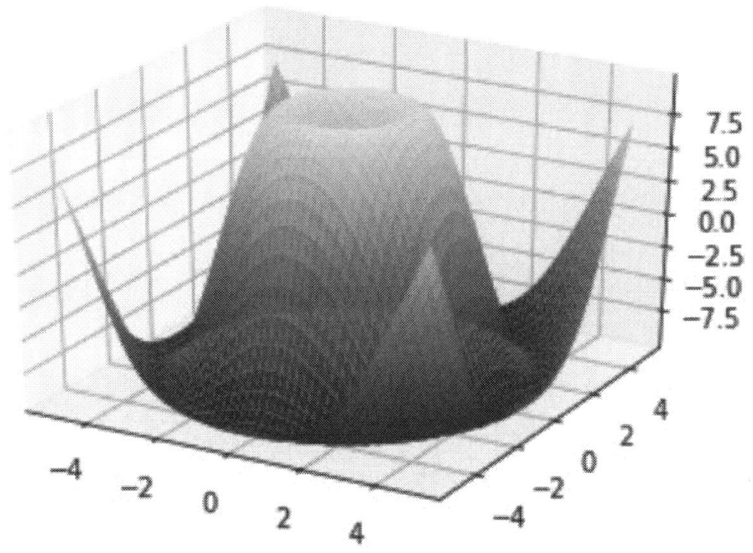

Figure 11.25: A complicated 3D surface

Perform the following steps to find the area:

1. Let's put the function into our area program and see what we get:

```
from math import sin, cos, sqrt
def surface(x,y):
    return 10*sin(sqrt(x**2+y**2))
print("Area of wave surface:",area(surface,-5,5,-5,5))
```

2. Run the program to see the output:

```
Area of wave surface: 608. 2832236305994
```

Looking at the preceding code, we can clearly see how easy it is to find the area of even complicated surfaces in just a few lines of code using Python.

> **NOTE**
>
> To access the source code for this specific section, please refer to https://packt.live/3gwd6kr.
>
> You can also run this example online at https://packt.live/2ZpgwOQ.

EXERCISE 11.07: FINDING THE AREA OF A 3D SURFACE – PART 2

Find the area of the surface $f(x,y) = 3\cos(x) + 2\cos(x)\cos(y)$ *with* $0<x<2\pi$ *and* $0<y<2\pi$.

Here's how the surface looks:

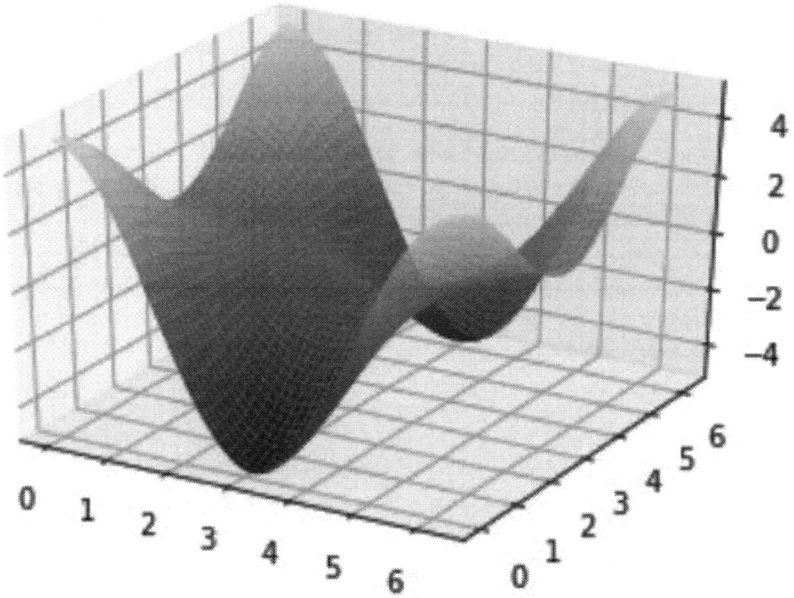

Figure 11.26: Another 3D surface

Perform the following steps to find the area:

1. Define our surface function to return the expression:

```
def surface(x,y):
    return 3*cos(x)+2*cos(x)*cos(y)
```

2. Run the **surface** function to get the value:

```
print("Area of surface:",area(surface,0,6.28,0,6.28))
```

The output is as follows:

```
Area of surface: 99.80676808568984
```

The area of this 3D surface is **99.80676808568984**.

> **NOTE**
>
> To access the source code for this specific section, please refer to https://packt.live/2VCaObq.
>
> You can also run this example online at https://packt.live/2NPXvQo.

EXERCISE 11.08: FINDING THE AREA OF A SURFACE – PART 3

Find the area of the surface $f(x,y) = \sqrt{1+\sin(x)\cos(y)}$ *with* $0<x<2\pi$ *and* $0<y<2\pi$.

Here's how the surface looks:

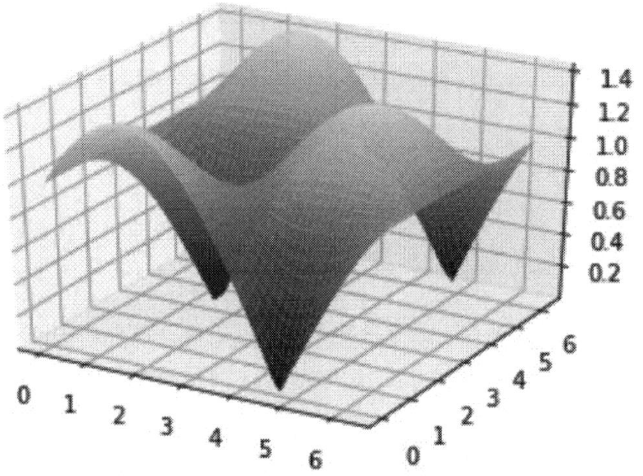

Figure 11.27: The surface of $f(x,y) = \sqrt{1+\sin(x)\cos(y)}$

Perform the following steps to find the area:

1. Define our surface function to return the new expression:

```
def surface(x,y):
    return sqrt(1+sin(x)*cos(y))
```

2. Run the **surface** function:

```
print("Area of surface:",area(surface,0,6.28,0,6.28))
```

The output is as follows:

```
Area of surface: 42.80527549685105
```

The area of this surface is **42.80527549685105**.

> **NOTE**
>
> To access the source code for this specific section, please refer to https://packt.live/3gwdLlV.
>
> You can also run this example online at https://packt.live/3dUNWdt.

INFINITE SERIES

Mathematicians have often run into functions that are too complicated for them to solve or otherwise deal with, and approximations have always been an important component in doing math. For mathematicians trying to take derivatives and integrals algebraically, many expressions have no nice neat solutions, derivatives, integrals, and so on. In general, no differential equations that scientists come across in real life have algebraic solutions, so they have to use other methods. More on differential equations later, but there's an important family of approximations that use *easy* functions to approximate *hard* ones.

POLYNOMIAL FUNCTIONS

It's easy to solve, differentiate, and integrate polynomial equations—ones such as $y = x^2$ and even the following equation:

$$f(x) = 3x^5 - 12x^4 + 7x^3 - 5x^2 + \frac{x}{6} + 11$$

Figure 11.28: A polynomial equation

The terms are all added (or subtracted) one after the other, and there are no trigonometric, logarithmic, or exponential functions involved to make things difficult. Here's the formula for approximating a *hard* function with an *easy* polynomial:

$$f(x) \approx f(a) + \frac{df}{dx}(a)(x-a) + \frac{1d^2f}{2dx^2}(a)(x-a) + \frac{1d^3f}{3!dx^3}(a)(x-a) + \cdots$$

Figure 11.29: The Taylor series

This formula is named Taylor series: any function (which is derivable) can be approximated with a certain precision in a specific point using only polynomials with a certain page.

SERIES

Mathematicians have a notation to represent adding together a bunch of numbers that follow a pattern:

$$\sum_{i=1}^{10} i = 1 + 2 + 3 + \cdots + 10$$

Figure 11.30: Formula for calculating series

The big symbol that looks like an *E* is actually the Greek letter sigma, or *S*, which represents the sum of the numbers. The equation below the sigma is where the variable starts (in this case, 1) and above the sigma is the last integer value for *i* (in this case, 10). To the right of the sigma is an expression for what to do with the variable. In this case, we're just adding *i*, the variable, as it goes from 1 to 10. This is almost exactly how you'd write a list comprehension in Python. Here's how:

```
s = sum([i for i in range(1,11)])
```

The first term in the list comprehension is what you see in the sigma series expression—in this case, *i*. For example, the series for the sum of the squares of the integers up to *n* would be as follows:

$$\sum_{i=1}^{n} i^2 = 1^2 + 2^2 + 3^2 + \cdots + n^2$$

Figure 11.31: Series for sum of squares of integers from 1 to n

In Python, we'd write it like this:

```
s = sum([i**2 for i in range(1,n+1)])
```

An old but useful series is the arctangent series. It calculates the angle (in radians) that has the given tangent; for example:

$$\tan\left(\frac{\pi}{6}\right) = \frac{1}{\sqrt{3}}$$

Figure 11.32: Equation of an arctangent series

From the preceding equation, the equation for arctan will be as follows:

$$arctan\left(\frac{1}{\sqrt{3}}\right) = \frac{\pi}{6}$$

Figure 11.33: Equation of an arctan

The series is calculated by this pattern:

$$arctan(x) = 1 - \frac{x^3}{3} + \frac{x^5}{5} - \frac{x^7}{7} + \cdots$$

Figure 11.34: Equation for series of arctan

Here is the sigma expression:

$$\sum_{i=1}^{\infty} \frac{(-1)^{i-1} x^{2i-1}}{2i-1}$$

Figure 11.35: A sigma expression

By plugging in the tangent for *x*, we can calculate a close approximation to the angle:

$$arctan\left(\frac{1}{\sqrt{3}}\right) = 1 - \frac{\left(\frac{1}{\sqrt{3}}\right)^3}{3} + \frac{\left(\frac{1}{\sqrt{3}}\right)^5}{5} - \frac{\left(\frac{1}{\sqrt{3}}\right)^7}{7} + \cdots$$

Figure 11.36: Substituting the value of x in the equation

That's quite a bit of calculation for a mathematician centuries ago, but here's the Python equivalent. Notice how close the first part of the list comprehension is to the preceding sigma expression:

```
def arctan(x,n):
    """Returns the arctangent of x using a series of n terms."""
    return sum([((-1)**(i-1)*(x**(2*i-1)))/(2*i-1) \
                              for i in range(1,n+1)])
print(arctan(1/1.732,10))
```

So, after 10 terms, we get the following:

```
0.523611120446175
```

This is very close to $\frac{\pi}{6}$.

CONVERGENCE

Mathematicians wanted to simplify the arctan series to easily calculate π using the fact that:

$$\tan\left(\frac{\pi}{4}\right) = 1$$

Figure 11.37: Trigonometric function of a tangent

From the preceding equation, the equation for arctan will be as follows:

$$arctan(1) = \frac{\pi}{4}$$

Figure 11.38: Formula to calculate arctan

They figured replacing *x* with *1* in the arctan series would make calculating π a walk in the park. Here are the first few terms:

$$\frac{\pi}{4} = 1 - \frac{1}{3} + \frac{1}{5} - \frac{1}{7} + \cdots$$

Figure 11.39: Substituting x = 1 in the arctan series

This expression gives the approximation for *pi*:

$$\sum_{i=1}^{\infty} \frac{(-1)^{i-1}}{2i-1}$$

Figure 11.40: Equation to find the approximate value of pi

We just write the code for the part to the right of the sigma, add code for the range of *n*, and sum them up:

```
for n in range(1,10):
    print(4*sum([((-1)**(i-1))/(2*i-1) for i in range(1,n+1)]))
```

We can show the progress toward approximating *pi* in the output:

```
4.0
2.666666666666667
3.466666666666667
2.8952380952380956
3.3396825396825403
2.9760461760461765
3.2837384837384844
3.017071817071818
3.2523659347188767
```

This is not very close to π. How about skipping up to higher numbers of terms? Let's change code for the loop:

```
for n in [100,1000,1000000]:
```

This is the output:

```
3.1315929035585537
3.140592653839794
3.1415916535897743
```

After 1 million terms, it only gets us five correct decimal places. This series *converges* to (that is, gets very close to or *tends toward*) π/4 too slowly for any practical use. So, for centuries, mathematicians have looked for better and better series to approximate π.

EXERCISE 11.09: CALCULATING 10 CORRECT DIGITS OF π

In 1706, English mathematician and astronomer John Machine used his improved series to calculate 100 decimal places of *pi*. Here's the series:

$$\frac{\pi}{4} = 4\ \arctan\left(\frac{1}{5}\right) - \arctan\left(\frac{1}{239}\right)$$

Figure 11.41: An arctan function

Use the preceding arctan function to calculate 10 correct digits of π. Follow these steps to do this:

1. Simply call our arctan function. 10 terms should be sufficient:

```
print(4*(4*arctan(1/5,10)-arctan(1/239,10)))
```

2. Run the preceding code to see the output:

```
3.1415926535897922
```

We get a pretty good approximation using 10 terms. It gives even more than 10 correct digits.

> **NOTE**
>
> To access the source code for this specific section, please refer to https://packt.live/3dPjVvD.
>
> You can also run this example online at https://packt.live/3dVlTKR.

EXERCISE 11.10: CALCULATING THE VALUE OF π USING EULER'S EXPRESSION

The great German mathematician Euler came up with the following expression:

$$\frac{\pi^2}{6} = 1 + \frac{1}{2^2} + \frac{1}{3^2} + \frac{1}{4^2} + \cdots$$

Figure 11.42: Euler's expression

Use this expression to approximate π. Does it converge more quickly than the adjusted arctan formula?

Perform the following steps:

1. Here's the code for approximating π using Euler's series:

```
from math import sqrt

for n in [100,1000,1000000]:
    print(sqrt(6*sum([1/(i**2) for i in range(1,n+1)])))
```

2. Does it converge more quickly? Run the preceding code to see the output:

```
3.1320765318091053
3.1406380562059946
3.1415916986605086
```

It doesn't seem like it converges any quicker. After 1 million terms, you'll still only have five correct decimal places.

> **NOTE**
>
> To access the source code for this specific section, please refer to https://packt.live/2NRnnLD.
>
> You can also run this example online at https://packt.live/38lHXgm.

A 20TH CENTURY FORMULA

Here is the brilliant Indian mathematician Ramanujan's formula to approximate π:

$$\frac{1}{\pi} = \frac{2\sqrt{2}}{9801}\sum_{k=0}^{\infty}\frac{(4k)!(1103+26390k)}{k!^4\left(396^{4k}\right)}$$

Figure 11.43: Ramanujan's formula to approximate π

Here's how to code that in Python:

```
from math import sqrt, factorial

one_over_pi = 2*sqrt(2)/9801*sum([(factorial(4*k)*(1103+26390*k))/ \
              (((factorial(k))**4)*(396**(4*k))) for k in range(10)])

print(1/one_over_pi)
```

The output after 10 terms is as follows:

```
3.141592653589793
```

That's very accurate!!

INTERVAL OF CONVERGENCE

The range of values for which a series converges (tends toward a value) is called the interval of convergence. Using Python, finding this interval is rather straightforward: you run some numbers through the series, and if they get infinitely large, they're not in the interval. If they produce a number, they're in the interval. For example, let's have a look at a very common textbook question and solve it using Python.

EXERCISE 11.11: DETERMINING THE INTERVAL OF CONVERGENCE – PART 1

Determine the interval of convergence for the following power series:

$$\sum_{n-1}^{\infty} \frac{(-1)^n n}{4^n}(x+3)^n$$

Figure 11.44: A power series

Perform the following steps:

1. Enter the sum into Python:

```
    def mystery_sum(x):
        return sum([(((-1)**n)*n)/(4*n)*(x+3)**n for n in \
                         range(1,1000000)])
```

   Since we can't use the number "infinity," we find the sum of all the terms from n = 1 to 1 million.

2. Run all the integers from -10 to 10 to see if there is any converge to a number:

```
for x in range(-10,11):
    print(x,mystery_sum(x))
```

3. When you run this, you'll get an **`OverflowError`**:

```
OverflowError: int too large to convert to float
```

All this means is that some of the numbers got became large, which is what we expected. We need to add a condition so that if we get that error, it'll simply return **`Infinity`**. This is done with a **`try...except`** block.

4. Let's tell Python to try a line of code. If it throws a specific error (in this case, **`OverflowError`**), don't stop the program, just do this instead:

```
def mystery_sum(x):
    try:
        return sum([(((-1)**n)*n)/(4*n)*(x+3)**n \
                                  for n in range(1,1000000)])
    except OverflowError:
        return "Infinity"
```

5. Now, the output gives us some infinities and some actual values:

```
-10 Infinity
-9 Infinity
-8 Infinity
-7 Infinity
-6 Infinity
-5 Infinity
-4 249999.75
-3 0.0
-2 -0.25
-1 Infinity
0 Infinity
1 Infinity
...
```

It looks like our interval of convergence is $-5 < x < -1$. This means we can use the series to get useful values if *x* is in the interval. Otherwise, we can't use it.

> **NOTE**
>
> To access the source code for this specific section, please refer to https://packt.live/38k30A2.
>
> You can also run this example online at https://packt.live/31AtmMU.

EXERCISE 11.12: DETERMINING THE INTERVAL OF CONVERGENCE – PART 2

Determine the interval of convergence for the following power series:

$$\sum_{n=0}^{\infty} \frac{nx^n}{5^{2n}}$$

Figure 11.45: A power series

Perform the following steps:

1. Define the sum in Python:

```
def mystery_sum(x):
    try:
        return sum([n*x**n/(5**(2*n)) for n in range(1,10000)])
    except OverflowError:
        return "Infinity"

for x in range(-30,30):
    print(x,mystery_sum(x))
```

2. Here's some of the output:

```
-30 Infinity
-29 Infinity
-28 Infinity
-27 Infinity
-26 -1.0561866634327267e+174
-25 -5000.0
-24 -0.24989587671803576
-23 -0.24956597222222246
-22 -0.24898143956541371
-21 -0.24810964083175827
-20 -0.24691358024691298
...
18 9.18367346938776
19 13.194444444444444
20 19.999999999999993
21 32.812499999999964
22 61.11111111111108
23 143.74999999999983
24 599.9999999999994
```

```
25 49995000.0
26 5.3728208568640556e+175
27 Infinity
28 Infinity
29 Infinity
```

All the output for *x* between -25 and 25 stayed small (between 0 and 600), no matter how many terms we used, so we'll call the interval of convergence $-25 < x < 25$.

> **NOTE**
>
> To access the source code for this specific section, please refer to https://packt.live/38pwuwC.
>
> You can also run this example online at https://packt.live/2YS46jl.

EXERCISE 11.13: FINDING THE CONSTANT

In this exercise, we will express an infinite series in Python and find the sum. We will use a famous constant, which is defined as the sum of the series:

$$\sum_{n=0}^{\infty} \frac{1}{n!}$$

Figure 11.46: Sum of the series

What is the value of this famous constant? Let's follow these steps to determine this value:

1. Import the factorial module and convert the preceding equation into Python, as follows:

```
from math import factorial
print(sum([1/factorial(n) for n in range(10000)]))
```

2. Run the preceding code to see the output:

```
2.7182818284590455
```

The famous constant is *e*, the base of the natural logarithms.

> **NOTE**
>
> To access the source code for this specific section, please refer to https://packt.live/2AoyubH.
>
> You can also run this example online at https://packt.live/2BZ4aVw.

ACTIVITY 11.01: FINDING THE MINIMUM OF A SURFACE

A major task in machine learning is minimizing a function. When you're training a neural network, you're changing values in a matrix or tensor to see which ones provide a better approximation of your test data. At every value in your network, you can see how much it contributes to your error. This sounds like the partial derivatives at different points on a surface, doesn't it?

An example of this is the process of gradient descent. Let's consider that we want to find the location of the minimum value of our function. Every point in our surface has a partial derivative, and we can use those to move a little bit toward a lower value. We'll start somewhere random, calculate the partial derivatives at that point, and then move in the direction that lowers the value of *z*, that is, the up-down value. So, if the partial derivative of *z* with respect to *x* (which we call *dz_dx*) is negative, that means *z* is decreasing as *x* is increasing, and we'll want to move in the positive *x* direction. If *dz_dx* is positive, that means *z* is increasing as *x* is increasing, so we'll want to go in the opposite direction, so we'll move in the negative *x* direction. We'll do the same for the *y* direction. This will look as follows:

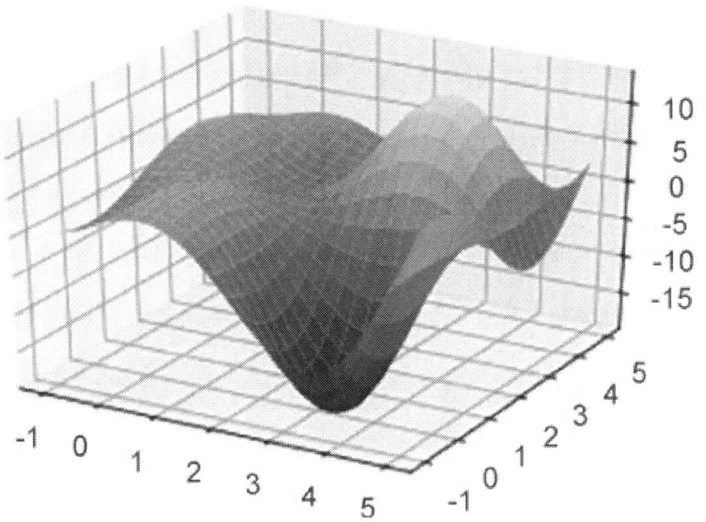

Figure 11.47: The path of descent to a minimum value

The first part of this activity is to create a function that finds the minimum point of a surface. This function can be written by following these steps:

1. Write a function that will create a random (x, y) location on a surface. You can call the **`uniform`** function of the **`random`** module to generate these values.
2. Calculate the partial derivatives of *z* with respect to *x* and *y*.
3. Change *x* and *y* by the negative of the partial derivatives, multiplied by a tiny *step* amount in case the partial derivative is large.
4. Calculate the partial derivatives at this new location and keep looping until the partial derivatives are both really small (less than 0.0001) or the location is off the surface.

5. Run the function on a bunch of random locations, saving the minimum *z* values to a *mins* list.

6. Finally, print the minimum of the mins list.

Once you have written the function, test it on a function that you already know the value of to verify that it works as intended. You can then run it on a function that you don't already know the minimum point of, in order to determine this unknown location. The steps for this are as follows:

1. Test your function on the surface $f(x, y) = x^2 + y^2$. Your function should find that the minimum value is 0, at the point (0, 0).

2. Once you're confident in your function, use it to determine the minimum of $f(x, y) = 3\cos(x) + 5x\cos(x) * \cos(y)$ with $-1 < x < 5$ and $-1 < y < 5$.

You should find that, depending on your starting point, your function will converge to different minimum points—a local minimum and a global minimum.

> **NOTE**
>
> The solution for this activity can be found on page 696.

SUMMARY

In the previous chapter, we learned the power of derivatives and integrals, so in this chapter, we built on those tools to solve some pretty difficult problems, such as the length of a spiral and the area of a 3D surface. We even extended derivatives and integrals to three dimensions by introducing partial derivatives. In a calculus class, we would be using lots of algebra in order to use these tools, but by using Python, we modeled the situation and tested our functions. We created variables that will contain our changing values and looped through the calculations millions of times, if necessary. To the mathematicians of previous centuries, this would have seemed like some kind of magic lamp.

In the next chapter, we'll deal with more changing rates and amounts and avoid a lot of algebra by using Python. We'll find out how much salt is in an ever-changing mixture, when and where a predator will catch its prey, and how long we'll have to invest our money to make 1 million dollars.

12

INTERMEDIATE CALCULUS WITH PYTHON

OVERVIEW

By the end of this chapter, you will be able to solve problems when given equations dealing with the change in a variable. In this chapter, you'll use numerical methods to model populations and temperatures and use differential equations to calculate their past values or predict their future values. You'll learn how to use binary search to *guess and check* your way to a very accurate solution when you know it's in a specific range of numbers. You'll also model situations where objects move and solve for their future positions when given differential equations for their velocity.

INTRODUCTION

Math students often complain that there's no real-world application for the kinds of problems arising in algebra and geometry, such as factoring polynomials or bisecting angles, but the same can't be said for differential equations. Using the tools, you'll learn about in this chapter, you will be able to model and solve real-life problems in physics, electronics, and engineering with differential equations. Python is the perfect tool for mathematicians and scientists who want to be able to crunch numbers and solve problems but don't want to have to get another degree in computer science to do so. Python is one of the most popular programming languages due to its ease of use and lack of unnecessary abstraction.

By the 1600s, mathematicians had modeled the motion of falling objects with mathematical equations and had set their sights on the planets in outer space. Newton modeled their motion and the equations he came up with referred not only to unknown numbers but also the changes in those numbers. For example, his equations didn't only contain an unknown angle, but the change in that angle (its angular velocity) and even the change in the change in the angle (its acceleration)! There were no tools for solving those equations, so he had to invent the tools himself. These tools became known as calculus.

DIFFERENTIAL EQUATIONS

Solving an equation in a math class usually involves an unknown number, *x*. The equation hides the value but gives you hints as to how to find the value, such as $2x+5=13 \; or \; \cos 2x=\frac{1}{2}$. But to solve a differential equation, you're only given information regarding the derivative of a function, and you're expected to find the function. It could be something as simple as the following:

$$\frac{dy}{dx}=2$$

Figure 12.1: Finding a function with derivative 2

This means *find a function whose derivative is 2.* This can also be written as follows:

$$y'=2$$

Figure 12.2: Alternative way to represent derivative of the function

By simple integration, we can find functions that work in this equation because we know the function $y = 2x$ has a derivative of 2. In fact, many related functions, such as $y = 2x + 1$, $y = 2x + 2$, $y = 2x + 3$, and so on, all have a derivative of 2. So, we write a general form, that is, $y = 2x + C$.

Things get more complicated when we don't have much to go on, like in this equation:

$$y' = y$$

Figure 12.3: Derivative of a function whose value is the function itself

This is asking for a function whose derivative is the function itself.

To understand how differential equations are used, let's start with simple functions, and ones involving things in the real world, such as money.

INTEREST CALCULATIONS

There's a crucial tool in the study of differential equations that originated in the study of interest calculations in the middle ages. Let's take a look at the following exercise.

EXERCISE 12.01: CALCULATING INTEREST

A savings account pays 2% annual interest. If $3,500 is invested, how much money is in the account after 5 years?

The formula for simple interest is as follows:

$$I = Prt$$

Figure 12.4: Formula for simple interest

Here, *I* is the interest, *P* is the principal or the original amount invested, *r* is the rate of interest or growth, and *t* is the time the amount has been invested for. By this formula, the interest earned on the amount is *I = (3500)(0.02)(5) = $350*. Follow these steps to complete this exercise:

1. This is a good opportunity to start a program that will take in an initial amount, interest rate, and time and output the interest earned using the preceding formula:

```
def amount(p0,rate,t):
    """Returns the amount after t
    years starting at p0 and growing
    at the given rate per year"""
    return p0*rate*t
```

2. As you can see in the docstring of the **amount** function, it will take a starting amount and a rate of growth and return the amount of the investment after the given number of years. Let's see the interest earned in 1-5 years:

```
for i in range(1,6):
    print(i,amount(3500,0.02,i))
```

Here's the output:

```
1 70.0
2 140.0
3 210.0
4 280.0
5 350.0
```

But this isn't really how interest works. A few times every year, we calculate the interest earned for that fraction of the year, add it to the principal, and the new principal is higher. The next interest calculation is on the higher number, hence the name *compound interest*. The formula for the amount after *t* years, given *n* compounding per year, is as follows:

$$A=P\left(1+\frac{r}{n}\right)^{nt}$$

Figure 12.5: Formula to calculate the amount after t years

3. Let's change our **amount** function to the following:

```
def amount(p0,rate,t,comps):
    """Returns the amount after t
    years starting at p0 and growing
    at the given rate per year
    compounded comps times per year"""
    for i in range(int(t*comps)):
        p0 += p0*rate/comps
    return p0
```

In this function, we added the interest earned in the fraction of the year given by the number of compounding. If we only compound the interest once a year, it looks like this:

```
for i in range(1,6):
    print(i,amount(3500,0.02,i,1))
```

This is what we get:

```
1 3570.0
2 3641.4
3 3714.228
4 3788.51256
5 3864.2828112
```

So, at the end of 5 years, we've earned $364, not just $350. Compounding more often, even with the same interest rate, makes the amount grow more quickly. If we changed the compounding to 12 per year (compounding monthly), we'd end up with $3,867 after 5 years, a little more than compounding annually.

> **NOTE**
>
> To access the source code for this specific section, please refer to https://packt.live/3dUWz7C.
>
> You can also run this example online at https://packt.live/3iqUKCO.

EXERCISE 12.02: CALCULATING COMPOUND INTEREST – PART 1

$2,000 is invested in a savings account that earns 5.5% annual interest, compounded monthly. How long will it take for the amount to grow to $8,000? Follow these steps to work this out:

1. We'll print out the first 5 years of the investment using our **amount** function from the previous exercise:

```
for i in range(1,6):
    print(i,amount(2000,0.055,i,12))
```

   The output is as follows:

```
1 2112.815720771071
2 2231.9951349686903
3 2357.8972049231984
4 2490.9011412619493
5 2631.4075450724245
```

2. After 5 years, the amount is only $2,631. To get to $8,000, we'll have to go to 20 or 30 years:

```
for i in [5,10,15,20,25,30]:
    print(i,amount(2000,0.055,i,12))
```

   The output is this:

```
5 2631.4075450724245
10 3462.1528341320413
15 4555.167544964467
20 5993.251123444263
25 7885.343112872511
30 10374.775681348801
```

   Sometime between 25 and 30 years, we'll get to $8,000. The way to get more exact is to guess smarter.

3. We'll cut the range in half and guess higher or lower based on what we get out. For example, the average of 25 and 30 years is 27.5, so we enter the following:

```
print(amount(2000,0.055,27.5,12))
```

The following is the output:

```
9044.814313545687
```

So, we'd reach $9,000 in 27.5 years. The time to get to $8,000 must be less than that.

4. We'll calculate the average of 25 and 27.5 and plug that in:

```
def average(a,b):
    return (a+b)/2
print(amount(2000,0.055,average(25,27.5),12))
```

The following is the output:

```
8445.203624219383
```

5. Let's write a program to keep doing this until we find our answer. This is called a **binary search**. Let's create a **bin_search** function that will take the name of the function we're using, the lower and upper bounds of the range we're searching over, and the target output—in this case, 8,000—as parameters:

```
def bin_search(f,lower,upper,target):
    for i in range(20):
        avg = average(lower,upper)
```

6. Here's the critical line. It plugs the average into the function, using all the other required parameters, and assigns the output to the **guess** variable. We'll check whether that variable is equal to our target or whether we have to guess higher or lower:

```
        guess = f(2000,0.055,avg,12)
        if guess == target:
            return guess
        if guess > target:
            upper = avg
        else:
            lower = avg
    return avg
```

7. We'll plug the lower and higher ends of our range into our function, as well as our target number, to get our approximation:

```
bin_search(amount,25,30,8000)
```

The output is as follows:

```
25.333333015441895
```

8. Looks like we'll get to $8,000 in **25 years and 4 months**. Let's check that:

```
amount(2000,0.055,25.334,12)
```

Sure enough, the balance after that compounding is just over $8,000:

```
8030.904658737448
```

We'll use the binary search again, but for now, let's use our code to find a rather important mathematical constant that comes up often in differential equations.

> **NOTE**
>
> To access the source code for this specific section, please refer to https://packt.live/3iq95PV.
>
> You can also run this example online at https://packt.live/2BpdbHI.

EXERCISE 12.03: CALCULATING COMPOUND INTEREST – PART 2

How much would you make if you invested $1 at 100% interest for 1 year, compounded continuously?

Remember that the more frequently you compound the interest, the higher the final amount will be. How much do you think it will be? $1.50? $2? The principal, rate, and time are all 1, but what is the **comps** variable? Follow these steps to complete this exercise:

1. To approximate compounding continuously, we'll compound the interest every second (*365*24*60*60* times per year):

```
print(amount(1,1,1,365*24*60*60))
```

The output is as follows:

```
2.7182817853606362
```

This is around $2.72. That number, 2.71828..., is the number *e*, which is the base of natural logarithms. It's very useful for modeling populations in the natural world since animals, plants, and microorganisms don't wait until the end of the month to reproduce—they do so continuously. So, when interest is compounded continuously or when a population is growing naturally, we'll use this formula:

$$A = Pe^{rt}$$

Figure 12.6: Formula to calculate compound interest

2. Let's create a function to do this quickly. First, we'll need to import *e* from the **`math`** module for our continuous compounding:

```
from math import e
```

3. Create a **`pert`** function that will plug in the initial amount or population, the growth rate, and the time, and return the final amount:

```
def pert(P,r,t):
    return P*e**(r*t)
```

We will return to this function throughout this chapter. For now, let's answer some more investment questions.

> **NOTE**
>
> To access the source code for this specific section, please refer to https://packt.live/2D2Q1r0.
>
> You can also run this example online at https://packt.live/31G5pDQ.

EXERCISE 12.04: CALCULATING COMPOUND INTEREST – PART 3

A person borrows $5,000 at 18% annual interest compounded monthly. How much will the person owe after 1 year? Follow these steps to complete this exercise:

1. We can just put it into our function call:

```
amount(5000,0.18,1,12)
```

   The output is as follows:

```
5978.090857307678
```

   For comparison, let's see what would happen if the interest was compounded continuously.

2. We'll use our **pert** function to input **P = 5000**, **r = 0.18**, and **t = 1** as values:

```
print("Continuous:",pert(5000,0.18,1))
```

   The resulting amount is as follows:

```
5986.096815609051
```

> **NOTE**
>
> To access the source code for this specific section, please refer to https://packt.live/31ES5Qi.
>
> You can also run this example online at https://packt.live/3f5j0s4.

EXERCISE 12.05: BECOMING A MILLIONAIRE

How long would it take to become a millionaire if you invested $1,000 at 8% annual interest compounded daily? What if the initial amount is $10,000? Follow these steps to complete this exercise:

1. First, let's define the **bin_search** function, as follows:

```
def bin_search(f,lower,upper,target):
    for i in range(20):
        avg = average(lower,upper)
        #Be sure to change this line
        #if the principal, rate or
        #compounding changes:
```

```
        guess = f(1000,0.08,avg,365)
        if guess == target:
            return guess
        if guess > target:
            upper = avg
        else:
            lower = avg
    return avg
```

2. Let's take some wild guesses and see what we would get if the $1,000 were invested for these numbers of years:

```
for i in [10,20,30,40,50]:
    print(i,amount(1000,0.08,i,365))
```

Here's the output:

```
10 2225.34584963113
20 4952.164150470476
30 11020.277938941583
40 24523.929773205105
50 54574.22533744746
```

3. After 50 years, you still would only have $54,000, not a million. But after 100 years, you'd have almost 3 million:

```
amount(1000,0.08,100,365)
```

Here's the output:

```
2978346.0711824815
```

4. The answer must be somewhere between 50 and 100. Looks like a job for our binary search:

```
print(bin_search(amount,50,100,1000000))
```

We get this output:

```
86.3588809967041
```

5. This shows that after 86.36 years, we'll have 1 million dollars. If the initial investment is $10,000, then update the **`guess`** variable in the **`bin_search`** function:

```
        guess = f(10000,0.08,avg,365)
```

Here's how we'll print out the output we want:

```
for i in [10,15,20,30,40,50,60]:
    print(i,amount(10000,0.08,i,365))
```

The output is as follows:

```
10 22253.458496311334
15 33196.803971077774
20 49521.64150470513
30 110202.77938941623
40 245239.2977320514
50 545742.2533744735
60 1214465.2585152255
```

6. So, we reach 1 million dollars in somewhere between 50 and 60 years. Let's change **1000** to **10000** in our binary search function and check it:

```
print(bin_search(amount,50,60,1000000))
```

We get this output:

```
57.57260322570801
```

Just over 57.57 years to reach a million dollars.

So, we've started off learning about differential equations by studying compound interest. An initial amount of money had a rate of interest applied to it at intervals of a year, a month, or a day.

> **NOTE**
>
> To access the source code for this specific section, please refer to https://packt.live/31ycoPg.
>
> You can also run this example online at https://packt.live/2NMT9sX.

Now, we'll extend the same reasoning to amounts of people, animals, bacteria, and heat, which change constantly, or *continuously*.

POPULATION GROWTH

Differential equations are useful for finding a formula for the population of people, animals, and bacteria at a certain time; for example:

$$\frac{dy}{dt} = ky$$

Figure 12.7: Differential equation to calculate population at time t

This differential equation means the rate of change of *y* is proportional to *y*, or the population grows proportional to its amount. This is the definition of population growth rate: a fraction or percentage of the population. The solution is similar to our interest problems involving continuous compounding:

$$y = y_0 e^{rt}$$

Figure 12.8: Differential equation to calculate the rate of change

EXERCISE 12.06: CALCULATING THE POPULATION GROWTH RATE – PART 1

In the 1980s, the annual population growth rate in Kenya was 4%. At that rate, how long would it take for the population to double? Follow these steps to complete this exercise:

1. No matter what the starting population, we're looking for *t*, which makes the factor e^{rt} equal to 2. We can use our **pert** function and our binomial search function, with a little tweaking:

```
def bin_search(f,lower,upper,target):
    for i in range(40):
        avg = average(lower,upper)
        guess = f(1,0.04,avg)
        if guess == target:
            return guess
        if guess > target:
            upper = avg
        else:
            lower = avg
    return avg
```

2. We're looking for the time, *t*, that will, with a growth rate of 4%, turn our initial population of 1 into 2. We estimate it will be somewhere between 1 and 100 years:

```
print(bin_search(pert,1,100,2))
```

The output is as follows:

```
17.32867951408025
```

We can check that with algebra. We take the log of both sides of the equation and solve *t*:

$$e^{0.04t} = 2$$

$$\mathrm{In}\,(e^{0.04t}) = \mathrm{In}\,2$$

$$0.04t = \mathrm{In}\,2$$

$$t = \frac{\mathrm{In}\,2}{0.04} = 17.3$$

Figure 12.9: Equation to solve for time (t)

3. This means that in just over 17 years, the population of Kenya will have doubled. We can check this with our **`amount`** function. In 1989, the population of Kenya was 21,000,000:

```
print(amount(21000000,0.04,17.3,1000000))
```

The following is the output:

```
41951845.46179989
```

Yes, using a million compoundings a year, the population grows to almost 42 million in 17.3 years.

In response to this, the Kenyan government made a big push to promote *family planning*. Did it work?

> **NOTE**
>
> To access the source code for this specific section, please refer to https://packt.live/2BxsfCT.
>
> You can also run this example online at https://packt.live/2Zuoy9c.

EXERCISE 12.07: CALCULATING THE POPULATION GROWTH RATE – PART 2

In 2010, the population of Kenya was 42.0 million. In 2019, it was 52.5 million. What is the population growth rate per year for that range?

Once again, we can use our binary search function to return a growth factor, *r*, given the initial population (in millions), the time, *t*, and the target population (in millions) after 9 years.

In the **bin_search** function, change the time to **9**:

```
        guess = f(1,avg,9)
```

Then, we'll find the annual growth rate for those 9 years. We know it's between 0 and 2:

```
print(bin_search(pert,0,2,52.5/42))
```

The value that is printed is as follows:

```
0.024793727925498388
```

The family planning program must have worked! Kenya reduced its population growth rate to 2.5%.

> **NOTE**
>
> To access the source code for this specific section, please refer to https://packt.live/3eWKzDW.
>
> You can also run this example online at https://packt.live/31EKPUq.

HALF-LIFE OF RADIOACTIVE MATERIALS

Much like population problems, half-life problems concern a population, but one of atoms of radioactive materials where half the atoms change over time into atoms of a different substance. For example, Carbon-14 decays into Nitrogen-14, and it takes about 5,730 years for half the carbon to decay. This makes *radiocarbon dating* a crucial tool in everything from archaeology to detecting forged artworks.

EXERCISE 12.08: MEASURING RADIOACTIVE DECAY

Radium-226 has a half-life of 1,600 years. How much of the radium in a given sample will disappear in 800 years?

The differential equation meaning "*the rate of decay of a substance is proportional to the amount of the substance*" is expressed like this:

$$\frac{dy}{dt} = -ky$$

Figure 12.10: Differential equation for calculating rate of decay of a substance

The solution is similar to that for our population problems, except that the decay factor is negative, since the amount decreases:

$$y = y_0 e^{-rt}$$

Figure 12.11: Calculating rate of change with negative decay factor

This means the final amount is equal to the initial amount of time, *e*, to the product of a decay factor, *r*, and time, *t*. We can use our binary search function as if this were a population problem. We're looking for the growth rate, *r*, that cuts our population in half in 1,600 years. Follow these steps to complete this exercise:

1. Change *t* in the **`guess =`** line in the **`bin_search`** function to **`1600`**:

```
        guess = f(1,avg,1600)
```

2. Then, search for the growth factor, which we figure is going to be between -2 and 0. Our target amount is ½ of the starting amount:

```
print(bin_search(pert,-2,0,0.5))
```

The following is the output:

```
-0.0004332169864937896
```

3. That's the decay factor, *r*, for Radium-226. All we have to do to find out the percentage of the sample left after 800 years is plug that into our **pert** function:

```
pert(1,-0.0004332,800)
```

The following is the output:

```
0.7071163910309745
```

So, around 71% of the sample remains after 800 years.

> **NOTE**
>
> To access the source code for this specific section, please refer to https://packt.live/2YSzQ84.
>
> You can also run this example online at https://packt.live/2ByUwJj.

EXERCISE 12.09: MEASURING THE AGE OF A HISTORICAL ARTIFACT

A sample of cloth is radiocarbon-tested for age. This means the scientists measure how much Carbon-14 (half-life 5,730 years) has decayed into a more stable isotope. They find the amount of Carbon-14 remaining is 10 times that of Carbon-13. How old is the cloth?

If Carbon-14 takes 5,730 years for half its amount to decay, we need to find the rate, *r*, for our Pert formula:

$$0.5 = e^{-5780r}$$

Figure 12.12: The Pert formula

Follow these steps to complete this exercise:

1. We use our binary search function to solve *r*:

```
def bin_search(f,lower,upper,target):
    for i in range(40):
        avg = average(lower,upper)
```

2. This is the line that's changed. We put a beginning amount of **1** into the **pert** function, *r* will be **avg**, and **5730** will be the target time:

```
        guess = f(1,avg,5730)
        if guess == target:
            return guess
        if guess > target:
            upper = avg
        else:
            lower = avg
    return avg

print(bin_search(pert,-2,0,0.5))
```

The following is the output:

```
-0.00012096809405193198
```

r = -0.000120968, so our Pert formula becomes as follows:

$$y = y_0 e^{-0.000120968t}$$

Figure 12.13: Substituting the new value of r in the Pert formula

This means *x* grams of Carbon-14 decayed, and 10x grams, 10 times as much, remains. So, the decayed amount is 1/11*th* or 0.091 of the whole sample. The ending amount is 1 – 0.091. That makes our Pert equation as follows:

$$0.91 = e^{-0.000120968t}$$

Figure 12.14: Pert equation with ending amount

3. The only unknown in our equation is *t*, so we're changing our **bin_search** function to guess and check strategically for the correct *t*. Go back to your **bin_search** function; the beginning should look like this:

```
def bin_search(f,lower,upper,target):
    for i in range(40):
        avg = average(lower,upper)
```

4. Here's the line we're changing. We're plugging in 1 for the original amount, the long decimal is our *r*, and the average of our time range is used for the time. The target is 0.091 of the sample, and this will keep guessing and averaging until it returns the exact number of years to get to the target:

```
        guess = f(1,-0.000120968,avg)
        if guess == target:
            return guess
```

5. Since it's a decreasing function, if the guess is less than the target, we'll have overshot it and the **upper** number will be replaced by the average:

```
        if guess < target:
            upper = avg
        else:
            lower = avg
    return avg
print(bin_search(pert,1,100000,0.91))
print(pert(1,-0.000120968,5730))
```

6. Notice we changed the **if guess < target:** line. We're looking for the number of years it'll take the amount to decay from 1 to 0.91 at the given rate. We suspect it's somewhere between 1 and 100,000 years. The second **print** line is just a check that our **pert** function confirms that after 5,730 years, the amount left is exactly half the original amount. Here's the output when we run our code:

```
779.633287019019
0.5000002702800457
```

According to our calculations, the cloth is around **780 years** old.

So, we originally wrote this code to measure the amount of money left in an investment that grew at a given rate for a certain time. In this section, we applied this to the amount of radioactive material left in an object after decaying at a known rate for an unknown amount of time. This is how scientists calculate the age of archaeological artifacts.

> **NOTE**
>
> To access the source code for this specific section, please refer to https://packt.live/3eOJJJv.
>
> You can also run this example online at https://packt.live/38mESgn.

Next, we'll use the same idea but apply it to the change in the temperature of objects such as a cup of coffee or a human body.

NEWTON'S LAW OF COOLING

Did you ever wonder how the **Crime Scene Investigator** (**CSI**) with the latex gloves on police shows can tell the time of death of the victim? Isaac Newton is credited with figuring out that the cooling of substances follows a differential equation:

$$\frac{dT}{dt} = -k\left(T_0 - T_{env}\right)$$

Figure 12.15: Differential equation for rate of change of temperature

See how this differential equation is slightly different than the ones we've seen before? Instead of the rate of change of the temperature of the substance being proportional to the temperature of the substance, this says *"the rate of change of the temperature of a substance is proportional to the difference between the temperature of the substance and the temperature of the environment."* So, if a cup of hot coffee is left in a hot room, its temperature is going to change less quickly than if it's left in a very cold room. Similarly, we know the starting temperature of the body of the victim on the police show: 98.6° F.

EXERCISE 12.10: CALCULATING THE TIME OF DEATH

An investigator arrives at the scene of the crime and measures the temperature of the environment and the body. If the environment is 65° and the body is 80°, the investigator notes the time and waits an hour. The difference between the temperatures of the body and the environment is 15. An hour later, the environment is still 65° and the body has further cooled to 75°. The difference in temperatures is now 10°. When did the victim die?

With this information, she can set up the following equation:

$$10 = 15e^{-r(1)}$$

Figure 12.16: Equation for calculating the time of death

Follow these steps to complete this exercise:

1. We can use our binary search to find out what the decay rate for the temperature is. We'll need to import **e** and make sure we have our **pert** and **average** functions:

```
from math import e

def pert(P,r,t):
    return P*e**(r*t)

def average(a,b):
    return (a+b)/2
```

2. The first part of our **bin_search** function is the same as before:

```
def bin_search(f,lower,upper,target):
    for i in range(40):
        avg = average(lower,upper)
```

3. Here's the important change: our original amount (the temperature difference) is 15 degrees, and we want to know *r*, the rate of change in our Pert formula:

```
            guess = f(15,avg,1)
            if guess == target:
                return guess
            if guess > target:
                upper = avg
            else:
                lower = avg
        return avg
print(bin_search(pert,-2,0,10))
```

Here's the output:

```
-0.4054651081078191
```

That's the rate of decay for this situation, so we know the beginning difference between the temperature of the body and the environment (98.6 – 65), as well as the final difference (10) and the rate of decay. Here's a graph of the situation:

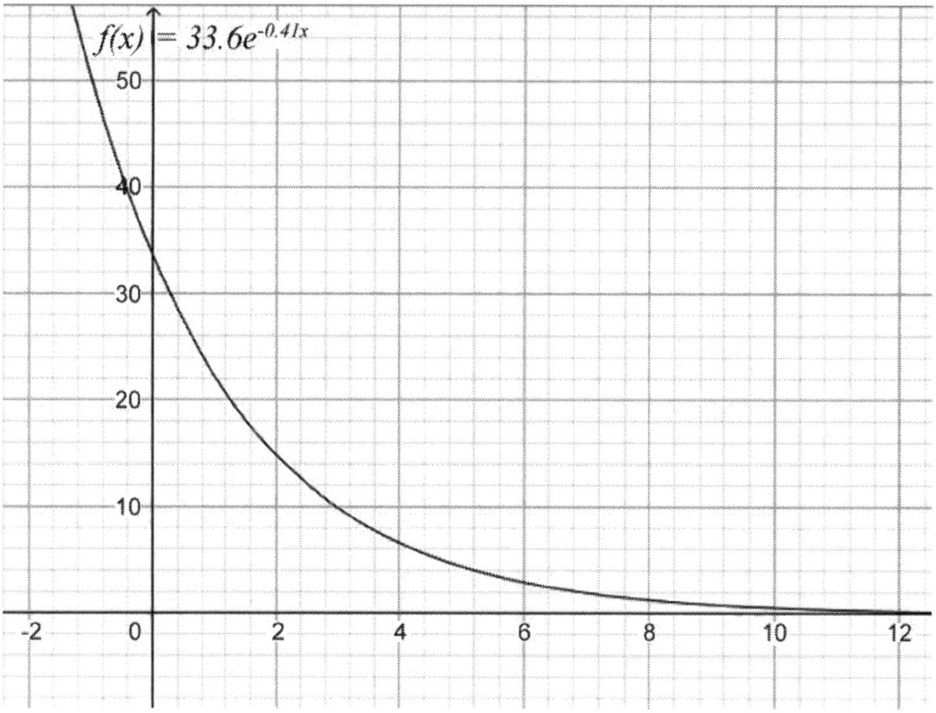

Figure 12.17: A graph of the cooling body

All we need to know is the number of hours it took for that difference to decay to 10. Our equation is as follows:

$$10 = 33.6e^{-0.4055t}$$

Figure 12.18: Number of hours taken for the difference to decay to 10

4. We change our binary search function to get the time:

```
def bin_search(f,lower,upper,target):
    for i in range(40):
        avg = average(lower,upper)
        guess = f(33.6,-.4055,avg)
        if guess == target:
            return guess
        if guess > target:
            upper = avg
        else:
            lower = avg
    return avg
```

But if the time is too low, the difference will be too high. The easiest way to get around this is to make the higher *t* the *lower* part of the function call and the lower *t* the *upper* end of the range to search.

5. The investigator figures the time has to be between 0 and 5 hours:

```
print(bin_search(pert,5,0,10))
```

The output will be as follows:

```
2.9887570258370033
```

Almost exactly 3 hours. That looks close to the time when the *y*-value of the curve in the preceding graph is 10.

6. Let's check that in our **pert** function. Start at a difference of 33.6 degrees with *r* = *-0.4055* and *t* = *3.0*. Hopefully, we end up with 10:

```
pert(33.6,-0.4055,3)
```

The following is the output:

```
9.954513505592326
```

So, now, when the star detective arrives on the scene at 2:30 a.m., the investigator can say, "The time of death was around 11:30 pm."

> **NOTE**
>
> To access the source code for this specific section, please refer to https://packt.live/38jN68K.
>
> You can also run this example online at https://packt.live/3gefegi.

EXERCISE 12.11: CALCULATING THE RATE OF CHANGE IN TEMPERATURE

A cup of coffee at a perfect temperature of 175° F is left in a 72° room. We wait 15 minutes and measure the temperature of the coffee to find it has changed to 140°. At this rate, what will its temperature be 1 hour from the start? Follow these steps to complete this exercise:

1. The difference starts at 103° (175-72). In 0.25 hours, it's changed to 68° (140-72). Now, we can set up an equation:

$$68 = 103e^{-r(0.25)}$$

Figure 12.19: Equation for calculating difference in the coffee's temperature

2. We can change our binary search function to reflect this situation. Change the **guess=** line in the **bin_search** function to this:

```
        guess = f(103,avg,0.25)
```

3. Run it to find what *r* between -2 and 0 will give us a difference of 68°:

```
print(bin_search(pert,-2,0,68))
```

   Here's the output:

```
-1.6608851322143892
```

4. That's fast! Put that into our Pert formula with *P = 103* and *t=1*:

```
pert(103,-1.6608851322143892,1)
```

   The following is the output:

```
19.566987911888482
```

That's the difference in 1 hour. If the room is 72°, that means the coffee will be *72 + 19.5 = 91.5°*.

> **NOTE**
>
> To access the source code for this specific section, please refer to https://packt.live/3gl5p0i.
>
> You can also run this example online at https://packt.live/2YTdCmw.

MIXTURE PROBLEMS

In algebra, there are word problems where you have to figure out how much material you have to add to a mixture to get a certain concentration or amount. In calculus, naturally, the problem has to be harder: for example, the mixture is changing; material is going into the mixture, and material is going out. You have to find out how much mixture or how much of the solvent is present after a specific amount of time. Let's look at the following exercise to better understand this concept.

EXERCISE 12.12: SOLVING MIXTURE PROBLEMS – PART 1

A tank contains 82 gallons of brine in which 18 pounds of salt is dissolved. Brine containing 3 pounds of dissolved salt per gallon flows into the tank at the rate of 5 gallons per minute. The mixture, which is kept uniform by stirring, flows out of the tank at a rate of 2 gallons per minute. How much salt is in the tank at the end of 39 minutes?

As you can imagine, this kind of problem leads to some complicated differential equations, and only after pages of algebra do you get an equation (usually involving *e* to some power) into which you can plug the time and get your final amount. However, using programming, we can simply start with our given starting solution and add and subtract whatever material the problem calls for. It's a matter of keeping track of solution and solute. Follow these steps to complete this exercise:

1. Let's create a function to find the salt content after `t` minutes, given our initial conditions:

```
def salt_content(t):
    salt = 18 #pounds
    brine = 82 #gallons
```

2. Then, every minute, 5 more gallons of brine is being added, containing 15 pounds (5 gallons at 3 pounds of salt *per gallon*) of salt:

```
for i in range(t):
    brine += 5
    salt += 15
```

3. Now, 2 gallons of the brine flows out every minute, but how much salt is in it? That requires us to find the concentration of each gallon of brine:

$$\text{concentration} = \frac{\text{pounds of salt in the tank at time t}}{\text{gallons of brine in the tank at time t}}$$

Figure 12.20: Formula to calculate the concentration of each gallon of brine

This can be easily converted into code, as follows:

```
    concentration = salt/brine
```

4. So, the salt leaving the tank every minute will be the number of gallons of solution flowing out, times the concentration of salt:

```
    salt_out = 2*concentration
    salt -= salt_out
    brine -= 2
```

5. After the loop finishes, we can print out the final amounts of brine and the salt:

```
print(i,brine,salt)
```

6. To solve our problem, we simply run our **`salt_content`** function with *t=39*:

```
salt_content(39)
```

The output is as follows:

```
38 199 469.2592152141211
```

That means we end up with 469 pounds of salt after 39 minutes. That number is very close to the analytical solution, but it's not exact. What could we do to get more accurate results? Remember, the idea behind *e*, the base of natural logarithms, is that it simulates constant change in a value, and we're only calculating our changes in our solution once every minute.

7. Let's introduce a variable, **frac**, that will let us calculate our changes in fractions of a minute:

```
def salt_content(t,frac=0.001):
    salt = 18 #pounds
    brine = 82 #gallons
```

8. The **frac=0.001** value in the parameters means we'll calculate the changes a thousand times per minute. That means we'll multiply the times we loop by 1,000, or 1/**frac**, and we'll multiply the change in our amounts by **frac**:

```
    for i in range(int(t/frac)):
        brine += 5*frac
        salt += 15*frac
        concentration = salt/brine
        salt_out = 2*concentration*frac
        salt -= salt_out
        brine -= 2*frac
    print(i,brine,salt)

salt_content(39)
```

The output changes to the following:

```
38999 198.99999999966812 470.74539697793307
```

470.7 pounds of salt is even closer to the analytical solution, and using smaller fractions of a minute doesn't change the output much.

> **NOTE**
>
> To access the source code for this specific section, please refer to https://packt.live/2BlX2Tn.
>
> You can also run this example online at https://packt.live/3dSrEcm.

Let's use this function on other problems.

EXERCISE 12.13: SOLVING MIXTURE PROBLEMS – PART 2

A tank contains a solution of 10,000 L of brine with a concentration of 1 kg of salt per 100 L. Brine with 2 kg of salt per 100 L flows into the tank at a rate of 20 L per second. The (uniform) mixture leaves at a rate of 10 L per second. Find out how much salt is in the tank in 5 minutes. Follow these steps to complete this exercise:

1. So, we need to do a little arithmetic to find out our initial amount of salt, but 1 kg of salt per 100 L is 100 kg of salt in 10,000 L, and it's 0.4 kg of salt in 20 L, which is flowing into the tank. Here's our new function:

```
def salt_content(t,frac=.001):
    salt = 100
    brine = 10000
    for i in range(int(t/frac)):
        brine += 20*frac
        salt += 0.4*frac
        concentration = salt/brine
        salt_out = 10*concentration*frac
        salt -= salt_out
        brine -= 10*frac
    return salt
```

Now, let's call the **salt_content** function:

```
print(salt_content(5*60))
```

The output when we call the function is as follows:

```
183.0769053279811
```

(Remember, our numbers are all in seconds, and we want 5 minutes, hence the **5*60** parameter.)

The output tells us there's 183 kg of salt in the solution in 5 minutes. This is very close to the analytical solution.

2. We can simplify our task by changing the hardcoded numbers to variables, so when we have a problem with a different initial amount of brine, for example, we can just enter a different number into the function call. We'll need variables for the initial amount of brine (or any solution), the initial amount of solute (so far, we've been using salt), the velocity of brine in, the velocity of salt in, and the velocity of brine out. Here's how to change the function:

```
def salt_content(t,salt_0,brine_0,salt_in,brine_in,v_out,frac=.001):
    salt = salt_0 #pounds
    brine = brine_0 #gallons
    for i in range(int(t/frac)):
        brine += brine_in * frac
        salt += salt_in* frac
        concentration = salt/brine
        salt_out = v_out*concentration* frac
        salt -= salt_out
        brine -= v_out* frac
    return salt
```

3. Now, to solve the last problem, our function call would have more arguments:

```
salt_content(300,100,10000,0.4,20,10)
```

The output is as follows:

```
183.0769053279811
```

As you can see, the output should be the same as in *step 1*. Let's apply this to more problems.

> **NOTE**
>
> To access the source code for this specific section, please refer to https://packt.live/3gkTWOd.
>
> You can also run this example online at https://packt.live/3eSWF17.

EXERCISE 12.14: SOLVING MIXTURE PROBLEMS – PART 3

A vat contains 100 L of a sugar-water mixture with 900 g of sugar. A sugar-water mixture containing 5 g of sugar per L enters the vat at a rate of 2 L per minute. Another mixture containing 10 g of sugar per L flows into the vat at a rate of 1 L per minute. The vat is kept mixed, and the resulting mixture is drained from the vat at 3 L per minute. Find the amount of sugar in the vat in 1 hour. Follow these steps to complete this exercise:

1. The only trick here is that the total solution entering is 3 L per minute, and the total solute entering is 20 g per minute. Here's the function call:

```
salt_content(60,900,100,20,3,3)
```

2. The output will be as follows:

```
705.2374486274181
```

The amount of solute is 705 g.

> **NOTE**
>
> To access the source code for this specific section, please refer to https://packt.live/2YRWNIl.
>
> You can also run this example online at https://packt.live/2YRWKfD.

EXERCISE 12.15: SOLVING MIXTURE PROBLEMS – PART 4

What if we added pure water? Would that make it harder or easier? Let's try this one.

A tank contains 1,200 L of a brine mixture of water and 18 g of salt. Fresh water enters the tank at a rate of 15 L per minute and the tank is mixed to remain uniform. A pipe drains the mixture at a rate of 10 L per minute. How much salt is in the tank after 15 minutes? Follow these steps to complete this exercise:

1. We can use our **salt_content** function, but the **salt in** variable will be set to **0**. This makes the following function call:

```
print(salt_content(15,18,1200,0,15,10))
```

2. The output for the salt content after 15 minutes is as follows:

```
15.944648402124784
```

The salt content has decreased from 18 g to 15.9 g.

> **NOTE**
>
> To access the source code for this specific section, please refer to https://packt.live/2ZsLTIs.
>
> You can also run this example online at https://packt.live/2AnLrT8.

So, we've seen several topics from differential equations that normally require a lot of algebraic manipulation to find an equation for the situation so that (presumably) we can plug in a variable and get the temperature, position, or amount we're looking for. Modeling using Python and running simulations as we have has saved us a lot of algebra and still got us very accurate answers.

EULER'S METHOD

In undergraduate math classes, you're taught all these algebraic methods for taking derivatives and integrals and solving differential equations. We didn't mention Laplace transforms, which are even more complicated ways of solving differential equations algebraically. Now, for the dirty secret about differential equations they don't tell you in school, unless you major in engineering: most differential equations you come across in real life have *no analytical solution*.

The good news is there have been numerical methods for avoiding messy algebra for hundreds of years, and with the invention of computers, these methods have become standard. Even when there is an analytical solution, numerical methods can be almost as accurate for practical purposes as the analytical method and take a fraction of the time to get a solution.

The idea of Euler's method is very simple:

1. Start at the known point.
2. Calculate the derivative at this point using the differential equation. This is the direction the curve is taking at this point.
3. Move a tiny step in the direction you calculated.
4. Repeat until you get to the end of the desired range.

EXERCISE 12.16: SOLVING DIFFERENTIAL EQUATIONS WITH EULER'S METHOD

You're given the differential equation $y'=y$. You want to know the output of the function *y = f(x)* at a specific value of *x*. You're given one point on the graph: *f(0) = 1*. This means, *"the derivative of this function at every point is the y-value of the function at that point."* Remember, the derivative is the slope or the direction that point on the graph is heading. Euler's method is to start at the initial value, in this case, at (0,1), and calculate the direction to the next point using the differential equation. The **Differential Equations** (**DE**) states the slope is the *y*-value, so we take a small step in the positive *x*-direction:

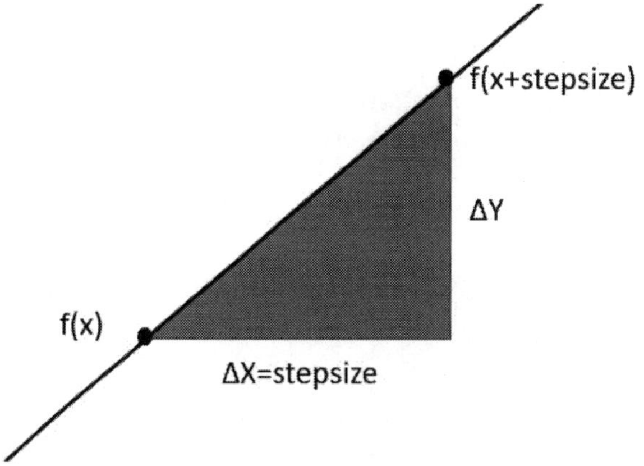

Figure 12.21: Taking a small step (hopefully) in the right direction

The derivative is as follows:

$$y'=\frac{\Delta y}{\Delta x}$$

Figure 12.22: Derivative of the function

So, *ΔY* becomes the following:

$$\Delta y=y'\Delta x$$

Figure 12.23: Formula to calculate ΔY

It's the product of the derivative and the stepsize. To find the next *y*-value, we add *ΔY* to the previous *y*-value. At the new point, we repeat this process: calculate the slope of the function at this point, multiply by the stepsize, and add that to the present *y*-value. Follow these steps:

1. Let's write a Python function to do that:

```
def euler(x0,y0,target_x,stepsize):
    x,y = x0,y0
    while x<target_x:
        slope = y #from diff eq
        x += stepsize
        y += stepsize*slope
        print(x,y)
    return y
```

2. So, we know the initial **x** and **y**. We want to know **y** when **x=2**; the stepsize can be ½:

```
print(euler(0,1,2,0.5))
```

The following is the output:

```
0.5 1.5
1.0 2.25
1.5 3.375
2.0 5.0625
5.0625
```

3. We no longer need the **print** statement inside the **euler** function, so comment it out:

```
        #print(x,y)
```

4. The first line is the result of calculating the slope, which is simply the *y*-value, 1, multiplying that by the stepsize, ½, and moving up that distance. If the derivative had been negative, we'd have moved down. On the second line, we multiplied the *y*-value, 1.5, by the stepsize, 0.5, and got 0.75. We moved up from 0.75 to 2.25 and so on. Taking small steps in the x-direction until we got to our target x-value, 2, we ended up at a *y*-value of 5.0625. We no longer need to print out each step, but let's cut the stepsize in half 10 times:

```
for n in [0.5**i for i in range(10)]:
    print(n,euler(0,1,2,n))
```

The following is the output:

```
1.0 4.0
0.5 5.0625
0.25 5.9604644775390625
0.125 6.583250172027423
0.0625 6.958666757218805
0.03125 7.166276152788222
0.015625 7.275669793128417
0.0078125 7.3318505987410365
0.00390625 7.3603235532692795
0.001953125 7.374657160341845
```

So, the smaller the stepsize, the closer we seem to be getting to 7.37. Here's a graph of the paths of the approximations:

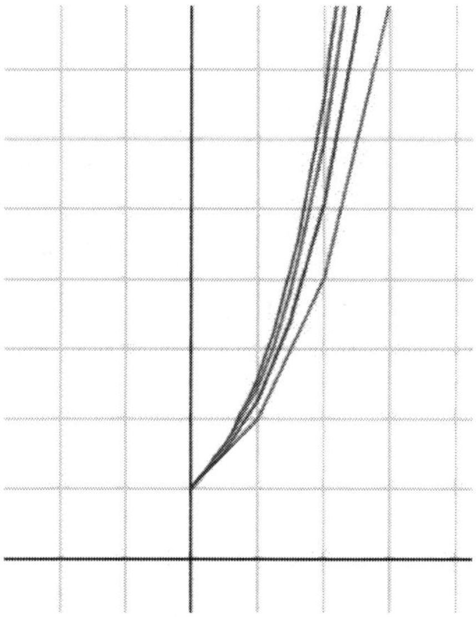

Figure 12.24: Better approximations with a smaller stepsize

The fourth curve (the curve to the right) is the path of our approximations with stepsize 1. The third graph has stepsize ½, the second curve ¼, and the first curve 1/8. We choose the $y = e^x$ differential equation because we know the algebraic solution.

When x is 2, $e^2 = 7.389$. Adding the actual curve of $y=e^x$ (the first curve on the left), we can see that the smaller the stepsize, the closer the approximations get to the actual curve:

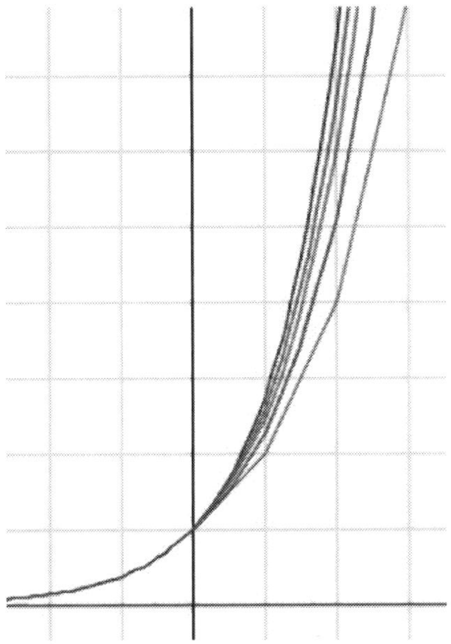

Figure 12.25: The actual curve added to the left side of the first curve

But the last approximation, with stepsize 0.001953125, took 1,024 steps between 0 and 2. It's easy to see why Euler's method wasn't preferred to algebraic methods before the invention of the computer.

> **NOTE**
>
> To access the source code for this specific section, please refer to https://packt.live/2VEQiaa.
>
> You can also run this example online at https://packt.live/2ByZvtv.

EXERCISE 12.17: USING EULER'S METHOD TO EVALUATE A FUNCTION

Use Euler's method and stepsize 0.001 on the **initial value problem** (**IVP**):

$$y' = x + y^2$$

Figure 12.26: Euler's method on initial VP

Here, $y(0) = 1$ in order to calculate the approximate solution $y(x)$ for when $x = 0.3$:

1. In the **euler** function, enter the differential equation in the **slope=** line:

```
def euler(x0,y0,target_x,stepsize):
    x,y = x0,y0
    while x<target_x:
        slope = x+y**2 #from diff eq
        x += stepsize
        y += stepsize*slope
    return y
```

2. Enter the proper parameters in the function call:

```
print(euler(0,1,0.3,0.001))
```

The output should be as follows:

```
1.4869555619353322
```

This means that by taking tiny steps from our known point (0,1) going in the direction specified by the differential equation, we were able to predict that 1.49 is the approximate *y*-value corresponding to the x-value 0.3.

> **NOTE**
>
> To access the source code for this specific section, please refer to https://packt.live/3inHj6S.
>
> You can also run this example online at https://packt.live/2VFLEbF.

RUNGE-KUTTA METHOD

Since Euler's method is based only on the derivative at each point, it has the problem of always overshooting or undershooting the true curve. Not surprisingly, in the centuries since Euler's method was invented, improvements have been made to offset its drawbacks. One such improvement is the **Runge-Kutta** (**RK**) method, which averages together four approximations, one of which is Euler's method, using the beginning of the interval, another using the end of the interval, and two other approximations using the midpoint of the interval. When averaged together, the approximations at the midpoint are given a higher weight.

Here are the equations when the DE is given, *f(x,y)*, the starting *x* and *y*, x_0 and y_0, and the step size, *h*:

$$k_1 = h * f\left(x_n, y_n\right)$$

$$k_2 = h * f\left(x_n + \frac{h}{2}, y_n + \frac{k_1}{2}\right)$$

$$k_3 = h * f\left(x_n + \frac{h}{2}, y_n + \frac{k_2}{2}\right)$$

$$k_4 = h * f\left(x_n + h, y_n + k_3\right)$$

Figure 12.27: Equations when f(x,y) is given

For the next *y*, we average together the four preceding approximations, with double the weight on k_2 and k_3:

$$y_{n+1} = y_n + \frac{1}{6}\left(k_1 + 2k_2 + 2k_3 + k_4\right)$$

Figure 12.28: Formula for averaging the 4 preceding approximations

Then, of course, *x* is incremented by *h*:

$$x_{n+1} = x_n + h$$

Figure 12.29: Incrementing x by h

This is a lot to code, but its power is impressive.

EXERCISE 12.18: IMPLEMENTING THE RUNGE-KUTTA METHOD

Use the Runge-Kutta method and stepsize 0.2 on the IVP:

$$y' = x^2 + y^2$$

Figure 12.30: Runge Kutta method with stepsize 0.2

1. First, we define the differential equation. Let's call it **deriv(x,y)**:

```
def deriv(x,y):
    return x**2 + y**2
```

2. Now, we'll define the Runge-Kutta method, calling it **rk4**:

```
def rk4(x0,y0,target_x,h):
    while x0 <= target_x:
        print(x0,y0)
        k1 = h*deriv(x0,y0)
        k2 = h*deriv(x0 + h/2, y0 + k1/2)
        k3 = h*deriv(x0 + h/2, y0 + k2/2)
        k4 = h*deriv(x0 + h, y0 + k3)
        #These are the values that are fed back into the function:
        y0 = y0 + (1/6)*(k1 + 2*k2 + 2*k3 + k4)
        x0 = x0 + h
```

3. When we start at *y(0) = 0* and we want *y(1)* using a stepsize of 0.2, here's what we call:

```
rk4(0,0,1,0.2)
```

Our progress is printed out as follows:

```
0 0
0.2 0.0026668666933346665
0.4 0.021360090381533078
0.6 0.0724512003541295
```

```
0.8 0.17409018097333867
1.0 0.35025754914481283
```

4. The same problem using the same stepsize, but using Euler's method, is less accurate. In the **euler** function, change the **slope=** line to match the new differential equation:

```
        slope = x**2 + y**2
```

5. Now, we print out the solution using Euler's method:

```
print(euler(0,0,1,0.2))
```

The following is the output:

```
0.2428567456277198
```

This isn't very close to the Runge-Kutta solution. However, the Runge-Kutta improvement may have been more useful before computers, because we can simply decrease the step size in Euler's method and get a much better approximation. This is the same output for Euler's method with a stepsize of 0.001:

```
print(euler(0,0,1,0.001))
```

The following is the output:

```
0.34960542576393877
```

This has been a brief look at the *numerical methods* used to solve equations, not by doing algebra but by feeding the starting point into a computer program and taking small steps in the direction indicated by the differential equations. This is an enormous field of calculus, especially now that free software and programming languages, coupled with fast computer processors, make easy work of previously laborious calculations.

> **NOTE**
>
> To access the source code for this specific section, please refer to https://packt.live/3eWxF95.
>
> You can also run this example online at https://packt.live/3dUlkkg.

PURSUIT CURVES

A big topic in calculus is the pursuit curve, which is the path traced by an agent pursuing a moving target. Since the pursuer moves directly toward its target, and then the target moves, this situation leads to all kinds of differential equations. The algebra can get very ugly, and that's why calculus professors love the topic. However, as we know, differential equations are usually about finding a general algebraic solution, that is, a function, not a number. In theory, we then plug values into the function to find the location of a particle or the temperature of a room at a specific time. Using Python, we skip the algebraic step by modeling the situation and finding a numerical solution. What we lose in generality, we gain in ease of computation.

EXERCISE 12.19: FINDING WHERE THE PREDATOR CATCHES THE PREY

A rabbit starts at (0,0) and runs in the positive *y*-direction at 1 unit per second. A fox starts at (20,0) and pursues the rabbit, running 1.5 times as fast as the rabbit. At what *y*-value does the fox catch the rabbit?

Perform the following steps:

1. First, we'll need some functions from the **math** module to measure distance and angles:

```
from math import sqrt, atan2,sin,cos
```

2. We'll write a function to measure the distance between the predator's position and the prey's position using the Pythagorean Theorem:

```
def dist(x1,y1,x2,y2):
    """Returns distance from (x1,y1) to (x2,y2)"""
    return sqrt((x1-x2)**2 + (y1-y2)**2)
```

3. The key is that the change in *y* over the change in *x* between the locations of the prey and the predator represents the tangent of the angle we want. We know their locations, so we use the inverse tangent function, called **atan2**, to calculate the angle so that the predator points directly at the prey. All we really want is to know how much to change the predator's *x*- and *y*-coordinates for them to move 1 unit toward the prey. To turn the predator toward the prey, we need to find the angle between the two points, as shown in the following diagram:

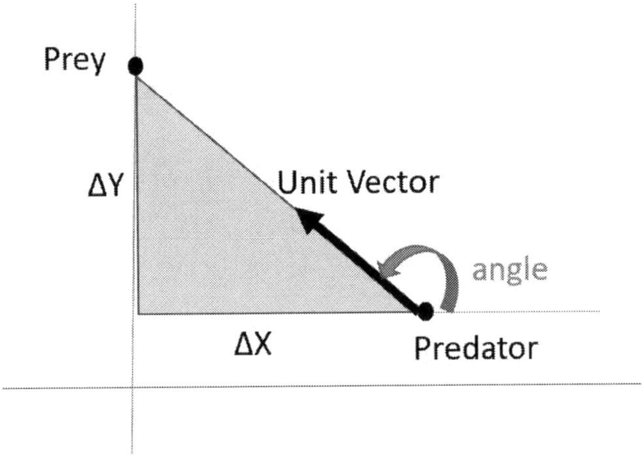

Figure 12.31: The angle between predator and prey

4. Once we know the change, we can multiply the vector by whatever velocity we want:

```
def towards(x1,y1,x2,y2):
    """Returns unit vector in [x,y] format from point
    1 to point 2"""
    dx,dy = x2-x1,y2-y1
    angle = atan2(dy,dx)
    return [cos(angle),sin(angle)]
```

   We calculate the change in **x** and **y**, calculate the angle using the **arctangent** function, and then we use cosine and sine to find the corresponding changes in the predator's *x*- and *y*-coordinates so that it walks one unit toward the prey.

5. Now, the chase can begin. We start the predator and prey at their stated locations. Then, we start a loop where we move the prey one unit (or an increment of that for more accuracy):

```
def chase():
    predator_x,predator_y = 20,0
    predator_v = 1.5 #prey is 1
    prey_x,prey_y = 0,0
    inc = 0.001
    while dist(predator_x,predator_y,prey_x,prey_y) > 0.001:
        prey_y += 1*inc
        p_vec = towards(predator_x,predator_y,\
                        prey_x,prey_y)
        predator_x += predator_v*p_vec[0]*inc
```

```
        predator_y += predator_v*p_vec[1]*inc
        #print(dist(predator_x,predator_y,prey_x,prey_y))
    return predator_y
```

6. Now, we run the chase and print out the *y*-value where the predator catches the prey:

```
y = chase()
print("Y:",y)
print("dist:",dist(1,1,4,5))
print("towards:",towards(1,1,2,2.732))
```

The output is as follows:

```
Y: 23.997299988652507
dist: 5.0
towards: [0.5000110003630132, 0.8660190526287391]
```

This is extremely close to the theoretical value of 24.

> **NOTE**
>
> To access the source code for this specific section, please refer to https://packt.live/3f6x44Z.
>
> You can also run this example online at https://packt.live/2NO1A7v.

EXERCISE 12.20: USING TURTLES TO VISUALIZE PURSUIT CURVES

In this exercise, we'll visualize the path of the predator and prey, which is called the *pursuit curve*. There's a built-in module in Python, based on the virtual turtles of the Logo programming language, that makes it easy to create virtual agents that can walk around the screen according to the code we write. Follow these steps to complete this exercise:

1. First, we import the functions from the **turtle** module:

```
from turtle import *
```

2. We set up the size of the screen according to the desired lower-left point, which we'll make (-30, -30), and the upper-right point, which we'll make (40,40):

```
setworldcoordinates(-30,-30,40,40)
```

3. Setting up the predator and prey means creating a **Turtle** object and setting its color, position, and speed. The turtle leaves paths when it walks, so we tell it **penup** to keep it from drawing until it gets to its starting location. Then, we tell it **pendown** so that it will start drawing:

```
#set up predator
predator = Turtle()
predator.color("red")
predator.penup()
predator.setpos(20,0)
predator.pendown()
predator.speed(0)
```

4. We set up the prey by making the turtle green and giving it the shape of a turtle:

```
#set up prey
prey = Turtle()
prey.color("green")
prey.shape("turtle")
prey.setheading(90)
prey.speed(0)
```

5. The **pursue** function should look familiar, but it has built-in functions to calculate the distance and even for pointing at another turtle:

```
def pursue():
    inc = 0.05
    while predator.distance(prey)>0.05:
        predator.setheading(predator.towards(prey))
        prey.forward(inc)
        predator.forward (1.5*inc)
    print("y:",predator.ycor())
```

6. We'll execute the **pursue** function and then once it prints the output, we'll tell it the program is done so that the graphics window doesn't freeze:

```
pursue()
done()
```

7. If you run this, you can watch the chase. Here's what the final output should look like:

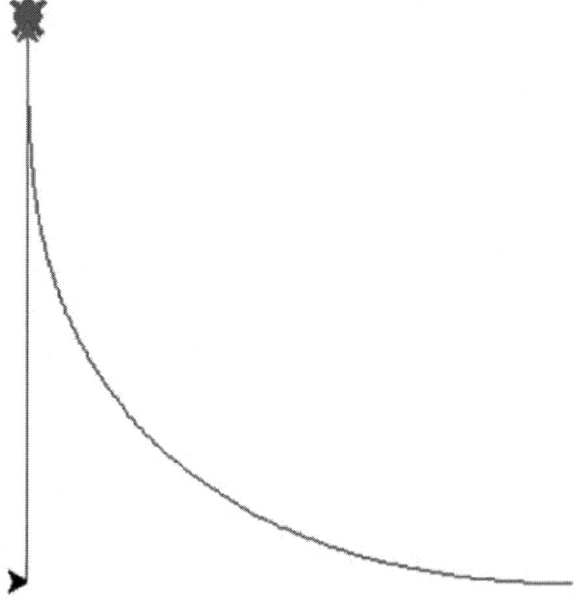

Figure 12.32: The path of the predator is a logarithmic curve

8. **Extension**: Change the prey's path into a circle. After the line to make the prey move forward, add this line:

```
prey.left(.3)
```

This will make the prey turn left a fraction of a degree every step. But if the turn is the same every time, it'll eventually make a circle. The resulting path looks like this:

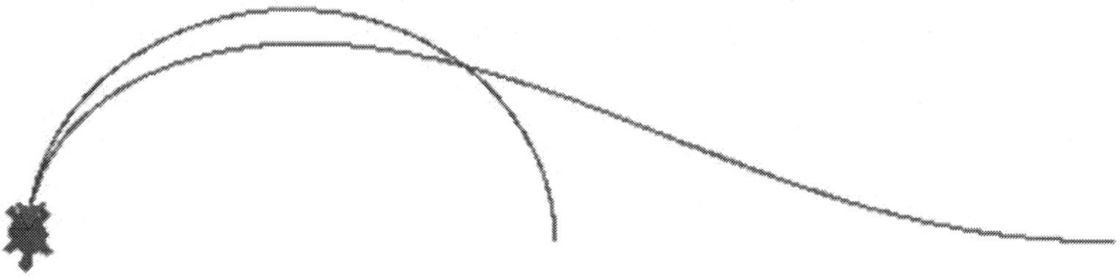

Figure 12.33: The pursuit curve when the prey is fleeing in a circular path

> **NOTE**
>
> To access the source code for this specific section, please refer to https://packt.live/3dWHDG6.
>
> This section does not currently have an online interactive example and will need to be run locally.

POSITION, VELOCITY, AND ACCELERATION

Differential equations are often used to study the paths of projectiles, and this can be said to be the origin of calculus. Newton invented the tools of calculus to solve the differential equations that resulted from his study of the movements of the planets and showed that falling objects on Earth are subject to the same laws of physics as orbiting planets.

EXERCISE 12.21: CALCULATING THE HEIGHT OF A PROJECTILE ABOVE THE GROUND

A ball is thrown upward with an initial velocity of 29 m/s. How long before it hits the ground? Follow these steps to complete this exercise:

1. In algebra class, we're led to calculate the height of a projectile using an equation:

$$h = h_0 + v_0 t - \frac{1}{2} g t^2$$

Figure 12.34: Formula to calculate the height of a projectile

Here, h_0 is the initial height, v_0 is the initial upward velocity, t is the number of seconds elapsed, and g is the acceleration due to gravity, around 32 feet or 9.8 meters per second. But projectiles don't calculate their position using equations; they simply travel in the direction their derivative indicates.

2. Let's model that:

```
v = 29
g = 9.8
h = 0
t = 0
```

So, for the first second, the ball will be thrown up at 29 meters per second but will be slowed down by gravity 9.8 meters per second, meaning after a second, it's only going *29 – 9.8 = 19.2* meters per second. So, after a second, the ball should be 19.2 meters up in the air. We repeat that every second until its height is 0.

3. Here's what the **height** function should look like:

```
def height(v0,h0,t):
    """Calculates the height a projectile given the
    initial height and velocity and the elapsed time."""
    v,h = v0,h0
    for i in range(1,t+1):
        v -= g
        h += v
    return h
```

4. The velocity and height are assigned their starting values, v_0 and h_0, and then the velocity is updated by *g* and the acceleration (due to gravity), and then the height, *h*, is updated by the velocity. We repeat our calculation every second and check to see when the ball's height returns to zero:

```
for j in range(1,10):
    print(j,round(height(v,h,j),1))
```

The following is the output:

```
1 19.2
2 28.6
3 28.2
4 18.0
5 -2.0
6 -31.8
7 -71.4
8 -120.8
9 -180.0
```

It looks like the ball hits the ground somewhere between 4 and 5 seconds. But when we put $t = 5$ into the preceding formula, we get the following:

$$h = 0 + (29)(5) - \frac{1}{2}(9.8)(5)^2 = 145 - 122.5 = 22.5$$

Figure 12.35: Substituting the values in the formula for calculating the height of a projectile

5. After 5 seconds, the ball should still be 22.5 meters in the air. What's wrong with our code? As you should know by now, the ball doesn't only change its velocity once every second. Its velocity is changing constantly. Just like compound interest, we need to calculate the new velocity many times a second. That's easy for Python. We'll just introduce an **inc** variable for the increment in time. Remember that this increases the number of times we loop through the calculations, so the **for i in range** line changes too. Then, *g* and *v* are multiplied by the increment. We'll recalculate every half a second:

```
def height(v0,h0,t):
    """Calculates the height a projectile given the
    initial height and velocity and the elapsed time."""
    inc = 0.5
    v,h = v0,h0
    for i in range(int(t/inc)):
        v -= g*inc
        h += v*inc
    return h
```

6. Run this using the same code to execute:

```
for j in range(1,7):
    print(j,round(height(v,h,j),1))
```

The output is now as follows:

```
1 21.7
2 33.5
3 35.6
4 27.8
5 10.3
6 -17.1
```

7. The ball is in the air for longer, and at 5 seconds, it's 10.3 meters in the air. If we make the increment very small, it should get much closer to 22.5 meters at 5 seconds. Change **inc** to 0.001, run it again, and you'll get this output:

```
1 24.1
2 38.4
3 42.9
4 37.6
5 22.5
6 -2.4
```

8. To answer the question of when the ball hits the ground, we'll have to do a binary search between 5 and 6 seconds. As in previous searches, we use our **bin_search** function and change the **guess** = line to reflect the number we're *guessing*:

```
def bin_search(f,lower,upper,target):
    def average(a,b):
        return (a+b)/2
    for i in range(40):
        avg = average(lower,upper)
        guess = f(29,0,avg)
        if guess == target:
            return avg
        if guess < target:
            upper = avg
        else:
            lower = avg
    return avg
```

9. All we had to change was the **guess** = line with the parameters of the **height** function. The last parameter, *t*, is what we're searching for, so that's what we're averaging. The binary search function will plug in values between 5 and 6 and return the value of *t* that returns 0:

```
print(bin_search(height,5,6,0))
```

Here's the output:

```
5.918000000000575
```

Now, we solve the quadratic equation:

$29t - 4.9t^2 = 0$

For t, we get $t = 0$ and 5.9184. Of course, the height of the ball was 0 before we threw it, and the second value is very close to what we got. Here's what the graph of the function looks like. Neglecting air resistance, the graph of the particle's height over time follows a parabolic path:

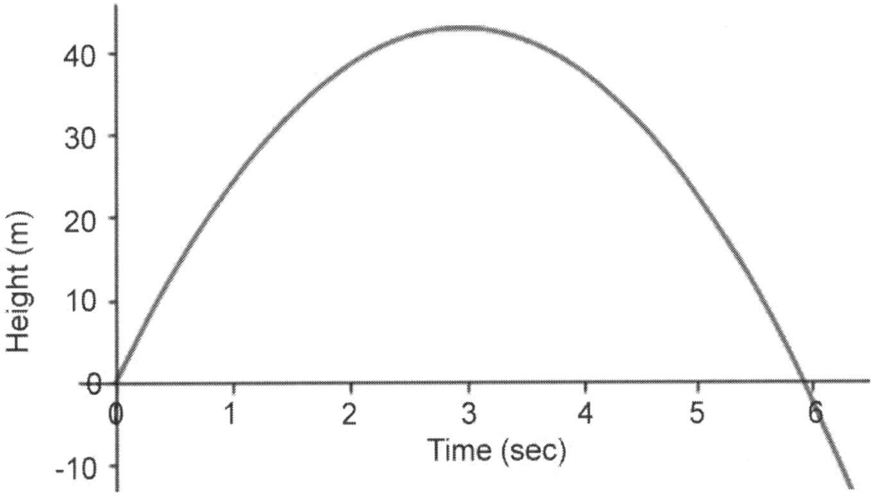

Figure 12.36: The path of a projectile without air resistance

This was a test of our code because we had a nice formula to check our output. Now, we will move on to harder calculus problems involving velocity and acceleration where there isn't a formula to help us check the answers.

> **NOTE**
>
> To access the source code for this specific section, please refer to https://packt.live/2VEAkN4.
>
> You can also run this example online at https://packt.live/2Bzpz7Z.

AN EXAMPLE OF CALCULATING THE HEIGHT OF A PROJECTILE WITH AIR RESISTANCE

Math students are forced to study particles traveling in perfect parabolic paths from algebra through calculus. Unfortunately, that's not how real particles travel. In real life, objects travel through some medium such as air or water and are slowed down depending on the density of the medium, their cross-sectional area, and other factors. This makes for a complicated equation for the force that's applied to a projectile. In the simplest of terms, *the force on a projectile is the acceleration due to gravity and deceleration proportional to the square of its velocity*. The equation looks like this:

$F = mg - kv^2$

With air resistance, we'll need to know the mass, *m*, of the projectile. The acceleration due to gravity, *g*, is 9.8 m/s^2. The *k* variable is a combination of at least three different factors, but the value $k = 0.27$ yields realistic results for this situation.

As in the previous exercise, we calculate the acceleration and use it to update the velocity. Then, we update the position of the projectile according to the velocity.

The force on the projectile is made up of two parts: the usual acceleration due to gravity and a drag component. Let's write a Python function to calculate that:

```
def force(v,mass,g,k,inc):
    """Returns the downward force on a
    projectile"""
    gravity = mass*g*inc
    drag = k*(v**2)*inc
    if v > 0:
        return gravity + drag
    return gravity - drag
```

Many times, our values are multiplied by **inc**, the increment variable, so that we can take smaller steps to get better approximations, as we did before. The **gravity** and **drag** variables are taken directly from the force equation. Notice that if the velocity is greater than 0, the projectile is traveling upward, so the downward force is the sum of the gravity and drag forces. Otherwise, the projectile is traveling downward, so the force of gravity is still downward but the drag is slowing it down, so we use the difference of the gravity and the drag.

Now, we'll adapt our **height** function from the previous exercise to calculate the time it takes for the height to equal 0 and add in a call to our **force** function:

```
def height(v0,h0):
    """Calculates the time it takes a projectile given the
    initial height and velocity to hit the ground."""
    inc = 0.001
    v,h = v0,h0
    t = 0
    while h >= 0:
        v -= force(v,1,9.8,0,inc) #test with k=0
        h += v*inc
        t += inc
    return round(t,1),round(v,1)
```

It's the **v -=** line that's doing the heavy lifting in this function. The velocity will be acted on by the downward force. When we run this using *k = 0*, we should get the same time and ending velocity as in the previous problem, with no air resistance:

```
print(height(29,0))
```

The output is as follows:

```
(5.9, -29.0)
```

Yes; in the previous exercise, the projectile took 5.9 seconds to reach the ground. When there's no air resistance and the ending height is the same as the initial height, the ending velocity will be the same as the initial velocity, only in the opposite direction, so –29 m/s.

Now, let's put in our more realistic value for *k*, **0.27**, and see how long it takes the particle to reach the ground and how fast it will be going. What do you predict?

Change the **v -=** line in the **height** function to the following:

```
        v -= force(v,1,9.8,0.27,inc)
```

The output when you run the program will be as follows:

```
(2.2, -5.9)
```

So, the projectile went up and back down in only 2.2 seconds, and the final velocity was –5.9 m/s. If we juxtapose the graphs of the heights of the projectiles with and without air resistance, we certainly get a lot less height with air resistance:

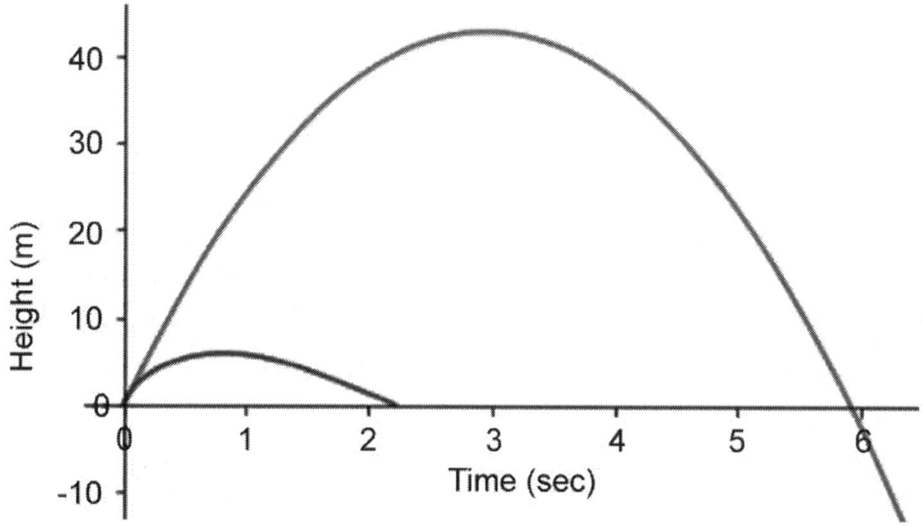

Figure 12.37: The height of a projectile, with air resistance (the inner curve)

That sure is a lot of resistance. Play around with different values for *k*, the constant of drag, to get different ending times and ending velocities. This leads us to a very interesting idea in math and science, known as **terminal velocity**, when the downward and upward forces on a projectile equal out and it no longer accelerates.

EXERCISE 12.22: CALCULATING THE TERMINAL VELOCITY

If your projectile started at an initial height of 3,000 meters and jumped out of a plane (downward velocity of 0), what velocity would it reach? Would it simply continue accelerating until the projectile hits the ground?

Change the mass to 80 kg, an average weight for a human, and *k* to **`0.27`**. Follow these steps to complete this exercise:

1. Make sure you have your **`force`** function from the previous example.
2. Change your **`height`** function so that it looks like this:

```
def height(v0,h0):
    """Calculates the velocity of a projectile given the
    initial height and velocity and the elapsed time."""
    inc = 0.001
```

```
    v,h = v0,h0
    t = 0
    for i in range(500):
```

3. Here's the important line where we tell the **`force`** function the mass, the value of *k*, and so on:

```
        v -= force(v,80,9.8,0.27,inc)
        h += v*inc
        if i % 50 == 0:
            print("v:",round(v,1))
        t += inc
```

4. We go through 500 loops but only print out the velocity every 50th loop. Let's run it with this line:

```
height(0,3000)
```

This is the output we receive:

```
v: -0.8
v: -34.1
v: -48.6
v: -52.6
v: -53.6
v: -53.8
v: -53.9
v: -53.9
v: -53.9
v: -53.9
```

The velocity starts at 0 and gets more and more negative until it stops decreasing. It evens out around 54 m/s (negative because it's downward), which is around 120 miles per hour, the terminal velocity for a human body in free fall. Here's a graph of the velocity over time:

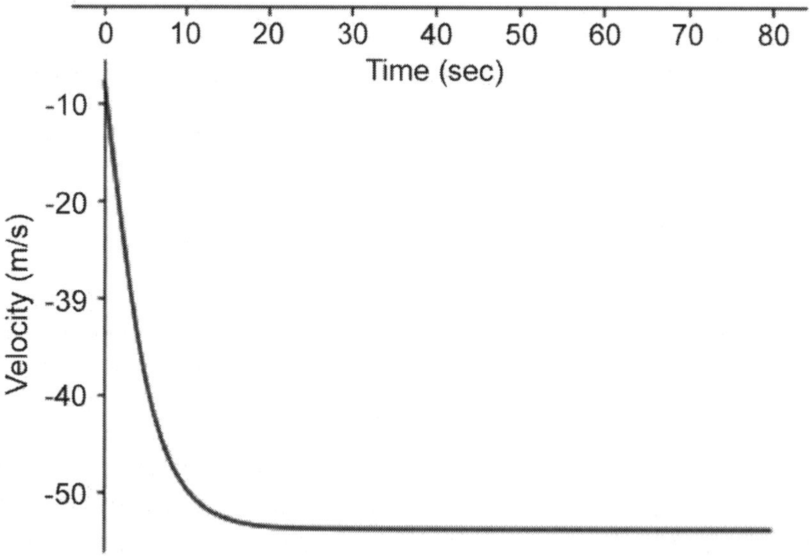

Figure 12.38: The velocity of a body in free fall with air resistance

> **NOTE**
>
> To access the source code for this specific section, please refer to https://packt.live/2NNmWBM.
>
> You can also run this example online at https://packt.live/2BUuXCp.

Now, let's complete an activity to test what we have learned in this chapter.

ACTIVITY 12.01: FINDING THE VELOCITY AND LOCATION OF A PARTICLE

The velocity vector of a particle moving in the *x-y* plane has the following components:

$$\frac{dx}{dt} = 1 + 3\sin\left(t^2\right) \text{ and } \frac{dy}{dt} = 15\cos\left(t^2\right)\sin\left(e^t\right)$$

Figure 12.39: Differential equation for the velocity vector of a particle

Find all the times (and coordinates) at which the line tangent to the curve is horizontal, and then find the speed of the particle at *t = 1*.

Perform the following steps to complete this activity:

1. Write functions for *dx/dt* and *dy/dt*.
2. Loop through the output to find where the derivative is 0 by finding the values where the derivative goes from positive to negative or vice versa. Then, use binary search to find more accurate approximations.
3. Create a `position` function and take incremental steps of time using loops, changing the position of the particle according to the derivatives (the *change in position*) given previously. The function should stop at the desired elapsed time and print out the *x-y* coordinates.
4. Plug the times you found in *step 2* into the `position` function to find the *x-y* coordinates of the particle when the derivative is 0.
5. You're asked for the speed of the particle at time *t = 1*. Find the vertical and horizontal components of the particle's velocity using the differential equations you're given, and also find the hypotenuse of the right triangle created with those components acting as the legs.

> **NOTE**
>
> The solution for this activity can be found on page 702.

SUMMARY

Calculus is a very powerful set of tools for modeling real situations, from the transfer of heat to the motion of planets. It has enabled us to calculate the rate of change of a function in an instant and the area under complicated curves (tasks that seemed impossible using only the tools of algebra and geometry). In this chapter, we've been able to deal with the rate of change of a value (the derivative) as a value in itself, and we've calculated some very accurate results using Python loops and functions. Modeling situations that lead to differential equations, such as the paths of projectiles, was what drove the development of the first electronic computers.

Math classes may still emphasize algebraic solutions to equations, even differential equations, but as we've seen in this chapter, using a computer is a straightforward way to model a real-life situation such as a predator pursuing its prey. We changed variables such as the amount of money in an investment, the amount of salt in a mixture, and the direction a predator was facing thousands of times, recalculating amounts and distances every step, and got very accurate results. Python was the perfect tool to set some starting conditions and let the program run until a projectile hit the ground or reached a terminal velocity. Python also helped us avoid laborious algebraic manipulations and let us *brute force* an answer by creating a simple model of a falling object or a predator pursuing its prey. This was *simple* because we didn't have to repeat the calculations thousands of times—the computer did. Plus, these numerical methods are already used on differential equations that have no simple algebraic solution, and they even work on those equations that do. Hopefully, this chapter has proven the power of using a computer to model and analyze complicated real-world situations.

Now, you've learned how to build on Python's loops, variables, conditionals, functions, and lists to solve complicated problems in statistics, probability, and calculus. You've also learned how to time the execution of your code and plot your output. You've used Python's state-of-the-art numerical package, **`numpy`**, to speed up calculations and manipulate arrays for a host of applications. You've also seen Python programming being applied to every math topic under the sun, and now you'll be able to apply it to any real-life situations you encounter in the future.

APPENDIX

CHAPTER 01: FUNDAMENTALS OF PYTHON

ACTIVITY 1.01: BUILDING A SUDOKU SOLVER

Solution

1. First, we define the **Solver** class to store its input puzzle in its **cells** attribute, as follows:

```
from copy import deepcopy
class Solver:
    def __init__(self, input_path):
        # Read in the input file and initialize the puzzle
        with open(input_path, 'r') as f:
            lines = f.readlines()
        self.cells = [list(map(int, line.split(','))) \
                      for line in lines]
```

2. The helper method that prints out the puzzle in a nice format can loop through the individual cells in the puzzle while inserting the separating characters **'-'** and **'|'** at the appropriate places:

```
    # Print out the initial puzzle or solution in a nice format.
    def display_cell(self):
        print('-' * 23)
        for i in range(9):
            for j in range(9):
                print(self.cells[i][j], end=' ')
                if j % 3 == 2:
                    print('|', end=' ')
            print()
            if i % 3 == 2:
                print('-' * 23)
        print()
```

3. The **get_presence()** method can maintain three separate lists of Boolean variables for the presence of numbers between 1 and 9 in individual rows, columns, and quadrants. These Boolean variables should all be initialized as **False** at the beginning, but we can loop through all the cells in the input and change their values to **True** as appropriate:

```
        """
        True/False for whether a number is present in a row,
```

```
    column, or quadrant.
    """
    def get_presence(cells):
        present_in_row = [{num: False for num in range(1, 10)}
                          for _ in range(9)]
        present_in_col = [{num: False for num in range(1, 10)}
                          for _ in range(9)]
        present_in_quad = [{num: False for num in range(1, 10)}
                           for _ in range(9)]

        for row_id in range(9):
            for col_id in range(9):
                temp_val = cells[row_id][col_id]
                """
                If a cell is not empty, update the corresponding
                row, column, and quadrant.
                """
                if temp_val > 0:
                    present_in_row[row_id][temp_val] = True
                    present_in_col[col_id][temp_val] = True
                    present_in_quad[row_id // 3 * 3 \
                                    + col_id // 3]\
                                    [temp_val] = True
        return present_in_row, present_in_col, present_in_quad
```

It can be tricky to index the quadrants. The preceding code uses the formula **`row_id // 3 * 3 + col_id // 3`**, which effectively results in the count where the top-left quadrant is indexed at **0**, the top-center **1**, the top-right **2**, the middle-left **3**, ..., the bottom-center **7**, and the bottom-right **8**.

4. The **`get_possible_values()`** method can call **`get_presence()`** and generate the corresponding lists of possible values for the remaining empty cells:

```
    # A dictionary for empty locations and their possible values.
    def get_possible_values(cells):
        present_in_row, present_in_col, \
        present_in_quad = get_presence(cells)
        possible_values = {}
        for row_id in range(9):
            for col_id in range(9):
                temp_val = cells[row_id][col_id]
```

```
            if temp_val == 0:
                possible_values[(row_id, col_id)] = []
                """
                If a number is not present in the same row,
                column, or quadrant as an empty cell, add it
                to the list of possible values of that cell.
                """
                for num in range(1, 10):
                    if (not present_in_row[row_id][num]) and\
                       (not present_in_col[col_id][num]) and\
                       (not present_in_quad[row_id // 3 * 3 \
                       + col_id // 3][num]):
                        possible_values[(row_id, col_id)]\
                        .append(num)
    return possible_values
```

5. The **simple_update()** method can be implemented in a fairly straightforward manner, in which we can have a flag variable (called **update_again** here) to indicate whether we would need to call the method again before returning:

```
# Fill in empty cells that have only one possible value.
def simple_update(cells):
    update_again = False
    possible_values = get_possible_values(cells)
    for row_id, col_id in possible_values:
        if len(possible_values[(row_id, col_id)]) == 1:
            update_again = True
            cells[row_id][col_id] = possible_values[\
                                    (row_id, col_id)][0]
    """
    Recursively update with potentially new possible values.
    """
    if update_again:
        cells = simple_update(cells)
    return cells
```

6. The **recur_solve()** method contains multiple instructional components, but the logical flow is simple to implement:

```
# Recursively solve the puzzle
def recur_solve(cells):
    cells = simple_update(cells)
```

```
            possible_values = get_possible_values(cells)
            if len(possible_values) == 0:
                return cells  # return when all cells are filled

            # Find the empty cell with fewest possible values.
            fewest_num_values = 10
            for row_id, col_id in possible_values:
                if len(possible_values[(row_id, col_id)]) == 0:
                    return False  # return if an empty is invalid
                if len(possible_values[(row_id, col_id)]) \
                   < fewest_num_values:
                    fewest_num_values = len(possible_values[\
                                            (row_id, col_id)])
                    target_location = (row_id, col_id)

            for value in possible_values[target_location]:
                dup_cells = deepcopy(cells)
                dup_cells[target_location[0]]\
                         [target_location[1]] = value
                potential_sol = recur_solve(dup_cells)

                # Return immediately when a valid solution is found.
                if potential_sol:
                    return potential_sol
            return False  # return if no valid solution is found
```

7. Finally, we place all of these methods inside the **`solve()`** method, which calls **`recur_solve()`** on **`self.cells`**:

```
    # Functions to find a solution.
    def solve(self):
        def get_presence(cells):
            ...

        def get_possible_values(cells):
            ...

        def simple_update(cells):
            ...
```

```
        def recur_solve(cells):
            ...
        print('Initial puzzle:')
        self.display_cell()
        final_solution = recur_solve(self.cells)
        if final_solution is False:
            print('A solution cannot be found.')
        else:
            self.cells = final_solution
            print('Final solution:')
            self.display_cell()
```

8. Print out the returned solution as follows:

```
solver = Solver('sudoku_input/sudoku_input_2.txt')
solver.solve()
```

A section of the output is as follows:

```
Initial puzzle:
-----------------------
0 0 3 | 0 2 0 | 6 0 0 |
9 0 0 | 3 0 5 | 0 0 1 |
0 0 1 | 8 0 6 | 4 0 0 |
-----------------------
0 0 8 | 1 0 2 | 9 0 0 |
7 0 0 | 0 0 0 | 0 0 8 |
0 0 6 | 7 0 8 | 2 0 0 |
-----------------------
0 0 2 | 6 0 9 | 5 0 0 |
8 0 0 | 2 0 3 | 0 0 9 |
0 0 5 | 0 1 0 | 3 0 0 |
-----------------------
```

NOTE

To access the source code and the final output for this specific section, please refer to https://packt.live/3dWRsnE.

You can also run this example online at https://packt.live/2BBKreC.

CHAPTER 02: PYTHON'S MAIN TOOLS FOR STATISTICS

ACTIVITY 2.01: ANALYZING THE COMMUNITIES AND CRIME DATASET

Solution:

1. Once the dataset has been downloaded, the libraries can be imported, and pandas can be used to read in the dataset in a new Jupyter notebook, as follows:

```
import pandas as pd
import numpy as np

import matplotlib.pyplot as plt

df = pd.read_csv('CommViolPredUnnormalizedData.txt')
df.head()
```

We are also printing out the first five rows of the dataset, which should be as follows:

```
In [1]: import pandas as pd
        import numpy as np

        import matplotlib.pyplot as plt

In [2]: df = pd.read_csv('CommViolPredUnnormalizedData.txt')
        df.head()

Out[2]:
```

	communityname	state	countyCode	communityCode	fold	population	householdsize	ra
0	BerkeleyHeightstownship	NJ	39	5320	1	11980	3.10	
1	Marpletownship	PA	45	47616	1	23123	2.82	
2	Tigardcity	OR	?	?	1	29344	2.43	
3	Gloversvillecity	NY	35	29443	1	16656	2.40	
4	Bemidjicity	MN	7	5068	1	11245	2.76	

5 rows × 147 columns

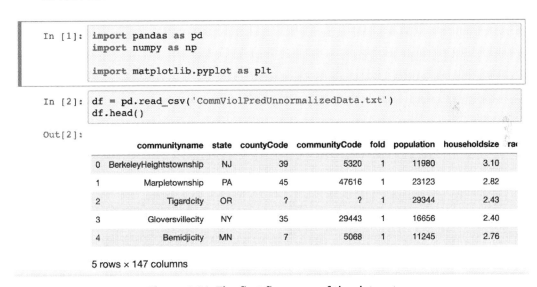

Figure 2.21: The first five rows of the dataset

2. To print out the column names, we can simply iterate through **`df.columns`** in a **`for`** loop, like so:

```
for column in df.columns:
    print(column)
```

3. The total number of columns in the dataset can be computed using the **len()** function in Python:

```
print(len(df.columns))
```

4. To replace the special character **'?'** with **np.nan** objects, we can use the **replace()** method:

```
df = df.replace('?', np.nan)
```

5. To print out the list of columns in our dataset and their respective numbers of missing values, we use a combination of the **isnull().sum()** methods:

```
df.isnull().sum()
```

The preceding code should produce the following output:

```
communityname          0
state                  0
countyCode          1221
communityCode       1224
fold                   0
                    ...
autoTheftPerPop        3
arsons                91
arsonsPerPop          91
ViolentCrimesPerPop  221
nonViolPerPop         97
Length: 147, dtype: int64
```

6. The numbers of missing values of the two specified columns can be accessed and displayed as follows:

```
print(df.isnull().sum()['NumStreet'])
print(df.isnull().sum()['PolicPerPop'])
```

You should obtain **0** and **1872** as the output.

7. To compute and visualize the counts of unique values in **'state'** using a bar plot (as well as to adjust the size of the figure), the following code can be used:

```
state_count = df['state'].value_counts()

f, ax = plt.subplots(figsize=(15, 10))
state_count.plot.bar()
plt.show()
```

This should produce the following graph:

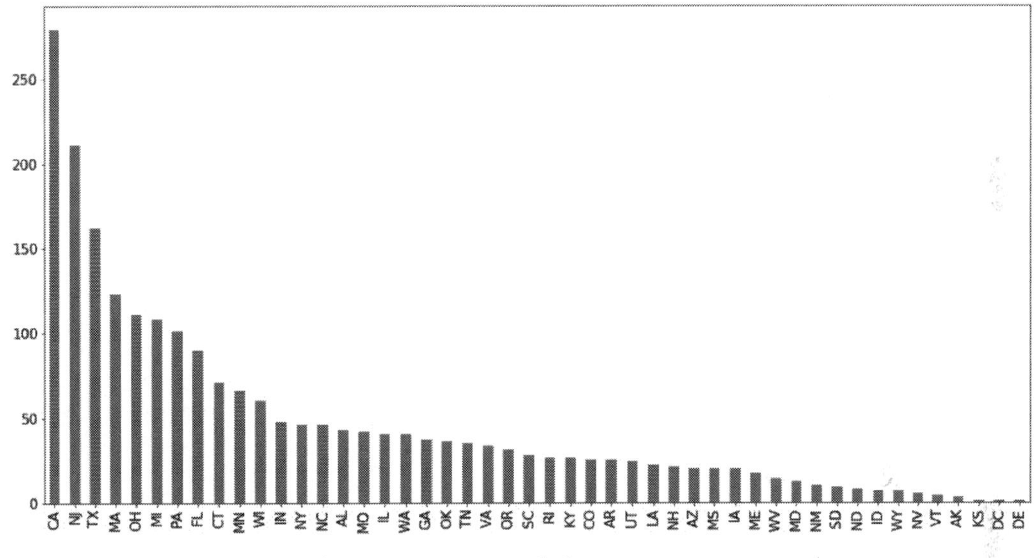

Figure 2.22: Bar graph for state counts

8. To compute and visualize the same information using a pie chart, the following code can be used:

```
f, ax = plt.subplots(figsize=(15, 10))

state_count.plot.pie()
plt.show()
```

The following visualization will be generated:

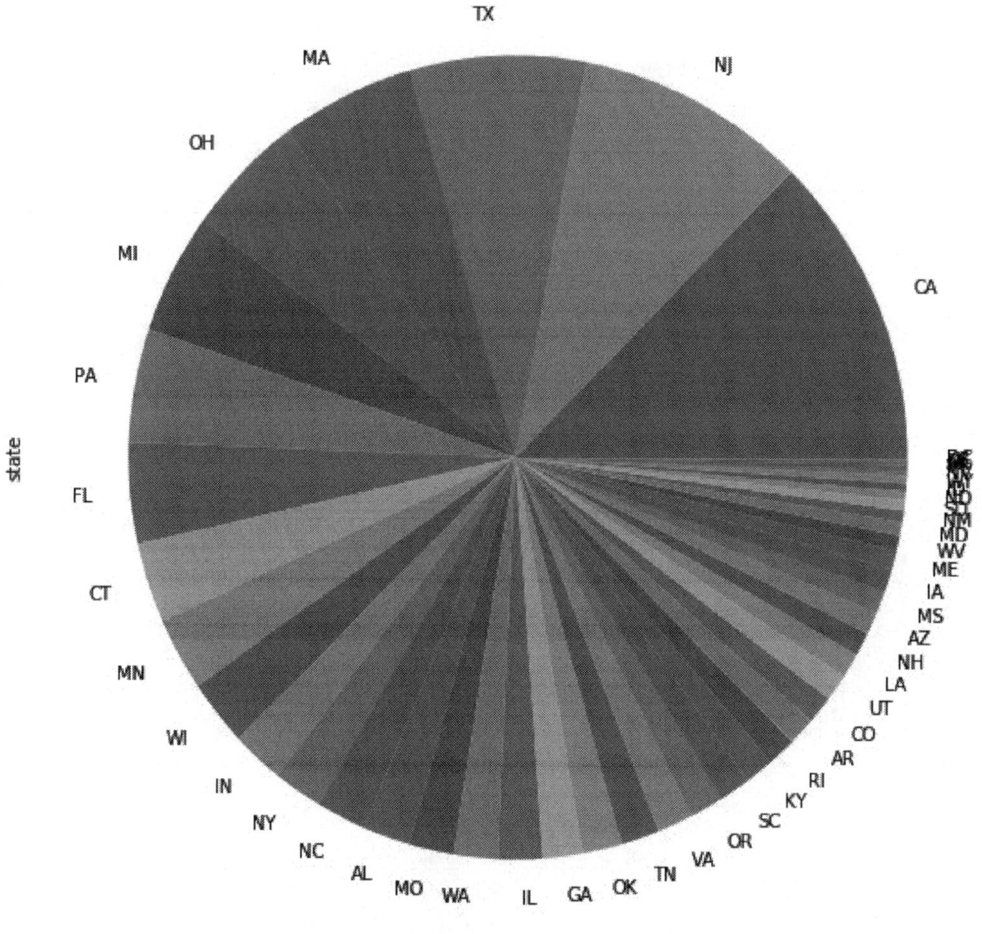

Figure 2.23: Pie chart for state counts

9. To compute and visualize the population distribution using a histogram, the following code can be used:

```
f, ax = plt.subplots(figsize=(15, 10))

df['population'].hist(bins=200)
plt.show()
```

This should produce the following graph:

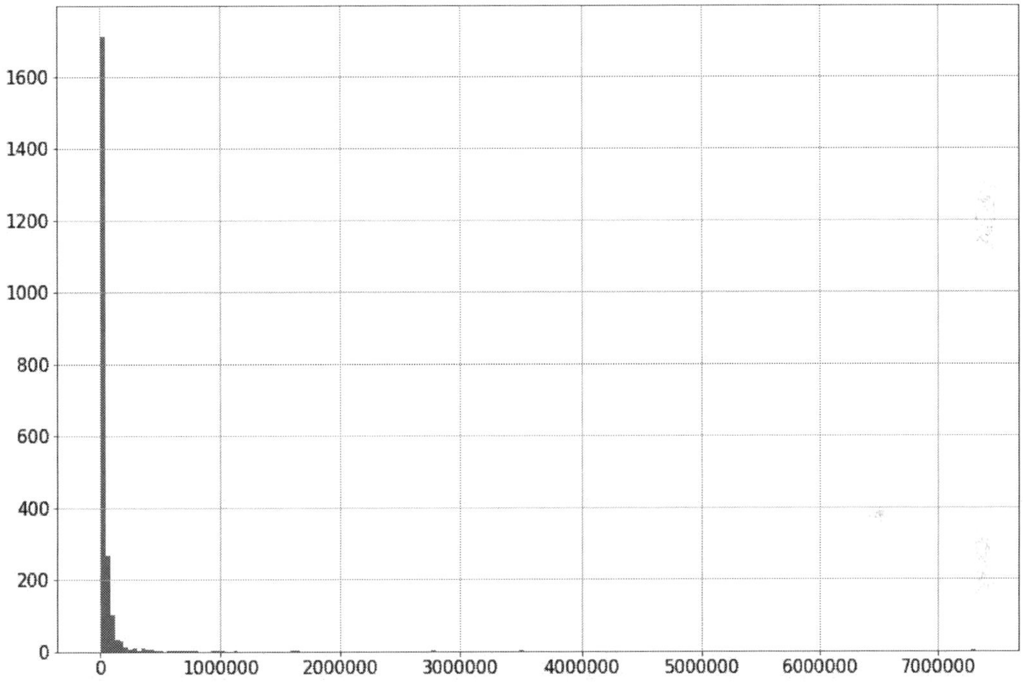

Figure 2.24: Histogram for population distribution

10. To compute and visualize the household size distribution using a histogram, the following code can be used:

```
f, ax = plt.subplots(figsize=(15, 10))

df['householdsize'].hist(bins=200)
plt.show()
```

This should produce the following graph:

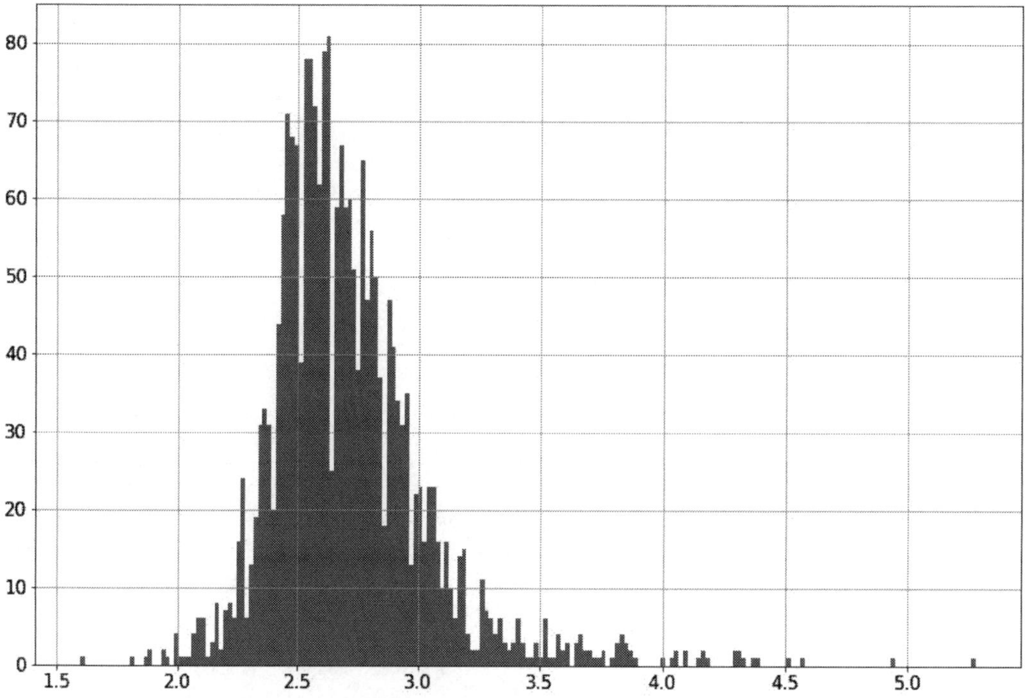

Figure 2.25: Histogram for household size distribution

> **NOTE**
>
> To access the source code for this specific section, please refer to https://packt.live/2BB5BJT.
>
> You can also run this example online at https://packt.live/38nbma9.

Chapter 03: Python's Statistical Toolbox

Activity 3.01: Revisiting the Communities and Crimes Dataset

Solution

1. The libraries can be imported, and pandas can be used to read in the dataset as follows:

```
import pandas as pd
import numpy as np

import matplotlib.pyplot as plt
import seaborn as sns

df = pd.read_csv('CommViolPredUnnormalizedData.txt')
df.head()
```

Your output should be the following:

```
In [2]: df = pd.read_csv('CommViolPredUnnormalizedData.txt')
        df.head()
Out[2]:
```

	communityname	state	countyCode	communityCode	fold	population	householdsize
0	BerkeleyHeightstownship	NJ	39	5320	1	11980	3.10
1	Marpletownship	PA	45	47616	1	23123	2.82
2	Tigardcity	OR	?	?	1	29344	2.43
3	Gloversvillecity	NY	35	29443	1	16656	2.40
4	Bemidjicity	MN	7	5068	1	11245	2.76

5 rows × 147 columns

Figure 3.29: The first five rows of the dataset

2. To replace the special character with the **np.nan** object, we can use the following code:

```
df = df.replace('?', np.nan)
```

3. To compute the actual count for the different age groups, we can simply use the expression **df['population'] * df['agePct...']**, which computes the count in a vectorized way:

```
age_groups = ['12t21', '12t29', '16t24', '65up']

for group in age_groups:
    df['ageCnt' + group] = (df['population'] * \
                            df['agePct' + group]).astype(int)

df[['population'] \
  + ['agePct' + group for group in age_groups] \
  + ['ageCnt' + group for group in age_groups]].head()
```

Note that we are rounding the final answers to integers using **astype(int)**. The first five rows of these newly created columns should look like the following:

```
In [4]: age_groups = ['12t21', '12t29', '16t24', '65up']

        for group in age_groups:
            df['ageCnt' + group] = (df['population'] * df['agePct' + group]).astype(int)

        df[['population'] + ['agePct' + group for group in age_groups] + ['ageCnt' + group for group in
```

Out[4]:

	population	agePct12t21	agePct12t29	agePct16t24	agePct65up	ageCnt12t21	ageCnt12t29	ageCnt16t24	ageCnt65up
0	11980	12.47	21.44	10.93	11.33	149390	256851	130941	135733
1	23123	11.01	21.30	10.48	17.18	254584	492519	242329	397253
2	29344	11.36	25.88	11.01	10.28	333347	759422	323077	301656
3	16656	12.55	25.20	12.19	17.57	209032	419731	203036	292645
4	11245	24.46	40.53	28.69	12.65	275052	455759	322619	142249

Figure 3.30: Actual count of different age groups

4. The expression **df.groupby('state')** gives us a **GroupBy** object that aggregates our dataset into different groups, each corresponding to a unique value in the **'state'** column. Then we can call **sum()** on the object and inspect the columns in question:

```
group_state_df = df.groupby('state')
group_state_df.sum()[['ageCnt' + group for group in age_groups]]
```

This should print out the count of the different age groups in each state. The first five columns of this output should be the following:

```
In [5]: group_state_df = df.groupby('state')
        group_state_df.sum()[['ageCnt' + group for group in age_groups]]
```

Out[5]:

state	ageCnt12t21	ageCnt12t29	ageCnt16t24	ageCnt65up
AK	3971927	8302160	3835631	1059150
AL	26531311	48598259	25509908	20155405
AR	12457357	23201471	11819576	10139231
AZ	37010700	74073284	36542705	24874683
CA	313751289	655608220	320917351	205368238

Figure 3.31: Count of different age groups in each state

5. Using the **`df.describe()`** method, you can obtain the following output:

```
In [7]: df.describe()
```

Out[7]:

	fold	population	householdsize	racepctblack	racePctWhite	racePctAsian	racePctHisp	agePct12t21	agePct1
count	2215.000000	2.215000e+03	2215.000000	2215.000000	2215.000000	2215.000000	2215.000000	2215.000000	2215.00
mean	5.494357	5.311798e+04	2.707327	9.335102	83.979819	2.670203	7.950176	14.445837	27.64
std	2.872924	2.046203e+05	0.334120	14.247156	16.419080	4.473843	14.589832	4.518623	6.18
min	1.000000	1.000500e+04	1.600000	0.000000	2.680000	0.030000	0.120000	4.580000	9.38
25%	3.000000	1.436600e+04	2.500000	0.860000	76.320000	0.620000	0.930000	12.250000	24.41
50%	5.000000	2.279200e+04	2.660000	2.870000	90.350000	1.230000	2.180000	13.620000	26.78
75%	8.000000	4.302400e+04	2.850000	11.145000	96.225000	2.670000	7.810000	15.360000	29.20
max	10.000000	7.322564e+06	5.280000	96.670000	99.630000	57.460000	95.290000	54.400000	70.51

8 rows × 108 columns

Figure 3.32: Description of the dataset

6. The boxplots visualizing the count of various crimes can be generated as follows:

```
crime_df = df[['burglPerPop','larcPerPop',\
               'autoTheftPerPop', 'arsonsPerPop',\
               'nonViolPerPop']]

f, ax = plt.subplots(figsize=(13, 10))
sns.boxplot(data=crime_df)
plt.show()
```

This should produce the following graph:

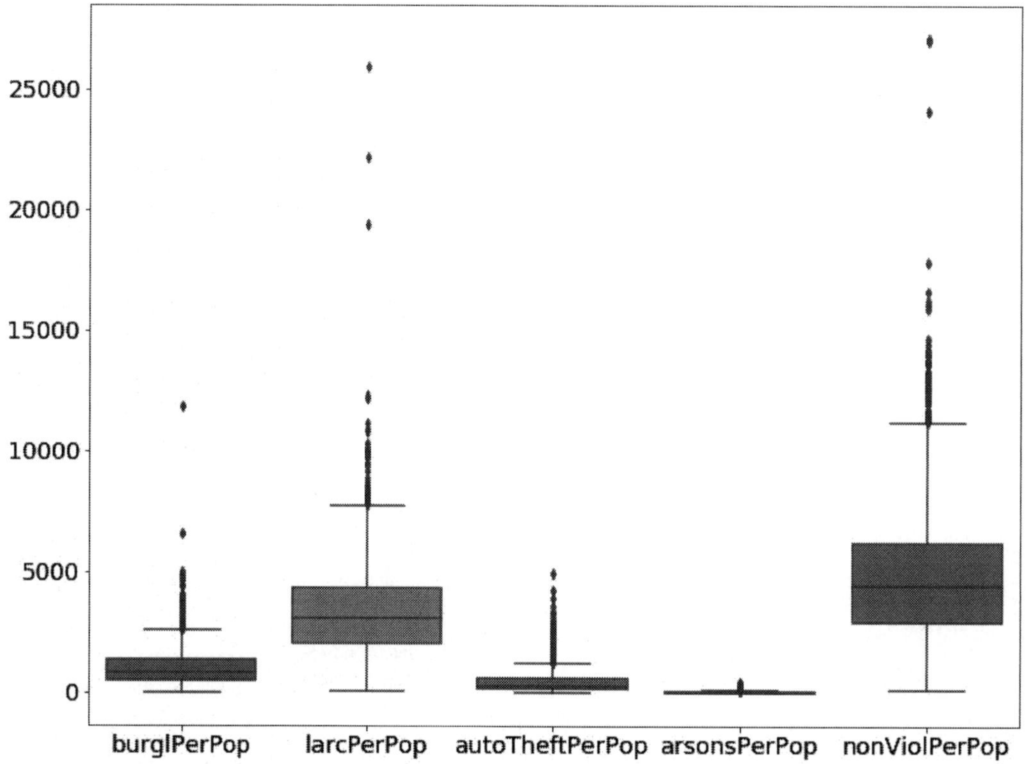

Figure 3.33: Boxplots of various crime counts

7. From the graph, we see that non-violent crime is the most common out of the five, while arson is the least common.

8. A heatmap for the correlation matrix that corresponds to the given columns can be used to visualize the information that was asked for:

```
feature_columns = ['PctPopUnderPov', 'PctLess9thGrade', \
                   'PctUnemployed', 'ViolentCrimesPerPop', \
                   'nonViolPerPop']

filtered_df = df[feature_columns]

f, ax = plt.subplots(figsize=(13, 10))
sns.heatmap(filtered_df.dropna().astype(float).corr(), \
                                 center=0, annot=True)
```

```
bottom, top = ax.get_ylim()
ax.set_ylim(bottom + 0.5, top - 0.5)

plt.show()
```

This should produce the following heatmap:

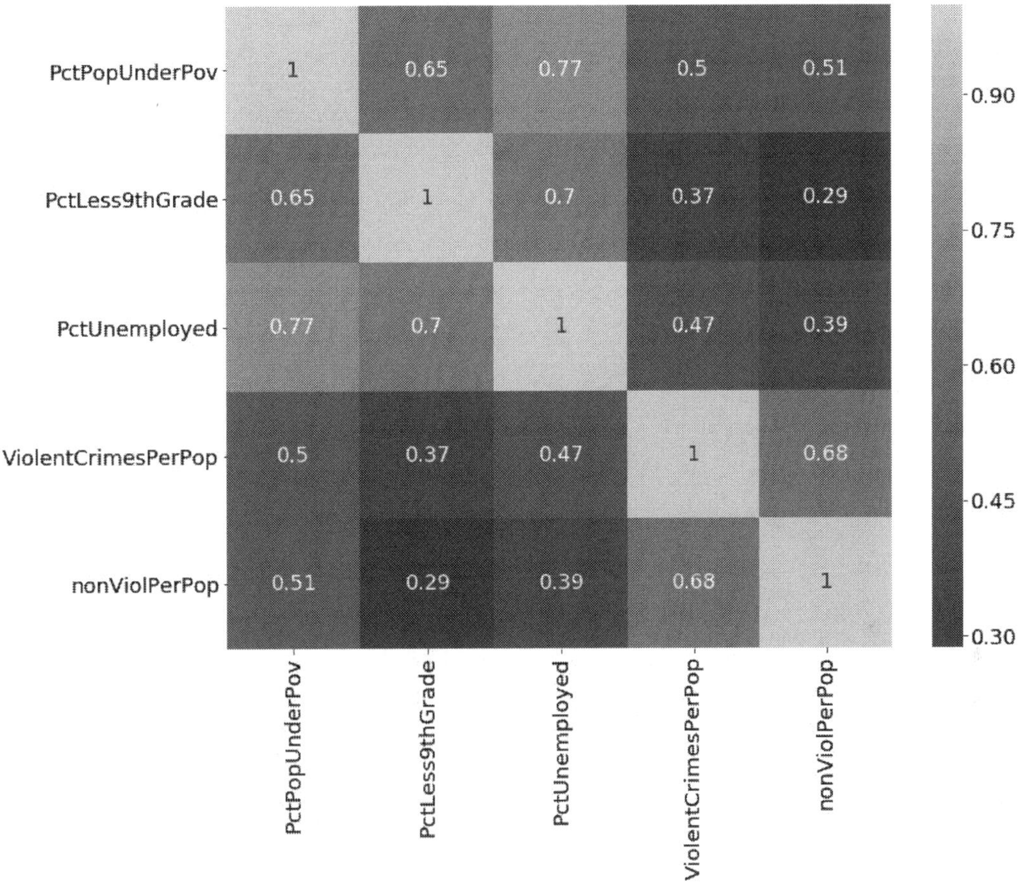

Figure 3.34: Heatmap for various population features

From the graph, we see that the percentage of the population under the poverty level and the percentage of unemployed are highly correlated (`0.77` being the correlation coefficient). This is an understandable yet telling insight into how various crime-related factors are connected to each other.

> **NOTE**
>
> To access the source code for this specific section, please refer to https://packt.live/3f8taZn.
>
> You can also run this example online at https://packt.live/3ikxjeF.

CHAPTER 04: FUNCTIONS AND ALGEBRA WITH PYTHON

ACTIVITY 4.01: MULTI-VARIABLE BREAK-EVEN ANALYSIS

Solution:

1. Let *x* be the number of burgers that the restaurant produces each month and *y* be the price of each burger. Then, the monthly revenue will be *xy*, the cost will be *6.56x + 1312.13*, and finally, the total profit will be the difference between the two: *xy - 6.56x - 1312.13*.

2. To break even, the number of burgers produced, *x*, must be equal to the demand, which gives us the equation: *x = 4000/y*. Furthermore, the total profit should be zero, which leads to *xy - 6.56x = 1312.13*.

   Overall, we have the following system of equations:

$$\begin{cases} xy - 6.56x = 1312.13 \\ x = \dfrac{4000}{y} \end{cases}$$

Figure 4.48: System of equations

3. From the first equation, we can solve for *x = 409.73628*. Plugging this into the second equation, we can solve for *y = 9.76237691*.

   To solve this system in Python, we first declare our variables and constants:

```
COST_PER_BURGER = 6.56
FIXED_COST = 1312.13
AVG_TOWN_BUDGET = 4000

x = Symbol('x')  # number of burgers to be sold
y = Symbol('y')  # price of a burger
```

Then we can call the **solve()** function from SymPy on the corresponding list of functions:

```
solve([x * (y - COST_PER_BURGER) - FIXED_COST,\
       x * y - AVG_TOWN_BUDGET])
```

This code should produce the following output, which corresponds to the actual solution of the system:

```
[{x: 409.736280487805, y: 9.76237690066856}]
```

4. The most challenging point about this function is that if the number of burgers produced by the restaurant, *x*, exceeds the demand, *4000/y*, their revenue remains at *4000*. However, if the number of burgers is low, then the revenue is *xy*. Our function therefore needs to have a condition to check for this logic:

```
def get_profit(x, y):
    demand = AVG_TOWN_BUDGET / y
    if x > demand:
        return AVG_TOWN_BUDGET - x * COST_PER_BURGER \
                                   - FIXED_COST

    return x * (y - COST_PER_BURGER) - FIXED_COST
```

5. The following code generates the specified lists and the corresponding plot when the price of each burger is $9.76:

```
xs = [i for i in range(300, 501)]
profits_976 = [get_profit(x, 9.76) for x in xs]

plt.plot(xs, profits_976)
plt.axhline(0, c='k')

plt.xlabel('Number of burgers produced')
plt.ylabel('Profit')

plt.show()
```

The output should look like the following:

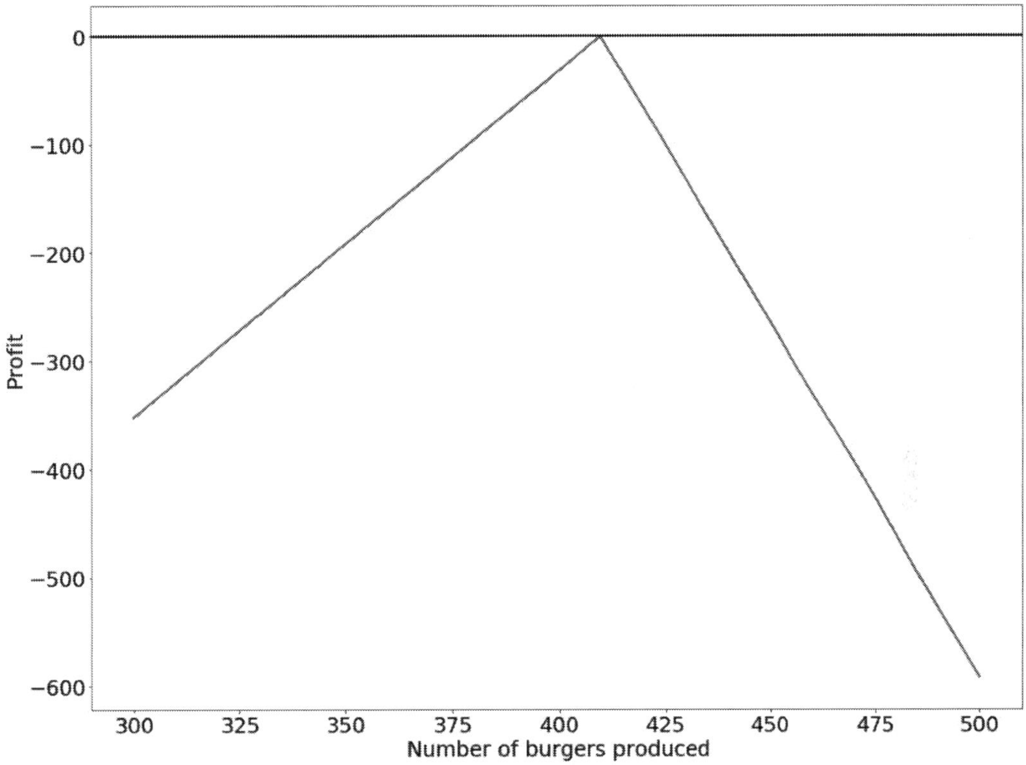

Figure 4.49: Break-even graph for a price of $9.76

The intersection of the upside-down V-shaped profit curve and the horizontal line at **0** denotes the break-even point in the analysis where the price of each burger is fixed at $9.76. The *x* coordinate of this intersection is somewhat above **400**, which roughly corresponds to the break-even solution in *step 3*, when *x* is approximately **410** and *y* is approximately 9.76.

6. The following code generates the specified lists and the corresponding plot when the price of each burger is $9.99:

```
xs = [i for i in range(300, 501)]
profits_999 = [get_profit(x, 9.99) for x in xs]

plt.plot(xs, profits_999)
plt.axhline(0, c='k')

plt.xlabel('Number of burgers produced')
```

```
plt.ylabel('Profit')

plt.show()
```

The output should look like the following:

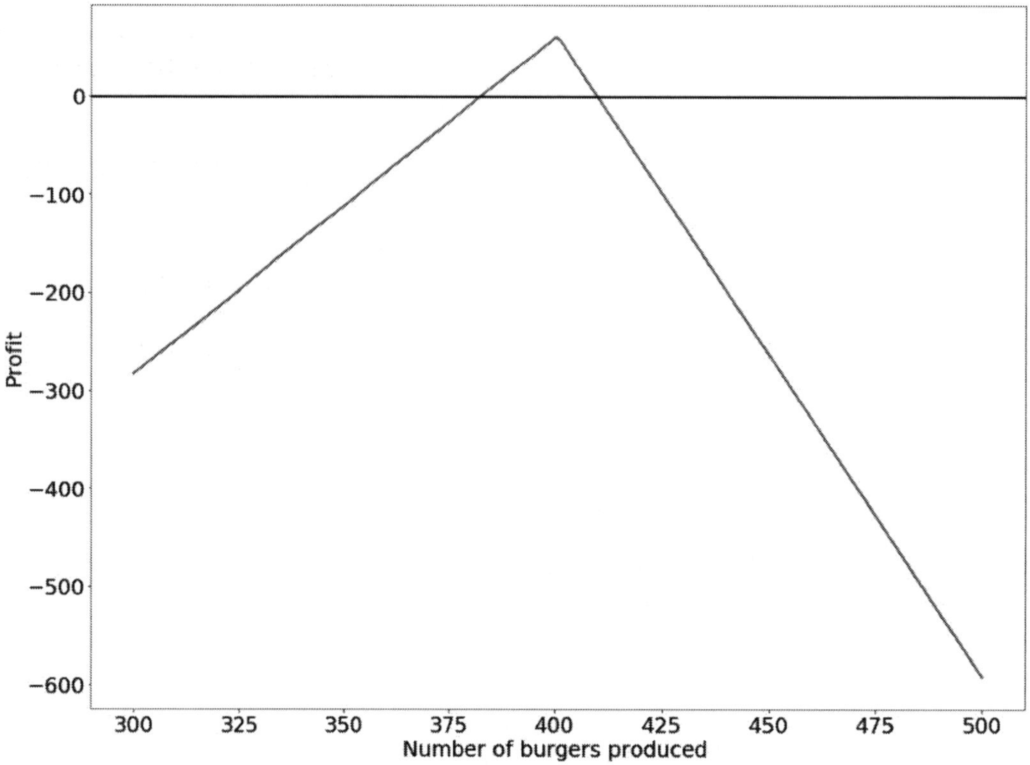

Figure 4.50: Break-even graph for a price of $9.99

Similarly, the two intersections of the profit curve and the horizontal line at **0** denote the break-even points in the analysis where the price of each burger is fixed at $9.99.

We see that as the number of burgers produced increases, the profit of the restaurant grows linearly. However, after this number meets demand and the profit curve peaks, the curve starts to decrease linearly. This is when the restaurant over-produces and increasing the number of products is no longer beneficial.

7. The following code generates the specified lists:

```
xs = [i for i in range(300, 501, 2)]
ys = np.linspace(5, 10, 100)

profits = [[get_profit(x, y) for y in ys] for x in xs]
```

`profits` is a two-dimensional list that is rather large in size, but the first few elements in that list should look like the following:

```
In [11]: xs = [i for i in range(300, 501, 2)]
         ys = np.linspace(5, 10, 100)

         profits = [[get_profit(x, y) for y in ys] for x in xs
         profits

Out[11]: [[-1780.13,
           -1764.9784848484849,
           -1749.8269696969696,
           -1734.6754545454546,
           -1719.5239393939391,
           -1704.3724242424241,
           -1689.2209090909091,
           -1674.0693939393939,
           -1658.9178787878789,
           -1643.7663636363636,
           -1628.6148484848484,
           -1613.4633333333334,
           -1598.3118181818181,
           -1583.160303030303,
           -1568.008787878788,
           -1552.8572727272726,
           -1537.7057575757576,
           -1522.5542424242426,
           -1507.4027272727271,
           -1492.2512121212121,
```

Figure 4.51: Two-dimensional list of profits

8. The specified heatmap can then be generated using the following code:

```
plt.imshow(profits)
plt.colorbar()

plt.xticks([0, 20, 40, 60, 80],\
           [5, 6, 7, 8, 9, 10])
plt.xlabel('Price for each burger')
plt.yticks([0, 20, 40, 60, 80],\
           [300, 350, 400, 450, 500])
plt.ylabel('Number of burgers produced')

plt.show()
```

The output should look like the following:

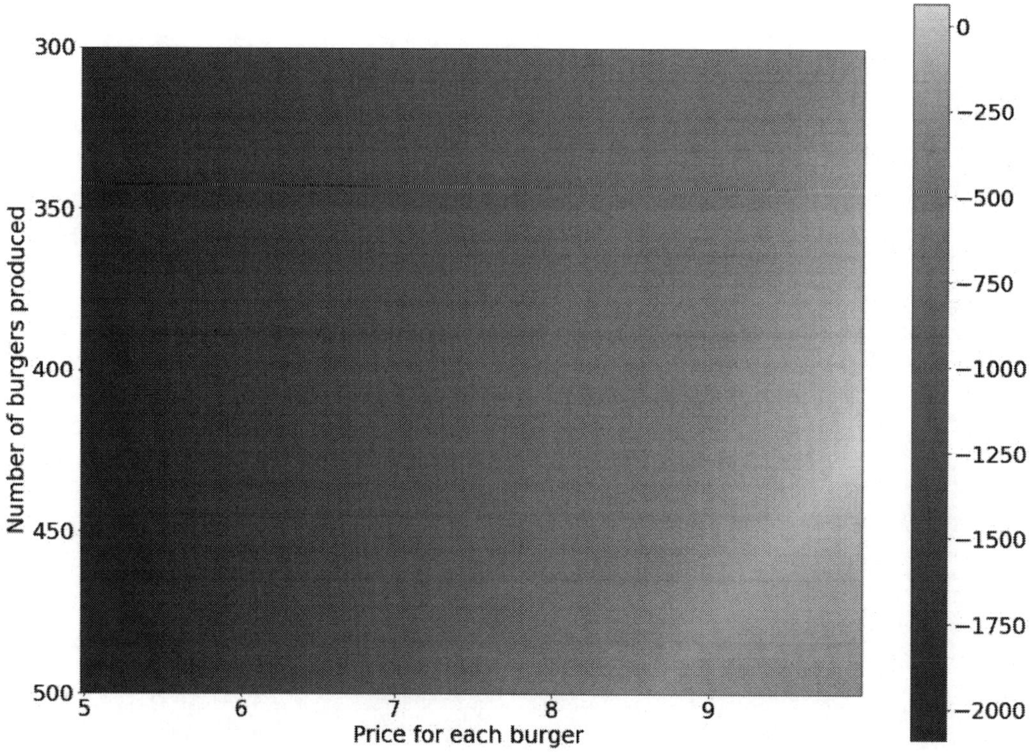

Figure 4.52: Heatmap of profit as a function of production and price

From the plot, we see that there are specific combinations of *x* and *y* that control the behavior of the profit of the restaurant.

For example, when the price of each burger is low (the left region of the map), the total profit is significantly lower than 0. As we move to the right of the plot, the brightest region represents the combinations of the two variables that will result in the highest profit.

> **NOTE**
>
> To access the source code for this specific section, please refer to https://packt.live/2C6dKWz.
>
> You can also run this example online at https://packt.live/2NTfEwG.

CHAPTER 05: MORE MATHEMATICS WITH PYTHON

ACTIVITY 5.01: CALCULATING YOUR RETIREMENT PLAN USING SERIES

Solution:

Perform the following steps to complete this activity:

1. First, we need to identify the input variables and note that the problem boils down to calculating the *n*-term of a geometric sequence with a common ratio (1 + interest) and scale factor for the annual salary.

   annual_salary and the percentage, *contrib*, of it is what we contribute toward our plan. **current_balance** is the money that we have at year 0 and should be added to the total amount. **annual_cap** is the maximum percentage that we can contribute; any input value beyond that should be equal to **contrib_cap**. **annual_salary_increase** tells us how much we expect our salary to increase by per year. **employer_match** gives us the percentage amount the employer contributes to the plan (typically, this is between 0.5 and 1). Lastly, the current age, the duration of the plan in years, the life expectancy in years, and any other fees that the plan might incur are input variables. The **per_month** Boolean variable determines whether the output will be printed as a per-year or per-month amount of the return.

2. Define the first function, **retirement_n**, to calculate the nth term of our sequence, which returns the contribution and employer's match as a comma-separated tuple:

```
def retirement_n(current_balance, annual_salary, \
                 annual_cap, n, contrib, \
                 annual_salary_increase, employer_match, \
                 match_cap, rate):
    '''
    return :: retirement amount at year n
    '''

    annual_salary_n = annual_salary*\
                      (1+annual_salary_increase)**n

    your_contrib = contrib*annual_salary_n
    your_contrib = min(your_contrib, annual_cap)
    employer_contrib = contrib*annual_salary_n*employer_match
    employer_contrib = min(employer_contrib,match_cap\
```

```
                            *annual_salary_n*employer_match)

    contrib_total = your_contrib + employer_contrib

    return your_contrib, employer_contrib,
        current_balance + contrib_total*(1+rate)**n
```

The input, as shown here, is the current balance and the annual salary in absolute values. We also define the contribution, the contribution cap (that is, the maximum value allowed), the increase of the annual salary, the employer match, and the rate of the return as relative values (floats between 0 and 1). The annual cap is meant to be read as an absolute value too.

3. Define the function that will sum up the individual amounts for each year and calculate the total value of our plan. This shall divide this number by the number of years over which the plan is to be used (payback duration) so that the per-year return of the plan is returned by the function. As inputs, it should read the current age, the duration of the plan, and the life expectancy (the duration of the payback is found by subtracting **`current_age + plan_years`** from **`life_expectancy`**):

```
def retirement_total(current_balance, annual_salary, \
    annual_cap=18000, contrib=0.05, \
    annual_salary_increase=0.02, employer_match=0.5, \
    match_cap=0.06, rate=0.03, current_age=35, \
    plan_years=35, life_expectancy=80, fees=0, \
    per_month=False):

    i = 0
    result = 0
    contrib_list = []; ematch_list = []; total_list = []

    while i <= plan_years:
        cn = retirement_n(current_balance=current_balance, \
              annual_salary=annual_salary, \
              annual_cap=annual_cap, n=i, \
              contrib=contrib, match_cap=match_cap, \
              annual_salary_increase=annual_salary_increase,\
              employer_match=employer_match, rate=rate)

        contrib_list.append(cn[0])
        ematch_list.append(cn[1])
```

```
        total_list.append(cn[2])

        result = result + cn[2]
        i+=1
```

The main operation of the preceding function is to set a loop (**while** iteration) where the previous function is called and the value of the plan is found at each year, *n* (we call it *cn* here for brevity). The result is the sum of the values of all the years and is stored in the **result** variable. We slice *cn (cn[0], cn[1], cn[2])* since the **retirement_n** function returns a tuple of three quantities. We also store the values of the contribution (employee), match (employee), and total in three individual lists. These will be returned from this function.

4. Lastly, subtract any fees that might need to be included and return the result:

```
    result = result - fees

    years_payback = life_expectancy - (current_age + plan_years)

    if per_month:
        months = 12
    else:
        months = 1
    result = result / (years_payback*months)
    print('You get back:',result)


    return result, contrib_list, ematch_list, total_list
```

5. Check our function and the output:

```
result, contrib, ematch, total = retirement_total(current_
balance=1000, plan_years=35,\
                     current_age=36, annual_salary=40000, \
                     per_month=True)
```

The output is as follows:

```
You get back: 3029.952393422356
```

6. Plot your findings. It is always good practice to plot what has been calculated since it helps you digest the main message. Also, the functions can be checked for potential errors:

```
from matplotlib import pyplot as plt

years = [i for i in range(len(total))]
plt.plot(years, total,'-o',color='b')

width=0.85
p1 = plt.bar(years, total, width=width)
p2 = plt.bar(years, contrib, width=width)
p3 = plt.bar(years, ematch, width=width)

plt.xlabel('Years')
plt.ylabel('Return')
plt.title('Retirement plan evolution')

plt.legend((p1[0], p2[0], p3[0]), ('Investment
returns','Contributions','Employer match'))
plt.show()
```

The plot will be displayed as follows:

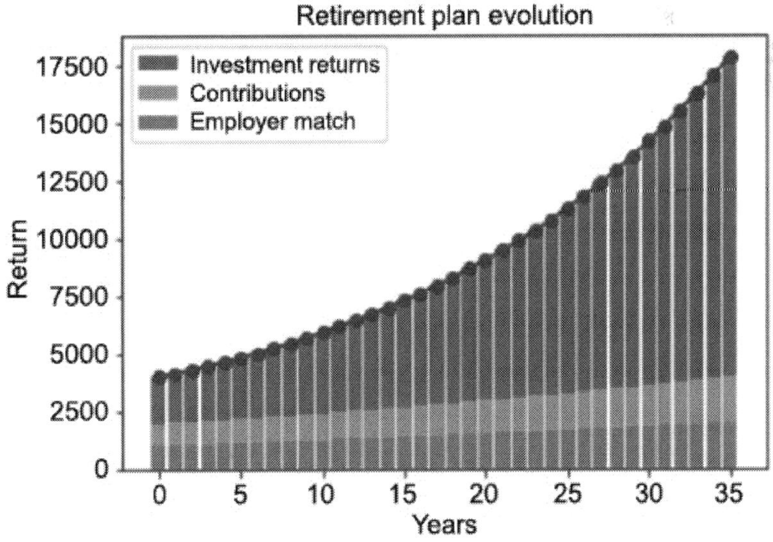

Figure 5.26: Retirement plan evolution plot

With that, we have created a Python program that calculates the per-month or per-year return of a retirement plan based on the current contributions and a set of other parameters. We have seen how our knowledge of sequences and series can be applied to a real-life scenario to yield results regarding financial and social interest.

> **NOTE**
>
> To access the source code for this specific section, please refer to https://packt.live/2YVgQWE.
>
> You can also run this example online at https://packt.live/38rOHts.

CHAPTER 06: MATRICES AND MARKOV CHAINS WITH PYTHON

ACTIVITY 6.01: BUILDING A TEXT PREDICTOR USING A MARKOV CHAIN

Solution:

There are a few ways to approach this problem, and it is worth mentioning that the approach we will be taking is perhaps the easiest way in which text prediction is used. In actual practice, text predictions are far more complicated and have many other factors that affect them, which we will briefly cover at the end of the activity.

1. We will be using the transcript of the speech given by Winston Churchill at the House of Commons after the soldiers of the Allied forces were rescued from Dunkirk during World War II. The speech by itself is worth a read and can be easily found online if you are interested.

> **NOTE**
>
> You can download the transcript from https://packt.live/38rZy6v.

2. This list is stored in a text file named **churchill.txt**. Read through that text file:

```
# Churchill's speech
churchill = open('churchill.txt').read()
keywords = churchill.split()
print(keywords)
```

We save this in a string object called **churchill** and then use the **split()** function in string to tokenize the text we have and store it in a list called **keywords**. The output of this will be as follows:

```
['The', 'position', 'of', 'the', 'B.', 'E.F', 'had',
 'now', 'become', 'critical', 'As', 'a', 'result', 'of',
 'a', 'most', 'skillfully', 'conducted', 'retreat',….]
```

3. Next, we iterate through the list and append the elements to a new list, which will store the keyword and the word following it:

```
keylist = []
for i in range(len(keywords)-1):
    keylist.append( (keywords[i], keywords[i+1]))
print(keylist)
```

This produces the following output:

```
[('The', 'position'), ('position', 'of'), ('of', 'the'),
 ('the', 'B.'), ('B.', 'E.F'), ('E.F', 'had'), ('had',
 'now'), ('now', 'become'), ('become', 'critical'),
 ('critical', 'As'),….]
```

> **NOTE**
>
> The list here is already initialized and is a list of tuples that can be converted to a list if you so desire, but it is not necessary.

4. After that, initialize a dictionary, **`word_dict`**. Once we have the dictionary, we iterate through the preceding **`keylist`** array and add words to the left in the preceding tuple as keys in the dictionary, and words on the right as values in that dictionary. If the word on the left is already added to the dictionary, we simply append the word on the right to the respective value in the dictionary:

```
# Create key-value pairs based on follow-up words
word_dict = {}
for beginning, following in keylist:
    if beginning in word_dict.keys():
        word_dict[beginning].append(following)
    else:
        word_dict[beginning] = [following]
print(word_dict)
```

This produces the following output:

```
{'magnetic': ['mines'], 'comparatively': ['slowly'],
 'four': ['hundred', 'thousand', 'days', 'or', 'to'],
 'saved': ['the', 'not'], 'forget': ['the'],….}
```

5. Having done this, we are now ready to build our predictor. First, we define a NumPy string, which takes a random word as a selection from the preceding set of keywords, and this will be our first word:

```
first_word = np.random.choice(keywords)
while first_word.islower():
    first_word = np.random.choice(keywords)
```

The second part of the preceding code is designed to make sure that we begin our sentence with a word that is capitalized. Without understanding in too much depth how natural language processing works, it is simple enough if we understand that the capitalized word used in the original transcript will pave the way to build a more comprehensive statement. We can also specify a specific word here instead of choosing it randomly as long as it is present in the corpus of keywords that we use.

6. Add this word to a new list:

```
word_chain = [first_word]
```

The first word here is generated randomly from the corpus of words present in the text file that we use, using the **random** function.

We will then append other words based on the dictionary we established previously.

7. Typically, we will be looking at the word we have freshly appended to **word_chain**, beginning with the first word in the list. Use this as the key in the dictionary we have created and follow it randomly with the list of values for that particular key from the dictionary we created previously:

```
WORDCOUNT = 40
for i in range(WORDCOUNT):
    word_chain.append(np.random.choice(word_dict[\
                                       word_chain[-1]]))
```

Note the use of the static variable, **WORDCOUNT**, that we have initialized, which specifies how long we want our sentence to be. If you are not in the habit of using nested Python functions extensively, simply start solving from the innermost function and use the value for the **outer** function.

8. Finally, we will define a string variable called **sentence**, which will be our output:

```
sentence = ' '.join(word_chain)
print(sentence)
```

> **NOTE**
>
> Since both the first words chosen here and the values in the dictionary are chosen randomly, we will get a different output every time.

Let's look at some of the outputs that we will generate:

```
Output 1:
British tanks and all the New World, with little or fail. We have
been reposed is so plainly marked the fighters which we should the
hard and fierce. Suddenly the sharpest form. But this Island home,
some articles of all fall

Output 2
That expansion had been effectively stamped out. Turning once again
there may be very convenient, if necessary to guard their knowledge
of the question of His son has given to surrender. He spurned the
coast to be held by the right

Output 3:
Air Force. Many are a great strength and four days of the British and
serious raids, could approach or at least two armored vehicles of
the government would observe that has cleared, the fine Belgian Army
compelled the retreating British Expeditionary

Output 4
30,000 men we can be defended Calais were to cast aside their native
land and torpedoes. It was a statement, I feared it was in adverse
weather, under its main French Army away; and thus kept open our
discussions free, without

Output 5
German bombers and to give had the House by views freely expressed
in their native land. I thought-and some articles of British and in
the rescue and more numerous Air Force, and brain of it be that Herr
Hitler has often
```

> **NOTE**
>
> To access the source code for this specific section, please refer to https://packt.live/3gr5uQ5.
>
> You can also run this example online at https://packt.live/31JeD2b.

CHAPTER 07: DOING BASIC STATISTICS WITH PYTHON

ACTIVITY 7.01: FINDING OUT HIGHLY RATED STRATEGY GAMES

Solution:

1. Load the **numpy** and **pandas** libraries as follows:

```
import pandas as pd
import numpy as np
```

2. Load the strategy games dataset (in the **dataset** folder of the chapter):

```
games = pd.read_csv('../data/appstore_games.csv')
```

> **NOTE**
>
> You can download the dataset from the GitHub repository at https://packt.live/2O1hv2B.

3. Perform all the transformations we did in the first section of the chapter. Change the names of the variables:

```
original_colums_dict = {x: x.lower().replace(' ','_') \
                        for x in games.columns}

games.rename(columns = original_colums_dict,\
             inplace = True)
```

4. Set the **'id'** column as **index**:

```
games.set_index(keys = 'id', inplace = True)
```

5. Drop the **'url'** and **'icon_url'** columns:

```
games.drop(columns = ['url', 'icon_url'], \
           inplace = True)
```

6. Change **'original_release_date'** and **'current_version_release_date'** to **datetime**:

```
games['original_release_date'] = pd.to_datetime\
                                  (games['original_release_date'])
games['current_version_release_date'] = \
pd.to_datetime(games['current_version_release_date'])
```

7. Eliminate the rows where **'average_user_rating'** is null from the DataFrame:

```
games = games.loc[games['average_user_rating'].notnull()]
```

8. Keep in the DataFrame only the rows where **'user_rating_count'** is equal or greater than **30**:

```
games = games.loc[games['user_rating_count'] >= 30]
```

9. Print the dimensions of the dataset. You must have a DataFrame with **4311** rows and **15** columns. You should get the following output:

```
(4311, 15)
games.shape
```

10. Impute the missing values in the **languages** column with the string **EN** to indicate that those games are available only in English:

```
games['languages'] = games['languages'].fillna('EN')
```

11. Create a variable called **free_game** that has the value of **free** if the game has a price of zero and **paid** if the price is above zero:

```
games['free_game'] = (games['price'] == 0).astype(int)
                     .map({0:'paid', 1:'free'})
```

12. Create a variable called **multilingual** that has the values of **monolingual** if the **language** column has only one language string, and **multilingual** if the **language** column has at least two language strings:

```
number_of_languages = games['languages'].str.split(',') \
                                        .apply(lambdax: len(x))
games['multilingual'] = number_of_languages == 1
games['multilingual'] = games['multilingual'].astype(int)
                        .map({0:'multilingual', 1:'monolingual'})
```

13. Create one variable that contains the four combinations from the two variables created in the previous step (**free-monolingual**, **free-multilingual**, **paid-monolingual**, and **paid-multilingual**):

```
games['price_language'] = games['free_game'] + '-' \
                        + games['multilingual']
```

14. Calculate how many observations we have of each type in the **price_language** variable. You should get the following output:

```
games['price_language'].value_counts()
```

The output will be as follows:

```
free-monolingual      2105
free-multilingual     1439
paid-monolingual      467
paid-multilingual     300
Name: price_language, dtype: int64
```

15. Use the **groupby** method on the **games** DataFrame, group by the newly created variable, then select the **average_user_rating** variables and calculate the descriptive statistics:

```
games.groupby('price_language')['average_user_rating']\
                                    .describe()
```

The output will be as follows:

price_language	count	mean	std	min	25%	50%	75%	max
free-monolingual	2105.0	4.129216	0.634426	1.5	4.0	4.5	4.5	5.0
free-multilingual	1439.0	4.227589	0.525904	1.5	4.0	4.5	4.5	5.0
paid-monolingual	467.0	4.064240	0.657693	1.5	3.5	4.0	4.5	5.0
paid-multilingual	300.0	4.251667	0.486435	2.5	4.0	4.5	4.5	5.0

Figure 7.35: Summary statistics grouped by the price_language categories

> **NOTE**
>
> To access the source code for this specific section, please refer to https://packt.live/2VBGtJZ.
>
> You can also run this example online at https://packt.live/2BwtJNK.

CHAPTER 08: FOUNDATIONAL PROBABILITY CONCEPTS AND THEIR APPLICATIONS

ACTIVITY 8.01: USING THE NORMAL DISTRIBUTION IN FINANCE

Solution:

Perform the following steps to complete this activity:

1. Using pandas, read the CSV file named **MSFT.csv** from the **data** folder:

```
import pandas as pd
import numpy as np
import scipy.stats as stats
import matplotlib.pyplot as plt
%matplotlib inline

msft = pd.read_csv('../data/MSFT.csv')
```

2. Optionally, rename the columns so they are easy to work with:

```
msft.rename(columns=lambda x: x.lower().replace(' ', '_'),\
            inplace=True)
```

3. Transform the **date** column into a proper **datetime** column:

```
msft['date'] = pd.to_datetime(msft['date'])
```

4. Set the **date** column as the index of the DataFrame:

```
msft.set_index('date', inplace = True)
```

5. In finance, the daily returns of a stock are defined as the percentage change of the daily closing price. Create the **returns** column in the MSFT DataFrame by calculating the percent change of the **adj close** column. Use the **pct_change** series pandas method to do so:

```
msft['returns'] = msft['adj_close'].pct_change()
```

6. Restrict the analysis period to the dates between **2014-01-01** and **2018-12-31** (inclusive):

```
start_date = '2014-01-01'
end_date = '2018-12-31'
msft = msft.loc[start_date: end_date]
```

7. Use a histogram to visualize the distribution of the returns column. Use 40 bins to do so. Does it look like a normal distribution?

```
msft['returns'].hist(ec='k', bins=40);
```

The output should look like this:

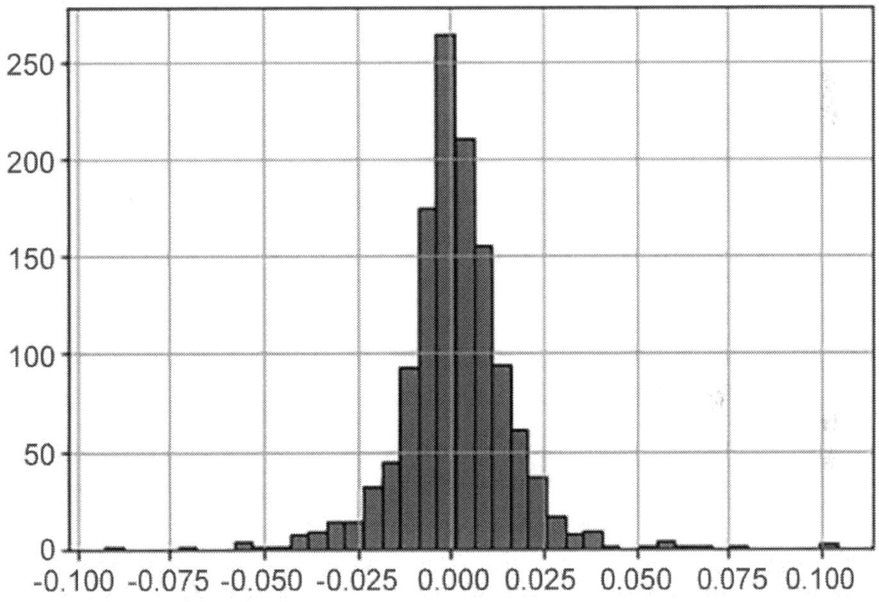

Figure 8.24: Histogram of returns of the MSFT stock

8. Calculate the descriptive statistics of the **returns** column:

```
msft['returns'].describe()
```

The output is as follows:

```
count    1258.000000
mean        0.000996
std         0.014591
min        -0.092534
25%        -0.005956
50%         0.000651
75%         0.007830
max         0.104522
Name: returns, dtype: float64
```

9. Create a random variable named **R_rv** that will represent *The daily returns of the MSFT stock*. Use the mean and standard deviation of the return column as the parameters for this distribution:

```
R_mean = msft['returns'].mean()
R_std = msft['returns'].std()

R_rv = stats.norm(loc = R_mean, scale = R_std)
```

10. Plot the distribution of **R_rv** and the histogram of the actual data. Use the **plt.hist()** function with the **density=True** parameter so both the real data and the theoretical distribution appear in the same scale:

```
fig, ax = plt.subplots()

ax.hist(x = msft['returns'], ec = 'k', \
        bins = 40, density = True,);

x_values = np.linspace(msft['returns'].min(), \
                       msft['returns'].max(), num=100)
densities = R_rv.pdf(x_values)
ax.plot(x_values, densities, color='r')
ax.grid();
```

The output is as follows:

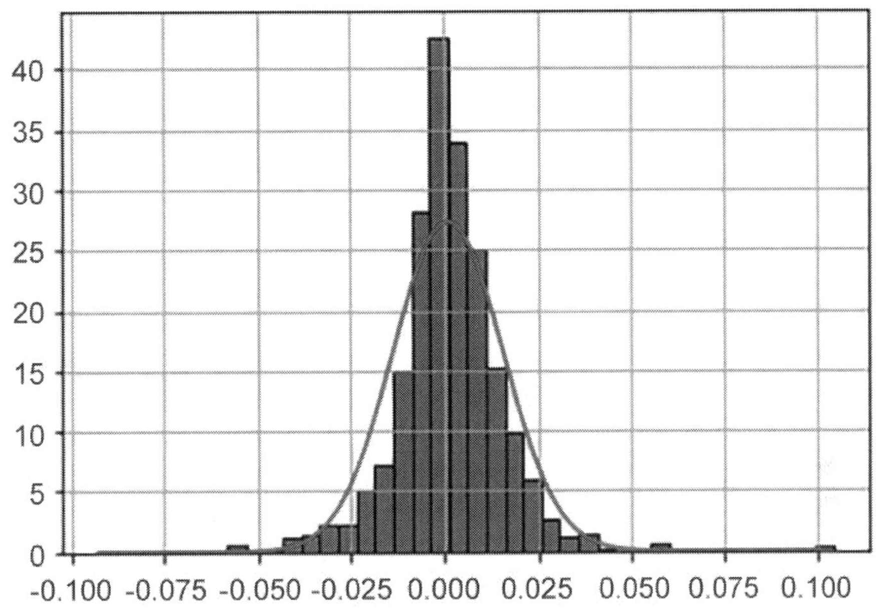

Figure 8.25: Histogram of returns of the MSFT stock

> **NOTE**
>
> To access the source code for this specific section, please refer to https://packt.live/2Zw18Ah.
>
> You can also run this example online at https://packt.live/31EmOg9.

After looking at the preceding plot, would you say that the normal distribution provides an accurate model for the daily returns of Microsoft stock?

No. The normal distribution does not provide a very accurate approximation regarding the distribution of stocks because the theoretical distribution does not completely follow the general shape of the histogram. Although the histogram is symmetric with respect to the center and "bell-shaped," we can clearly observe that the frequency of the values around zero is much higher than we would expect in a normal distribution, which is why we can observe that the bars are well above the red curve in the center of the plot. Also, we can observe many extreme values (little bars on the left- and right-hand sides) that are unlikely to be present in a normal distribution.

CHAPTER 09: INTERMEDIATE STATISTICS WITH PYTHON

ACTIVITY 9.01: STANDARDIZED TEST PERFORMANCE

Solution:

1. We are going to use the t-confidence interval function that we created earlier to calculate a 95% confidence interval. I have recreated it here for completeness:

```
# We will use the T-Confidence Interval Function
# we wrote earlier in the Chapter

print("For Math:")
t_confidence_interval(list(data['Math']),0.95)
print("For Reading:")
t_confidence_interval(list(data['Reading']),0.95)
print("For Science:")
t_confidence_interval(list(data['Science']),0.95)
```

The output for this code should be the following:

```
For Math:
Your 0.95 t confidence interval is (448.2561338314995,473.686980454214
8)
For Reading:
Your 0.95 t confidence interval is (449.1937943789569,472.800788478185
95)
For Science:
Your 0.95 t confidence interval is (453.8991748650865,476.979010849199
2)
```

It looks like we can say with 95% confidence that the mean score in math for a country is between **448.3** and **473.7**, between **449.2** and **472.8** for reading, and between **453.9** and **477.0** for science.

2. We are going to divide the dataset into two different datasets; one where there are more than **50** internet users per **100** people, and another where there are **50** or fewer internet users per **100** people:

```
# Using A Hypothesis Test, evaluate whether having
# widespread internet infrastructure could have an
# impact on scores
# We need to divide the data set into majority
# internet (more than 50 users out of 100) and
# minority internet(50 users or less)
```

```
data1 = data[data['internet_users_per_100'] > 50]
data0 = data[data['internet_users_per_100'] <= 50]

print(data1)
print(data0)
```

Here are the two datasets, **data1** and **data0**. Notice how **data1** has all the countries where we have more than 50 internet users per 100 people, and **data0** has 50 or fewer internet users per 100 people:

```
                internet_users   Math       Reading    Science
                _per_100
Country Code
ALB             63.252933        413.1570   405.2588   427.2250
ARE             90.500000        427.4827   433.5423   436.7311
ARG             68.043064        409.0333   425.3031   432.2262
AUS             84.560519        493.8962   502.9006   509.9939
AUT             83.940142        496.7423   484.8656   495.0375
...             ...              ...        ...        ...
SWE             90.610200        493.9181   500.1556   493.4224
TTO             69.198471        417.2434   427.2733   424.5905
TUR             53.744979        420.4540   428.3351   425.4895
URY             64.600000        417.9919   436.5721   435.3630
USA             74.554202        469.6285   496.9351   496.2424

[63 rows x 4 columns]
                internet_users   Math       Reading    Science
                _per_100
Country Code
DZA             38.200000        359.6062   349.8593   375.7451
GEO             47.569760        403.8332   401.2881   411.1315
IDN             21.976068        386.1096   397.2595   403.0997
PER             40.900000        386.5606   397.5414   396.6836
THA             39.316127        415.4638   409.1301   421.3373
TUN             48.519836        366.8180   361.0555   386.4034
VNM             43.500000        494.5183   486.7738   524.6445
```

3. Since we are going to compare two samples with likely different variances, we are going to use the 2-sample t-test function from the **scipy.stats** package. Our significance level is going to be 5%. Since we want to test to see whether the internet users' majority mean is higher, this will be an upper-tailed test. This means that we will have to divide our p-value by 2 and only accept the results as significant if the test statistic is positive. The following code will run our test (note—this is a truncated version of the code; the complete code can be found in the GitHub repository):

```
import scipy.stats as sp

math_test_results = sp.ttest_ind(data1['Math'],\
                    data0['Math'],equal_var=False)

print(math_test_results.statistic)
print(math_test_results.pvalue / 2)

reading_test_results = sp.ttest_ind(data1['Reading'],\
                       data0['Reading'],equal_var=False)
print(reading_test_results.statistic)
print(reading_test_results.pvalue / 2)

science_test_results = sp.ttest_ind(data1['Science'],\
                       data0['Science'],equal_var=False)
print(science_test_results.statistic)
print(science_test_results.pvalue / 2)
```

The results are as follows:

```
For Math: (note - statistic must be positive in
    order for there to be significance.)
3.6040958108257897
0.0036618262642996438
For Reading: (note - statistic must be positive
    in order for there to be significance.)
3.8196670837378237
0.0028727977455195778
For Science: (note - statistic must be positive
    in order for there to be significance.)
2.734488895919944
0.01425936325938158
```

For math, reading, and science, the p-value (the second number) is less than 0.05, and the test statistic (the first number) is positive. This means that for all three tests, there is a significant increase in test scores between the majority internet users' group over the minority internet users' group.

> **NOTE**
>
> Results like this always bring up a famous saying in statistics—correlation does not imply causation. What this means is that just because we found a significant increase in the mean score of the internet majority group, that does not mean that the internet caused the increase in the scores. There could be some third unknown variable that could be causing the difference, known as a **lurking variable**. For example, wealth could be behind the increased scores and internet usage.

4. For our final task, we will build a linear regression model that describes mathematics scores in terms of reading and science scores. First, let's extract the scores from our DataFrame and put the mathematics scores in their own DataFrame separate from the reading and science scores. We will use the **`LinearRegression`** function from **`sklearn.linear_model`** and assign it to its own variable. Then, we will fit the model using the smaller DataFrames. Finally, we will print the intercept and the coefficients of the regression equation:

```
#import sklearn linear model package
import sklearn.linear_model as lm

# Construct a Linear Model that can predict math
#    scores from reading and science scores
y = data['Math']
x = data[['Science','Reading']]

model = lm.LinearRegression()
model.fit(x,y)

print(model.coef_)
print(model.intercept_)
```

The results are as follows:

```
[1.02301989 0.0516567 ]
-38.99549267679242
```

The coefficients are listed in order, so science is first and then reading. That would make your equation as:

$$\widehat{math} = 1.02301989 * science + 0.0516567 * reading - 38.99549267679242$$

Figure 9.23: Formula for mathematics scores in terms of reading and science scores

5. Finally, we will graph the points and the regression and notice that the linear model fits the data well:

```
import matplotlib.pyplot as plt
from mpl_toolkits import mplot3d
import numpy as np

threedee = plt.figure().gca(projection='3d')
threedee.scatter(data['Science'], data['Reading'],\
                 data['Math'])
threedee.set_xlabel('Science Score')
threedee.set_ylabel('Reading Score')
threedee.set_zlabel('Math Score')

xline = np.linspace(0, 600, 600)
yline = np.linspace(0, 600, 600)
zline = xline*1.02301989 + \
        yline*0.0516567-38.99549267679242
threedee.plot3D(xline, yline, zline, 'red')

plt.show()
```

The results are as follows:

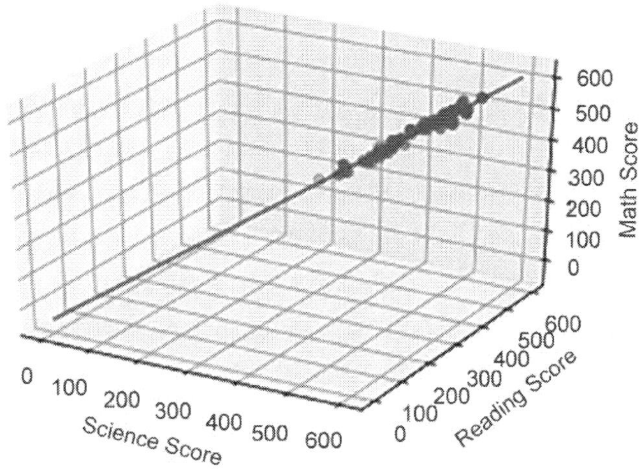

Figure 9.24: The linear equation seems to fit our data well

> **NOTE**
>
> To access the source code for this specific section, please refer to https://packt.live/3is2GE8.
>
> You can also run this example online at https://packt.live/3dWmz2o.

CHAPTER 10: FOUNDATIONAL CALCULUS WITH PYTHON

ACTIVITY 10.01: MAXIMUM CIRCLE-TO-CONE VOLUME

Solution:

1. To find the volume of the resulting cone, you need the height of the cone and the radius of the base, as in the figure on the right of *Figure 10.33*. First, we find the circumference of the base, which is equal to the arc length AB in the cut circle on the left. You can set *R* to **1** since all we're interested in is the angle.

   Radian measurements make finding arc lengths easy. It's just the angle left over from the cut, which is $2\pi - \theta$ times the radius *R*, which we're setting to **1**. So θ is also the circumference of the base of the cone. We can set up an equation and solve *r*:

$$2\pi - \theta = 2\pi r$$

$$r = \frac{2\pi - \theta}{2\pi}$$

Figure 10.34: Formula to calculate the radius

2. We'll code that into our program. We'll need to import a few things from Python's **math** module and define the **r** variable:

```
from math import pi,sqrt,degrees
def v(theta):
    r = (2*pi - theta)/(2*pi)
```

3. The height of the cone can be found using the Pythagorean theorem, since the hypotenuse, the slant height of the cone, is the radius of the original circle, which we set to **1**:

$$r^2 + h^2 = 1$$

$$h = \sqrt{1 - r^2}$$

Figure 10.35: Formula for calculating the hypotenuse

The volume of a cone is:

$$V = \frac{1}{3}\pi r^2 h$$

Figure 10.36: Formula for calculating the volume of a cone

4. So, we'll add that to our function:

```
    h = sqrt(1-r**2)
    return (1/3)*pi*r**2*h
```

Not so hard, is it? This is all we have to do when using Python. If we were doing calculus the old-fashioned way, we'd need an expression for the volume *V* in terms of only one variable, *θ*, the angle we cut out. But we have an expression for *r* in terms of *θ*, an expression of *h* in terms of *r*, and an expression for volume in terms of *h* and *r*. Our program will calculate the volume nearly instantaneously.

5. Now we can run that through our **find_max_mins** function. Theta is measured in radians, so we'll check from **0** to **6.28** and print out the degrees version:

```
find_max_mins(v,0,6.28)
```

The output will be as follows:

```
Max/Min at x= 1.1529999999999838 y= 0.40306652536733706
```

So, the optimal angle to cut out of the original circle is 1.15 radians, which is around 66 degrees.

> **NOTE**
>
> To access the source code for this specific section, please refer to https://packt.live/3iqx6Xj.
>
> You can also run this example online at https://packt.live/2VJHIqB.

CHAPTER 11: MORE CALCULUS WITH PYTHON

ACTIVITY 11.01: FINDING THE MINIMUM OF A SURFACE

Solution:

1. We need to import the **random** module to use its **uniform** function, which chooses a random decimal value in a given range:

```
import random
from math import sin, cos,sqrt,pi
```

2. Create a function that will provide us with partial derivative of **f** with respect to **u** at (**v**,**w**):

```
def partial_d(f,u,v,w,num=10000):
    """returns the partial derivative of f
    with respect to u at (v,w)"""
    delta_u = 1/num
    try:
        if u == 'x':
            return (f(v+delta_u,w) - f(v,w))/delta_u
        else:
            return (f(v,w+delta_u) - f(v,w))/delta_u
    except ValueError:
        pass
```

3. Next, we'll need a function for the surface, a range for *x*, a range for *y*, and a step size:

```
def min_of_surface(f,a,b,c,d,step = 0.01):
```

4. We'll call the **uniform** function of the **random** module to generate an **x** and a **y** value for the starting point:

```
    x,y = random.uniform(a,b),random.uniform(c,d)
```

5. We might as well print out the starting point for testing purposes. If we simply say **print(x,y,f(x,y))**, we'd get unnecessarily long decimals, so we'll round everything off to *two* decimal places when we print:

```
    print(round(x,2),round(y,2),round(f(x,y),2))
```

6. 10,000 steps will probably be enough. We could also make it an infinite loop with **while True**:

```
    for i in range(100000):
```

7. Calculate the partial derivatives at (x,y):

```
        dz_dx = partial_d(f,'x',x,y, 10000)
        dz_dy = partial_d(f,'y',x,y, 10000)
```

8. If the partial derivatives are both really close to 0, that means we've descended to a minimum value for *z*. It might be a local minimum, but taking more steps won't get us anywhere for this random starting point:

```
        if abs(dz_dx) < 0.001 and abs(dz_dy) < 0.001:
            print("Minimum:", round(x,2),round(y,2),round(f(x,y),2))
            break
```

9. Take a tiny step in the *x* direction, opposite to the value of the partial derivative. That way, we're always stepping down in the *z* value. Do the same for *y*:

```
        x -= dz_dx*step
        y -= dz_dy*step
```

10. If *x* or *y* goes outside the range of values we gave them, print **Out of Bounds** and break out of the loop:

```
        if x < a or x > b or y < c or y > d:
            print("Out of Bounds")
            break
```

11. Finally, print out the value of the location we ended up at, as well as its *z* value:

```
    print(round(x,2),round(y,2),round(f(x,y),2))
```

12. Let's test this on a surface that we know the minimum value of: a paraboloid (a 3D parabola), whose minimum value is 0, at the point (0,0). We'll test it for values between -5 and 5. Here's the equation for the surface:

$$f(x,y) = x^2 + y^2$$

Figure 11.48: Equation for the surface of 3D parabola

13. In Python, it will look like this:

```
def surface(x,y):
    return x**2 + y**2
```

Here's what the surface looks like:

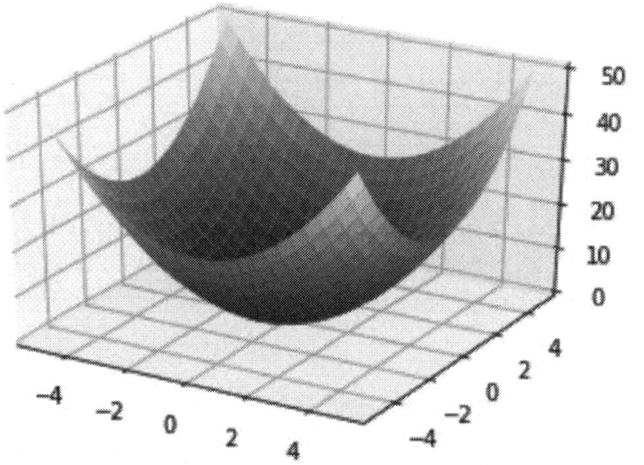

Figure 11.49: The graph of a paraboloid

14. We chose this one because, similar to its 2D equivalent, the minimum point is at (0,0) and the minimum *z* value is 0. Let's run the **min_of_surface** function on the paraboloid:

```
min_of_surface(surface,-5,5,-5,5)
```

The output is as follows:

```
-1.55 2.63 9.29
Minimum: -0.0 0.0 0.0
```

The random point that was chosen was (-1.55, 2.63), which produced a z-value of 9.29. After its walk, it found *the minimum point at (0,0) with a z-value of 0*. If you rerun the code, it'll start at a different random point but will end up at (0,0).

15. Now that we're confident the **min_of_surface** function works, let's try another surface:

$$f(x,y) = 3\cos(x) + 5x\cos(x) * \cos(y)$$

Figure 11.50: Equation of another surface

We'll use *-1 < x < 5* and *-1 < y < 5*.

16. First, we redefine the surface function and then run the **min_of_surface** function for the range specified:

```
def surface(x,y):
    return 3*cos(x)+5*x*cos(x)*cos(y)
min_of_surface(surface,-1,5,-1,5)
```

The output will be as follows:

```
-0.05 4.07 3.14
Minimum: 1.1 3.14 -1.13
```

It looks like the minimum point found from this random point is at (1.1,3.14) and that the minimum *z* value is **-1.13**.

17. When we rerun the code to make sure everything is correct, sometimes, we get an **Out of Bounds** message and sometimes, we get the same result, but significantly often, we end up at this point:

```
3.24 0.92 -12.8
Minimum: 3.39 0.0 -19.34
```

18. Let's put the **min_of_surface** into a loop so we can run a number of trials:

```
for i in range(10):
    min_of_surface(surface,-1,5,-1,5)
```

Here's the output:

```
1.62 4.65 -0.12
Out of Bounds
2.87 0.47 -15.24
Minimum: 3.39 0.0 -19.34
2.22 0.92 -5.91
Minimum: 3.39 0.0 -19.34
-0.78 -0.85 0.32
Out of Bounds
```

```
1.23 3.81 -0.61
Minimum: 1.1 3.14 -1.13
1.96 -0.21 -4.82
Minimum: 3.39 -0.0 -19.34
-0.72 3.0 4.93
Out of Bounds
2.9 -0.51 -15.23
Minimum: 3.39 -0.0 -19.34
1.73 -0.63 -1.58
Minimum: 3.39 -0.0 -19.34
2.02 2.7 2.63
Minimum: 1.1 3.14 -1.13
```

Every time the program produced a **`Minimum`**, it was one of the two points we've already seen. What's going on? Let's take a look at a graph of the function:

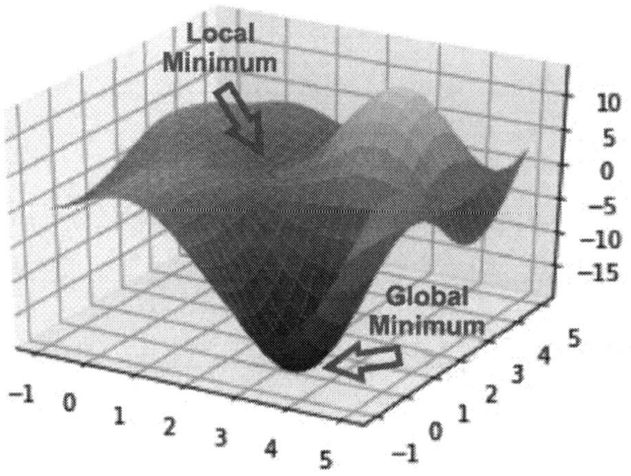

Figure 11.51: A graph of $f(x, y) = 3\cos(x) + 5x\cos(x) * \cos(y)$

What the graph shows is that there's more than one minimum. There's a global minimum, where the function goes deep into the negative numbers, and a local minimum, where any point in that *valley* will simply descend to the point (1.1, 3.14) and not be able to get out.

> **NOTE**
>
> To access the source code for this specific section, please refer to https://packt.live/2ApkzCc.
>
> You can also run this example online at https://packt.live/2Avxt1K.

CHAPTER 12: INTERMEDIATE CALCULUS WITH PYTHON

ACTIVITY 12.01: FINDING THE VELOCITY AND LOCATION OF A PARTICLE

Solution:

1. For the first part, we only have to find where $\frac{dy}{dt} = 0$. Let's write functions for *dx/dt* and *dy/dt*:

```
from math import sqrt,sin,cos,e

def dx(t):
    return 1 + 3*sin(t**2)

def dy(t):
    return 15*cos(t**2)*sin(e**t)
```

2. Now, we can loop from 0 to 1.5 and see where *dy/dt* goes from positive to negative or vice versa:

```
t = 0.0
while t<=1.5:
    print(t,dy(t))
    t += 0.05
```

   Here's the important part of the output:

```
1.0000000000000002 3.3291911769931715
1.0500000000000003 1.8966982923409172
1.1000000000000003 0.7254255490661741
1.1500000000000004 -0.06119060343046955
1.2000000000000004 -0.3474047235245454
1.2500000000000004 -0.04252527324380706
1.3000000000000005 0.8982461584089145
1.3500000000000005 2.4516137491656442
1.4000000000000006 4.5062509856573225
1.4500000000000006 6.850332845507693
```

   We can see *dy/dt* is zero somewhere between 1.1 and 1.15 and, again, between 1.25 and 3 since that's where the output changes its sign.

3. Let's use binary search to narrow down those ranges. This is identical to the previous **bin_search** function except for the **guess =** line. We're simply plugging the average into the **f** function to get our guess:

```
def bin_search(f,lower,upper,target):
    def average(a,b):
        return (a+b)/2
    for i in range(40):
        avg = average(lower,upper)
        guess = f(avg)
        if guess == target:
            return guess
        if guess < target:
            upper = avg
        else:
            lower = avg
    return avg

print(bin_search(dy,1.1,1.15,0))
```

The answer is **t = 1.145**.

4. For the other range, you have to change **if guess < target** to **if guess > target** and call the function this way:

```
print(bin_search(dy,1.25,1.3,0))
```

The answer is **t = 1.253**. But that was too easy. The challenge is to find the exact *x-y* location of the particle at those times.

5. We need a **position** function that will take tiny steps, like in our ball problem:

```
def position(x0,y0,t):
    """Calculates the height a projectile given the
    initial height and velocity and the elapsed time."""
```

6. First, we set up our increment variable and set a variable called **elapsed** to **0**:

```
    inc = 0.001
    elapsed = 0
```

7. Our initial values of **vx** and **vy** will be the derivatives at 0, and **x** and **y** will also start off at 0:

```
    vx,vy = dx(0),dy(0)
    x,y = x0,y0
```

8. Now, we start the loop and run it until the elapsed time reaches the desired **t**:

```
    while elapsed <= t:
```

9. We calculate the horizontal and vertical velocity, then increment **x** and **y** and the loop counter:

```
        vx,vy = dx(elapsed),dy(elapsed)
        x += vx*inc
        y += vy*inc
        elapsed += inc
    return x,y
```

10. Now, we'll put the times we found into the **position** function to get the position of the particle at the times we know the derivative is 0:

```
times = [1.145,1.253]
for t in times:
    print(t,position(-2,3,t))
```

The output gives us the following:

```
1.145 (0.4740617265786189, 15.338128944560578)
1.253 (0.9023867438757808, 15.313033269941062)
```

Those are the positions where the vertical velocity is 0.

11. For the second part, where we need to find the speed of the particle at $t = 1$, the speed will be the hypotenuse of the right triangle formed by the vertical speed and the horizontal speed:

```
def speed(t):
    return sqrt(dx(t)**2+dy(t)**2)

speed(1.0)
```

The output is as follows:

```
4.848195599011939
```

The speed of the particle is 4.85 units per second.

> **NOTE**
>
> To access the source code for this specific section, please refer to https://packt.live/3dQjSzy.
>
> You can also run this example online at https://packt.live/3f0IBCE.

INDEX

T

U

V

W

Made in the USA
Monee, IL
24 October 2020

45999611R00407